Flaubert

Flaubert

MICHEL WINOCK

Translated by Nicholas Elliott

The Belknap Press of Harvard University Press

Cambridge, Massachusetts | London, England

2016

This book was originally published as *Flaubert*,
© Éditions Gallimard, Paris, 2013.

English translation published with the support
of the Centre national du livre.

Library of Congress Cataloging-in-Publication Data

Names: Winock, Michel, author.
Title: Flaubert / Michel Winock ; translated by Nicholas Elliott.
Other titles: Flaubert. English
Description: Cambridge, Massachusetts : The Belknap Press of Harvard
    University Press, 2016. | "This book was originally published as
    Flaubert, (c) Éditions Gallimard, Paris, 2013"—Title page verso. |
    Includes bibliographical references and index.
Identifiers: LCCN 2016012077 | ISBN 9780674737952 (alk. paper)
Subjects: LCSH: Flaubert, Gustave, 1821–1880. | Novelists, French—
    19th century—Biography.
Classification: LCC PQ2247 .W5613 | DDC 843/.8—dc23 LC record
    available at http://lccn.loc.gov/2016012077

Contents

Preface

Why write yet another biography of Flaubert? I first read *Madame Bovary* and *Sentimental Education* during my high school years, but without much pleasure. I only truly discovered Flaubert while studying literature at the Sorbonne. The program for the French literature certificate included *Sentimental Education*, which had previously done so little to satisfy me. But I was brought around by rereading the novel, enriched by several scholarly works: the masterpiece had been revealed to me. I was not alone. I remember an afternoon in the Luxembourg Gardens preparing for the end-of-year exam with a few classmates, reciting passages from the *Education*—laughter vied with admiration. Having defected from literature and converted to history, I convinced my professor Louis Girard, a great specialist of the nineteenth century, to allow me to write a dissertation on "Flaubert: Historian of His Time." I have never stopped rereading Flaubert since. The catalyst for this book came in 2007, when the Bibliothèque de la Pléiade published the fifth and final volume of Flaubert's brilliant correspondence, a scholarly edition prepared by Jean Bruneau, with the assistance of Yvan Leclerc.

In writing this volume, it has not been my intention to compete with, much less join, those cohorts of qualified Flaubert specialists in France and abroad who have for decades tirelessly contributed new studies, released the master's unpublished works, and delivered virtuoso efforts in what is called "genetic criticism." Among them, I would particularly like to thank Yvan Leclerc and his team at the Flaubert Center at the University of Rouen, whose generous help and warm welcome I so appreciated.

My only aim in these pages is to share with readers my interest in the "hermit of Croisset," by depicting the life of a man in his century. It is a biography written for pleasure, but it remains a historian's biography.

The life and work of Gustave Flaubert are part and parcel of France's great century of democratic transition, which is defined by the end of the society of orders of the Ancien Régime and its replacement by a society of classes; the growing demand for equality; the implementation of universal male suffrage; the secularization of society; the industrial revolution; the birth of the proletariat and the spread of socialist doctrines; the gradual liberation of the press; the development of public education (established by the Guizot law of 1833 and the Ferry laws of the 1880s); the progress of literacy; and accelerated technical transformations in the fields of transportation and printing. This lasting democratic transition unfolded after the July Revolution of 1830 and under the domination of a single class: "The leveling process which began in 1789 and made a fresh start in 1830," wrote Balzac in *The Peasantry*, "has in reality paved the way for the muddle-headed domination of the bourgeoisie and delivered France over to them."

Flaubert unequivocally disparaged this historical process, but his many diatribes bear witness to its reality. He was not a reactionary like the counter-revolutionary philosopher Joseph de Maistre, pining for the alliance of Throne and Altar. Flaubert did not harbor the slightest monarchical or clerical sympathy. What he repudiated was the rise in power of the *majority* as a result of expanded suffrage, or what his contemporary Tocqueville called "democratic society"—the principle of equality which undermined the legitimacy of the elite and denied the superiority of the intellect over the vulgar masses.

His hatred for his era settled on the bourgeoisie, which in his eyes embodied the debasement of mind, mores, and taste. This criticism reveals some contradictions because Flaubert himself belonged to this class; but for him, the bourgeois was first and foremost the modern man, made stupid by utilitarianism, bloated with preconceptions, deserted by grace, and impervious to Beauty. Caught in a historical movement he abominated, empyrean Flaubert held fast to an eternal truth: Beauty and Art do not belong to any era. Paradoxically, by making the art of writing transcendent and placing it above everything that the modern world stood for, Flaubert became the most modern writer of his time.

Flaubert

CHAPTER I

The Time and the Place

Born during the reign of King Louis XVIII (1821) and buried during the presidency of Jules Grévy (1880), Gustave Flaubert spent most of his life in the era of Monsieur Prudhomme. Prudhomme, a comic character created by the playwright and actor Henri Monnier in 1830 and a "monstrously true type," according to Baudelaire, embodied bourgeois complacency and stupidity.[1] I certainly do not share the opinion of those who characterize the nineteenth century as a mix of occultism, sentimental mushiness, and raving utopianism.[2] I recognize the achievements of a period that was innovative on every front; but nonetheless, one must admit that the century also witnessed the triumph of a greedy, self-satisfied, and sententious bourgeoisie. Flaubert defined his constant target in a famous turn of phrase that was purely moral rather than sociological: "I call *bourgeois* anyone who thinks in a base manner."

Gustave Flaubert began life and spent his youth in a historical air pocket. For a quarter of a century, France had been ablaze with the fires of the Revolution and the suns of the Empire. France was torn between civil war and foreign war, the great principles were proclaimed to the universe, the soldiers of Napoleon's Old Guard pounded European soil all the way to Moscow, and defeats had become as spectacular as victories. All of Europe had gathered in a coalition against the French Caesar and managed to eliminate Napoleon, but only once the flamboyant saga of the Hundred Days had played out at Waterloo.

The Battle of Waterloo took place six years before Flaubert's birth. With the help of the Allies, Louis XVIII, brother to the guillotined king, restored the monarchy, winning over the French people with a new constitution that was no more than a mess of pottage, despite its promises that absolutism had not returned, that the regime would be liberal and parliamentary, that freedom would replace censorship, and that from now on citizens would be able to sleep in peace. Indeed, peace reigned for forty years. When France rid itself of the last of the senior branch of the Bourbons, Charles X, with the July Revolution of 1830, the era of the bourgeois monarchy was established under the reign of Louis Philippe and the influence of François Guizot, the intellectual behind the July Monarchy.

Looking back, we don't lack affection for this period. After all, it was during this era that the French grew accustomed to the processes of representative government; to peace in international relations; to the momentum of the industrial revolution, as symbolized by the first railroads; and to Romantic art and literature. But the younger generations of the time did not see it that way. Alfred de Musset, Flaubert's senior by a decade, eloquently described this passage from the epic to the trivial in his novel *The Confession of a Child of the Century:* "A feeling of inexpressible unease began to ferment in those young hearts. Condemned to be docile by the kings of the world, given over to pedants of all kind, to idleness and boredom, the young saw the foaming waves against which they had strengthened their arms ebbing away from them. In the depths of their souls, those oiled gladiators felt unbearably wretched. The richest among them turned into libertines; those possessed of modest fortune took up professions, the law perhaps, or the army; the poorest feigned enthusiasm for causes, fell in love with big words, threw themselves into the perilous sea of action without direction." In this work, which was published in 1836 and read by Flaubert at the age of fifteen, Musset found a single word to sum up the situation: "The effect was a rejection of everything that exists in heaven and on earth. It could be termed disillusionment or, if you prefer, *despair.* It was as if humankind was in a coma and had been pronounced dead because it had no pulse."[3] Flaubert's future friend Maxime Du Camp would later describe Musset's juniors as follows: "The artistic and literary generation to which I belonged had a wretchedly sad youth, a sadness without cause or object, an abstract sadness inherent in the person or the period."[4]

And what a period it was. While the Empire's soldiers were sidelined, speculators like Balzac's Birotteau, Camusot, and Nucingen triumphed. The lean gave way to the fat. These parvenus were rarely the conquering bourgeois of capitalist innovation, the captains of industry, the entrepreneurs whose names are etched in the outlines of epic history, or those men whose grandeur was celebrated by Marx, the prophet of socialism. Instead, these men were merchants, notaries, magistrates, attorneys, and public defenders—that whole world of the courts depicted by Daumier—as well as doctors, apothecaries, and the legions of property owners and people living off interest, reassured once and for all about the national assets that they or their ancestors had acquired and which had briefly seemed to be imperiled by the Restoration. Even the top bankers were involved in insurance and making loans to merchants rather than stoking industry. Though Rouen had a cotton industry and spinning mills, its people were for the most part not major entrepreneurs. They were prudent, thrifty, conservative, suspicious, barely practicing Catholics, exemplary of a dull provincial bourgeoisie that was practical, hardworking, and a little stingy. These people were content with the world as it was. They were not short on small pleasures, the safest of which was to watch their nest eggs grow.

Faced with this materialism or with their idea of it, young people, according to Musset, "by affecting despair, found an outlet for their unused strength. Scoffing at military glory, religion, love, at everything under the sun, is a great consolation for those who do not know which way to turn. In behaving thus, they mock themselves: they put themselves in the right by justifying everything they say."[5]

The Notables of the Hôtel-Dieu

Gustave's family owed its position in the bourgeoisie to annuities and merit. Gustave's father, Achille-Cléophas Flaubert, was a native of the Aube region southeast of Paris, born in 1784 to an old family of veterinarians. After receiving his secondary education at the Collège in Sens, he was one of the privileged few to attend medical school in Paris, where he was so successful—he was top of his class every year he was enrolled—that the government reimbursed his education expenses under the Consulate regime of Napoleon Bonaparte. Having received the third highest mark on his internship entrance exam and begun his residency under Guillaume Dupuytren, one of the eminent figures of French medicine and surgery, he was exempted from military service in 1806 due to "pulmonary phthisis." Dupuytren, who appreciated and vaunted his skill, had him appointed to the Hôtel-Dieu in Rouen, the city's principal hospital, as a "provost in anatomy" under the supervision of chief surgeon Jean-Baptiste Laumonier. His new supervisor introduced him to Caroline Fleuriot, whom he would marry in 1812, soon after defending his thesis.[6]

Little by little, Achille-Cléophas Flaubert became both a renowned surgeon and a professor of medicine. At the time, Rouen did not have a medical school; Dr. Flaubert taught at a preparatory "secondary school" within the hospital. After Laumonier's death in 1818, Dr. Flaubert became chief surgeon. His growing reputation owed more than a little to the subject of his thesis, "The Way to Treat Patients Before and After Surgical Operations." He was as interested in people as in their illnesses. The eminent Dr. Larivière in *Madame Bovary* is largely inspired by Dr. Flaubert: "He belonged to that great surgical school created by Bichat—that generation, now vanished, of philosopher-practitioners, who cherished their art with fanatical love and applied it with enthusiasm and sagacity."[7] Devoted, selfless, and sympathetic to the struggles of penniless wretches (he started the practice of offering free outpatient consultations), he was also a remarkable practitioner whose reputation spread far beyond Rouen. Gustave would have the opportunity to verify this during his trip to Egypt, when the French consul in Suez told him that he had "heard a great deal" about his father.[8] By 1826, a Paris medical directory described Achille-Cléophas Flaubert as "one of France's leading doctors." Like Achille-Cléophas's students, the young Gustave admired and venerated the great man. Gustave inherited from his father a mindset that was nonconformist and Voltairean, during an era of alliance between Throne and Altar. A police memorandum written to the government when Dr. Flaubert was a candidate to the Royal Academy of Medicine in 1824 and published by the scholarly periodical *L'Intermédiaire des chercheurs et des curieux* in January 1910 noted his "liberal opinions," while recognizing that "his excellent moral qualities have earned him public esteem and respect."

Yet the great man's selflessness had its limits—Achille-Cléophas amassed a not insignificant fortune. The partial suffrage system then in place gave voting rights to only a minority of the French population (approximately 100,000 people under the Restoration, a little more than twice that under the July Monarchy), restricted to men who could pay a certain minimum tax. In 1820, Dr. Flaubert paid 1,349 francs in taxes. With the tax quota for voting rights under the Restoration at 300 francs, he was one of only 3,700 electors in Seine-Inférieure, a department of close to 700,000 inhabitants. He was even eligible for office, which required payment of 1,000 francs and was a privilege afforded to only 17,300 French citizens under the Restoration. By 1846, the year of his death, his tax payment had risen to 2,145 francs—tenfold what was required by the July Monarchy. As these figures reveal, the Flauberts' fortune guaranteed them a position in Rouen's high society. Achille-Cléophas left an estate worth approximately 800,000 francs, which consisted primarily of the property at Croisset and land in the regions of Aube (Nogent-sur-Seine) and Calvados (Pont-l'Évêque).⁹ This estate would ensure Gustave a comfortable living after he discontinued his studies.

Flaubert's parents' affluence did not prevent them from embracing a certain nonconformism. In a letter to his mistress Louise Colet a few months after the death of his father, Flaubert described a scene that, however anecdotal, illustrates both of his parents' freethinking ways. While they were in Le Havre, Achille-Cléophas Flaubert learned that "a woman he had known in his youth, when he was seventeen, lived there with her son. . . . He got it into his head to go and see her again. This woman whose beauty was famed in her region had once been his mistress. He did not do what many bourgeois would have done; he did not hide the fact. He was better than that. So he went to visit her. My mother and the three of us [the children] waited in the street for him, the visit lasting close to an hour. Do you think that my mother was jealous or piqued in the slightest? No, and yet she loved him, she loved him as much as a woman has ever been able to love a man, and not only when they were young, but up to the last day, after thirty-five years of marriage."¹⁰

Gustave's mother, Anne-Justine-Caroline Fleuriot, was the daughter of Jean-Baptiste Fleuriot, a health officer like Charles Bovary (i.e., someone who practiced medicine but was not accredited as a medical doctor), and Caroline Cambremer de Croixmare, who was from a family of ship-owners. Anne-Justine was orphaned quite early in life. Her mother died while giving birth to her, and her father died in January 1803, when she was nine years old, after which she was taken in by Dr. Laumonier and his wife, her godmother, at the Hôtel-Dieu. She was living there when she was asked to marry twenty-seven-year-old Dr. Flaubert. At the time, Anne-Justine was eighteen years old and had just finished boarding school. The young couple married in 1812 and initially settled on rue du Petit-Salut where, Madame Flaubert would tell her granddaughter, she had "the best years of [her] life." When Laumonier died and was replaced as chief surgeon by Achille-Cléophas, the couple moved into the Hôtel-Dieu, in the wing known as the *Pavillon*—now a museum devoted to the Flaubert family and the history of medicine. Dr. Flaubert's waiting room was on the ground floor, next to the kitchen where the Flauberts' faithful servant Julie busied herself. On the second floor was the parents' bedroom and, most importantly, a billiards room, the legendary *Billard* that Gustave and his friends used as a theater. The children's rooms were on the third floor. The Flauberts had six children, but in that age of high infant mortality, three were lost at a young age following the birth of the eldest, Achille, in 1813. Gustave was born in 1821, followed by his sister Caroline in 1824.

The age difference between Achille and Gustave, combined with Achille's move to Paris to study medicine, created a distance between the two brothers that only grew with time. They also had very different personalities. Gustave formed a more intimate bond with his sister Caroline. From the age of ten, he performed plays with her in the *Billard*. Later, when his trips took him far away from her, he addressed her by many tender names in his letters: "my good little rat," "pretty rat," "kid," "my good Caroline." She answered that she was his "golden rat" for life and that she thought about him "continually." Gustave had become her Pygmalion, loaning her his books and reading long passages aloud that enchanted her, made her laugh, and impressed on her his tastes and mocking attitude. When Caroline left the family home to marry Émile Hamard in April 1845, Gustave's heart was broken.

Flaubert was initially educated by his mother, as was common at the time in bourgeois households. Free-spirited, affectionate, discreet, a little wild, and courageous, she had not absorbed much piety at the Laumoniers; her son later wrote that she became an atheist after the deaths of her husband and daughter. Gustave described her as a "good woman, upright and open-minded." But he got his precocious passion for literature neither from her nor from his father. The first person to initiate him into the marvel of stories was Julie, the maid. While bedridden for a year with an illness, Julie had spent her idle hours reading, which enabled her to fill her beloved little Gustave's head with stories and legends. The other initiator was old Mignot, Gustave's friend Ernest's great-uncle, who lived across from the Hôtel-Dieu and read him stories. Mignot passed on his love for *Don Quixote*, one of the future writer's major reference points.

Neither his father nor his mother gave Gustave a religious education, even though the restored monarchy was very Christian. He was baptized, a ritual that couldn't be avoided, but religion would never be central to his life. In this regard, the Flaubert family was not atypical in Rouen, a city where the bourgeoisie was readily turning to anticlericalism, particularly under the Restoration. Additionally, Normandy had been experiencing "dechristianization" since the eighteenth century, as attested to by the low birth rate, the reduced observance of Lent, and the feminization of the Catholic religion through the expansion of female religious orders. It was a region from which the Lord was vanishing.[11]

More than the church, it was the hospital that made up Flaubert's child-hood world. Once he became a writer, he often evoked its macabre atmo-sphere. "The Hôtel-Dieu's autopsy room," he told Louise Colet, "looked out onto our garden. How many times my sister and I climbed on the trellis and, hanging from the vines full of curiosity, looked at the exposed cadavers! The sun shone on them; the same flies that flitted about on us and on the flowers landed there, came back, buzzed! . . . I can still see my father looking up from his dissection and telling us to go away."[12]

Life in the Hôtel-Dieu was his familiar landscape. A world of doctors, male nurses, nuns in wimples, and especially the sick taking their walks or lying on stretchers, shadowed by death. He watched them from his bedroom and observed their pale faces pushed up against the ward windows. He would re-spond to Louise Colet's surprise at his pessimism with this gloomy explana-tion: "I always sense the future, the antithesis of everything is always before my eyes. I have never seen a child without thinking of a grave. The sight of a naked woman makes me imagine her skeleton."[13]

This morbid environment's imprint on Flaubert's vision of the world, his fascination for funereal proceedings, and his despair—all have possibly been exaggerated, including by the man himself. A different sensibility might have been less affected. But by coming in contact with suffering and misery at an early age, Flaubert internalized the finitude of life. He was confronted with death from the day he was born.

The Collège Royal

In February 1832, Gustave began school in the eighth form (equivalent of the U.S. fourth grade) at the Collège Royal de Rouen, first as a day student, then, beginning in May 1832, as a boarder. The Revolution of July 1830 had recently ended the reign of the Bourbon king Charles X and enthroned Louis-Philippe d'Orléans in the Tuileries Palace. The oldest building of the Collège Royal had been built in the sixteenth century; Corneille had studied there. Under Napoleon, it became an imperial high school (*lycée impérial*). It was renamed the Collège Royal under the Restoration and remained so until 1873, when it became the Lycée Corneille under the Republic. Enrollment ranged from five hundred to six hundred students. Gustave would stay there through his *classe terminale de philosophie*, a year of post-secondary education that pre-pared students for the top universities.

Attending a *lycée* or a *collège royal* was a privilege available to only two percent of children. Schooling was expensive: room and board cost about 700 francs, while a teacher's salary at the time was no more than 500 francs a year.[14] Life at boarding school was harsh. The premises were poorly heated and rudimentary, hygiene left much to be desired, and discipline was rigorous. Dictation was taken "on your knees, your body doubled up, holding your notebook and your inkwell with one hand, and your quill with the other."[15] Student insurrections were not uncommon; the Collège Royal de Rouen had witnessed such an incident only a few months before Gustave's arrival. Far fewer hours were spent in class than in study hall, doing written homework under the supervision of a monitor. The most important subject remained Latin, which was practiced through translation, discourse, and versification.

In *Les Mémoires d'un fou* [*Memoirs of a Madman*], written in 1838, Flaubert related his grim memories of the school: "I attended *collège* beginning at the age of ten and contracted an early and profound aversion to mankind." An aversion to youth, in particular: a world of prejudices, egotism, and the tyranny of the strong. "I was abused there for all my preferences: in the classroom for my ideas; in the schoolyard for my penchant for solitary unsociability." He depicts himself as shut away in his solitude, "hassled" by his schoolmasters and "ridiculed" by his classmates. Gustave hated the regulated life that began at dawn with a drum roll and the set times signaled by the bell: "This regularity may be well suited to the masses, but in the case of the poor child who sustains himself on poetry, dreams, and chimeras, who thinks about love and all that foolishness, it constantly awakens him from that sublime reverie, it does not leave him a moment of rest, it suffocates him by bringing him back to an atmosphere of materialism and common sense that horrifies and disgusts him."[16]

Flaubert lays it on a little thick here; though he was isolated from his classmates, he did find the time to read and write. Not all academic exercises were unpleasant to him. And he met at least two teachers at school who inspired him and had a positive influence. Beginning in the fourth form (equivalent of U.S. eighth grade), Gustave's taste for history was stimulated by Adolphe Chéruel, a graduate of the École Normale Supérieure, licensed history teacher (a disciple of Jules Michelet), and future professor at the Sorbonne. Chéruel had Gustave read numerous ancient and modern works and gave him free-writing assignments. In a letter to his friend Ernest Chevalier, the facetious student called his teacher "a dickhead of the highest rank," but also "a historian of the highest merit." Chéruel was then working on his *Histoire de Rouen sous la domination anglaise au XVᵉ siècle* [*History of Rouen under English Domination in the Fifteenth Century*], which would be published in 1840.

The other schoolmaster to influence Flaubert was Honoré Gourgaud-Dugazon, who was his literature teacher beginning in the fifth form (equivalent to U.S. seventh grade). Gourgaud-Dugazon also suggested books to read—he may have been responsible for Flaubert's discovery of Byron—and narratives to write. Having discovered a particularly talented student in Gustave, he kept track of his progress and encouraged him. In a letter to his former teacher dated January 22, 1842, Flaubert wrote how impatient he was to see him again: "Hours pass quickly when we are together; I have so many things to tell you, and you listen so well!"[17] He was addressing a friend, a confidant to whom he could reveal his insecurities and present his first attempts at a novel.

He was less appreciative of "old Magnier," his teacher when he got to the *classe de rhétorique*, the last year of secondary education. Flaubert's fellow student François Bouquet reports that Magnier unleashed "comical furies" against the romantic fever he detected in his most ardent students. "The dramas of Dumas and Hugo had just been performed on the Rouen stage," Bouquet explains, "and the presence of [the great actress] Marie Dorval had given these performances a particular vividness. . . . While old Magnier inveighed against *Richard Darlington* and *Marie Tudor* from his pulpit, the fanatics displayed their new faith by wearing cravats à la Antony."[18]

Flaubert's academic record at the Collège was neither poor nor exceptional. His end-of-term reports describe a student whose behavior was a little frivolous but whose morals were good. He attended to his religious duties, and his progress was regularly judged "quite satisfactory."[19] He was awarded academic prizes only in history and natural history. He was less interested in the classroom than in his personal projects in historical narrative and literature, which he began very early, before he even had a firm grasp on spelling and grammar. His letters bear traces of this early passion for writing and composing plays. He was nine years old when he wrote to his friend Ernest, "I will send you notebooks I have begun to write, and I would be grateful to you to send them back to me, if you want to write something inside you will make me very happy."[20]

Born near the small Norman town of Les Andelys a year before Flaubert, Ernest Chevalier was his first great friend. The two children met before

Flaubert enrolled in school. Ernest's maternal grandparents, the Mignots, lived across from the Hôtel-Dieu; the two boys got to know each other through this neighborly happenstance. "Yes," Gustave wrote to Ernest in 1830, "friend from birth until death." Though only nine, he already venerated friendship. He expressed his reverence in no uncertain terms, with little regard for conventional syntax: "for you and I are bound by a love that can be called fraternal. Yes, I, who have deep feelings, yes I would walk a thousand leagues if necessary to be reunited with my best of friends, for nothing is so sweet as friendship oh sweet friendship . . . without attachment how could we live."[21] The two boys spent their Thursdays and Sundays together. Gustave entrusted Ernest with his writing projects and worries. He told him about his political convictions and discussed the latest literary and theatrical news. The theater was the principal entertainment for the people of Rouen, who were diligent theatergoers. There were several theaters, the most distinguished of which was the Théâtre des Arts, which was reserved for polite society; Flaubert would send Emma Bovary there. Young Gustave had even paid several visits to a Parisian theater near the Porte Saint-Martin when his family stopped in Paris on the way to visit Achille-Cléophas's brother-in-law François Parain ("Uncle Parain") in Nogent-sur-Marne. He would later tell Louise Colet that he had had "an unbridled taste for the stage" in his youth.

At an early age, Gustave even prided himself on having political opinions. At nine, the tempestuous boy celebrated the Poles, who had won their independence from the Russians.[22] At twelve, he resolutely declared himself a republican. When Louis Philippe and his family came to visit "the city that saw the birth of Corneille" in September 1833, Gustave was bothered by the expense of the trip and mocked the gawking citizens of Rouen, who rushed in and spent hours waiting, "and for whom? For a king! Ah!! the world is so stupid. Personally I saw nothing—not the review, not the arrival of the king, not the princesses, not the princes."[23] In August 1835, Gustave was outraged by a bill aimed at restricting freedom of the press and the theater following the assassination attempt on Louis Philippe by Giuseppe Fieschi (the bill was passed in September): "Yes, this law will be passed, for the representatives of the people are nothing but a filthy lot of sold-out wretches, they see only their own interests, their natural bent is toward baseness, their honor is a stupid pride, their soul a lump of mud; but some day, a day that will come before long, the people will unleash the third revolution: kings' heads will roll, there will be rivers of blood."[24] That same August, he commented on the trial of the "accused of April [1834]," a group of workers who had led riots in Lyon, and elevated the men responsible for the riot at the Saint-Méri cloister and the rue Transnonain (an incident immortalized by Daumier) to the rank of heroes of the century: Marc Caussidière, "with the terrible masculine face," and Charles Lagrange, "one of these men with high ideas."

The paths of these two friends who had spent so much time playing, laughing, and chatting together would later diverge. Ernest would become a magistrate, marry, and adopt a bourgeois life. The charms of a childhood friendship sworn to be eternal were lost. "Good old Ernest!" Flaubert wrote to his mother on December 15, 1850: "There he is, married, established—and a magistrate to boot! What a perfect bourgeois and gentleman! How much more than ever he'll be the defender of order, family, property! But then he has followed the normal course." Long gone was the teenager with whom Gustave had shared enthusiasms and declarations of friendship, his fervor for Victor Hugo, and his schoolboy bawdiness. Ernest had swapped the "serious-ness of comedy" for the "comedy of seriousness": "My heart bleeds to think of it. Now I'm sure that down where he is he's thundering against Socialist doctrines, talking about the 'edifice,' the 'basis,' the 'helm of State,' the 'hydra-headed monster.' As a magistrate, he is reactionary; married, he'll be a cuckold; and so spending his life between his female and his children on the one hand, and the turpitudes of his profession on the other, there he is, the perfect example of a man who has managed to attain everything life has to offer."[25]

The second friend young Flaubert made was Alfred Le Poittevin, who was five years his senior. Gustave would remain passionately attached to him until Alfred's premature death. The friendship really took hold in 1837, once Al-fred had moved to Paris to study law. He was the son of Paul Le Poittevin, a wealthy cotton manufacturer, and Victoire Thurin, a childhood friend of Flau-bert's mother. Alfred was the oldest of three children, followed by Laure, who was born the same year as Flaubert and later married Gustave de Maupas-sant, father of the future writer. The Le Poittevin and Flaubert families were close. Alfred joined Gustave and Ernest Chevalier in the theater in the *Bil-lard*, where his plays were performed along with Flaubert's.

Alfred was a lover of literature and also wrote—especially poetry. He was an impassioned reader of Goethe and Shakespeare. Gustave learned a great deal from him. Romantic and sensitive to the highest degree, Alfred instilled some of his pessimism in Flaubert or, to quote Musset, some of his "despair."

An unhappy love affair had driven him to a frantic quest for pleasure and regular visits to brothels, to which he initiated his young friend. Their relationship consisted of long conversations, shared secrets and ideas, walks, rowing on the Seine, and mutual pledges. The boys spent vacations together at the Flauberts' country house in Déville-lès-Rouen, at the Thurins' country house, and at Les Andelys with the Chevaliers. Flaubert submitted his writings to this much-admired friend. Once he became a student in Paris, Alfred recommended houses of ill repute, enriching his tips with countless spicy comments.[26] Flaubert was disappointed when Alfred got married, and was shattered when he died in April 1848. He sat with his friend's body for two nights before kissing him goodbye in his coffin. He reported that the memory of this dear friend would accompany him everywhere.[27] He admitted to his correspondent Mlle Leroyer de Chantepie that Alfred De Poittevin was the man that he "had most loved in the world": "I never knew anyone (and I know many people) with such a transcendental mind as the friend I am telling you about. We sometimes spent six hours at a stretch talking about metaphysics. We reached a high level a few times, I assure you."[28] In 1862, he told Laure de Maupassant of the "large" place her brother had in his life: "That memory never leaves me. Not a single day passes, I dare to say almost not an hour, without my thinking of him." He revealed to her that he was "dazzled" by Alfred, going so far as to admit that "when he married, I suffered torments of jealousy: it was a rupture, an uprooting! . . . With delight and sadness mingled I think of our interminable conversations, talks made up of everything from farce to metaphysics—the books we read, our dreams, our high aspirations! If I am worth anything, it is certainly because of those things. I have retained a great respect for that part of the past: we were not commonplace, and I have done my best not to fall short."[29]

After Alfred Le Poittevin's death, Louis Bouilhet became Flaubert's closest friend. Gustave had met him at school, but the two young men did not become friends until after Alfred's marriage in 1846. Louis had initially chosen to become a doctor, and he had studied with Dr. Flaubert before giving up on the profession. Gustave and Louis supported each other in their literary endeavors. Together, they read aloud and wrote outlines. Bouilhet would become Flaubert's most trusted adviser and his most demanding proofreader. Shortly after Bouilhet's death in 1869, Flaubert told George Sand: "In losing my poor Bouilhet I lost my midwife, the person who saw into my thinking more clearly than I do. His death has left me with a void that I'm more aware of every day."[30]

Boredom and Pranks

Early on, Flaubert developed an inclination for mockery that would inspire permanent theatrics. He created an imaginary character, the Garçon (the Boy), with his friends Chevalier and Le Poittevin and his sister Caroline. The Garçon was a kind of marionette that was at the same time both a Louis-Philippe-loving bourgeois and a prankster always ready to laugh at the king. In Flaubert's correspondence, the Garçon comes alive, yelling and laughing; each of the young people was responsible for inventing new wickednesses for the *Billard*. They talked about the Garçon as if he were a real person. The Goncourt brothers give a report on him:

> It was a heavy, obstinate, patient, continuous, heroic, eternal joke, like a small-town or German joke. The Garçon had his own movements, which were those of an automaton, a halting, strident laugh, which was no laugh at all, and enormous physical strength. Nothing provides a better idea of the strange creation that truly possessed and captivated them than the attack they launched each time they passed a cathedral in Rouen. One would immediately say: "How beautiful this Gothic architecture is, it elevates your soul!" Immediately, the one playing the Garçon rushed out with his laugh and his gestures: "Yes, it's beautiful ... and so is the Saint Bartholomew's Day Massacre! And the Edict of Nantes and the *Dragonnades* are beautiful too."[31]

The Goncourts suggest that the pharmacist Homais in *Madame Bovary* was a "reduced figure" of the Garçon. During Flaubert's trip to Egypt, the Garçon would encounter competition from the Sheikh, a new character concocted by Flaubert and his traveling companion Maxime Du Camp. "The Sheikh," Gustave explained to his mother, "is an inept old man with a private income, respected, very well established, and ancient, who asks us questions about our trip along the following lines:—'And in the cities you passed through, was there a little society? Is there a club where one can read the newspapers? Is the development of the railroad beginning to be felt? Is there a major rail line? And socialist doctrines, thank God, I hope, have not yet made inroads in the vicinity.' "[32] From these childhood games, an obsession emerged that would be at the heart of his future body of work: the hatred of stupidity.

There was a facetious spirit in Flaubert's personality that balanced out his precocious boredom and gloomy view of the world. He had proudly lost any illusions about human nature at an early age. Beginning at age nine, he wrote down examples of adults' foolishness. At twelve, he confessed to Ernest Chevalier that had he not planned to write, he would be totally disgusted by his existence and that a bullet "would have delivered him from this farcical joke called life." While there was obviously some posturing in his juvenile, Romantic declarations, the sentiment is constantly echoed in his writing. At sixteen: "I have now come to see the world as a spectacle and to laugh about it. What do I care about the world?" Behind every great ideal that was proclaimed, he detected vanity, bad faith, emptiness, and corruption. Religion gave him no comfort: "I can't believe that our body, composed as it is of mud and shit and equipped with instincts lower than those of the pig or the crab-louse, contains anything pure and immaterial, when everything around it is so polluted and ignoble."[33] In his eyes, both the metaphysical future and the future of his own life were shams. So he learned to laugh at the vacuity and absurdity. Young Flaubert remained a pleasant companion, a lover of pranks and an unbridled joker. But, as he admitted to Ernest Chevalier, "I am more of a clown than I am cheerful." When he reached his final year at the Collège, he wondered what he would do after his schooling ended. Full of irony, he resigned himself to becoming like everyone else: "An honest man, settled down and all the rest if you please, I will be just like anyone else, like everyone else, just like I'm supposed to be, a lawyer, a doctor, a sub-prefect, a notary, an attorney, a common judge, a stupidity like every other stupidity, a man of the world or the office, which is even dumber. . . . Well, I've chosen, I've decided, I'll go study law which instead of leading to everything leads to nothing. I'll spend three years in Paris getting syphilis and then what?"[34] This was Gustave's self-description as a youth without "conviction, enthusiasm, or belief."

In the meantime, he had to pass his baccalaureate exam. Unfortunately, he was expelled from the Collège in his last year. The previous year, while struggling with his Latin verses, he had told Ernest: "Oh good God, when will I be clear of these bastards? I can't wait for the day when I tell the Collège to go to hell." His wish was granted earlier than anticipated. When the popular philosophy teacher Monsieur Mallet was replaced by a certain Bezont, a hornet's nest was stirred up in the student body. The substitute complained that he had been interrupted by some pupils, including Gustave Flaubert. After the third warning, he imposed a general punishment: one thousand verses for the entire class. "My intention," Bezont wrote to the headmaster on December 11, 1839, "was also to take advantage of the first moment of silence to exempt them from the extra homework, but since the disorderliness continued, I had to maintain the punishment."[35] The school's directors confirmed the punitive assignment. Punished along with all his fellow students, Flaubert led the initiative for a class-wide refusal. He explained himself in a letter to the headmaster signed by twelve of his classmates, including Louis Bouilhet and his future brother-in-law Émile Hamard: "Dear Headmaster, We were told that we were children, that we were behaving like children; through our moderation and loyalty, we will try to convince you of the contrary."[36] Ultimately, Flaubert, the top student in philosophy composition, was expelled along with two other headstrong pupils. He began preparing for the exam alone at home. Although he was not worried about philosophy or physics, he dreaded mathematics and Greek. Chevalier, who had gotten his baccalaureate the previous year, gave him his assignments and class notes to read. Gustave was lonely but rose to the challenge, wearing himself out studying from morning to night and learning Demosthenes and two books of the *Iliad*. The dreamer had put on the Benedictine's habit. Then it was done: by mid-August 1840, he had passed his baccalaureate—a diploma only four thousand French boys of his age (1 percent) received that year. He could now enroll in medical or law school. But did he have a taste for it?

CHAPTER 2

"Oh! To Write"

"You may not know what a *pleasure* it is to compose! To write, oh! to write, is to take hold of the world. . . . It is to feel one's thought be born, grow, live, stand up on its pedestal, and remain there forever."[1]

Gustave Flaubert composed this hymn to writing at the age of fourteen. It came at the end of the tale "Un parfum à sentir ou Les Baladins" [A Scent to Smell, or The Street Artists], which he described as a "strange, bizarre, incomprehensible book." The joy of writing allowed the young boy to transcend that loathing of the world that he expressed early in his letters, as well as his dark view of society and the despair which formed the backdrop of his mental landscape: "Let us intoxicate ourselves with ink, since we lack the nectar of the gods."[2] What is surprising here is not the attitude, which is quite common among sensitive teenagers, but its staying power: there is ample evidence of it throughout Flaubert's life. The antithesis between the disgust with life and the exaltation of writing took shape early. On one side was the world that filled him with boredom, the dreary repetition of the days, the pitiful spectacle of imbeciles playing at being honest folk, wearing their Legion of Honor rosettes and white ties; he was astonished that the sun could still rise on such insignificance. But fortunately, there was another life, in which it was possible to make one's salvation: the quest for "the beautiful in the infinite" (*Memoirs of a Madman*). But one should not be deceived: Flaubert did not write simply to "escape," to stave off boredom or dodge dreadful reality; he aspired to the Absolute, which he wrote with a capital A. He would later discuss his "aesthetic mysticism" with Louise Colet. His juvenilia reveal its seeds.

Flaubert was a writer both precocious—which is not so unusual—and extraordinarily prolific—which is rarer. Though his exacting writing standards prevented him from publishing his first novel, *Madame Bovary*, until 1856, when he was nearly thirty-five, he had already produced an abundant body of unpublished work; one gets a sense of its breadth in the thick *Bibliothèque de la Pléiade* volume devoted to his juvenilia. Though he had been a little slow learning to read, by the age of nine he was sending Ernest Chevalier "notebooks [which he had] started to write." His early comedies for the *Billard* have vanished, but what remains of his childhood and youthful creations reveal an apprentice writer who exercised his talents in every genre: the historical narrative, short story, speech, play, and novel. Also at nine, he tackled "liberal constitutional and political speeches," all of which have been lost. Amédée Mignot, Ernest Chevalier's uncle and an attorney at the Rouen bar, came across some of Gustave's short works when the boy was barely ten and had him autograph a few under the title "Three Pages of a Schoolboy's Notebook." A brief "Éloge de Corneille" [In Praise of Corneille] has survived. It consists of an academic exercise in which the young Rouen native compares his compatriot to Racine: "Some argue your merits versus those of Racine, and I proudly reply: Who has the most merit? He who removes thorns from a path, or he who then plants flowers? Well! you are the one who removed the thorns, which is to say the difficulties of French versification! Corneille, you get the prize. I salute you!"[3]

Once enrolled at the Collège, the thirteen-year-old boy founded a newspaper, *Les Soirées d'étude* [*Study Evenings*], which was to appear "every Sunday" and was described in a subheading as a "Literary Journal." It lasted only two issues. At the time, Gustave wrote abundantly, without restraint, never crossing out a word, moving forward at high velocity—the polar opposite of the future artist endlessly sculpting his work. Later, he would mock fame as nothing but a harlot; but now, he dreamed of applause: "Author! Author!" This was why he loved the theater, starting with Shakespeare, who spurred him to learn English. In 1830, the year of his first known correspondence, the battle over Victor Hugo's play *Hernani* erupted, pitting outraged "classicists" against the "Romantics" behind Hugo. For Flaubert, there was no question: Victor Hugo was his "great man." The select circle of playwrights he admired included Alexandre Dumas, whose *Antony* and *La Tour de Nesle* enchanted him, Alfred de Vigny for his *Chatterton,* and Goethe for his *Faust.* His passion for the dramatic arts soon led him to write his first drama, the lost *Frédégonde.* He soaked up the works of Chateaubriand and, as he got older, those of Montaigne and Rabelais, whom he considered the fountainheads of French literature and culture. At seventeen, he declared that he only had profound esteem for "two men, Rabelais and Byron, the only two who have written in a spirit of malice toward the human race and with the intention of laughing in its face."[4] His copy of Rabelais was "crammed with notes and comments philosophical, philological, Bacchic, erectile etc."[5] It was his bible. As for Byron, he discovered him at fifteen, mostly thanks to Alfred Le Poittevin. The English poet, killed in 1824 at Missolonghi while fighting alongside the Greek revolutionaries, had been acclaimed by Goethe, Hugo, Vigny, and Lamartine and become the herald of the Romantic soul. In Byron, young Gustave and his friend Alfred found an amplified echo of their gift for despair.

Was it the spirit of the times? Or a singularly melancholic temperament? In either case, Flaubert's juvenilia are steeped in pessimism and boredom. As a youth, Flaubert displayed an acute sensitivity to the miseries of human nature, the lies of social and political life, the hypocrisy of notables, and the void of existence. In "Agonies," a piece he composed at sixteen and dedicated to his friend Alfred, he laid out the essence of skepticism: "Virtue is a mask, vice is the truth . . . ; the good man's home is a mask, the brothel is the truth; the nuptial bed is a mask, the adultery consummated within is the truth; life is a mask, death is the truth."[6]

The blank page and the quill were his only resources for the possibility of re-enchantment.

Under the Auspices of Clio

Gustave's taste for history was equally precocious. History was then fashionable, and not clearly distinguished from literary works—Augustin Thierry, the author of the *Récits des temps mérovingiens* [*Tales of Merovingian Times*], admitted that Chateaubriand's *Les Martyrs* [*The Martyrs*] had decided his vocation. This national sensibility had been kindled by the Revolution and the Empire. Michelet began publishing his vast *History of France* in 1833. The following year historian and minister of education François Guizot established the Comité des travaux historiques (Committee for Historical Work), which aimed to bring to light a collection of unpublished documents of French history. In 1835, Guizot founded the Société de l'histoire de France (Society for the History of France), which was devoted to publishing archives. Meanwhile, authors relied on the muse Clio to inspire their novels and dramas, with Vigny (*Cinq-Mars*), Hugo (*Cromwell, Hernani, Marion Delorme, The Hunchback of Notre-Dame*), Alexandre Dumas (*Henri III et sa cour, La Tour de Nesle*), and Musset (*Lorenzaccio*) among the leading lights of the trend. Small papers, journals, and literary magazines opened their pages to historical tales, which were highly in vogue during the 1830s, when young Flaubert was making his first literary sallies.

Before he had even enrolled in school, the nine-and-a-half-year-old boy wrote a short biography of Louis XIII, dedicated "To Mommy on her name day." This was no ordinary present. Its few pages were probably drawn from Michaud's *Biographie universelle* [*Universal Biography*], but however meager the child's creative contribution, they are a testament to Gustave's penchant for history. He even supplemented the text with a chronology beginning in 1614: "Marie de Médicis ordered work begun on the Luxembourg Gardens and planted the Champs-Elysées."

Flaubert read the journals that arrived at the Hôtel-Dieu and received the much-appreciated instruction of his teacher Adolphe Chéruel beginning in the fifth form. Although Chéruel was still young when Flaubert met him, he was already highly accomplished. He had founded the *Revue de Rouen*, been elected to the city's scholarly academy, and joined the Société des antiquaires, a historical and archeological organization, while waiting to climb the ladder of a great academic career in Paris. Chéruel was not only a scholar but a spirited educator, lecturing without notes in a "clear, loud, resonant" voice that captivated his students.[7]

Under his influence, Flaubert read the great chroniclers of the Middle Ages and Renaissance—Jean Froissart, Philippe de Commynes, Pierre de l'Estoile, and Brantôme—as well as the scholarly works of Abel-François Villemain, Claude Fauriel, and Jean de Sismondi. At his professor's request, he wrote survey papers such as "The Influence of Spanish Arabs on Medieval Society" and "The Struggles Between the Priesthood and the Empire." For Flaubert, history would serve primarily as an inexhaustible reservoir of narrative themes, the veracity of which was not his most pressing concern.

Like Hugo and Dumas, Flaubert used his historical tales to pursue an interest in episodes and characters of the past—particularly medieval and Renaissance times—which had imprinted the excitement of blood and horror in the collective memory. In these tales, one dies by means of the sharp dagger of an enemy or a traitor, after a life dominated by cruelty, sexual depravity, and the infamies of the will to power. Gustave's story "Dernière Scène de la mort de Marguerite de Bourgogne" [Final Scene of the Death of Marguerite de Bourgogne], about the debauched queen strangled at Château-Gaillard in

1315, is a prime example of this genre: "Twenty-six years old! and she was Marguerite de Bourgogne, Marguerite of the bloody orgies in the Tour de Nesle; Marguerite of the nights of insomnia and the dreams of blood; Marguerite, the queen of France." She was nothing at all in the hands of her executioner, who strangled her with her own hair: "A muffled groan was heard, a body fell to the ground, and Marguerite was a corpse!"

Another historical death had dominated the newspapers' cultural pages since Paul Delaroche had exhibited his soon-to-be-famous painting *Assassinat du Duc de Guise* [*Assassination of the Duke of Guise*] at the Salon of 1834. Flaubert, who had just finished his play *Frédégonde,* also wrote on the murder of the Duc de Guise—perhaps at the behest of Gourgaud, his literature teacher. Aside from Michaud's *Biographie universelle,* he drew his facts from Louis-Pierre Anquetil's *Histoire de France* [*History of France*], which was a goldmine for him. Anquetil had previously inspired Chateaubriand's take on the same subject in his *Analyse raisonnée de l'histoire de France* [*Rational Analysis of the History of France*]. Flaubert also borrowed from Prosper de Barante's 1826 *Histoire des ducs de Bourgogne* [*History of the Dukes of Burgundy*]. At fourteen, the young writer already had a good handle on telling a story, as is plain in "Deux Mains sur une couronne" [Two Hands on a Crown], a tale of the madness of Charles VI: "In Paris that day all was commotion. The city had a festive air, and the old façade of the Louvre even seemed to brighten up with pride. . . . Paris was a sea of people, a dark hive of men, women, beggars, and soldiers." Charles enters the city on his white horse, riding beside his wife: "The queen! Oh! as soon as she was seen in the streets, cries of exultation, whirling of feet, hurrahs without end, a rain of flowers; from time to time she turned to Charles and her big black eyes seemed to tell him, 'I'm happy,' and her smiling mouth, 'I love you.'" This opening is reminiscent of the beginning of Dumas's tale "La Belle Isabeau" [The Beautiful Isabeau]. But the celebrations, embraces, and politeness were all an illusion—it would end in a bloodbath.

For a time, Flaubert was also inspired by the Spanish Golden Age. In 1836, not yet fifteen, he took an interest in Philip II, King of Spain and Navarre, in "Un Secret de Philippe le Prudent" [A Secret of Philip the Prudent]. He describes the confrontation between the king and the grand inquisitor, Don Olivarès, in a controlled style: "It was a matter of who would be the most clever and the most cunning, who would best serve God, who would be the most ferocious and fanatical in his ministry. But it was always the same one that yielded to the other, and it was the Crown that lowered itself before the

Church." We will never know Philip's "secret," for the narrative was left unfinished after a single chapter of seventeen pages. It is a pity, for aside from a few clichés, the adolescent Flaubert already expressed himself uncommonly well.

Also in 1836, he wrote a "Chronique normande du Xe siècle" [Norman Chronicle of the 10th Century]: "Do you know Normandy, that old classical land of the Middle Ages where each field has had its battle, each stone holds on to its name and each piece of debris a memory?" It is the story of the Normans' resistance to the French king Louis IV, who planned to annex Normandy by kidnapping and killing Richard, the twelve-year-old heir to the kingdom. The setting is the year 952 in Rouen. The king enters the city to acclamation, cheers, and cries of joy. But his designs are brought to light by Richard's tutor Osmond: "No, no, the people will not let themselves be deceived this way, they will take arms." Soon the city's hurrahs have become jeers and threats: "Yet the very same people had come with flowers and cries of love the other day! Now he was stamping his feet with impatience and rage, like a man in a delirium. They hollered for 'The king! The king!' and their thousand arms waved pikes, axes, halberds, daggers, spears, and closed fists in the air." Louis IV starts to tremble in the face of this assault. He is waiting for reinforcements, but his vassal Bernard refuses to supply them. He is forced to give up; Normandy will remain Norman. The king returns Richard to the people, and once again the cheers are heard.

When he was sixteen and a half, Flaubert took his writing to another level with the five-act play *Loys XI*. The play was composed in fifteen days, after two months of research, notably in the memoirs of Philippe de Commynes and the *History of the Dukes of Burgundy*. Philippe was a character appealing to Romantics: he was deceitful, cruel, superstitious, and Machiavellian but had a lofty idea of his kingdom and of the authority he aimed to extend over his vassals, beginning with the Duke of Burgundy. "I had been deeply taken," Flaubert wrote in his introduction to the play, "with Louis XI's features, placed like Janus between two halves of history: he reflected its colors and indicated its horizons. A mix of the tragic and the grotesque, of triviality and loftiness, you'll admit that for a sixteen-year-old imagination that loved the severe forms of history and drama it was tempting to set that head face-to-face with Charles the Bold's."[8]

The phrase "mix of the tragic and the grotesque" shows that Gustave had read Victor Hugo's resounding manifesto to his *Cromwell* in 1827: he had written not a tragedy, but a "drama." At the time, Flaubert passionately admired Hugo. In his correspondence, he referred to him as the "great author of [The Hunchback of] *Notre Dame*": "Is not V. Hugo as great a man as Racine, Calderón, Lope de Vega and many another long admired?"[9] The final two scenes, where we see Louis XI facing death as a poignant supplicant, imagine a confrontation between the king, pleading for his life, and the holy man who has come to confess him and remind him of his crimes. Commynes sorrowfully comments: "Ah! A head so political and so vast!" Before dying, the king becomes more human and admits to his moral dereliction: "Everything bores me now; however much I work, it is in vain. . . . Well, Commynes, my head is as empty as a cleaned and swept scaffold. . . . Such a life is so boring, always calm and cold like the sleep of a tomb." This was the very boredom that Gustave constantly experienced. A few months after finishing his drama, he wrote to Ernest Chevalier: "I have lived, that is, I have been bored."

Aside from his keen interest in the Middle Ages, Flaubert was also fascinated with antiquity. Posing as a provocative apostle of decadence, he did not hesitate to repeatedly proclaim his fervor for Nero, "the towering man of the ancient world." In 1839, he described the Roman Empire's path to ruin in the short, eight-page text "Rome et les Césars" [Rome and the Caesars]. Probably one of the last assignments he handed in to his teachers at the Collège Royal, it is a truly memorable text. "Rome's work was the conquest of the world. Once the world was conquered, it had only to get drunk and go to sleep; bursting with warm blood, wine, voluptuousness, rolling in its gold, it staggered and fell down exhausted." By a shortcut true to the Romantic inspiration, he outlined a history of the death throes of the Roman Empire "in a five-century feast." In short, congenital decadence. Throughout these pages, one feels the pleasure the young writer takes in recounting obsessions with blood, sensual pleasures, and death, three key terms later associated with the French nationalist Maurice Barrès, but already requisitioned by the fledgling historian. "At the time," he wrote, "history was a bloody orgy."[10]

Gustave was under the dual influence of the historical fiction made fashionable by Romanticism and the "serious" history then becoming institutionalized and embodied by his up-and-coming teacher Chéruel. The young Flaubert navigated on the mingled streams of Alexandre Dumas, who dressed up history to make it more exciting, and the pioneers of a scholarly, critical history initiated by Edward Gibbon in late-eighteenth-century England.

An Anthology of Despair

The juvenilia of the writer later seen as the paragon of the realist novel reveal a young author whose mind was full of Romanticism. His Romantic bent was first expressed in his taste for history, a discipline in which the most extreme passions were unleashed. The rest of his juvenilia, which include philosophical and fantastic tales, sketches, short stories, speeches, and portraits, also attest to this interest.

Whether mundane or supernatural, death haunts his early compositions. Many pieces' titles speak for themselves: "Voyage en enfer" [A Trip to Hell]; "La Fiancée et la Tombe" [The Fiancée and the Tomb]; "La Grande Dame et le Joueur de vielle ou La Mère et le Cercueil" [The Grande Dame and the Hurdy-Gurdy Player, or The Mother and the Coffin]; "La Dernière Heure" [The Last Hour]; "Rêve d'enfer" [Dream of Hell]; "La Danse des morts" [The Dance of the Dead]; "Les Funérailles du docteur Mathurin" [The Funeral of Doctor Mathurin]. One cannot help thinking that the fact that the young Gustave was so used to seeing the passage from life to eternal rest may have led him to place death both at the center of his life and at the heart of his work, just as it was at the heart of the Hôtel-Dieu. In a short story entitled "La Peste à Florence" [The Plague in Florence], he evoked his father's hospital by referring to "something moist and sepulchral, similar to the odor of a dissection amphitheater." During the night of June 1 to June 2, 1836—a most fruitful year—he wrote a meditation in verse on death, which he entitled "La Femme du monde" [The Woman of the World]: "My name is cursed on earth; yet the misfortune, despair, and envy that reign over it as tyrants often call me to their rescue." The speaker reveals its identity in the twenty-seventh and last verse: "I still love to detail all the suffering endured by those whom I take in my embrace./Now do you recognize me? I have the head of a skeleton, hands of iron, and in those hands a scythe./They call me Death."

Death inhabits all his tales as the only tangible truth of existence. In "Rage et impuissance" [Rage and Impotence], he tells the story of a man who is buried alive and, through chattering teeth, calls on God to deliver him. God remains silent, and the man eventually blasphemes him, while above him, the air is rent by the barking of his lost dog. In "La Dernière Heure," Flaubert relates the final moments of a nineteen-year-old man who has decided to commit suicide following the death of his "beautiful little sister with big blue eyes" and "a night of tears and sobbing by the light of two funeral candles." Once again, Flaubert's quill gives rise to imprecation, revolt, and anger at God's silence. One thinks of Cain's revolt—Cain as seen by Byron, that victim of fate. The figure of the dark, desperate poet, the cursed exile fallen into debauchery in Venice before conspiring with the secret revolutionary societies of the Italian *carbonari* and dying for the cause of independence in Greece was, as Musset put it, "deeply inspired by melancholy," but was also its inspirer.

This profoundly pessimistic vision of humanity and its destiny is disseminated throughout most of his dramatic and fantastic tales. The boredom he experienced was that of a creature grappling with the emptiness of being on earth, suffering from his incompleteness and loneliness. As in Gothic novels, his dark thoughts drove him to the macabre. We admire a beautiful woman; he invites us to confront the truth: "This angel of beauty will die and become a corpse, that is to say a stinking carcass, and then a little bit of dust, the void ... fetid air imprisoned in a tomb. There are people whom I always see as a skeleton and whose yellow complexion seems to me to be mixed with the soil that will contain them." He expressed a similar idea in the short story "Quidquid volueris," which is subtitled "a psychological study" but is actually one of his best fantastic tales. This rather long story—about one hundred pages—was written before his sixteenth birthday. It tells the story of the impossible love between a half-man, half-monkey monster and a beautiful girl. The tale is not unrelated to romantic disappointment, a kind of emotional prison that Gustave was already familiar with. The monster Djalioh, who is mute but has human feelings, is driven mad by his forbidden love for Adèle, the young woman of the house where he lives. He eventually rapes and kills her. In Flaubert's hands, the exhumation is like a trip to hell: "[Adèle] was buried, but after two years she had lost much of her beauty. For she was exhumed to be buried in the Père Lachaise cemetery, and she stank so much that a gravedigger became ill." Though propriety was among the rules of classical literature that the pupil had learned in school, it no longer had its place in the poetics of the new literature. In the preface to *Cromwell*, Victor Hugo had forged the neologism "*bégueulerie*"—itself derived from "*bégueulisme*," which Stendhal had invented to describe excessive prudishness in his *Racine et Shakespeare* [*Racine and Shakespeare*]—to refer to the classics' powdery style. Did Flaubert compel himself to follow this recommendation to say everything "without prudishness"? He embraced bad taste and would continue to do so, though more discreetly, in his future masterpieces.

In his manifesto, Hugo urges the rehabilitation of the body, too often forgotten in the name of the sublime and good taste. In young Flaubert's narratives, the protagonists' bodies are subjected to multiple realistic variations. His short story "Passion et vertu" [Passion and Virtue] was inspired by a news item in *La Gazette des tribunaux,* a newspaper that specialized in court cases. A desperate love affair drives the heroine Mazza to call for Satan and death and to commit suicide without remorse or hope. The passion she experiences drives her to, wild, delirious actions: "Mazza bit him in the chest and sank her nails into his throat." Her lover Ernest has chosen to separate from her, but "when thinking about her and her burning embraces, her fleshy bottom, her white breasts, her long black hair, he missed her."[11]

In more autobiographical works such as "Agonies" and *Memoirs of a Madman,* the expression of the impossibility of faith in God and a supernatural life is particularly evident: "I searched and I found nothing." The priests encountered by his heroes are shameless liars who preach good morals and visit prostitutes, or nice, down-to-earth fellows who, when asked for advice, can only think of the grub they are warming up—one is reminded of Matthew Lewis's Gothic novel *The Monk,* which had caused a scandal at the end of the previous century. His was a world without God, without hope, dominated by tyranny, poverty, injustice, skullduggery, vanity, the bustling of courtiers around the throne, and the stupidity of honest folk. What could one expect from it? Before Flaubert was seventeen, he already seemed to have lost every illusion: "Man's life is like a curse that emerges from the chest of a giant and goes crashing from rock to rock, gradually dying out with each vibration that reverberates in the air."[12] Nihilistic professions of faith are overabundant in the pages written by this teenager who could objectively have been called happy but whose mind had been penetrated by the misfortune of being. History is but a "road of blood," he wrote in "La Danse des morts."

One can already find all of Flaubert in these sketches: an utterly dark vision of humanity, life, and the world. Young Flaubert's maxims, which were undoubtedly in keeping with the literature of his time, and particularly Byron's poetry, would make a beautiful anthology of melancholy. His attitude was also inspired by a feeling of revolt against the era in which he was living, "this good civilization, this agreeable slut who invented railroads, poisons, clyster pumps, custard pies, royalty, and the guillotine." This was obviously literary posturing: Gustave was not suicidal in the fashion of Werther, but the darkness of his mental world would never relent. At the advanced age of seventeen, he announced his plan: "If I ever do take an active part in the world it will be as a thinker and demoralizer."[13]

The God Yuk

For the task of demoralizing the dupes, posers, and naïve people preaching virtue and happiness, Flaubert honed a weapon: his sense of the grotesque. Victor Hugo had sung the praises of the grotesque in his manifesto on Romantic drama: "It penetrates everywhere," he wrote, "for in the same way that the most vulgar people have their many bouts of sublimity, the most elevated frequently pay tribute to the trivial and the ridiculous."[14] For Hugo, it is a matter of balancing the sublime, which represents "the soul purified by Christian morality," with the grotesque, which "plays the part of the human beast." For Flaubert, however, the grotesque unequivocally dominates everything. In his short story "Smar," he turns it into a god, the god Yuk.

"Smar," a tale both philosophical and fantastic, was inspired by Edgar Quinet's *Ahasvérus*, which had itself been suggested by the legend of the wandering Jew. *Ahasvérus* is a long prose poem, a modern epic—a "sacred representation"—about the "universal tragedy played out between God, man, and the world." With its long sweep, its quest for the absolute, mythologies of history, and allegories, *Ahasvérus* is the ambitious work of an uneasy visionary. "A strange sickness torments us today," Quinet wrote, with a reference to the hero of Chateaubriand's *René*: "What would I call it? It is no longer only yours, René, the sickness of ruins; ours is sharper and more bitter. It is the sickness of the future. What kills us is more than the weakness of our thought; it is the weight of the future to be borne in the void of the present." Gustave Flaubert wrote "Smar" in 1839, when he was in the *classe de rhétorique*, his second-to-last year at the Collège. In this "old mystery," as he called it, God has vanished and Satan is in charge. Smar, who represents humanity, is transported to the heavens by the Devil and put to the test through a series of peregrinations. Initially happy, Smar soon discovers that "creation is cruel," life is "full of pain," and the mysteries of the universe are unfathomable. Satan makes him experience every passion, every misery, and every successive illumination of despair. In the end, Satan and Smar fall in love with the same woman—who is none other than Truth. Will she choose the man or the Devil? Neither one nor the other: victory belongs to Yuk, the god of the grotesque, and "everything ends in a monstrous coupling."

The god Yuk laughs at everything, including death. He embodies Flaubert's lifelong conviction that stupidity has the world in its grip. Satan had initiated Smar into the misery of the world: "What! You have never before felt all that was false in life, all that was narrow, petty, and lacking in existence? Did nature seem beautiful to you, with its wrinkles and wounds, its lies? Did the world seem to you to be full of harmony, truth, and grace—the world with its cries, its running blood, its madman's drool, its rotten scoundrels?"

Lucidity demands that one laugh about it like Yuk does, with a "Homeric," "inextinguishable" laugh, a laugh as "indestructible as time." Here one thinks of Yuk's predecessor the Garçon, whose laughter was so great that Flaubert had to coin the term *hénaurme* to describe it. Yuk is essential to the world: he penetrates institutions, mores, beliefs, systems, theories—everything that lives and everything that dies.

Nothing is spared, not even love. To Louise Colet, Flaubert would admit that "the grotesque aspects of love have always kept me from indulging in it."[15] Both in his juvenilia and in his great works, derision and irony never lose their right to vengeance. Pettiness and triviality are always hiding beneath the noble bearings he observes. One of his first texts was entitled "La Belle Explication de la 'fameuse' constipation" [The Beautiful Explanation of the "Famous" Constipation]. In the few lines extant, one learns that "constipation is a tightening of the *merdarum* hole." Ultimately, Flaubert always wrote as a child of the Hôtel-Dieu. In a less medical and more sociological manner, his "Leçon d'histoire naturelle" [Natural History Lesson], a pastiche of a zoology treatise published in the little Rouen paper *Le Colibri*, depicts the "clerk genus." Monographs dedicated to individual social types were then fashionable and would become even more popular in the 1840s under the name of "physiologies," a trend launched by Balzac with his *Physiologie de l'employé* [*Physiology of the Employee*]. One could find in bookstores and newspapers such titles as *Physiologie du bas-bleu* [*Physiology of the Bluestocking*], *Physiologie du barbier coiffeur* [*Physiology of the Barber Hairdresser*], and *Physiologie de l'étudiant* [*Physiology of the Student*]. Flaubert was ahead of the curve by publishing his physiology of the "clerk" in 1837. This work was a generic caricature whose romantic inspiration is apparent in its blatant contempt for the conformist and gullible petit bourgeois, an aspect in which one can detect the irony later wielded by the author of the *Dictionary of Accepted Ideas*. Those who have read Flaubert will recognize the figures of Homais and Bouvard and Pécuchet in this prosopography. The life of the clerk—who must be addressed as "Mister Employee" in order to avoid offending him—is regulated down to the slightest detail and repetitive in its vacuity. But the clerk is happy, and Flaubert cheerfully describes his imbecilic joy, with many picturesque observations on the clerk's clothing, his pen-pusher's work, his leisure activities, his customs, his language, and his movements. The function mechanizes and makes idiotic those who are reduced to it.

Most of Flaubert's early works display a similar level of satirical verve. In "Quiquid volueris," he provides the following description of Adèle, the monkey-man's beloved: "Her gaze was blue and moist, her complexion was pale; she is one of these poor girls who was born with gastritis, drinks water, taps out Liszt's music on a noisy piano, loves poetry, sad reveries, and melancholic love affairs, and has stomach aches."[16] Beneath the vaporous and ethereal, one finds the vulgar protestations of a digestive system. Flaubert's irony is not only directed at people of small means, but also the "superior classes"—rich philanthropists, dandies, priests, servile ministers, and even the king himself. Of a notable in his tale "Ivre et mort" [Drunk and Dead], he writes that "he had no other merit than in having only a little conscience, a good tailor, a beautiful watch chain, and a skillful wife, which he had used as beggars use their wounds, to make a living from a deception that enabled him to have an income, a farm, and rent." All these important people put on airs while actually living with masks, aping virtue and profundity, responsibility and honesty in a social comedy in which each plays his part and sticks out his pompous, solemn, and decorated chest. They must be slain!

In "Étude sur Rabelais," written shortly before he turned seventeen, Flaubert admires the liberating mockery of the great manipulator of words and beings. He follows Pantagruel's journey as he visits "all the nations" and nowhere encounters "what is good." What prevails is "an eternal laughter, immense, muddled, the laughter of a giant, which deafens the ears and makes one dizzy; monks, soldiers, captains, bishops, emperors, popes, nobles and peasants, priests and laymen, all pass before the colossal sarcasm of Rabelais, who flagellates and stigmatizes them, and they all come out from under his quill mutilated and bleeding." Rabelais the "destructor" is the example to be followed. The word *grotesque* recurs several times in Flaubert's text. And if Rabelais assailed the society of his time, what would he say today? "You no longer have Christianity. So what do you have? Railroads, factories, chemists, mathematicians. Yes, the body is better off, the flesh suffers less, but the heart still bleeds."[17] Universal skepticism, dreary boredom, blathering politics—if Rabelais were back, "his book would be the most terrible and sublime that has ever been written."

In the genre-spanning collection of writings making up his juvenilia, Flaubert had become the follower of a cult he would never relinquish: that of the god Yuk. On September 8, 1871, he would confess to George Sand that "mankind is displaying nothing new. Its irremediable wretchedness has embittered me ever since my youth."[18] From one tale to another, all these despairing cries create the picture of an adolescent whose pessimism was more powerful than his dreams. The disenchantments of love would only add their gloomy touch to his representation of the world and of existence. Over the course of a childhood spent between a school where one died of boredom and a hospital where one died plain and simple, Gustave's personality took shape by reacting against the platitudes of society under Louis Philippe, the illusions of religious belief, and, more generally, the established order of universal stupidity. The temperament revealed at a young age is that of a sensitive soul whose inaccessible dreams had been wounded, even mutilated. Like Baudelaire's Poet, he would have come to resemble the albatross, "exiled on the ground, hooted and jeered [at],"[19] had he not had the resources of a double balm: Rabelais's destructive laughter, and the quest for Beauty through writing.

CHAPTER 3

To Love

What did this young man whose tales dwelt on "the inconvenience of being born" really have to complain about? He was among the privileged few who had the means to get an education; his parents were notables who could guarantee him a comfortable future; he had a delightful sister and good friends with whom he could satisfy his love of the stage and his taste for farce. He was handsome and healthy, he liked to laugh and make others laugh: could the habitual ill temper he indulged in have been a pose? After befriending him in Paris, Maxime Du Camp would reproach Flaubert for this: "You have beside you, close at hand, all the desired elements for happiness and you are not happy. Dear Gustave, do you not deceive yourself, do you not, by a quirk too common in the human heart, force yourself to be unhappy in order to feel sorry for yourself?"[1]

Nonetheless, Flaubert's two early autobiographical works, *Memoirs of a Madman* (1838) and *Novembre* [*November,* 1841–42], like his fictional works, were etched in darkness. This time the subject was love—and while Gustave's experience with love from the age of fourteen to eighteen had the effect of a magic spell, it did not deliver him from melancholy. On the contrary.

Mad for Élisa

If one is to believe Flaubert, he experienced love only once in his life, at the age of fifteen, on a beach in Normandy. Stated so bluntly, it sounds foolish. Can the wounds of an adolescent love really tyrannize one forever? To the point that one never recovers? That one believes the only possible love to be an impossible one? This is exactly the nice story that has been passed on by Flaubert scholars, beginning with Émile Gérard-Gailly.

The Flaubert family was in the habit of going to Trouville at least every second summer to meet with Achille-Cléophas's brother-in-law François Parain, whom Gustave adored, and other members of the family. Mme Flaubert owned property in the area of Pont-l'Évêque, less than six miles from the sea. In Trouville, the Flauberts stayed at L'Agneau d'Or, the only inn in town, which was "run by old Madame David," as Flaubert noted in "Un Coeur simple" [A Simple Heart]. Morning swims were followed by afternoon excursions over rolling terrain "with the donkey," then the wait on the dock for the fishermen to return in their small boats, which "slipped through the lapping waves to the middle of the port, where the anchor suddenly dropped."

One morning in the summer of 1836, Gustave was taking his usual walk along the beach at low tide. Suddenly, he noticed a red coat with black stripes on the sand. "The tide was rising," he wrote in *Memoirs of a Madman*, "the shore was adorned with foam; a large wave had already soaked the coat's silk fringe. I moved it to place it farther along; its fabric was soft and light, it was a woman's coat."

Later, at the inn, someone called out to him to thank him for his "gallantry." This portentous scene is well known, but it played such an important role in the writer's life and work that it bears repeating in his own words:

> I turned around; it was a young woman sitting at the next table with her husband.
>
> "Excuse me?" I asked her, concerned.
> "For picking up my coat; wasn't it you?"
> "Yes, Madame," I continued, embarrassed.
> She looked at me.
>
> I lowered my eyes and blushed. What a gaze, indeed! How beautiful this woman was! I can still see that ardent pupil beneath a black brow settling on me like a sun. She was tall, dark with magnificent black hair that fell in braids over her shoulders; her nose was Greek, her eyes burning, her eyebrows high and admirably arched, her skin was glowing and as if brushed with gold; she was slender and shapely, one could see azure veins snaking across that brown, rouged bosom.

Thirty years later, in *Sentimental Education*, Frédéric Moreau would meet a woman with black tresses, big eyebrows, and splendid dark skin: "It was like an apparition." She is sitting on the deck of a boat sailing from Paris to

Nogent-sur-Seine, with a "long shawl with purple stripes" hanging behind her, over the rail. "Now the fringe was pulling it down, and it was on the point of falling into the water when Frédéric leapt forward and caught it. She said: 'Thank you, Monsieur.'"[2]

Though the description of love at first sight in *Memoirs of a Madman* may be more naïve, Flaubert's great novel of 1869 is not markedly different in its content. Each morning, the narrator of *Memoirs of a Madman* returns to the beach to exult in the sight of this woman coming from her swim and to brush past her "half naked" body wearing the "scent of the waves." His heart beats violently: "I was immobile with astonishment, as if Venus had come down from her pedestal and started to walk. It was because for the first time I could feel my heart; I felt something mystical, something strange like a new sense. I was bathed in infinite, tender feelings; I was cradled by hazy, vague images; I was taller and prouder all at once." Flaubert pushes any idea of sensual pleasure aside, repeating the word *mystical*: "it was some kind of mystical sensation."

For the first time, Gustave encountered what he had dreamed of during the hours of boredom at school: a woman who captivates you with her beauty, whom you want to hold in your arms indefinitely, lavish love on, and cover in kisses. A woman from whom you would become inseparable. The "great nuptial flight." Ecstasy.

This woman, whom he called Maria in *Memoirs of a Madman*, was Élisa Foucault. Her married name was Schlésinger. She had a young daughter, whom she nursed herself, allowing Gustave to discover a woman's bare breast—"that pulsating bosom" that he would forever remember. The young man quickly hit it off with Élisa's husband, liking his demeanor as a pleasant fellow and bon vivant who played to the gallery. He saw him as a man who was "part artist and part traveling salesman." Gustave soon became close friends with the couple. They went horseback riding together and talked about literature. Gustave was pleased to learn that he and Élisa had mutual tastes. One day Maurice, the husband, invited Gustave to join them for an excursion in a rowboat. Gustave discovered powerful new emotions by being so close to her: "I was drunk with love."

"Monsieur Maurice," as Flaubert called him, was a pleasant character, both forthright and colorful. Just shy of forty, with an impressive mustache, he was physically attractive, forceful in his judgments, and an overflowing source of eloquence. A shrewd businessman, he had become a master at deceiving his clients. He was full of schemes, a con man familiar with the courts, but also jovial, quick to laugh, and a born seducer of women. He had made a reputation for himself in Paris as a successful music publisher. Maxime Du Camp described him as "a man who constantly stirred up business and had a hand in twenty operations at once, heading an important establishment in Paris, sniffing out truffles from a distance, and abandoning his wife to chase after the first petticoat to appear on the street corner, a past master at getting publicity, throwing gold coins out the window and bending over to pick up a penny."[3] One recognizes many of the traits Flaubert would give Jacques Arnoux, the publisher of *L'Art industriel* in *Sentimental Education*.

Thanks to his Prussian background (he had previously been established in Berlin), Schlésinger was acquainted with a number of German musicians, including Giacomo Meyerbeer, through whom he had met Wagner. At his store on rue de Richelieu, he also welcomed the Pole Heinrich Panofka, the Hungarian Franz Liszt, and the French composers Ludovic Halévy and Hector Berlioz. He paid poorly or not at all, but musicians let themselves be cheated because he could help them become well known in Paris. In 1834, he had launched the music journal *Gazette musicale de Paris*. Within a year, he had annexed its rival and precursor *Revue musicale*. He now headed the *Gazette et revue musicale de Paris*, which featured contributions from writers such as Eugène Scribe, Jules Janin, George Sand, Alexandre Dumas, and Balzac. Dumas had told him about the charms of Trouville, where he was a regular visitor, prompting Maurice's arrival there by post-chaise with his wife. The young Flaubert fell in love with Élisa, but he may have been equally fascinated by this man who was so familiar with litterateurs and artists, a real-life version of Balzac's "Illustrious Gaudissart," the hyperactive super-salesman who embodied the spirit of the July Monarchy.

Élisa's personality contrasted starkly with that of her profligate husband. This fervent Catholic woman inspired respect through her majestic beauty and a reserved attitude that gave her an aura of mystery. Yet when Gustave made the acquaintance of the twenty-six-year-old Élisa in Trouville, she was in fact not Madame Schlésinger but Madame Judée. Émile Gérard-Gailly's research has revealed that at the time of the dazzling first encounter in 1836, Élisa was still the legitimate wife of Émile-Jacques Judée, a lieutenant with the Train des équipages, the branch of the French army responsible for transport, whom she had wed in Vernon on November 22, 1829.[4] Their conjugal idyll had been brief: the next year, Judée, then only a sub-lieutenant, left

France for Algeria, from which he would not return until November 1835. By then, Élisa and Maurice were living together as husband and wife, and Élisa was six months pregnant. What did Judée do? Did he act like a soldier protecting his honor and ask Schlésinger to make amends? Not at all. He accepted the fait accompli and did not breathe a word of it to anyone until he died in 1839.

This story has a logical explanation. A young married man mindful of his career decides to leave for Algeria to move up the ranks through the battles of conquest, and a neglected young wife falls into the arms of a man who is passing through and impresses her with his volubility, his Parisian style, and his open admiration of her beauty. Once back in Vernon, Judée, who has been away from Élisa for five years, accepts the separation—not divorce, which was no longer legal—in exchange, one supposes, for a payment provided by her infatuated common-law husband. On this matter, René Dumesnil states categorically: "Élisa was the object of a deal; she was sold."[5]

Gérard-Gailly and his followers do not accept this chronicle of a failed marriage. They argue, first, that Élisa's religious piety makes it "impossible" to believe that she would commit the sin of adultery and, in addition, give birth to an illegitimate child. True, this is exactly what took place—but there were extenuating circumstances. For, second, why would the proud infantryman passively accept the sullying of his honor as a husband and soldier? In answering this double question, Flaubert scholars who agree with Gérard-Gailly's theory have hypothesized that on the day after his wedding, Judée committed "a major transgression, a transgression that compromised his career and reflected poorly on his wife and in-laws"—this is Dumesnil's explanation, following Gérard-Gailly almost word for word. What kind of transgression? No one knows. And how does Schlésinger's taking Élisa as his wife and having a child with her save her and her parents' "honor"? Wouldn't the "honorable" thing be to quietly wait for her husband to return? As for Élisa's virtue, its reputation rests solely on hearsay. After being abandoned by her husband for years, even the most pious woman might conceivably succumb to the charms of a gallant man who comes along to lavish gifts on her and declare his indestructible love, along with other tempting promises. It is as if in the eyes of the inventors of the "great love," Élisa has to be above any suspicion and be respected as a victim, even if that means defending poorly founded hypotheses. For it has been decided that Élisa was and would remain Flaubert's only love—that beautiful, great, and only love whose object must be a "pure" woman, above suspicion and exceptional. An icon.

When she gave birth, Élisa had to hide her name—public records identified Judée as her husband and would therefore have identified him as the father of her child. Consequently, her daughter's birth certificate read: "Marie-Adèle-Julie-Monina Schlésinger, daughter of Maurice-Adolphe Schlésinger and an unnamed mother, born April 19, 1836, in Paris, rue de Richelieu, no. 97." Élisa did not have legal guardianship of her daughter. Yet she remained under the protection of the unfaithful "Monsieur Maurice." Everything seems to indicate that she never loved him and was aware of his escapades, but that she was grateful to him for keeping the illegitimacy of their union a secret and presenting her as his lawful wife.

This was where the couple stood when Gustave Flaubert befriended "M. and Mme Schlésinger." It was only upon Judée's death in 1839 that Élisa, now a widow, was able to make the union official by marrying Schlésinger incognito, following his conversion from Judaism to Catholicism. They had a second child, Adolphe, in January 1842.

In the summer of 1836, Gustave spent a few weeks of pure joy with his new friends, under the spell of this dazzling woman whom he claimed to love without erotic arousal, though this contradicts other statements he made. The Schlésingers had a Newfoundland dog called Nero. Since the young woman liked to pet her dog, the teenage Flaubert transferred the affection he felt for the mistress to the animal: "At fifteen I wished I were a certain Newfoundland that was kissed between the ears by a lady of my acquaintance. I don't know what boneyard that doggie's skull is rotting in. But long ago it was the object of powerful lust for me, such that even an emperor's diadem might not have aroused a more ardent desire."[6] Sometimes Schlésinger's friend Panofka, who had joined him in Trouville, enlivened their evenings with his violin and left Gustave feeling languid. There were also receptions and balls, where the young man never took his eyes off that woman who moved among the guests while he wished to keep her forever by his side.

Alas! "We had to leave; we separated without being able to bid her goodbye. She left the baths the same day we did. She left in the morning, we in the evening; she left, and I did not see her again." Once the apparition had dissipated, Gustave felt "chaos" in his heart, but remained inhabited by the obsessive image of Élisa.

Back in Rouen, everything seemed "deserted and lugubrious." He returned to Trouville during other summers and looked for Élisa, in the grips of an overwhelming desire to see her again, but she had disappeared—for all time, he believed. He responded with a despairing farewell cry in *Memoirs of a Madman:*

> Do you know that I have not spent one night, not a day, not an hour, without thinking of you, without seeing you again as you came out from beneath the waves, with your black hair on your shoulders, your dark skin with its pearls of salt water, your dripping clothes and your white foot with pink nails sinking into the sand, and that this vision is always present, and that it always whispers to my heart? Oh! no, all is empty.

As was his habit, Flaubert attempted to ridicule the memory of the "sublime thing" in his tale. The buffoonery of love! Strolls by moonlight, sighs, declarations: "I believed a woman was an angel ... Oh! how right Molière was to compare her to a bowl of soup!" But *Memoirs of a Madman*'s overall tone is that of an elegiac song, touched with a "vague sadness, something indefinable and dreamy, like dying resonances."

Yet the story of Élisa does not end here. Gustave saw her again during his student years in Paris, between 1840 and 1843. He had become a man by then, a seductive one, blessed with "heroic beauty," according to Maxime Du Camp. Flaubert echoed his friend's opinion in a letter to Louise Colet: "from seventeen to nineteen . . . I was splendid . . . , sufficiently so to attract the attention of an entire theater audience—it was in Rouen, the first night of *Ruy Blas*."[7] Unhappy in her marriage, Mme Schlésinger might have been charmed by a declaration on the part of the student. His frequent visits to the Schlésingers, his constant attendance at their Wednesday gatherings, and the anonymity of the big city itself made possible a less compromising relationship than in Trouville. Did Flaubert remain a silent lover? Du Camp, who only received partial confidences from his friend, thought so: "He later found them again in Paris, persisted in admiring the husband, persisted in looking at the wife, and persisted in keeping quiet."[8] His two novels entitled *Sentimental Education,* bearing the same name but written more than twenty years apart, both feature a heroine based on Élisa but do not have the same conclusion. In the first, Henry and Emilie become lovers, while in the second, Frédéric and Mme Arnoux obey the prohibitions: moral scruples, religious obstacle, missed opportunity. Flaubert scholars are divided about which conclusion better matches reality. Émile Gérard-Gailly and René Dumesnil consider the second *Education* to be closer to the truth, while Jean Pommier,

Claude Digeon, and Jean Bruneau conjecture that Flaubert and Élisa did become lovers, finding evidence in a letter Maxime Du Camp wrote to Flaubert on June 24, 1844 ("You loved once; the second time, and it will happen, you will make yourself grow in an extraordinary fashion") and a letter Flaubert wrote to Louise Colet on October 8, 1846 ("I had only one true passion").[9] But neither letter is conclusive, and Maxime Du Camp's memoirs report that Flaubert kept mum on the subject during his years in Paris. The mystery remains. At any rate, the relationship's significance lies elsewhere. Whether consummated or not, this first love, Flaubert's "great love," remained so deeply rooted in him that it would inspire the 1869 masterpiece, the second *Sentimental Education*, and this final scene where the aging Mme Arnoux comes to say her goodbyes to Frédéric:

> Frédéric suspected that Madame Arnoux had come to offer herself to him; and once again he was filled with desire, a frenzied, rabid lust such as he had never known before. Yet he also had another, indefinable feeling, a repugnance akin to a dread of committing incest. Another fear restrained him—the fear of being disgusted later.[10]

While Élisa's fictional fate is not debatable, one can legitimately seek to determine the relationship between literary creation and real life. Flaubert scholar Jacques-Louis Douchin has questioned the idea of the "great love."[11] A reader of *Memoirs of a Madman* might already pick up a contradiction: while the narrative initially describes love at first sight, the author ultimately lets slip that the illuminations of love only came to him after the fact, once Maria/ Élisa had walked away. Douchin also aptly points out that while the enraptured lover of Élisa wrote to his friends about everything under the sun, he never said a word about her. And why did he wait more than two years to find her after enrolling at law school in Paris in 1841? What a quiet passion! As an admiring reader of *The Sorrows of Young Werther*, wouldn't the adolescent Flaubert have dreamed of loving a Charlotte to the point of losing his mind? Could it be that it was love of love rather than love of Madame Schlésinger that drove him to create the legend of a romantic love—an impossible but oh-so-poetic love, which he would marvelously exploit in his fiction, culminating with his 1869 masterpiece? In his 1909 book on Flaubert, René Descharmes expressed early doubts about this *amour fou:* "He found in himself the feelings described in books. . . . Perhaps he had endeavored to experience them, to model his passion after those of Byron's, Goethe's, and Chateaubriand's heroes, to give himself the illusion that he shared their state of being and that, like them, he endured love in its most complete form."

In any case, this combination of embellished memory and romantic imitation remained a source of inspiration for Flaubert. His poetic bent would make the most of it in the otherwise highly ironic *Sentimental Education*.

Sexual Education

After the departure of Maria/Élisa, *Memoirs of a Madman* turns to Flaubert's love games with Caroline-Anne Heuland, a young Englishwoman who attended boarding school with his sister Caroline. Jacques-Louis Douchin notes that the pages of *Memoirs of a Madman* devoted to Caroline-Anne appear more credibly authentic than the passages on the "great love": "One day she lay down on my couch in a very ambiguous position; I was seated close to her and didn't say a word." On another occasion, she calls to him from her window while her mother is away and asks him to come upstairs. In short: "She was alone, she threw herself into my arms and kissed me effusively; it was to be the last time, for she has since married." A brief fling: "Maria's gaze overshadowed any memory of that pale child."

Flaubert tells us that vanity drove him to lose his virginity while he was still at the Collège Royal: "They mocked me for my chastity, I blushed, I was ashamed of it, it weighed on me as if it were some kind of corruption." The account in *Memoirs* is discreet, only describing the remorse after the rite of passage: "A woman presented herself before me, I took her; and I came out of her arms full of disgust and bitterness . . . as if Maria's love were a religion I had profaned." Some of the details have been filled in by the Goncourt brothers, whom Flaubert would regularly visit and confide in during his stays in Paris. Their *Journal* for the date February 20, 1860, reveals that Flaubert had "[lost] his innocence with his mother's chambermaid."[12] Always a sleuth, Jacques-Louis Douchin wondered about the identity of this chambermaid, who is not mentioned anywhere else. Perhaps Flaubert had been ashamed to admit that his first lover was a professional in a Rouen brothel? "Disgust" or, at the very least, disappointment, are likely if one believes Flaubert's confidences to Ernest Chevalier: "I went to the brothel for some fun and was merely bored."[13]

Yet in *November,* the autobiographical novel he wrote in 1842, he recounts the anticipation of sex in passionate, nearly purple prose. He took pleasure in brushing against prostitutes, in visiting the streets they frequented, and in occasionally talking to them, but never went further. He surrendered to dreams of lust and sank into a "bottomless despondency." Driven by the violence of desire, seized with the need to love, fascinated by "adultery," he was saddened that he could not take a woman into his arms. In smoldering passages, he describes the desire that came out of "all his pores," the way he stared at the women he met and was permeated by their odor. "Though they were clothed, I immediately decorated them with a magnificent nudity." In her introduction to *November*, Claudine Gothot-Mersch notes that "it is striking how this twenty-year-old boy is able to analyze the awakening of sexuality in the adolescent he has barely left behind."[14]

An allusion to rue de la Cigogne in his *Cahier intime* [*Intimate Notebook*] suggests that the successful baccalaureate candidate paid a visit to a brothel located on that Rouen street. But it was probably in Marseille, in late October 1840, that Gustave finally experienced the sensual pleasures of which he had dreamed.

After his undoubted disappointment at his offspring's expulsion from the Collège Royal, Achille-Cléophas Flaubert was so pleased that Gustave had passed his baccalaureate that he treated him to a long trip through the south of France and Corsica from August 22 to November 1, 1840. Though the surgeon sometimes fell asleep while Gustave read his prose to him, he was not a philistine interested only in his field. While on vacation in Nogent-sur-Seine a week after Gustave's departure, he wrote to his son: "I am pleased to see that diligence did not tire you and that you are lively of body; do what it takes to ensure this continues and that your mind always remains gay and your heart as good as we know it to be. Take advantage of your trip and remember your friend Montaigne, who wants us to travel principally to bring back nations' humors and their manners, and to rub 'our brains against other people's.' See, observe, and take notes; do not travel as a grocer or a traveling salesman."

Though his advice was probably superfluous, it shows that this somewhat distant father was no stranger to Gustave's education and his intellectual standards. The other striking aspect of the correspondence between Flaubert and his family over the course of the trip is the gentle affection that prevails. The mother's tender words, his sister "Caro's" teasing affection, and the traveler's own messages reveal the extent to which Gustave was a deeply loved son and brother—which his autobiographical tales hardly suggest. Before the great bereavements that would affect him, the young Flaubert seemed to have everything necessary to be happy, as Du Camp had told him. We know today that he was not happy, but he pulled the wool over everyone's eyes with his buffoonery, his impersonations, and his tall tales. This is how his mother liked to think of him; she wrote him that in Nogent the "big nonsense-talker" was missed, along with his "pranks," which she admitted some found "tedious," but hastened to add: "As for me, I will never have enough and you can be sure that when you return I will continue to laugh, like a silly fool, at everything you say."[15]

Flaubert did not set off on this journey alone. His guide, Dr. Cloquet, was a former student of Dr. Flaubert and now a professor of clinical surgery in Paris. A few years earlier, he had taken the eldest of the Flauberts' sons, Achille, on an expedition to Scotland. This mentor was accompanied by his sister Lise and his friend Father Stefani, an Italian priest. Aside from the few surviving letters written by the young tourist, we have the travel narrative that he began in Bordeaux and finished after his return to Rouen, *Pyrénées– Corse 22 août–1er novembre 1840* [*Pyrenees–Corsica August 22 to November 1st, 1840*]. Other allusions to the trip were made in his *Intimate Notebook* of 1840–1841.

At the time, the French railroad was still in its infancy—it would only fully develop under the Second Empire. The travelers left for Bordeaux by stage-coach, passing through Tours and Angoulême. "Bordeaux resembles Rouen in its stupid and bourgeois sides," Flaubert wrote to his "good rat," his sister Caroline. The Garonne had muddy water, the porcelain factory exploited children and young women who were crammed in beneath its window panes, and the graves in the cemetery were "more stupid than the deceased living." Ultimately, what he most appreciated about the capital of the department of Gironde was that its municipal library gave him access to Montaigne's manuscript—the "Bordeaux copy"—of the *Essays*. He touched it with "as much veneration as if it were a religious relic."

After Bordeaux came Bayonne, which he "adored," and the Adour River under a setting sun. He wanted to see Biarritz, which he had heard was beautiful. The stopover took a dark turn when the travelers found a swimmer on the beach calling for help for two drowning men. Gustave immediately removed his coat and unbuttoned his ankle boots with the assistance of a sobbing mother dressed in black. Bearing her blessings, he plunged into the water and swam as fast as possible toward the spot he had been shown. Gustave was an excellent swimmer, but the waves were too strong for him. His efforts proved in vain. The two bodies were later brought to shore, to the great despair of the woman in black. People surrounded Flaubert, lent him a pair of peasant trousers, and then forgot him after ten minutes. "As I deserved," he modestly added.[16]

From Bayonne, the travelers took a side trip to Spain along the Bidasoa River, which led them to Hondarribia, then back up to Irun. The rest of the itinerary brought them to Pau and Cauterets, with excursions to Gaube Lake and Gavarnie—the "most beautiful" thing Flaubert saw in the Pyrenees. He squabbled a little with Dr. Cloquet, a strict follower of the *Guide du Voyageur* guidebook: "Is it my fault if I'm bored by what is called *interesting* and annoyed by the *most curious?*"[17] But the quartet got along fairly well. It was a comfortable, bourgeois trip, far from a backpacker's adventure. They slept in nice inns and often dined at the homes of Dr. Cloquet's friends, who treated the visitors to generous meals. Then came Bagnères-de-Bigorre, Saint-Bertrand-de-Comminges, and Bagnères-de-Luchon, on the way to Toulouse. Once there, the travelers embarked on the Canal du Midi, passed through Castelnaudary, Carcassonne—where they stopped over—Narbonne, Nîmes, the Pont du Gard, and Arles. "You cannot imagine the Roman monuments, my dear Caroline, and the pleasure I derived from the sight of the Arena." He became increasingly enchanted by the trip, which found the little group arriving in Marseille on September 27. Two days later they headed to Toulon, and from there, to Corsica.

The Mediterranean filled Gustave with joy—the azure sky, the sea's limpid water, the warm air, the people's kindness. "I like the Mediterranean. There is something grave and tender about it that evokes Greece, something immense and voluptuous that evokes the Orient."[18] In terms of beauty, the best was yet to come. Corsica would reveal itself to him like Venus rising from the clear waters of the Aegean. Flaubert was dazzled. Having landed at Ajaccio, the travelers were welcomed by Prefect Jourdan, who had administered the department for ten years and knew it like the back of his hand. He offered endless advice, corrected their preconceived notions, and gave them a foretaste of the hospitality they would enjoy throughout their trip across the island. Early in the morning of October 7, they left on horseback with their guide Captain Laurelli, following twisting and turning paths through the maquis, and arrived in Vico after a ten-hour journey.

Flaubert's narrative of the crossing of Corsica via Corte is noteworthy not only for its description of fragrant landscapes and near-virgin nature. Flaubert speaks of the Corsicans as an ethnologist, with a quality inherent to the profession: sympathy. "One must not judge Corsican customs with our petty European ideas," he wrote, forgetting that Corsica was part of France. After Mérimée and before Maupassant, he brought an aesthete's fascination to his discovery of local customs—the fierce honor of Corsican bandits, which drove them to vendettas, trials in absentia, and clandestine wandering, the hardness of local traditions, daughters married off without being consulted, and men's lives spent hunting, "a life of laziness, pride, and grandeur."[19] Here was the "noble savage," the resistance to civilization. And what an explosion of light, of scents, of beauty! Having returned via Bastia, Flaubert would never forget this immersion in the island's natural beauty.

On the way home, Flaubert had his first sexual encounter while staying with his companions at the Hôtel Richelieu in Marseille. Of the several descriptions of this amorous encounter, the account he gave to the Goncourt brothers is the most precise:

> He happened on a little hotel in Marseille where some women from Lima had arrived with sixteenth-century ebony furniture inlaid with mother-of-pearl at which everyone who saw it marveled. Three women in silk dressing-gowns falling in a straight line from the back to the heels, together with a little Negro dressed in nankeen and wearing Turkish slippers. . . .
>
> One day, coming back from a bathe in the Mediterranean and bringing with him all the life of that Fountain of Youth, he was invited into her bedroom by one of the women, a magnificent woman of thirty-five. He gave her one of those kisses into which one puts all one's soul. The woman came to his room that night and started by sucking him. There followed an orgy of delight.[20]

The young woman had brought him to previously unknown transports of pleasure. But it was only to last one night.

Several of Flaubert's texts deal with his encounter with this woman, Eulalie Foucaud, who managed the hotel with her mother. Strangely, through an unlikely coincidence, or "objective chance," the enchantress's family name was almost the same as that of Élisa—Foucaud and Foucault. One had revealed love to him; the other now introduced him to flesh: "Oh! flesh, flesh!" he wrote in his *Intimate Notebook*, "a demon who constantly returns, tears the book out of your hands and the gaiety out of your heart, makes you dark, fierce, egotistical, and *sui gaudens* [self-satisfied]; we repel him, he returns, we drunkenly give in to him, we rush in, we spread out, the nostril flares, the muscle draws tight, the heart throbs, we fall back with our eyes wet, dismayed, shattered. That's life: hope and disappointment."[21]

Flaubert would not forget Eulalie. As for her, she was taken with the young man and wrote him ardent letters, four of which have survived: "Why were we granted to love each other, to know the heavens' felicity through each other, since we were so soon to leave each other, and especially since you were so quick to forget me."[22] Flaubert would explain his answer to her in a letter to Louise Colet in 1846: "When I was eighteen, back from a trip to the Midi, I wrote similar letters for six months to a woman I didn't love. I did it to force myself to love her, to play a role with conviction."[23] Louise Colet's cousin needed to travel to Marseille; Gustave imprudently requested that Louise ask her cousin to check whether Madame Foucaud still lived there. The previous year, he had passed through Marseille on his way to Italy and seen that Eulalie and her mother no longer ran the Hôtel Richelieu, which was now dilapidated. He had looked no further, but spurred on by memory, wanted to entrust Louise's cousin with a letter. Louise was concerned. Gustave should have known better—he knew her well enough! "Why are you taking offense in advance about a note I intend to send to Madame Foucaud? . . . I'm telling you: look, this is who I loved in the past, and you are the one I love now." Whether out of trust or perversity, he had Louise read the letter, while confessing, "I fear you will be saddened by it again. I obeyed the impulse to write to this woman." And once she had read it, he was surprised: "So you found my letter a little tender? I hadn't suspected it." And repeated: "When I wrote her with the faculty I have of being moved by my quill, I took my subject seriously but *only while I wrote*." Louise Colet came back to the charge; he had to promise her that he had *"never loved her."*[24]

Yet this non-love for Eulalie was so significant a memory that it would resonate in his work on several occasions, beginning with *November*. In this autobiographical novel, Eulalie became Marie—a courtesan with the Romantic traits of the "ideal whore" (Goncourt), pure and virtuous despite the profession into which she had fallen. As in real life, the encounter between the narrator and Marie is brief but intense. Physically, she resembles Maria, who was inspired by Élisa: the same olive skin, the same black hair, the same large, arched eyebrows. But this time the story goes beyond feverish, innocent swooning:

Her hot, trembling skin stretched beneath me, and shivered; from head to toe, I felt covered in sensuality; my mouth stuck to hers, our fingers laced together, rocked by the same thrill, intertwined in the same embrace; inhaling the smell of her hair and the breath of her lips, I felt myself die deliciously. I paused for a time, gaping, savoring the beating of my heart and the last quiver of my agitated nerves; then it seemed to me that everything was extinguished and disappeared.

The narrator only sees Marie once more, on the evening of their first encounter, exactly as in the Marseille episode. Aside from the "splendors of the flesh," she offers him a long confession, explaining how she became a lady of the night through a vain quest for love: "I hoped that one day, someone would come ..." She kisses him, holds him tight: "I felt pulled into a hurricane of love." The narrative comes to an abrupt end: "I never saw her again"—an improbable narrative twist, but one that echoed what had really happened in Marseille when Flaubert had had to leave with his traveling companions the morning after his initiation night.

November was an important step in Flaubert's work. The novel would remain unpublished; its weaknesses were blatant even to the author, who criticized it for lacking in stylistic coherence. Yet despite poor dialogue, romantic clichés, and the clumsy use of two narrators (the second narrator discovers the first one's manuscript after his death), many passages are successful—particularly that of the narrator's arrival at the prostitute's place—and the psychological analysis is subtle.[25] Flaubert specialists have seen *November* as the maturation of an author writing with increasingly frequent but intermittent beauty. As its title suggests—the name of a month heralding winds, dark skies, and winter fogs—*November,* which is inspired by Goethe's *Werther* and Chateaubriand's *René,* is still haunted by his obsession with loneliness, boredom, and death. "Why," Flaubert asked himself, "is man's heart so big and life so small?"

CHAPTER 4

A Change of Direction

Once Flaubert had passed his baccalaureate, there was no escaping the fate he dreaded: he had to leave for Paris to study law. Those who knew him thought he might aim for the Council of State, France's supreme court of appeal for administrative law courts. His friend Ernest Chevalier was on his way to the magistracy. He could also seek to become a lawyer, a notary, or a bailiff, the professions from which most parliamentary deputies were recruited. A political career was conceivable. But Paris was also the citadel of literary and artistic ambition. The "cold prison of the provinces" (Balzac) stifled strong souls, bold spirits, and daring hearts. It did not deaden passions—small-town rivalries could be fierce—but it set limits to one's dreams. In this respect, France was unique. Paris dominated the country and sucked all the blood out of the provinces. This was the product of an old story stretching back over centuries, from the Capetian monarchy to the Napoleonic empire. Its chapters were the successive steps in the rise of a city chosen as the country's capital, a city where everything would eventually be concentrated: political bodies, cultural hubs, and the boldest economic ventures. Even the least ambitious worked the obligatory move to Paris into their plans. Balzac, a key historian of the great Paris centrifuge, sums up the situation in the preface to *Le Cabinet des Antiques* [*The Collection of Antiquities*]:

> In the provinces there are three kinds of superior types who quickly leave for Paris, inevitably impoverishing provincial society, which is powerless before this constant misfortune. Aristocracy, Industry, and Talent are eternally attracted to Paris, which thus swallows up the capacities that are born at every point in the kingdom and uses them to compose its strange population, parching the national intelligence in its own favor. The provinces bear

most of the guilt for this impetus that despoils them. Should a young man appear and raise great hopes, he is immediately told: to Paris![1]

Paris was also reputed for being a sprawling city in which one could escape the monitoring of fellow citizens, the leagues of virtue, and the gossip of neighbors, all of whom saw the capital as a new Babylon where debauchery reigned supreme and perdition was guaranteed. "Paris is a truly dangerous place for the young."[2] Strutting one's stuff in the foyers of the Opéra or the Théâtre des Funambules, taking mistresses, having orgies with courtesans, losing oneself in a maze of pleasures: this was what fed the dreams of young provincial people who one fine day took the royal messenger service stagecoach and landed with heart aflutter in that center of sin, decried by morality and religion.[3] Their steps were guided by freedom as much as ambition.

But Gustave was not like Balzac's determined Rastignac. In a letter sent to Ernest before he had even earned his baccalaureate, he wrote: "To go to Paris, all alone, to study law, lost among lockpickers and ladies of the night, where you'll probably buy me a coffee at the *Colonnades dorées* or some dirty whore at *La Chaumière*. No thank you. Vice bores me as much as virtue."[4]

To Paris

Fourteen months passed between Flaubert's return from Corsica in early November 1840 and his departure for Paris, though there is little to explain this delay. In January 1841, Gustave again told Ernest Chevalier how little enthusiasm he harbored for the education to which he had resigned himself: "You tell me to tell you what my dreams are?—Not one!—My plans for the future!—None. What do I want to be? Nothing, following a maxim of the philosopher who wrote: 'Hide your life and die.' I am tired of dreams, annoyed by plans, sick of thinking about the future. And as for being *something*, I will be as little as possible."

These qualms were not the only reason for his slowness. If we are to believe a letter sent to the same friend on July 7, 1841, Gustave's health may have been responsible for his extended stay in the family home. He refers to the physical transformation he is undergoing and reports that he has become colossal, enormous, fat: "All I do is pant for breath, . . . sweat, and slobber. I am a chyle-machine, a device that makes blood to strike and lash my face and shit that stinks and smears my ass." He was as bored as ever as he followed the family routines: Les Andelys in April, Trouville in August, Nogent-sur-Seine to visit his uncle Parain. Deprived of sun and love, he continued to amuse Caro and his mother, but his heart wasn't in it. Early in January 1842, having escaped from military service by the luck of a random draw, he said his goodbyes to the family and took the stagecoach to Paris (the Paris-Rouen rail line did not open until May 1843). He reached the capital on the morning of January 8 and checked in to the Hôtel de l'Europe, on rue Le Peletier. He finally found more permanent accommodations in July, when he moved in to Ernest Chevalier's former apartment at 35, rue de l'Odéon after his friend had received his doctorate in law and begun his career in the magistrature. In the meantime, Flaubert traveled back and forth between Paris and Rouen. He purchased law books but did not study them, choosing instead to busy himself with Greek and Latin and continuing work on *November*, which he would complete in late October. He confessed to his former teacher Gourgaud-Dugazon that he did not see himself as a future lawyer destined to argue cases about shared walls. "When people speak to me about the bar, saying 'This young fellow will make a fine trial lawyer,' because I'm broad in the shoulders and have a booming voice, I confess it turns my stomach. I don't feel myself made for such a completely materialistic, trivial life."[5] He remained obsessed with only one thing: writing!

His life in Paris began with idleness. The two versions of *Sentimental Education*, in which Flaubert probably put much of his own experience, provide quite a clear picture of this period. Like Gustave, Henry, the first version's protagonist, studies law and is far from diligent about attending class. He roams the streets, visits the Jardin des Plantes, takes walks in the Palais Royal by day and on the boulevards by night, lingers by the stalls of the second-hand booksellers along the Seine, stops by the street peddlers on the Champs Elysées, crosses Paris by omnibus, dallies in cafés, and ends his day in front of his fireplace. In the 1869 *Sentimental Education*, Frédéric Moreau experiences a similar lack of activity in the first days after his arrival. Yet Gustave soon developed a taste for society life, thanks to his former guide Dr. Cloquet and other friends of the family. He was reunited with the Schlésingers, who ran an open house, and dined at their home every Wednesday. He enlarged his circle of acquaintances and got back in touch with former classmates from Rouen, including Hamard, his future brother-in-law.

In July, while his family enjoyed Trouville, Gustave laboriously crammed for his law examination. It took three years to earn a degree. The first-year curriculum included the Civil Code and the *Institutes* of Justinian. He wrote to his sister that "the lowing of steers is undoubtedly more literary than the law professors' lessons; the torn clothes of fishermen, restitched with blue and white thread, are more beautiful than the ermine-fringed robes of doctors of law." Studying the Code was killing him, stupefying him, making him "sweat blood." He couldn't take it anymore. He grumbled, he moaned, he groused. Soon he learned that despite his best efforts he might not even pass the first exam: to do so, he needed to present a certificate attesting that he had faithfully attended classes, which would be hard to do given that he had regularly played hooky. Nonetheless, he continued to slave away through July and found solace in writing to his dear Caro, who gave him news from the seaside. He predicted that when she saw him next, she would only find "a residue of Gustave." Then came failure: his papers were not in order, he would have to take the exam in December. He immediately took off for Trouville.

Delighted to be back by the sea, he swam, smoked his pipe, stretched out in the sun, swam again, and delved back into Ronsard, Rabelais, and the literary journals. He continued to deplore what awaited him with the start of the school year: "Oh usufruct, oh servitude, how I screw you today but how you will soon re-screw me." He spent the early fall in Rouen, where he told Ernest that he had just caught crabs. In November, he was back in Paris. He moved in to an apartment on rue de l'Est, which he set about furnishing with Hamard, a gifted haggler. This time, he attended his classes and slogged away, but he continued to dine out, notably at the home of the Colliers, English family friends who lived on the Champs Elysées. Caroline had met them in Trouville in July 1842, and Gustave liked to flirt with their two daughters, Gertrude and Henriette. For his regular meals, he made a deal with a cheap neighborhood restaurant, where he ate mediocre daily fare. Though his dining arrangement was economical, his moving expenses had left him short of money. He asked Caroline to appeal to their father to send him a money order. A few weeks before the exam, a horrible toothache reduced him to tears. Coirac, a dentist on rue du Mail, warned him that he had not felt the last of his dental pains: he would probably soon lose all of his teeth. "I want to send law school packing once and for all," he wrote to his "good rat" Caroline, "and never set foot there again. Sometimes it makes me break out into a cold sweat that could kill a man. Good God, what fun I'm having in Paris, and what an enjoyable young man's life I lead here!" Enough with the toothaches, the crummy restaurant's leathery beef and acidic wine, and the law drilling that was turning him into a halfwit! Caro tried to cheer him up by sending tender letters; he answered that he was still thinking about the Garçon and that he had invented entirely new things for him to do, "destined to have the greatest success." But she should realize that Paris was not a land of plenty for everyone! This time, his mortification, torture, and insomnia paid off: on December 28, Flaubert passed his first-year law exam.

He was glad to be reunited with his family in Rouen for New Year's Day. How happy they were together, laughing, playing dominos, telling stories by the fire. But he could not avoid returning to Paris on February 8, 1843, to begin the second year of his degree. That year's curriculum consisted of the next part of the Civil Code, criminal law, and the criminal procedure code. Gustave balked again, choosing instead to begin a new novel, which he entitled *Sentimental Education*.

Maxime Du Camp

Of the new friends Flaubert made in Paris, Maxime Du Camp was undoubtedly the one who best distracted him from his dreary existence. Like Gustave, young Maxime was a nonchalant law student who was crazy about literature. They met in March 1843, at the home of their mutual friend Ernest Le Marié, a former classmate at the Collège Royal de Rouen. Du Camp was the same age as Flaubert and was preparing to embark on a literary career. Over the following year, he began to publish columns and serials in various newspapers. The portrait he left of Gustave in *Souvenirs littéraires*, the literary memoir he published after Flaubert's death, suggests a personality that, however lyrical and romantic, has little in common with the gloomy hero of Flaubert's autobiographical novels: "He was heroically beautiful. . . . With his white skin and slightly pink cheeks, his long flowing hair, his broad-shouldered tall stature, his abundant golden-blond beard, his enormous sea-green eyes sheltered under black eyebrows, with his voice resounding like a trumpet, his exaggerated gestures and ringing laugh, he resembled those young Gallic chiefs who fought the Roman armies."[6] In other words, a young man poorly suited to law studies, to which he devoted himself so as not to upset his father, but without attention or method. At home, he mechanically copied over the books on the curriculum, without retaining a word; in the lecture hall, he took notes just as mechanically, discovering that they were incomprehensible when he later reread them. Life was elsewhere, first and foremost in friendship. Aside from Alfred Le Poittevin and Maxime Du Camp, Gustave befriended Du Camp's friend Louis de Cormenin, whose father, a deputy from Ain and a confirmed liberal, wrote pamphlets under the pseudonym of Timon. The four young men dined together and spent long evenings discussing everything from theology to literature, with the exception of politics. Flaubert continued to curse Louis Philippe and his bourgeois regime, but he was nevertheless not a republican, contrary to what he had once proclaimed; he openly mocked Guizot's and Lamartine's speeches before the Chamber of Deputies. Du Camp soon marveled at the knowledge of this young Norman who had read everything, could remember everything, and was a one-man "living dictionary." Gustave amused his friends with his jokes and also with his remarkable gift for impressions. Still a theater lover, he delighted them with his imitations of the actress Marie Dorval, whom he had seen in *Antony* in Rouen. In short, he was the perfect companion, the life of the party, who hid his fundamental gentleness under a mask of thundering fierceness. As for women, who found him physically attractive, he claimed to be done with them.

One evening, Flaubert asked Du Camp to come up to his apartment. He needed to talk to him about something. He had never admitted to Maxime that he wrote. That night, he invited him to discover *November,* reading it aloud to him in a single sitting. His friend was enthralled, charmed, admiring: "Finally," he wrote, "a great writer is born to us, and I was receiving the good news." From that day on, the two friends were inseparable. They shared every enthusiasm and plan. According to Du Camp, Flaubert had two literary masters at the time: Chateaubriand, for his *René,* and Quinet, for his *Ahasvérus,* from which he could recite entire monologues. Du Camp already noticed his preoccupation with harmony, even at the cost of good grammar: "What we say is nothing, the way that we say it is everything; a work of art that seeks to prove something is nothing for that reason alone."[7]

At the same time, Flaubert was thirsty for knowledge, to the point that he and Du Camp seriously considered writing an encyclopedia, beginning with *Les Transmissions du Latin* [*The Transmissions of Latin*], a dictionary that would provide every derived meaning of Latin words in all the European languages that had adapted them. This was not the first manifestation of Gustave's craving for erudition—though it did not extend to the Civil Code.

His law studies suffered from his enthusiasms; once again, he was skipping classes, particularly since he continued to socialize outside of his quartet of friends. He enjoyed visiting James Pradier, a neoclassical sculptor and relative of Dr. Cloquet who was an acquaintance of the Flaubert family; Pradier would later create busts of Caroline and Dr. Flaubert. In his *Souvenirs*, the often sharp-tongued Du Camp reports a friend's bon mot: "Every morning, Pradier sets off for Athens, but he stops along the way and never gets any further than Notre-Dame-de-Lorette." But Flaubert, who called him Phidias, considered him "a great artist, yes, a great artist, a real Greek, the most ancient of all the moderns."[8] Pradier is responsible for the statues representing Lille and Strasbourg on the Place de la Concorde in Paris and the statue of Rousseau in Geneva. The lively Mme Pradier entertained on Sundays; Gustave enjoyed her soirées and made new acquaintances there. It was here that he would meet his future mistress Louise Colet, but first the Pradiers introduced him to Victor Hugo: "What can I tell you?" he wrote to his sister Caroline on December 3, 1843. "He is a man who looks like any other, with a rather ugly face and a rather common appearance. He has magnificent teeth, a superb forehead, no eyelashes or eyebrows. He talks little, gives the impression of being on his guard and not wanting to give himself away; he is very polite and a little stiff. I greatly like the sound of his voice. I enjoyed watching him from close by; I looked at him with astonishment, as I would at a casket of gold and royal diamonds, thinking of everything that has come out of him—that man who was sitting on a little chair beside me; I kept looking at his right hand, which has written so many splendid things."[9] To Flaubert, there was only one "great poet" of the century, and that was "Father Hugo." He would later qualify his judgment, but at the time it was unreserved. The two men would begin a correspondence in 1853, when Hugo was a political exile on the isle of Jersey. Flaubert was still unknown, but Louise Colet was a recognized woman of letters, and she asked Hugo to write to her care of Flaubert. In June 1853, Gustave received the first of two envelopes to deliver to Louise. He did not fail to remind Hugo that he had met him at the Pradiers': "There were five or six of us; we drank tea and played 'the game of the goose'; I even remember your large gold ring, with its engraved lion rampant, which we used as a stake."[10] They would meet again.

During his stays in Paris, Gustave never forgot about Caro, Carolo, Caroline, the good little sister, the darling whom he missed. One cannot help being moved by the big brother's tender feelings expressed for the "good rat" in their spontaneous, merry letters. Caro reports to him on doings with the family and in Rouen; he sends her his Parisian review. Yet in both their cases, sadness sometimes shows through the witticisms and jokes. The Schlésingers come up: Caroline reads Maurice's musical review, and Gustave is invited to their home for lavish meals that he cannot fully enjoy because of his teeth, those painful teeth that force him to chew on one side of his jaw. The siblings constantly remind each other of their next chance to see each other: "You cannot imagine," she writes, "what the house is like without you."

On May 4, 1843, the sun rose on a big day: the railroad between Paris and Rouen was to be inaugurated. A banquet was prepared, tents were raised, and Caroline wanted to be sure not to miss any of the spectacle: jousts, equestrian displays, races, fireworks, thousands of people squeezing in. From Paris, her big brother told her what poison the railroad was: people spoke of nothing else. "Never had the capital of Neustria caused such a stir in Lutetia," he wrote, using the Frankish terms for Normandy and Paris. Flaubert saw the railroad as an instrument of the modernity he loathed. He would take the train—one had to live in one's time—but would always seize the opportunity to inveigh against it. His father barely lived long enough to use it, but it inspired a fear in him that would also be expressed by contemporary savants such as the physicist François Arago. Dr. Flaubert was so fearful of the train that, though he did take it to Paris a few times, he would disembark at the station in Rolleboise and ride a cart to the next station to wait there for another train, so as to avoid a tunnel between the two stations.[11]

For the moment, Gustave crammed like a maniac, went back to his lectures but did not listen, moped around in criminal law, dreamed of the grass and copses of his Normandy, and dulled the torments of law school by remembering happy times he had spent with his sister: "You, for example, my good baby rat, I have in my ears your resounding and gentle laugh, that laugh for which I could kill myself with buffoonery, for which I would give my last prank, my last drop of saliva. To the extent that sometimes when I am alone in my room, I make faces at myself in the mirror or let out the Garçon's cry, as if you were there to admire me."[12]

Although he was tempted to return to Rouen for a few days now that his native city was a mere two hours from Paris by railroad, Gustave resisted: if he went, he would have too much trouble getting back to work. But then again, why not. It would be too dumb to miss out on "a few enjoyable quarters of an hour." He went for the feast of Saint-Jean, then darted back to Paris to wear himself down studying for the August exam. His toothaches, probably due to neuralgia, were giving him hell. Finally, he learned he would take the test on August 21.

According to Maxime Du Camp, Flaubert spent extravagantly in Paris; he regularly had to ask his father for "pocket change." In July, Achille-Cléophas gently scolded his son: "You're a fool twice over, first to let yourself be swindled like a hick who allows himself to be taken in by captains of industry and courtesans, who should only prey on simpletons and senile imbeciles (and thank God you are neither stupid nor old); your second fault is not to have confidence in me."[13] He asked him to go a little easier on his resources, but especially to tell him straight out what he was spending his money on. As Gustave wrote to Carolo, it was time for all this to come to an end.

Unfortunately, it all came to a bad end. On the day of the test, Flaubert asked Maxime Du Camp to encourage him with his presence. "He put on the gown," writes Du Camp, "slipped the neckband under his golden beard and did not feel reassured. It was a pathetic performance. . . . He was most distressed. He said: It's a memory problem. Not at all. That brain, crammed full of art and poetry, had been unable, despite his efforts, to assimilate arbitrary maxims whose mere form upset and exasperated him." That very evening, Gustave left Paris seething with rage and joined his parents in Nogent-sur-Seine.

The Turning Point

In the fall, he returned to the infernal capital to attempt to pass his end-of-year exam. We do not know the details of that test, other than that it also ended in failure. Though Gustave already felt that his law studies had come to an end, it took a serious health problem in January 1844 to make Dr. Flaubert relent. The doctor had acquired a plot of land in Deauville on which to build a cottage. His two sons had gone to inspect the property. On the trip back, while he was driving the cabriolet, Gustave was struck by what he would refer to in one of his letters as a "cerebral congestion." Nearly a decade later, he reminisced about the incident in a letter to Louise Colet: "The last time I passed this way was with my brother, in January '44, when I fell, as if struck with apoplexy, into the bottom of the cabriolet I was driving, and for ten minutes he thought I was dead." Achille carried him to a house by the road and immediately bled him, then brought him back to Rouen. "They bled me in three places at once and I finally opened my eyes," he wrote to Ernest Chevalier on February 1. "My father wants to keep me here a long time and observe me carefully; my morale is good, however, because I don't know what worry is. I'm in a rotten state; at the slightest excitement, all my nerves quiver like violin strings, my knees, my shoulders, and my belly tremble like leaves."[14] He went back to Paris, but had another attack in February and returned to his family. The young man was put on a strict diet, denied tobacco, oppressed by constant bloodletting (as was still advised by the Broussais school), and prescribed leeches and orange-flower water. He was miserable but put on a brave face. Du Camp reports that one day when his father "had just bled Gustave and the blood was not appearing in the vein in his arm, he had hot water poured on Gustave's hand; in their alarm, they did not notice that the water was nearly boiling, and the poor soul was given a second degree burn from which he suffered cruelly." There was no longer any question of returning to Paris any time soon, other than to collect his belongings and give his landlord notice. But first he would go to take in the sea air at Tréport; the entire family set out on April 25.

Over the years, many questions have been raised about Flaubert's illness. The January 1844 attack was followed by others, occurring sporadically. Maxime Du Camp reported witnessing some of these attacks. Gustave would suddenly become very pale, run to lie down, and be seized with convulsions: "This paroxysm in which his whole being was trembling was invariably succeeded by a deep sleep and an aching stiffness that lasted several days. . . . He only felt safe at home."[15] With time, the fits became rarer, but it is not impossible that his death in 1880 was due to such an incident. It was later determined that he suffered from epilepsy, or fits of an "epileptiform nature."[16]

Did Flaubert's illness have an effect on his literary work? Some, including Du Camp, have maintained that it was responsible for the extreme slowness with which he wrote his books: "It was from this moment that his inconceivable difficulty with working dated, a difficulty which he seemed to apply himself to intensifying, and which he ultimately took pride in." Behind this judgment one might suspect the ill-will and jealousy of Gustave's old friend, who concludes: "Gustave Flaubert was a writer of rare talent; without the nervous illness that struck him, he would have been a man of genius."

In fact, Flaubert's nervous illness, which would diminish over the following years, played an entirely different role in shaping his life. From then on, he was relieved from studying a subject that horrified him and tormented him with the idea that he would become a public prosecutor or lawyer. Thanks to his parents' fortune, he was a man of independent means who could devote himself to literature. The most radical interpretation on this subject is the one put forward by Jean-Paul Sartre in *The Family Idiot*. Sartre dismisses the epilepsy diagnosis and replaces it with that of neurosis, as had previously been suggested by René Dumesnil, who thought Flaubert suffered from hysterical-neurasthenic neurosis.[17] Sartre concurred, but added that the neurosis should be understood as the "murder of the father." It resolved the dilemma that Gustave was faced with—the conflict between the necessary obedience to the paterfamilias and the impossibility of devoting himself to work (his law studies) that repulsed him, ate away at him, killed him. The contradiction hardened: "His passive obedience robs him of any possibility of refusing the activity his father imposes on him, but this increasingly difficult passivity, and his basic distaste for the future being prepared for him, succeed in making it impossible. Impossible to obey, impossible to refuse obedience."[18] Neurosis pulled Gustave out of the impasse; it showed the father that he was completely wrong about his youngest son and that he was responsible for his illness. Gustave's body delivered his message to Achille-Cléophas. According to Sartre, a process of somatization resolved many years of a dominance-submission relationship between father and son and ultimately freed the young man.

Sartre's many pages on the incident of January 1844 and Flaubert's neurosis are probably debatable from a psychiatric and neurological point of view. However, they have the merit of underlining the importance of the turn Flaubert's life took after this "nervous attack," whose etiology is in the relationship between father and son. Whether it was epilepsy or neurosis, it made it possible for the writer to be born. Flaubert would later explain his illness to Louise Colet: "Had my brain been sounder, I would not have fallen sick from studying law and being bored. I would have turned those circumstances to my advantage, instead of being hurt by them. My unhappiness, instead of remaining confined within my mind, overflowed into the rest of my body and sent it into convulsions. It was a 'deviation.'"[19]

Another event that occurred in 1844 contributed to establishing Gustave as a solitary writer: after Dr. Flaubert's property in Deauville was expropriated for the construction of the Rouen-Le Havre railroad, he purchased a house at Croisset. It was a large eighteenth-century country residence located two and a half miles from Rouen in the commune of Canteleu, on the right bank of the Seine and separated from the river only by a towpath. A park, tall trees, a magnificent view of the river crisscrossed by sailboats—it was in the serenity of this new home that Flaubert would write his major works, transforming a row of lime trees into the "*gueuloir*," or "shouting parlor," in which he checked the musicality of his sentences. Today nothing remains of the residence other than a garden house that has been converted into a museum.

During his convalescence, and perhaps as early as his stay at Tréport, Flaubert returned to the novel that he had interrupted to prepare for his 1843 exam; he completed it in January 1845. This initial *Sentimental Education* would only become known to the public in 1910, thirty years after its author's death, for Flaubert had assessed it with his typically harsh self-criticism. Yet it comes as no surprise that the novel is neither uninteresting nor lacking in beauty. Although Flaubert abandons autobiography in this work, he entrusts the narrative to an anonymous narrator who does not hesitate to say "I," pass judgment, and address the reader—three devices that the experienced Flaubert would replace with impersonal narration. The dialogues are too long, there is no shortage of inconsistencies, and the narrative's logic is sometimes deficient. But Flaubert's art of description is already evident, his sense of irony is confirmed, and the minor characters are clearly drawn.

The novel deals with two principal themes through two characters, Henry and Jules, to whom the author gave many of his own personality traits. The first story, which is Henry's, is a story of love followed by loss of love. A law student in Paris, Henry boards at the Renaud home with other students who receive lessons from the master of the house. He falls in love with the master's wife, Émilie, whose physical description, it has been noted, is reminiscent of Élisa. Like Élisa, Émilie does not love her husband and is attracted to the young man. After a few weeks of banter, confidences, and hesitations, Henry and Émilie become lovers under the master's own roof. Redoubling their daring, the lovers secretly embark for America, where the young man is finally able to put bread on the table by writing for newspapers and giving lessons. There follows the long but irresistible decline of passion; love erodes, wears out, and is reduced to the banality of the quotidian—a depoeticization that the lovers become aware of when each confesses to the other a desire to return to Europe. They return by ship and, after spending a few days together in Paris, gently separate: no conflicts, no scenes, no tears, they just separate, period, because it's over. And Henry, having become downright realistic, if not cynical, launches into a career like Balzac's.

Jules follows a different path. In the first part of the novel, he is only present through the letters he sends his friend Henry from the provincial town where he has stayed for lack of money to pursue higher education. The character mostly gains depth in the book's final part. Jules has also had a great love, but he has not had time to experience its eventual decline because Lucinde, the actress he loves, has left him. Though tremendously distressed, after a few twists and turns he finds the road to salvation in art. While Henry's beginnings in life are reminiscent of Gustave's romantic adventure with Élisa, there is no doubt that Jules more deeply embodies Flaubert's moral and intellectual development: far from wishing to conquer Paris as his friend has, Jules devotes himself ascetically to literature.

Yet these two characters, with their divergent life stories, share a common trait: the failure of love. Jules's failure is described in the novel's twentieth chapter: "Great moral suffering, like physical fatigue, leaves you so exhausted that the mind is incapable of formulating a desire or the body of rousing itself to any kind of action. To anyone who has wept a lot or shed a great deal of blood, there is even a certain pleasure in the numbness that sets in when his wound stops smarting and his heart is no longer torn; only those who have cried their hearts out appreciate how sweet it is just to moan."[20] Further along, one finds a reflection that could only have been expressed after the nervous attack of January 1844: "This was the stage, which I will call *considered despair*, that . . . poor Jules suddenly attained when, in a single day, like a starving wolf carrying off a whole flock of sheep in a night, fate robbed him of his love and everything he hoped for."[21] This "considered despair" finds an equivalent when Henry gives up in chapter 24: "It would be untrue to say that Henry had stopped loving Mme Renaud; he still did, but in a more tranquil way, less abundantly, less ardently. His love had become staider and more serene, at once the corollary of its predecessor and its antithesis, without either passionate outbursts or inner qualms."[22]

Mme Schlésinger was no longer anywhere in sight; though Flaubert would eventually see her again, it would be without any hope of winning her over. She now aroused a "sweet," "considered" passion stoked by memories rather than the future, and which would inspire the admirable character of Marie Arnoux in the second *Sentimental Education*. He would have other loves, starting with the imminent stormy affair with Louise Colet, but his heart would remain occupied by the luminous image of Élisa.

The great turning point of 1844 (the nervous illness, the end of his law studies, his father's acquisition of Croisset) propelled Flaubert into another life, in which studious retreat would be as chosen as it was imposed. His spiritual solitude was soon reinforced by the March 1845 marriage of his sister Caroline, the loving Caro, the beloved Carolo, who married his former classmate Émile Hamard—particularly since the newlyweds were to settle in Paris. "What can I tell you about it?" he wrote to Ernest Chevalier, who had just been appointed deputy public prosecutor to Corsica. "Whatever you want. Say whatever you please. It can all be summarized by the two letters I spoke when I learned of it: AH!" As enigmatic as they may be, these two letters do not express joy.

CHAPTER 5

Death on the Horizon

Regrets, worry, and sadness—Flaubert's "AH!" was probably the most concise remark that could be heard in Rouen regarding his sister Caroline's marriage. There is no question that the wedding was a heartrending event for Gustave. The ceremony was held on March 3, 1845, after which the couple would settle in Paris on rue de Tournon. And, naturally, they would honeymoon in Italy. In Flaubert's *Dictionary of Accepted Ideas*, the entry on Italy reads: "Should be seen immediately after marriage."[1] The newlyweds were following the norm. However, they would travel not alone, but with M. and Mme Flaubert and Gustave. Achille was the only member of the family to remain in Rouen. "Family" honeymoons like these were not unusual, though in this case Dr. Flaubert may have wanted to accompany his daughter because of her fragile health. And while the entire family set out for Genoa together, it had been agreed that if everything went well the lovebirds could travel on to Naples alone.

The trip was not an entirely pleasant one for Gustave. He was certainly delighted to discover Italy, but the company weighed on him. He had a different sensibility than his parents; he dreaded their comments. The small group traveled by stagecoach from Nogent-sur-Seine to Chalon, where they boarded a steamboat to go down the Saône River to Lyon; then they journeyed to Marseille in several stages on the Rhône. From Marseille, Gustave wrote to Alfred Le Poittevin: "Alfred, I conjure you in the name of heaven, in my own name, never travel with anyone! Anyone!" He did manage to slip away to the Hôtel Richelieu. He wanted to see Eulalie Foucaud again: "It will be singularly bitter and farcical, especially if I find her having become ugly, as I expect." Always the optimist, Flaubert. And always haunted by the inexorable decay of the flesh. But he laughed at the word "disillusionment," such a bourgeois term. Wasn't disillusionment poetic, one thousand times more poetic than illusion? He was saddened to find the hotel closed down, "empty and echoing like a great tomb." Eulalie was truly no more than a memory. Yet in Marseille he could not keep from reminding his confidant Alfred of the "blissful interludes" he had spent with her. He could have made an effort to find her new address, but the information he was given was unclear. More importantly, he confessed to lacking "eagerness."[2]

From Marseille, they followed the coast through Fréjus, Antibes, and Nice to Genoa. Here, Flaubert was dazzled by the palaces, the hotels, the gardens flooded with roses, the marbles: "I go into many of the churches, listen to the singing and the organ, watch the monks, look at the chasubles, the altars, the statues."[3] He had brought with him a history of the Republic of Genoa by Émile Vincens, which gave him the idea for a drama about an episode of the Corsican War. The company was supposed to split up here, but the newlyweds would not go any further: Caroline had been having kidney trouble since Toulon. The entire family thus returned home via the Simplon Pass and Geneva, making stops in Milan and Turin. From Milan, Flaubert wrote to Alfred about his powerful discovery of Brueghel's painting *The Temptation of Saint Anthony* at the Balbi Palace. He had lingered before the canvas a long time, examining every detail. He told his friend that he could see the subject being adapted for the theater. In his travel notes, he wrote:

In the background on both sides, on each of the hills [are] two monstrous devil heads, half living, half mountain—bottom left, Saint Anthony between three women, and turning his head away to avoid their caresses. They are naked, pale, they smile and are about to envelop him in their arms.—Facing the viewer, all the way at the bottom of the painting, Gluttony, naked from the waist up, thin, her head bearing red and green ornaments, sad face, inordinately long and taut neck, like a crane's, curving toward the nape—prominent collar bones, presenting to the viewer a tray laden with colorful dishes.—Men on horseback, in a barrel—heads coming out of the animals' stomachs—frogs with arms and leaping in the fields—man with red nose on a misshapen horse surrounded by devils—winged dragon gliding—everything seems to be on the same plane.

The whole picture swarms, teems, and snickers in a grotesque, fiery way, beneath the innocuousness of each detail. The painting initially appears muddled, then it becomes strange for most, funny for some, something more for others—for me it erases the entire gallery where we stand. I do not remember the rest.[4]

In September 1849, Flaubert would complete the first of several versions of his "passion play," *The Temptation of Saint Antony.*

In Geneva, he managed to slip out again, cigar in mouth, to visit little Rousseau Island, in the Rhône River right in front of the family's hotel. He wanted to see the statue of Rousseau by his friend Pradier. Standing at the foot of the statue, he suddenly heard music and found himself stirred by the sound of trombones and flutes. He was also deeply moved to discover Byron's name carved into one of the pillars of the Chillon prison. Then, in Ferney, by Voltaire's bedroom; in Coppet, by Mme de Staël's chateau; and later, in Besançon, by the house where Victor Hugo was born. Despite his frustrations, Flaubert came back from this trip with a host of notes and descriptions recorded throughout the journey and completed upon his return in early June 1845. It would later become clear that the greatest benefit of this family trip was the impression left by Brueghel's painting on Flaubert's retina: *The Temptation of Saint Antony* had him in its grip. He would need to write three versions of it to exhaust the subject. The trip also reinforced the taste for Antiquity that Chéruel and Michelet had already instilled in him, and which he carried, as he wrote to Alfred, "in my entrails." In his imagination and in terms of aesthetics, he tried to "live in the ancient world." This Antiquity was no longer pure fantasy now that he had learned to read the Roman inscriptions and observe the vestiges of vanished civilizations. Some have seen this journey as the moment when Flaubert, leaving behind his subjectivity and lyricism, began trying to achieve an "objective vision" of the world.[5] To see, to observe, to immerse yourself in reality by leaving yourself behind: that was the way.

"I Have Drawn Away from Women"

Over the months that followed the nervous attack of January 1844, Flaubert's health slowly improved, but he remained on the alert, always at risk. He was sometimes overcome by anxiety, which could lead to more convulsions: his body stiffened, he suddenly went pale, and then he lost consciousness and started violently shaking. The fits came and went quickly, but left the sick man feeling very weak. There were agonizing consequences if he had bitten his tongue. During the trip to Italy, he regained his appetite and wondered how a fellow as solid as he was could suffer from nervous illness. Upon his return, he revealed to Ernest Chevalier that he had experienced two more nervous fits while away: "If I'm recovering, I'm not recovering quickly. Which is neither news nor comforting to me. Shit! I've said it. With this big word, we console ourselves for all the human miseries, so I like to repeat it: shit, shit." [6] Medicine was tentative, groping; he was now prescribed quinine instead of valerian.

Did epilepsy directly or indirectly cause Flaubert's lack of sexual appetite over the next two years? Was it exhaustion of the libido? Or voluntary continence? He frequently raised the subject in his letters to friends: they were used to talking about sex, often in bawdy terms that would later lead Ernest Chevalier, a magistrate on his way to becoming a conservative deputy, to destroy some of Flaubert's letters for the sake of respectability. But enough of the letters to Chevalier have survived, along with those to Le Poittevin, to give us an idea of the lull in his erotic life.

Before leaving for Italy in April 1845, Flaubert reported to Alfred Le Poittevin about his recent brief stay in Paris. He had attempted to see Schlésinger again, but "Monsieur Maurice" was in London. He did not say a word about Schlésinger's wife, the woman who had been Flaubert's "great love." He did obtain Mme Pradier's address on rue Laffitte and went to see her, as he put it, as if drawn by a "lost woman." The Pradiers had just separated following misconduct on Louise's part. Known as Ludovica, she was now living alone, a thirty-year-old woman denied access to her children and watched by the police. Gustave visited her out of friendship and compassion, but his account to Alfred also makes clear that he was attracted to her. After all, Louise was a beauty and a liberated woman. Nothing happened between them that day, except that Louise invited Gustave to come for lunch the next time he was in Paris. Flaubert's letter then reports that he went to the boulevard but "did not do anything obscene."

Having learned of his visit to Mme Pradier, Alfred encouraged him to accept her invitation. Gustave replied: "As you recommend, and as I promised, I will go and lunch with Mme Pradier, but it is doubtful that I'll do more than that, unless she invites me *very* openly. Sex games have nothing more to teach me. My desire is too universal, too permanent, too intense, for me to have desires. I don't use women as a means to an end: I do what the poet in your novel does—I use them only as objects of contemplation."[7] This suggests that Flaubert chose to be chaste, and that the cause was not a sudden fit of virtue but indifference: "It's a singular thing," he wrote to Alfred, "the way I have drawn away from women." He was as bluntly candid as ever: "It is now two years since I last had coitus; and, in a few days, a year since I performed any lascivious act." This situates the beginning of the chaste period earlier than January 1844, indicating that Flaubert's "impotence" (the term used by certain commentators) was not a result of his epilepsy. "I must have fallen very low, since the sight of a brothel inspires me with no urge to enter it."[8]

Flaubert seemed to want to escape from common impulses. Upon his return from Italy, he confided to Alfred that he was "still prey, sometimes, to strange yearnings for love, although I am disgusted by it down to my very entrails." Pradier's suggestion that he take a mistress was probably good advice, but he would not follow it. He gave his friend this strange explanation: "Normal, regular, rich, hearty copulation would take me too much out of myself, disturb my peace. I would be re-entering active life in the physical sense, and that is what has been detrimental to me each time I've tried it."[9] Everything proceeded as if he had decided to live as a hermit, in a regulated, calm, industrious way. As he told Ernest Chevalier, "since what I dread is passion, movement, I believe that if happiness is to be found it is in stagnation. Ponds do not have storms."[10]

Even once he returned to an active sex life, he would sometimes deliberately abstain, "as a matter of principle," in order not to damage an impression, a sensation, the very beauty of a situation. He refused to surrender to the influence of the senses: art is always sublimation. Thus in his letter from Marseille, he had explained to Le Poittevin that after having chatted with "a whore from the brothel opposite the theater," he did not "go upstairs": "I didn't want to spoil the poetry of it."[11]

"Calamity Is Upon Us"

In early January 1846, Dr. Flaubert developed a deep abscess in his thigh. Running a high fever, he was operated on by his son Achille. By then, it was probably already too late. Achille-Cléophas, barely sixty-four years old and still active at the Hôtel-Dieu, died of blood poisoning. This twist of fate devastated the Flaubert family. "You knew the good, intelligent man we have lost," Gustave wrote to Ernest Chevalier, "the tender, noble soul that is gone."[12] Father and son had been opposites in every way. One was positive-minded, a straightforward thinker, and a renowned surgeon beloved by his fellow citizens. The other swore only by art and literature. Knowing that, it would be easy to believe that the doctor preferred Achille, who had followed in his footsteps, to Gustave, who had failed his law studies and did not seem to know what he wanted. Maxime Du Camp bore witness: "Flaubert Senior was humiliated [by Gustave] and did not hide it; he was bewildered, as if he were faced with an unknown pathological case. He only understood action. The son of a Nogent-sur-Seine veterinarian, he had become a surgeon—an eminent surgeon—and he could not accept that his son could be what he called a *grimaud*, or a bad writer, a pencil pusher." This explains the title of Sartre's book on Flaubert, *The Family Idiot:* "With the best intentions, Achille-Cléophas made himself his youngest son's persecutor." According to Sartre, Dr. Flaubert took a different tone when he addressed his eldest son, Achille: "He speaks to him man to man." As for Gustave, he would never be anything but a child in his father's eyes. Sartre uses these ideas as a foundation for his psychological analysis in three dense volumes that explain the "Flaubert case": poor neglected Gustave, the black sheep suffering from a terrible inferiority complex vis-à-vis his brother, of whom he is inevitably jealous. Yet this brilliant demonstration is not entirely convincing: the correspondence shows that Gustave loved and admired his father. In 1869, he praised his father's humaneness in a letter to George Sand: "It's true that I'm the son of a man who was extremely humane, and sensitive in the good sense of the word. The sight of a dog in pain brought tears to his eyes. Yet this didn't impair his efficiency as a surgeon. He even invented some operations that were quite dreadful."[13] If he felt crushed and scorned by his father, he certainly never complained about it. Nonetheless, communication between Flaubert and the great surgeon was never easy. As he admitted to Louise Colet, "How many times, without wanting to, I brought tears to the eyes of my father, who was so intelligent, so perceptive! But he understood nothing of my idiom. . . . I have the infirmity of being born with a special language, to which I alone have the key."[14] One can question whether he truly made his father cry, but what is interesting here is his confession of the failure of communication between the surgeon and the future writer.

In any case, Gustave took to Rouen's two newspapers to make a call for funding to erect a statue of his father—which he insisted should be by Pradier.

He also did everything he could to ensure that his father's place be taken by Achille, whom rival doctors wanted to remove from the Hôtel-Dieu. In late January 1846, he informed Ernest Chevalier that he had been to Paris, probably to lobby Dr. Cloquet and the Ministry of Education, and rejoiced that "up to now there can be no doubt that [Achille] will succeed his father in everything." For someone who did not like the bourgeoisie, Flaubert shared its embrace of family loyalty. And it would be difficult to interpret his behavior as that of a younger brother jealous of his elder, unless it was precisely by being active and devoted to his brother that Gustave took his revenge—by taking on the role of protector of the family, Gustave was stepping into his father's shoes. A noble, apparently selfless role, but one whose chivalrous nature put the older brother in the younger brother's debt.

Eventually, a compromise was reached: Dr. Émile Leudet, a former student of the deceased who had hoped to succeed him, became chief surgeon, with Achille as deputy surgeon. The two men shared teaching duties, taking a semester each. Achille would live in his father's quarters at the Hôtel-Dieu, while Gustave and his mother would spend most of the year at Croisset and the four winter months in a new apartment in Rouen, rue Crosne-hors-Ville.

Yet the Flauberts were not to know any respite from misfortune. Having given birth to her daughter Désirée-Caroline shortly before her father's death, Caroline now fell sick—an "outbreak of pernicious fever that gave us the most serious concerns." On March 15, Flaubert wrote to Maxime Du Camp that his sister was losing her memory, that her mind was muddled, that she could no longer tell him apart from his brother Achille, that she was surprised not to see her father, and that she moaned and cried out. Gustave was desperate: he expected the worst. Ten days later he informed his friend that the young woman had died. She was laid out in her wedding dress with a white bouquet, and Gustave sat by her all night. Then he piously had her death mask cast: "I saw the great paws of those louts touching her and covering her with plaster. I shall have her hand and her face. I shall ask Pradier to make me her bust and will put it in my room. I have her big colored shawl, a lock of her hair, her table and writing-desk. That is all—all that remains of those we love!"[15]

The funeral was bleak. The grave was too narrow for the coffin, so the gravediggers had to use a spade and crowbars to force it down. One climbed on the casket, just over the dead woman's head: "I was standing at the side, holding my hat in my hand; I threw it down with a cry."[16] Caroline's husband Hamard dropped to his knees and wept, throwing kisses to his dead wife. Dazed, Flaubert felt tremendous pain and "terrible injustice."

The previous day, Gustave's little niece had been baptized in a ceremony that seemed unreal. A priest still flushed by his lunch reeled off prayers and the verger poured the water, replying "Amen" according to an old ritual that seemed to Flaubert to come from a very ancient religion with "insignificant symbols." "Undoubtedly the most intelligent things there were the stones, which had once understood all of this and may have retained something of it."

Gustave was worried about his mother: how would she get over these repeated calamities? He brooded about her imminent death, wanting to protect himself from any surprise. Happily, Mme Flaubert had a reason to survive: to raise and protect Caroline's little girl. As for Gustave, he clenched his fists, withdrew into silence, and settled into affliction. Caroline, dead! The one he had loved and pampered, with whom he had spent so many exquisite hours in the *Billard* theater, reading aloud, having literary conversations. He had been her guide and teacher. She agreed with his ideas, admired him, laughed at his pranks, charmed him by playing Beethoven and Mozart on the piano. In the Flaubert family, she was his ally, his partner in crime, the one who understood, admired, and loved him. The memory of his "poor rat" would never leave him: "I still have an empty place where she was in my heart," he wrote to his mother, "and nothing will fill it."[17] He was overcome with remorse when he thought that he had let her marry Hamard, "such a vulgar man, from his boot to his hat."

Also in 1846, Gustave was struck by another piece of bitter news. Though it was of a different nature, it drove him a little further into solitude: his friend Alfred Le Poittevin was getting married. In July, Gustave had told Alfred that without him, he would have nothing left. Alfred was his most intimate friend, the only superior mind he had found with whom to make common cause and share common projects. They had read the same authors, with Alfred usually ahead of Gustave, initiating him and introducing him to countless treasures; they had talked for hours, for entire nights; they had exchanged letters full of knowledge and emotion. Flaubert was heartbroken by news of the marriage because it meant the end of this intimacy: "Are you sure, oh great man," he asked him in a letter dated May 31, 1846, "that you'll not end up becoming a bourgeois? In all my artistic hopes, I was at one with you. It is that aspect that distresses me."[18] Alfred was getting married, he was moving away, everything was disappearing. On July 16, Le Poittevin married Louise de Maupassant; Gustave Flaubert was disconsolate.

Stoicism

The deaths that devastated Flaubert anchored him in the new life he had chosen. His illness had reinforced his decision to stop pretending to live like everyone else by allowing him to give up both the law curriculum he detested and a bourgeois future. He would be able to devote himself to studying and writing. After his father's and Caroline's deaths, his future seemed clear: he would live for Art. Sartre does not beat around the bush, coolly making a statement that breaks with propriety but is not any less believable for it: "On January 15, 1846, Gustave had a life-changing stroke of luck: he lost his father." The author of *The Words* may have been thinking of his own life, but no matter: "Achille-Cléophas let his son have the last word." In May 1846, Gustave told Maxime Du Camp: "The internal life I have always dreamed of is finally beginning to appear."[19]

What has been called Flaubert's two-year "impotence" contributed to this "conversion." He did not want to be a victim of romantic passion again. He even feared short-lived affairs. No yoke! No influence! "Like Saint Augustine giving up on women to become Christian," writes Jean Bruneau, "Flaubert stopped living to make art."[20] Yes, he would have other mistresses and enjoy dinners, social traditions, and trips, but he had convinced himself that anything that distracted him from literary work was of secondary importance. One had to choose between life and art. This is why he was so upset by Alfred Le Poittevin's marriage: he felt that Alfred was lost to art. One had to give up on happiness, or rather to know that happiness, for him and for Le Poittevin, for "people of our kind," was in the *idea*—or so he thought.

He threw himself into his work with a vengeance. The previous year, he had poked fun at his lot in a letter to Ernest Chevalier: "While my life is pleasant, it is not rich in laughs. Yet I desire no other life for myself for the next few years. I even want to buy a beautiful bear (painting), to have it framed and hung in my room after writing underneath it *Portrait of Gustave Flaubert*, to indicate my moral disposition and social humor."[21] He read, studied, wrote, "toiled." He analyzed Voltaire's plays, not because he liked them—"it is tedious"—but because Voltaire had a feeling for structure. He continued to decipher Shakespeare with undiminished admiration. He dove into the ancient writers, notably Quintus Curtius's enormous *History of Alexander*, which satisfied his taste for columns and togas. He studied Buddhism. He did not neglect the literature of his own era. He judged Stendahl's *The Red and the Black* to have a "distinguished spirit" but wondered about style, the "true style" that it lacked. He read or wrote eight to ten hours a day, marveling at the fact that he was finally living his inner life, his real life. He continued to exhort Alfred to devote himself to Art, the only means to avoid being unhappy. He aggressively asked Chevalier, who had become a deputy public prosecutor in Calvi, whether he ever looked at himself in the mirror, and if so, whether the sight made him laugh. Life for him was now in the physical confinement through which he hoped to scale the heights of artistic creation. He had lost his former cheerfulness, but also his sadness: "I am mature," he said. For he had broken with the outside world, the bustle of humans, and the immediate concerns of the bourgeois. He was elated by the voluntary demarcation of his life.

While his loved ones' deaths had distressed him, he now felt immune to misfortune, which had already struck him so hard: he had become a fatalist.[22] In May 1846, he confided to Maxime Du Camp that he was now "in an inalterable state." Reality had to be accepted as it was; one could not revolt against it. Of course, one could become dehumanized by such an attitude. Flaubert himself reported that Mme Flaubert was disturbed to see the frenzy for sentences wither his heart.[23] He was tickled: his mother had made "a sublime remark." Despite this, he remained convinced that "he still [had] juice in his heart."

Over a period of two years, Flaubert had become a literary hermit. His illness served as justification; his father's death eased what remained of his guilty conscience. His life was no longer swayed by indecision: he would do nothing. But of this nothing he would make everything, a body of work. Admittedly, he was not yet certain of his genius; he had already written many pages that he hadn't published. But since he did not aspire to social success, he had time. There was something of Pascal's gamble in his resolution: he bet on the uncertain absolute rather than the mediocre, relative satisfactions of bourgeois life. The inevitable compromises with that life were to be kept to an essential minimum. Only the vagaries of life could make him falter—vagaries like falling in love.

CHAPTER 6

Louise

On July 28, 1846, Flaubert was in Paris visiting his friend James Pradier, who was to make a bust of Caroline. Pradier was in the habit of entertaining artists and writers in his studio near Place Pigalle. When Flaubert arrived, he found Pradier's guests busily conversing, glasses in hand. His gaze was immediately drawn to a beautiful young woman. This woman, who was unknown to him, was the thirty-five-year-old poet and writer Louise Colet. They exchanged glances, then were introduced. The mutual attraction was immediate.

Fully aware of her powers of seduction, Louise Colet had written her self-portrait in a diary she had begun the previous year:

> I am now thirty-four, no more, no less. I have gained weight, my figure is no longer svelte, but it is still elegant and very shapely. My bosom, neck, shoulders, and arms are very beautiful. [My] thick hair (light brown, but it was very blond when I was a child), artfully arranged by a hairdresser every day, draws many compliments. . . . I have a high forehead, very attractive, very expressive, thick and finely drawn eyebrows, dark blue eyes, big, very beautiful when they come alive with the shock of thought or sensations, but often tired by work and by tears.[1]

Louise's contemporaries confirmed her self-praise on many occasions. Witness Théodore de Banville: "Supremely beautiful, with an imposing and charming head styled with long golden locks, enchanting the gaze with the vivid flush of blossoming lips, a queen thanks to her superb neck and her white hands with pink nails, she was both a poet and a subject for poetry."[2]

As we have seen, Flaubert had long abstained from sexual relations. According to Sartre, his father's death put an end to this "hysterical castration."

"It is just as if Achille-Cléophas had been the actual castrator."[3] Once the father was gone, desire returned. Dazzled by this woman known as the Muse, Flaubert dashed to Louise Colet's home the very next day, knowing that she had a salon but not caring that it was held on a different day of the week. It was not hard to break the ice: they were both passionate about literature. Louise had already published a great deal, notably poems; he had published nothing but had written abundantly and spoke about literature as a connoisseur. He put Shakespeare above everything else; as it happened, Louise had translated *The Tempest* in verse. She read him part of her translation. She was attracted to this twenty-four-year-old man, so handsome and tall and apparently so confident in his opinions. Yes, they would see each other again, no later than the next day.

The Muse

Born in 1810 in Aix-en-Provence, Louise Colet had enjoyed reading since childhood and began writing verse at a young age. Her father, Antoine Revoil, head of the city's postal service, died in 1826. The youngest of six children, she was primarily educated by her mother, Henriette, née Le Blanc, a cultured woman to whom she was very attached and who died in 1834. In the meantime, the young woman, raised on Romantic literature and a great admirer of George Sand, devoted herself to poetry and was introduced to the salon of the novelist, singer, and tragedienne Julie Candeille in Nîmes, where she often went to visit her sister Marie. But this patroness died the same year as Louise's mother. Living in the family home at Servane, close to Mouriès and not far from Avignon, with her unmarried brothers and sisters, she was misunderstood by her siblings and subjected to their sarcasm and cruelties. She dreamed of leaving for Paris. Her opportunity came in December 1834 when she married Hippolyte Colet, a musician who had studied at the Conservatoire in Paris. Having been offered a position as a flute teacher in the capital, Colet moved there with his young wife. His ambition was to become a composer, while her own dream was of literary fame.

She initially sought to write for newspapers, whose numbers had grown exponentially since the Revolution of 1830 and the new freedoms of the press allowed under Louis Philippe. Her efforts bore fruit: several of her poems were printed in *L'Artiste*, which also published George Sand and Eugène Delacroix. Thanks to her persistence, energy, a handful of new connections, and the stunning beauty that was her most reliable asset, Louise managed to be introduced into Charles Nodier's salon at the Bibliothèque de l'Arsenal, where she met Émile and Delphine de Girardin, who wielded considerable influence through Émile's daily newspaper *La Presse*. Louise soon resolved to collect her poems in a volume entitled *Fleurs du Midi* [*Flowers of the South of France*]. Never lacking in self-confidence, she asked no less a luminary than Chateaubriand for his support. The great writer elegantly sidestepped her request by recognizing the beauty of some of her poems, but advising her to seek sponsorship from a poet: "Choose among those who have glory, they will be honored to predict yours." Louise unscrupulously took Chateaubriand's letter and placed it at the beginning of her collection, which was published in 1836. Though he initially greeted the collection coldly, the esteemed critic Charles-Augustin Sainte-Beuve finally published a review of *Fleurs du Midi* in the *Revue des deux mondes*. He was not sparing in his criticism, but allowed a word of encouragement to slip through: "this effort . . . heralds a real and uncommon ability."

Louise made sure to send a copy to Louis Philippe and his daughter Marie d'Orléans, who was moved by her poetry and arranged for her to receive a modest four-hundred-franc pension from the Ministry of Education. Though the couple still had to live quite frugally, Louise was offered a potential lucky break by an acquaintance from Provence, François-Auguste Mignet, a historian of the French Revolution and member of the Académie Française. Mignet advised her to compete in the Académie's biennial poetry contest. The subject for 1839 was the Château de Versailles. Why not? She hurried over to the palace built by Louis XIV, wrote the poem on the spot, sent if off and— miracle!—was awarded the prize over about sixty other competitors. Mignet had backed her submission, as had her acquaintance Népomucène Lemercier, who was not indifferent to her charms. The critics tore her to shreds, but she didn't care: she had won the prize's two thousand francs and made new connections. As was customary, she visited the Academicians to thank them, beginning with Victor Cousin, a member of France's Chamber of Peers and senior lecturer at the Sorbonne. Cousin, who was considered one of the greatest living philosophers and drew delighted crowds whenever he lectured, fell for the prizewinner's beauty and soon took her as a mistress. With a patron like him, she would go far.

Cousin chaperoned her and gave her literary advice. He arranged for Hippolyte's salary at the Conservatoire to be raised and Louise's pension to be tripled. He introduced her to the editors of the periodicals; she soon became a personality on the Paris literary scene. In 1841, she opened her salon on rue Bréra, close to Place Pigalle, and became known as the Muse. The same year, she published her new collection, *Penserosa*. This time, Sainte-Beuve's polite sourness turned to praise—probably because he had his eye on the Académie: "An elegant and brilliant volume which now promises her a place among our muses. It is impossible to deny that these verses display harmony, sparkle, assurance, a large and sonorous touch."[4] Louise's pension now rose to three thousand francs a month.

Yet the path to the top was scattered with thorns. The humorist Alphonse Karr targeted Victor Cousin and Louise Colet in his satirical monthly *Les Guêpes:* "It is now perfectly certified at the ministry of education that to have a pension as a man of letters, one must be a beautiful woman." More damaging was that Karr, who knew that Louise was pregnant (she would give birth to a daughter in August 1840), unsubtly alluded to the fact that the philosopher, who had been appointed Minister of Education on March 1, 1840, was probably the father ("a sting from Cousin"). Louise ordered her husband (who was likely the actual father) to demand redress from the insulter, but courage was not one of Hippolyte Colet's leading qualities. A finer flutist than a fencer, Colet copped out. Venturing to avenge her besmirched honor with her own hands, the impetuous Muse grabbed a kitchen knife, went to Alphonse Karr's home, and attempted to drive the blade into his back. The knife slipped, and the insulter disarmed the lady. To keep the scandal under control and avoid a court case, Cousin asked Sainte-Beuve—who still aspired to the Académie—to persuade Karr to leave it there. The humorist settled for ironically recounting the incident in the following issue of *Les Guêpes*, while Sainte-Beuve was appointed custodian of the Bibliothèque Mazarine, the library at the Institut de France.

During the period from the birth of her daughter Henriette to Gustave Flaubert's arrival in her life, Louise Colet consolidated her status as a woman of letters and salon hostess. She wrote both in verse and in prose about a wide variety of subjects: *Penserosa*, *Poésies nouvelles* [*New Poems*], *Funérailles de Napoléon* [*The Funeral of Napoleon*] (1840, on the occasion of the return of the emperor's ashes), *La Jeunesse de Mirabeau* [*The Youth of Mirabeau*] (initially serialized in *La Presse*), *Charlotte Corday*, *Madame Roland*—all works that bear witness to her sympathies with the Girondists, the more moderate camp during the French Revolution. She always sent copies of her works to George Sand, who congratulated her but chided her for her historical preferences: "Either hate equality," Sand wrote to Colet, "or respect those who proclaimed it!" The illustrious author was then at the height of her radical period, before her political convictions moderated. For the time being, she lectured her young rival: "You are making war on the principle of the people's sovereignty . . . you refuse to understand the Revolution!"[5]

Another woman played a more generous role in Louise's life: Juliette Récamier, muse to Chateaubriand, who invited her to her salon at the Abbaye-aux-Bois, a former Benedictine convent on the Left Bank. Here, Louise was soon admired for her beauty, her eagerness to support audacious positions, her cultural breadth, and her participation in every conversation. The friendship between the two women would be unfailing. Later, Louise would take an apartment on rue de Sèvres to be close to Juliette, who would entrust her with a treasure, the letters from her former suitor Benjamin Constant.

In 1843, Louise participated in the Académie's poetry contest, the subject of which was the Molière fountain recently inaugurated on rue de Richelieu. Helped by the advice of her friends Béranger and Victor Cousin, she won the two-thousand-franc prize for a second time, with no more critical success than before. The same year, she published *Les Cœurs brisés* [*The Broken Hearts*], a collection of short stories.

Still facing financial difficulties, she spared herself no effort and wrote profusely. But she did not work herself to the bone merely to get paid: she had political convictions. She had become closer with the feminists and socialists, which led her to support Flora Tristan's paper *L'Union ouvrière*. Her collection of short stories in two volumes, *Saintes et folles* [*Saints and Madwomen*], published in 1845, attested to her commitment to the women's cause. The following year, she published *Chants des vaincus* [*Songs of the Defeated*], in defense of the "nationalities" movement then threatening empires. In a similar vein, *Le Réveil de la Pologne* [*The Awakening of Poland*] called for the independence of Poland, a cause dear to all republicans.

As we can see, Flaubert did not fall in love with an ordinary woman. Though genuinely passionate about literature, she was probably even more devoted to fame. Seductive and enterprising, she advanced more through her boldness and beauty than her actual literary talent. Not that her writing was without merit: among her abundant productions, one finds beautiful verses and nice prose pieces, but none of her works have stood the test of time. She hosted and was hosted, was protected and courted, and always made sure she was appealing. By the time she met Flaubert, she had separated from her mediocre husband and had distanced herself from Victor Cousin after a short-lived affair with a Pole. She was unattached and available.

The Misunderstanding

It is not surprising that the couple met at James Pradier's. Louise was a regular there, and the sculptor was responsible for the Molière fountain that had earned Louise her second poetry prize. Flaubert, who had long socialized with Pradier, hoped that aside from sculpting Caroline's bust, his friend would be chosen by the city of Rouen to make a statue of his father—and indeed, he was. Pradier's wife Louise d'Arcet was still serving as his hostess at the time, though she would stop once the couple separated.

What we know of the affair between Flaubert and Louise Colet, which was to last close to eight years with one long interruption, comes primarily from Gustave's letters to Louise. Very few of Louise's letters have survived; they were probably burned by Flaubert (or his legatee). Of the first part of the correspondence, which began during the night of August 4 to 5, 1846, and was temporarily interrupted on August 25, 1848, we know of one hundred and four letters from Flaubert and only one from Louise Colet. During the first phase of their affair, the hermit of Croisset wrote to his mistress nearly every day; she responded at the same rate. Conveniently, the new Paris-Rouen railroad made it possible for a letter mailed in Rouen before 11 AM to reach its addressee the same afternoon—a feat nearly unimaginable to those using the postal service in the twenty-first century. The rapidity of communication intensified the exchange of impressions and emotions; one could answer on the spur of the moment, and the response to the response followed instantly.

Along with Flaubert's letters, there are a few other sources, such as the account of the affair by Maxime Du Camp, who often served as a postmaster to Louise when he was in Paris. (When he was away, Flaubert sent his letters care of General Delivery.) What do the letters and additional documents tell us? Admittedly, we are dealing with a one-sided source, but in the rapid epistolary dialogue between the two lovers, Flaubert often quotes his correspondent, and her attitudes are quite clear. Yet readers of Flaubert must be wary of the near uniqueness of the sources, which impel us to always consider things from Gustave's point of view, to the detriment of Louise's perspective. It is with this caution in mind that I have attempted to reconstruct their love affair, the first part of which is discussed in this chapter.

Gustave Flaubert and Louise Colet truly loved each other—one could even say passionately loved each other—though it must immediately be added that they did not share the same definition of love. After Flaubert seduced the Muse in the days following their first encounter at Pradier's, he returned to Croisset, where he instantly initiated the magnificent correspondence that gives us such insight into his personality. The sincerity of his love for Louise is clear from the outset: "Yes. I desire you and I think of you. I love you more than I loved you in Paris. I can no longer do anything; I keep seeing you in the studio, standing near your bust, your long curls on your white shoulders, your blue dress, your arm, your face—everything" (August 6, 1846).[6] Two weeks later: "Yes, my beautiful one, you've enwrapped me in your charm, infused me with your very self. Oh! If I have perhaps seemed cold to you, if my sarcasms are harsh and hurt you, I want to cover you with love when I next see you, with caresses, with ecstasy. I want to gorge you with all the joys of the flesh, until you faint and die."[7] When Louise expresses the slightest doubt, he protests: "Yes, I love you, I love you. Do you hear? Must I shout it even louder?" (August 31). Yes, again: "All the little stars of my heart converge around your planet, oh my beautiful celestial body" (September 17). His love was not merely sensual: "As I said, I have been loved before, but *never the way you love me,* nor has there ever been between a woman and myself the bond that exists between us two" (September 18).[8] If Louise's letters were late to arrive, Gustave was distraught: "Not a word since Thursday morning. Pray answer me right away. I am terribly worried. . . . I've been burning with impatience and anxiety for four long days" (October 20). Anyone who has loved knows the anxiety experienced while awaiting a letter not written or gone astray. What joy when the letters arrive in a batch, delayed by a wrong address or an error on the part of the mail carrier. Flaubert had felt that fear: "Never tell me that I do not love you, since you put me through melancholy like I have never felt before" (December 2).

The reason Louise Colet doubted this oft-proclaimed love was her lover's voluntary absence, the fact that he was always away from her, locked up in his solitary Norman retreat, only rarely allowing her the pleasure of a face-to-face encounter. During the first phase of their affair, which lasted close to two years, Gustave and Louise met only four times after their initial encounter. There were three brief encounters in Paris and one day of passion at an inn in Mantes, halfway between Paris and Rouen. Louise was passionate, ardent, full of desire. She relished the carnal harmony they shared and was filled with admiration for Gustave, yet she did not understand the attitude of this ardent lover who repeated that he loved her but only allowed her to see him in those rare moments allowed by his whims. Her letters were filled with a permanent protest, a desperate call, and constant tears. Though he always replied to her, it was as if he were satisfied to make love by mail. She responded with sadness, pain, suffering, and finally anger: what did this evasion mean? "Anger!" Flaubert exclaimed, "Good God! Vituperation, invective! Lurid language. What does it mean? That you like disputes, recriminations, all the bitter daily wrangling that ends by making life a real hell?" (August 30, 1846).[9]

How did Flaubert explain to her that he could not come to Paris more often, that he could not live in Paris, and that she herself could not come to see him at Croisset? His principal justification was the presence of his mother, a sad, inconsolable hypochondriac, wild with worry about his fragile health and attacks, which continued to frighten her despite the fact that they were less frequent. She needed him: "Yesterday and the day before, my mother was in a frightful state; she had funereal hallucinations. I stayed by her side. You don't know what it is, the burden of such despair that has to be borne alone" (August 8–9, 1846).[10] He felt responsible for her, for keeping her alive: "My life is bound to another one, and it will be so as long as this other one lasts" (August 27).

Louise found it difficult to accept this explanation: Paris was now so close to Rouen, Gustave only needed to come up with the kind of excuse he sometimes already used, like the need to consult a volume at Paris libraries such as the Bibliothèque Royale or the Bibliothèque Sainte-Geneviève. And his mother was not alone, after all: her other son, Achille, practiced medicine in Rouen. The very idea that a man of twenty-six needed an "excuse" to go to the capital was hard to swallow. In many of his letters, Flaubert informs his mistress that he has a marvelous plan, an excellent opportunity to see her in ten days, a week, one month. One such plan gradually becomes comical. The municipality of Rouen had decided to assemble in Paris a commission of various personalities to choose the artist to execute the sculpture of Achille-Cléophas. Flaubert, still supporting his dear Pradier's candidacy, committed to joining the commission, which would provide him with numerous opportunities to travel to Paris. He could thus promise Louise that he would see her again. But the commission kept delaying, its secretary was dilly-dallying—the man needed a kick in the pants. Then the members were on vacation, Gustave and Louise would have to wait patiently: "Oh! the fools, and my mother who isn't well!" (October 13, 1846). They waited. "No news from the commission." The meeting was postponed until November. So he decided for himself: "If it isn't done by November 1, I'm leaving." Louise didn't fall for it, and Gustave defended himself: "I'm not talking about the commission, since you accuse me of using it to cover my delays and of making it into a shield against you, nor of when I'll come *for business*. First of all, I have no business in Paris other than you" (October 21). It seemed hopeless. But finally he kept his promise, and on November 8 he told Louise that he would arrive in Paris the next day. Flaubert stayed four or five days, but his relationship with Louise Colet had turned sour. He was not always a tender man; in fact, he had even been a boor on some occasions (recall the letter to Eulalie Foucaud), and sources of friction had multiplied. So she spoke very harshly to him and refused his kiss goodbye. He left with a heavy heart and wrote to her immediately: "You think that all I want from you is pleasure. Do I like pleasure? Do I have senses? And you accuse me of being heartless. So I have nothing left; maybe that's possible—what do I know? Well, I wanted to write you a long letter, but I can't find anything to say. I am troubled, agitated, the memory of your grief and the grief that I caused you is there like a ghost that attracts me and frightens me. But is it my fault?" (November 13).

The relationship between Flaubert and Louise Colet limped along, and only because Louise was devoted to it. She gave herself over to this love with all her passion; she was disturbed, she questioned herself, and soon she bridled at this recluse who claimed to love her but had to ask his mother's permission to see her: "So they guard you like a young lady?" But if he couldn't come to Paris as often as she wanted, she said, she could come to see him at Croisset. Her suggestion was immediately rejected with horror: what would the neighbors think, his friends, not to mention his mother? Madness! "It's impossible. The entire region would know by the next day. It would lead to an endless, odious fuss." Did the fear of what people would say really have such a powerful grip on this sworn enemy of the bourgeois?

The truth was something else entirely. Flaubert finally told his mistress the idea he had formed of love. He had initially fallen sway to his physical attraction to Louise, who had become his mistress during the course of two days and two carriage rides around the Bois de Boulogne. This flattered his pride: he, an untitled young man from the provinces, had seduced a celebrated literary woman. But he had not met the expectations of a woman lost in love, who could not accept his distance, the rarity of their meetings, and certain sentences in his very first letters: "Your love has made me sad. I can see you are suffering; I foresee I will make you suffer. Both for your sake and for my own I wish we had never met, and yet the thought of you is never absent from my mind."[11] Years earlier, Gustave Flaubert had chosen his path. He was inhabited, haunted, invaded by a single idea, that of the great work he was going to write. Nothing was to distract him from that. He had refused to let himself get caught up in the snare of *illusion* once and for all. The love of a woman was sometimes delightful but always dangerous in its devouring form. It must remain incidental. Yet despite his best efforts, his life had been turned upside down by meeting Louise, by her appeals and demands. He was always glad to see her, but in the days that followed he would describe himself as wiped out, unable to work. Louise Colet's biographer Joseph Jackson notes that if the two lovers had lived close to each other and seen each other regularly, "the profound differences that separated them would quickly have become obvious and the affair would have lasted a few weeks at most."[12] Yet Flaubert did not want to break up: "I could go a year without seeing or writing to you, still my feeling would not cool by one degree" (September 28, 1846). Distance does not prevent love: "Across space our desires meet like clouds and blend together in a single breath" (October 25). Better yet: "When two persons love, they can go ten years without seeing each other and without suffering from it" (late December 1846).[13] One can only imagine Louise's reaction to this manifesto. He constantly repeated that he loved her, but in his own way. The problem was that it was not her way. Since she pushed him to it, he made his point explicit: "You want to know if I love you. Well, as much as I can love, yes, which is to say that for me *love is not the first thing in life, but the second*" (January 21, 1847; italics added).

Flaubert was even brusquer when he wrote to her from Paris on the eve of his trip to Brittany with Maxime Du Camp: "For me, love is not and should not be in the foreground of life; it should remain in the back room. Other things in the soul take precedence over it—things which seem to me nearer the light, closer to the sun. So, if you look upon love as the main dish of existence, the answer is No. As a seasoning, Yes."[14]

A Trip to Brittany

Flaubert's trip to Brittany with his friend Du Camp shows that when he wanted to, Gustave could free himself from maternal supervision—though Mme Flaubert and her granddaughter and nanny did come spend a few days with the travelers in Brest at one point during the three-month trip. In Louise Colet's eyes, the trip was an admission and a betrayal. Some have seen Flaubert's taste for friendship, even intimacy, with young men (first Le Poittevin, now Du Camp, soon Bouilhet) as a sign of homosexual leanings. It is true that in his youthful correspondence and the later letters describing his trip to the Orient, Flaubert refers to homosexual experiences. In the confession of Louise Colet that Julian Barnes imagined in his novel *Flaubert's Parrot*, Louise refers to Du Camp as Gustave's "ambitious catamite"[15]—perhaps vindictively. We also know that Flaubert and Du Camp agreed to burn most of their youthful correspondence, which they considered potentially compromising. So? What is certain is that like most men of his era, Flaubert preferred masculine company: separation of the sexes was the rule, and school customs created a certain complicity between young men in which sex certainly played a part, but most often in the form of bawdy tales, pornographic jokes, and gossip about bordello exploits.

In any case, Gustave set off with Maxime on May 1, 1847, planning for a long journey starting in Blois with a visit to the chateaux of the Loire. Leaving Paris by train, occasionally riding in horse-drawn carriages, and using ferries and boats when necessary, they intended primarily to walk, with their bags on their backs and their sticks in their hands, braving fatigue, wind, rain, and sun: "It seemed to us," wrote Du Camp, "that we were escaping from civilization, and we were entering the wilderness; we were inclined to admire everything, the ruins in which wild radish blossomed, rocks covered in kelp, and the moors under a golden carpet of gorse."[16] At night, the two travelers stayed at hotels, inns, or guestrooms, but might also find themselves in a convent or a stable. When they liked a place, they stayed several days and took the opportunity to have their boots resoled. They daydreamed, sang, and marveled at their future works. Flaubert, who had meticulously prepared the whole trip, recounted for his friend the history of the local monuments and people with that taste for the past he would never lose. Sometimes the two young men seemed too offbeat to the locals and were stopped by gendarmes or customs officials asking to see their passports. One day, Flaubert, always ready for a prank, whispered into a sergeant's ear: "Tell the king not to come here; the area is not safe, royalist insurgents are still about!"[17]

Louise was appalled by this trip. Gustave had refused to see her on his way through Paris, from which he wrote her the disconcerting letter about love as a "seasoning." He was aware of her dismay. He wrote again from Nantes, on May 17, 1847, and urged her to reply, failing which it would be goodbye for good, "as if one of us had left for the Indies and the other for America." She replied. From Quimper, he explained that the trip was necessary: he "needed air," he "was suffocating." Once again, he worried when he didn't receive a response. From Saint-Brieuc, he wrote, "Why this silence?" It was simply that the mail was also traveling and took its time to arrive.

Their reconciliation would not last. Having returned from his trip in early August, Flaubert joined his mother and niece in a house at La Bouille, a dozen miles from Rouen, where the women had taken refuge to escape an epidemic in the city. This gave rise to new recriminations from Louise: he hadn't even sent her a bouquet for the anniversary of their first meeting on July 29. "You have not been able to resign yourself to accepting me with the weaknesses of my position," he replied, "with the demands of my life. I gave you the substance, you also wanted the surface, the appearance, the care, the attention, the trips, everything I exhausted myself to make you understand I could not give you" (August 6). There followed new outbursts, new diatribes on Louise's part, and new sidesteps on Gustave's. In the month of September 1847, he had another attack: "My nerves are at it again." Could it have been sparked by the growing tension with his mistress? Flaubert had the feeling that the slightest ironic word, the slightest joke, the slightest memory caused her suffering and protests.

He himself was often clumsy, cutting, or abrupt in the name of honesty. In a letter dated November 7, 1847, he recounts a memory that clearly illustrates his hierarchy of values—art as essential, love as incidental. He reminds Louise that one day in Mantes, under the trees, she told him that she "wouldn't exchange her happiness for the fame of Corneille." Her "hyperbole" upset him: "If you knew how those words shocked me, how they chilled the very marrow of my bones." He accuses her: "I have always seen you lump art together with other things—patriotism, love, what you will—a lot of things which to my mind are alien to it and, far from augmenting its stature, in my opinion diminish it. This is one of the chasms that exist between you and me."[18] For once, Louise's biting reply, dated November 9, has survived: "No, no, my good friend; and if I really did speak that lover's hyperbole, it was probably to answer some tenderness on your part that I was foolish enough to believe you truly felt. Don't you have a little hyperbole on your conscience yourself? Didn't you once write me that you wanted to buy the carriage in which we took our first outing? Wasn't that, as far as tender feelings go, unintelligent and indeed quite ridiculous? And now you won't spend 16 francs to come and see me?" The counterattack continued: "Now if you were to offer me one hundred nights like the one in Mantes in exchange for the satisfaction of having finished my drama [at the time Louise was writing the play *Madeleine*], I would answer: I prefer my drama, my dear, I prefer my drama."

This fierce game was coming to an end. Flaubert, who had returned to Rouen after the quarantine in La Bouille, had gotten to work on his account of the trip to Brittany. Letters between Flaubert and Louise Colet became less frequent. She did not know that he was unfaithful to her with Ludovica in the spring of 1847; he did not know that she was unfaithful to him with a young Polish man named Franc. In March 1848, with the revolution in full swing in Paris, Louise let Gustave know that she was pregnant and that he could not be the father: they had not seen each other in over a year.[19] Flaubert had faced the possibility of fatherhood in August 1846. Louise had told him that her period was late, which they both referred to by the colorful term "the English," in reference to the English Guard's red coats. Flaubert had reacted to her joy at the idea of bearing his child by describing her wish as "an appalling threat to my happiness."[20] But a few days later, he reassured her: "How could you think I would love you the less if you had a child by me? On the contrary, I would love you more. A thousand times more."[21] More "hyperbole"? In any case, it was a false alarm. There was another scare in December, but on the eighth he was reassured: "It's a good thing that the English have landed." His relief was obvious.

But now she really was pregnant, and he had nothing to do with it. The news of the pregnancy seems to have triggered the separation that had been brewing for some time. In any case, in that month of March 1848, Flaubert wrote to Louise Colet what appears to be a farewell letter:

Why all your preambles to telling me the "news"? You could have given it to me outright from the beginning. I spare you the reflections it inspires in me and the feelings it arouses. There would be too much to say. I pity you, I pity you greatly. I suffered for you, and—more to the point—"I have seen it all." You understand, don't you? It is to the artist that I speak.

Whatever may happen, count on me always. Even though we may no longer see each other or write, there will always be a bond between us that will not be effaced, a past whose consequences will endure. My "monstrous personality," as you so amiably call it, does not obliterate in me every last decent feeling—"human" feeling if you prefer. One day you will perhaps realize this, and regret having expended so much vexation and bitterness on my account.

Adieu, je vous embrasse.[22]

In the same letter, Flaubert reproaches Louise for her "persistence" in criticizing Du Camp, with whom he was then the closest of friends. No longer troubling themselves with Louise, the two ramblers got to work on a joint effort, the account of their tour of Brittany, *Par les champs et par les grèves* [*Over Strand and Field*], which would not be published until 1885, on the initiative of Flaubert's niece Caroline; its authors had considered it too aggressive and digressive.[23] The book was composed of twelve chapters based on their notes from the road, with Flaubert writing the odd-numbered chapters and Du Camp the even ones.

Flaubert wanted to make a work of art, not a hastily written, formulaic travel narrative. It took him three-quarters of a year. He poured all his desire for style into it, having "difficulty writing the most simple things." The speed with which he wrote his juvenilia and the spontaneity of his correspondence were long gone. Now he devoted himself to long hard hours of toil in order to be worthy of the "masters," particularly the ancient ones, whom he read constantly and practically worshipped. "It is the first thing I wrote with difficulty," he would write to Louise Colet. This asceticism, the acceptance of suffering, the relentless dedication to work, his permanent dissatisfaction with the sentences he wrote, his despair at not being able to *render,* as he put it—all of which was completely incomprehensible to someone like Louise Colet—delayed publication for years. He crossed things out, polished them, refined them, tortured himself to find the right word, to hear in his mind the harmonious succession of sentences. His travel narrative contains an abundance of showpieces, some of which seem like style for style's sake; but more often, the reader admires his art of description, colorist's palette, and grasp of the picturesque. He wants to show everything: the landscapes, sunken paths, fields lying fallow, the slaughterhouses in Quimper, the Carnac dolmens, the flocks of birds in churches, the sea, the sunsets, the people encountered—traveling salesmen, fishermen, beggars, Breton bagpipe players ... He mentions the food, omelets everywhere they went, ubiquitous veal, but also Daoulas strawberries and Cancale oysters. He describes the ugliness and marvels of Catholicism: the bad local religious art, the Romanesque abbeys, the

Gothic cathedrals, the processions, the beautiful chasubles and the blessed sacrament in gold, the fresh flowers and the candles lit on the altars of the Virgin. He gives equal attention to the "infamous" streets of Brest, where he notes the "thick caresses of the men of the people." He is outraged by the prudishness that distorts works of art. "Isn't what people want today," he writes, "the opposite of nakedness, simplicity, and the truth? Fortune and success go to those who know how to cover and dress things! The tailor is the king of the century, the fig leaf its symbol; laws, arts, politics, everything is covered up!"[24] It comes as no surprise that the word "stupid" appears constantly in his writing, sparing no one and nothing. But he also expressed his fervor, as in his description of the trip to Combourg, René Chateaubriand's birthplace, which the two friends visited to honor the aging writer: "Nothing sounded in the deserted room where once, at this time of day, the child René had seated himself on the edge of the window." But everything was dilapidated: "The ceiling beams, which you can touch with your hand, are worm-eaten with age; the laths are visible beneath the plaster of the high wall, which has big dirty spots; the window panes are obscured by spider webs and their frames encrusted with dust. This was his room. It faces west, toward the setting sun." There follows a long meditation on "this man who started here and who filled a half century with the clamor of his pain."[25] Irony does not preclude admiration: "Not satisfied with being grand, he wanted to appear grandiose, and yet it transpired that this vain compulsion did not erase his true grandeur."

These pages in the form of a requiem were prescient: Chateaubriand died on July 4, 1848, less than a year after their visit to Combourg. Shortly thereafter, Louise Colet sent Flaubert a lock of Chateaubriand's hair, accompanied by a poem. Flaubert replied on August 25:

> Thank you for the gift.
> Thank you for your very beautiful poem.
> Thank you for the remembrance.
> Yours, G.

To him, Louise Colet belonged to the past.

CHAPTER 7

1848

As a woman inspired by the history of the Revolution, an activist for the emancipation of women, and an apostle of the people's cause, Louise Colet tried on several occasions to interest Gustave Flaubert in politics. She was surprised to learn that he did not even read the papers. He answered her in no uncertain terms: "Yes, newspapers disgust me profoundly—I mean the ephemeral, things of the moment, what is important today and won't be tomorrow. This is not insensitivity. It is simply that I sympathize as much, perhaps even more, with the past misfortunes of those who are dead and no longer thought of—all the cries they uttered, now unheard. I feel no more pity for the lot of modern working classes than for that of the ancient slaves who turned the millstone. I am no more modern than I am ancient, no more French than Chinese; and the idea of *la patrie*, the fatherland—that is, the obligation to live on a bit of earth colored red or blue on a map, and to detest the other bits colored green or black—has always seemed to me narrow, restricted and ferociously stupid."[1]

Yet despite this declaration of timelessness in the name of the sacred nature of Art, whose only purpose is Beauty and which he forbids to be "useful" or "moral," Flaubert could not overcome the limitation of his own life, which was rooted in a single country and a specific era. Whether or not he read the newspapers, current events came knocking at his door. When the Revolution of 1848 burst out in Paris and shook the provinces, it did not wait for his permission to create repercussions all the way to Rouen. In fact, in December 1847 Flaubert even decided to spend an evening in Rouen at one of the reformist banquets that led up to the revolution. These banquets were born of a movement launched by the opposition to Louis Philippe and his prime minister François Guizot, which demanded the reform of the electoral law that granted suffrage to only 240,000 electors in a country of 35 million inhabitants (roughly 1 elector per 30 citizens), or about double—but only double—the number of voters under the Restoration. At a time when democratic momentum was gaining and spreading across the nation, Guizot defended this severely limited suffrage tooth and nail. To avoid the ban on public meetings, the protesters came up with the idea of organizing a series of banquets in every region. The banquets would provide an opportunity to eloquently express their demand for expansion of the electoral base and put mounting pressure on Paris. From July 9, 1847, to February 22, 1848, seventy banquets were held, attended by 17,000 people.

On December 20, 1847, Flaubert told Ernest Chevalier, now a magistrate in Ajaccio, that he was preparing to participate in the reformist banquet in Rouen: "The powers that be will take a dim view of me, *I will be put down in the registers,* and this will set an unfortunate precedent for me, when in the future you wield the sword and scales of justice against the one who sends you his best." Despite his joking tone, he really went, accompanied by Maxime Du Camp and Louis Bouilhet; curiosity carried the day. The three friends listened but did not applaud. Later, while coming home along the Seine, they mocked the pompous exhortations and resounding proclamations they had heard, never considering the campaign's actual results. Soon after, Gustave sent Louise his account of the banquet, which had been held on Christmas Day: "I attended a reformist banquet! What taste! What cuisine! What wines! And what speeches! Nothing has given me more absolute contempt for success than to consider the price at which it is obtained. I remained cold, feeling sick with disgust amidst the patriotic enthusiasm drummed up by the helm of state—the abyss we are charging into, the honor of our flag, the shadow of our standards, the brotherhood of peoples, and other claptrap of the same type." He made fun of "M. Odilon Barrot's virtuous hollering" and the "tearful lamentations of Maître Crémieux regarding the state of our finances": "And after this 9-hour session spent sitting before cold turkey and suckling pig in the company of my locksmith—who whacked me on the shoulder whenever something good was said—I came home frozen down to the entrails. Whatever poor opinion you have of man, bitterness takes hold of your heart when such unbelievable nonsense, such muddled stupidity is spread out before you."

Flaubert's raillery was Olympian. Though he was no supporter of Louis Philippe, Guizot, or the bourgeoisie attached to the July regime, the opposition seemed equally ridiculous to him, with its overblown eloquence, its audience of traveling salesmen, and its ad nauseam repetition of quotations from the popular songwriter Béranger, "that boiled meat of modern poetry—everyone can eat it and find it good." He was convinced that the artist must remain above such trivial agitation. But he also believed the artist should not prohibit himself from observing it: "from the perspective of art" it could be interesting to witness what transpired. There are scenes, faces, and flashes of eloquence that the imagination alone is powerless to devise and that can be sources of inspiration when found in life. For that very reason, he decided to travel to Paris as soon as he heard news of the revolutionary February days of 1848.

"In Revolt"

"In revolt": the expression is borrowed from the title of the chapter on the Revolution of 1848 in Maxime Du Camp's literary memoirs. A slightly misleading title, if truth be told, given that neither he nor Flaubert truly *participated* in the events other than as enthusiasts of spectacular performances and colorful tumult, asking for nothing more than to gape at the confusion of cries, chants, gunshots, and stampedes. With his friends Louis de Cormenin, Maxime Du Camp, and Louis Bouilhet, Flaubert *watched* the revolution. The young men, especially Flaubert, took the detached attitude of the spectator. "You ask my opinion about what has just taken place," he wrote to Louise Colet in a letter of March 1848, "Well, it is all very funny. The expressions on the faces of the discomfited are a joy to see. I take the greatest delight in observing all the crushed ambitions."[2] In his view, comedy vied with nonsense in the upheaval of the street and the defeat of the throne; the loquacity on one side and the fear on the other were indeed very "funny."

However, the four friends did see nearly everything that took place over those days in February. In his *Souvenirs de l'année 1848* [*Memoirs of 1848*], Du Camp recounts their wanderings through the feverish streets. Having arrived at Du Camp's apartment on February 23, Flaubert and Bouilhet accompanied him to the Palais Royal, the boulevards, and the Tuileries, joining an exultant crowd: "Long live reform!" "Down with Guizot!" After a firing squad killed several people on Boulevard des Capucines, they saw the demonstrators' bodies placed in wagons and carried around Paris by torchlight to the cry of "Revenge! They're slaughtering our brothers!"[3] They heard the alarm sound, saw the gun shops pillaged and the barricades built. On the morning of February 24, Bouilhet predicted that Louis Philippe was lost, but the others were skeptical. Louis de Cormenin, who had come to fill them in about the previous evening, left to go speak with a few deputies. Maxime, Louis, and Gustave set off again, following the insurgents as artistic onlookers. During a period when they lost sight of Bouilhet, Maxime and Gustave witnessed the taking of the Tuileries. The crowd invaded the palace, which was soon "sacked and pillaged from top to bottom." "We heard a few shots," wrote Du Camp; "they were breaking mirrors by firing at them. The genie of destruction, who torments children and victors, was entering the palace." Once outside, he and Gustave managed to save the lives of a disarmed group of mounted munic-ipal guards: "Having arrived two feet from us, these men took off their po-lice hats and saluted, their faces drawn in a forced smile." Hearing guns being cocked, the two friends rushed over to the guards, took them in their arms, and called them their "lost brothers." A few "good people" followed suit, and the guards were saved.

Gustave and Maxime returned to Du Camp's place exhausted, their minds swimming with the incredible scenes they had witnessed, and found Louis Bouilhet waiting for them. He had been forced to help build barricades and had only escaped by intentionally dropping a cobblestone on his foot. After dinner, Louis de Cormenin took them to the Hôtel de Ville, where the Re-public was to be proclaimed. "So Flaubert, Louis, and I set off again, leaving Bouilhet half lame by the chimney." Their path was interrupted by countless barricades through which they had to negotiate passage. Cormenin took care of the parleying by using his father's name: "We were allowed to cross the cobblestones, the barrels full of sand, and the upside-down carts."[4] Having reached the Hôtel de Ville, they witnessed the proclamation of the provisional government "in the name of the sovereign people."

Flaubert returned to Croisset after experiencing the furies and enthusiasms of the Paris revolution that pitted the moderate republicans behind Alphonse de Lamartine against the socialist revolutionaries led by Louis-Auguste Blanqui, and after seeing the extraordinary number of demands carried in a cortege to the provisional government's seat at the Hôtel de Ville. What he had witnessed confirmed his disdain for politics, but the images of the people "in revolt" would remain etched in his memory and be indelibly described in his second *Sentimental Education*.

In the following weeks, Flaubert was primarily occupied with private con-cerns. He was devastated to learn of his friend Alfred Le Poittevin's death of a heart ailment on April 3. For two entire nights he kept watch over the body, and then he wrapped Alfred in his shroud and kissed him goodbye. He described his friend's final moments to Maxime, who had stayed in Paris after being called up by the National Guard: "At daybreak, about four o'clock, the attendant and I began our task. I lifted him, turned him, covered him. The feeling of the coldness and rigidity of his limbs stayed in my fingertips all the next day. . . . He was carried to the cemetery on men's shoulders. It was almost an hour's walk. From behind, I saw the coffin swaying like a rolling boat. The service was atrociously long. In the cemetery the earth was muddy. I stood by the grave and watched each shovelful as it fell: there seemed to be a hundred thousand of them. When the hole was filled, I walked away, smoking."[5] Le Poittevin, that dear beloved friend, the admired elder who had been his guide and his fraternal confidant, was no more.

While the revolution continued into April and one demonstration came after another in Paris, life at Croisset seemed quiet. Yet Flaubert had also been called up to the National Guard, and he told Ernest Chevalier that he had done his first watch after marching to plant a Liberty tree, a ritual carried out throughout France in a fairly conciliatory spirit, given that these republican symbols were planted with the blessing of a priest. "Love is stronger than hate," went the song by Pierre Dupont, one of the most popular songwriters of the time. France was still in a phase of "lyrical illusion," short-lived reconciliation, and apparent agreement between "sleeping republicans" and "morning-after republicans." However, after the extreme left called for demonstrations on April 16 to postpone the elections, dissension grew and the inclination to fraternize was lost. Flaubert did not seem to pay any attention. In May, he began writing his *Temptation of Saint Anthony* and kept at it until he was distracted by the news of the terrible June days in Paris.

The provisional government had passed a decree proclaiming the right to work and pursued its fight against unemployment with the creation on February 26 of the Ateliers Nationaux, "national workshops" where the unemployed were given two francs a day for menial construction work. To the dismay of the radicals and socialists, the elections for the Constituent Assembly held on April 23 under universal male suffrage were won by a majority of "morning-after republicans." The ballot box had failed to appease the conflict between the revolution's vanguard, which vehemently expressed itself in the political clubs that had been springing up since February, and the Assembly's bourgeois majority. On May 15, close to one hundred and fifty thousand people marched in a demonstration backed by Armand Barbès,

François-Vincent Raspail, and Blanqui to protest France's policy not to intervene in favor of the Poles massacred by the Prussians and Austrians. The Assembly was occupied for several hours and a new provisional government proclaimed at the Hôtel de Ville. Meanwhile, the Executive Commission that had replaced the previous provisional government called up the National Guard, the mobile guard, and the army and put an end to the insurrection.

The worst was yet to come. Due to the economic crisis, unemployment was growing, as was the number of people registering with the National Workshops: they numbered 115,000 on the day after the events of May 15. The poorly organized workshops provided piddling work, at best, to these craftsmen and workers, who were becoming increasingly politicized in their idleness and were starting to be swayed by socialist doctrines. The workers began to hold meetings on the boulevards in favor of "a democratic and social republic." The majority in the Assembly took fright and sought to abolish this institution that was not only expensive, but was creating revolutionaries. Enough! On June 21, it was decided that the National Workshops would be dissolved: men under twenty-five would have to join the army, and the others would be sent to work sites in the provinces. After negotiations failed, barricades were erected in the capital's eastern quarters under ad hoc leaders. The social war dreaded by some and judged inevitable by others had begun. It would rage over three days of relentless battle. "Give us bread or give us death!" In his memoirs, Alexis de Tocqueville describes the insurgents' "strategic science," attributing it to the fact that most of them had had a military education: "Half of the workers in Paris have served in our armies, and they are always ready to take up arms again."[6] Governmental forces (the National Guard from the western quarters, reinforced by battalions rushed in from the provinces, mobile guards, and soldiers of the line) under Minister of War Louis-Eugène Cavaignac lost one thousand men; the insurgents lost several thousand, including fifteen hundred who were sent to the firing squad without a trial. Maxime Du Camp commented: "Victory rested with civilization, and for a few weeks General Cavaignac was proclaimed the savior of the nation."[7] Ever the courageous defender of civilization, Maxime paid his share with a wound to the leg received while wearing the National Guard shako. He wrote to Flaubert, still at Croisset, that the street fighting was not over: "Paris is in a state of siege. One hears nothing but the firing of cannons. Yesterday our company attacked the barricade at the Barrière Rochechouart. I was shot in the leg. The bullet went in 2 inches above the knee and came out in the middle of the calf. . . . I'm in a lot of pain, but there isn't the slightest danger."[8]

Flaubert was worried, but was prevented from rushing to his friend's bedside by an unfortunate family situation at Croisset. His brother-in-law Hamard, showing signs of dementia (Gustave wrote to Chevalier that he was "completely mad"), had gotten it into his head to take back his daughter Caroline, who was being raised by Mme Flaubert. Hamard had served a summons to his mother-in-law: "Consider, my poor Ernest, the state I am in. What an existence! I do nothing, I can neither read, nor write, nor think." The court would eventually rule that little Caroline could remain under Mme Flaubert's care, but Gustave was kept busy by the twists and turns of the affair throughout the weeks of revolution and civil war in Paris. In October, he confessed to Ernest: "Oh! family is such a pain in the ass! A mire! A hindrance! How it swallows you up, rots you to the bone, and drains the life out of you."

Yet nothing, neither family, nor revolution, nor concern about his friend's wound, could tear Flaubert away from his work on *The Temptation of Saint Anthony*, which he had been thinking about since the trip to Italy: "My book comes first." He was gradually becoming convinced by Maxime, who was slowly recovering, to embark on a long trip to the Orient, but he was determined not to leave before he had finished writing his "mystery." In December, Louis-Napoléon Bonaparte was elected president of the Republic with a comfortable lead over Cavaignac in the first round. Flaubert did not bother to vote: "Flaubert, Bouilhet, and I," wrote Du Camp, "were in Rouen by the fire reading Philippe Desportes's *Amours d'Hippolyte* [*Loves of Hippolytus*], going into ecstasies over the Icarus sonnet and hardly thinking that we had a duty to fulfill. Caesar or Brutus, what did we care!" The three friends were bored by politics, for they were "cut off from anything that did not relate to art or literature."[9]

Paris could burn and power could shift from the Orléans family to Bonaparte for all Flaubert cared: his mind was in Thebaid, the region of Upper Egypt where Christians had sought shelter from the persecution of Emperor Decius in the middle of the third century. According to legend, it was here that the future Saint Anthony resisted concupiscence and the other temptations sent by the Devil. Flaubert's *Temptation of Saint Anthony* was inspired not only by Brueghel's painting, but by Edgard Quinet's *Ahasvérus*. In September 1849, the manuscript was finished. Maxime Du Camp and Louis

Bouilhet were invited to Croisset to listen to a reading of the work. The author had not breathed a word of his project to them, "neither of the general plan, nor of the work itself," writes Maxime, who devotes several pages of his memoirs to the thirty-two hour reading session: "He read for four days, without stopping, from noon to four, and from eight to midnight." The two listeners had promised not to speak until the end. Throughout these long hours, Flaubert read his prose, convinced that he would make his friends gasp with enthusiasm, that he would move them; he finally had the masterpiece for which he had so long and desperately hoped. Unfortunately, as one "temptation" came after another, his friends' faces became increasingly stony. This succession of characters playing the same scene over and over was altogether too static. "His efforts were wasted on us! We did not understand, we could not guess what he was getting at, and, in truth, he was getting nowhere. Three years of labor collapsed without any result; the work went up in smoke. Bouilhet and I were distressed. After each part of the reading, Flaubert would ask us: 'So?' We did not dare to answer."

Having reached the end of the book, Flaubert urged his friends to deliver their verdict. Bouilhet and Du Camp had conferred and agreed that it was their duty to prevent their friend from heading down this slippery slope on which he would spoil his vast talent—a talent of which they had no doubt. And so Flaubert was dumbfounded to hear them confess that he had been mistaken—that his work was a failure. This admission, this judgment that was so difficult to express to a beloved friend, was a powerful proof of their friendship. They did what they had to. Flaubert was initially surprised, then miffed and disappointed, but he accepted their criticism.

"Flaubert balked; he would reread certain sentences and tell us: 'Yet it's beautiful!'" Yes, but the beauty of these sentences did not change the fact that the entire book needed to be rewritten or thrown in the fire: "There are excellent passages, exquisite reminders of Antiquity," the friends told Flaubert: "but all that is lost in the exaggeration of the language; you wanted to make music but you made nothing but noise."

Many lovers of Flaubert consider his friends' severity excessive or even incomprehensible. Witness René Dumesnil: "What remains inexplicable is that a few cluttered passages hid the brilliant beauty of many other pages from them. One has to think that Flaubert read very poorly ... or that they listened very distractedly."[10] According to Du Camp, he and Bouilhet advised their friend to choose a down-to-earth subject, in the style of Balzac.

Bouilhet allegedly suggested he tell the story of Delamare, a country doctor who had committed suicide after his wife had been compromised by her escapades and killed herself. This news item is generally mentioned as one of the sources of *Madame Bovary*, the novel to which Flaubert, following his friends' advice, would soon devote himself. As for *The Temptation*, Flaubert hid it away in a drawer but did not abandon it: he would tackle the subject twice more before publishing the definitive version in 1874.

Writing the Revolution

Flaubert's apparent indifference to the fateful days that began with the February 1848 revolution and continued to the 1851 coup d'état that put Louis-Napoléon in power stands in stark contrast to the attention he gives these events in *Sentimental Education* and, to a lesser degree, *Bouvard and Pécuchet*. The former novel's protagonist, Frédéric Moreau, is plunged into the heart of these events, along with the characters surrounding him. The attention Flaubert devotes to immersing his characters in the flow of historical events leads him to be as scrupulous as a historian: fiction must be embedded in reality without ever betraying it. To this end, Flaubert went all out to gather rich and varied documentation. Without neglecting oral sources—having personally witnessed some of the Paris events of 1848, he also interviewed George Sand, Jules Duplan, Ernest Feydeau, and Maurice Schlésinger—Flaubert also made use of Maxime Du Camp's *Souvenirs de l'année 1848*, consulted newspapers (*La Presse, Le National, L'Illustration, Le Journal des débats,* etc.), and read the abundant literature on the subject, beginning with the book *Histoire de la révolution de 1848* [*History of the Revolution of 1848*] by Daniel Stern, alias of Marie d'Agoult.[11] As Gilbert Guisan has shown, some passages from *Sentimental Education* are taken directly from Stern's book. For example:

> FLAUBERT: "And nobody knew if the banquet would be held, if the Government would carry out its threat, or if the National Guard would appear."[12]
>
> DANIEL STERN: "Was it truly cancelled? Would it be held? Would the National Guard come? Would the government carry out its threat?"

Basing his work on abundant, in-depth research, Flaubert activated his characters and made them react according to their temperament, their political leanings, and their birth, creating contrasting types that included the fervent revolutionaries, the opportunists, and the provisionally defeated. In *Sentimental Education* we encounter Citizen Regimbart, who is driven by his single-minded hatred of the government, living off his wife and admired by the café owners in whose establishments he spends his days ranting and vaunting the revolution; Sénécal, driven by socialist ideals, a school monitor who dreams of an ethically just society; and Dussardier, an assistant in a firm of carriers, the embodiment of the people, a devoted and courageous man proud to spend time with gentlemen. Dussardier is driven by an illusion particularly characteristic of the lyricism of that February: "The Republic has been proclaimed! We shall all be happy now! I heard some journalists saying just now that we're going to liberate Poland and Italy. No more kings! You understand what that means? The whole world is free! The whole world!"[13]

Beside these fervent characters, we find the opportunists, powerfully rendered in the character of Deslauriers, a lawyer without a cause who "looked forward impatiently to a great upheaval in which he confidently expected to make a niche for himself."[14] After the events of February, he manages to get himself appointed as one of the commissioners who replaced the prefects. Deslauriers fits the social and historical type of those young people, often with university degrees and sometimes talented, who were refused employment, honors, and even the right to vote by the regime that was put in place in July. Many of the non-proletarian participants in the uprisings were driven by ambition for a place in the sun and desire for revenge against society; the educated, the semi-educated, and those revolted by the injustice of their lot dove into a political movement which they expected to promote them.

If Frédéric can be included in this opportunistic phalanx, it is for a different reason. Frédéric is an heir, a former law student who has become a person of independent means, leading an idler's life with a few vague desires to write. The revolution provides him with spectacle, adventure, and—Why not?—the chance to be on the front line of politics. This gives Flaubert the opportunity to write a legendary scene, one of the funniest in *Sentimental Education:* pushed by his friends, weak-willed Frédéric finally decides to stand for election in April 1848. Flaubert describes his protagonist's introduction to one of the clubs that sponsored candidates, a responsibility shared by the clubs and the newspapers in this period without organized political parties. Flaubert maliciously names this club the "Club de l'Intelligence." The session Frédéric attends is a classic, and a delight for historians. In a dozen pages of fierce irony with occasional flashes of sympathy, Flaubert captures better than anyone what was called the "spirit of 1848," a blend of illusions, pipe dreams, aspirations to fraternity, and even religiosity. While preparing his book, he had been struck by the role Christianity played in elaborating socialist doctrines: "I noticed," he wrote, "in the so-called men of progress, starting with Saint-Simon and extending to Proudhon, the strangest quotations. All of them speak of religious revelation." Coming in the midst of the Industrial Revolution, the Christian dimension of the Revolution of 1848 was quite far from the spirit of the Revolution of 1789 and even more so from the heavily anti-clerical Revolution of 1830. The fact that it added *fraternity* to republican dogma is now a widely accepted fact, but Flaubert, who was observing without interpreting, was one of the first to highlight it. He also emphasized the tendency to mimic the revolutionaries of 1789, an aspect mentioned in Tocqueville's *Souvenirs* and personified in *Sentimental Education* by the dogmatic character Sénécal, chairman of the club session, a former member of secret societies who has risen to a position of power: "as it was customary for every person in the public eye to model himself on some famous figure, one copying Saint-Just, another Danton, and yet another Marat, he himself tried to resemble Blanqui, who in his turn imitated Robespierre."[15] As the meeting of the Club de l'Intelligence turns into a farce, Frédéric gives up on running for office.

There were also those who were defeated by the Revolution: the upper bourgeoisie, along with its parasites and clients. Flaubert describes their fears. M. Dambreuse, a middle-class deputy, banker, chairman of several companies, and renowned lord of the Faubourg Saint-Honoré, singlehandedly stands for Important People. In his view, the February revolution makes no sense: "This new state of affairs not only threatened his fortune but, far worse, contradicted his experience. Such a splendid system! Such a wise king! What could have happened?"[16] The flight of Louis Philippe had left him and those of his ilk completely distraught. Despite their anger and fear, they tried to adapt, covering up their distress. M. Dambreuse quickly curbs the external signs of his wealth, dismisses three servants, sells his horses, and buys a soft hat. To better understand this unexpected situation but especially to flaunt his sudden support for the ideas of the day, he affects to read the newspapers he had previously loathed. He goes so far as to purchase a revolutionary painting he would have considered grotesque the previous season. Flaubert's pleasure at lacerating the image of the bourgeois is palpable: "[Dambreuse] had enthusiastically adopted 'our sublime motto: Liberty, Equality, Fraternity,' for he had always been a Republican at heart." Of course, if Dambreuse had voted with the ministry under the previous regime, it was simply to accelerate its unavoidable downfall. Dambreuse even lashes out at M. Guizot, "who—you can't deny it—has landed us in a fine mess!" Better yet: "he declared his sympathy for the workers—'for after all, we are all workers, more or less.' And he carried his impartiality to the point of admitting that there was some logic in Proudhon."[17] Dambreuse doesn't mind what happens to the Orléans and the Orleanist regime, so long as he can cut his own losses and wait for better days. It is a devastating portrait.

Always attentive to the paradoxes of the great movements of history, Flaubert noted a more unexpected victim of the Revolution: the kept woman, teetering on the edge of despair because the revolutionaries' attack on the bourgeois order threatened women of easy virtue. Rosanette spits a working-class girl's hatred of the Revolution in the face of Frédéric, the law student waiting for his inheritance, "blaming him for everything that had happened in France during the last months, accusing him of having started the Revolution; it was his fault if everybody was ruined, if the rich were leaving Paris, and if she died later on in the workhouse."[18] The heyday of incorruptible revolutionaries was not beneficial for whores.

Published twenty years after the fact, in 1869, *Sentimental Education* was Flaubert's way of participating in a revolution he had "missed," though he had been old enough to be a part of it. The crisis of 1848 was undoubtedly the historical event that had the biggest impact on him, despite the fact that he appeared uninterested as it unfolded. There is further evidence of its significance in *Bouvard and Pécuchet*, written ten years later and set in the provinces, in Chavignolles. The astonishment of the bourgeois in the provinces is as great as it was in Paris. And their rallying to the Republic is just as speedy. In the provinces as in the capital, Liberty trees are planted and blessed by the clergy—in this case, by a priest nurtured on the counter-revolutionary philosopher Louis de Bonald, who, "after thundering against the kings" in his speech, "glorified the Republic."[19] One is not surprised to find the "progressist" Dr. Vaucorbeil among the unanimous citizens. More astonishing is the rallying of the Count de Faverges, but his hatred for the usurper Louis Philippe is greater than his dislike of the Republic: "Everything for the people," he proclaims, dreaming of the imminent return of the Bourbons. Even the notary has become a republican, but only to avoid whatever one might fear from the workers streaming by singing *La Marseillaise*.

The provinces diligently imitate the capital, and begin by massively subscribing to republican newspapers. They have the same concerns: the faithful of '89 dream of liberating Poland, but the bourgeois are afraid of tax increases. The Republic is not yet called into question, though Mme Bordin, who hates it, does offer five francs to fund the National Guard's equipment. The surprising phenomenon, noted by Flaubert, is the sudden ascent of the working class in the esteem of the bourgeois: "The powerful fawned upon the lower classes."[20] People sing: "Hats off before the cap! On your knees before the workman!"[21] But beginning in May 1848, the reactionaries begin to be roused. Chavignolles's bourgeois inhabitants delight in the most absurd gossip about Louis Blanc and Ledru-Rollin. The Count de Faverges predicts the imminent accession to the throne of the Count de Chambord, the Bourbon pretender, while Heurtaux, a former captain of the Empire, hopes that Louis-Napoléon Bonaparte will soon take power. For their part, the workers want work—unemployment has spread. Chavignolles's municipal council pulls together its own version of the "national workshops," which a clumsy councilor calls "charity workshops," drawing the ire of the "smocks." The workers are dispersed by being ordered to build a pathway.

In *Sentimental Education*, Flaubert's characters are mobilized by the Assembly's closing of the National Workshops and the insurrection that follows. Aside from the socialist theorist Sénécal, who will be deported to the island of Belle-Île, everyone sides with the National Guard carrying out the repression, including Dussardier, the man of the people. He fights the insurgents to defend the Republic but goes about it as one accomplishes a painful duty, like the "man of probity" in *Les Misérables*, who "from very love of the people opposes them. But he deeply understands their reason, and does so with respect."[22] It is no different in *Sentimental Education:* for Dussardier, the situation is tragic. The euphoria of February is long-forgotten, and once the workers are defeated, their brother Dussardier sees that the victors "hated the Republic" and realizes he has made a terrible mistake.

The novel continues to show the terrible revenge of the rich. Père Roque arrives in Paris with the troops from Nogent; like many other provincial members of the National Guard, he had answered the call to defend order. Once the danger passes, Roque swaggers and guards the prisoners at the Tuileries with his compatriots. To exorcize the fright the workers gave him, he hurls abuse at them through the basement window, then shoots a prisoner asking for bread point blank. Flaubert did not make up any of this ferocity; he found an account of it in a "historical notice" published in the newspaper *La Commune de Paris* in March 1849.

Aside from Dussardier, who is filled with remorse, and Sénécal, who is imprisoned and defeated, all of the characters in *Sentimental Education* are pleased with the outcome of the events of June. M. Dambreuse has recovered his self-confidence and can once again open his doors to his posh friends, who are still reeling from the insurrection, but soothed by the return to order. They give free rein to their hatred—if dreams were weapons, Louis Blanc and Proudhon would drop dead. Pellerin, the failed painter who had gotten nothing from the Republic and had seen the socialists mock his art, takes a violent turn toward royalism. Hussonnet, the hack journalist in the service of any winner, starts writing reactionary pamphlets that open Dambreuse's doors to him. Frédéric, true to his inconstant nature, has forgotten his recent republican fervor and expands his new ambitions by courting Mme Dambreuse. As for Deslauriers, now a commissioner in the provinces, he finds himself between a rock and a hard place, threatened equally by the conservatives and the socialists. He too has gone back on his ideas: he hates the workers now, and, sensing that the future belongs to the bourgeoisie, he has Frédéric introduce him to the Dambreuses, who only a few weeks earlier had been among the defeated. Flaubert records the long-winded, reassured banalities of this polite society back on its feet following a bad time.

Order reigns in France. In Paris, the Dambreuse home has become an "annex to [the Orleanist headquarters on] the rue de Poitiers": everyone there attacks the Republic and even the recently passed constitution. They crack jokes all day long, write pamphlets, indoctrinate the mistreated clergy, and send emissaries to the provinces. In the Paris of *Sentimental Education,* as in the Chavignolles of *Bouvard and Pécuchet*, those who adulated General Cavaignac, who was known as the butcher of the insurrectionists, now bitterly reproach him for his republican convictions and prefer Changarnier, the head of the National Guard. The future is not yet entirely certain, but it's on the right track. At the Dambreuse home, guests are delighted with Adolphe Thiers's latest book, *De la propriété* [*On Property*], and jeer at socialist ideas with an enthusiasm proportionate to the fear that recently struck their hearts. Flaubert's eloquence redoubles when it comes to Thiers, about whom he wrote to George Sand: "I shall try, in the third part of my novel (when I reach the reactions that followed the June Days) to slip in a panegyric of said gentleman, apropos of his book on Property, and I hope he'll be pleased with me."[23] As for the socialists, they were disappointed in the people. Sénécal considers the masses still immature and incompetent: "A dictatorship is sometimes indispensable. Long live tyranny, provided the tyrant does good."[24]

This principle of authority is on everyone's lips. The conservatives are split regarding the political solution—Orléans, Chambord, or Bonaparte—and debate it in the "ladies' salons," which allows Rosanette an opportunity to host her "soirées." When the coup d'état of December 2, 1851, is announced, of all those who had ardently hoped for the Republic, only one man remains true to his wishes—Dussardier. Sénécal sides with law enforcement and kills his former comrade, who falls dead off the barricade where he had proclaimed "Long live the Republic!" His death is the product of a sinister historical to and fro: in June 1848, Dussardier had been with the National Guard and Sénécal on the other side; in December 1851, they find themselves on opposite sides again, but Sénécal is now with the police. The workingman's hope and illusions die with Dussardier.

In *Bouvard and Pécuchet*, Flaubert shows that the coup d'état and the resulting advent of the Empire were also imposed without any difficulty in rural towns like Chavignolles. In December 1848, "all the citizens of Chavignolles voted for Louis Napoleon."[25] "The great party of order" takes shape and asserts itself; it is led by the parish priest, the mayor, the notary, and the legitimist count. The Liberty trees have lost their leaves and are chopped down. The terrible fright experienced by the wealthy is replaced by their triumph and leads to the passing of educational laws that reassert the clergy's influence. This is when the community school appears in the novel, followed by Flaubert's description of its poverty and forced submission to the parish priest. M. Petit, the schoolmaster, has remained true to his republican ideals, but the law and lack of resources force him to kowtow to the reproachful Abbé Jeufroy, who considers that Petit gives short shrift to sacred history and catechism. All the notables believe liberty went too far and that what is needed now is an "iron fist." On December 3, they learn that the French have inherited a strongman. Everyone seems delighted.

February 22, 1848–December 2, 1851: between those two dates, the history of France as told by Flaubert's novels is that of a road full of potholes. The 1848 Revolution was in vain. Yes, Louis Philippe fell, but society did not change: the rich stayed rich and the poor stayed poor, that is, when they didn't die on the barricades, like Dussardier. The upper bourgeoisie, which had initially been horrified by a revolution that caught it unawares, was able to gradually detach itself from the republican regime and work toward its downfall. Each in their own way, *Sentimental Education*'s Dussardier, Deslauriers, and Sénécal embody the failure of republican and socialist hopes. Despite his naiveté, Dussardier, who aimed so high, is spared by Flaubert; his soul remains pure from the beginning to the end of the story. Deslauriers is open to any movement that will ensure him a position. As for Sénécal, he represents Flaubert's idea of the hidden face of socialism: authoritarianism. "Isn't the socialists' ideal state," Flaubert asked, "a kind of vast monster absorbing any individual action, any personality, any thought, and that will direct and do everything?" The Dambreuses claim authority, as does Sénécal. Things have come full circle: from one end of society to the other, people have been brought to their knees. All servile, all groveling! As for the rest, all those who applauded the Revolution, they have returned to serving their personal interests: not one of them defended the Republic. It seems Flaubert's judgment on these events was not unlike Pécuchet's exclamation after the coup d'état: "Since the bourgeois are vicious, the workers jealous, the priests obsequious, and the masses ultimately accepting of any tyrant, so long as he leaves their snouts in the trough, Louis Napoleon did the right thing! Let him gag the people, crush them underfoot, wipe them out—it would serve them right for their hatred of the law, their cowardice, their ineptitude, and their blindness!"[26]

For Flaubert, the contradiction was obvious. He detested those in power. According to him, the best government was one "in the death throes." Yet he was inclined to accept the restoration of the Empire because of the little regard he had for humanity in general and the fact that his contempt for the revolutionaries was equal to his disgust for the rich and powerful. If he was an anarchist, he was a right-wing anarchist. Yet the only character worthy of respect in his heavily researched account of the Revolution of 1848 is Dussardier, a pure person and a republican hero, which somewhat mitigates Flaubert's very dark conception of the people. Collectively, the people are ugly, dirty, and stupid, but it is among them that one can find the signs of a contemporary holiness or a lay heroism. The character of Félicité in *A Simple Heart* would later confirm this view.

CHAPTER 8

A Longing for the Orient

"I was dreaming of distant voyages in the lands of the South; I saw the Orient and its vast sands, its palaces crossed by camels with their bronze bells; I saw the mares leaping toward the horizon reddened by the sun; I saw the blue waves, a pure sky, silver sand; I smelled the perfume of the warm oceans of the South; and then, close to me, under a tent, in the shade of a large-leafed aloe, a woman with brown skin and an ardent gaze, wrapping her arms around me and speaking to me in the language of the houris."

These words are spoken by the narrator of Flaubert's *Memoirs of a Madman*, written in 1839. Clearly, the long journey that Flaubert and his friend Maxime Du Camp embarked on ten years later was not an impromptu affair. Flaubert refers to his dream of Oriental new horizons on several occasions in his juvenilia. It was a dream he shared with many of his contemporaries. "Today," he wrote in the *Intimate Notebook* of 1840–41, "my ideas of a great journey came back stronger than ever. It's still the Orient. I was born to live there."[1] The Romantic generation was fascinated by the Orient. The term "orientalism" was coined in 1799, both in English and in French, and was added to the Académie Française's dictionary of the French language in 1838. In his dictionary of art and archaeology, the art historian Louis Réau explained its origin: "Orientalism began in the eighteenth century with the fashion for Turkish and Chinese art and artifacts, but grew rapidly at the beginning of the nineteenth century with the Egyptian campaign, the struggles for Greek independence, and the conquest of Algeria." The term refers both to the scientific movement launched by Napoleon's expedition to Egypt and the aesthetic, cultural, literary, and artistic enthusiasm that followed. Egyptomania reached its peak in the 1820s after Jean-François Champollion caused a sensation by discovering the secret of hieroglyphics and, as a result, the method for deciphering them. In 1831, a chair in Egyptology was created for Champollion at the Collège de France. It was also his idea for the French government to ask Muhammad Ali, viceroy of Egypt, to give one of the two obelisks of Luxor to France, in recognition of excellent Franco-Egyptian relations. The viceroy replied: "I have done nothing for France that France did not do for me. I offer her the remains of an ancient civilization in exchange for the new civilization that she has sown the seeds of in the Orient. May the obelisk of Thebes safely arrive in Paris and eternally serve as a link between the two cities."[2] A specially adapted ship named the *Louxor* was built for this exceptional cargo. Its long journey—via the Nile, the Mediterranean, the Atlantic, the English Channel, and the Seine—was a spectacular event. On September 14, 1833, the ship arrived at its port of call in Rouen. The Seine was too low for it to continue to Paris until December 11, giving the young Flaubert plenty of time to admire it. The monument was finally erected on the Place de la Concorde on October 25, 1836, before a jubilant crowd.

Literature and painting brought to life the themes of a mythical, mysterious, colorful Orient. In 1829, Victor Hugo published *Les Orientales,* noting in his preface that "today . . . we are far more occupied with the Orient than we have ever been before." Eugène Delacroix was among the most notable painters to embrace the fashion, beginning with his *Massacre at Chios* (1824) and later *The Death of Sardanapalus* (1827).[3]

Parallel to this artistic and literary movement, scientific developments were also advancing. Another now legendary feature of the push to the Orient was the arrival in Egypt of the Saint-Simonists in 1833, led by Father Prosper Enfantin. Planning to help Muhammad Ali in his efforts to modernize Egypt, these apostles of industrialization conceived of the Suez Canal, a "marital bed" between Orient and Occident. The rage for the "Orient" in the first half of the nineteenth century was also expressed in fashion, interior design, and a wide variety of objects, all of which referred to an Orient that began in Athens, which was liberated from the Turks in 1829, and extended through the Ottoman Empire and all the areas over which Constantinople had more or less administrative control: Egypt, Syria, Palestine, and, further on, legendary Persia, so coveted by the European powers.

A great number of people, especially writers, responded to what one could refer to as "the call of the Orient." In 1811, Chateaubriand reported on his travels from Paris to Jerusalem in *Itinéraire de Paris à Jérusalem* [*Journey from Paris to Jerusalem*]. Some twenty years later, Lamartine provided his own account of the Orient in *Souvenirs, impressions, pensées et paysages pendant un voyage en Orient* [*Memories, Impressions, Thoughts, and Landscapes during a Trip to the Orient*]. In 1848, Gérard de Nerval published his lesser-known but equally revealing *Voyage en Orient* [*Journey to the Orient*]. These travelers were not all looking for the same thing. In *Itinéraire,* Chateaubriand states that he was primarily seeking traces of the past, which was the setting for his prose epic *Les Martyrs*. By aiming for Jerusalem, he was following on from his *Genius of Christianity*. According to him, the Orient was sinking into decadence, and the barbarians—that is, the non-Christians—were responsible. The spirit of the Crusades lived on in Chateaubriand. Religious motivations also played a part in the journey of Lamartine, who set off in search of "traces of God in the Orient"—in other words, to investigate the biblical sites of the Holy Land, the "land of testimony, still imprinted with the traces of the ancient and the new commerce between God and man." In fact, his religious convictions developed along the course of the trip, particularly after the death of his daughter in Beirut; he shifted from a conformist Catholicism to a kind of deism or non-dogmatic Christianity. As for Gérard de Nerval, when he left Marseille in January 1843 he was hoping to escape the dark obsessions that followed the death of his beloved Jenny Colon. The account of his journey was initially published in the periodicals *L'Artiste* and the *Revue des deux mondes*. Did Gustave and Maxime read these excerpts? If they did, they did not mention them, and the complete version of Nerval's narrative would not be published until after their return, in 1851.

Maxime was the more eager of the two travelers. He was anxious to take off again after a first trip in 1846, which had inspired a travel narrative dedicated to Gustave, *Souvenirs et paysages d'Orient, Smyrne, Éphèse, Magnésie, Constantinople* [*Recollections and Landscapes of the Orient, Smyrna, Ephesus, Magnesia, Constantinople*]. He now wanted to write a travel book that would stand out from all previous publications by its scientific thoroughness and literary elegance. Flaubert did not share his ambition. His desire was more vague. He had once considered traveling with Alfred Le Poittevin, before he had settled into being a homebody. One might even wonder if he would have embarked on this adventure at all if his friend hadn't suggested it. Yet his desire for the Orient had not diminished—he leapt at the opportunity Maxime presented him. Their journey was to last from late October 1849 to July 1851. It was far more than a little jaunt across the sea.

What We Know

The details of this trek are well known, thanks to the two travelers' own writings. The first and richest source is Flaubert's correspondence. Excluding the last letters written to his mother from Paris before their departure, but including the first one sent from Lyon, there are no less than eighty letters. The principal addressee is Mme Flaubert, for whom Flaubert strives to describe every step of his journey, both to entertain her and to reassure her. And also, perhaps, to record his impressions, with the knowledge that he would find the letters upon his return. It took a great deal of effort and a few misleading assurances to make Flaubert's mother accept this long separation and an expedition whose many dangers she feared. Her consent was won by a ruse. She was told that her beloved son, still subject to his nervous attacks, needed heat and light—in other words, the warm climate of the Orient.[4] As the doctor in the family, Gustave's older brother Achille played along in helping to convince their mother. Most importantly, Gustave went to Paris to consult his friend Dr. Cloquet, his former mentor in Corsica, who confirmed the prescription with the full weight of his medical authority. Mme Flaubert could not oppose such a recommendation for her son's well-being. Nonetheless, unbeknownst to Gustave, she tried to persuade Maxime that a lengthy stay in Madeira would be just as beneficial as this potentially dangerous trip to the Orient. Du Camp was inflexible, and Mme Flaubert did not insist.[5] Throughout his travels—and as much as the unpredictable mail would allow—Gustave did his best to send reassuring news and tender words:

> I constantly think of you, the idea of you accompanies me everywhere. Yes, my poor dear, keep up your hopes; I will tell you beautiful tales of travel, we'll chat about the desert by the fire; I will tell you about my nights under the tent, my treks under the hot sun. . . . We will tell each other: "Oh! Do you remember how sad we were?" and we will kiss each other, remembering our initial anxiety.

He calls her his "poor old dear," his "poor beloved mother," his "poor darling." He pampers her, encourages her to follow his journey on the map and to read books about Egypt, and eventually suggests that she join him at the end of his tour, in Italy—which she did. These travel letters are infinitely valuable: alongside his delicate expression of intensely tender feelings, possibly haunted by a guilty conscience, Flaubert narrates, relates, exposes, describes, and details all his discoveries in this fabulous Orient. He tells her about every topic—with the exception of his health and his sex life.

These gaps—particularly regarding sex—are filled in by his letters to a correspondent from whom he has nothing to hide, Louis Bouilhet. Flaubert's former classmate Bouilhet didn't become his close friend until early in 1846, several years after they had passed their baccalaureate exams. Bouilhet had studied medicine and interned at the Rouen hospitals but had been dismissed for insubordination. He chose to abandon his medical studies and wholly devote himself to poetry, while earning a meager living as a tutor.[6] Flaubert described his friend to Louise Colet: "He's a poor fellow who gives lessons here for a living and who is a poet, a true poet, who writes superb and charming things and will remain unknown because he lacks two requirements: bread and time."[7] This letter was written in 1846. Three years later, Bouilhet decided to start a cram school in Rouen with three friends, while continuing to write poetry. Meanwhile, Gustave and Louis had become close friends, both consumed by the art of writing. They wrote plays together, including the five-act tragedy in verse *Jenner ou La Découverte de la vaccine* [*Jenner, or the Discovery of Vaccination*], of which a few fragments have survived. Every Sunday, Bouilhet came to Croisset to share ideas and jokes (both men were pranksters), and he read his verses to Flaubert deep into Monday morning. They were totally uninhibited about criticizing each other, as evidenced by the way Louis and Maxime tore apart the first *Temptation of Saint Anthony* after Gustave read it to them. A deep friendship had taken root and would last until Bouilhet's death in 1869. The two writers had a profound influence on each other. In the travel letters to Bouilhet, one already sees Flaubert at work, dissecting, correcting, praising, or criticizing the verses his friend sent him. Although Bouilhet's letters to Flaubert from the period have been lost, we have about a dozen that Gustave sent to him. It is here that one finds the best complement to his letters to Mme Flaubert; Gustave told Louis everything of his erotic trials and tribulations between the Nile and the Dead Sea, frequently in crude terms.

Flaubert's travel notes, long unpublished but now well known, are another precious source. These notes belie the allegations of Maxime Du Camp in his *Souvenirs littéraires* that throughout the journey Flaubert was bored, distracted, daydreaming, and more absorbed by his memories than the discoveries to be made ("If he could, he would have liked to travel lying immobile on a couch, seeing the landscapes, the ruins, and the cities passing before him like a panoramic canvas being mechanically unveiled"). In fact, Gustave took voluminous daily notes. He even attempted to put these sketchy notes into readable form in his *Voyage en Egypte* [*Journey to Egypt*], though he did not intend to publish this text. In 1910, his niece published an expurgated, censored version designed not to offend the sensibilities of good people with the vulgar tales of her uncle, who had since become a great writer. The original manuscript changed hands several times among collectors and was finally published unabridged by Pierre-Marc de Biasi in 1991.[8]

Maxime Du Camp also took numerous notes, which can be found in the posthumous volume *Voyage en Orient (1849–1851)* [*Journey to the Orient (1849–1851)*], published in 1972.[9] During his lifetime, Du Camp published an edited travel narrative entitled *Le Nil* [*The Nile*] in 1853. Strangely, Du Camp uses "I" instead of "we," making Flaubert conspicuous by his absence. Du Camp's *Souvenirs littéraires* also includes three chapters on the trip to the Orient.

In *Souvenirs littéraires*, Maxime Du Camp shows how well he got along with Gustave Flaubert. There was only one unfortunate incident, resulting from Gustave's love of a good joke. In the heart of the desert, somewhere between the Red Sea and the Nile, their caravan accidentally lost its water tank. Dying of thirst, Gustave had the misguided idea of talking about the "marvelous lemon ice cream you get at Tortoni's [café in Paris]," going on and on with the joke until Max was exhausted and could dream of nothing else than to kill his friend. They did not speak for forty-eight hours. But overall they made excellent traveling companions—though it must be said that they rarely spent time alone together. They clearly delighted in Gustave's comic genius, which was not always so inopportune. We know, for example, that they invented a character called the Old Sheikh, the Garçon of the sands, who exemplified their penchant for derision.

Two Envoys on a Mission

The two friends did not set off on this long journey lightly. Maxime, who was the more practical of the duo and had plenty of useful connections, took care of all the preparations while Gustave finished writing his *Saint Anthony*. The journey would require a considerable amount of equipment, particularly since the two friends had no intention of roughing it, as they had in Brittany. They intended to have every comfort: a tent, naturally, but also guns, saddles for the horses, archaeological tools, spyglasses, a medicine chest, warm-climate clothes, maps, guidebooks, and many other items. They would also take along photographic equipment for Maxime, who was thinking ahead to his book and wanted to distinguish himself by offering readers a travel narrative enriched by real images.

Photography was a recent art, invented by Nicéphore Niépce in 1827. The first daguerreotype was made in 1838, and a few subsequent improvements had reduced the amount of equipment required. But the undertaking remained novel and demanded tremendous patience on the part of the photographer.[10] Du Camp rose to the challenge, photographing everything that drew his interest, from ruins and monuments to landscapes. Before his departure, he perfected his technique through a few lessons with the professional photographer Gustave Le Gray. Le Gray taught him about the calotype, a new process invented by the British photographer Henry Fox Talbot in 1841, which was the first to provide a negative. From Egypt, Flaubert wrote to his mother: "Max's days are entirely absorbed and consumed by photography. He is doing well, but grows desperate whenever he spoils a picture or finds that a plate has been badly washed. Really, if he doesn't take things easier he'll crack up. But he has been getting some superb results."[11]

Mme Flaubert provided for all these advance purchases, as well as those the two friends made once they arrived—in short, for all the expenses of the trip. One could even say that she bled herself dry. Du Camp had hoped he might inherit some money from his grandmother, who had died in September, but the estate hadn't been settled yet. So the "beloved dear old lady" of Croisset gave her son a first installment of 16,000 francs upon his departure—a considerable sum of money—and supplemented that with three later installments totaling 11,000 francs, for a total of 27,000 francs.[12] This was not a regular tourist budget, but a magnificent gift deriving from a mother's love.

In return, Maxime took care of all the arrangements. As the author of a previous travel book and an officer of the Legion of Honor who had been decorated for the wound he received in June 1848, he enjoyed a certain credibility, which he put to use to solicit "instructions" for his "trip to Egypt, Persia, and Syria" from France's Académie des Inscriptions et Belles Lettres, a learned society devoted to history and archaeology. On September 12, following a report from the commission appointed by the academy, he received information about various sites and was encouraged to report on his conquests "for philology, archaeology, and art."[13] Better yet, he managed to be assigned a mandate from the Ministry of Education, addressed both to him and his traveling companion:

> I wanted our journey to be surrounded with every comfort, and I had asked the government to assign us a mission that would serve as a recommendation to the diplomatic and commercial agents that France maintains in the Orient. Need I mention that this mission had to be and was absolutely free of charge? We were not denied. Gustave Flaubert—it's hard for me not to smile here—was charged with collecting, in the different ports and various caravan meeting points, whatever information seemed to him to be useful to communicate to the chambers of commerce.[14]

One can easily imagine how much zeal Flaubert applied to this mission; writing to Bouilhet, he laughed about his ministerial instructions, "which seem to be waiting impatiently for the day I'll use them as lavatory paper."[15] Later, he asked Bouilhet: "Can you see me in every town, informing myself about crops, about production, about consumption? 'How much oil do you shit here? How many potatoes do you stuff into yourselves?' And in every port: 'How many ships? What tonnage? How many arrivals? How many departures?' And ditto, ditto. *Merde!* Ah, no! Frankly—was it possible?"[16] Nonetheless, both young men were treated as quasi-official figures and were met with open arms by consuls and embassy attachés wherever they went.

Aside from the assistance of diplomatic personnel, Gustave and Maxime enjoyed personal recommendations to numerous French citizens in the Near East. They would also make new acquaintances, receiving a warm welcome at every stop of their journey from expatriates delighted to meet travelers bringing news of the old country. Upon arriving in Alexandria, Flaubert wrote to his mother: "My darling—I am writing you in white tie and tails, pumps, etc., like a man who has been paying a call on a prime minister: in fact we have just left Artin Bey, Minister of Foreign Affairs, to whom we were introduced by the consul and who received us splendidly. He is going to give us a *firman* with his seal on it for our entire journey. It is unbelievable how well we are treated here."[17] This excellent treatment continued throughout their ramble in Egypt and elsewhere. Sometimes they enjoyed unexpected hospitality, which allowed them to deepen their knowledge of the country. Gustave was even able to discuss his beloved Saint Anthony in the very place where the anchorite had lived, thanks to a Catholic priest he met at their host's home in Medinet el-Fayum.

While this assistance did not do away with the journey's challenges, such as bad weather and health problems, the two friends were certainly taking off on a high-end expedition, one crucial aspect of which included the hiring of two servants. In May, they started looking for these two rare birds. One of them would be specifically assigned to help Maxime with his photography and to watch over Gustave, in case he experienced convulsions. The other would be an Arabic-speaking dragoman who would serve as an interpreter and take care of anything else that came up. In a letter to his uncle Parain dated May 12, 1849, Flaubert listed the job requirements as taking care of the tent, the weapons, and the clothing, and noted that the candidate should be aware that there would be various dangers: "shortages of necessary items, excessive heat, bad food very often, illnesses, gunfire, seasickness, etc." And also a near total lack of "females." Maxime ended up making the final choice. The first man selected to accompany them was Sassetti, a former dragoon from Corsica, "a strange fellow troubled by nothing and knowing everything." They had more difficulty finding the dragoman, but eventually lucked into Joseph Brichetti, an intelligent and devoted servant who knew his way around Egypt: "We have a perfect dragoman," Flaubert wrote to his mother, "a man of about fifty, an Italian who is three-quarters Arab, a tall funny phlegmatic type who knows every nook and cranny of Egypt." He spoke enough pidgin French to make himself understood and would eventually be able to interpret for Flaubert during his conversation with the priest in Medinet el-Fayum. Once in Egypt, the two travelers would also occasionally hire local guides, sailors, cameleers, and other interpreters—they were never caught unprepared.

On October 22, 1849, Flaubert took leave of Croisset and boarded the train to Paris, where he and Maxime Du Camp spent a few busy days dealing with final preparations and saying their goodbyes to friends, including Dr. Cloquet and also Maurice Schlésinger, with whom Gustave spent an evening at the Opéra-Comique without making any mention of Élisa. To soften the cruel blow of their separation, Gustave took his mother to spend some time at the home of his paternal uncle Parain and his cousins the Bonenfants in Nogent-sur-Seine. Their leave-taking was heartrending: "How she screamed when I closed the door of the living-room behind me!"[18] In the train back to Paris he began to cry, asking himself at every station whether he should get out and return to Nogent. Once in Paris, he arrived distraught at Maxime's, where he was to spend the night. Sobbing all evening, he experienced "anguish such as no separation ever caused me."[19] Du Camp got home late to find his friend stretched out in front of the bookcase looking distressed: "I thought he was asleep, but then I heard him sigh. I have never beheld such a state of prostration, and his size and appearance of physical strength made it all the more remarkable. When I questioned him he replied with lamentations: 'Never again will I see my mother or my country! This journey is too long, too distant; it is tempting fate! What madness! Why are we going?' I was dismayed. He told me that he had left his study at Croisset exactly as though he were going to return to it the next day—on the table a book open at the last page he had read, his dressing-gown thrown over a chair, his slippers near the sofa. 'It is unlucky to take precautions,' he told me; and then, referring to the death of my grandmother, said cruelly: 'You are lucky; you leave no one behind.'" The next day, Maxime assured Gustave that he was free to give up on the trip: "The struggle was brief. 'No!' he cried. . . . The arrival of Bouilhet and my friend Louis de Cormenin, who came to keep us company during the last days, was a diversion for him. He threw off his languor and was himself again."[20]

The next two days were devoted to "huge dinners, quantities of wine, whores." Flaubert explained that his "poor tortured nerves needed a little relaxation."[21] He also accompanied Maxime to the Louvre to see the Assyrian bas-reliefs brought from Nineveh by Paul-Émile Botta, whom they would later meet in his position as French consul to Jerusalem. On October 28, Gustave was happy to meet the writer Théophile Gautier, who was a friend of Maxime's. Maxime and Gustave treated Gautier to dinner at Les Trois Frères Provençaux in the Palais-Royal, where they were joined by Bouilhet and Cormenin. After dinner, Gustave said his goodbyes to Paris his way, by taking Bouilhet to "la Guérin," a well-known brothel. The next morning, he accompanied his friend to the train station: "Thank God it's over—no more saying goodbye to anyone."

On October 29, a bright day, Gustave and Maxime left Paris by stagecoach. The trip from Paris to Marseille was still difficult at the time: there were only a few sections of railroad, where the stagecoach was hoisted onto a rail car. "Near Fontainebleau," wrote Flaubert, "a few small flames flew away from the locomotive and one landed in the coupé and was quietly burning my coat, when I woke to shrill cries of terror coming from under the hat of the woman sitting beside me; she could already see us all burned alive . . . and blamed our cigars, though our good manners had led us to abstain." He saw that blazing shards of coal were actually flying about on both sides of the tracks. In the evening, they stopped for dinner at Ancy-le-Franc, in Burgundy. The next day, they took a boat from Chalon-sur-Saône to Lyon. Closely observing everyone he met, Flaubert was drawn to "a young and svelte creature," then by a lady who could have been her mother, and later by "a handsome little man with a curved and pointed mustache." "Despite myself," he wrote, "an invincible curiosity makes me wonder what kind of life is led by the passersby I encounter." The novelist in Flaubert began to imagine what the stranger's life and feelings must be like, and what brought him to be standing on the deck of this boat.

In Lyon, the two travelers were happy to run across one of their friends, the painter Charles Gabriel Gleyre, who convinced them that Egypt, which he had visited, would be the most beautiful part of their trip; that they should linger there and travel all the way to Nubia, which had been conquered in 1821 by Muhammad Ali. Flaubert wrote to his mother about the encounter with Gleyre: "Following his advice, we may stay in Egypt longer than we had planned, even if it means giving up or rushing the rest of our trip." The next morning, around 5, Gustave and Maxime boarded a boat to sail down the Rhône. The boat was delayed by fog. At 4 PM, they were still only in Valence. But they spotted a stagecoach leaving for the south, jumped in and rode to Avignon, where they boarded the train that finally brought them to Marseille. They were alone in a compartment with a gentleman who smiled each time they passed another train, invariably repeating: "How about that? Isn't human industry something?" And with this banality, so began Flaubert's never-completed *Dictionary of Accepted Ideas* ("RAILROADS: One must exclaim over their invention"). Then, finally, Marseille. It had taken four days to get from Paris to the Mediterranean.

Being in Marseille again brought up the delectable memory of Eulalie, who had disappeared once and for all but was still alive in Flaubert's mind. He wanted to visit the hotel where they had met, but the establishment was still closed. While waiting for their boat for Alexandria to sail, he and Maxime hung around, went to song and dance cabarets, and saw a performance of Eugène Scribe and Fromental Halévy's *La Juive* [*The Jewess*] at the opera. They also visited a colorful character, Dr. Clot, known as Clot Bey, who could take credit for organizing Muhammad Ali's health system and founding several hospitals and medical schools in Egypt. Following the death of Muhammad, who had just been succeeded by his grandson Abbas Pasha, Clot Bey had returned to France with a fine collection of Egyptian antiquities that he was about to donate to the state. Famous in Egypt, he gave the two friends letters introducing them to various Egyptian personalities, "engineers, generals, beys, pashas, etc." They lined their pockets with every safe-conduct imaginable.

The Messageries françaises freight company had had regular connections to the Orient, which were made easier by the steam engine, since the late 1830s. On November 4, the two friends embarked on the *Nil;* on November 7, they landed in Malta. The ship had four classes: Maxime and Gustave traveled in first class, the two servants in second class. Flaubert marveled that he wasn't seasick: "I haven't been seasick (except for the first half hour after leaving Marseille, when I vomited a glass of rum I had drunk to *prevent* my being sick). For the rest, for the entire duration of the crossing, from Sunday morning to this evening, I've been one of the most lively, if not the most lively, of the passengers." Maxime, however, could not say as much: he spent the crossing clinging to the rail. The Orient was drawing closer: "Women of Malta, generally small, pale complexion, aprons over their head. Already close to the veil." Their initial attempt to leave Malta went awry due to a storm; the ship had to turn back. "As for me, I felt a movement in my stomach that deconstipated me once and for all. It was not fear, but emotion—there was no apparent danger—it was the unhappy idea of losing ourselves on the rocks of Malta by night." During this second stay on the island, the friends took an excursion with a guide. The sky cleared, the sea calmed down, and once again they left for Alexandria. Flaubert had recovered his cheerfulness: "I am cherished on shipboard, I make many jokes, I am seen as a very witty man." But the sea swelled again, and some passengers were afraid: "Despite myself from time to time I laugh at the grotesqueness of what is happening—people throwing a fit and throwing up—the ship creaking—wandering mutts—M. and Mme Codrika arguing—with each swell the boat sinks to starboard and comes back up bottoming out."[22] Flaubert took advantage of the good weather's return to chitchat with passengers: he did not miss a word when Codrika, whom he had already mentioned in his notes, told him about his romantic misfortunes. He was always on the lookout for stories, colorful individuals, and, naturally, cosmopolitan nonsense. "After eleven days of rolling and pitching, of wind and heavy seas," wrote Du Camp, "we sighted the shore of Egypt, and on Saturday the fifteenth of November, 1849, we disembarked at Alexandria."[23] It was actually on a Thursday that the pair disembarked from a small boat and settled at the Hôtel d'Orient, the finest choice available. Bright sunshine, palm trees, camels—they had arrived. "Landing took place amid the most deafening uproar imaginable: negroes, negresses, camels, turbans, cudgelings to right and left and ear-splitting guttural cries. I gulped down a whole bellyful of colors, like a donkey filling himself with hay."[24]

Egypt had just come out of a long period under the rule of Muhammad Ali, who, after having fought Napoleon at the head of Albanian troops, had taken power in Cairo in 1804. With the assistance of the English and French, he had largely emancipated himself from the Ottomans, who had finally granted him the title of viceroy. From 1805 to 1849, Muhammad Ali had done a great deal to develop his country, including reforming the administration, launching major irrigation works, promoting cotton and sugarcane culture, building a navy, and recruiting foreign, particularly French, engineers. He had also built a modern army with the support of Joseph Sève, a French military commander known as Suleyman Pasha, whom Gustave and Maxime would soon meet. Abbas Pasha, the mediocre successor to the man rightly known as the founder of modern Egypt, had just come to power when Gustave Flaubert and Maxime Du Camp set foot in Alexandria, determined to be filled with wonder.

CHAPTER 9

From the Pyramids to Constantinople

Arriving in Egypt did not free Flaubert from his worries. Not only did he feel guilty for subjecting his mother to this long separation, but he also remained profoundly disturbed by Louis Bouilhet and Maxime Du Camp's harsh judgment of his *Temptation of Saint Anthony*. In March 1850, he opened his heart to Bouilhet: "What am I to do once back in the old lodgings? Publish or not publish? What will I write? Will I write at all? The *Saint Anthony* business dealt me a heavy blow, I don't mind telling you."[1] The following September, he wrote his friend that for "the first four months" of his trip he was sick from the "terrible blow" dealt by his failure.[2] One can deduce that Egypt, which he traveled through for over eight months, from mid-November 1849 to mid-July 1850, helped him to get over his disappointment and pain.

Egyptian Splendor

Gustave and Maxime's plan was to travel through the Nile Delta and Cairo, up the Nile to Nubia, back down the Nile to Cairo again, and finally to Alexandria, where they would embark for Beirut. They had not determined how much time they would devote to this part of the journey, since they would have to adapt to factors beyond their control: lack of wind, sandstorms, devastating illness, or, looking on the bright side, the desire to linger in an enjoyable place. The first shock for the travelers, despite the fact that they had expected to be impressed, was the sight of the Sphinx and the Pyramids, which they reached from Cairo—Maxime, Gustave, and Sassetti on horseback, and Joseph on a donkey. Flaubert wrote that as they approached, "I could no longer contain myself, I rode my horse at full gallop, Maxime followed suit, and I reached the foot of the Sphinx. Seeing that (which is indescribable, it would take ten pages, and what pages!) made my head spin for a moment, and my companion was as pale as the paper I write on." At nightfall, they raised their tent for the first time; Flaubert smoked his pipe under the stars, contemplating the sky while a jackal howled in the distance. The next morning, the travelers climbed up the Pyramid of Cheops, pushed and pulled by the Arabs in their escort. At the top, they waited for the sun to rise, an event which Flaubert would describe again and again—with chromatic variations—throughout the journey:

> The sun was rising just opposite; the whole valley of the Nile, bathed in mist, seemed to be a still white sea; and the desert behind us, with its hillocks of sand, another ocean, deep purple, its waves all petrified. But as the sun climbed behind the Arabian chain the mist was torn into great shreds of filmy gauze; the meadows, cut by canals, were like green lawns with winding borders. To sum up: three colors—immense green at my feet in the foreground; the sky pale red—worn vermillion; behind and to the right, a rolling expanse looking scorched and iridescent, with the minarets of Cairo, *canges* passing in the distance, clusters of palms.[3]

They were filled with wonder.

For their expedition on the Nile, Gustave and Maxime rented a large *cange*—a long sailboat with oars. Flaubert described it to his mother: "It is painted blue; its *raïs* [captain] is called Ibrahim [Abraham]. There is a crew of nine. For quarters we have a room with two little divans facing each other, a large room with two beds, on one side of which there is a kind of alcove for our baggage and on the other an English-type head; and finally a third room where Sassetti will sleep and which will serve as storeroom as well. The dragoman will sleep on deck."[4] They traveled up the Nile by sail after a difficult departure due to lack of wind. The crewmen had to jump into the river with ropes and swim to shore to tow the boat. "When they're not towing, they are pushing from the riverbed with long boathooks." When sandstorms struck, the travelers had to stay cooped up inside. Flaubert took the opportunity to write; his efforts yielded a few pages of his *Journey to Egypt* entitled "The Cange," but he soon gave up.

While the plan was to save extended visits for the trip back down the Nile, the travelers did make some brief stops on shore. Guns in hand, they went off on the hunt. "It makes me laugh damn hard!" Flaubert wrote to his mother, "Me, a hunter! You'll call me an infamous joker if I tell you that last Saturday we killed 54 pieces of game. All turtledoves and pigeons." Joseph prepared the game for them to eat. For the rest of the meal, they ate jam made of dates, oranges, and figs and drank water. Once Bedouins sold them a gazelle, which fed them for two days. They also hunted for crocodiles, but "the rascals die hard." It was hot, but the light was sublime, exposing the entire color spectrum over the course of the day, a spectacle to "make any painter faint away."[5]

Once past Aswan, the expedition continued toward Nubia. In order to ascend a cataract where violent rapids rushed between the rocks, they hired two special chiefs and a Nubian pilot to accompany them to Wadi Halfa, the terminus of the trip upriver. It took no less than one hundred Nubians—half on the rocks to pull a cable from the boat and half on board to haul a rope attached to the shore—to make it past this obstacle unscathed. The next day, Flaubert set out for the cataract alone on a donkey "to kill the jackal we saw last night near the dead crocodile,"[6] but could not find it. Around noon, the traveling company turned back, as Du Camp wrote in *Le Nil:* "My *cange* is now set for the descent of the river. The two masts and the yards have been taken down, strong thole-pins have been inserted in the gunwales, the oars are in place and we are ready to leave."[7]

On the way back down the river, they systematically visited all the ancient sites, the succession of temples sometimes boring Flaubert stiff: "Are they going to become like the churches in Brittany, the waterfalls in the Pyrenees? Oh necessity! To do what you are supposed to do."[8] In his *Souvenirs,* Du Camp comments that "[the] temples seemed to [Flaubert] always alike, the mosques and the landscapes all the same."[9] In fact, Flaubert was creating a hierarchy of what he admired, while Du Camp wanted to exhaust the entire inventory of monuments, notably by photographing them. Thebes, Luxor, and Karnak had the same effect on Flaubert as the Pyramids and, on the other bank of the Nile, the tombs of the Valley of the Kings. "The most beautiful thing I saw," he would write to Dr. Cloquet from Damascus, "was first and foremost the Pyramids . . . then Thebes, the palace of Karnak and the tombs of the Kings, then a dancer in Cairo, a great unknown artist called Hassan el-Bilbeis, something very sad, very ancient about her." Indeed, while there is no doubt of his (selective) admiration for antiquities, Flaubert proved more attentive to the people he encountered and was always curious to go behind the scenes. He was more sensitive to people than to stones.

These people came from every walk of life—the powerful, the nobodies, the slaves, the pashas on their divans surrounded by black Africans, the Greek

Orthodox priest with his long beard and his mule, the Copt in a black turban, the Persian in a fur-trimmed coat, and the desert Bedouin: "There is much jostling and arguing and fighting and rolling on the ground," he wrote from Cairo, "much cursing of all kinds and shouting in all languages; the harsh Semitic syllables crack in the air like whiplashes. You brush against all costumes of the Orient."[10] Flaubert talked with those in positions of power, the consuls and pashas who hosted them, as well as representatives of the various religions. With a Coptic bishop, he addressed questions "concerning the Trinity, the Virgin, the Gospels, the Eucharist."[11] In Cairo, he spent hours talking about Islam and the other religions of the Orient with the learned Halim Effendi: "We speak with priests of all the religions. The people here sometimes assume really beautiful poses and attitudes. We have translations of songs, stories and traditions made for us—everything that is most folkloric and original."[12] Flaubert as ethnologist! He discovered culinary customs, learned to eat with his hands, and sang the praises of Turkish cuisine and the excellent local pastry (fritters, cakes, sweet dishes, etc.). He appreciated the gentle manner and kindness of the Egyptians and sat through an interminable service at an Armenian church.

He was also struck by a variety of upsetting sights, such as the boats full of slaves that he glimpsed on the way up the Nile. On each boat, he saw "a few old negresses who make the trip over and over again to encourage the new women, to make sure they do not get too discouraged and do not make themselves sick with sadness." He was not indifferent to the question of slavery. Like Nerval before them, Gustave and Maxime visited the "slave bazaar" in Cairo: "The contempt in which human flesh is held is something to behold." Other acts of violence fascinated him. In Wadi Halfa, he met the provincial tax collector, who collected his due "with a great many whacks of the stick, by arresting and chaining people up." They followed him for four days: "A village had not wanted to pay, he grabbed the sheik, chained him, and took him away in his *cange*. When it passed close to us, we saw the poor old man lying on the bottom of the boat, bareheaded under the sun and duly locked up. From the bank, men and women followed and yelled." He describes another incredible scene near a Coptic convent. Looking for alms, monks would spot a boat on the Nile and immediately clamber down from the rocks, throw themselves naked into the water, and swim to the boat, shouting as loud as they could: "*Baksheesh, baksheesh, cawadja christiani*" ("Give us money, Christian sir"). One of the sailors tried to chase them away by showing them his penis and his ass, "pretending to piss and shit on their heads (they were clinging to the sides of the *cange*). The other sailors shouted insults at them, repeating the names of Allah and Mohammed. Some hit them with sticks, others with ropes; Joseph rapped their knuckles with his kitchen tongs. It was a *tutti* of cudgelings, pricks, bare asses, yells and laughter. As soon as they were given money they put it in their mouths and returned home via the route they had come."[13]

In the desert between the Nile and the Red Sea, he admired the procession of pilgrims headed for Mecca, long caravans advancing in single file or in a broad front. "At Koseir we saw pilgrims from the depths of Africa, poor negroes who have been on the march for a year, even two years."[14] Stranger yet, in Cairo he discovered an "ascetic priest" who urinated in public to help sterile women who wanted children. The women placed themselves under the "parabola of urine" and rubbed "this liquid" on themselves. All of this Flaubert described without indignation, false prudery, or moral judgment, but with tireless curiosity, always on the lookout for the picturesque.

Sex Tourism

The Orient was a sexual fantasy; the harem unleashed Western imaginations, and women's veils seemed to conceal intoxicating charms. The heat, the languor of the streets, the spices, and the dance of the *almeh*, the Egyptian belly dancers—everything seemed designed to allure the tourist. Throughout their journey, Flaubert and Du Camp visited many prostitutes. The dancers of Cairo were legendary for their favors, but they had been exiled to Upper Egypt. The two partners in crime thus experienced the same disappointment mentioned by Gérard de Nerval: "All that was available here were *almeh* ... male *almeh*."[15] Indeed, the dances the two friends saw in Cairo were performed by male transvestites. But everywhere the travelers went, touts led them to bordellos, or children offered up their own mothers. Flaubert tried out coitus in silence, except when he brought his dragoman Joseph along to hold the candle and interpret. He was surprised by the "shaved cunts [which] make a strange effect."[16] Sometimes the encounter took place in a filthy rat hole, which did not seem to disgust the enthusiast: "When the brain sinks," wrote Flaubert, "the prick rises."[17] Contempt for women is expressed shamelessly; misogyny was a matter of course. The code of virility, shared by most writers of the time, situates Flaubert's crudity in the masculine mores of an era dominated, in historian Alain Corbin's words, by the "necessary mani-festation of sexual energy."[18] The letters of Mérimée, Stendhal, and Gautier are identical in manner with those exchanged by Le Poittevin, Du Camp, and Flaubert: they routinely display a bawdy tone, recommendations for bordellos, tales of triumphant conquest, confidential updates on the state of their gen-ital organs, conspicuous mocking of sentimentality, and an obsession with sexual potency. "Of course," Corbin writes, "boasting incites one to inform the correspondent of the extent of one's scores, the number of screws had in a night or over the course of a stay."

The single exception to this out-and-out cynicism was Gustave's awed en-counter with Kuchuk Hanem at Esna. A tout escorted by a muzzled sheep led the friends to the home of this famous courtesan, who captivated them with her beauty ("a regal-looking creature") and her striptease dances. Gustave's night with her was memorable because sensual pleasure finally mixed with romantic tenderness: "We loved each other, or at least I think so." The first encounter was on the trip up the Nile. He returned to see her on the way back down: "The result of all this—infinite sadness; like the first time, she had per-fumed her breasts with rosewater. This is the end; I'll not see her again, and gradually her face will fade from my memory."[19] But maybe not, for as he later confessed to Louis Bouilhet in a letter from Constantinople: "Why have I a melancholy desire to return to Egypt, to go back up the Nile and see Kuchuk Hanem? All the same, it was a rare night I spent there, and I tasted it to the full."[20] There would be echoes of this night in *Salammbô* and the end of his tale "Herodias." Bouilhet was also taken with the idea of the fabulous Orient but could not afford to visit. Though he knew nothing of Kuchuk Hanem other than what Flaubert had told him, he wrote a poem about her:

In your house in Esna, what are you doing now,
Dark-haired Kuchuk Hanem, seated by the river.

Sometimes Flaubert preferred to soak in what he saw and smelled ("odors of spices") in the whores' quarter rather than sowing his wild oats: "Well, I abstained deliberately, in order to preserve the sweet sadness of the scene and engrave it deeply in my memory. In this way, I went away dazzled and have remained so. There is nothing more beautiful than these women calling you. If I had gone with any of them, a second picture would have been superimposed on the first and dimmed its splendor."[21] A ceasefire in exchange for a tableau vivant: the artist was on the lookout.

Several passages in the letters to Bouilhet again raise the question of Flaubert's homosexuality. He reports that in Egypt sodomy is an "accepted" practice and that everyone refers to it as a natural thing. It takes place at the baths, for "all the bath-boys are bardashes."[22] Flaubert confides in Bouilhet that he wants to experience it for himself, and returns to the subject in a letter dated June 2, 1850: "You ask me whether I've enjoyed the work of the baths. Yes, and on a young fellow marked by smallpox, and who had an enormous white turban. It was a laugh, that's all. *But* I'll do it again. For an experience to be done well, it must be repeated."

This experience has led some to the hasty conclusion that Flaubert was homosexual. His earlier correspondence, reaching quite far back into his youth, offers no shortage of expressions that could lead one to believe it, as do Alfred Le Poittevin's letters: "I'll definitely come see you on Monday, one o'clock. Are you hard?"—"Goodbye, old pederast!"—"I kiss your Priapus."— "Goodbye, old man, a kiss on the cheek while I Socratize you." Sartre's opinion on the matter: "It appears to me that the epistolary use of these 'turns of phrase' clearly indicates that they did not refer to any real practices."[23] These expressions are in the register of "banter," Sartre continues, but are reminders—as Flaubert would himself write to Louise Colet—that at the time of his friendship with Alfred, Gustave was "reputed to be a pederast" (September 18, 1852). Jacques-Louis Douchin clarifies the point: "Homosexuality? No. Pederasty? Yes, but only at a certain period and in clearly defined circumstances. . . . It was during his trip to the Orient that Flaubert acquainted himself with pederasty, in my opinion, purely out of curiosity, and also 'to be like everyone else.'"[24] Flaubert did what he did out of curiosity, for amusement and a taste for the picturesque and local color—"and that's all," writes Douchin. For Flaubert, "ethnological" curiosity knew no bounds.

What can be stated with certainty is that Flaubert caught syphilis in the whorehouses. He became aware of his condition in Rhodes, initially believing he had been infected in Beirut. Pierre-Marc de Biasi contests the idea that the disease first appeared on this trip, citing a passage from an expurgated letter to Ernest Chevalier dated May 6, 1849, six months before Flaubert's departure: "I'll have you know that your friend is apparently consumed by a pox as old as life itself. Despite how you treat the symptoms—which can be cured—it reappears here and there. My nervous illness, which I sometimes still feel and which cannot be cured in the environment I live in, may well be caused by it."[25] However, the word "apparently" casts some doubt on the diagnosis. In any case, Flaubert first described his illness when he was in Constantinople, suspecting it was a gift from a Maronite woman. Morning and night, he dressed his "wretched prick."[26] He later recounted his misadventure in the Galata quarter of Constantinople, where he was horrified by the "disgusting" prostitutes offered to him by a madam. As he was about to leave, the woman offered him her own daughter, who was reserved for "special circumstances." Once she was alone with him, the young girl asked in Italian to "examine [his] tool" to make sure he wasn't sick. "Well! Since on the lower part of my glans I still have an induration, and was afraid she would see it, I acted the Monsieur and jumped down from the bed, saying loudly that she was insulting me, that such behavior was revolting to a gentleman; and I left, very annoyed not to have fired such a pretty shot and thoroughly humiliated to think of myself as having a nonpresentable prick."[27]

Whatever the date and place of contamination, Flaubert did contract syphilis. While Flaubert takes it lightly in his letters, Jacques-Louis Douchin quotes Dr. Germain Galérant's suggestion that the main reason the two friends cut their journey short and gave up on visiting Persia may have been so that Flaubert could "see the famous Paris syphilis doctor Ricord as soon as possible."[28] The hypothesis is debatable, given that Flaubert first mentions Dr. Ricord in his private correspondence with Louis Bouilhet in August 1854, which indicates that he was not in a big hurry to see him. Additionally, he only referred to the great venereologist to tell his friend that he wouldn't go for a consultation because he lacked the money and considered it "of little use." In the meantime, he was losing clumps of hair and soon found himself suffering from debilitating weakness.

New Horizons

On July 19, 1850, the two traveling companions boarded a ship in Alexandria for Beirut, Ottoman Syria's port town. They reached Beirut under a blue sky and discovered its white houses running down to the clear sea, surrounded by mulberry trees and parasol pines.[29] "Then, on the left," wrote Flaubert, "Lebanon, meaning a mountain chain with villages in the wrinkles of its small valleys, crowned with clouds and snow on the peaks."[30] More than the city itself, wrote Du Camp, it was the setting and the surrounding countryside that filled them with awe: "the forest of parasol pines, the paths lined with Barbary figs, myrtles, pomegranate trees overrun with chameleons" and those "wooded peaks of Lebanon whose pure lines are defined against the sky."

The travelers were welcomed by the French consul Lesparda and his family, along with a small group of French locals. "Indeed," Flaubert explained to his mother, "these exiles are delighted to find people to whom they can talk about their world and their studies. We brought them Paris and something of what they had all left there." Among them was Camille Rogier, the director of the postal service, who was a painter and a friend of Théophile Gautier. Rogier hosted the two friends for most of their meals and also provided them with house-calls from "nymphets," to be taken before lunch and after dessert.

From Beirut they left for Jerusalem with five horses (one of which carried the animal feed), mules, and a donkey for the head mule-driver. They visited Tyre ("a city surrounded by medieval ramparts like Aigues-Mortes"), Sidon ("filled with a smell of incense"), Mount Carmel, Acre ("desolate, empty"), Jaffa, and Ramallah ("big, empty, and dirty"). Flaubert admired the variations in the landscape, which stood in contrast to the monotony of Egypt. But once they finally reached Jerusalem, the two friends were disappointed: "a charnel house surrounded by ramparts. Everything in it is rotting, the dead dogs in the streets, the religions in the churches."[31] The Holy Land was not so holy:

> The Holy Sepulcher is the agglomeration of all possible maledictions. In so small a space there are an Armenian church, a Greek church, a Latin church, a Coptic church. Each insulting the others, cursing them from the bottom of its soul, encroaching on their rights to candlesticks, rugs, and pictures—such pictures! It is the Turkish pasha who has the keys to the Holy Sepulcher; when you want to visit it, you apply to him. I find that titillating; as a matter of fact, it is for humanitarian reasons, for if the Holy Sepulcher were given over to the Christians they would massacre each other without fail.[32]

What Flaubert described is an Ottoman provincial capital in which the Christians were in the process of regaining their footing. The representatives of the different religions struggled bitterly to control the holy sites—and even to dream up new ones. Flaubert did not fail to take note. Maxime Du Camp corroborates his friend's observations in his own account: "Luckily, the Muslims are here." In his notebook, Gustave recorded that "[one] thing stood out above all others for me, which was the sight of the full-length portrait of Louis Philippe decorating the Holy Sepulcher—oh, you grotesque man, so you are just like the sun, dominating the world with your splendor—your light shines all the way into the tomb of Jesus Christ."[33] The genius of Christianity was not to be found here. Flaubert, however poor a Christian, returned to his hotel feeling revolted, for these holy places were "disgustingly whorish. Hypocrisy, greed, falsification, impudence—there is plenty of those, but of holiness not a trace."[34] In the garden of Gethsemane at the Mount of Olives, he saw three Franciscans having a pleasant chat with two young women "whose white breasts were gleaming nakedly in the sun."[35] Laughable! To comfort himself, he reread the sermon on the mount from the Gospel According to St. Matthew. He had to get out of there, breathe in fresh air; for the country itself was "harsh and spectacular," "on a level with the Bible."

The French consul in Jerusalem was Paul-Émile Botta, one of the founders of Assyriology and a former student of Dr. Flaubert at the Rouen medical school. Du Camp wrote that Botta was "as hospitable as a Bedouin chief, erudite, a discerning archaeologist, spoke all the languages of the Orient, as thin as an ascetic, uneasy, nervous, a music lover, opium eater, and charming." Yet his gentle demeanor was combined with ultra-Catholic convictions that could lead him to lose his temper with anyone who contradicted him, which would be the cue for him to pick up his cello and "play a Schubert melody to calm himself, just as Saul was calmed by David's harp."

After two weeks in the holy city, from which they made trips to Bethlehem ("It's beautiful—it's true—it lifts one with a mystic joy") and to the Dead Sea, the entire company headed off again, "asses nearly always on the saddle, wearing boots and spurs, armed to the teeth." They returned to Beirut via Damascus and Tripoli. They stopped at watering holes and slept in the open under the trees, while the mules' bells tinkled and the riders scratched their flea bites. They reached Damascus via Nazareth and the Sea of Galilee. It was so hot that the travelers gave up on wearing socks inside their boots. In Baalbek, Joseph, the good dragoman, came down with a fever and began vomiting shortly before they were to cross Mount Lebanon. The company was forced to split up: Flaubert and Sassetti crossed Lebanon with the caravan, while Maxime returned to Beirut to entrust Joseph to Dr. Suquet, a member of the French colony, and to find a replacement. Du Camp reunited with Flaubert at the Lazarist house in Ehden. Now Sassetti became sick. At the time, quinine sulfate was the cure-all: it had more or less put Joseph right, and now put Sassetti back on his feet after a period of about ten days, during which Flaubert feared he would die. Yet despite his servant's illness, during this part of the adventure Flaubert enjoyed "galloping with his horse in the full sun," with "the majestic appearance of a pasha."

Upon returning to Beirut, Maxime Du Camp busied himself preparing the rest of their trip to Persia, which they intended to reach via Antioch and Baghdad. The very evening of his arrival, after he had hired a new dragoman, a Greek polyglot, and picked up a crate of clothing and linens sent from Paris, the French consul general handed him a letter from Mme Flaubert. The letter, wrote Maxime in his *Souvenirs*, contained "six pages that can be summarized as follows: 'Instead of going further away, come closer. I am dying of worry at the idea that Gustave will cross the Euphrates and will make me spend months waiting for news from him. Persia frightens me: what difference does it make to you whether you are in Persia or Italy?' "[36] Maxime gave it some thought and accepted Mme Flaubert's argument. When he told Gustave, he was visibly relieved, though he added: "I would have gone to Persia with you if you wanted."

From Beirut, the two companions boarded the Austrian ship *Stamboul* on October 1, 1850, headed for the island of Rhodes. The ship was full of Turks traveling from Syria to Turkey: "The entire port side of the deck was occupied by the harem, white and black women, children, cats, dishes, all sprawled higgledy-piggledy on mattresses, vomiting, crying, yelling, and singing." After stopping in Cyprus for a few hours, they landed in Rhodes on October 4. The weather had changed; the cold was upon them. Quarantine regulations forced them to spend the first few days in a lazaretto. Then they visited the island, starting with the city: the former church of Saint John, now a mosque, the Grand Master's Palace, the Saint-Nicholas Tower, and the ramparts full of cannons, many of which were decorated with the French fleur-de-lis. Next they spent five days riding mules around the island, traveling from one village to the next, among the strawberry trees, myrtles, rhododendrons, giant heather, fig trees, pines, and olive trees. They visited Greek churches, ruins, and fortresses.

From Rhodes, they left by *caïque* to sail to Marmaris in Anatolia, from which they traveled by caravan for about two weeks toward Smyrna, passing through Ephesus: "Ah! It's beautiful! Orientally and antiquely splendid! It is reminiscent of lost luxuries, purple coats embroidered with gold. Herostratus!

How good it must have felt! The Diana of Ephesus!"[37] They reached Smyrna on October 26. The rain was pouring down, and it had turned cold. They stayed locked up in their rooms. But thanks to the gentlemen at the consulate they still had local connections and visits to make. They did not much care for Anatolia—the landscape was "heavy" and the mountains "[looked] dumb," Maxime noted. He came down with an intermittent fever that lasted thirteen days. Flaubert devotedly tended to his friend, hurrying to a reading room to find a book to read to him and administering trusty quinine sulfate.

From Smyrna, they embarked for Constantinople, where they landed on November 13, 1850. Here they bid goodbye to gloominess: Constantinople seemed admirable, and the setting was spectacular. "The whole thing is built like an amphitheater in the mountains," Flaubert told his mother, "and is full of ruins, bazaars, markets, mosques, with snow-covered mountains on the horizon, and three seas bathing the city." It was enormous, teeming, cosmopolitan, picturesque. They visited the mosques, Hagia Sophia, and the seraglio, they glided over the Bosporus aboard *caïques*, lingered in the bazaars and haggled with the merchants as was the custom, admired the whirling dervishes and the port with countless birds soaring above it, and went to the theater to see the ballet *Le Triomphe de l'Amour* [*The Triumph of Love*]: "This is a strange city, where one leaves the dervishes to go to the Opera! The two worlds are still more or less mixed, but the new one is prevailing; even in Stamboul, European garb dominates, admittedly only for men."[38] Flaubert saw the bardashes dance, but there would be no pederasty: "These gentlemen," he wrote to Bouilhet, "have lovers at court, or some such. They are reserved for the pashas. In short, it was impossible for us to sample them. Which I am not in the least sorry about, for their dance made me deeply disgusted with them." They did visit the Greek and Armenian ladies "chez Antonia," however. Gustave was happy; he was finally receiving his mother's letters after having been deprived of them for so long. He initiated an extensive epistolary back-and-forth to convince her to join him in Italy. Would she come alone? Maybe with little Liline (his niece Caroline)? Or why not with Uncle Parain? Flaubert, who prided himself on having become a good rider, roamed the streets and countryside on horseback, riding around the city walls. He was enchanted. While sailing up the Golden Horn in a *caïque*, he was carried away by his Oriental dream: "This was where one would live with the abducted odalisque: this crowd of veiled women, mute, with their big eyes looking at you, this whole unknown world, that is so foreign to you; children and young people on horseback, galloping—they make a dreamy sadness take hold of you. We return to Constantinople without saying a word. The fog settles over the masts, the minarets, the sea."³⁹

On December 18, after spending five weeks in Constantinople, they sailed again, headed for Piraeus, where they were quarantined once more and had to spend five days in the lazaretto. Flaubert was sad: "Adieu, mosques! Adieu, veiled ladies! Adieu, good Turks in the cafés!"⁴⁰ In Athens they lodged at the Hôtel d'Angleterre. After years of studying Greek, Flaubert was bowled over by the Acropolis: "The sight of the Parthenon is one of the things which has most profoundly penetrated me in my entire life."⁴¹ They visited Eleusis, Marathon, Salamis, and unforgettable Delphi. It was the inclement season, it rained often, they had to cross rivers on horseback. Snow followed rain, they were soaked, got lost, struggled to find shelter, and eventually came to a village hotel where the hostess served them an omelet. Flaubert was morose: there was no doubt he was losing his hair, and he felt he was getting old (though he wasn't even thirty). His opinion of the country suffered the effects of his mood: "Greece is wilder than the desert; it is entirely given over to poverty, filth, and a state of neglect."

Back in the capital, the two friends went to the French School at Athens for dinner. The next day, they visited Konstantinos Kanaris, the hero of Greek independence to whom Victor Hugo had dedicated one of his *Orientales*. This small man with a square face did not impress them. The heroes of independence were tired; he was a senator now, a "real bourgeois." In short, a "sad visit." The rest of the Greek jaunt took place in the Peloponnesus: Megara, Corinth, Mycenae, Argos, and so on. In Sparta, they became the center of attention. They were followed everywhere they went by a huge crowd, including into a café, where they were surrounded by a circle of curious onlookers when they sat down.

On January 24, 1851, the two friends left Athens; two days later they landed in Brindisi. From there, they headed to Naples, where Flaubert bought razors to remove his beard: "My poor beard, which I bathed in the Nile, which the desert blew through, and which was so long perfumed by Tombac tobacco. Beneath it I discovered an *enormously* fattened face; I'm disgusting, I have a double chin and jowls." While in Naples, they paid a long visit to the Museum of Antiquities and made trips to Herculaneum and Paestum. Their appetite for discovery did not diminish. Maxime had sold his camera, but both he and Flaubert constantly took detailed notes on everything they encountered. In late March, they traveled to Rome, where they were to separate. Flaubert was initially disappointed by the city: "Seeking the Rome of Nero," he wrote to Bouilhet, "I found only that of Sixtus V. . . . The gown of the Jesuits has covered everything with a gloomy, seminarist murk." Yes, but there was also sixteenth-century Rome, Michelangelo's Sistine Chapel, the paintings, the statues: "Rome is the most splendid museum in the world."[42]

The great journey was coming to an end: Maxime returned to Paris, and Gustave welcomed his mother, who arrived alone in Rome with her chambermaid. Together, they visited Florence and Venice and returned to Paris in June.

What Now?

During this long journey, Flaubert wrote very little other than an abundance of notes and the fairly brief text "La Cange," which he would include in his *Journey to Egypt*. Yet he spent a great deal of time reflecting about himself, his art, and his future. He responded to his mother's concerns by telling her how little he cared about fame: "At the present moment," he wrote from Cairo, "I certainly see no reason (even from a literary point of view) to do anything to get myself talked about."[43] Should he set his sights on a job, as she suggested? No; "when one does something, one must do it wholly and well."[44] This was the privilege of a man of independent means: he would not have to look for a *position*. Nor would he marry. He did not want to "participate actively in life," for this would prevent him from seeing it clearly; it would make him suffer too much or enjoy himself too much. "The artist, to my way of thinking, is a monstrosity, something outside nature." It was decided: upon his return, he would live as he had lived since he had quit law school, far from everything: "I care nothing for the world, for the future, for what people will say, for any kind of establishment, or even for literary renown, which in the past I used to lie awake so many nights dreaming about."[45]

As we have seen, he had accepted Maxime Du Camp and Louis Bouilhet's criticism of *The Temptation of Saint Anthony* and been shaken by its failure. But he had not in any way given up on writing and on the prospect of achieving something that resembled his idea of perfection. He continued to uphold the doctrine to which he had adhered when he was eighteen: Art for Art's Sake.[46] The contemporary trend was for utilitarian literature: socialist doctrines proliferated, and there was a collective desire for writers to express humankind's hope for the future. But he had no interest in the future: "What do we care what tomorrow will look like?" His position was clear: "Stupidity consists in wanting to reach conclusions. We are a thread, and we want to know the whole cloth."[47]

He also told his mother that the trip had developed his "contempt" for humanity. Not that he had lacked it before! Everywhere he went, he had encountered human weakness, human stupidity, "and all this, the landscapes and roguery, produce a calm and indifferent pity in you, a dreamy serenity that casts its gaze about without attaching itself to anything, because it's all the same to you and you feel yourself liking the animals as much as the men, and the pebbles on the beach as much as the houses in the city." Flaubertian impersonality is rooted in this view of a world that can only be saved from utter mediocrity by art. He discovered that one should not draw conclusions or judge, only observe things and transcribe them in a style entirely devoted to beauty. From Cairo to Athens via Constantinople, Flaubert experienced this way of staying outside of things without ever passing judgment in order to better *render* them: detachment would be the rule.

It follows that Flaubert did not care about politics. As we have seen, he adhered neither to the stubborn conservatism of the bourgeoisie nor to the utopianism of those who planned the future. In his *Souvenirs littéraires*, Maxime Du Camp, who shared Flaubert's ideas at the time, describes how he and Gustave greeted their friend Louis de Cormenin's news from Paris. Cormenin, the son of a deputy of 1848 and president of the constitutional commission, told them that by a law passed on May 31, 1850, the heavily conservative Assembly had restricted universal male suffrage, notably under the influence of Thiers, who had used the expression "vile multitude." "Those people," wrote Cormenin, "think they can win an advantage by killing the republic; they are fools following their momentary passion: the May 31st law will chase out those who imagined the republic and will crown the president [Louis-Napoléon Bonaparte]; when you return, there may be eagles on our flagpoles." Cormenin was not far off—all he got wrong was the date. But Du Camp had the same reaction as Flaubert: "I read all that without paying much attention, for politics was of no interest to me."[48]

Flaubert did not return from his journey with any kind of model of civilization in mind. In his view, the Orient "was even sicker than the Occident," and he predicted that Egypt would be colonized by England. But he had accumulated a stock of images, landscapes, colors, and scenes from life that had enriched his imagination and from which he would draw in the future: the dream of the Orient would haunt him to his dying day. Maxime Du Camp published a travel narrative illustrated with remarkable photographs.[49] In October 1852, the Académie des arts et métiers, industries et belles lettres presented Du Camp with a diploma and a gold medal for his "archaeological work." After its initial publication in *La Revue de Paris,* Du Camp's *Le Nil* was reprinted five times in the nineteenth century. As for Flaubert, he would wait a few more years before coming out of the shadows.

CHAPTER 10

Louise (Last and Final)

During his travels, Flaubert had succeeded in escaping the political news from France. But his return in June 1851 plunged him into a country in turmoil. Louis-Napoléon Bonaparte had been elected to a four-year term as president of the Republic in 1848. He wanted to serve another term, but the Constitution limited the office to one term. Backed by a campaign of petitions, he sought to amend the Constitution. The Assembly voted on the matter on July 19, but the proposed amendment did not get the requisite 75 percent of votes in favor. Only the naïve thought Bonaparte would leave it at that. On December 2, the anniversary of the Battle of Austerlitz, the prince-president and his minister of war Saint-Arnaud crossed the Rubicon—the name they gave to their operation—and seized all power. Republicans attempted to rise up everywhere—in Paris, and particularly in Lyon, Marseille, and the southeast. The crackdown was relentless. The National Assembly was dissolved, and representatives Victor Hugo and Edgar Quinet were forced into exile. The coup d'état had succeeded; France had fallen under the dictatorship of Bonaparte. One year later, on December 2, 1852, the Empire was re-established with Louis-Napoléon—now Napoleon III—at the helm, a restoration that was validated by referendum. Those now in power intended to prove their legitimacy through universal suffrage.

Flaubert happened to be in Paris during the coup d'état. Writing to his English correspondent Henriette Collier on December 8, he told her that "one would have to be made of bronze to remain calm," but nothing more. A month later, he wrote to his uncle Parain about his satisfaction at having witnessed the events: "Providence, which knows I am a lover of colorful events, always takes care to send me to opening nights when they are worthwhile. This time I wasn't cheated; it was elegant."[1] In June 1852, admitting that he felt himself "a foreigner in the midst of his countrymen," he expressed his liking for the prince-president "who restores this noble France under the soles of his boots. I would even go and kiss his ass to thank him personally, if the spot weren't already taken by such a crowd."[2] But when he attended a first communion in Normandy in June 1852, he was outraged to see that the "priest found a way to sing the praises of Napoleon in his sermon. That gives you a sample of the general baseness reigning in France."[3]

Wherever he looked, he saw nothing but poverty, filth, stupidity. To express this relatively constant state of mind, he quoted a saint and martyr, Polycarp, a second-century bishop of Smyrna who would become one of its patron saints: "Saint Polycarp," he wrote in August 1853, "was in the habit of saying, 'Oh Lord, what a century you brought me into!' while covering his ears and fleeing wherever he was. I am becoming like Saint Polycarp." In his seminar at the Collège de France in the 1970s, Roland Barthes referred to this fiercely antimodern attitude as "Polycarpism." Deploying his taste for hyperbole, Flaubert made a Polycarpist declaration of faith at the beginning of the Second Empire: "'89 demolished the royalty and the nobility, '48 the bourgeoisie, and '51 *the people*. There is *nothing* left but a roguish and idiotic rabble.—We have all sunk to the same level of shared mediocrity. Social equality has entered the sphere of the Mind. We make books for everyone, art for everyone, science for everyone, just as we build railroads and public shelters. Humanity has a rage for moral debasement.—And I am angry with it, because I'm also part of it."[4]

One corollary of Polycarpism was an aristocratic attitude: "Well, yes, I am becoming an aristocrat, an enraged aristocrat. . . . I strongly detest my fellow men and do not feel like their fellow." The democratic society announced by Tocqueville made the dinosaur shudder. "What the hell do Art, poetry, and style do for the masses? They don't need all that."[5] His disgust for the modern was aroused by economic development, industry, and mechanization: "As work is broken down into compartments, men-machines take their places beside the machines themselves."[6] Industrialism fostered ugliness on an inordinate scale. The only way to survive was to "regard the human race as a vast association of cretins and scoundrels." This hatred of the herd, of regulations, of a common standard, led to Flaubert's need for solitude and his refusal to belong to any organization, academy, or corporation: "Bedouin, to your heart's content; citizen, never."[7] This "discriminating" individualism explains his passive but genuine rallying behind Napoleon III, who was known by the nonsense name Badinguet: "I am thankful for Badinguet. Bless his heart! He brought me back to contempt for the masses, and hatred of what is popular."[8]

Over the years that followed his return from the Orient, Flaubert, far from the masses, set to work on *Madame Bovary,* the novel whose formal beauty was to transfigure the mediocrity of its subject. This stubborn desire to shun the world would alienate him from Maxime Du Camp. Yet, unexpectedly, he experienced a return of his passion for Louise Colet, who had never stopped loving him.

Maxime and Louis

Maxime Du Camp was ambitious and had never made a secret of his eagerness to succeed. He did not understand how his friend Gustave could spill ink over pages and pages in his Norman sanctuary, indifferent to literary fame and ignoring the newspapers and periodicals that allowed one to develop a reputation. As it happens, Maxime had joined Théophile Gautier, Arsène Houssaye, and Louis de Cormenin at the head of the new periodical the *Revue de Paris.* His tale "Tagahor" was published in its first issue, dated October 1, 1851. He offered to publish fragments of Flaubert's *Saint Anthony,* but the bear of Croisset felt "neither the need nor the desire" to do so. Du Camp, who pressed Flaubert to settle in Paris, to participate in literary life, to rub shoulders with those at the heart of it, in short to follow his example, grew irritated with the resistance put up by this recluse bogged down in a province inhabited only by ruminants. He lectured him in a superior tone, to the point that Gustave grew tired of his "same old song." Du Camp tried to explain himself: "It seems to you that my behavior lacks dignity; it seems to you that I should have thrown my prose out there and patiently waited with folded arms for admirers to come to me. No! Since I started this, since I want to make it, I will not fail to reach my goal. I am off—*bon voyage!*" *To make it:* this expression was not in Flaubert's vocabulary. "I am simply a bourgeois living retired in the country, occupying myself with literature, and asking nothing of others, neither consideration nor honor nor even esteem."[9]

Flaubert could have been more understanding; he could certainly have been more grateful that his former travel companion had published poems by his friend Bouilhet in the November 1, 1851, issue of the *Revue,* particularly since the issue was dedicated to his recently deceased friend Pradier. But Flaubert was inflexible. His judgment of Maxime's works was increasingly harsh, notably in the case of his autobiographical *Livre posthume* [*Posthumous Book*], which he deemed "pitiful," "odious in its character and in pretensions of every kind."[10] In January 1853, Du Camp was made an officer of the Legion of Honor. "How immensely ironic it all is! And how honors swarm where there is no honor!"[11]

Maxime was not part of Gustave's life anymore. Gustave had certainly cared for him: together they had sown their wild oats and traveled countless miles. But Maxime was no longer a jolly fellow; he was a socialite, hosted by the minister of the interior, full of himself, bouncing his Legion cross on his chest—laughable! When Du Camp published the beginning of *Le Nil* in the *Revue de Paris*, Gustave deemed it a botched book with an "ultra-flat" style borrowed from Champollion-Figeac's *L'Égypte ancienne* [*Ancient Egypt*]. Nothing about Maxime found favor in his eyes anymore. On December 21, 1853, he confessed to Louise Colet: "Deep down I still love him, but he has irritated, repulsed, and denied me so much and done such odious dirty tricks that for me 'it is as if he were already dead.'"

Flaubert's judgment of Du Camp was shared by Louis Bouilhet, who was now his dearest friend. Louis was still teaching at his cram school in Rouen and was living with Léonie, the daughter of Norman farmers, and her son Philippe. Every Sunday, Bouilhet traveled to Croisset to visit, talk, and read with his friend Gustave. Louis read him his poems, notably *Melaenis,* which had been published in the *Revue de Paris:* "To summarize," Flaubert wrote to Louise Colet, "*Melaenis* is the last echo of the many cries we have let out in solitude; it assuages the mass of appetites that were ravaging our hearts." Flaubert would read Louis the pages of *Madame Bovary* that he had written during the week. They advised and corrected each other without deference, shared their enthusiasm for books they both read, and encouraged and comforted each other. Life at Croisset would have been bleak for Flaubert without these Sundays devoted to friendship and shared work. He was heartbroken when Louis Bouilhet left to settle in Paris in October 1853: "The old Sundays are over. I am going to be alone now, alone, alone." But this gave Flaubert a reason to go to Paris more often.

Love Returns

The major romantic event of Flaubert's life in the years between the end of his trip to the Orient and the spring of 1854 was the return of his passion for

Louise Colet. Louise initiated the reconciliation. Unlike Gustave, who had put the affair behind him, Louise, despite her occasional lovers—or perhaps *because* of these lovers, whom she could compare to Flaubert—had never stopped loving the giant of Croisset. The rough draft of a letter she wrote to Flaubert in June 1851, when he was back in Paris after his trip, has survived. She writes that she is upset that he has not been in touch or visited her, demands that he return her letters, wants to return his, and is clearly hoping to see him again. We do not know if this epistle was ever sent, but Louise did better: with her typical resolve, she decided to set out for Croisset, which Flaubert had always forbidden her to do.

In her journals, which were later published under the title *Mémentos* [*Mementos*], Colet reports that on Thursday, June 26, she took the train for Rouen. She had just reread her former lover's letters: "Devastating emotion, tears, regrets; he loved me. To love each other so much and not see each other! To burn with desires and never satisfy them, is that possible? I was suffering too much, I was irritated, excessive, with little idea of how to seduce him." She did not resign herself; full of audacity, she went for broke. Once in Rouen, she took a room at the Hôtel d'Angleterre and wrote a note to Gustave: "Pressing necessity compels me to see you." She went down to the embankment and hired a boatman to take her to Croisset, right to the Flaubert home, which was only separated from the Seine by a fence and the towpath. The front gate was open. She went in, walked to the house and gave her note to a servant, who promptly returned with the recipient's answer: "M. Flaubert cannot see Madame, he will write her." Monsieur was dining with guests; Madame should leave her address, and he would visit her at eight o'clock that evening. Louise was preparing to return to her small boat when Gustave appeared:

"What do you want from me, Madame?"
"I must speak to you."
"That is truly impossible here. I will join you in Rouen at eight o'clock by the steamboat."

And so they were reunited in Rouen. "He seemed so strange to me in his Chinese outfit," wrote Louise; "loose pants, calico smock, yellow silk tie with gold and silver stripes, a long and droopy mustache. His hair has become sparse and his forehead is slightly wrinkled, though he is only thirty." At the

Hôtel d'Angleterre, they opened up to each other. Louise confessed that she was prepared to live "in some village, or here," where Gustave could come see her whenever he wanted. His reply was blunt: "I would be a contemptible wretch to deceive you. But I can do nothing for your happiness." She cried, became agitated, admitted that she had made mistakes—"mistakes due to a nature overexcited by those daily letters, letters of passion that excited my senses and my imagination without ever satisfying them." She continued: "He listened to me with kindness, he would move the candle forward to see me better and sometimes took my arms in his hands. I tried to smile so I would not look too defeated." As Gustave was taking his leave, Louise gave him the manuscript of her play *Madeleine*, which she had just finished; he promised to read it and to come to Paris to return it to her: "I embraced him, he returned my caress, and our last words were: see you soon."

Louise had succeeded in breaking through Gustave's reserve, but she would have to wait to win him back. While on a trip to England, she received a letter from him and read it "with a pang." When they saw each other in Paris in September, their reconciliation seemed to be decided; Louise appreciated his "gentleness," his "kindness," but still experienced "the bitter sadness of possessing him so little and having so little influence on his nature."[12]

One can certainly understand her doubts upon reading the letter she received from Flaubert on October 23, 1851: "Yes: I do wish that you did not love me, and that you had never known me; and in so wishing I think I express a regret that concerns your happiness."[13] He was singing the same tune he used to sing in the old days: I love you the best that I can, I appreciate your company, I desire you, but don't ask me for more—I have my novel to write. "My feeling for you is a mix of friendship, attraction, esteem, emotional tenderness, and intellectual understanding, which makes a complex whole. I do not know its name, but it appears solid."[14] Yet in the following months, Flaubert's letters become more tender. He repeatedly tells her that he loves her and that the only reason he comes to Paris is to see her. These trips are "oases in which I come to drink and shake off onto your knees the dust from my labor." He promises that in a year or eighteen months, he will take a place in Paris and come more often.

Flaubert sent Louise the first *Sentimental Education* and *Saint Anthony*. She was full of praise, writing in her *Mémentos* that he was "a genius." Her entry for March 14, 1852, reads: "He loves me, I think he will no longer be able to do without me, just like I cannot do without him." The "hours of exhilaration" experienced in Paris and in a small hotel in Mantes revived their mutual desires. The next month, Flaubert was worried that "the English" were late: "The possibility of giving life to someone makes infernal angers roar in the depths of my heart."[15] They had another scare in December of the same year, and again Flaubert was anxious at the idea of becoming a father; he did not want to pass on to anyone "the boredom and ignominies of existence." He was soon reassured by the return of the "Redcoats."

While there is no doubt that Gustave's physical attraction to his mistress was the driving force of their renewed union, in Louise he also found intellectual qualities, an ear attentive to his ramblings, and even a fellow writer. From 1852 to 1854, he wrote her his most beautiful letters: "Your love penetrates into me like a warm rain, and I feel soaked in it to the depths of my heart. Don't you have everything I need to love you—body, mind, tenderness? You are simple in soul and strong of mind, very little "*pohétique*" and very much a poet. There is nothing in you but good, and all of you is like your bosom, white and soft to the touch."[16] Or in July 1853: "Do you know that on Thursday you wrote me a burning letter that awakened my senses? Oh dear volcano, how I love you and am thinking about you."

Louise sent her verses to Croisset, and Gustave diligently corrected them with Bouilhet, who was delighted that the three of them formed "a bundle that no one can separate." Louise was touched by her lover's extraordinary devotion to improving her poems. He bluntly made her cut bad verses or suggested she change a word with a severity that she had the intelligence to appreciate. There was no room for vanity in the face of the "genius's" judgment. He reprimanded her for her comedy L'Institutrice [The Schoolmistress]: it was written in a "vulgar" style, was careless, "painful to read," with an "interminable monologue." When she responded that her friend Mme Roger had liked the play, he replied: "If Mme Roger likes your comedy, too bad for her. Either she has poor taste, or she is deceiving you to be polite, unless I am completely blind." She had to take it in stride, but what joy when the master—who was still unpublished, we should recall, though Louise never doubted him—sang her praises upon reading a poem such as the long piece La Paysanne [The Peasant Woman].

Grateful, she attempted to "launch" Bouilhet after Gustave introduced the two of them in Paris in January 1852. On March 11, the Muse, who still hosted her salon on rue de Sèvres on Thursdays despite her financial difficulties, gathered her guests in honor of Louis and his Roman poem Melaenis. Mme Edma

Roger des Genettes, who would briefly become Bouilhet's mistress, read the fourth canto to a large, appreciative crowd. "You did something for Bouilhet," Flaubert wrote to Louise on March 20, "that went straight to my heart. That was very good (and very clever?) of you. It will have been poor Bouilhet's first success. He will remember that little evening his whole life. My inner muse blesses you for it and sends your soul its most tender kiss."[17]

The resumption of his relationship with Louise gave Flaubert an opportunity to become closer to Victor Hugo, whom they both admired. Louise had sent some of her verse to the great exile and initiated a correspondence with him. She began to serve as his mail carrier, aided and abetted by Gustave. In order to keep Hugo's letters from being seized at the border by the censor, Louise and Gustave developed a system by which Hugo sent his mail in a double envelope from Jersey to the London address of Mrs. Farmer, the former teacher of Gustave's sister Caroline. Mrs. Farmer then sent the mail to Flaubert, who forwarded the letters not directly addressed to him to Louise Colet, who distributed them to their addressees. The mail sent by the Muse followed the same path in reverse, via Flaubert. Hugo was grateful for Flaubert's help. The two men started to correspond. We know of fourteen letters from Hugo and two letters from Flaubert to the writer he called "the Grand Crocodile." In the first of Flaubert's surviving letters, the hermit of Croisset reminds Hugo that they had been introduced at Pradier's in the winter of 1844 and confesses his "admiration" for his "genius." In the other letter, dated July 15, 1853, he thanks Hugo for a photo by his son and waxes enthusiastic on a subject he usually avoided—politics:

> Private infamies proceed from political turpitude, and it is impossible to take a step without treading on something unclean. . . . But since you extend your hand to me across the ocean, I take it and grasp it. I grasp it proudly, the hand that wrote *Notre-Dame* and *Napoléon le Petit*, the hand that has hewn colossi and fashioned bitter cups for traitors, that has culled the most glorious delights from the loftiest reaches of the intellect, and that now, like the hand of the biblical Hercules, alone stays raised amid the twofold ruins of Art and of Liberty![18]

The rather pompous prose is unlike Flaubert's usual style. Should it be considered ironic? There is no question that Gustave had admired Hugo since childhood and that his compliments were sincere. What was less sincere was to lead the Hercules of the Channel Islands to believe that he shared his republican convictions. Flaubert caught himself bending the truth to impress the great man, then sought to correct himself. In September of the same year, he wrote to Louise: "I simply cannot let him go on thinking that I'm a republican, that I admire the people, etc."[19] He promised to admit everything: "I cannot lie to be pleasant to him." But we do not know whether this confession was ever written, and if so whether it arrived in Jersey. In 1854, Hugo sent Flaubert his *Châtiments* [*Punishments*] one page at a time to avoid police surveillance. He thanked him for his "good graces" and sent him his "most affectionate regards," which suggests Flaubert had not kept his promise to enlighten him about their divergent political views.

Bovary Underway

One of the most valuable aspects of Flaubert's correspondence with Louise Colet during this period is his regular account of the slow germination of *Madame Bovary*.

On September 20, 1851, as he was preparing to leave for London with his mother the following Thursday to visit the Great Exhibition, Gustave wrote to Louise: "Last night I began my novel."[20] He had a title: *Madame Bovary*. According to Maxime Du Camp's *Souvenirs littéraires*, Gustave was standing before the second cataract of the Nile when he cried out: "I will call her Emma Bovary!" In any case, the first reference to Flaubert's novel is found in a letter dated July 23, 1851, in which Maxime asks Gustave if he is working on "the story of Mme Delamare, which is so beautiful."[21] (Delphine Delamare was the protagonist of a news item that may have inspired the plot of *Madame Bovary*.) After the failure of *The Temptation of Saint Anthony*, the author had decided to replace a "noble" subject with a "trivial" story: "What I should like to write, is a book about nothing, a book dependent on nothing external, which would be held together by the internal strength of its style."[22] To subdue his lyricism, he chose not a sublime, fantastic, or heroic subject, but a dull bourgeois story. From the beginning of his project, he set himself the imperative of *impersonality*. The author would no longer intervene as in traditional novels—he could not give his opinion or comment on his narrative: "No lyricism, no reflections; the author's personality is absent." The task was to seek reality, to closely observe the most ordinary details: "It is a long way from the mythological and theological extravagances of *Saint Anthony*."[23] He had discovered his trade secret: "Impersonality is the sign of Strength."[24] His art would be to expose, not to discuss: "Literature will increasingly come to resemble science; it will primarily *expose*, which does not mean it will be didactic." It would also be like scientific work in that the author would not systematically search for what was singular or extraordinary, but for what was general. When Louise was writing *La Servante* [*The Maid*], he gave her a piece of advice: "If your generality is powerful, it will overcome, or at least compensate for, the particularity of the anecdote.—Think as much as possible of all maids."[25]

Yet literature remained an art, and its objective was still Beauty; it could only exist through its style. This explains Flaubert's relentless attention to the sentence, his obsession with finding the right word, the rooting out of repetition and assonance, the avoidance of *that* and *which* (*qui* and *que*) "tangled together," and the quest for musical harmony. His ear served as his inspection tool. In his *gueuloir*, he read his prose out loud, on the alert for false notes and bad rhythm: "A good prose sentence," he wrote to Louise, "should be like a good line of poetry—*unchangeable*."[26] Flaubert revised over and over again, working with ascetic intensity. He wrote ten pages to keep one that satisfied him. Like a modern Sisyphus pushing his rock, he moved forward, went back, crossed out sentences, reached new heights, plummeted, and endured "atrocious pain" in his attempt to whittle down, extend, shorten, prune, and restrain his prose: "The grand turns of phrase, the broad, full periods surging like rivers, the multiplicity of metaphors, the dazzling bursts of style, in short everything I like, will not be found in it."[27] He often took two days to finish two sentences. Time and again, he wrote to Louise that he had spent "four hours without writing *one* sentence!" Time and again, he wrote that he was on the verge of collapse, ready to "vomit with fatigue": "My head is spinning and my throat is burning from looking for one sentence, grinding away at it, digging into it, turning it over and over, rummaging in it, and yelling it out a thousand different ways until it has *finally* been completed.—It is good. I guarantee it; but it was not without difficulty."[28]

Sometimes he became discouraged and swore never to write this kind of book again, for it was painful for him to go so far against his natural inclination—"the dithyrambic and puffed up style." It was hard for him to handle the distance he had established between his common, bourgeois, and mediocre subject and the demands of the style he imposed on himself: "The vulgarity of my subject sometimes makes me nauseous, and the prospect of the difficult task of writing so many more common things horrifies me."[29] In these cases, he spoke of the "agony of art" and ranted: "*Bovary* is wearing me out"; "What trouble my *Bovary* is still giving me!";[30] "My damn *Bovary* is tormenting me and exhausting me."

There has been much discussion of Flaubert's slowness as a writer. According to Maxime Du Camp, his illness was to blame. His fits continued during these years, though they were less frequent than at the beginning. Flaubert probably sought shelter at Croisset in part because he did not want his weaknesses to be on display. On August 15, 1852, Louise Colet described in her *Mémentos* a fit she had witnessed: "His fit at the hotel, my terror. He begs me not to call anyone; his efforts, his gasping, the foam coming out of his mouth, my arm bruised by his contracted fingernails. After about ten minutes, he comes around, vomiting. I assure him that his spell only lasted a few seconds and that his mouth did not foam."[31]

Some contemporary neurologists have tried to diagnose Flaubert's disease and its obsessive characteristics. Let's consider the evidence. Was it "cerebral atrophy with left temporo-occipital predominance caused by a hypothetical neonatal affliction"? Or perhaps, "if we consider that Flaubert died of a subarachnoid hemorrhage, the most probable etiological diagnosis is that of a vascular malformation that caused epilepsy and ruptured."[32] Whether the cause of his illness was neurotic, organic, or hysterical, researchers have postulated a link between the "bradyphrenia" (sluggish mental processing) that explains the slowness of Flaubert's creative process and the "absence of libido" that explains his solitary retreat. According to this line of thinking, the effect of his illness was a double impotence, both when he was faced with the blank page (which made him puff and pant) and with a woman ("overall hyposexuality").[33]

While I am not an expert, I will counter this medical theory with some common-sense observations. First, the drop in libido. One of the neurologists quoted above attributes it to "the bromide he took for his epileptic fits." Anyone with knowledge of Gustave and Maxime's tour of brothels in the Middle East might have some doubts about this. Louise's *Mémentos* also inform us that while Gustave was certainly too occasional a lover, he was an exhilarating one: on August 24, 1852, she describes him as "more passionate than ever." On January 1, 1853, she writes: "This past year has been the sweetest, the best of my life. Gustave loved me well, and through him I tasted art and love better than ever before."

As for his creative slowness, Flaubert himself explained it: it had taken only eighteen months for him to write *The Temptation of Saint Anthony,* but this swiftness dated from before his commitment to impersonality, which was a response to the failure of *Saint Anthony.* "It takes a great deal of effort for me to imagine my characters and then to make them talk, for they deeply disgust me. But when I write something from my *guts,* it goes quickly."[34] The letters attest to the fact that he could write pages and pages at a time, for hours on end, without striking out a single word. But "to write the mediocre well" was a crushing task. Additionally, while Flaubert constantly revised his writing, his friend and adviser Bouilhet proved equally demanding: "B. has made me rewrite the same paragraph three times now . . . we do not spare each other." Recall his old motto: "aesthetic mysticism." His work was like that of the monk illuminating a manuscript, a perfectionist who never came to the end of his task. One might consider him "obsessive" or hypothesize that his illness accentuated his compulsive traits, but one must seriously doubt that he was impotent. The fact of the matter is that Flaubert used his illness to choose the kind of life that seemed most suitable to his creative work. He suffered to bring *Madame Bovary* into the world because it was what he chose to do. "This book is exhausting me, I am wearing out what remains of my youth on it. Too bad! It must be done."[35]

Maxime Du Camp did not understand the revolution that Flaubert was performing on the modern novel. The impersonality he adopted was a demanding novelty: style had to *suggest* what novelists before him had traditionally analyzed and explained from the writer's perspective. The point was not to write in a "beautiful style" but to entrust the words linked together in a sentence, the descriptions, and the images with the mission of meaning—a demanding task for the future reader and even more so for the author writing the novel. Flaubert was not *slow*—he wrote thousands of pages. But he was creating a new art of the novel.

"I Shall Never Be In"

Read in parallel to Flaubert's letters and in the absence of her own letters, Louise Colet's *Mémentos* reveal that there was a dark side to the renewal of great love. Louise constantly felt that Gustave did not love her enough, that he was indifferent to her financial situation, and that he remained a selfish man more concerned with his novel than with her. "Perhaps it was bad luck that

I found him again. There is nothing inside this man," she wrote on November 18, 1851. Though in the following months she repeatedly wrote that she was happy—particularly late in 1852—the same causes produced the same effects: Gustave's remoteness, his refusal to live in Paris, the way he curbed his romantic feelings to focus on his literary obsessions were all things she had previously experienced. Despite her resolution not to whine and Flaubert's satisfaction that they had gotten back together, she could not truly be happy: "Gustave only loves me for himself, as a total egotist, to satisfy his senses and read me his work."[36] Most importantly, she understood that she could not conceive of a shared future with him. Hadn't he advised her to marry Victor Cousin, her daughter Henriette's alleged father? "Doesn't that amount to telling me that his future and mine are not linked? That I should not count on him?"

Louise was constantly worried about money. A widow, she survived on her modest pension from the Ministry of Education and the small pension Victor Cousin paid for the care of Henriette; she supplemented her income with whatever royalties she could get for her articles and books. She considered Gustave inattentive to her needs; she even referred to his "avarice." In July 1852, he asked her to tell him frankly about her financial problems, and he offered on several occasions to give her five hundred francs, but she refused, finding the way he made his offer offensive. He protested: "You seem to consider me niggardly because I don't offer assistance when I am not asked. But when did I ever refuse? . . . You say I never feel a spontaneous urge to be generous? I say that is not true, that I am quite capable of such impulses." If only Gustave loved her more, she thought, he would be much more devoted.

She had another grievance: he refused to introduce her to his mother, despite the fact that Louise constantly asked to visit her at Croisset or to meet her in Paris. He feigned not to understand her persistence. Finally, he gave in—it was agreed, he would do everything he could for the two women to meet; but, he said, "I can't imagine why it's so important to you."[37] Though Mme Flaubert and her granddaughter Caroline spent time in Paris in December 1853, the introduction Louise had hoped for did not take place. She spoke to Louis Bouilhet, entrusting him with her grievances. Bouilhet did not hesitate to report back to his friend: "Do you want me to say straight out what she is after, with her visits to your mother, with the comedy in verse, her cries, her tears, her invitations and her dinners? She wants and expects to become your *wife!*"[38] So that was why she refused to marry Cousin!

Bouilhet recognized that in the past the Muse had been obliging to him—she had launched him in Paris, found him an apartment when he decided to settle there, and even had a brief fling with him—"but it was all done for so obvious a purpose that I am ashamed."[39] Solidarity between men had its rules; it took precedence over gratitude.

Louise was also inclined to fits of jealousy, for which Gustave had little tolerance. She did not tell him that she sometimes "wanted to kill him rather than see him go to another woman,"[40] but she reproached him in retrospect for his affair with Kuchuk Hanem after she requested that he show her his Egyptian travel notes. He had to reassure her: "The Oriental woman is a machine, and nothing more; she does not make any distinction between one man and the next."[41] But was Louise herself faithful? In 1852, she began a relationship with Alfred de Musset, who had just been elected to the Académie Française and was thus in a position to help her win another poetry prize. Naturally, this made Musset attractive to her, though she was disgusted by the fact that he was an alcoholic wreck. Finally, she took him to bed, only to discover that he was "impotent."[42] One night while they were riding in a carriage, he became vulgar and frightened her. She wanted to jump out of the carriage. He challenged her to do it, and she fell out:

> We were on the Place de la Concorde across from the Pont de la Chambre. The carriage came to a halt, the driver came over to me. He says: "The gentleman has sent me to see if you are hurt." I answer: "Tell him you couldn't find me." He says: "He's a scoundrel and you're a good woman, I can see that. Do you want me to leave him here and take you home? Oh! Poor women, poor women!" I tell him: "No, go back to him, tell him you didn't see me."

Musset was dead drunk. Louise gave Gustave a slightly expurgated version of the scene. He got upset and wanted to beat up the poet: "Oh, my poor Louise! You, you in that situation! For a moment I saw you dead in the street, with the wheel rolling over your stomach, a horse's hoof in your face; in the gutter, you, you, and because of him!" Five days later, he reflected about Louise's adventure and his reaction: "Was I jealous about all that?—Possibly. Yet upon reading the account in your long letter, when I felt so furious, it was not jealousy, but two feelings, that of my impotence, my inanity (I wasn't there, I told myself) and a sense of scandal, of personal affront, like the swallowing of an ignominy being intoned to me."[43] Yet Louise let bygones be bygones and saw Musset again. He was sometimes odious, sometimes charming, "practically impotent"; she said she was "in love with his genius." She both admired and despised him. During the same period, she rejected the advances of François Villemain, literary historian and permanent secretary of the Académie, who hovered around her, pressured her, went down on his knees before her, kissed her hair, and read her love poetry: "His [Villemain's] goal is now to seduce me by making me hope for the prize next year: a vile rogue!" Deep down, she knew very well that none of this would happen if Gustave were truly with her: "Gustave hurts me so much by leaving me alone like this."[44]

In 1853, Gustave traveled to Paris about every two months. His relationship with Louise was primarily epistolary, which did not satisfy her. His long letters were too much like literary dissertations, on Lamartine (whom he detested), Leconte de Lisle (whom he liked), Stendhal (whom he didn't much care for), and his great enthusiasms: Shakespeare, Hugo, Rabelais, Cervantes, Montaigne ... He continued to correct her writings and to give her lessons in style; she appreciated his seriousness, his talent, his vast knowledge, but all this prose that would delight future readers did not provide her with what she was looking for: feeling, passion, exhilaration. Once again she complained about his absence, and once again he explained that he needed to live at Croisset, no longer because of his mother, whom he did not mention as often, but for his work: "I will never write well in Paris, I know it." Her "diatribes" started up again, annoying Flaubert. He softened but stuck to his guns: "I make you suffer, poor dear Louise. But do you think I do so out of principle, or pleasure, and that I don't suffer to know that I am making you suffer?" He promised to come see her more often, that he would take an apartment in the capital, only later. Pleasure and bitterness alternated throughout 1853. "One day I find you happy with me. Then the next day, it's something else." Flaubert resigned himself to a separation, as he confided to Bouilhet in December: "She makes me very sad, our poor Muse. I don't know what to do about her. I assure you that this grieves me in all kinds of ways. How do you think things will end? I suspect her of being thoroughly tired of me. And for her own piece of mind it would be best if she broke with me."[45] The severity with which he spoke to her about her poem *La Servante* did not improve their relationship: "I find this work malicious in intent, cruel, and poorly executed." Meanwhile, she reproached him for his "sepulchral detachment." The pace of their letters slowed: "I think that at bottom she is tired of me,"[46] he wrote to Bouilhet. He maintained that his feelings for her had not changed: he had told her time and again that love was but an *accompaniment* in life, but she stubbornly refused to believe him.

During the winter of 1853–54, Flaubert took up with a new mistress, the actress Béatrix Person, a friend of Marie Durey, a fellow actress who was Louis Bouilhet's mistress. According to Louise Colet's biographer Joseph Jackson, "Béatrix Person participated in foursomes with Flaubert, Bouilhet, and Marie Durey."[47] In March 1854, Louise Colet began an affair with Alfred de Vigny, also a member of the Académie. She had sent him her poem *La Paysanne*, to which he responded enthusiastically: "You are admired, you are loved, and you have not yet been lifted high enough." Louise did not tell Flaubert about her new love; she remarked only that she had become friendly with Vigny. "I'm glad you've found Vigny," he answered. "May that old nightingale amuse you!" Gustave was not the jealous type. It was as if he could foresee that Vigny would give him the opportunity to end his relationship with Louise. On March 19, he told her that his "jealousy rests easy." He was delighted when she told him that Vigny, the rapporteur for the Académie's poetry prize, had read her poem *L'Acropole* [*The Acropolis*] to his fellow academicians: "This Vigny seems like an excellent man to me!" In April, their letters took a harder tone, as Gustave reproached Louise for her "injustices." She accused him of lacking certain feelings and not liking children. He protested: he cherished his niece, taking care of her and giving her history and geography lessons: "My heart is *human* and if I don't want to have children myself, it is because I feel I would be too *paternal*."[48]

Arriving in Paris a few weeks later, Flaubert finally learned that Louise was Alfred de Vigny's mistress. He used this confirmation as a pretext and returned to Croisset without seeing her. Their correspondence came to an abrupt end. In March 1855, as she was preparing for a trip abroad, Louise sent Flaubert a note asking to see him before she left. Back in Paris, Flaubert rudely turned her down on March 6:

Madame: I was told that you took the trouble to come here to see me three times last evening.

I was not in. And, fearing lest persistence expose you to humiliation, I am bound by the rules of politeness to warn you that *I shall never be in*.

Yours,

G.F.

This note, which can be seen at the Musée Calvet in Avignon, includes a hand-written addition by Louise Colet: "poltroon, coward, cur."[49]

Ultimately, the second and final act of Gustave Flaubert and Louise Colet's relationship was like the first. It ended the same way, too, following a similar logic. To him, she had been someone to take interest in because she was beautiful and desirable, shared his literary culture, and was receptive to his ideas. He was probably initially drawn to her by a mimetic desire that maintained his fervor: after all, she was at the heart of a masculine world that welcomed, pampered, published, and desired her. He was nothing; she was the Muse, rewarded by the Académie. How many women could claim such distinctions at the time? Then, voluntary separation and the rarity of their encounters contributed to stoking the flames of a love that was ultimately destined to die out. Too many hard-line defenders of Flaubert have considered it their duty to inventory each of the lovers' faults and come down hard on Louise Colet.[50] Yet her attitude was understandable. If one can judge a person by the object of their passions, it must be said that Louise Colet had not made a bad choice in falling for this unknown man and becoming an early discoverer of his genius. If truth be told, there was a disparity between her immoderate love and Gustave's "accompanying" love. She dreamed of them becoming a couple; all he saw ahead was his endlessly restarted work. The hourglass was empty for a second time: their days of love had always been numbered.

CHAPTER II

Emma

"It's over with the Muse," Flaubert announced to Bouilhet, not realizing that he hadn't heard the last of Louise Colet. "In 1863, after the publication of *Salammbô*," wrote Maxime du Camp in his literary memoir, "there was such applause surrounding Flaubert that she attempted to get hold of him again and adorn herself with him; he resisted and forever kept his door shut to her." Du Camp's account is questionable, if we are to believe the judgment Louise made in a contemporary letter to a female friend: "He can no longer make my heart leap or my senses quiver. I find him ugly, common, and completely malicious toward me. I will never shake the hand of that cunning Norman. But I recognize the very great, very real, authentic talent in the book."[1] Flaubert had not disappeared from her life, despite the "absolute contempt" in which she now held his personality. In 1856, she had made him a character in her novel *Histoire d'un soldat* [*Story of a Soldier*], in which Léonce—aka Gustave—appears at the theater flanked by two practically naked women: "His red face was puffed up as if he had had too much to drink, and his body jiggled in his white vest; he no longer had his beautiful shiny eyes, but heavy eyes lacking brightness." In 1859, the year George Sand published *Elle et lui* [*She and He*], an account of her affair with Alfred de Musset, to which Musset's brother Paul soon responded with his own *Lui et elle* [*He and She*], Louise, still feeling slighted, published the novel *Lui*, in which Flaubert is again depicted as Léonce and subjected to pointed attacks. Now that Louise had stopped crying over the relationship, she took her revenge. She even glorified the image of Alfred de Musset (Albert in the novel), who had once been so odious, the better to destroy the memory of Flaubert: "One by one I had seen the arrogant and haughty solitary man disavow all of his doctrines on art and love and turn his opinions into a currency for the basest covetousness." A lover's rancor rarely makes for good literature. "I had been crushed," she wrote in *Lui*, "by an inert, brutal stone arm, not at all concerned about my misery." It was true.

For his part, Flaubert had once again put the relationship behind him. His mind had returned to his roots. In September 1855, during a brief stay with his mother on the coast, he wrote to Louis Bouilhet that he was "completely wide-eyed by my old memories of Trouville, which the *sight of the places* has reawakened." A year later, he received an invitation sent from Germany by "old Maurice [Schlésinger]" to attend his daughter Maria's wedding in Baden. Élisa added her own personal letter of invitation. On October 2, the very day after the first pages of *Madame Bovary* were published in the *Revue de Paris*, Gustave wrote to her to apologize that he would not be available, allowing himself a nostalgic, tender reminder of the good old days in Trouville. "And please believe, dear Madam, in the steadfast fondness of your devoted friend, who affectionately kisses your hand." Élisa had not disappeared from his mental landscape, but he did not want to see her again. "He was scared to see Élisa again," contends Jacques-Louis Douchin. "He did not want Élisa to destroy his dream."[2] Douchin considers that Flaubert had never loved Mme Schlésinger, that she was only a tool used by the artist. I believe, on the contrary, that the teenage Flaubert deeply loved the lady of Trouville, but that he later turned this first love into a myth and made good use of it as an artist.

For the time being, his love life was devoid of romance. Outside of his brief encounters with the actress Béatrix Person when he was in Paris, he remained secluded at Croisset. Writing to Bouilhet, he confessed his fantasies about his niece Liline's British teacher, Isabel Hutton, informed him of his solitary pleasures, and comforted his friend about his romantic mishaps with one of those professions of faith he lavishly dispensed: "One should stick to Prostitution, no matter what the socialists and other hypocrites of the same ilk say." This despite the fact that he was suffering the consequences of that practice in the form of a case of syphilis whose treatment was torture: "It is probable that I am so saturated with mercury that I can tolerate no more. . . . Do you know that the head of my penis is *slate-gray?*—what a joke!"[3] He eventually had to consult his brother, who reassured him.

Little Liline was growing up, and Uncle Gustave energetically supplemented her teacher's lessons. In April 1856, he wrote her an affectionate letter from Paris, asking her to take good care of her grandmother, her "*bonne maman.*" "Next year," he added, "you'll receive your first communion. That's the end of childhood. You will become a young person. Just think of that!

It's the time to have every virtue. Did the priest in Catelau think you were good at catechism?" These are surprising questions, coming from Flaubert the unbeliever. It was not that he had found God, but that there was nothing sectarian about him. When it came to the education of young girls, the well-born young man resurfaced. In any case, Gustave's affection for his niece would never waver.

After Louis Bouilhet left for Paris, Flaubert resumed writing to him, encouraging and protecting him from a distance. From time to time he gave him news of Louis's mistress Léonie, who had remained in the area. But most importantly, he offered him the advice of a zealous literary agent exclusively at his service. Bouilhet wanted to stage his drama in verse, *Madame de Montarcy*, and was despairing that he would ever find anyone to do it. He moaned and groaned: nothing was going his way. "Every day I slip down a dark and fatal slope; I no longer think, I no longer act." Flaubert lectured him, encouraging him to go out and about and meet influential people: "*You must bother the world*, do not let go, do not give up." He bullied him, reproached him for his "moronism," and told him he wanted to "kick him in the ass." There could be no rest; he had to put his nose to the grindstone, move heaven and earth, and avoid any hesitation: "As long as you're jerking your brain off about your personality, be assured that your personality will suffer." If his play was turned down at the Comédie Française, he should go to the Opéra! Find out who is on the reading committee, "don't neglect anything, goddamn it, better to make fifteen attempts than one." Yet Flaubert realized that he was advising his friend to do what he himself had always rejected: "You will have thought of a comparison, that between me and Du Camp. Four years ago he was criticizing me about more or less the same things I'm criticizing you about now."[4] No matter, Gustave continued to harass Louis and eventually had the pleasure of learning that *Madame de Montarcy* would be produced at the Théâtre de l'Odéon. The play would be a significant hit in December 1856, just as the final installments of *Madame Bovary* were being published in the *Revue de Paris*. Gustave had promised Louis it would happen: "We'll have our turn, don't worry."[5] Simultaneously serving as impresario, cheerleader, and PR man, Flaubert enthusiastically took care of promoting his dear friend Louis. "Our friend Louis is now considered a first-rate poet among literary people, and to some extent among the public too."[6]

Between writing letters to Louis Bouilhet and finishing his novel, Flaubert read the daily paper *La Presse* and took a very distant interest in the news.

The war in Crimea briefly caught his attention; he was enthused about the taking of Sebastopol. But what really stirred him up was a failed assassination attempt on Napoleon III that occurred on the same day that Sebastopol fell: "Thanks be to God who saved him for us, for France's good fortune. What is deplorable is that the wretch is from Rouen. It's a dishonor for the city. One will no longer dare to say one is from Rouen." Ultimately, the imperial regime suited him well: under Badinguet's leadership, the republicans and socialists had stopped whining, the country was calm, and one could work in peace. Well, too bad for the exiled Victor Hugo! Polycarpism was still his credo: "I feel waves of hatred against the stupidity of my era suffocating me. Shit is rising into my mouth, as with a strangulated hernia."[7] The man who claimed to detest power made the best of authority: in a contemptible world, a strong political grip protected the artist's tranquility.

In October 1855 he took an apartment in Paris, as he had long told Louise Colet he would do, though he was no longer doing it for her. During his previous visits to Paris, he had usually stayed at the Hôtel du Helder or the Hôtel Sully; now he settled at 42, boulevard du Temple. His mind had been made up by Bouilhet's move to the capital and the imminent completion of *Madame Bovary*. He would spend increasingly long stretches in Paris, though Croisset remained his base, the place where he could be with his mother and niece. "I have acted like a fool in doing as others do, in deciding to live in Paris, in wanting to publish. As long as I was writing for myself alone, I lived in a perfect serenity of art. Now I am full of doubts and uneasiness."[8] This was the anxiety of the writer about to step out of the shadows.

Bovary Arrives

"People think I am enamored with reality, when in fact I loathe it," Flaubert wrote to one of his correspondents; "for I undertook this novel out of a hatred of realism. But I detest false idealism no less."[9] Yet encyclopedias and literary histories tell us that Gustave Flaubert is the most distinctive representative of the realist school, whose chief theorist was the writer Jules Champfleury. In 1854, Flaubert read Champfleury's novel *Les Bourgeois de Molinchart* in serial form in *La Presse*. The novel happened to deal with a story of adultery in the provinces—a thematic similarity that briefly worried Flaubert. But he was reassured by an aspect he considered crucial: "As for the style, not strong, not strong." Like Champfleury, the author of *Madame Bovary* grappled with the dullest reality, but in his case it was to realize a work *of style*. The undertaking was paradoxical. He kept saying that "all the things I love are not in it": he gave up on long lyrical passages, ringing phrases, and epic descriptions. "I persecute metaphors, and completely banish moral analyses," he wrote, signaling a break with the old school and the Romanticism of his youth. He wanted to base his work on reality—he valued "style above all else, and after that, Truth."[10]

He hunted down this truth with the persistence of his obsessive nature, forcing himself to "attentively observe the dullest details." There is evidence that he researched everything that could be objectively verified. Thus, while he was in Paris writing the famous scene of the visit to the Cathedral of Rouen, in which Emma and Léon grudgingly follow the Swiss guard who is guiding them, he asked his friend Alfred Baudry for details about the cathedral's chapels, stained-glass windows, and tombs. He devoted the same care to attempting to master the system of promissory notes by which Emma seals her fate, asking a family notary, Frédéric Fovard, to answer a whole series of questions. Similarly, he asked his friends about issues relating to anatomy and chemistry. He refused to describe Madame Bovary's agony in vague terms: it had to be precise, credible, *real*. This commitment to exact details required a professional's vocabulary. Medical language came easily to him; he described with a surgeon's skill the unfortunate Charles Bovary's operation on a young man with a clubfoot. Why was it necessary for a master of style to be so exacting about the authenticity of what he described? It was Flaubert's notion of aesthetics: write as an artist, describe as a historian. Though he believed in art for art's sake, his art was based on the requirements of truthfulness. Emma is an imaginary character, like all the other players in her tragedy, but she is *representative*. One of the novel's admirers, Mlle Leroyer de Chantepie, would tell Flaubert: "From the beginning, I recognized and loved her as a friend that I might have had. . . . No, this story is not fiction."[11]

Haunted by the double imperative of making beauty and adhering to reality—however common the reality—Flaubert worked relentlessly: "I am going slowly, very slowly." It was now to Louis Bouilhet instead of Louise Colet whom he wrote about the sentence-by-sentence obstacle course: "*Bovary* is coming along *pianissimo*." "After five or six pages, I sometimes eliminate sentences that took me *several* entire days." He had to force himself to reject exuberance: "And that is what charms me, exuberance." "I am in the middle of *Bovary*'s financial affairs. It is atrociously difficult. It's time this was finished, the burden is killing me." "I am profoundly weary of this work. It is a real chore for me now."

The impersonality on which he prided himself had its limits. The material for his novel was taken not only from his research but from aspects of his own life. To take an insignificant example, when Emma goes to the Théâtre des Arts in Rouen to meet Léon, it is to see Gaetano Donizetti's *Lucia di Lammermoor*, the very opera that Flaubert and Maxime Du Camp had seen at the Constantinople Opera on November 13, 1850.[12] Many other details from Flaubert's life found their way into the novel, though naturally he never said a word about it.

As for his style and metaphors—of which there are many, despite what he says—the fact that Proust could make a pastiche of them proves that there is a Flaubert touch and that it is an original touch. Its most characteristic aspect is the often savage irony with which the little world of Yonville-l'Abbaye is depicted, along with the art of comedic framing. Recall the two scenes in which Rodolphe, and then Léon, declare their love. The first takes place in the middle of the agricultural fair, as Flaubert alternates between the pompous oratory of the notables on the rostrum and the seducer's tender words. The second happens in the Cathedral of Rouen, where Léon sighs while the Swiss guard bores the future lovers with his historical explanations. The author is undoubtedly present; he does not speak, say "I," comment, or judge, but his personality shines through in every paragraph. His images, descriptions, portraits, analyses, and dialogues reveal a conception of the world that is purely his own. As Jean Bruneau points out, Flaubert is not stingy with "general maxims," which is another "manner in which the writer can speak up in his work."[13] Flaubert is certainly audible in the statement "of all the icy blasts that blow on love, a request for money is the most chilling and havoc-wreaking."[14] And surely he is the one complaining that "human speech is like a cracked kettle on which we tap crude rhythms for bears to dance to, while we long to make music that will melt the stars."[15] This "impersonal" novel even contains a "we" at the beginning—the "we" of the Rouen high school students watching the bumbling Charles Bovary enter their classroom. Although this "we" quickly disappears, it serves to introduce the author into the narrative.

Flaubert finally achieved his ends: in late May 1856, *Bovary* was completed. It would be published in two stages: first as a serial in the *Revue de Paris*, where his friend Maxime served as a go-between, then as a single volume whose publisher remained to be found. By April 1856, he had already made an agreement with the *Revue*, which would publish the novel in six installments. The forthcoming publication was announced in the issue of August 1, with a typo: "*Madame Bovary* (*Moeurs de province*) by Gustave Faubert." Flaubert reacted by saying: "Gustave Faubert is the name of a grocer in the Rue de Richelieu, opposite the Comédie Française! This debut seems far from auspicious to me. . . . Even before I appear, they skin me."[16] He wasn't out of the woods yet. He still had to contend with the demands and whims of the *Revue*'s editor-in-chief, Léon Laurent-Pichat, who obviously didn't understand the author's intentions and wanted to significantly alter the text. On July 14, 1856, a sententious Maxime Du Camp wrote to his friend, "Let us take full charge of the publication of your novel in the *Revue;* we will make the cuts we think indispensable; and later you will publish it in a volume of whatever form you choose, that is your affair. . . . You have buried your novel under a heap of details which are well done but superfluous."[17] An outraged Flaubert scribbled the word *gigantesque* ("priceless") in the margins of this vulgar laundry list. In a letter to Laurent-Pichat, he bluntly stated: "*I will do nothing:* I will not make a correction, not a cut; I will not suppress a comma, nothing, nothing! But if the *Revue de Paris* thinks that I am compromising it, if it is afraid, the simple thing to do is to stop publication of *Madame Bovary* at once. I wouldn't give a damn."[18] On October 1, 1856, after Flaubert had finally agreed to a few trims, *Madame Bovary* began to appear in the *Revue de Paris;* the last installment was published in the December 15 issue. There had been plenty of friction between the two parties along the way.

On November 19, Maxime Du Camp told Flaubert that the carriage scene in which Léon makes love to Emma was *impossible*: "They get in the carriage and come out later, that can pass, but the details are truly dangerous, and we are retreating simply out of fear of the Imperial Prosecutor." Flaubert gave in but demanded that the *Revue* publish a note to the reader: "The editors find themselves obliged to omit from this installment a passage which they consider unsuitable for publication in the *Revue de Paris*. They hereby advise the author of their action and take full responsibility for it."[19] Shortly before the final installment ran on December 15, Flaubert was told of additional cuts. He had reached his limit. He consulted his lawyer, Jules Sénard, about taking the *Revue* to court for abuse of power. Finally, the periodical agreed to print a note to the reader from the author: "Considerations which it is not in my province to judge compelled the *Revue de Paris* to omit a passage from the issue of December 1; its scruples having been again aroused on the occasion of the present issue, it has thought proper to omit several more. In consequence, I hereby decline responsibility for the lines which follow. The reader is therefore asked to consider them as a series of fragments, not as a whole."[20]

The Portrait of a Woman

Flaubert's portrait of a woman was so convincing that it inspired the term *bovarysme* (Bovarism), which remains in use to this day. The novelist coined the term in his correspondence, though he did not give it the pathological sense it would later acquire. The word would enter common French usage after the publication in 1902 of Jules de Gaultier's book *Le Bovarysme*. De Gaultier describes the psychological notion of Bovarism as "the power man has to conceive of himself as other than he is and, by extension, to escape a mediocre reality through a fanciful, romantic, imaginary world." Seen in this light, Bovarism is found throughout the ages, like mythomania or hysteria. Flaubert's talent is all the more admirable for having yielded a universal type; Emma, however, is a pure product of the nineteenth century that he loathed.

Emma Bovary is undoubtedly a singular character, with her own gifts and weaknesses, but she is also a social type: "My poor Bovary," Flaubert wrote, "without a doubt, is suffering and weeping at this very hour in twenty villages of France."[21] The Goncourt brothers reported Bishop Dupanloup's response to the novel: "A masterpiece, yes, a masterpiece for those who have heard confessions in the provinces."

Education plays a major role in Emma's tragedy. At the age of thirteen, Emma, the daughter of a farmer who has become affluent, is sent to a convent. Education for girls is mediocre: at the Couvent des Ursulines, Emma studies dance, geography, drawing, tapestry, and piano. In *De l'amour* [*On Love*], Stendhal noted that, "A woman of thirty in France has not the acquired knowledge of a boy of fifteen, nor a woman of fifty the logic of a man of twenty-five."[22] And as Balzac wrote, "the gates of the cloister set the imagination ablaze." Of love and marriage, Emma learns nothing from her teachers, leaving her to glean what she can from clandestine reading and the kindness of housekeepers. Like her classmates, Emma listens to an old spinster who works in the linen room and teaches them "eighteenth-century love songs," as well as surreptitiously lending them novels.[23] Romanticism, illusions, "Lamartinian meanderings"—the expression is Flaubert's.

Emma's Christian education also leaves a lot to be desired. Admittedly, there is no shortage of "prayers, retreats, novenas and sermons"[24]—on the contrary. But what about the crux of the matter? Flaubert emphasizes the sensual aspect of this religious education: "The metaphors constantly used in sermons—'betrothed,' 'spouse,' 'heavenly lover,' 'mystical marriage'—excited her in a thrilling new way."[25] The Countess d'Agoult (known under the pen name Daniel Stern) described her experience of a convent education: "In this alleged religious instruction I was given, I learned neither the connections between faith and reason nor those between law and conscience, nor the just discernment of duty and right in human relations."[26] Morality was reduced to its precepts.

In Emma's case, this education proves all the more harmful given that she is not a proper young lady, but the daughter of a farmer. By being schooled above her social class, she becomes disgusted with the rural environment to which she is condemned. Once she returns to live among ordinary people, her veneer of education, the time spent with posh schoolmates, and especially the dreams and illusions born of her seclusion and romantic readings give her a feeling of superiority over her native milieu, accompanied by melancholy and even nostalgia for her years at the convent. From here on out, dream and reality will constantly clash.

Marriage is an escape: by marrying the country doctor Charles Bovary, Emma breaks free from the peasant milieu and imagines that she is reaching that other world of bourgeois distinction. Her union is not forced upon her, which is a piece of good fortune not enjoyed by all of her contemporaries, many of whom are at the mercy of family interests. Nonetheless, like these less fortunate women, she barely knows her future husband: never having been alone with him, she lulls herself with illusion and marries a mediocre man *without knowing it*. While Flaubert exaggerates Charles Bovary's dullness, the disappointment Emma soon experiences is that of many young women of her time, women who often wed older men more concerned with their work than with their wives' personal development.

Charles is deeply in love with his wife, but his blundering and awkwardness are too glaring for her to return the favor. Though disappointed by this spouse so far below her hopes, this man without luster or ambition, she initially attempts to put a brave face on it: she draws, plinks on the piano, makes jam. Her boredom becomes crushing; a leaden routine regulates all of Charles's actions, including kisses, which are dispensed "only at certain times . . . like a dessert that could be counted on to end a monotonous meal."[27] The young woman comes to ask herself: "Why—*why*—did I every marry?"[28]

Pleasures and entertainment are rare; the people who surround her, mediocre. She becomes acutely aware of this mediocrity when the Bovarys are invited to the Château de Vaubyessard. In this aristocratic setting where the silver cutlery sparkles and each piece of lacework is more beautiful than the next, where the grace of those dancing the waltz is rivaled only by the women's elegance, Emma, who has surrendered herself to "the splendors of this night,"[29] feels at her very core that this is the life she should have lived, she who is bogged down in triviality. Her invitation to the ball at Vaubyessard "had opened a breach in her life."[30] She will not let herself forever stagnate in Tostes, the small town where Charles has his practice. Through a chance encounter, she discovers the escape of adultery with the young clerk Léon, who is a little bland but can join her in enthusing over an insipid romanticism. Her hopes come to a sudden end when the clerk leaves to finish his studies in Paris. Seeing his wife sinking into melancholy, the ever-obliging Charles attempts to cure her nervous illness by taking over the practice of a colleague in the slightly larger town of Yonville-l'Abbaye.

In this new home, Emma gives birth to a daughter, whom she calls Berthe, a name she heard at the Château de Vaubyessard. Motherhood does not change the banality of her existence. Berthe is sent to be cared for by a nurse, as is the custom. Boredom returns; Yonville seems just as far from the superior life to which she aspires as Tostes did. Then comes the wealthy man who will satisfy her craving for enchantment. With the spirited and charming Rodolphe, she believes she has finally found love. She is initially transported by their erotic relationship. But, after hoping that he will permanently rescue her from quotidian mediocrity and believing that she has convinced him to leave with her, she discovers the cynicism of her lover, who has no desire to abandon his comfortable life. Emma is devastated. Bovary, distressed to see her falling back into depression, accepts the pharmacist Homais's idea that she amuse herself by going to an opera in Rouen. Here she runs into Léon, who has returned from Paris, and makes him her second lover. With Léon, she rediscovers the frenzy of her secret encounters with Rodolphe. She is once again elated and as an "experienced" woman she gives herself over to "the intimacies of passion." "She was the *amoureuse* of all the novels, the heroine of all the plays, the vague 'she' of all the poetry books."[31] Alas! After a while, she discovers that "adultery could be as banal as marriage."[32] No, this peacock will not be able to quench her constant thirst for romantic passion. Finally, drowning under an accumulation of credit notes and debts that threaten to destroy her household, she asks for Léon's help, then even Rodolphe's. Faced with the incapacity of one of them and the selfishness of the other, she realizes that her entire life has been a vast deception. Harassed by money-lenders, her head spinning, devastated by her lost illusions, she kills herself, finding in death the only way to put an end to vile reality.

Flaubert is famously said to have remarked, *"Madame Bovary, c'est moi!—D'après moi."* "Madame Bovary is me!—According to me." But in fact, there is no written record of this statement, and it may be apocryphal. Nonetheless, it has constantly been repeated and commented upon since René Descharmes reported it in 1909: "An individual who knew Flaubert's correspondent Mlle Amélie Bosquet very well recently told me that after asking the novelist where he had found the character of Mme Bovary, Mlle Bosquet was clearly and repeatedly told: 'Madame Bovary is me!—According to me.'"[33] Let's consider the remark authentic. Flaubert was the same age as his heroine. Like her, he had known boredom and the permanent clash between dream and reality. They both belonged to the last Romantic generation and both harbored vague and grandiose ideas that were inevitably disappointed by the coarseness of life. Baudelaire sheds a different light on the fusion between the artist and his character, both prisoners of "a society that has renounced spiritual love once and for all." He underlines Emma's androgyny, that of a woman whose femininity is counterbalanced by "the energy of action," the "rapidity of decision-making, the mystical fusion of reason and passion, which characterizes men created to act." The novel tells us that Léon "was becoming her mistress, far more than she was his."[34] For his part, Flaubert created Emma with the desire to "rid himself (as much as possible) of his sex and make himself a woman." Referring to Emma Bovary's heartbreak, Baudelaire says: "Here is a Caesar at Carpentras; a woman in pursuit of the ideal."[35] And how could one avoid hearing Flaubert's voice in her final disillusionment: "Why was life so unsatisfactory? Why did everything she leaned on crumble instantly to dust? . . . Everything was a lie! Every smile concealed a yawn of boredom; every joy, a curse; every pleasure, its own surfeit; and the sweetest kisses left on one's lips but a vain longing for fuller delight."[36] A few years later, Flaubert would confess to the Goncourt brothers that he had twice vomited while writing about Emma's suicide by arsenic.[37]

This empathetic merging was not total, however, for Emma Bovary, unlike Flaubert, participates in the bourgeois world of accepted ideas. A mediocre woman whose imagination is inspired by maudlin romance, she only seems profound in comparison with the vacuity of those surrounding her. Her words do not avoid the standard language found in literature for young women. Her "Lamartinian" outpourings pitifully echo the definitions in the *Dictionary of Accepted Ideas*, the old project that Flaubert continued to keep alive. Standing by the sea, Emma asks Léon: "Don't you have the feeling . . . that something happens to free your spirit in the presence of all that vastness?"[38] Compare this with the entry for *sea* in the *Dictionary:* "Is bottomless. Image of the infinite. Confers great thoughts."[39] As Pierre-Marc de Biasi puts it: "At no time is anyone safe from the irony that circulates throughout this novel."[40]

A New Molière?

The supporting characters in *Madame Bovary* make up a world often depicted in Flaubert's letters, that bourgeois world—in this case the provincial bourgeois world—that imbues collective experience with an invariable stupidity. The *Dictionary of Accepted Ideas* serves as the semiological treatise for this world.

Flaubert, the doctor's son, accurately represents the medical world and its hierarchy in his sociological novel. At the bottom of the ladder, we find health officer Charles Bovary. Because Napoleon had created a large corps of military doctors, medical practitioners under the Restoration fell into two groups: medical doctors trained in faculties, and health officers who had been in the army and acquired largely practical skills. The hierarchy between these two groups persisted under the July Monarchy; health officers were no longer exclusively trained in the military, but they had shorter schooling. Thus, we learn that young Bovary leaves collège by his third year to study medicine. Though his curriculum is condensed, he is frightened by the number of required subjects. He initially fails, then manages to pull through, "like a mill-horse that treads blindfolded in a circle, utterly ignorant of what he is grinding."[41] Once his diploma is in hand, Bovary practices "his art" in the small town of Tostes. His life is hard, his patients are scattered, and his rounds on horseback sometimes drag on until midnight. He is not exactly a thinking man, but by working hard he manages to make an honest living. The move to Yonville ruins him, not only because of his wife's extravagant spending, but also because of a lack of patients owing to illegal competition from the pharmacist.

The health officer's life varied according to location but was hard everywhere. Patients were not abundant; often they did not even have the means to consult a doctor. There were no set fees, and it was not unusual to be paid in kind, with poultry or ham. Medical science was still in its infancy, and the medical doctors were more highly regarded. For difficult cases, health officer Bovary calls on Dr. Canivet, who looks down on these auxiliaries who dishonor the profession. But doctors like Canivet bow down before leading lights such as Dr. Larivière, who rushes to Yonville when Madame Bovary commits suicide. Flaubert used his father as the model for Larivière: "Disdainful of decorations, titles and academies, hospitable, generous, a father to the poor, practicing Christian virtues although an unbeliever, he might have been thought of as a saint if he hadn't been feared as a devil because of the sharpness of his mind."[42] This "great talent" is practically the only character in the novel who escapes stupidity, but he only passes through.

The political and philosophical opinions of the medical profession of the time are well known. Under the Restoration, Balzac had already described a multitude of materialist doctors for whom "everything came down to liver and spleen, brains and lungs."[43] Flaubert confirmed as much: in the first half of the nineteenth century, doctors were the representatives of scientific positivism and the props of the liberal left. The entry for *doctor* in the *Dictionary* reads "All doctors are materialists."[44] As for Charles Bovary, he has no political ideas for the simple reason that he has no ideas at all. Flaubert exaggerates his mind's lifelessness to highlight his wife's boredom: " 'It's pathetic!' she whispered to herself, despair in her heart. 'What a booby!' "[45] In his preparatory manuscript, Flaubert noted: "Intimate coarseness down to the way he cautiously folds his napkin,—and eats his soup.—In winter he wears knit vests and gray wool socks with white trim ... Good boots. In the habit of picking his teeth with the tip of his knife and trimming the stoppers of bottles to make them fit inside." This is a neat summary of all the details Flaubert found loathsome and that he used to reveal Emma's aversions. Poor Charles does not get to put his best foot forward.

The pharmacist Homais, also a medical professional and a self-described man of science, is a more solid citizen. A proponent of maternal breastfeeding and vaccination, he holds forth in his pedantic, peremptory way about his love of progress and hatred for the clergy. Critic Jean Cassou considers him "one of those brilliant figures, like those of Cervantes and Molière, in which the great poets, who are both great realists and great dialecticians, are able to paint a social type and at the same time depict the conflict of an ideal with its own caricature."[46] In Homais, we find two complementary characters: the apothecary and the intellectual. As apothecary, he serves as the unofficial town doctor; as such, he has "violated the law of 19th Ventose, Year XI, Article I, which forbids anyone not holding a diploma to practice medicine."[47] His convivial courtesy quashes any protestations certified doctors might make, while his poise and constant loquacity ensure his reputation among the country people: he is believed to be a master. Three other doctors, after Bovary, will be ruined by this state of affairs. But Homais is first and foremost the small town's intellectual, the local correspondent for the *Fanal de Rouen*, the paper to which he sends off his overblown articles with the faith of a lay missionary. In his pantheon, Voltaire and Rousseau are reconciled. As a deist, he believes in the Supreme Being and is violently hostile to priests wallowing in "squalid ignorance." He does not believe a word in the Bible. The apothecary drives the point home, denouncing the "mummeries" and "tricks" of Catholicism, the celibacy of priests, rural superstitions, and "the monstrous days of the Middle Ages."[48] Additionally, Homais advocates the strictest morals, rails against the Old Testament's bawdiness, and angrily reprimands his servant, whom he has caught learning about the mysteries of marriage in a book hidden from his master. The only disciplines worthy of admiration are the arts, the sciences, philosophy, and history—all so rich in glorious human examples. It would be "a medievalism worthy of that abominable age when they imprisoned Galileo" not to consider theater as one of the schools for virtue.[49] It behooves a learned man to listen to "what science has to say," and better yet if he himself is a scholar, like Monsieur Homais, who is the author of a seventy-two-page essay on the manufacturing of cider. He delves into his well-stocked library to find the technical vocabulary for his speeches, which are equal parts demonstration and diatribe. As an occasional poet, he venerates Pierre-Jean de Béranger (whom Flaubert despised) and sometimes sings out his verse. But this progressive citizen also believes in law and order. His supreme ambition is to be awarded the cross of the Legion of Honor. His wish eventually comes true; he makes sure history is on his side.

Religion's representative pales into insignificance beside this eloquent prophet of a new era. The priest, Abbé Bournisien, is sometimes outraged by the pharmacist's diatribes but does not have the intellectual baggage to best him. Flaubert sets an oratorical sparring match (then frequent in French villages) between Homais and Bournisien during a wake: What could be a more suitable place for philosophizing than the bedside of a dead woman, in this case Emma Bovary? They discuss the celibacy of priests, the constant hobby horse of the anti-clericalists. The pharmacist inveighs against it in the name of morals. To which the priest can only answer with this pathetic justification: "How would you expect anyone who was married to be able to keep the secrets of the confessional, for example?"[50] The clergyman's intellectual shortcomings are bad enough; worse yet is his failure to help his tormented parishioners. At the onset of her moral crisis, Emma turns to the priest for support: she finds a simpleton without the slightest sense of human psychology. Flaubert describes Bournisien thus in his correspondence: "he thinks only of the physical side (the sufferings of the poor, no bread, no firewood), and has no inkling of my lady's moral lapses or her vague mystical aspirations; he is very chaste, faithfully performs all his duties."[51]

This is the parish priest as seen by Flaubert. He is a priest who follows a routine, gracelessly dispenses the good word, and mechanically distributes the sacraments. He is equally ignorant in the religious and secular realms, disoriented by the anti-clericalist's arguments, and unable to soothe his parishioners' moral distress and spiritual doubts, all despite his exemplary conduct and unquestionable good will. He is a man left behind by history and a symbol of the collapse of the church, of which Flaubert had no doubt. The novelist would side with Homais, if the pharmacist weren't so grotesque. At Madame Bovary's death bed, the priest throws the Voltairian apothecary a line: "We'll be good friends yet!"[52] The two types of nonsense—clerical and anti-clerical—sign a pact over Emma's coffin. After the Revolution of 1848, the Voltairian bourgeois followed Thiers's example and entered a new alliance with the church: law and order first!

Some have criticized Flaubert for his caricatural approach to his supporting characters: Bovary, Homais, Bournisien, the lady-killer Rodolphe, the inexperienced fool Léon, the money-lender Lheureux, the tax collector Binet, the libidinous notary Guillaumin—beneath every outfit, wrote the novelist Jules Barbey d'Aurevilly, is "the same imbecile." A century later, François Mauriac added: "A defect in his mind forced him to see only people's appearances.

What existed for him was the combination of pretentions, mannerisms, compulsions, and attitudes that first strikes us about a man, and of which [Jean de] La Bruyère made the most."[53] In fact, La Bruyère's *The Characters* was among Flaubert's bedside books.[54] Flaubert's one-dimensional figures should be seen in light of his desire to "reproduce types."

Nonetheless, these characters' remarks are not always stupid. We sometimes hear Flaubert speaking through them. Even Rodolphe, that backwater Casanova, has his flashes of brilliance, however driven by his desire to seduce: "Our duty is to feel what is great and love what is beautiful—not to accept all the social conventions and the infamies they impose on us."[55] In his break-up letter, Rodolphe sounds like Flaubert in his hypocritical treatment of Louise Colet: I never should have loved you, etc. Even Homais's pseudo-scientific decoctions provide the reader with food for thought.

Yet we must accept that Flaubert had no desire to provide his supporting characters with the ambivalence, complexity, and contradictions of living beings. One only finds advanced psychology in the portrait of Emma Bovary. She is the center around which the bourgeois and petit bourgeois flail, chatter, and maneuver in that infernal pantomime that ends in a danse macabre.

Once *Madame Bovary* was in print in the *Revue de Paris*, Flaubert became convinced that his novel was a "failure." "This book," he wrote to Louis Bouilhet, "reveals far more patience than genius, far more work than talent." He repeated this assessment in a letter sent to his friend Jules Duplan on October 11, 1856: "Contrary to what I expected, I found the first reading of my printed work extremely unpleasant. I only noticed the misprints, three or four repetitions of words, which shocked me, and one page with an abundance of the word *which*—as for the rest, it was *black* and nothing more." After the initial phase of postpartum sadness, he found reassurance in the novel's reception. On December 12, he wrote to his cousin by marriage Louis Bonenfant that "*Bovary* is a success beyond what I had hoped." But the censor was watching, and the courts were lying in wait.

CHAPTER 12

Fame

On December 24, 1856, Gustave Flaubert signed a publishing contract with Michel Lévy, a publisher whose rapidly growing house had become a rival to the three major houses, Hachette, Garnier frères, and the Librairie nouvelle of Jaccottet and Bourdilliat. Although these established publishers had let Maxime Du Camp know of their interest in *Madame Bovary*, Flaubert chose Lévy, in large part because Lévy had made an agreement with Louis Bouilhet to publish his play *Madame de Montarcy*, which had recently been produced at the Odéon. Michel Lévy also had a reputation for not making his authors wait around to have their books published and to receive their payment. He offered Flaubert 400 francs (a little over $1,600 in today's dollars) for each of *Madame Bovary*'s two volumes, a standard amount for a first book with a print run of 6,000 copies sold at 1 franc per volume.[1] At the time, writers were not paid based on the number of copies sold, as they are today. Book rights were sold for a set fee and a determined period of time—in this case, five years. The first edition was published in April 1857 and quickly sold out. Two reprints followed, raising the number of copies sold to 30,000.[2] As early as the second printing in May, Flaubert began to feel that he had been had: "15,000 copies have now sold; in other words, 30,000 francs have slipped through my fingers."[3] The publisher would make a profit of over 26,000 francs, since Flaubert had been promised only a 500-franc bonus for each additional printing. Though he considered that he had been "swindled," this was standard practice, which publishers justified by the many loss-makers they printed. Flaubert did not protest to Lévy—he had signed the contract with full knowledge of the facts—but he had reason to be surprised to see so little income from his novel's commercial success. The advantage of his success was that he could demand significantly more money for his next contract: in 1862, when he renewed the publication rights for *Madame Bovary* and sold the rights to *Salammbô*, he was able to command 10,000 francs. This still seems modest compared with the 250,000 francs that Lamartine earned from the sale of the twelve-year rights to his *Histoire des Girondins* [*History of the Girondins*] to the publisher Furne. Yet for the first time, at thirty-five, Flaubert was making money.

Unfortunately, *Madame Bovary* would cost him far more than he earned, as a result of legal expenses related to the court case brought against the novel shortly after its publication in the *Revue de Paris*.

The Trial

In late December 1856, Flaubert was summoned to the office of the examining magistrate, facing accusations that his novel was an "outrage to public morals and religion." He was convinced—and would long remain so—that his book was only being used as a pretext to "demolish the *Revue de Paris*," which had already received two warnings in April 1856. This was what he told his brother Achille, whom he mobilized in preparation for the criminal trial ahead, along with all his acquaintances. On January 25, he visited Lamartine, who promised his support. When Achille offered to come to Paris to help him, Gustave wrote him to explain his defense strategy, which was to emphasize their familial and bourgeois distinction:

> Everything you have done is good. The important thing is to bring pressure to bear on Paris by way of Rouen. An indication of the influential position which Father had and which you now have in Rouen is our best means of preventing the thing from coming to a head. They thought they were attacking some penniless devil, and when they learned that I had something to live on they opened their eyes. The Ministry of the Interior must be made to learn that we are, in Rouen, what is called "a family"—that we have deep roots in the city and the department, and that in attacking me, especially on grounds of immorality, they will offend many people.

He concluded his letter: "Try to have it *adroitly* said that it would be dangerous to attack me, to attack *us*, due to the coming elections."[4]

It was more or less unprecedented for Flaubert to invoke his rank, lay claim to his honorability, and call on his lineage. He must have enjoyed believing that the minister of the interior might worry that an attack against the son of Achille-Cléophas Flaubert could affect the elections. In any case, through Achille and on his own initiative, Gustave alerted anyone who could influence the authorities and flattered himself that he had "*very* powerful protectors." He was delighted to have the support of men of letters—and not just them: "The police have blundered," he wrote to Achille on January 20, 1857. "They thought they were attacking a run-of-the-mill novel and some ordinary little scribbler, whereas now (in part thanks to the prosecution) my novel is looked on as a masterpiece; as for the author, he has for defenders a number of what used to be called 'grandes dames'; the Empress, among others, has twice spoken in my favor; the Emperor said, the first time, 'They should leave him alone'; and despite all that the case was taken up again. Why? There begins the mystery."[5]

A mystery? Really? If he had been more attentive to the political situation, Flaubert would have been aware of the nature of the regime that had established itself under Napoleon III. In this phase, referred to by historians as "authoritarian," the Empire leaned on the traditional forces of society, of which the Catholic church was the pillar. In the eyes of the church, whose "total support of the coup d'état" had been declared by Pope Pius X himself, "bad books" were more dangerous than ever during this time of rapidly growing literacy. Freedom could only be conditional, for man, marked by original sin, is not naturally good—the temptation of evil weighs on him at every moment. Censorship aimed to avoid freedom's effects on the social order, which in the eyes of the ruling class was also a moral order. By the decree of February 17, 1852, newspapers were subject to restrictive measures (such as prior authorization, the obligation to run government announcements, and a five centime tax stamp per copy), and correctional courts, which did not have juries, replaced the court of assize for trying misdemeanors. Organs of the press were threatened with suspension and suppression through a process of official warnings wielded by prefects or, in Paris, the minister of the police. In 1852, the Goncourt brothers were brought before the Sixth Correctional Chamber for a newspaper article accused of corrupting morals and encouraging debauchery. The censor also kept a close eye on the theater and the publishing world. In February 1856, Xavier de Montepin, author of the novel *Les filles de plâtre* [*Ladies of Plaster*], was sentenced to three months in jail and a fine of 500 francs for outrage of public morals and moral standards. This explains why Laurent-Pichat had requested cuts to the serial publication of *Madame Bovary*—self-censorship is the natural outcome of censorship. Yet Flaubert was wrong in thinking that the powers that be were using his novel as a "pretext" to go after the *Revue de Paris*. In fact, he really was the target—or rather the target was his text, his heroine, and his depiction of the "patterns of provincial life," as the subtitle has it. In 1857 alone, two other authors bore the consequences of this intellectual repression: Eugène Sue for his *Mystères du peuple* [*Mysteries of the People*] and Baudelaire for *Les Fleurs du Mal*. Under Napoleon III, France had been plunged back into a law-and-order regime far more uncompromising than what it had known under the Restoration and the July Monarchy. The disorder of Yonville-l'Abbaye and the adultery, madness, and suicide of Madame Bovary were deemed detrimental to the tranquility of the emperor's subjects. There could be no tolerance for a modern literature infected with vices.

There is no denying that *Madame Bovary* is permeated by a scandalous aura that is now difficult to perceive due to the ubiquity of eroticism—even pornography—in today's newspapers and books and on screen. In the thousands of pages of plot outlines, notes, and rough drafts that preceded the final writing of the novel, Flaubert makes abundant use of obscene terms, lewd descriptions, and very crude scenes, which he knew would not be in the final text but would underpin it. "Everything seems to indicate," writes Yvan Leclerc, "that Flaubert felt the need to note these crude words, to imagine these frank scenes in order to 'rev up his noggin,' as he put it, to create an orgy and a riot of words inside his mind, 'to make harems in his head' before writing a text that was chaste on the surface, but beneath which there burned that which was willingly self-censored yet persists . . . . 'The carnality must be in the emotion.'"[6] Strictly speaking, the judge would have difficulty identifying what he felt when he read the novel—an indefinable erotic charge. In his preparatory manuscript, Flaubert jotted down the word "suggest" *(faire comprendre)*. "Suggest" for the purpose of avoiding censorship, but also because it is more powerful to suggest than to describe. This was yet another stylistic challenge.

At 10 AM on January 29, 1857, Gustave Flaubert stood trial in the Sixth Correctional Chamber, defended by his lawyer Maître Sénard. He faced the charges with two other defendants, Laurent-Pichat, manager of the *Revue de Paris*, and the printer Auguste-Alexis Pillet. For his judges, Flaubert had written a summary of his case in which he compared the censured sentences from his book with the works of various great authors:

My justification is in my book. Here it is. Once the judges have read it, they will be convinced that far from having made an obscene and irreligious novel, I have on the contrary composed something that has a moral effect.

Does a literary work's morality consist in the absence of certain details that, when looked at in isolation, can be incriminated? Shouldn't we instead consider the impression that results, the indirect lesson that stands out? And if due to an inadequacy of his talent the artist has only been able to produce this effect through an entirely superficial brutality, are passages that seem at first glance reprehensible not for that very reason all the more indispensable? Though it is impudent to evoke great men to talk about small works, before you judge me, remember Rabelais, Montaigne, Régnier, all of Molière, the Abbé Prévost, Lesage, Beaumarchais, and Balzac.

Honest books sometimes have salutary bitterness. For my part, I only fear honeyed literature that is absorbed without disgust and that poisons without scandal.

Until now I had believed that the novelist, like the traveler, enjoyed the freedom of description. Like many others before me, I could have chosen my subject from the exceptional or ignoble classes of society. Instead, I took it from the most numerous and the dullest. I grant you that its reproduction is unpleasant, but I deny that it is criminal.

In fact, I do not write for young girls, but for men, men of letters.

The trial opened with the indictment of Flaubert by the deputy imperial prosecutor, Ernest Pinard. He began by summarizing the novel, which he believed would have been more aptly titled, "Story of the Adulteries of a Provincial Woman." In his view, the book was characterized by a "lascivious tone" from beginning to end. "Did he try to show [Madame Bovary] from the perspective of intelligence? Never. From the perspective of the heart? Hardly. From the perspective of the mind? No. From the perspective of physical beauty? Not even that. Oh, I am well aware that there is a brilliant portrait of Mme Bovary after adultery; but the picture is lascivious first and foremost, the poses are voluptuous, Mme Bovary's beauty is a provocative beauty." The adultery in question is less condemnable in and of itself than its praise by the protagonist: "She sings a hymn to adultery, to its poetry and pleasures." Pinard was grateful to the *Revue* for sparing its readers the carriage scene, but while "the *Revue de Paris* draws the carriage's blinds, it allows us to enter the room where rendezvous are held."

The prosecutor praised Flaubert's talent, but only to point out that it was this talent that was dangerous. To support his argument, Pinard referred to the descriptions of the temptations of Saint Anthony which had just appeared in the journal *L'Artiste* (with Théophile Gautier's help, Flaubert had published revised passages of his *Temptation of Saint Anthony* in *L'Artiste* in January 1857). "He likes to depict temptations, especially the temptations to which Mme Bovary gave in."

Flaubert was guilty, far more so than the periodical that published him: "Lighten Pillet's sentence as much as you want; even be indulgent with the manager of the *Revue;* as for Flaubert, the principal culprit, it is with him that you must be severe!"

Now the floor was given to Maître Jules Sénard, who had been the president of the National Assembly in 1848. A friend of the Flaubert family (he was the father-in-law of Frédéric Baudry, Gustave's former classmate), he had since become a star of the Paris bar. His plea began with a defense of Emma expressed as if she were a real person; he showed what was poignant about her situation. As for "M. Flaubert," where did he draw his inspiration from? Well, this writer with a "lascivious tone" was "steeped in Bossuet and Massillon." No less! Sénard continued: "His name is Flaubert, he is the second son of M. Flaubert; he wanted to make a path for himself in literature, by profoundly respecting morality and religion." The lawyer emphasized Flaubert's respectability, his literary talent, and the tributes he had received from other writers. Particularly Lamartine. Ah, Lamartine! Sénard asked whether the court knew what the great poet had said to his client about Mme Bovary's demise: "The expiation is disproportionate to the crime; you have created awful, dreadful death!" When Flaubert had asked him if he understood why he was being charged by the correctional court, Lamartine answered: "I believe that throughout my entire life, I have been the man who, both in his literary works and his other accomplishments, best understood public and religious morality; my dear child, it is impossible that there is a court anywhere in France that will sentence you."

His plea was brilliant, indignant, clever, and full of powerful images. To hear him, one would imagine that Flaubert was a valiant writer who, guided by the most eminent authorities, had never thought of anything but morals and religion. All is fair in love and war! There was nothing Flaubert was less interested in than edifying French youth: he had always said that art should not have a moral or practical goal. But faced with an accuser leaning against the confessional and sanctifying the family, it would have been suicidal to advocate the autonomy of literature and the defense of art for art's sake. Flaubert agreed that it was better to turn to Bossuet and Massillon: "Maître Sénard's speech was splendid," he wrote to Achille on January 30. "He crushed the attorney from the Ministry of Justice, who writhed in his seat and made no rebuttal. We flattened him with quotations from Bossuet and Massillon, smutty passages from Montesquieu, etc. The courtroom was packed. It was marvelous, and I was in fine form."[7]

The verdict was announced on February 7. All three defendants—the author, the manager of the *Revue*, and the printer—were acquitted, but the court harshly reprimanded Flaubert, "for literature's mission must be to beautify and refresh the spirit by elevating the intelligence and refining mores, rather than to instill disgust for vice by presenting a picture of the disorders that may exist in society."

Initially overjoyed by his acquittal, Flaubert soon worried about the future: "What can I write," he asked Louise Pradier, "that could be more inoffensive than my poor *Bovary*, dragged by the hair into criminal court like a harlot?" He had become a "suspect author." Would he be able to get *The Temptation of Saint Anthony* published after Pinard's allusions? And now advice started flooding in about how to cut out various parts of *Madame Bovary* for its publication in book form. He informed Michel Lévy that he no longer wanted his book to appear and that his only wish was to return to the silence and solitude of the countryside. In any case, he refused to cut the passages of his novel attacked by the prosecution. So what if the public prosecutor still had two months to appeal! Michel Lévy refused to back down. He pressed Flaubert to authorize publication, and Gustave did not know what to do. Finally, his publisher convinced him. *Madame Bovary* appeared in bookstores on April 18, 1857.

The Reception

"The result was not what the administration had sought," wrote Maxime Du Camp. "Thanks to this persecution, to the trial in criminal court, and the indictment of the imperial prosecutor, *Madame Bovary* was a colossal success; Gustave Flaubert became famous overnight."[8] Curiosity about a novel said to be immoral and written in a "lascivious" style undoubtedly played its part. But Flaubert's real success was not so much in his sales, however impressive, as in the reception that his book immediately received from the finest writers and the fact that he was welcomed into the ranks of the greats. His patience, tireless work, and refusal to make public his earlier writings had suddenly paid off. Yet there were also plenty of blows.

The first significant attack came from the *Revue des deux mondes* on May 1, 1857. In this influential publication, the new novelist was panned in Charles de Mazade's column: "In his novel, M. Flaubert imitates M. de Balzac, just as he imitates M. Théophile de Gautier in a few other recently published fragments [*The Temptation of Saint Anthony* in *L'Artiste*]. One can see that the author of *Madame Bovary* belongs to a literature that believes it is innovative but is nothing new, alas—and that is in fact not even young, for youth, by drawing inspiration only from itself, has less experience, less technical skill, and more freshness in its inspiration." There was more to come: in the *Revue des deux mondes'* supplement dated May 15, 1857, the criticism was reiterated by a certain Deschamps. Flaubert was surprised by the *Revue's* relentlessness.

On May 4, 1857, however, he was thrilled to read a highly laudatory article by Sainte-Beuve in *Le Moniteur universel*. The fifty-three-year-old literary authority praised the book and recognized in *Madame Bovary* those "new literary signs: science, spirit of observation, maturity, strength, a little hardness." He called its author "one of the leaders of the new generation," concluding with a line that would often be repeated: "Anatomists and physiologists, I find you everywhere."

Sainte-Beuve's article displeased Paulin Limayrac, who delivered an unexpected attack six days later in *Le Constitutionnel:* "Let the love of the ideal come back quickly, along with a sense of admiration, that fertile source of beautiful thoughts, and let the spirit of denigration disappear, like a nocturnal bird when the sun rises. There is no lack of promising signs, if one is willing to look closely, and our hopes double when we consider there is a great writer on the throne."[9] Cut to the quick, Sainte-Beuve replied with a note addressed to Minister of State Achille Fould, for the affair was becoming political and the famous critic did not intend to let himself be ranked with the opposition: "Since December 2 and before, M. Sainte-Beuve has endeavored to prove that one can be an honest, independent man of letters and highly approve of the French government. Given that he has been as helpful as he could be in his line of work, is it any way to thank him to have him publicly criticized by one of the writers who find their inspiration at the Ministry of the Interior and the Ministry of Education?"

In his letter of thanks to Sainte-Beuve, Flaubert sought to clarify where he stood: "I do not belong to the generation you speak of: at least, not in ways of feeling. I insist that I belong to *yours*—I mean the good generation, that of 1830. It represents everything I love. I am a rabid old Romantic—or a fossilized one, whichever you prefer."[10] This was not the last time Flaubert would deny that he was the leader of the realist school. Nonetheless, he was delighted with Sainte-Beuve's article, which was so long and detailed and, on the whole, so favorable.

On June 26, *L'Univers,* an inflexibly Catholic and ultramontanist newspaper, published an article in which Léon Aubineau discussed *Madame Bovary* without mentioning its title or its author's name, but whipped himself up into a frenzy against Sainte-Beuve:

> It is said that M. Sainte-Beuve's article on the book we're discussing, and the full, excessive, and warm praise it contains, led *Le Moniteur* to do without the famous critic's contributions.[11] If this decision is true, we can only applaud, and be glad for this kind of moral administrative sanction. There is something more precious for *Le Moniteur,* more useful, that it must more carefully acquire and preserve than the talent and contribution of M. Sainte-Beuve, which is the agreement of upstanding minds, of hearts attached to morality. The public spirit would be doubly affected if such works, after having escaped the sword of justice, were glorified by the government's official organ.

Other critics thought they were being insightful by describing the author of *Madame Bovary* as a follower of Champfleury, whose periodical *Le Réalisme* had been founded in 1856. Anatole Claveau, a columnist for the *Courrier franco-italien,* elucidated the filiation as follows: "Champfleury style (that says it all), common as can be, trivial, without strength or scope, without grace or subtlety. Why should I fear highlighting the most prominent fault of a school that also has its qualities? The Champfleury school, to which M. Flaubert clearly belongs, considers that style is too green for it; it turns its nose up at it, it despises it, it can never be too sarcastic about those authors *who write.* To write! What's the point?" One can imagine Flaubert's stunned response to this utter misinterpretation.

On May 23, the journal *Rabelais* published a positive review of *Madame Bovary* by Émile Desdemaines, who insisted on the hypocrisy of the self-righteous: "M. G. Flaubert has refused to put fig leaves on his statue; he was right to do so, we like it better this way. Our era is too prudish to be honest. Never have we preached so much and practiced so little; it is not sermons we are lacking, but examples. In the evening we go to see the chaste comedies of M. Ponsard—a poet who has put catechism into verse—and at night we read the novels of the Marquis de Sade." The May 26 edition of the *Journal des débats* ran a review by the less inspired Cuvillier-Fleury: "One could say that for the last ten years novels and plays have given us the same woman. Emma Bovary is the Marguerite of *La Dame aux camélias* [*The Lady of the Camellias*], the duchess of *La Dame aux perles* [*The Lady with Pearls*], the Suzanne of the *Demi-monde,* and all the heroines of M. Dumas fils, with a new name."

On June 25, *Le Correspondant,* a Catholic periodical more liberal than *L'Univers,* published an article by Armand de Pontmartin, "Le Roman bourgeois et le roman démocrate: MM. Edmond About et Gustave Flaubert" [The Bourgeois Novel and the Democratic Novel: MM. Edmond About and Gustave Flaubert], in which one could notably read: "*Madame Bovary* is the pathological exaltation of the senses and of the imagination in a discontented democracy." In the September 20 issue of *L'Artiste,* Xavier Aubryet responded to Pontmartin, who "severely criticizes Flaubert for depicting a heartless woman. Well, a heartless woman is exactly what Flaubert wanted to depict: had Madame Bovary been virtuous, it would have been a different novel." Looking back today, it is hard to imagine this time when journalists and critics could viciously quarrel over a novel and send each other epigrams.

In October, two articles joined Sainte-Beuve's piece as the most remarkable reviews of *Madame Bovary* to appear in its year of publication and to achieve posterity. On the 6th, Jules Barbey d'Aurevilly, the author of *Une vieille maîtresse* [*An Old Mistress*], applauded the novel in *Le Pays:* "Never was a success more legitimate." He cleared up a misunderstanding regarding the claim that the book was "immoral": "No, the author of *Madame Bovary* was not immoral. Nor was he moral. He was only unmoved ... A most peculiar originality! There are novelists who love their heroes, who glorify them, who justify them or feel sorry for them. There are others who detest them, who condemn or curse them, which is also a way of loving them. But all or nearly all come to life before the figures they have created. It is repellant to man's nature to have a subject in hand without being passionately for or against him. But M. Flaubert escapes this custom, which seems to be a law of the human spirit." The book's coolness is due to this "poverty of sensitivity." Sainte-

Beuve had raised a similar issue in his detailed article in the *Moniteur,* which was the story's total lack of a positive hero, as it would be called in the era of socialist realism. "One criticism I would level at the book," he wrote, "is that good is too absent; it is not represented by a single character." This did not prevent Barbey from being convinced that "M. G. Flaubert is of the true breed of novelists; he is an observer more occupied with others than with himself. . . . *Madame Bovary,* studied, scrutinized, and detailed as she is, is a superior creation, who alone earns her author the title of novelist."

The most gratifying article for Flaubert was published in *L'Artiste* on October 18. It was by Charles Baudelaire, whose own *Les Fleurs du Mal* had been published on June 21. Flaubert had congratulated him for the collection of verse in a note dated July 13, remarking on his particular admiration for the sonnet *La Beauté* [*Beauty*]: "To sum up," he told him, "what I love above all in your book is that in it Art occupies first place. Furthermore, you write of the flesh without loving it, in a melancholy, detached way that I find sympathetic. You are as unyielding as marble and as penetrating as an English fog."[12] In August, *Les Fleurs du Mal* was in court, with thirteen poems under attack. Once again, the indictment was entrusted to Pinard. Unfortunately, Baudelaire did not have as talented a lawyer as Sénard to defend him. Six poems were suppressed from the collection, and their author was sentenced to a 300-franc fine for outrage to public morality. Flaubert sent him his support. The two writers were exact contemporaries and shared a pessimistic outlook on the society in which they lived: "A poet," wrote Sainte-Beuve, "who comes to shake us out of our hypocritical or indolent satisfaction, scares us or irritates us."[13] The affinity between his way of seeing the world and Flaubert's led Baudelaire to write the year's most perceptive article on *Madame Bovary* and its central character. He dismissed Sainte-Beuve and Barbey's reservations and criticisms:

> A number of critics have opined: this work, truly beautiful for the minuteness and the vividness of the descriptions, contains no single character who speaks for morality, who is the mouthpiece for the author's conscience. Where, oh! where is the proverbial and legendary character whose duty it is to point the moral of the tale and to guide the reader's understanding? In other words, where is the accusing finger?
>
> Rubbish! Eternal and incorrigible confusion of functions and art forms. A true work of art has no need of an indictment. The logic of the work itself

is equal to all the postulates of morality, and it is up to the reader to draw the conclusions from the conclusion.[14]

Flaubert warmly thanked Baudelaire: "You entered into the arcana of the book as though my brain were yours. It is understood and felt to its very depths."[15]

Aside from the articles in the press, which were regularly sent to him by his devoted friend Jules Duplan, Flaubert received a tremendous amount of mail, including notes or letters from Michelet, Champfleury, Edmond About, and Victor Hugo: "You have made a beautiful book, Monsieur," wrote Hugo on August 30, "and I am happy to tell you so. . . . You are, Monsieur, one of the driving spirits of the generation to which you belong. Continue to [keep] high before her the torch of art. I am in the darkness, but I have the love of light. To say that is to tell you that I love you. I take your hands in mine."

Many letters came from unknown admirers. One of the most interesting is from a Reims notary, Emile Cailteaux: "You show us real life in a new and gripping way! . . . Your eminently interesting book is full of charming and deeply true portraits, descriptions, stories, and speeches. What a personality Emma has! What truth! What passion! And yet what simplicity! Sadly, Monsieur, there are in our provinces too many women with Madame Bovary's personality. We call them the *misunderstood*."[16] Flaubert responded to his correspondent's inquisitiveness by telling him that the novel and the character were "pure inventions" and that the characters were "completely made up and Yonville-l'Abbaye itself is a place *that does not exist*." He wanted not to make portraits, but to "reproduce types."

Among these strangers who wrote to him, the most engaging and most remarkable was a woman, Marie-Sophie Leroyer de Chantepie, with whom a long correspondence would ensue.

An Unusual Friendship

On December 18, 1856, Mlle Leroyer de Chantepie sent Flaubert an enthusiastic letter, written shortly after she finished reading the last part of *Madame Bovary* in the *Revue de Paris*. She called the novel "a masterpiece of naturalness and truth." A resident of Angers who had herself written three novels, she confessed to Flaubert that no book had ever left "such a deep impression on her" and told him of the "violent commotion" it had caused: "it is the scalpel applied to the heart, to the soul; it is, alas, the world in all its hideousness. The characters are true, too true, for none of them lift the soul, and nothing is consoling in this tragedy, which leaves us with vast despair but also a severe warning." Flaubert replied to her on February 19, 1857, after recovering from the fright caused by his trial: "This *Bovary,* whom you love, has been dragged like the lowest lost woman into the dock with the criminals. True, she was acquitted, the grounds for my verdict are honorable, but I nonetheless remain a *suspicious* author, which is a mediocre glory." His correspondent was encouraged to immediately respond with a long letter, in which she combined personal confidences with further appreciation for the "masterpiece" and its admirable scenes and descriptions "that leave Balzac far behind." She told Flaubert that she experienced the same deadly ennui as Emma and that she, too, faced loneliness in wondering about the meaning of her life. She praised Flaubert's perspicacity in reading the souls and thoughts of women. And that pharmacist and priest were so real! "Never has anything seemed to me as real, as admirable as *Madame Bovary.* Though I have suffered too much to cry easily, well, I cried for three days after finishing it. I think about it constantly and associate all the locations in it with this story, whose heroine truly exists for me. I loved her like a sister; I wanted to throw myself between her and her misfortune, to advise her, to console her, to save her! I will never forget her! I am convinced this story is true! Yes, one has to have been a participant in or a witness of such a tragedy to write it with such truth! No author, no matter how talented, could create anything as true and as perfect!" She explained to him that she lived in the countryside "amidst absurd prejudices, injustices of every kind," and that she suffered habitually from melancholy. Two weeks later, she told him that she was going to write a review for *Le Phare de la Loire.* It was published on June 25, 1857.[17]

This time Flaubert replied to her right away. He dissuaded her from believing he had told a true story: *Madame Bovary* was "totally invented." "Into it I put none of my own feelings and nothing from my own life. The illusion (if there is one) comes, on the contrary, from the *impersonality* of the work. It is a principle of mine that a writer must not be his own theme." He gave her the secret of his aesthetic: "Art must rise above personal affections and neurotic susceptibilities! It is time to banish anything of that sort, and give it the precision of the physical sciences. Nevertheless, the capital difficulty for me remains style, form; the indefinable Beauty *resulting from the conception itself*—and which is, as Plato said, the splendid raiment of the Truth."[18] He also revealed something about himself: like her, he had lived alone in the countryside, he had traveled the world a little and knew Paris. But nothing "beats a good read by the fire." He followed with a short self-portrait: "I am thirty-five, five feet six inches tall, I have the shoulders of a porter and the nervous irritability of a little schoolmistress. I am single and solitary."

Touched by this letter, the lady from Angers replied to Flaubert practically by return mail,[19] with a long missive that delved further yet into her secrets. She was an "old maid," twenty years older than the author she so admired, "the only daughter of the second marriage for both father and mother," of the poor minor aristocracy, suffering from "excessive sensitivity" due to "her mother's frights during the Revolution." She had been educated by nuns. "My health was entrusted to an ignorant doctor, my soul to a fanatical priest, helped by an even more fanatical old maid. These people did me irreparable damage." She had been loved but had never encountered "that ideal of perfection that is so impossible to attain." She poignantly confesses that she finds nothing to console her in the profoundly disagreeable province she inhabits.

Flaubert replied quickly, addressing her as his "dear colleague": "Your letter is so honest, so true, and *so intense;* it moved me so much that I cannot prevent myself from replying to it immediately." Somewhat indelicately, he thanks her for telling him her age: "That puts me at ease. We will chat together like *two* men." Yet Flaubert is not cold-hearted. He is so sensitive to the distress that has been revealed to him that he writes a long letter in which he intertwines words of comfort with the story of his own life. He has recognized this wounded soul as a soul mate: "Write me all that you want, at length and often, even if I sometimes do not answer you for a while, for starting yesterday we are old friends. I know you now and I love you." He continues: "I have the greatest sympathy for your mind and your heart." He speaks to her of her religion, Catholicism, which he does not believe in but respects, and points out the contradiction between the "liberalism" of her mind and the "old stuff" of dogma. He advises her to "hang on to science" and recommends therapeutic reading such as *Examen des dogmes de la religion chrétienne* [*Examination of the Dogma of the Christian Religion*] by Patrice Larroque, "a complete refutation of Catholic dogma." As for his political position, he wants to be clear: "I am not sympathetic to any political party, or, to put it better, I loathe them all, because they all seem to me to be equally narrow-minded, fake, puerile, concerned with the ephemeral, without a sense of the big picture, and never rising above the *useful*. I hate all despotism. I am an enraged liberal. This is why socialism seems to me a pedantic horror that will be the death of all art and all morality. As a spectator, I have witnessed nearly all the riots of my time."

In this letter and the ones that followed, Flaubert set about becoming a spiritual adviser and psychological counselor ("Read Montaigne! Work!"). He sent her a copy of *Madame Bovary;* she sent him her novels, including *Angélique Lagier,* an appeal in favor of divorce and against the death penalty. He read her books and wrote to her about them, skillfully praising her and pointing our her weaknesses. As the correspondence continued, the breaks between letters grew increasingly shorter. Mlle Leroyer disputed some of Flaubert's positions, on socialism, compulsory schooling, and Catholicism, for instance, but considered him "the ultimate good and sensible man." In this correspondence between the humble novelist of Angers and the newly minted great writer, which would last until 1876, one sees concern for another person and a sustained surge of kinship—characteristics that many of Flaubert's critics and contemporaries would have been surprised to find in this champion of "impersonality." Was his sensitivity to the misfortune of a solitary soul due to the fact that he could recognize in her his own circumstances? He wrote to her that he did not like to see "as beautiful a nature as yours sink into grief and idleness." These epistolary exchanges, treasures of an improvised body of work, are all the more surprising in that the two friends were never to meet.

CHAPTER 13

Life in Paris

Madame Bovary propelled Gustave Flaubert's name into literary history. It also changed the author's life. Suddenly people wanted to meet him, and he was invited all over town. He was now one of the top literary figures in the nation. Paris opened its arms to him; the hermit could become a socialite. He had an additional reason for traveling to the capital more frequently, which was that his mother often accompanied little Caroline to her Paris boarding school. And now that he had set to work on his new novel, *Salammbô*, Flaubert needed a tremendous amount of research material that could only be found in Paris libraries such as the imperial library on rue de Richelieu.

While Flaubert was sometimes the subject of newspaper articles, there was a line he refused to cross: he would not write for newspapers and periodicals. "I'd sooner drive a coach than *write for money*."[1] Since he could get by without chasing after freelance work the way so many other writers had to, he devoted himself entirely to the book he was writing, preferably at Croisset rather than in Paris. Five long years would pass between the publication of *Madame Bovary* and that of *Salammbô*, during which Flaubert spent at least a third of his time in the capital—between three and four months a year, ideally in winter and spring. At Croisset, on the banks of the Seine in which he liked to swim on mild days, Flaubert remained the fierce writer, always dissatisfied, bellowing his sentences out, constantly revising, rooting out assonance and repetition, and searching for the right metaphor until it was time to take the train to go dip into the scholarly works he did not have on hand. He was leading the life of a monk, but a monk who also knew how to have a good time.

A New Environment

Flaubert quickly blended into the literary scene and the theater world. He had already campaigned in 1856 for his friend Bouilhet, who had finally had a hit at the Odéon with his play *Madame de Montarcy*. Now living in Mantes with his common-law wife Léonie, Bouilhet entrusted Flaubert with his play *Hélène Peyron*, which Gustave also succeeded in placing at the Odéon. In 1860, Flaubert once again busied himself to place Bouilhet's new play, *L'Oncle Million;* it was a flop, but that only served to strengthen Gustave and Louis's friendship. Bouilhet regularly traveled to Croisset to spend hours with Flaubert, reading and revising the manuscript of *Salammbô*.

Their relationship had come to include a new friend, Ernest Feydeau, whose son Georges would become a famous playwright of popular farces. Ernest was himself a writer and made a living as an outside broker on the Paris stock exchange; Flaubert met him at the offices of *L'Artiste*, where he had published excerpts from *Saint Anthony*. In 1858, Feydeau had a hit with his novel *Fanny*. The two men quickly became close friends, and Ernest and his wife sometimes came to lunch at Croisset. He asked Flaubert to read his new novel, *Daniel*. As was his wont, Flaubert did not beat around the bush: "I have read two hundred pages of *Daniel*. I will finish reading it tonight. I think there is much that is *very good*. But I am very often appalled by the repetitions and the stylistic carelessness, of which there is a lot. What a savage you are! Next to *superb* things it is stuffed with unforgivable vulgarities." There was no changing him: in his eyes, honesty was the golden rule of friendship. In his letters, one admires the meticulousness with which he analyzes the manuscripts sent to him, finding what is good or not quite right in each part, applauding here, seething with anger there, hunting down clichés and stock phrases, and giving copious advice, often with a streak of humor: "As for the doctor [a character in the novel], I ask you for his death as a personal favor."[2] In his letters to Ernest, Flaubert sometimes sounds like the schoolboy he never quite outgrew: "Well, well," he wrote to Feydeau while his friend was on a trip to the South of France, "you old lech, you old Valmont, you filthy Noireuil and Père Jérôme, are you defiling the department of Haute-Garonne? Are you filling the gullies with the ejaculations of your untamable knob? How many goats have you brought shame upon, how many chambermaids have you seduced, how many shepherds raped and dinner tables dazzled? You must be feeling good down there, speaking *javanais* [an argot of bordellos], with your big gaiters and your Spanish suit." The passage of time had not dulled the kid in him.

In Paris, where he already knew Théophile Gautier, Flaubert became acquainted with Baudelaire, Michelet, Sainte-Beuve, Ernest Renan, the columnist Paul de Saint-Victor, and Jules and Edmond Goncourt. The Goncourt brothers became his close friends, and he is often mentioned in their *Journal*. With all these colleagues, Flaubert proved to be an enjoyable companion, a passionate conversationalist who could also clown around after dinner. In January 1862, Baudelaire had the curious idea of putting himself up as a candidate for the Académie Française. He asked Flaubert to try to convince Jules Sandeau to give him his vote. Flaubert, who was highly scornful of the Académie, wrote to Sandeau without hesitation: "Do it! Appoint him! It will be beautiful." For him, "a friend's first duty is to help a friend." Baudelaire was full of gratitude: "My dear Flaubert, you are a real warrior. You would have deserved to be part of the Sacred Band. You have the blind faith of friendship, which implies real politics." Baudelaire never had the slightest chance of being elected to the Académie, but this hopeless enterprise was a triumph for friendship.

Flaubert had a more ambiguous relationship with Jules Michelet, whose works he had pored over in his youth. In a letter to Gautier, he tore apart Michelet's book on love, *L'Amour:* "All he talks about is [the womb], all he dreams of is ovaries, breastfeeding, placentas, and constant coupling. It's the apotheosis of marriage, the idealization of the conjugal fart, the frenzy for pot-au-feu." Next he read *La Femme* [*Woman*] and wrote to Feydeau: "What an old babbler! Honestly, he's overindulging in chatter." But then Michelet sent him his new book, *La Mer* [*The Sea*]. "How can I thank you, Sir and dear Master, for sending me this book? How can I describe the enchantment I experienced in reading it?" The Garçon could be as polite as a society lady when he needed to be. He told Michelet that he had devoured his books as a high school student. Delighted, Michelet thanked him and expressed his admiration: "Such a letter is even better than the book—a beautiful and rare event that I so rarely see: a superior man who loves what is produced by others and is sympathetic to it."[3] In June 1861, Flaubert was once again enchanted with Michelet's new book, *Le Prêtre, la Femme, et la Famille* [*The Priest, the Woman, and the Family*]: "There is no one now who can ignore you, who can escape the influence of your genius, who can avoid living with your ideas." Quid pro quo, the "old babbler" warmly congratulated Flaubert upon the release of *Salammbô*. Flaubert replied in kind: "For eight days now I've wanted to come see you to talk to you about your prodigious *Sorcière* [*Witch*], which I devoured in one overnight sitting." It was decided now: in Flaubert's eyes, Michelet was a master, and it would never be contested again.

It was also in the offices of *L'Artiste* that Flaubert met the Goncourt brothers, in 1857. They immediately hit it off. He invited them for meals at his apartment, visited them, and got in the habit of calling them *"mes bichons"* ("my pets"). Through endless talks, shared secrets, and long meals, Flaubert and the brothers established a real connection. But this did not prevent the Goncourts from making countless nasty comments about Flaubert in their *Journal*. Flaubert congratulated his friends for their *Maîtresses de Louis XIV* [*Mistresses of Louis XIV*] and marveled at their *Soeur Philomène* [*Sister Philomène*], but true to his usual frank approach, he also raised questions and objections about their work and identified the weak points. The brothers responded, explained themselves, justified their choices. When he was apart from them and their letters became too infrequent, he protested and begged them to write. In short, an intense friendship had formed between Gustave and the two gossips of French letters. They described him thus in the *Journal:* "Very tall, very strong, with big prominent eyes, swollen eyelids, full cheeks, a rough drooping mustache, complexion blotched with red." They depicted him making his passionate declamations, "his eyes bulging out of his head, his face bright, his arms raised as if to embrace a lady." He made the *bichons'* heads spin with his way of talking about style, the masters, and his book. They reported how he spoke about his fascination with the Marquis de Sade: "He is the last word in Catholicism. . . . Let me explain: he is the spirit of the Inquisition, the spirit of torture, the spirit of the medieval Church, the horror of Nature. There isn't a single tree in Sade, or a single animal."[4] Yet the *Journal* is full of criticism of Flaubert. Did the Goncourts even truly consider him a friend? They wrote of him:

> Ultimately, this frank, loyal, open, furiously blooming nature lacks the right chemistry to lead from an acquaintance to friendship. We are at the same stage that we were the first day we saw him, and when we ask him to come over for dinner, he expresses his deep regrets, but at night he must only work. Oh, what an amusing error! These men—whom the bourgeois always imagines at parties, orgies, living twice as much as other men—unable to give up an evening to friendship and society! Solitary and hidden laborers, living far from life, with their thought and their work of art![5]

This evaluation clearly resulted from the brothers' pique at Flaubert's turning down a single invitation and does not reflect the reality of his life in

Paris. He was constantly parking himself with someone or other at the Café Anglais, Tortoni's, or the Trois Frères Provençaux. The bear allowed himself furloughs from the den. And fame had improved his skills as a seducer, particularly with actresses. As we have seen, there was the affair with Béatrix Person, "that excellent creature" who eventually married the agricultural landowner Jules-Émile Godefroy—one could always rely on the land. Flaubert's love affair with the actress and singer Suzanne Lagier was more boisterous. She is primarily known to us through the Goncourts' *Journal*, which depicts her as a real tart. The Goncourt brothers' Suzanne Lagier is plump and outspoken, a booming loudmouth with an acid wit, hopping from one bed to the next: "a big old lady with a big old voice; like a good Newfoundland dog, she must sell her ass for a penny." "Madame, her maid used to say, is like a gentleman who is always hard." At soirées, she was lively, funny, and alluring, with an endless supply of dirty anecdotes. She brought a touch of gaiety to every party. "No comedy of the time equaled that woman, no merriment was as amusing as that life of the party and that delightful loudmouth, the most beautiful dish of any supper, a woman to be served in watercress like a Regency mistress."[6] The brothers recount several lunches at Flaubert's place with an ever more baroque, crude, and cynical Lagier. Her off-and-on relationship with Flaubert bumped along for several years, with multiple break-ups and reconciliations. Only one letter from Flaubert to the actress has survived: it is an 1871 missive concerning a plan to have her play Mademoiselle Aïssé, the title role in Louis Bouilhet's posthumous drama.

Flaubert's theater conquests did not stop there—or so we are led to believe by allusions in his letters to "la Ramelli" and other women, though there is not much else to go on. We know more about his affairs with high society Parisian "pets," kept women who sometimes hosted salons. He is known to have had at least one fling with Esther Guimont, who had been the mistress of Prince Napoleon and Napoleon III himself. The relationship appears to be attested by a note that was written by Guimont, discovered by a collector, and published in the newspaper *L'Intransigeant* on March 2, 1939, though it must be said that it reads like a drunken parody: "I commit," wrote the lady, "to deliver myself to sir Gustave Flaubert, to use and abuse me as he pleases, once the bathroom at the house I am having built at rue de Chateaubriand is ready." These courtesans, humorously immortalized in the plays of Georges Feydeau, were girls from modest backgrounds whose only credentials were beauty and low standards. Once their bed and board was provided by a rich, aging protector, they could receive whatever lovers they pleased free of charge. Gustave used his experience with these women to create Rosanette in *Sentimental Education*.

Flaubert probably also had a dalliance with Jeanne de Tourbey, another leading figure of the Empire demimonde, though we do not know when it occurred. He met her in 1857, when her protector, Marc Fournier, wanted to produce a stage adaptation of *Madame Bovary*. De Tourbey held a literary salon frequented by Mérimée, Renan, Sainte-Beuve, and now Flaubert. Since she lived on rue Vendôme (now rue Béranger), just a step away from the boulevard du Temple, Flaubert called her his "dear neighbor." She became the Comtesse de Loynes through her marriage in 1871 and went on to host the most famous anti-Dreyfus salon of the fin de siècle, giving her lover, the renowned critic Jules Lemaître, a place to pontificate. But in the late 1850s, she was still a very young woman and the subject of Flaubert's attentions, as can be seen in a letter he sent her on May 15, 1858, while on a trip to Tunis. He claims to think of her "nearly continually." He lays it on thick: "And yet I thought I had left all that behind! What vanity on my part! The heart is like these palm trees, it grows back as it is stripped." Flaubert delivers other gallant remarks to his "dear and beautiful neighbor":

> Is it in the boudoir at rue de Vendôme that your panther's grace and demonic spirit are found? How often I dream of all that! I follow you, in my thoughts, coming and going everywhere, gliding over your carpets, lounging in your armchairs, taking exquisite poses!
>
> But there is a problem with this picture—the number of gentlemen surrounding you (good fellows for that matter). It is impossible for me to think of you without seeing the tails of black coats at your feet. It looks to me like you are walking on mustaches, like an Indian Venus on flowers. What a sad garden!

Other letters to this "exquisite person" followed, all of which were more respectful than those he sent to Aglaé Sabatier, a woman better known as *"la Présidente."* Sabatier was just five months younger than Flaubert. She was supported by a Belgian industrialist, Alfred Mosselman, but was also Baudelaire's "Muse and Madonna." Flaubert came to her Sunday literary dinners on rue Frochot whenever he was in Paris, rubbing shoulders with Théophile Gautier, Ernest Feydeau, Henri Monnier, and Maxime Du Camp, among others. His first known letter to Aglaé Sabatier is dated March 1, 1856, and concerns a dinner invitation. The following year, he sent her a copy of *Madame Bovary*, inscribed, "To the charming wit, the ravishing woman, the excellent friend, our beautiful, good, and unmoved President, Mme Aglaé Sabatier, a paltry homage from her devoted Gve Flaubert." The few surviving letters from Flaubert to Aglaé are fairly risqué and suggest that the two were *very* close. In the summer of 1859, he wrote to her: "Are you staying in Paris all summer? Has it been hot the last two months? And I imagine you have plunged your beautiful feminine body into the flow of the Seine many times. Oh how that lesbian must have climaxed beneath you! And how I would have liked to be in her place! Forgive me, I believe I've uttered an obscenity. It is a cry from the heart." And this: "Adorable President, 'I take my pen to write you' (and *just between us* it is not my pen I want to take)." Maxime Du Camp would later recognize Aglaé in the character of Rosanette; the President had become the Marshal. The Goncourt brothers describe her as follows: "A biggish woman with a coarse, hearty manner; a courtesan with something common about her. This rather vulgar creature endowed with classical beauty left me with the impression of a camp-follower for fauns."[7] Though we have no further details of Flaubert's Paris courtships of the time, it is fair to say that he got around.

Juliet

A smooth talker, backstage privateer, and mustachioed seducer, Flaubert seemed to embrace the codes of virility in his new Parisian life: the company of women and girls was a necessity to which feelings were incidental. Yet Flaubert had other ways of relating to women. There was friendship, for instance, as attested by his correspondence with his fellow Norman Amélie Bosquet. After publishing *La Normandie Romanesque et merveilleuse* [*Romantic and Marvelous Normandy*], Bosquet had begun writing novels under the pseudonym of Émile Bosquet. Flaubert first met her at the Rouen municipal library. He may initially have considered seducing her, but once she turned him down, the relationship developed and Flaubert diligently read her work, encouraged her, spent long hours discussing her writing, and approached publishers on her behalf. In October 1862, he wrote to her: "Do you know that during your last trip we had two sessions that remained not *on*, but *in* my heart? It seems to me that we were more intimate than usual; there was ... something I can't put my finger on. But something all at once good, powerful, and tender ... and like a gentle embrace. I like you very much when you don't laugh." In 1869, the relationship was permanently compromised when Amélie Bosquet, by then a contributor to the feminist journal *Le Droit des femmes* and author of the recently published *Le Roman des ouvrières* [*The Workingwomen's Novel*], read *Sentimental Education* and was outraged to discover that the character of Mlle Vatnaz ridiculed the feminist cause.

Another woman is the subject of a beautiful story told by Jacques-Louis Douchin in his *Vie érotique de Flaubert* [*The Erotic Life of Flaubert*]. Although Douchin pokes fun at Flaubert's "great love" for Élisa Schlésinger, he feels confident that there *was* a great love in Flaubert's life, but it was "censored." The beloved was Juliet Herbert, little Caroline's third governess, who had arrived at Croisset in the spring of 1855, when she was twenty-six, and stayed until 1857. Born to a distinguished but ruined English family, she had resolved to make a living as a private tutor. On May 9, 1855, Flaubert mentions her to Bouilhet without a trace of Romanticism: "Since I saw you excited by (and for) the governess, I am (excited) too. At dinner, my eyes gladly follow the gentle slope of her bosom. I think she notices, because she looks sunburned five or six times a meal." Their relationship took a decisive turn in the spring of 1857 when Juliet, still at Croisset, began to translate *Madame Bovary* into English under Gustave's supervision. Is Douchin correct in his supposition that they became lovers while working together? Flaubert told his publisher Michel Lévy that "this translation is a real masterpiece." Yet it would lead nowhere: the novel was not translated into English until 1886, and the version published was not Juliet's.

Partially thanks to Louis Bouilhet's correspondence, we know that after leaving France in 1857, Juliet Herbert returned to Croisset several times in the following years. In 1865, Flaubert stayed in London from June 26 to July 12, though the purpose of his trip has never been discovered. In his notebook no. 13, one finds the notes that confirm the relationship: an intimate dinner for two at a restaurant and "the evening, moonlight—Delightful return—long conversation." The very modesty of these notes leads Douchin to conclude that "for the first and only time in his life, Gustave Flaubert experienced love." We know Flaubert returned to London in 1866, but no letters from the purported correspondence between the novelist and the governess have survived. In her book *Flaubert and an English Governess: The Quest for Juliet Herbert*, the English scholar Hermia Oliver inquires into the role Juliet played in Flaubert's life.[8] It is known that the "English governess" provided him with some information for *Sentimental Education*. Though Gustave and Juliet would continue to see each other, their meetings were far apart. In a letter to his niece dated October 28, 1870, Gustave writes: "My life hasn't been pleasant these last eighteen months! Think of all those I've lost! (All I have left is you and *that poor Juliet*! And neither of you are here!)" (italics added). On September 8, 1872, he writes to his niece from Paris: "Once poor Juliet has left, I'll go for three or four days." In 1874, he inscribes the first copy of *The Temptation of Saint Anthony* to Juliet, his "dear companion." He uses the same expression to describe her in a letter to Caroline dated September 14 of the same year: "I think that in eight days *my dear companion* (I'm not talking about you) will come to see you." Further on in the same letter, he writes: "As soon as I return to Croisset, Laporte will bring my dog, for whom Juliet has given me a superb collar." On August 21, he had told Caroline he was leaving for Paris, where he would see "dear Juliet."

In 1967, the American historian Benjamin F. Bart suggested in his *Flaubert* that this affair "was surely the most tender and the longest and deepest of his many relations with women."[9] According to Douchin, "Juliet reigned supreme, leaving far behind all of Flaubert's other flings and romantic experiences."

To verify this, one would need to have access to the two lovers' letters. There is no doubt that the correspondence existed, first because they saw each other many times over many years but were most often apart, and second because Flaubert was a tireless letter-writer, and one cannot imagine that he would write less often to his "dear companion" than, for instance, to Mlle Leroyer de Chantepie. Unfortunately, no letters have been found. Is Caroline to blame? Douchin puts forward another, highly plausible hypothesis, which is that Juliet herself wanted the letters destroyed because they "bore witness to a love that she wanted to keep for herself." They were "a treasure too precious for future generations to prostitute in public." Perhaps Juliet's former pupil Caroline executed Juliet's wishes by destroying her side of the correspondence, while Juliet herself took care of Gustave's letters. It should be noted that many of Flaubert's letters from women have disappeared—starting with Louise Colet's. Could it be that the writer himself, this man so hostile to any publicity regarding his private life, weeded the secrets out of his posthumous life?

If there was a love story here, which is likely, it remains "the last great mystery of Flaubert's life," as Jean Bruneau has said, a great love that could tolerate long separations of over four years but that did not sweep away everything else in its path. In 1859, Flaubert could still write to Mlle Leroyer de Chantepie: "As for love, all that I have ever found in that supreme joy is turmoil, storms, and despair! Woman seems an impossible thing to me. And the more I study her, the less I understand her. I have always stayed as far away from her as I could. She is an abyss that attracts and frightens me." The fact remains that Flaubert could love at a distance: he seemed to enjoy his love much more when he was separated from its object. Juliet could have been the ideal love—the one that did not disturb the artist, that filled his imagination, and that was safely revived by the irregularity of their encounters.

To Carthage!

Even before the publication of *Madame Bovary*, Flaubert had set to work on a new novel, which he initially called *Carthage* and later retitled *Salammbô*. The plot was inspired by a story the Greek historian Polybius recounts about the Mercenary War that broke out in the Carthaginian Empire in 241 BCE after the first Punic War between Rome and Carthage, the two empires of the Mediterranean. The war lasted three years and four months, from fall 241 to late 238, and began when the mercenaries revolted against the Punic government for not paying their arrears. Carthage's troops were composed of a variety of Iberians, Gauls, Ligurians, and, especially, Libyans. The government moved them 125 miles from Carthage, to Sicca, where they were asked to forgo part of their pay. The Libyan Matho took the helm of the revolt, which was soon supported by the indigenous populations that were subjects of Carthage. Polybius calls the war that ensued "inexpiable": there were massacres, atrocities, and torture, as well as incidents of cannibalism among the starving prisoners. Eventually, the Carthaginians won. Matho was captured alive, and some of his companions were publicly tortured to death. Salammbô—to be written with two m's, Flaubert points out, to ensure that the name is pronounced "Salam" and not "Salan"—was the daughter of the Carthaginian chief Hamilcar. The rebel Matho had fallen in love with her, and she died upon witnessing his execution.

Carthage! What an idea! Flaubert had long been thinking about writing a historical novel set in Antiquity, whose epic images had entranced him as a child. His desire had been kindled by the journey to the Orient with Du Camp. Initially he thought of writing an "Egyptian" novel. Carthage, which was founded by the Phoenicians in the ninth century BCE, seemed more challenging because little was known of it aside from the three Punic Wars, the last of which ended with the razing of the city in 146 BCE. The lack of knowledge about the city-state excited Flaubert's imagination. After Yonville and triviality, he would turn to the saga of Carthage. Yet he stayed faithful to his method, rejecting dreamed-up exoticism. He strove to reproduce what was real, or if that was impossible, what was "probable." He borrowed the principle that Ernest Feydeau had applied to his *Histoire des usages funèbres et des sépultures des peuples anciens* [*History of the Funeral Customs and Sepulchers of the Ancient Peoples*]: "As for my archaeology," he wrote Feydeau, "it will be 'probable,' that's all. As long as no one can *prove* that I've written absurdities, that's all I ask."

In the same letter to Feydeau, Flaubert talks in concrete terms about the ongoing tension in his mind between beauty and reality: "A book can be full of enormities and blunders, and be no less splendid for that. Such a doctrine, once admitted, would be deplorable, I know, especially in France, where pedantry and ignorance reign. But in the opposite tendency (which is mine, alas!) I see a great danger. Concentration on costume makes us forget the soul. I would give the demi-ream of notes I've written during the last five months and the ninety-eight volumes I've read, to be, for only three seconds, really moved by the passion of my heroes."[10]

Flaubert left no stone unturned in his research. He enlisted his friends to help him unearth information. He approached Félicien de Saulcy, an Orientalist he had met in Constantinople, to provide him with facts about Carthage; asked for the help of Alfred Maury, the librarian at the Institut de France; wrote to Eugène Crépet, whose Catholic encyclopedia he had consulted, to request engravings and useful drawings; sent Bouilhet's acquaintance Jean Clogenson, who had just visited Tunis and Carthage, a list of questions to forward to his friends in Tunis; pressed the Comte de Saint-Foix, whom he had met on his journey and who was now an assistant consul in Tunis, to explain to him how the Psylli captured and trained their snakes. Louis Bouilhet was initially somewhat skeptical about this endeavor, "so difficult that it scares me." But seeing his friend determined to rise to the challenge, he could not resist his enthusiasm. Here was Flaubert, plunging into massive volumes, some of which were utterly unexpected, as he told Jules Duplan: "My desk is so cluttered with books that I get lost.—I rush through them without finding much. However, I am committed to *Carthage* and I will write this colorful romp no matter the cost. I would like to start in a month or two. But first I have to devote myself by induction to a formidable archaeological task. I am currently reading a 400-page in-quarto on the Mediterranean cypress, because there were cypresses in the courtyard of the Temple of Astarte. That can give you an idea of the rest."[11]

In his letters to Ernest Feydeau and Jules Duplan, Flaubert detailed the countless books he read. Duplan, whom he had met in 1851 through Maxime Du Camp, was the brother of his notary, Ernest Duplan. Now that they were close friends, Flaubert did not hesitate to ask for his help finding books. Duplan had already provided him with all the press clippings about *Madame Bovary*. Like Bouilhet, he had initially had his doubts about *Carthage*. "No, old boy," Flaubert answered him on May 20, 1857, "despite your advice I will not abandon *Carthage* to start again on *Saint Anthony* because: I am no longer in this circle of ideas and I would have to return to it, which is no small task for me. . . . I am in *Carthage* and I am going to try, on the contrary, to dig into it as deep as possible, and to become ex-*h*alted." By September 20, he was able to tell his friend that he had written fifteen pages. The novel had begun! But not without torment: "Frankly, I'm worried it will be *irritating*.—It seems to me I am turning to tragedy and that I am writing in a deplorable academic style!"

Now that he had begun writing, he was faced once again with anxiety, doubts, fears, migraines, pages written and abandoned, and the tasks of rooting out assonances, finding the right word, and digging up additional information as he went. "One has to be absolutely mad to undertake books like this! At every line, at every word, I overcome difficulties which no one will thank me for, and perhaps they will be right not to thank me. For if my system is wrong, the work will be a failure."

In April 1858, having decided to scout the settings for his novel, he left for Carthage via Algeria. While waiting for his boat in Marseille, he wanted once again to see the "famous house" where eighteen years earlier he had had that memorable encounter with Eulalie Foucaud: "All changed!" he wrote to Louis Bouilhet. "The ground floor, then the salon, is now a bazaar and upstairs is a barbershop. I went there twice to be shaved. I spare you any Chateaubrian-desque comments and reflections on the flight of time, on falling leaves and falling hair."[12] He may have loved Juliet the best, but the remembrance of both Eulalie and Élisa lived in his memory like a latent emotion that could be stirred by circumstance. He would always cherish these women he had loved—with melancholy.

From Tunis, he wrote to Bouilhet that "I know Carthage *thoroughly* and at every hour of day and night." What had he found there? Stones, remnants—essentially not much more than local color, the landscape and its inhabitants, whose way of life he adopted without hesitation: "The other day, on my way to Utica," he wrote to Ernest Feydeau, "I slept among dogs and chickens, be-tween two walls made of cow dung; all night I heard jackals barking."[13]

From there, he returned to Algeria by land, accompanied by a small escort—"a trip that few Europeans have taken," he wrote to Jules Duplan. "This way I will see *everything* I need for *Salammbô*." Since November 1857, he had found his definitive title: *Salammbô, Carthaginian Novel*. On June 3, he embarked for France at Philippeville.

While he assured his friends that he had been "chaste" on his trip, his travel notes reveal at least two exceptions. One was his encounter with a woman named Ra'hel in a filthy brothel near the leather souk. More significant was his visit to the "splendid" Nelly Rosemberg, a lady-in-waiting who appears to have inspired Salammbô's physical appearance: "long eyelashes, short lips, fleshy and prominent—some mustache, fan-shaped lashes.—her eyes more than black and extremely bright though languorous, rouged cheek-bones, yellow skin, splendid pupils drowned in sperm."[14]

For Flaubert, the most obvious result of this two-month trip was the cer-tainty that he had to start over from scratch: "I'll have you know," he wrote to Feydeau on June 20, 1858, "that *Carthage* must be entirely redone, or rather must be done. *I'm tearing it all apart.* It was absurd! Impossible! Fake!" Now he was off again, with his mind clearer, tackling his "colossal" task. In fact, he merely had to rework the three chapters he had already written. He wouldn't finish the manuscript until April 1862, after endless months of pain, doubt, and revision. In June, while deep into his corrections, he confessed to Jules Duplan: "My head is full of crossing-outs, I am exhausted, incensed, stupefied by *Salammbô*. The disgust of publication compounds the nausea provoked by the book; in short, merely the name of my novel bores the shit out of my very soul." As with *Bovary*, he had been able to count on Louis Bouilhet, the uncompromising friend he referred to as "Monseigneur," throughout the writing of *Salammbô*. Now he had to find a publisher for the book, but this time he swore he would not let himself enter into a … Carthaginian agreement. He had demands!

CHAPTER 14

Salammbô

In May 1862, Flaubert asked his notary, Ernest Duplan, brother of his friend Jules, to represent his literary interests. He began by informing him of his wishes. First—and perhaps surprisingly—he did not want the publisher, Michel Lévy, to read his manuscript: he was selling the book to him based on his name, his reputation, and the success of *Madame Bovary*. If Lévy were to read the manuscript, he would be able to disguise his individual opinion as popular opinion and, as a competent businessman, use any alleged concern regarding potential sales to subject Flaubert to his conditions. Second, he did not want any illustrations, "because the most beautiful literary description is swallowed up by the paltriest drawing." Third, he refused to be paid based on a percentage of sales, despite the fact that this was a potential method of remuneration, because there was no way of determining with accuracy the number of copies sold (indeed, Flaubert never learned how many copies of *Madame Bovary* were sold). Rather, he would sell his novel for a lump sum of 20,000 francs (approximately $85,000 in today's dollars). As one might expect, Michel Lévy resisted Flaubert's demands: he wanted to read the manuscript and refused to rule out illustrations. He also demanded that the deal include the rights for a future "modern novel" (set no earlier than 1750). And he considered that Flaubert was asking for too much money. Negotiations turned bitter; Flaubert threatened to look for another publisher.

Finally, both parties made concessions. Michel Lévy agreed to forgo illustrations and the second agreement binding Flaubert to offer him a modern novel. He would merely have a right of first refusal if Flaubert wrote such a novel, which he was not obliged to do. For his part, Flaubert sent Duplan a copy of *Salammbô* with which he could do as he pleased, including show it to Lévy. He also agreed to sell the book for half his initial bid: 10,000 francs for the rights for ten years. The agreement was signed on September 11, 1862.

Ever the clever businessman, Lévy let word get around in the press that *Salammbô* had been sold for 30,000 francs. The Goncourt brothers took offence at that: "Something suspicious about Flaubert has been revealed," they wrote in their *Journal*, "since he has become Lévy's accomplice for the fee of thirty thousand francs for *Salammbô*. What I had vaguely glimpsed under his frank nature has now become clear to me and I have come to mistrust this friend—who used to say that the true man of letters should work his whole life long on books for which he should not even seek publicity—now that I have seen him perform such clever acrobatics in selling his own." The two brothers were undoubtedly bitter that Michel Lévy had turned down their own book *Les Hommes de lettres* [*Men of Letters*] a few years earlier. As it happens, Gustave had nothing to do with this misleading promotional move. Yet he was ultimately pleased that he had stayed with Lévy, who published George Sand, Ernest Renan, Balzac, Stendhal, and many other celebrated writers, and was on the verge of signing a contract with Louis Bouilhet for his new play, *Dolorès*. The public response was gratifying: there would be five editions of *Salammbô* between 1862 and 1864.[1]

An "Archaeological Novel"

Flaubert's new novel was a new challenge. With *Salammbô*, he took his method of impersonality even further than he had with *Madame Bovary* by choosing a subject set in little-known Antiquity and escaping the "small passions and small people" of his own century. But the Carthaginian novel mystified many readers who had enjoyed *Madame Bovary*. Mlle Leroyer de Chantepie is a good test case: she thanked Flaubert for the copy she had received, congratulated him for his great talent, and told him she would write an article about *Salammbô*. Yet she did not manifest the slightest enthusiasm; she surely had none. How could the woman who had identified with Emma relate to this tale of battles between protagonists that were so distant from her? Flaubert had predicted as much in May 1857, at a time when he was being compared to Balzac: "As for Balzac, I'm sick of hearing about him. I'm going to try to put together something sparkling and loud, where the comparison won't be so easy. They're so stupid with their 'observation of mores'! I don't give a shit about that!"[2]

One quickly realizes that the "sparkling" and "loud" *Salammbô* is light years away from the psychological novel *Madame Bovary*. It is closer to an epic, peopled by characters who are more symbolic than real and are always surrounded by those anonymous masses who are the saga's main players. Love, which is to the novel what wind is to the mill, is reduced to its most simple expression. Yes, Matho, the head of the Mercenaries, has fallen in love with Salammbô, daughter of Hamilcar and priestess of the goddess Tanit, and one surmises that the siege of Carthage by Matho and his troops is actually an assault on Hamilcar's daughter, but Flaubert does not dwell much on the warrior's and the priestess's feelings. This lack of psychological interest and of a romantic dimension, along with an overabundance of war scenes, have certainly continued to discourage many readers. *Salammbô* is not moving. Émile Faguet confesses as much in his *Flaubert:* "It is very tiring, and it is as boring as it is tiring. I do not believe that a single reader can honestly say he has read *Salammbô* without putting it down several times for long stretches. You can read *Salammbô* in three days, but it is a tall order only accomplished with steady resolve, and it won't be done recklessly." Quoting Faguet, Albert Thibaudet protests: "How absurd! At sixteen or seventeen, I read *Salammbô* straight through as passionately as I read *Les enfants du Capitaine Grant* [*In Search of the Castaways* by Jules Verne] when I was twelve!"[3] To each his own Flaubert!

The book's greatness lies in an elevated style that is applied here not to describing a small town in Normandy in the nineteenth century, but to composing a vast epic poem full of sounds, colors, odors, and all sorts of breathtaking violence. In *Bovary*, Flaubert had turned the trivial into art; in *Salammbô*, he satisfied his need for beauty with horrifying and monstrous scenes. He describes the movement of armies, war machines, the din of assaults and the frenzy of counterattacks, chains of massacres, putrescent flesh, and suffocating deaths, all with a constant aesthetic attention to the picturesque, local color, and exoticism—intoxicating the reader with rare and exotic words, applying himself to detailing the combatants' weapons, clothes, jewels, and gestures, to recounting the massacres and most awful cruelties with an original vocabulary. He does not shy away from the kind of accumulation we find in this description of the march of the Mercenaries:

> Men from every nation were there, Ligurians, Lusitanians, Balearics, Negroes, and fugitives from Rome. You could hear beside the heavy Doric dialect the Celtic syllables ringing out like battle chariots, and Ionian endings clashed with desert consonants, harsh as jackal-cries. Greeks could be

recognized by their slender figures, Egyptians by their hunched shoulders, Cantabrians by their sturdy calves. Carians proudly tossed their helmet plumes, Cappadocian archers had painted great flowers on their bodies with herbal juices, and some Lydians in woman's dress wore slippers and earrings as they dined. Others who had daubed themselves ceremoniously in vermilion looked like coral statues.[4]

See, Flaubert seems to tell us, we've come a long way from the bourgeois people of Yonville—I promised to surprise you! To do something "new"! And also to make us shudder with the genre now known as "gore": there is an abundance of bloody scenes, cannibalism, crucifixions, deaths by thirst and hunger, and sadistic lynchings. We are spared nothing of the cruelty of the Carthaginians and the Barbarians. Both groups are merely representatives of a humanity that reveals its animalistic nature in surrendering to base instincts and death wishes. Even the animals participate in battle, notably a herd of elephants that stamp on the rank and file, flattening the foot soldiers, their roaring mixing with the crash of weapons and shields. Admittedly, war is boring, and as he reached the end of his novel, Flaubert worried about having written a book full of soldiers: "It seems to me that *Salammbô* is deadly boring," he wrote to the Goncourt brothers in July 1861. "There is an obvious excess of ancient grunts. Nothing but battles and enraged people. One wishes for leafy bowers and sweet cream. Berquin [an author of children's stories] will seem delightful after this." Yet even the most reluctant reader cannot remain indifferent to the writer's power in certain virtuosic passages.

In the chapter entitled "Moloch," the Carthaginians are entrenched behind their ramparts, lacking water. Their backs are against the wall. The Elders decide to reverse their fortune by sacrificing the children of the great families. Moloch's servants are sent to snatch the children. When they come to take little Hannibal, Hamilcar's own son, the leader hides his child and offers in his place the young son of a slave. The boy's trembling father comes to beg for his son's life:

> [Hamilcar] had never thought—so vast was the gulf separating the two of them—that they might have anything in common. Even that seemed a kind of outrage to him, as if it were an encroachment upon his privileges. He answered with a look colder and heavier than an executioner's axe; the slave, fainting, fell to the dust at his feet. Hamilcar stepped over him.

Finally, to ensure his silence, Hamilcar sends him "the best things from the kitchens; a joint of goat, beans, and pomegranate preserve. The slave, who had not eaten for a long time, pounced on it; his tears fell into the dishes."[5]

There follows the spectacular scene of the next day's sacrifice:

> The Rich, the Elders, the women, the whole crowd, were massed behind the priests and on the terraces of the houses. The great painted stars had stopped turning; the tabernacles had been set on the ground; and smoke from the censers rose straight up, like gigantic trees spreading out their blue branches amid the azure.
>
> Several people fainted; others became inert and petrified in their ecstasy. An infinite dread oppressed every breast. The last shouts died out one by one—and the people of Carthage panted, absorbed in its desire for terror.
>
> At last the high priest of Moloch ...[6]

This is chapter 13. The novel reaches its peak in the following chapter, "The Defile of the Axe," which describes the final confrontation between the Carthaginians and the Barbarians. One of the Mercenaries' armies is trapped in a gorge blocked on both ends by massive rock slides. Their only hope lies in the arrival of Matho at the head of his own army, but days pass, food and drink run out, and the emaciated men start to starve to death. At that point the cannibalism begins: "Then, as they had to live, as a taste for this food had developed, as they were dying, they slaughtered the water-carriers, the grooms, all the Mercenaries' servants. Each day some were killed. Some people ate a lot, regained strength and were no longer depressed." They finish off the wounded: "the dying, to make people believe they were vigorous, tried to stretch out their arms, raise themselves up, laugh." Later: "Thirst tortured them still more, for they had not a drop of water, the water skins being completely empty since the ninth day. To allay the need they put on their tongues the metal scales of their belts, ivory pommels, sword blades. Former caravan leaders tied ropes tightly round their bellies. Others sucked a pebble. They drank urine cooled in bronze helmets."[7] The entire chapter continues in this savage vein. Hope shifts from one camp to the other, horrors come one after the other, more and more clashes erupt, elephants frightened by the flames brandished before them throw themselves into the gulf, projectiles of all kinds whirl through the air, helmets, shields, and swords crash into each other, and even the lions are called in.

Having reached this point, just before the final chapter relating the deaths of Matho and Salammbô, the reader experiences, if not emotion, at least a visual sensation of barbaric grandeur, as well as admiration for Flaubert's art, the baroque power of his descriptions, and the vehemence of his blood-thirsty theater. Flaubert was showing the full extent of his creative powers—it is as if a contemporary filmmaker like Claude Chabrol went overnight from dissecting provincial life to directing a Cecil B. DeMille blockbuster. In a century that loved poetry and saw people fervently reading Victor Hugo's *La Légende des siècles* [*The Legend of the Ages*], Flaubert gave readers a true epic. It would be the talk of the town.

Friends and the Press

After *Salammbô*, no one could deny that Flaubert had become one of the major writers of his time. Of the many letters Flaubert received after the novel's publication (now in the Lovenjoul collection at the Institut de France), those that extend beyond mere courtesy are extravagantly laudatory.[8] Champfleury was sorry that Flaubert had not "indicated the gap between the two books, for this is what led bleating sheep to whine when they could not overcome the distance between *Madame Bovary* and *Salammbô*." But compliments poured in from the most prominent artists and writers of the day. Hector Berlioz: "Your book has filled me with admiration, astonishment, and even terror. . . . It frightened me, I've been dreaming about it these last few nights. Such style! Such archeological science! Such imagination!"[9] Eugène Fromentin: "I've just finished *Salammbô*. It is beautiful and robust, full of dazzling spectacle and an extraordinary intensity of vision. You are a great painter, my dear friend, better than that, a great *visionary*, for what else can we call the man who has created such vivid realities out of his dreams and has made us believe in them?" Victor Hugo praised the enduring beauty of the legendary married to the real: "It is a beautiful, powerful, and wise book. . . . Your erudition is the great erudition of the poet and the philosopher. You have brought back to life a vanished world, and you have combined this surprising resurrection with a poignant drama. Every time I find in a writer the double feeling of the real, which shows life, and the ideal, which shows the soul, I am moved, I am happy, and I applaud." Leconte de Lisle: "It is full of power and brilliance and is permeated above all with that singular genius, particular to our century, which reconstructs piece by piece the forceful and perfectly true aspects of past eras." Jules Michelet: "People will be struck dumb with surprise, dear Sir. I can see it from the beginning. It is a meteor . . . , but its effect, its greatness are enormous." While we do not have a letter from Baudelaire to Flaubert about *Salammbô,* the poet discusses Flaubert's novel in a letter to Auguste Poulet-Malassis written on December 13: "Big, big success. An edition of two thousand swept up in two days. . . . What Flaubert did, only he could do. Far too much bric-a-brac, but much epic, historical, political, even animal grandeur. Something astonishing in the gesticulation of all the characters."[10]

Published in November 1862, *Salammbô* was the subject of numerous articles beginning in December. Though the reception was mixed, Fortuné Calmets's article in *Boulevard* lifted Flaubert to the highest level from the outset: "There is today a writer who has enough power to create a *success* out of a work that displays the impertinent goal of interesting people through the sole power of Art, that is to say without the slightest help from any of the usual means of successful people: the *common plot,* the *useful fact, scandal."* Paul de Saint-Victor, a friend of the author, was unstinting with his praise in his article in *La Presse,* one of the leading dailies of the Second Empire, on December 15: "I no longer need to describe the success of *Salammbô:* its title is on everyone's lips, the book is in everyone's hands. . . . I am among those who admire it nearly without reservation and who think that the author has grown with his subject." He extols "the splendor of the tone and the breadth of the perspective," the "ethnographic genius," the "feeling of vanished races," "the restoration of abolished types, the ability to bring back to life the dead families of the ancient world." Flaubert was touched by this article: "A little more and he'd call me the Eternal Father." On December 22, *Salammbô* was celebrated by Théophile Gautier in *Le Moniteur:*

> Reading Salammbô is one of the most violent intellectual sensations one can experience. [Some have accused] M. Flaubert of ornamentation, flashiness, and tawdriness. Critics have been bothered by the overly Carthaginian appearance of a few words. With time, these excessively bright colors will fade on their own, these exotic words, more easily understood, will lose their strangeness, and M. Gustave Flaubert's style will appear for what it is: full, robust, sonorous, original in a way that owes nothing to anyone, colorful when necessary, precise, sober, and masculine when the narrative requires only ornament—in short, the style of a master. His book will remain one of

the greatest literary monuments of this century. To summarize in a single sentence our opinion of Salammbô: it is not a history book, it is not a novel: it is an epic poem.

Gustave was delighted. "What a beautiful article, my dear Theo, how can I thank you? If someone had told me twenty years ago that the Théophile Gautier who filled my imagination would write such things about me, I'd have gone mad with pride."[11] Flaubert could also count on George Sand, whom he did not yet know well, but who published an article on his novel in *La Presse* on January 27, 1863. She celebrated the "great artist" who had written this "strange and magnificent" book, full of "darkness and brilliance." A "completely original" work. "It was monstrous, this African Babylon, this atrocious Punic world, this great Hamilcar, a villain, this religion, these temples, these battles, these tortures, these vengeances, these feasts, these betrayals; all that, the poetry of cannibals, something like Dante's inferno." Yet in this very long laudatory article, George Sand did point out that the chapter entitled "The Defile of the Axe" was reprehensibly implausible: "There is no place that could be inaccessible to forty thousand men who all have weapons with which they could cut into any kind of stone, probably ropes for their carts, or at least animals whose hides could be used to make straps, a thousand devices to make clamps." In short, she does not believe that such an enormous army could have been trapped in that gorge. Flaubert's thank-you note to George Sand has not survived, but we have her reply, in which she explains that she wanted to right a wrong, for the reviews she had read of the novel seemed "unfair and inadequate." As for her criticism of "The Defile of the Axe," she admits that it was quite "puerile": "I let it stand because a reservation only brought out the sincerity of my admiration."[12] Michel Lévy exulted upon reading Sand's article: "Magnificent!" Her review inaugurated a friendship that would lead to an abundant correspondence between the lady of Nohant and the hermit of Croisset; for the time being, he asked for her portrait to hang "on the wall of my study."

Sand decided to write her article because she had been startled by the unfairness of certain attacks on *Salammbô*. Indeed, much of the press had shown its teeth, and not to smile with admiration. In *Le Monde*, Léon Gautier wondered whether it was a novel or a scholarly treatise: "Actually, they could have called this book: *Elements of Punic Archaeology*" (December 5, 1862). In *Le Siècle*, the other leading daily of the period, Taxile Delord criticized the novel for having an excess of details, to the detriment of feelings, love, and passion (December 8). In the *Journal des débats*, Alfred Cuvillier-Fleury denounced its "pompousness" and hyperbolic style (December 9). In the *Revue nationale*, Horace de Lagardie wrote of a "descriptive compulsion" (December 10). Armand de Pontmarin, who had already panned *Madame Bovary*, ridiculed *Salammbô* in *La Gazette de France:* "It is very probable that physicians will forbid this book to the more beautiful half of their clientele, who would come away from it not only with migraines, but with spasms and nervous fits. As for pregnant women, it's scary to think about: an absolute ban on *Salammbô*, for fear of giving birth to little monsters and compromising future generations" (December 21). The most common criticism was simply that the book was boring: "All of M. Flaubert's descriptive art," Benoît Jouvin wrote in *Le Figaro*, "will run the risk of giving those studious heads bent over his book nothing more than a violent headache. . . . Well, the book is boring; in France, that is a death sentence" (December 28). In *L'Union*, Georges Cadoudal wrote: "One comes out of it tired, broken, shattered with boredom and aches." He also accused the author of breaking with propriety: "There are things in human nature which we must keep far from view, images that must be veiled, areas forbidden to the curiosity of painters and poets." The *Revue des deux mondes*, which had not spared Flaubert at the time of *Madame Bovary*, came back to the charge, this time under the pen of Saint-René de Taillandier, who attacked him for his "openly displayed indifference, in this egotistical art that believes it is exempt of any human feeling once it has said 'I am realism.' Good and evil, momentum and resistance, debauchery and repentance, he describes everything in the same tone, with an icy impartiality. . . . Despite such keen talent, *Madame Bovary* inspired disgust; despite energetic effort, *Salammbô* has merely added fatigue and boredom to disgust" (February 15, 1863). The distinguished thinker Émile Boutmy published a more balanced study in the *Revue nationale et étrangère*, but criticized Flaubert's amorality: "M. Flaubert's characters have no moral consistency. They seem to be pushed or pulled here and there by their passions, never trying to resist them, without any personal energy, conscience, or freedom. To tell the truth, most of his heroes, those in the foreground, are real maniacs, madmen, idiots, and so on. Buried in the illusions of their blinkered minds or struggling against pathological appetites and without any genuine goal, they might attract scholarly curiosity; they do not attract sympathy. As has been aptly noted, Salammbô has no personality other than being hysterical" (May 10, 1863).

From the moment he began work on the Carthaginian novel, Flaubert had predicted that he would be "bawled out." In September 1861, he confided in the Goncourt brothers that he was already weary of "all the foolishness that will be said after publication of this book." To which he added: "Unless it falls flat. For where can one find people who are interested in all this?" This fear was unfounded: *Salammbô* met with popular acclaim. At the time, outside of paintings, only a book could offer unbridled exoticism with the sound of bugles, haunting battles scenes, and a triumphant profusion of oddities, all these *excesses* which were not to be found in everyday literature and which cinema would later turn into a twentieth-century genre.

Polemics

On December 8, 1862, Sainte-Beuve published the first part of a long article on *Salammbô* in *Le Constitutionnel*. The subsequent installments appeared on December 15 and 22. Sainte-Beuve had become the arbiter of French literature through his weekly "Causeries du Lundi" (Monday Chats) columns. From the outset, he notified readers that his friendship with Flaubert would not prevent him from coming to "a verdict based on careful reading; impartial, and unrestricted by conventional rules of politeness."[13] Sainte-Beuve did not like *Salammbô*, and he presents detailed arguments to explain why. Before he even begins analyzing the novel, one can feel his hesitance at Flaubert's shift from Yonville-l'Abbaye to Carthage: "He was tempted by the impossible and nothing else: we were expecting him here on our turf, in a field in Touraine, Picardy, or Normandy again: good people, you're in for a surprise—he was off to Carthage."

Sainte-Beuve conscientiously describes the novel in a highly detailed and remarkable summary that reveals a very close reading. Yet already, in the first article, he regrets that Flaubert's realism is attracted first and foremost by what is "awful and harsh." Archaeology, which was then in fashion, has drained history of its human substance; one does not believe in the story's characters: "We have long ridiculed those historical novels and tragicomedies that showed Alexander in love, Porus in love, Cyrus in love, or Genseric in love, but Matho in love, that African Goliath behaving like a wild man or a child in full view of Salammbô, does not seem any less false to me; he is as far removed from nature as from history." And there is so much that is improbable, so many unnecessary descriptions. "What we are dealing with here is an auctioneer having a good time. In the vault of precious stones, for example, he will enjoy enumerating all the unimaginable mineral marvels, up to and including carbuncles 'formed by lynxes' urine.' That is going too far, and letting the dabbling trickster show through. In this entire visit to underground warehouses, the author's goal is not to show Hamilcar's character, but only to show the warehouses." And what about all those strange words, presented without the help of a glossary? Worse—bad taste rules: "the paintbrush seems to be wielded by a surgeon; one recognizes all the forms and nuances of corruption, of cadaverous decomposition, according to race." Flaubert invents "torture methods, ways of mutilating bodies, singular, refined, vile horrors. An element of sadistic imagination is mixed into these descriptions": "a failing one must absolutely dare to highlight." Flaubert "cultivates atrocity."

In the last article, Sainte-Beuve shows his hand from the start: "There are so many battles in *Salammbô* that I am struck with the desire to start one myself." The critic drives home his point: there is nothing human in this tale, in which the author persists in "depicting horrors." The very idea that presided over this composition is an "error": Antiquity is too far from us, particularly since we know next to nothing about Carthage and the author "failed to give his work real interest and life." The entire novel "smells too much of oil and the lamp." Sainte-Beuve allows that we are dealing with a consummate craftsman. "I do see well-designed and well-built doors, walls, locks, and storerooms, each separate," but "nowhere do I see the architecture." Good paragraphs, yes, but "few good pages." To tell the truth, it all makes Sainte-Beuve yawn: "How do you expect me to get interested in this lost war, buried in the gorges and sands of Africa, in the revolt of these Libyan and other tribes against their Carthaginian masters, in these ugly little local hatreds between one barbarian and another? What do I care about the duel between Tunis and Carthage?" Flaubert wanted at all cost to escape what was common and familiar, so now we have him telling us about strange things like these "crushed fly legs . . . that are used in a young girl's cosmetics, and of so many other similar oddities." The verdict was scathing: Flaubert's enterprise was grandiose, but the result was a flop.

Flaubert was mortified by these three articles, these three "philippics." He sent Sainte-Beuve an "apologia": "Are you quite sure, first of all, that your general judgment isn't a little overinfluenced by your emotional reaction? The world I depict in my book—barbarian, Oriental, Molochian—is displeasing to you *in itself*." He replied to every objection in detail. For instance, regarding his vocabulary: "I could have bored the reader to death with technical terms. Far from doing so I was careful to translate everything into French. I used not a single special term without immediately furnishing an explanation. I except the names of coins, measurements, and the months, which are indicated by the context. But surely, when you encounter on a page such words as 'kreutzer,' 'yard,' 'piastre,' or 'penny,' they are not beyond your understanding? What would you have said had I called Moloch 'Melek,' Hannibal 'Han-Baal,' Carthage 'Karthadhadtha,' and if instead of saying that the slaves in the mill wore muzzles, I had written 'pausicapes?' As for the names of perfumes and precious stones, it is true that I had to take names that are in Theophrastus, Pliny, and Athenaeus. For plants, I used Latin names— 'commonly accepted names'—instead of Arab or Phoenician."

Flaubert justifies every detail that provoked Sainte-Beuve's skepticism and irony—from "bitches' milk" to the "carbuncles formed by lynxes' urine"— by citing his sources. Concerning the cruelties for which he was denounced, he does not appreciate Sainte-Beuve charging him with an "element of sadistic imagination." As a man who once "sat on a bench in Criminal Court, accused of offences against public decency," he cannot accept such an accusation. He lists the references for all the horror, cruelty, and barbarism in his scenes— he had invented nothing! He continues with a dig at the author of *Port-Royal* (a history of the Port-Royal abbey near Paris): "I regard the tattooed Barbarians as less inhuman, less 'special,' less ludicrous, less exceptional, than men living a communal life who address each other as 'Monsieur' to the end of their days. And it is precisely because they are remote from me that I admire your talent for making me understand them. For I *believe* your picture of Port-Royal, and I would enjoy living there even less than in Carthage. Port-Royal, too, was an exclusive group, unnatural, forced, all of a piece—and yet true. Why will you not allow two truths to exist, two diametrically opposed examples of excess, two different monstrosities?"

Flaubert ends his letter gracefully: "You have clawed me, but you have also given me the handshake of affection; and though you have mocked me a little you have nevertheless given me three great salutes—three long articles, very detailed, very distinguished, which must have been more painful for you than they are for me."[14] On December 25, Sainte-Beuve thanked Flaubert for his explanations and promised him that when the three articles were published in book form he would include Flaubert's "apologia" at the end of the volume, "with only these few words of reply from me. I had my say; you responded;

attentive readers will judge."[15] In a final note, Flaubert thanks him for making this commitment, but asks him to strike from the book version of his letter the entire paragraph containing the word "sadistic": "In rereading this passage, I find a certain sharpness that I do not like. There are things one says but does not write, others that one writes but does not care to see printed. It is *a criticism I am making of you*. I do not want it to be public. Do you understand me?"

Here, one should note a laudable side of Flaubert's personality. He continued to see and dine with Sainte-Beuve between the articles' publication dates: "Our friendly and cordial relations," wrote Sainte-Beuve, "did not suffer." Many other writers would have been angered by the great critic's severity and would have cut ties with him and possibly even sought redress. Of course, Flaubert had a great deal of admiration for this friend, whom he addressed as "dear Master," and was well aware of the influence he wielded. He was not as courteous with the Paris-based German archaeologist and museum curator Guillaume Froehner when he dared to put his scholarly knowledge to use to criticize *Salammbô*.

As Sainte-Beuve had pointed out, archaeology was in fashion. On May 1, 1862, a show opened at the Palais de l'Industrie, an exhibition hall built for the Paris World Fair of 1855, with more than eleven thousand works from the collection of a ruined Italian marquis, Giovanni Pietro Campana, that had recently been acquired by the emperor (in fact, the exhibition space was commonly referred to as the "Napoleon III museum"). The following year, the emperor donated the Campana collection to the Louvre. In an article entitled "Le Roman archéologique en France" [The Archaeological Novel in France] and published in the *Revue contemporaine* on December 31, 1862, Froehner examined with a fine-tooth comb the failings of Ernest Desjardins's introduction to the exhibition of Etruscan frescos in his brochure *Promenade au musée Napoléon-III* [*A Stroll through the Napoleon III Museum*], the fantasies of Théophile Gautier in his *Roman de la momie* [*The Novel of the Mummy*], published back in 1858, and, above all, the errors in *Salammbô*.

According to Froehner, M. Flaubert's failure was total:

Browsing his thick pseudo-Carthaginian volume, with a pompous title and an arrogant appearance, one does not quite know if it is the work of a fanciful mind who tried to create an impossible world, or if it is the desperate effort of a man of taste who is horrified by the increasing blandness of the modern novel, or finally if one should simply recognize it as an attempt on the part of the author of *Madame Bovary* to prove that he too could bore people after being ashamed by an easy success. On this important point, critics are at work. From our perspective, *Salammbô* is the illegitimate child of *Les Misérables* and the Campana museum.

Indeed, one comes across sublime sentences and colossal ideas here that bear the distinctive mark of Victor Hugo. However, there is also the same forced diction, the same fondness for atrocities and horrible scenes, and an unpleasant tendency to make them even more horrible.

Froehner asks what role the Campana museum may have played "in the laborious creation of this pathetic story." While M. Desjardins's brochures turned warehouses into novels, Flaubert's novel "has become a warehouse." The long article continues with a list of inaccuracies, fundamental errors, anachronisms, and topographic, religious, sartorial, historical, and other inventions: "The love of bizarre and unexpected elements has too often won out over the love of truth." And why is the heroine's name spelled "with two 'm's,' contrary to the elementary rules of Semitic grammar?" There is more Chinese than Carthaginian in this novel, which could be called a "*Carthachinoiserie.*" Froehner suggests that the author would have been better off consulting Fable and Dureau de la Malle before he started.[16] For that matter, the Carthaginians weren't all bad—they produced some great things. Why didn't Flaubert show any of them?

Flaubert's reply blazed across the pages of *L'Opinion nationale* on January 24, 1863, and the *Revue contemporaine* on January 31:

> Let me first ask you, Monsieur, why you so obstinately link me with the Campana collection, claiming that it was my source, my continual inspiration. The fact is that I completed *Salammbô* last March, six weeks before the opening of that museum. . . . I have no pretensions to archeology, . . . [however], I know enough to risk saying that you err completely, from the beginning of your article to the end, on every one of your eighteen pages, in every paragraph, and in almost every line.
>
> You reprimand me for not having consulted either Fable or Dureau de la Malle, from whom "I might have profited." A thousand pardons! I have read them—more often than you, perhaps, and amid the ruins of Carthage itself.[17]

Flaubert addresses the author's criticisms one by one, cites his sources, explains that the two 'm's' in Salammbô "were put there on purpose, so that the name would be pronounced Sala*m* and not as in Salan." The verve, precision, irony, and energy of Flaubert's reply reveal his talents as a scrapper; Froehner's objections are knocked down and his scholarship is destroyed, as Flaubert's merciless jubilation starts to show, along with his desire to leave his opponent speechless, like Pascal when he took aim at the casuists. His diatribe must have hit the bull's eye, as we can tell from Guillaume Froehner's reply, published by the *Revue Contemporaine* of January 31, 1863, and *L'Opinion nationale* of the following February 4. Froehner states he has been "mistreated" and refers to the "terrible epistle": "In this damning response, as it has been said somewhere, even I saw myself as astoundingly ignorant. . . . It must have been a great joy for M. Flaubert to see me hobbled and made a laughing stock for your forty thousand readers, while he enumerated my crimes for you, sometimes in Latin, sometimes in his swaggering French." The scholar is stunned, like a boxer on the mat. He tries to get back up by hanging on to an alleged error *Salammbô*'s author made in describing human sacrifices in Carthage. He closes his defense with an *ex professo* sentence on the "total lack of science" displayed by the novelist: "On a few points, the author confirms what I say while he thinks he is refuting me; on others, he takes perverse pleasure in distorting the meaning of my words to give himself the pleasure of an easy triumph; for all the rest, he administers the proof of his own incompetence."

Growing increasingly angry, Flaubert did not back down. On February 4, *L'Opinion nationale* published his final response, in which he noted that in replying to the twenty points of his refutation, the eminent scholar had remained brief. "I will pay no further attention to this gentleman. I withdraw a word that seems to have displeased him. No: M. Froehner is not *léger* [lightweight]. He is just the opposite. And if I 'chose him as a victim, from among so many writers who have disparaged my work,' it was because he had seemed to me the most serious. I was certainly mistaken. . . . You [the letter is addressed to Guéroult, the paper's editor] had given him the opportunity to apprise many people of his existence. This foreigner desperately wanted to become known. Now he is: to his—advantage."[18]

Salammbô's critics were probably not entirely wrong. Flaubert had set himself a major challenge by deciding to entirely reconstruct an ancient world of which little was known and to write a historical novel with few sources. His erudition may have allowed him to create an impression of authenticity, but in fact, fabrication was the dominant mode. Flaubert knew as much: "Furthermore," he wrote to his friend Félicien de Saulcy, "I can now no longer distinguish conjecture from authentic sources in my book."[19]

In a sense, *Madame Bovary* is far more "historical" than *Salammbô*. The characters are more believable, and the settings described, the words spoken, and the story itself all plunge us into the realities of rural life under the July Monarchy, including its "Bovarism." But did Flaubert really attempt a "historical novel" in writing *Salammbô?* Wasn't he rather trying to produce a work of art in keeping with his theory of impersonality? This time, since the truth he sought to achieve in tandem with beauty was located in a distant past, he forced himself to provide every piece of truth he could find in libraries. As a result, *Salammbô* is neither a history book—there are too many uncertainties, too many fabrications—nor a novel that touches, moves, or captivates the reader. It is a series of tableaus painted with bright colors; a prose poem whose length can be tiresome; at best, a kind of opera. In fact, its lyrical nature has inspired several composers, including Modest Mussorgsky, who based *The Libyan* (1864) on Flaubert's novel.[20] Yet Sainte-Beuve's advice was not lost on Flaubert: as soon as the fires lit by *Salammbô* had been extinguished, he set to work on the "modern novel" *Sentimental Education*.

CHAPTER 15

Caroline's Marriage

The publication of *Salammbô* and the subsequent polemics and public reception left Flaubert in a kind of daze: "I spent three very difficult months at Croisset," he wrote to Mlle Leroyer de Chantepie in June 1863, "without writing or reading a thing. That nearly always happens to me between two books." He did confide to his correspondent, however, that he had prepared "the outlines of two books." We know that he was referring to *Sentimental Education* and *Bouvard and Pécuchet,* though he would take years to write the former and would leave the latter unfinished. He also wanted to work with Louis Bouilhet on a *féerie,* a then-popular form of theatrical spectacular with supernatural elements. But for the moment, in June 1863, he traveled to Vichy to rest at the Hôtel Britannique while his mother took the waters. Seventeen-year-old Caroline accompanied Flaubert and his mother. She and her uncle took long walks together. He read while she drew, stopping to talk to her or recite some verse.[1] He did not have a clue that within a year his niece would be getting married.

A Paternal Feeling

Flaubert had transferred to Caroline his love for his sister, whose death had come right after the birth of the little girl who would bear her mother's name. His letters to her are full of tender nicknames: Caro, Bibi, Bichon, Chat, Loulou, Lolotte, Lilinne, Loup, and many others that reveal his unfailing affection. Recall that he had defended himself when Louise Colet accused him of trembling at the idea of having a child, writing: "My heart is *humane.* . . . I love my little niece as if she were my daughter, and I take care of her enough (*actively*) to prove that I'm not just saying that."

Flaubert was an eager participant in Caroline's education while she grew up at Croisset with him and her grandmother. Both Flaubert and his mother had feared that the child might be taken away from them by her father, Émile Hamard, the former classmate whom Gustave had reluctantly accepted as his brother-in-law. After his sister's death, Flaubert had worried that Hamard would go insane: he had gone into a state of emotional collapse, then become delusional, sworn that he would become an actor, announced that he would soon make his debut at the Comédie Française, and depleted his assets. "Throughout my childhood," Caroline wrote in her memoirs, "my father was a subject of shame and sorrow in my awakening consciousness." During a momentary return to sanity, he had attempted to reclaim his daughter—Mme Flaubert had hidden her in Forges-les-Eaux, and Hamard had taken his mother-in-law to court. The judge ruled in Mme Flaubert's favor, recognizing her as the legal guardian, with Émile's maternal uncle, Achille Dupont, as surrogate guardian. Hamard distanced himself, leaving Uncle Gustave to become Caroline's tender and affectionate surrogate father. Life at Croisset soon bored the teenage girl; Uncle Gustave was her lifeline.

He was also her teacher: "It is a joy for me, my poor Loulou, to have given you a taste for intellectual activities. Think how much boredom and nonsense it spares you! But in you I found fertile soil, and it was easy to cultivate it." Aside from the stories and reading with which he delighted her, he took it upon himself to teach her history and geography once she had learned to read and write from Mme Flaubert. Caroline's grandmother also recruited an English teacher to give her English and piano lessons. "My teacher [Miss Isabel Hutton] was not very friendly," writes Caroline; "she was very strict and we did not get along at all. The piano lessons were terrible, she had no patience. . . . I would run to take refuge with my uncle when I was scolded. His big arms opened up to receive me and I leapt into them. We were infinitely tender with each other, which on many occasions led to remonstrances from my grandmother. 'This is ridiculous, Gustave,' she would say. 'You spoil the child far too much.' "[2] Miss Hutton was let go in 1853; Juliet Herbert took her place from 1854 to 1857.

Until she turned seventeen, Lilinne took lessons from her uncle in his study at Croisset, in that den where maps, globes, and puzzles vied with books for her attention. "Once I turned ten, he made me take notes while he spoke. Once my mind was able to understand it, he started to make me notice the artistic side in everything, especially my reading." The passionate young girl adulated her uncle and followed all his advice. He taught her that once you open a book, you have to "devour it in one go" because that's the only way to see it as a whole: "Keep reading the *Histoire de la conquête* [*History of the Conquest of England by the Normans* by Augustin Thierry]. Do not get in the habit of starting to read something and leaving it for a while. . . . Get used to pursuing an idea. Since you are my student, I don't want you to have that *disjointed* aspect to your thoughts, that lack of follow-through, which is the *preserve* of people of your sex. This is some tedious (or *tedious*) advice for you, my pet, that smells of the sheik.[3]—But the letter you sent this morning is so sweet and so well drafted that I can talk to you as though you were a reasonable young man, which is the greatest praise I can give you." Flaubert, or How to Educate Girls.

In matters of religion, Caroline was as pious as the rest of the Flaubert family was indifferent. At nine, she followed tradition and took catechism lessons. As we have seen, Uncle Gustave, far from objecting, encouraged her to take catechism as seriously as her geography classes. "The occasion of my first communion was one of great excitement," Caroline writes. "In an environment where religious practice had no place, I felt very embarrassed to devote myself to all that my zeal suggested. I remember pilgrimages I invented into the orchards; I walked to the top of our property barefoot, on a deserted path that ran next to an old wall halfway up the hill, and in my bedroom I had a little chapel full of tiny candles I lit to say my prayers. My uncle was very tolerant—he never said anything about my feelings and never hurt them. I think he saw a certain poetry in them, which fit my age. It was entirely different with my uncle, Dr. Achille Flaubert. I was terrified to see him come to dinner on a Friday: when my two eggs [fasting menu] appeared, he never missed an opportunity to make one of those jokes that chilled me and that would have been enough to prevent me from liking him, even had I not had other reasons to do so later."[4] Despite the fact he was a nonbeliever, Gustave even agreed to accompany his niece to Sunday mass in Vichy while his mother stayed in her room.

The adolescent girl also took drawing lessons, and her surviving portraits show an obvious talent. She soon fell in love with her teacher, Johanny Maisiat, a painter twenty-two years her senior. In Paris, he took her to the Louvre; at Croisset, he had her admire the beauty of the landscape and the effects of the light. These extended times spent alone together awakened the young girl's first romantic feelings. Alas: "When I was about to turn eighteen, I was offered a suitable, honorable—in a word, bourgeois—marriage. It was as though I had been thrown off Parnassus."

Did Mme Flaubert and Gustave worry that the teacher and his student were becoming too intimate, that a passing romance could end up with a proposal? However much Gustave liked Johanny, he certainly did not think of him as a good match. The threat of a dalliance with the drawing teacher may have precipitated Mme Flaubert's desire to marry off her granddaughter.[5]

A Bourgeois Marriage

A young man had noticed Caroline at her cousin Juliette Flaubert's wedding to Adolphe Roquigny. His name was Ernest Commanville, and he was the twenty-nine-year-old son of a wood merchant. After confiding in his friend Roquigny that he found Caroline to his liking, he was encouraged to approach her. Commanville made an offer of marriage, Mme Flaubert agreed; as for Caroline, she was not charmed by him. She found her suitor quite handsome, tall, with good manners and nice eyes. Only his forehead "marred his head, it bulged above the eyebrows." A dapper-looking gentleman who had assets was not to be discounted, but Caroline did not feel attracted to him; her initial instinct was to say no. After meeting Ernest twice, she confided in her Uncle Gustave that she still wasn't sure. He answered her from Paris on December 23, 1863:

> So, my poor Caro, you're still in the same uncertainty, and perhaps now, after a third meeting, you've advanced no further? It's such a serious decision to make that I'd be in exactly the same state of mind were I in your pretty skin. Look, think, explore yourself heart and soul; try to discover whether this gentleman can offer you any chance of happiness. Human life feeds on more than poetic ideas and exalted sentiments. But on the other hand if bourgeois existence kills you with boredom, what to do? Your poor grandmother wants you to marry, fearing to leave you alone in the world, and I too, dear Caro, should like to see you united with a decent young man who would make you as happy as possible. The other night, when I saw you crying so bitterly, your distress nearly broke my heart. We love you dearly, my darling, and the day of your marriage will not be a merry one for your two old companions. Little jealous though I am by nature, I shall begin by having no liking for the fellow who becomes your husband. But that's not the question. As time goes on, I'll forgive him, and I'll love him and cherish him if he makes you happy.

Though he claims that he can't "pretend to advise" her, Uncle Gustave soon shows the direction in which he is leaning:

What speaks well for M. C[ommanville] is the way he has gone about things. Moreover, we are acquainted with his character, his background and connections, things it would be next to impossible to know in a Parisian milieu. Here in Paris you might perhaps find young men who are more brilliant; but charm—*l'agrément*—is almost exclusively the property of Bohemians. Now the idea of my poor niece being married to a man without means is so dreadful that I won't consider it for a moment. Yes, my darling, I declare I'd rather see you marry a millionaire philistine than an indigent genius. For the genius wouldn't be merely poor; he would be brutal and tyrannical, and make you suffer to the point of madness or idiocy.

Flaubert, who had spent years describing the slow agony of Emma Bovary, trapped in a bourgeois marriage, overwhelmed by loneliness among people who are her intellectual inferiors, reacted to this situation just like any of the good bourgeois folk he loathed would have done. This despite the fact that he had allowed his contempt for the bourgeois existence that "kills you with boredom" to show at the beginning of his letter. When all was said and done, he considered that the most important foundation was to have material security, comfort, and enough money to maintain a certain standard of living. In referring to more "brilliant" people, Gustave may have been thinking of his friend Johanny Maisiat, the painter that Caroline liked, who was almost certainly penniless. This horror for the "bohemian" is a good example of Flaubert's famous remark: "Live like a bourgeois, and think like a demigod."

Caroline had told her uncle that she would be bored living in Rouen, where she would have to settle if she married Commanville. Gustave sought to reassure her:

The bugbear of living in Rouen has to be considered, I know; but it's better to live in Rouen with money than to be penniless in Paris; and for that matter why shouldn't you move to Paris later if the business goes well?

I am like you, you see; I don't know what to think; I keep saying white one moment and black the next. It's hard to see straight in questions that concern one too deeply.

Yet he picked up his earlier argument: "It will be hard for you to find a husband who is your superior in mind and upbringing. If I knew one who had those qualifications and met all other requirements I'd set off and secure him for you very quickly. So you are faced with having to take a young man of good character who is nevertheless inferior. [Oh Emma!] But will you be able to love a man whom you'll inevitably look down on? Will you be able to live happily with him? That's the whole question. You'll doubtless be badgered to give a quick answer. Don't do anything in a hurry. And whatever happens, my poor Loulou, you know you can depend on the affection of your old uncle, who sends you a kiss."[6] Despite Flaubert's apparent perplexity, the wisdom of nations looms over his words: security first!

Caroline answered him by return mail. She was still in a state of uncertainty, still having the same thoughts: "This state of indecision cannot go on, I'm told it's starting to be known in Rouen; and I'm frightened to think that within a few days I will have to say yes or no. Certainly M. C (since that's how you refer to him) has a lot of things in his favor, we played some music together yesterday, he is a good musician. . . . While chatting with me, he told me that he had taken lessons with Bouilhet. I really wish you would talk to Bouilhet about him. See what he says about him, if he considers him an intelligent fellow; maybe Bouilhet won't remember him?"

She needs to know more, to ask around: "I'm ridiculous," she writes, "to make inquiries all around, but I'm so scared, so scared to make a mistake. And to leave you, dear old man, is an idea that makes me very sad. But you would still come to see me, wouldn't you? Even if you found my husband too *bourgeois*, you would still come to see your Lilinne? You would have a room in my house, with the kind of big armchairs you like."

One can feel that Caroline was on the verge of giving in to her grandmother's pressure. Finally, she said yes. Yet according to the rules, her suitor now had to ask her father, Émile Hamard, for her hand in marriage. Mme Flaubert wrote to Maître Fovard, the family notary in Paris, to inform him both of the intended marriage and that Caroline was leaving her eight-hundred-franc pension to Émile Hamard, which would serve to "properly" clothe her father; in addition, "we will rent him a furnished room, in a respectable hotel and the next time we come to Paris, M. Commanville will personally come to propose. Before then I hope you will be able to get Hamard to consent, by making a case for all the advantages his daughter will have by marrying a man who is rich, loves her, and accepts her without a penny."[7]

We do not know whether Commanville went to see the spruced-up Hamard; in any case, Caroline's father gave his power of attorney to Fovard to draw up the marriage contract.

There was a brief commotion at Croisset when it was thought that Commanville was not Ernest's real surname. In fact, his name was Ernest-Octave Philippe *dit* Commanville ("known as" Commanville). Yet through an oversight, his birth certificate did not include the surname "Philippe," which led the Flauberts to worry that Ernest was an illegitimate child. Having been notified, Caroline's paternal great-uncle Achille Dupont, her surrogate guardian, came to tell Caroline's grandmother that she had been hasty in choosing a husband for her granddaughter. From Paris, Gustave wrote to find out more: "All I understand is that Achille Dupont threw a fit in front of our poor old lady?" (January 26, 1864). Eventually everything was straightened out, and the name "Philippe" was added to the birth certificate by a judgment of the civil court at Le Havre on January 6, 1864.[8]

"Let's hope," Gustave wrote to Caroline on February 1, 1864, "that all our agitation is over and that calm will follow the storm." The future bride had become reconciled to her fate: "Not only did my fiancé pay a lot of attention to me, but I had suddenly become an important person for the entire family. I was stunned by the errands to run, the people to see, the things to decide: renting a house, buying furniture ... I admit that I developed a taste for receiving beautiful white bouquets sent from Paris every week with the fashionable florist's stamp. M. Commanville was open-handed, he acted generously. I was interested in my new situation. I was also occasionally a little thrilled to feel a man in love with me by my side, though deep down my heart still ached."[9]

On April 6, 1864, Caroline married Ernest Commanville. The newlyweds immediately left for Italy on their honeymoon. On the surface, everything seemed to be going well, but Flaubert was unaware of a dark secret that would cast a shadow over the marriage and which Caroline later revealed in her volume of memoirs, *Heures d'autrefois* [*Hours of Yesteryear*]. Caroline writes that she did not want children, though she does not say why. Her reluctance may have been due to her mother's death from puerperal fever shortly after giving birth. Another family incident, the death in childbirth of her great-grandmother, Mme Flaubert's mother, may have added to her fears. Infant mortality rates were particularly high at the time, and maternal mortality following childbirth was significant.[10] She may also not have wanted children because she wanted to avoid sexual relations, particularly with a man she did not love. We'll never really know the reason. In any case, she had told her grandmother that she refused to become a mother and had asked her to inform her fiancé. She may have been playing her last card with this request. If so, it was a failure: Mme Flaubert "smiled," she writes, "at what she must have considered a little girl's nonsense, yet promised to deliver this strange message. Some time later, I asked if it was agreed. 'Don't worry,' she answered, 'everything will be fine.'" In fact, her grandmother had not said a word to Commanville, which would later spark her granddaughter's resentment: "My grandmother was certainly an honorable and very distinguished person. How could she have acted so irresponsibly? How could she not have better understood the child she had raised? How could she not have balked before the responsibility of marrying me off, given such evidence of my absolute lack of love for my fiancé and my total lack of understanding of the duties of marriage? It is truly painful for me to criticize her memory, yet I have to state the extent to which I was sacrificed in the most important act of a woman's life, for it explains many events that would be incomprehensible without this first tragedy of my soul."[11]

There was no sex education for young girls at the time, even in a family of doctors. Husbands were left to initiate their wives. One can only imagine the young husband's surprise, disappointment, and bitterness when Caroline confessed at the beginning of the honeymoon that she did not want children.[12] Additionally, since the young woman had, as she writes, "a total lack of understanding of the duties of marriage," we can guess how the couple started out. Caroline is too discreet in her memoirs to tell us herself, but we know that in the nineteenth century the wedding night often turned into a nightmare. In *Une vie* [*A Life*], Maupassant describes the trials his protagonist Jeanne experiences when she finds herself alone in a room with her husband Julien, despite the fact that she loves him. Shortly before the wedding night, her father has tried to prepare her: "There are mysteries that we diligently hide from children, especially from girls, girls who must remain pure in spirit, irreproachably pure until that time when we put them in the arms of the man who will look after their happiness. He will be responsible for lifting the veil on the sweet secret of life." Jeanne does not understand a thing her father says; when Julien tries to take her, she wants to run away, "to lock herself up somewhere, far from this man."

What happened between the newlyweds in Italy? All we know from Caroline's account is that they clashed and that the honeymoon did nothing to awaken love in her heart. "The first time I felt the chasm between us was the day after we began our life together. As we were going up the Saint-Gothard [Pass], I admired the appearance of three *pifferrari* [wandering pipers from Abruzzo] who were begging at the door to the coach. I saw all the poetry of Italy and Antiquity in them. They are 'revolting vagabonds,' my husband interrupted; he refused to go any further. That was the chasm."

Gustave Flaubert knew nothing of this failure and bitterness. Driven by pride, Caroline kept up appearances. From Croisset, Gustave wrote to his niece on April 11: "So, my poor Loulou, my dear Caroline, how are you? Are you happy with your trip, your husband, and your marriage? How I miss you! And how I'm eager to see you and chat with your sweet self." On April 14: "It was about time your letter arrived, my dear Caro, for your grandmother was starting to lose her mind, despite the fact that we explained that the mail needs time to bring your news. There was nothing to be done, and if we hadn't gotten some today, I don't know how tomorrow would have gone. . . . You seem to be enjoying yourself, my poor Loulou? I would have liked to see you on a sled and on a mule! . . . But what interests me more than your trip is your P.S., namely that you really like your companion and that you're getting along well. Keep that up for another fifty years and you will have done your duty." In another letter written that April, Flaubert told his old friend Ernest Chevalier how pleased he was by Caroline's marriage: "I will tell you that my new nephew seems like an excellent fellow and that he adores his wife. That's the important thing. As for his profession, he has a mechanical sawmill in Dieppe, and brings in wood from the north, which he sells in Rouen and in Paris. He is highly regarded by the bourgeois as an honest man and a competent man in his business."

Once they returned from Italy, Caroline and Ernest moved in to a home at 9 quai du Havre in Rouen on April 23. They would later live in Neuville, near Dieppe, next to Commanville's sawmills. After a joyless childhood, Flaubert's niece entered a dreary matrimonial existence. Her uncle had no idea, for she continued to "put on an act of conjugal bliss."[13]

Unbeknownst to him and despite his best intentions, Flaubert had caused his beloved niece's unhappiness by joining his mother in pushing her to marry. After using all her authority to make the union happen, Mme Flaubert had purposely neglected to inform Ernest Commanville of her granddaughter's wish not to have children. Caroline's situation gives a stark picture of the misfortunes sometimes brought on by bourgeois marriages. On the one hand, there was the concern of parents eager to marry their daughter to a man suitable "in every respect," without any thought given to the young woman's deep feelings. On the other, there was the lack of communication between the betrothed; they required a go-between, who could be unreliable. Discretion has left us with no information about the sexual relations between Caroline and Ernest, but we can imagine his frustration and her discomfort. Divorce was prohibited. They had to resign themselves to live side by side, and they never had children. Though he was psychologically astute when it came to Emma Bovary, Flaubert did not realize what was afoot. Appearances were kept up. Under *household*, the *Dictionary of Accepted Ideas* warns: "Always speak of it with respect."[14]

Flaubert liked his nephew Ernest Commanville. He thought he had a good head on his shoulders, to the point that he decided to entrust Ernest with managing his fortune. Knowing his niece as well as he did, how could Flaubert have let himself be deceived? He probably did not want to know too much. Barely a year later, Caroline fell in love with Baron Ernest Leroy, the prefect, whom she had met at a ball in his home. Flaubert noticed that his niece and the baron were becoming closer: "Are you still delighting the salons of Rouen in general and of his honor the prefect in particular? The prefect in question seems charmed by you," he wrote her in February 1867. In April 1867, he wrote, "I know . . . that you are still adorning the prefect's soirées." For years, Caroline was enchanted by Leroy's attentions, the meetings, bouquets, and romantic messages. She found her admirer "without beauty" but with "intense eyes, a pale complexion, an irresistible face, as they say in novels."[15] Caroline assures us that this relationship never came to adultery: "The idea of being the cause of despair to the three people I considered myself as belonging to—my husband, my uncle, and my grandmother—prevented me from running away with the man I loved." At least she experienced some sweet comfort: "I was no longer alone." But in July 1872, the baron died. Caroline fell sick and was advised to take the waters at Luchon, where she was accompanied by her uncle. Here, he finally learned what had happened: "He learned of my pain," she writes. "I confessed everything to him, and he understood how little happiness there was in my union with M. C[ommanville] and to what little extent he cared for what was in my mind and heart."

More than ever, Caroline could be glad that she had a "good nanny," as she called her uncle. Nonetheless, in her case the fierce opponent of the bourgeoisie had conformed to the prejudices of a class that he loathed but that remained his own.

CHAPTER 16

The Hermit in White Gloves

When Gustave originally left for Paris to study law, he did not see himself as a social climber, like Balzac's Rastignac. Yet two decades later, the success of *Madame Bovary* and *Salammbô* had made him into a leading literary figure who was often in the papers—and not only for his books. Though he did not live extravagantly and continued to spend most of the year at Croisset, where he wrote, he began to extend his stays in the capital. He rubbed shoulders with the literary lights of the time and tried out society life at the salon of Princess Mathilde, cousin to the emperor. The hermit could now be seen in a black suit and white gloves.

The expenses associated with the life of a socialite or semi-socialite, the beau monde and the demimonde, dinner with friends at fine restaurants or at home, keeping a servant in a rented apartment, and taking occasional trips (to Baden, or to London to see Juliet), as well as those required for his new novel, soon exhausted the ten thousand francs that Flaubert had made on *Salammbô*. In February 1865, Gustave asked his friend and notary Frédéric Fovard for "a few effigies of the monarch in order to: 1. pay off my debts, 2. live in peace for a while, without thinking about damn money." Mme Flaubert was alarmed by "Gustave's position." The same month that Gustave asked Fovard for money, she wrote to the notary to tell him that her son had asked her for seven thousand francs. She alluded to the farm at Courtavant, which could be sold, but "this would take a few months, supposing we found a buyer." She added: "Also, if he collected his share of the proceeds on the farm, I fear that it would quickly be absorbed." She told Fovard that she counted on his friendship "to help us get your poor friend out of this tight spot."[1] In a letter dated the following March 2, she wrote to Fovard: "Gustave's affairs are putting me in a very difficult situation, for I cannot do without the 6 or 7 thousand francs he needs without overly depriving myself." Before she traveled to Paris, she asked Fovard to take stock of the bills from Gustave's suppliers and to put Courtavant up for sale. On April 7, Gustave sent Fovard a recap of his debts: he owed 2,728 francs to Touzan, the upholsterer who had redone his study at Croisset; 1,883 francs to Marguillier, his tailor in Paris; 498 francs to Guy, his glove merchant; and 500 francs to various other suppliers. The total came to 5,609 francs. Over the following days, he begged Fovard "to take care of everything": "There is nothing more tiresome than constantly asking my mother for money. Try to convince her that I do not engage in wild debauchery! Alas, I wish I did; I'd be more cheerful. And since she's decided to pay my debts, let her do it properly, *properly*, without too much recrimination."

Now forty-four years old and a famous writer, Flaubert was still living hand to mouth. This was partially a result of maintaining what he considered his honor, a stance made possible by his mother's generosity: he still refused to compromise his pen in journalistic activities, the kind of work that kept many of his fellow writers from ruin. Him, a mercenary pen? Never! Yet while he claimed that he didn't "engage in extravagant spending" and that his life was hardly all "fun and games," he maintained a certain standard of living, confessed to allowing himself certain "excesses," and only paid attention to his finances when his creditors raised the alarm. He asked Fovard to appeal to his publisher, Michel Lévy, a task he preferred not to do himself: "Try to get a *bonus* out of him, old man (honestly, he owes it to me), and failing that, an advance."[2] He told his faithful friend Jules Duplan that he could turn to his brother Achille, who would give him money right away: "But that's precisely what I don't want to do." Finally, Michel Lévy loaned him five thousand francs. And then too, the family had a significant amount of property, which led him to write to George Sand that he did "not have what are called money worries. My income is very limited, but secure."[3] It was just that he was a little short from time to time—small cash flow problems, which did not prevent him from offering his financial help to Sand. She declined, but thanked him "for the kind thought."

Other than these private difficulties, Flaubert was now on the same level as the writers who were the talk of the town. His circle grew beyond his old and dear friends Louis Bouilhet, Ernest Feydeau, and Maxime Du Camp: aside from Théophile Gautier, he befriended Hippolyte Taine and became close to Ernest Renan, whose scandalous *La Vie de Jésus* [*The Life of Jesus*] had led him to be dismissed from the Collège de France. He also became close friends with George Sand and met Ivan Turgenev (whose name he spelled Tour-gueneff) and Frédéric Mistral. When in Paris, he took over from Aglaé Sabatier's salons, hosting dinners every Sunday.

In the years following the release of *Salammbô*, he was fairly close with Michelet, who continued to send him his books. Flaubert never failed to respond with a token of his admiration: "You leave an indelible mark on everything you touch."[4] He went to see the great historian with the Goncourt brothers, whose *Journal* includes a description of "the big, bourgeois, nearly working-class house" of the man they called the "sleepwalker of the past": "On the third floor, a small door with a single panel, like a shopkeeper's door. A maid opens the door, announces our presence, and we waltz in to a little study."[5] Michelet invited the trio to his Thursday night soirées, where guests squeezed into the small study and could meet scholars such as Renan and the chemist Marcellin Berthelot. "This whole crowd of republicans and liberals," wrote the Goncourts, "look like professors: you'd think you were at a soirée at the home of the head of an academy in the provinces." Flaubert admitted to his friend Edma Roger des Genettes that he did not like all of Michelet's works: "The *Bible de l'humanité* [*Bible of Humanity*] is a bad book because the structure is vague, and because the author discusses a heap of things about which he knows nothing, starting with India. . . . What is atrocious about this latest book is the fragmentary approach, the lack of connections between ideas, the lack of proof beneath the facts." To the author, he sang a different song: "I have just read this marvelous book straight through, in ten hours. It has laid me out flat. Yet I think I clearly understand it as a whole. What breadth! What a circle! . . . What isn't beautiful in your work? Heart, imagination, and judgment, you shake everything inside us, with your powerful, delicate hands."[6] This show of hypocrisy was rare for Flaubert, who was ordinarily so frank. Like Victor Hugo, Michelet was a sacred cow; he could not be attacked.

Late in 1862, Flaubert's literary socializing began to focus on the Magny dinners, which were becoming a veritable institution on the Paris literary scene.

Dinner at Magny's

We do not know exactly who came up with the idea for the Magny dinners. It may have been the physician François Veyne, who treated the illustrator

Paul Gavarni and was a friend of the Goncourt brothers. In any case, the dinners began to be held in the fall of 1862 at the Café Magny, 3, rue de la Contrescarpe-Dauphine (now rue André-Mazet). Sainte-Beuve had become a regular at Magny's when he was appointed the librarian of the Bibliothèque Mazarine. The restaurant was owned by Modeste Magny, a restaurateur from the Champagne region who had apprenticed with a top local chef and was said to have invented "tournedos Rossini" and the Chateaubriand steak. The prestigious Joanne travel guide rated it one of the finest restaurants in Paris. Guests at the dinners ate in a private room, far from indiscreet ears. The fortnightly gatherings, initially held on Saturdays and later on Mondays, were successively known as the atheists' dinner (Barbey d'Aurevilly denounced them for being served "against God"), the Magny dinners, and, for a short time, the Gavarni society.

Paul Gavarni—whose real name was Guillaume Chevalier—was a well-known illustrator who had depicted the world of students, bohemians, and kept women in satirical magazines like *Le Charivari*. He had become famous for his illustrations in the weekly *La Mode* and was now nearing sixty. As the Goncourt brothers' former teacher and good friend, he frequently visited them at their apartment on rue Saint-Georges. By 1862, he had stopped drawing. His health was failing, and he had become bitter. It appears that Dr. Veyne, known as the "bohemians' doctor," dreamed up these regular dinners to entertain him.[7] The Goncourts' *Journal* serves as a chronicle of these meals held for writers and some of their friends, allowing an inside view of this society, to which new members were recruited by co-optation. Flaubert participated as of the second dinner, held on December 6, 1862; he was a regular whenever he was in Paris. At Magny's, Flaubert was exclusively in the company of men until George Sand joined in 1866. Members included Sainte-Beuve; Gavarni; Dr. Veyne; Philippe de Chennevières, a museum curator and future director of the École des Beaux-Arts; Charles-Edmond, a Polish refugee whose real name was Chojecki but who used only his first name for his books and articles; the theater critic Paul de Saint-Victor; Frédéric Baudry, a librarian at the Bibliothèque de l'Arsenal; Eudore Soulié, curator at the Musée de Versailles; Taine; Renan; Princess Mathilde's lover, the sculptor Émilien de Nieuwerkerke; Théophile Gautier; Auguste Nefftzer, a journalist and founder of the daily *Le Temps;* Marcellin Berthelot; and, of course, the Goncourt brothers. Sainte-Beuve established himself as the most commanding member of the assembly by a kind of birthright (he was fifty-eight in 1862), but also because he was then the most famous: he was a member of the Académie, the historian who had written *Port-Royal,* and the reigning authority on the literary scene with his famous Monday columns in *Le Constitutionnel.* Sainte-Beuve was overbearing and inclined to ranting. His head was stuffed with colorful memories, and he was eager to let loose and put down the greats. According to him, Balzac was "not real," Hugo was just a "joker," and Michelet was merely a hack who wrote schoolbooks. If Flaubert pleaded for Michelet or Hugo, Sainte-Beuve pounded his fist on the table, despite the fact that it might irritate his "inflammation of the joints."

The Goncourt brothers hated Sainte-Beuve and his bald man's skullcap, his "schoolboy outbursts," and his fits of anger and nostalgia: "The swollen head resulting from a deprived childhood, the libertinism of an old man who gets irritated and excited, the hot flashes and hallucinations of a diligent and hemorrhoidal scholar."[8] Gautier derisively called him "dear uncle" or "Uncle Beuve." Flaubert could easily have been tempted to scoff at the man who had panned *Salammbô,* but although he quibbled with him, he was never as hostile as the Goncourt brothers, who called him a "conversation sucker," a "bidet listener," a "confidant eager for quarrels," which he then used in his articles, and a man "who hid beneath beds to take notes for his memoirs." Some of the Goncourts' more substantive grievances against Sainte-Beuve would be repeated by Proust in *Contre Sainte-Beuve* [*Against Sainte-Beuve*]: "When discussing a book, his responses are never about the book, but always about the man—his connections, his position, and the role he played." He was also power-hungry and did not hide his desperate desire to be appointed to the Senate, where he would be paid thirty thousand francs to "properly look after a little woman, double his secretary's wages, and pay his governess's thousand *écus* of debt."

The violence of the Goncourts' criticism tells us a great deal about these dinners, where open fury vied with homicidal thoughts. At this table, Flaubert was one of the nice fellows, like Théophile Gautier, who could rant and rave without slandering anyone. Most of the time, there was little room for politeness in the Magny style of conversation. Coarse language abounded. While literature and fine arts were frequently on the agenda, there was nothing the assembled liked better than talk of women, love, and prostitution. "Thereupon Flaubert," the Goncourt brothers write, "with his face flushed and his eyes rolling, proclaimed in his booming voice that beauty was not erotic, that beautiful women were not meant to be bedded, that the only useful purpose they served was inspiring statuary, and that love was born of that mysterious element which was produced by excitement and only very rarely by beauty. He expatiated on his ideal, which turned out to be the ideal of an ignoble Turk. Chaffed about it, he went on to say that he had never really possessed a woman, that he was a virgin, and that he had used all the women he had had as the mattress for another woman, the woman of his dreams."[9]

The dinner in question focused on copulation and its necessity, giving rise to contradictions, swaggering assertions, and twisted but eloquent proofs. The scholar Taine discoursed on all this "like a Scottish preacher," always "English and Protestant." Théophile Gautier boasted that he had fathered seventeen children. Sainte-Beuve pounded his fist on the table, as usual, and declared that he liked filth. Saint-Victor was indignant about "the depilation of Oriental women." Nineteenth-century woman was in for a rough time at Magny's, whether it was through torrents of eloquence, explorations of sexual infernos, bragging contests, the constant harping of the sexually frustrated, or hymns to a future Eve.

One could count on similar verbal jousting if talk turned to religion and God; yelling contests broke out, and violence rubbed shoulders with science. "In the heat of the arguments and yelling, Taine gradually seems to take on a nearly fantastical appearance," the Goncourt brothers wrote. "He looks like an idea of Kant's embedded in a tale of Hoffmann. And he manages, in a frightening, supernatural way, to become so grotesque it's nearly threatening, with his blue glasses throwing thunderbolts and seeming to have become his real eyes." Naturally, Ernest Renan cannot help but join in the argument that is rattling the silverware. While apparently cowering, Renan has been paying close attention. He calls for order in his thin voice and dares to declare before his stunned colleagues that he admires Jesus Christ and that only one thing is true and beautiful in this world: holiness.

Despite the pervasive materialism of the age and the fact that most members were proud atheists, some diners were frightened if the number of people around the table ended up being an unlucky thirteen. Saint-Victor was particularly superstitious: he would not even consider staying if the dread number came up. There was an easy fix, however: they brought in Magny's son to be the fourteenth guest. The fact that he was a high school student did not stop them from "chatting about Hugo's copulations." Even that was subject to debate. While one guest said that Hugo was a stud, Sainte-Beuve—who had been Mme Hugo's lover—asserted that he had once been to a brothel with Mérimée, Musset, and Hugo, but that Hugo, with his military decorations and his brandenburgs (ornamental lapel trimmings), did not go up to a room. "The girls said: 'He's a young officer having a hot flash.'"

Though the diners were often sharp-tongued, the tone sometimes shifted to a confessional mood: people opened their hearts and revealed their melancholy. Despite their dislike of Sainte-Beuve, the censorious Goncourt brothers were briefly touched by the deep sadness the critic displayed when he spoke of his loneliness and ugliness and his desire to be handsome and seduce women. Yet they could not help but conclude that "there is a melancholy, disappointed satyr at the bottom of that little old man."[10] They were no more indulgent with Flaubert, despite the fact that he was a faithful and devoted friend to them. In their view, he was nothing but a provincial, puffed up with pride, stringing one incongruity after another, each more clumsy and tiresome than the last. There is something barbaric about this man, they wrote, who dreams of "heroic, savage times, tattooed with intense colors and loaded with cheap jewels." They portrayed him as a Viking on the loose from his longboat.

While the Magny diners did not talk much about politics, they could not ignore the legislative elections of June 1863. The opposition was making headway, particularly in the cities. In Paris, the nine deputies elected were all in the opposition, including eight republicans and Thiers, a proclaimed liberal. As proper reactionaries, the Goncourt brothers considered that "any government that reduces the number of illiterate people is going against its own principles." Flaubert missed the heated discussion at Magny's that day because he had accompanied his mother and niece to the spas of Vichy, where he did not make the slightest comment on France's political future. He was "outrageously" bored until he received Feydeau's new novel *Le Mari de la danseuse* [*The Dancer's Husband*] and turned to dissecting it in a long letter to Feydeau. Vichy was no fun, and neither was Croisset. Paris was so much more enjoyable! But Flaubert had the determination necessary to leave the bustle of the literary world and "slog away like a bear," far from the Paris scene.

Flaubert continued to attend the Magny dinners, but by their third year these noisy feasts had started to bore the Goncourt brothers: "We are beginning to feel contempt and disgust for the Magny diners. To think that this is the gathering of the freest minds in France! Certainly, they are mostly, from Gautier to Sainte-Beuve, talented people. But what a dearth of their own ideas, of opinions made with their own nerves and sensations! What a lack of personality, of temperament!" Edmond and Jules were nothing if not killjoys.

Evenings with the Princess Mathilde

There was no need for white gloves at the Magny dinners, but Flaubert's Parisian outings did not stop there. Beginning in January 1863, he became a regular at Princess Mathilde's salon. Mathilde, who was the daughter of the emperor's cousin Jérôme Bonaparte and the sister of Prince Napoleon, had married a Russian prince and separated from him four years later. She prided herself on her interest in art and literature and had established herself as a patron of writers, whom she invited to her home on rue de Courcelles or to Saint-Gratien, her summer home near the Lac d'Enghien. The Goncourt brothers, who had sent her their *Femme au XVIIIème siècle* [*Woman in the Eighteenth Century*], had begun attending her soirées in December, while Flaubert was still battling *Salammbô*'s critics. On January 21, 1863, the Goncourts brought Flaubert to meet the princess, who had loved his latest novel.

The princess entertained with her lover, Émilien de Nieuwerkerke, and her personal reader, Mme Defly, by her side. She showed her visitors the studio she used to paint watercolors, which was full of baubles. A casual, free-spirited woman, she was bursting with curiosity and had a talent for putting her guests at ease, asking about their work and sharing her opinions on the latest artistic and literary doings. While the Wednesday evening soirées were often intimate, Flaubert found a large crowd (at least one hundred and fifty guests) on his first visit with the Goncourt brothers. The guests wore breeches and silk stockings rather than trousers and included the emperor, who looked a little gloomy. Prince Napoleon was there, discussing the Roman Question concerning papal power, as were various ministers and newspaper editors. The party was in full swing. "The three of us," the Goncourt *Journal* reports, "form a group of oddballs. We are about the only three people who aren't decorated. And looking back at the three of us, I can't get it out of my head that we three were taken to court for offenses against public decency by the government run by that man there, by the justice system headed by the emperor sitting right there, whom we're practically rubbing elbows with. How ironic!"

And what about Flaubert? According to these two wicked tongues, he was bursting with vanity: "The empress spoke to him, she asked him for Salammbô's costume for a ball . . . , and he tells me he is planning to have made for himself a pair of tight breeches in the court style, like those the guests usually wear here." Clearly, the hermit was dazzled; he would be back. He would be invited to more intimate soirées, where conversation loosened up and the hostess theorized about art and literature. Flaubert returned with the Goncourt brothers and Sainte-Beuve on February 11.

In November, the prince—casually known as Plon-Plon—invited Flaubert to the Palais-Royal. The prince was seen as representing the progressive wing of the imperial family. As a deputy under the Second Republic, he had sat with the extreme left. As an anti-clericalist, he had defended the principle of Italian unification and stood up to Empress Eugénie, a staunch Catholic who worried about the pope. Since 1859, Napoleon III had been allied with Piedmont-Sardinia in support of the Italian national movement. His armies had defeated Austria at the battles of Magenta and Solferino, which had brought criticism from Catholics. The emperor later advised the pope to give up some of his states, which Pius IX refused outright. Ultimately, France received Nice and Savoy in exchange for allowing Piedmont to annex central Italy. The two areas' inhabitants confirmed the annexation with a plebiscite in 1860. But the Roman Question had not been settled. When Flaubert first set foot in the home of the emperor's cousin Prince Napoleon, who had ostensibly espoused the Italian cause by marrying Marie-Clotilde, daughter of Victor Emmanuel II, King of Sardinia, the imperial family was divided, with some joining Eugénie in supporting the pontifical party, while the others sided with Plon-Plon and favored Italian unification. Flaubert, who was not very involved in political issues, became friendly with the prince, encountering him not only at his home in the Palais-Royal, but at the apartments of his mistress Jeanne de Tourbey. In a letter to Caroline in December 1863, Gustave marveled that the prince called him "dear friend." Some time later, he was delighted to have attended the Opera Ball "in a grand imperial box" with Prince Napoleon and the ambassador of Turin. On May 15, 1865, Prince Napoleon made a major liberal speech at the inauguration of a statue of Napoleon I in Ajaccio. The Court was not pleased. From Croisset, Flaubert wrote to Jeanne de Tourbey: "Yesterday morning I read a truly beautiful speech, which moved and filled me with enthusiasm. It is beautiful and good, brave and true, elegant and sensible. You must be proud and happy." The emperor made his disapproval known, Plon-Plon replied in *La Presse*, and Flaubert expressed his delight in another letter to Jeanne de Tourbey: "I am very proud that such a man shakes my hand when I meet him." Flaubert reported that he was "flattered and touched" that the prince had sent him a printed version of his Ajaccio speech: "To have thought of me from a distance is a charming courtesy." Yet his ties with the prince did not make him any less cordial with the empress: in November 1864, during a visit to the imperial palace in Compiègne, he asked his trusty friend Jules Duplan to order a bouquet of white camellias, "the finest possible; I insist that it be ultra-chic. (One has to cut a fine figure when one belongs to the lower orders of society.)"[11]

In June 1867, he was invited to the great reception that Napoleon III held at the Tuileries for the Universal Exposition: "The sovereigns," he wrote to his niece, "desire to see me as one of France's most splendid curiosities, so I am invited to spend the evening with them next Monday." Flaubert's irony does not mask his pride.

The princess brought Flaubert into Napoleon III's circle of influence. Dinners at rue de Courcelles were interspersed with stays at Saint-Gratien, where he worked hard to show himself in a good light. Flaubert began a correspondence with Mathilde, who clearly reciprocated his friendship. On one occasion, she tells him she has sent one of her watercolors to Croisset, but that the package seems to be lost. He searches Rouen's train stations and finally unearths it. Thank you! Thank you! "I have just hung it on my wall," he writes, "in front of my desk, between a bust of my sister by Pradier and a mask of Henry IV, in dear and illustrious company, as you see." Was Flaubert in love? Could Mathilde have had a weakness for him?

The question did come up. In fact, the Goncourt *Journal* contains one or two allusions to the matter. On April 26, 1865, they report that the princess "only has eyes, a seat next to her, attention and interest for Flaubert. . . . Might she desire to take [him] as a lover?" In his preface to *Lettres inédites à la Princesse Mathilde*, a collection of Flaubert's letters to the princess published in 1927, Count Joseph Primoli describes a scene at Saint-Gratien between "Matho" (the hero of *Salammbô*) and Mathilde:

> The door opens: Matho comes in slyly, more like a shy schoolboy than a conquering warrior. . . . Without saying a word, he watches her work. . . . The princess feels this passionate gaze moving over her neck, her shoulders, her hand and ... she waits ... After a long silence, annoyed by the insistent gaze, she abruptly raises her head: "Well? What do you have to tell me that's so confidential, so pressing? We're alone, just as you wanted, and I am ready to hear everything." How astonished she is to see him turn very pale, then

bright red. The most diverse expressions pass over this distraught face: fear, anxiety, terror, despair ... Is he still haunted by the evocation of Matho? She hears him stammer a few incoherent words, then sees him hurriedly stand up, head for the door, and run away.[12]

A sentence in one of Flaubert's letters to Mathilde seems to confirm that his feelings for her were more than friendly: "I have embarked on it [the new novel] to make people take pity on these poor misunderstood men and to prove to ladies how shy they are."[13] Yet none of this adds up to conclusive proof. Make of it what you will.

The princess knew how to be useful to her friends and did not hesitate to intervene with the authorities on their behalf. In September 1864, she did everything she could to help Sainte-Beuve get his coveted appointment to the Senate; the appointment was made in April 1865. The great critic now had an opportunity to change some of his political positions. While he had previously been a conformist, his guaranteed income now allowed him to risk defending liberal ideas in the Senate, much to Flaubert's delight.[14] The princess also interceded with the minister of education, Victor Duruy, to have Flaubert awarded the Legion of Honor. The writer accepted without any qualms, though he would continue to proclaim that "honors dishonor." He told all and sundry that what he liked about receiving the red ribbon was "the joy of those who love me." A familiar tune, but readers of *Madame Bovary* may recall the last sentence of the novel, which underlines the irony of Homais's triumph: "He has just been awarded the cross of the Legion of Honor."[15]

What had become of the fierce, uncompromising Flaubert, the writer who ripped into the bourgeois, the solemn and important people, the suppliants, and the assistants to the assistants of power? Perhaps because he had so long repressed his desire for fame and recognition, once success came he felt that he was not betraying himself by accepting its social dividends. The lure of literary socializing had combined with a secret yearning for glory. Under this imperial regime where everything trickled down from the top, his friendship with Mathilde, her interest in him, his immoderate desire to please her, and his fascination with luxury finished off what remained of his spirit of sedition. The readiness of Flaubert and the Goncourt brothers to oblige the imperial regime is neatly summed up in a remark Edmond de Goncourt made to Princess Mathilde in 1874: "Oh! Princess, you don't realize how helpful you were at the Tuileries, how many hatreds and angers your salon defanged, what a buffer you were between the government and those who wield a pen ... As for Flaubert and me, if you had not bought us, so to speak, with your grace, your attention, your friendship, we would both have been violent critics of the emperor and the empress."[16]

Yet Flaubert did not become a servile soul. Maxime Du Camp reports that at the Château de Compiègne, Flaubert defended the shunned and exiled Hugo, a leading enemy of the usurping emperor: "Into that submissive and blinkered world," Du Camp writes,

> he carried the spirit of literary independence that was in him more than in anyone else. One evening, in the empress's private circle, someone spoke irreverently of Victor Hugo. I do not know if these words expressed a sincere conviction, or if they were merely an attempt at flattery. Gustave Flaubert intervened without moderation: "Stop right there! That man is the master of all of us, and one should only speak his name with respect." The person who had spoken insisted: "But won't you agree, Monsieur, that the man who wrote *Les Châtiments* ..." Flaubert, his eyes blazing, cried: "*Les Châtiments!* There are magnificent verses in it; I can recite them to you if you like!" It was not considered appropriate to continue on this path; the discussion was interrupted and one of the assistants hastened to take the conversation in another direction.[17]

"Les Bichons"

From 1860 to 1865, Flaubert's most intimate friends in Paris were Jules and Edmond de Goncourt. Edmond, the elder, was born in 1822 and was thus an approximate contemporary of Flaubert; Jules was born in 1830. Until Jules's death in 1870, the two brothers operated as a single person, signing their literary works with both their names, writing their *Journal* together, living and socializing together, and sharing a mistress: a rare twinning in French literary circles. They had met Flaubert in 1857, the year of *Madame Bovary*'s publication, at a time when they themselves had not yet published a significant book. They initially considered him a teacher, but eventually came to see him as a rival. As fellow worshippers at the altar of literature, the three men quickly became close. Beginning in 1860, the trio was inseparable whenever Flaubert was in Paris. Although the brothers began visiting Princess Mathilde before Flaubert did, the three of them were soon regular attendants at her salons, as well as at the Magny dinners. The brothers were always at Flaubert's Sunday dinners on Boulevard du Temple, Flaubert was often their guest at rue Saint-Georges, and the three of them frequently crossed paths at the homes of friends such as Théophile Gautier.

Yet their personalities were strikingly different. The brothers whom Flaubert referred to as his *bichons*—after the toy dog breed—were delicate creatures who were concerned with artistic ornamentation and collected knickknacks and autographs, whereas Flaubert, as soon as he left his hermitage, became a booming companion, demonstrative and assertive, who was not afraid of a crude joke. In the *Journal*, the Goncourts refer to him as "provincial," an insult coming from Parisians, and describe him as a "barbarian" with a "bellowing voice" and a "wild extravaganza of gestures." Flaubert confided in them about his childhood memories, the invention of the Garçon, and his affair with Louise Colet. The brothers' *Journal* is peppered with notes and anecdotes about their friend, many of which are mean-spirited, in contrast to the friendly, playful tone of his letters to them. They speak of Flaubert's "immense, secret pride," and the way in which he "quietly pushes himself forward, establishes relations with important people, creates a network of useful acquaintances, all the time pretending to be independent, lazy, and fond of solitude" (November 23, 1862).[18] One always senses a bitter tone between the lines, even when they are admiring.

While the brothers' jealousy was undeniable, so was their friendship. They often write "the three of us," as if Gustave were the third brother: "The three of us, who are melancholic," "the three who would ask not to be born," "the three of us who hold literature above all else." The Goncourts and Flaubert even consulted each other about their manuscripts. But were the brothers sincere? Flaubert was quicker to show his enthusiasm, even when he expressed reservations, as was typical of him in commenting on his friends' works. As for the Goncourt brothers, although they genuinely admired the author of *Madame Bovary*, they didn't hold back on criticizing him in their *Journal*. "*Salammbô* does not come up to what I had expected of Flaubert." It is "inflated, melodramatic, declamatory, luxuriating in over-accentuation."[19] When he read them the *féerie* he had recently written with Louis Bouilhet, *Le Château des coeurs* [*The Chateau of Hearts*], they tore into it behind his back. Was the friendship lopsided? One might come to that conclusion from reading the *Journal*, in which bottled-up criticism sometimes explodes into violent diatribe. Nonetheless, the Goncourts considered Flaubert their teacher and their ally: "With Gautier," Jules wrote to Gustave, "the three of us are the bastion of Art for Art's sake, of the morality of Beauty, of Indifference to politics—and of skepticism when it comes to joking. But everyone else attacks us! We need you in every respect."[20] They dedicated what they considered their most "personal" book, *Idées et sensations* [*Ideas and Sensations*], to Flaubert, who was delighted by this tribute.

The Goncourts and Flaubert had a mutual need to see each other, to share ideas and read each others' work. Flaubert wrote the brothers that "being in Paris without my *Bichons* seems bizarre to me, and leaves me *unhinged*." In October 1863, they finally accepted his invitation to come to Croisset. Their account of the visit remains the most detailed description of Flaubert's retreat:

> We find ourselves in this study devoted to stubborn, tireless work, a place that has seen so much toil and out of which came *Madame Bovary* and *Salammbô*.
>
> Two windows look out on the Seine with a view of the water and the boats passing; three windows open onto the garden, where a beautiful arbor seems to shore up the hill rising behind the house. Between the latter windows, oak bookshelves with helical columns are connected to the big bookshelf, which spans the entire back of the room. Facing the view of the garden, against white paneling, a fireplace is surmounted by a yellow marble clock, with a bronze bust of Hippocrates. Next to that, a bad watercolor, a portrait of a languid and sickly English girl whom Flaubert knew in Paris [Gertrude Collier]. Then box lids with Indian drawings, framed like watercolors, and the etching by Callot, a *Temptation of Saint Anthony*, which hang there like images of the master's talent.
>
> Between the two windows overlooking the Seine, on a square case painted bronze, there stands the white marble bust by Pradier of his dead sister, with two long ringlets, a pure and firm face that looks like a Greek face in a keepsake. Next to it, a daybed, consisting of a mattress covered by a Turkish fabric and loaded with pillows. In the middle of the room, close to a table with an Indian box decorated with colorful drawings and a golden idol on top of it, is the work table, a large round table with a green cloth, where the writer takes ink from an inkwell in the shape of a toad.

They note "a bric-à-brac of Oriental things: amulets with the green patina of Egypt, arrows, weapons, musical instruments, a wooden bench on which the people of Africa sleep, cut their meat, and sit, copper trays, glass necklaces, and two mummy feet that he tore out of the caves of Samoun, putting themselves in the midst of his papers with their Florentine bronze hue and the frozen life of their muscles. This interior is the man, his tastes and his talent: his true passion is for that vast Orient. There is something of the Barbarian inside this artistic nature."

While the portrait of Flaubert in the *Journal* shifts with the writers' moods and is added to, rectified, and clarified with every encounter, it is never truly flattering. Yet there is no doubt that the Goncourts viewed Flaubert as a major contemporary writer. He was also a dear friend whom they could count on in tough times. His loyalty was never clearer than when their play *Henriette Maréchal* was performed at the Théâtre-Français late in 1865. From Croisset, he carefully followed the ups and downs of rehearsals, soothed the authors' anxieties, sent his encouragements, and shared in their joy at staging their work. He was in the minority clapping and cheering while the rest of the audience for the public dress rehearsal heckled and booed. The youth of the day did not attack the play itself—which, incidentally, did not deserve much praise—but its authors, who were guilty of associating with those in power. The uproar continued over the following performances. Saint-Victor denounced a cabal in *La Presse*. Having returned to Croisset, Flaubert wrote several times to defend them: "Goodbye, my poor dear old friends. How tired and irritated you must be now! But, goddamn it, you are good fellows. You can say that to yourselves in the silence of your study.—And ours is a beautiful trade, after all, since it makes everyone furious, including the 'youth of the day.'"

When orders were finally given to shut down the production of *Henriette Maréchal*, the Goncourts suspected the decision came from the empress, who was jealous of Princess Mathilde, to whom they had made a rousing tribute in the preface to the printed version of the play published shortly before the ban: "What is really real about all this," they wrote to Flaubert, "is that we've had our neck broken by a very great lady of your acquaintance, who, according to what is currently being said in Paris, is jealous of the princess's salon." Early in January, they left their home at rue Saint-Georges for Le Havre. On the 6th, they dined with Flaubert at Croisset. "He really does work fourteen hours a day," they wrote in the *Journal*. "This isn't work, it's a Trap-pist monastery."

There is no doubt that the Goncourts saw Flaubert as a "thoroughbred" writer. Yet there was something about him that frightened them, something one might refer to as his *excesses*. There was his excessive approach to work, as they wrote, but also his excess of fancifulness, his resounding verbiage, banter, and contradictions. By calling them his *bichons*, Flaubert was affectionately underlining their differences in temperament. While warm feelings were gen-erally not the Goncourts' forte, and denigration was their second nature, their friendship with Flaubert was active and lasting. He merely treated them with a generosity that they were unable to reciprocate.

CHAPTER 17

Monseigneur

As Flaubert came and went from Paris throughout the 1860s, an important figure began to recede from his life: Louis Bouilhet, his best friend and alter ego. Bouilhet had left Paris to settle in Mantes in 1857, after Michel Lévy published his long poem *Melaenis* in book form. He had achieved recognition in Paris with his play in verse, *Madame de Montarcy*. But though the play had been much applauded during its run at the Odéon, it had been a struggle to get there—how many arias he had written before finally succeeding! Supported by Flaubert, his indefatigable advocate with theater managers, he had previously sustained two flops in a row and had grown discouraged by the time La Rounat, the Odéon's new manager, offered him his stage. Dropping everything, Flaubert took charge and, as excited as he was imperious, appointed himself the director of rehearsals. Maxime Du Camp describes the scene in his *Souvenirs littéraires:*

> He would stride across the stage, having the actors repeat the monologues, indicating the gestures to make, setting the tone, placing and replacing the characters, addressing everyone from the prop collectors to the actors, the prompter to the stagehands, in the familiar form; his storming presence filled the theater; he couldn't have worked harder to make Bouilhet's play a success if it had been his own. He had understood that this was a desperate game, and that if the play fell, Bouilhet fell with it, or rather fell back into provincial life, into Latin lessons, into moral poverty and discouragement.
>
> He was admirable in his ardor, devotion, and even skill, for despite the exterior ferocity of his nature, it was not for nothing that he was born in Normandy, and he did not lack for subtlety. Influential critics were courted, and young people from the schools, who were sometimes a formidable audience, were befriended; nothing was left to chance, and Flaubert relentlessly applied

himself to the task. Bouilhet allowed it to happen; he followed Gustave like a shadow, approved, but did not feel reassured.[1]

On November 6, 1856, Bouilhet attended the opening of his play in a state of extreme anxiety. Suddenly, he left the wings and dragged a friend outside to confide that he was panicking that the play would be a disaster, that he would be booed, and that he would have nothing left to do but throw himself into the Seine. He returned to the theater to an unhoped-for ovation for *Madame de Montarcy* and its author. The play was performed seventy-eight times—Bouilhet could claim victory. Yet in May 1857, he left Paris to settle in Mantes. Life in Paris was expensive, theater was at best an unpredictable source of revenue, and Bouilhet was fundamentally a pessimist. In Mantes, where he rented a small house and made a living as a tutor, he could be reunited with his companion Léonie Leparfait, who had stayed in Rouen, and Philippe, the son she had had with Philippe de Chennevières. He promised himself to lead the simple, quiet life needed to write. And since he was midway between Paris and Croisset (Flaubert and Louise Colet had had several rendezvous in Mantes), he told himself he wouldn't be separated from his dear Gustave. They would indeed see each other often, whether in Flaubert's hermitage, in the capital, or in Mantes. Most importantly, they would regularly write each other long letters in which they would continue to help each other with their work.

Once he settled in his retreat, Bouilhet got to work on the "modern" play, *Hélène Peyron*, while Flaubert was deep in *Salammbô*. The two friends encouraged each other. Gustave and his intimates had nicknamed Bouilhet *"Monseigneur"*—"your Grace." Caroline writes that the name referred to "his elegant appearance and his slightly sanctimonious manner." The idea might have come to Flaubert after a masked ball to which Bouilhet had worn a cassock. In any case, *Monseigneur* became common usage in Flaubert's circle, and Bouilhet took to using the name to sign his letters to Gustave, whom he in turn addressed as *"mon cher Vicaire général"*—"my dear Vicar general." Their bond never slackened. Flaubert had explained it to Louise Colet some ten years earlier: "In our respective work, we are like a kind of railroad indicator to each other, holding out an arm to show that the way ahead is the right one and that we can follow it."[2] Louis always told Gustave of his theatrical projects but also often moaned and groaned about being blocked, unleashing a veritable litany of complaints: "I'm at an absolute low"; "I'm singing an old tune nobody wants to hear"; "I wish I were dead"; "I've reached the lowest level of despair and discouragement"; "I feel like I'm stuck with an inescapable fate and relentless bad luck"; "I'm disgusted with myself"; "In fact, I would be so happy if I could promptly croak, and without pain, yes indeed!" Flaubert shook him out of it however he could, spurring him on, reassuring him, and kidding him in terms so unceremonious that he sometimes regretted his bluntness. He told his niece Caroline that he had had to apologize to him: "I had become like the vicar general shaking his bishop!" When Flaubert himself experienced similar fits of hypochondria and spleen, Bouilhet would faithfully reinvigorate him. Their correspondence is a constant exchange of complaints and encouragements: "My dear old man," Bouilhet wrote to Flaubert on October 22, 1864, "if ever our complete correspondence were to fall into the hands of a stranger, he would find in it a rather sad exchange of pain and despair. When one of us stops moaning for an hour, the other howls, and it's been this way for twenty years, which hardly suggests a shared foundation of wild cheerfulness. Indeed, we are not cheerful, but we should not have chosen this fatal profession, the most horrible one I know. As for changing our habits and our lives now, we should not think of it. We need to go forward, as you so aptly say, until death."

First and foremost among the pains discussed were the difficulties of their profession. For Louis, it was finding a good subject for a drama or a comedy and, once he had that, bending over backward to get the play staged: offering it to a theater, enduring one rejection after another, and then, once the play was accepted, making the corrections and changes requested by the theater; convincing the best actors; listening to the censor's opinion ("the voice of the official responsible for public decency, charged with making sure we don't cause people in this brothel we call a theater . . . to get too many hard-ons");[3] and, finally, attending the opening all atremble, hoping that favorable reviews would allow the play to run for a while. When Bouilhet was panned, his friend was there to comfort him: "Keep going, old man, listen to no one and follow your path."

For Flaubert, "the pangs of style" far exceeded the mania for research: he puffed and panted, struck a passage, rewrote it, wrote twenty pages to keep three sentences, searched for the elusive *mot juste*, wore himself out whittling down his sentences, rewriting his chapters, and rereading them aloud in his *gueuloir*, where he was rarely happy with the results. "You're still engaging in your unbridled search," Bouilhet told him, "that's very beautiful, but damn it, doctor! ... These long nights of work stir the blood, you'll give yourself pimples! Going to bed at six in the morning! ... It makes me shudder; do you want to destroy your temperament?" His words fell on deaf ears. At Croisset, Gustave was chained to his new novel, relentlessly pushing on: "Goodbye, dear old man," he wrote his friend, "it is nearly four in the morning. Which means I've had an eighteen-hour work day. That's reasonable. With that, I'm going to bed and sending you my best."

The two friends kept each other posted about their physical ailments: endless colds, bad flu, and above all, countless boils. They were also not prudish about discussing more intimate disorders. In March 1867, when Bouilhet wrote that there was pain and swelling "in Monseigneur's left testicle," Flaubert delivered his diagnosis: "Regarding monsieur's sicknesses, Cloquet, whom I had palpate my balls, claims I have a sickness 'common among ecclesiastics.' The remedy is to make your sprinkler spout." Bouilhet later replied that "the pain in my testicle comes and goes, I wore a supporter, which helps a lot." It was easier to discuss the body's aches and pains than the sorrows of the heart.

From his refuge in Mantes, Louis reproached Gustave for hanging around in Paris too much: "The more you go, the more you like society. I've developed in the other direction. Though I never liked it much, I now loathe it. You're concerned with Paris; I'm not. I know one always winds up there. But it's not on the sidewalk that we'll have any of our great days of old, Karaphon!" (Karaphon was one of Bouilhet's affectionate nicknames for Flaubert.) Gustave rejected Bouilhet's point. Didn't he spend most of the year at Croisset, quill pen in hand? Louis did not mean to offend him: "I'll start by sending you my apologies if I expressed myself so poorly that you thought that I found your life since 1851 too *sociable*. I simply wanted to say that your aspirations and desires toward high society are far stronger now than they were in that fabulous time when Du Camp was pressuring you to come live in Paris and you told him to take a walk."[4]

Bouilhet was not wrong. Part of Flaubert's life was now caught up in the capital, in salons and dinners—even if it was only for three or four months a year. Perhaps Monseigneur would have traveled to the city to visit his friend more often, but he did not have the means: "You always tell me, go to Paris, be there, put pressure on people, harass society. I have only one answer for you, but it is without appeal: 'I don't have the money, I don't have the means to go to Paris for eight days, because I barely have enough to live on until the end of the year.' I only tell you that so you'll stop accusing me of apathy and laziness in my working life. What I do, I am forced to do. That's all."[5]

Yet he sometimes had to resign himself to making the trip—his plays demanded it. He often stayed in Flaubert's third-floor apartment on Boulevard du Temple, which gave the two friends a chance to "get together a little more." Gustave took the opportunity to drag Louis to visit his friends at the home of Théophile Gautier or the Goncourt brothers or at the Magny dinners. Whenever Bouilhet's plays opened in Paris, Flaubert rushed from Croisset to distribute tickets to his friends and clap until his hands turned red. In the absence of his bishop, the vicar general hustled to defend Bouilhet's interests to the power players in the theater business, for there were always retractions, promises that needed to be refreshed, and all sorts of negligence. Each drama or comedy accepted was a victory, but nothing was guaranteed.

On Sunday, October 28, 1866, on the eve of the opening of *La Conspiration d'Amboise* [*The Ambois Conspiracy*], Flaubert introduced Louis Bouilhet to Princess Mathilde at her salon (naturally, she had an invitation to the opening). The Goncourt brothers were there too, as usual, and as usual they did not miss an opportunity for some backbiting: "Today Flaubert brought Bouilhet along to present him to the Princess. I cannot imagine what unfortunate inspiration that poet had had at lunch, but he stank like an omnibus! Coming upstairs, Nieuwerkerke said with a shudder: 'There's a writer down there who reeks of garlic!' The Princess for her part scarcely noticed it, and then only after everybody. It is amazing how imperceptive that woman is about so many subtle things, like the freshness of butter or fish! The best thing and the worst thing about her is that she is not entirely civilized."[6] The *bichons* just couldn't help themselves—they had to yap!

But most of the time Flaubert and Bouilhet got together at Croisset, just as in the old days, spending hours reading and rereading their manuscripts. In this era dominated by the *école du bon sens* (school of common sense) identified—and derided—by Baudelaire and represented by playwrights such as Eugène Scribe, François Ponsard, and Alexandre Dumas fils, Louis Bouilhet's theatrical career went against the tide. He remained faithful to the tradition of Victor Hugo and the historical drama in verse, which was seen as passé and dismayed theater managers by its reliance on sumptuous costumes and costly sets. Under Flaubert's influence, Bouilhet had given up on his juvenile Romanticism, his royalist and religious fervors, and the idea of the poet's social mission; he had converted to Art for Art's sake and the theory of impersonality. Clearly, Flaubert had more influence on Bouilhet than the reverse. He had convinced him to abandon the subjective, personal, sentimental literature to which he was originally devoted. The essential thing, Flaubert had taught him, was to describe "shared feelings" rather than telling autobiographical tales. Bouilhet's first major poem, *Melaenis,* which was inspired by Ancient Rome, was a forerunner to the poetry of Parnassians such as Charles-Marie Leconte de Lisle and José María Heredia. In 1854, he had published a "scientific poem," *Les Fossiles* [*The Fossils*], in the *Revue de Paris.* Flaubert had corrected the poem, and Gautier had encouraged the poet. Flaubert later described *Les Fossiles* as "the only scientific poem in all of French literature that remains poetry." With his attention to style and precise descriptions, his taste for history, and his relentless toil, Bouilhet was following in Flaubert's footsteps. He also provided his friend with the resource of his non-negligible critical faculties. A marvelous listener, he would identify all of Flaubert's wrong notes, lapses in taste, and syntactic errors. As Bouilhet advises in his *Art poétique* [*Poetic Art*], "Choose a solid and salutary critic." Flaubert was lucky to know him. Upon Bouilhet's death, he wrote, "I feel like I have suffered an amputation.—A big part of me has disappeared."[7]

Le Château des Coeurs

In the 1860s, Flaubert and Bouilhet also returned to the idea of working on a joint project. While he was still hesitating between several subjects for a novel, Gustave felt his old itch for the stage and suggested to Louis that they collaborate on a play in the then-popular theatrical genre of the *féérie,* in which fantastical, often supernatural subjects were given spectacular staging. During his stay in Vichy in the summer of 1862, Flaubert read many volumes of fantasy plays while taking a break from correcting the proofs of *Salammbô.* The form of the *féérie* was several centuries old and had been practiced by no less an artist than Shakespeare; it provided an opportunity to mix poetry and comedy, fantasy and drama. Flaubert's idea was to renew the tradition by taking the *féérie* in the direction of social satire: the bourgeois, always and forever down with the bourgeois! To do so, he would need Bouilhet's dramatic technique and trade secrets. While Bouilhet was open to Flaubert's offer, he suggested that it might be useful to invite a third party to participate in the collaboration. He was thinking of their friend Charles d'Osmoy, a witty fellow Norman, slightly younger than they were, whom they nicknamed the Idiot of Amsterdam. Though he was "tormented" by his Roman play *Faustine,* Bouilhet set to work on a plot outline in June 1863. He came up with a story in which fairies were deprived of their influence on man for one thousand years "because they had lost some talisman, which had been stolen by their enemies the gnomes." He set up a conflict between the ideal (fairies) and the powers of evil (gnomes), which took place every thousand years: "You understand that with this outline, we can joke with all of society. The gnomes, that is to say the practical and the prosaic, have controlled the world for a thousand years. As is readily apparent. They crushed the fairies during the last contest; that's why we don't find many fairies on the boulevards or even in our woods. Given how light and mobile they are, the fairies live in exile in cloudy, fantastic regions. When they want to come down to earth, which has been invaded by evil instincts, they can only come to the polar extremes or the unknown depths of Africa. This cannot go on any longer. Fairies love the earth. They were made for this planet. They want to reign here again."

Flaubert approved of this starting point. After they discussed and fleshed out the project, Bouilhet found the scheme that would provide their *féérie*'s title: "I will give the gnomes a vampire's instinct, I will suppose that their evil power needs *men's hearts* to feed and sustain itself. So the gnomes spend their time cheating humans, stealing their sensitive organ." Yet these mortals whose hearts have been ripped out are not dead, for the gnomes have outfitted them with an ingenious mechanism that makes blood. Bouilhet explained: "The *féérie*'s driving force will therefore be, not the search for a talisman, but the search for the place, like a warehouse, where the gnomes keep men's hearts, that is to say everything they had that was noble and good. From time to time they eat some, which does not make them better beings, because they do it out of irony and meanness." The idealistic protagonist Paul is on the verge of suicide when the Queen of the Fairies promises him that if he can deliver the hearts of men that are locked away in the gnomes' castle, she will give him "a love beyond the greatest dream."

The playwright got started with a first scene, which he described in detail in a letter to Gustave. The novelist replied with some objections. In late June, d'Osmoy agreed to collaborate on the play. Louis and the new recruit immediately began writing a full plot outline. It was understood that Flaubert would write the prose, while Bouilhet and d'Osmoy would take care of the verse, the poetry, and the ariettas. It was also agreed that "the fairies' goal was to find the hearts to give them back to the men." The scenes came in rapid succession as bourgeois idiocy was attacked and Paul was swept up in a multitude of twists and turns. After numerous trials, he managed to deliver the hearts. In reward he received the love of Jeanne, which was promised to last for eternity.

During the summer of 1863, Flaubert set to work on his scenes full of enthusiasm and optimism, while Bouilhet presented the scenario to Fournier, the manager of the Porte-Saint-Martin theater. Fournier returned the manuscript: "Would you believe," Bouilhet wrote to Flaubert, "that he's had enough of *fééries* because he loved them too much and like all excessive people he now abhors them." But neither Louis nor Gustave allowed himself to be discouraged: "We've started it, we have to finish. And once the play is written from start to finish it will undoubtedly have a better chance than in its current state, which is neither fish nor foul." On October 19, Flaubert told the Goncourt brothers that he had just finished *Le Château des coeurs* [*The Castle of Hearts*]. Characteristically, he added: "And I am *ashamed* of it. It seems like a vile, filthy thing." On October 26, he wrote to his regular correspondent Amélie Bosquet that "the absolute lack of distinction, an indispensable aspect for the stage, may be responsible for this lamentable impression. The play is not poorly made, but so empty! All this in no way dampens my hopes of success; on the contrary, it's a reason to believe in it. But I am interiorly humiliated: I made something mediocre, inferior."

The Goncourt brothers were called to the rescue. They showed up at Croisset on October 29 and stayed until November 3. Gustave and his brother Achille came to meet them at the train station and brought them to Croisset by carriage. The next day, Gustave read them his *féérie*—"a work," they wrote, "of which, in my esteem for him, I thought he was incapable. To have read every *féérie* only to write the most vulgar of all!" There is no record of what they told him, but it seems likely they expressed some gentle reservations. In any case, Gustave wrote to Caroline two weeks later that he felt it was "not working at all," contrary to the opinion of his two collaborators, with whom he squabbled "very intensely." He rewrote the end, which he declared "excellent." At the beginning of December, he traveled to Paris at the same time as Bouilhet, who was there to attend to his play *Faustine*. A copy of the *Château* was given to Hostein, the manager of the Théâtre du Châtelet. The newspapers got involved, mentioning the *féérie* and predicting it would be a success. Yet upon reading the manuscript, Hostein judged that it would be too expensive to stage. It was passed on to Noriac, the manager of the

Variétés theater. Victory! On January 26, 1864, Uncle Gustave told his niece: "The *féérie* is accepted. Rehearsals will begin in July, the stage has to be expanded etc., etc. Next Monday we have to fix a heap of things in the play." Alas! In March, the three authors learned that despite his promises, Noriac had changed his mind. "After holding on to the manuscript for two and a half months, they noticed that their stage was too small."[8] The authors had to resign themselves to the fact that *Le Château des coeurs* would not be performed. In 1880, a few months before his death, Flaubert would publish an illustrated version of the *féérie* in the short-lived periodical *La Vie moderne*.

The Last Glimmers of a Friendship

The warm reception given to the opening of Louis Bouilhet's new play *La Conjuration d'Amboise* at the Odéon on October 25, 1866, helped Flaubert get over the failure of *Le Château des coeurs*. Once again, he had rallied every last one of his friends. The play was a solid success: it was performed 105 times in Paris and toured extensively in the provinces, including to Rouen in December. It was even staged for the emperor and his family in the theater at the Château de Compiègne. In seventh heaven, Bouilhet wrote to Flaubert on December 1: "The papers all reported a huge success at Compiègne. I think that will give the box office a second wind in the coming days." The exhausted and delighted playwright was even introduced to Princess Mathilde.

Louis's joy was short-lived. In February 1867, he learned that his mother had died in Cany, where she lived with his two sisters. Bouilhet's relationship with his mother had always been tense. As a strict Catholic, she did not appreciate his anticlerical leanings, disliked his theater milieu, and reproached him for living with Léonie outside of marriage. Despite it all, Louis saw his mother and sisters quite regularly. Upon her death, he told Flaubert he was experiencing "a nearly physical pain, like a load of my entrails had fallen out." He rushed to Cany and organized the funeral. As he wrote to his friend, "the gentlemen ecclesiastics weren't too intolerable. On the other hand, you wouldn't believe the suppliers' greed. The candle merchant's bill, incredible! The demands of the home nurses, etc. My mother wasn't even buried yet when women selling mourning goods were knocking on the door, trying to beat each other to the sale."[9]

Despite his theatrical successes, he continued to be nagged by money problems. That spring, the death of the director of the Rouen municipal library in

April brought hope that Bouilhet might be able to put an end to his life of hardship in Mantes. If he were appointed as the librarian's replacement, he would be able to quit tutoring. While there was no lack of competition, the mayor of Rouen, Verdrel, assured Bouilhet that he had his support. He was told he needed a few recommendations from high up. Bouilhet thought of Princess Mathilde and Minister of Education Victor Duruy. Flaubert got to work. Bouilhet was appointed to the position on May 2, 1867, and took up his post on the twentieth. Now he was back in Rouen, not far from Croisset. Gustave was delighted: "Bouilhet's post brings him four thousand francs a year and lodging. Now he need no longer think of 'earning his living'—true luxury."[10] After the two friends started seeing each other more often, they came up with the idea of writing a farce called *La Queue de la poire de la boule de Monseigneur* [*The Stalk of the Pear of the Ball of His Grace*] about an archbishop's gluttonous exploits. But Flaubert, who hosted Bouilhet at Croisset every Sunday, noticed that his long face had returned. He was going in circles trying to find the subject for a new play. Flaubert turned to his friend Jules Duplan: "I'm not happy with Monseigneur. He seems very sick to me, but I couldn't say in what way. He coughs often and gasps continuously, like a whale. Add an invincible sadness. Monseigneur is turning to hypochondria, and the animal has more talent than ever! He writes superb self-standing pieces of verse, but cannot find a subject for a drama. That is what distresses him. He badmouths everyone." A long-overlooked text by Flaubert suggests that their friendship had cooled: "Over the last three years, he had changed, his mood, temperament, and ideas had changed; a certain narrow and provincial side of him had developed." But, he adds, "I had *rediscovered the old him*. The last time he came here, we worked on the last scenes of my novel."[11]

Around this time, Louis Bouilhet was contacted by a young man named Guy de Maupassant. He was the son of Laure, the sister of Gustave's beloved friend Alfred Le Poittevin. Guy was in his final year at the Collège in Rouen, where one of the supervisors had introduced him to Bouilhet's poetry. He decided to go and see him. Since Bouilhet knew his family, the connection was easily made. Soon Guy was showing him his own verse. They were sometimes joined by Flaubert. Bouilhet made Guy work hard; he had found a disciple. In September 1868, Flaubert noted that he had "livened up." He had found his subject and written the first act of *Mademoiselle Aïssé*. The play was finished late in May 1869 and accepted by the Odéon. That June, Flaubert was overjoyed: he and Bouilhet would revise the recently completed *Sentimental Education* sentence by sentence.

But Louis's health was deteriorating. In June 1869, Flaubert wrote to his niece that he found his formerly so cheerful friend "frail and sad." Late that month, Bouilhet left to take the waters at Vichy. "We don't know exactly what's wrong with him," Flaubert wrote to Jules Duplan; "maybe something very serious, for his *hypochondria*—which is total—must have a cause?" Flaubert tormented himself; he thought his friend had albuminuria, "a disease you don't recover from." The doctors in Vichy did not keep Bouilhet; he returned to Rouen and died there on July 18, 1869. Flaubert was overcome with despair. He buried his friend with empty eyes and "sobs in his gut." He described Louis's last moments in a long letter written to Maxime Du Camp five days later:

> I saw Bouilhet every other day and *found him improving*. His appetite was excellent, as were his spirits, and the swelling in his legs was subsiding. His sisters came from Cany to make scenes about religion, and were so disgusting that they shocked a decent canon from the cathedral. Our poor friend was *superb;* he sent them packing, telling them in so many words to go fuck themselves. When I left him for the last time, on Saturday, he had a volume of La Mettrie on his bed-table; it reminded me of poor Alfred reading Spinoza. No priest set foot in his house.
>
> His anger against his sisters was still sustaining him on Saturday, and I left for Paris hoping he might still live a long time.
>
> At five o'clock on Sunday he became delirious and began to compose aloud the plot of a medieval drama on the Inquisition. He kept calling for me, to show it to me, and was enthusiastic about it. Then he was seized with trembling, stammered, "Adieu! Adieu!," burying his head in Léonie's breast, and died very peacefully.[12]

Gustave had just lost his "adviser," his "guide," "an old companion of thirty-seven years." His life was "turned upside down." The deceased received tributes from Théophile Gautier in *Le Moniteur*, Théodore de Banville in *Le National*, and Edmond Villetard in the *Journal des débats*. But Barbey d'Aurevilly pulled no punches in *Le Gaulois:* "Poor Bouilhet will be forgotten once and for all." Flaubert's fervor would give him the lie.

Guy de Maupassant expressed his sorrow in verse:

Poor Bouilhet! Him, dead! So good, so paternal!
He who appeared like another Messiah to me
With the key to the heavens where sleeps poetry.
And now he is dead and forever gone
To that eternal world to which aspires genius.
But from up there, no doubt, he can see and read us
Read what was in my heart and how I loved him.[13]

Flaubert took it upon himself to honor his memory. He began by attending to his final play, *Mademoiselle Aïssé*. After making the necessary changes, he overcame many obstacles and managed to have the play staged in January 1872, with Sarah Bernhardt in the title role.[14] The same month, Flaubert published *Dernières Chansons* [*Last Songs*], a volume of Louis Bouilhet's verse, and prefaced it with a long manifesto on aesthetics. He also fought to have a statue of Bouilhet erected in Rouen. On January 26, 1872, *Le Temps* printed a "Letter to the Municipality of Rouen" in which the writer denounced the municipal officials' disgraceful refusal to finance the projected monument, "an idea for a fountain." The "Letter" was distributed as a brochure by Michel Lévy. When a new municipal council was appointed in 1874, Flaubert returned to the charge and won his case, but work on the monument did not begin until 1880.

Today Louis Bouilhet only lives on in literary culture through his unfailing friendship with Gustave Flaubert. In assessing his friend's work, Flaubert's affection had won out over critical lucidity. But while Bouilhet's dramas and comedies are no longer performed, Flaubert's legacy is inseparable from the man who helped his work take its final shape. These two men who resembled and helped each other and shared a literary ideal have left us with the example of a legendary friendship.

The literary critic Albert Thibaudet said of their relationship: "Friendship is more like love than we think, and in any pair of friends there is usually a masculine value and a feminine value. An artist with feminine nerves, a Bovary with a mustache . . . like Flaubert needs to find in friendship what he lacks, what completes him, and what he envies: that will, that resolution, that masculine solidity that together make men of action." One might question this interpretation based on the determination with which Gustave supported his friend's career in the theater. Louis could lift Gustave's spirits, but the favor was often reciprocated. Theirs was a flawless literary collaboration, grounded in a common aesthetic ideal that was the basis of this unsinkable relationship. They were fond of each other, but would not have had such a solid connection if they had not needed each other for their creative pursuits. The friendship was based on equality, despite the fact that one has been remembered as a master and the other as a minor poet.

In 1912, during a stay at Croisset, Henri de Régnier wrote his own interpretation of the friendship on the first page of a guestbook in the Flaubert home:

Flaubert, Bouilhet, your names are united in glory
For your hearts beat with the same love of beauty.
No matter that as winners of a common victory
To defeat dark oblivion and death without memory
One got the spark and the other the torch!

CHAPTER 18

Frédéric Is Not Me

Sainte-Beuve had recommended it; Flaubert did it. He set to work on a "modern novel," despite how pained he was by his era's triviality. The initial idea stemmed from his adolescent passion for Élisa Schlésinger. Referring to Flaubert's "great love" for Élisa as a passion that transcended the years is both true and false. False, because while the adolescent Flaubert had once been overcome by this impossible love, life had unraveled it. By his own admission, it was over by the time he was twenty.[1] The statement is true, however, if we accept the idea that our former loves endure in our memory. We are no longer in love, but we still harbor an emotion that is always ready to reactivate the old enchantment. In Flaubert's case, there was more at play than the contingencies of his life: he cultivated the memory of this first love and embellished it in order to establish it as the primal scene of his sentimental education. As he wrote to Louise Colet: "People say the first love is the strongest. I remember that one, though it is very ancient history, so old that I have the impression that it was not me who lived it."[2]

After his friend Bouilhet withdrew to Mantes, he learned that "Madame Maurice" might be living there. He asked Louis if he could confirm her presence, to tell him if he had seen her. There would be no follow-up to his request—Louis Bouilhet never encountered Mme Schlésinger. But Flaubert's curiosity has attracted the attention of biographers who wish to draw conclusions from a possible meeting between Flaubert and Élisa at this juncture. Such a reunion, they imagine, could have inspired the poignant scene between Frédéric and Mme Arnoux in *Sentimental Education*'s second-to-last chapter: they had loved each other but could not be together and now it was too late. But this encounter did not take place, either in Mantes or anywhere else: Flaubert did not see Mme Schlésinger throughout the entire period that he was working on the novel.[3]

Thus the starting point for the "modern novel" to which Flaubert dedicated himself after *Salammbô* was the impossible love he first felt for Élisa Schlésinger, née Foucault, on the beach at Trouville, a love whose changing image, enhanced by separation, was never fully erased. Yet the author of *Madame Bovary* was a different man from the young novelist who wrote *Mémoires d'un fou*, which exalted his youthful love through the figure of Maria. He had since developed a theory of impersonality, most clearly illustrated in *Salammbô*. "I am not attracted to anything that has to do with me personally," he wrote Louise Colet.[4] How would he combine an autobiographical project—a conceit he loathed—with the self-imposed precepts of the cool gaze? One solution he found was the use of irony, which allowed for self-detachment.

In 1863, while he was working on *Le Château des coeurs*, Flaubert was still hesitant about the subject of his next novel. He made outlines for two potential stories. One was *Les Deux Commis* [*The Two Clerks*] or *Les Deux Cloportes* [*The Two Woodlice*]—the future *Bouvard and Pécuchet*—and the other was *Sentimental Education*, a title he took from his unpublished 1845 novel. A letter from Louis Bouilhet suggests that by March 1863 Flaubert was leaning toward *Sentimental Education:* "As you say, a story about romantic feeling would be something newer and more successful coming from you, because it would be more unexpected." By April, he could tell Jules Duplan that his scenario for *Sentimental Education* was "beginning to take shape," but added that "its general design is bad! It doesn't form a pyramid! I doubt that I'll ever become enthusiastic about this idea. I'm far from cheerful."[5] In October 1864, he announced to Mlle Leroyer de Chantepie that he had gotten started: "Here I am, harnessed now and for the past month to a novel about modern life, which will be set in Paris. I want to write the moral history of the men of my generation—or more accurately, the history of their *feelings*. It's a book about love, about passion; but passion such as can exist nowadays—that is to say, inactive. The subject as I have conceived it is, I believe, profoundly true, but for that very reason probably not very entertaining."[6]

Flaubert worked relentlessly until May 1869, when he completed the book. Since the novel's central storyline took place from 1840 to the end of 1851, and the love story was closely tied in with historical events, he read countless historical works, period newspapers, and memoirs. As usual, he called on his network of friends and acquaintances to find references, specific details, the perfect little fact, often getting only a few lines out of each inquiry. More than ever before, he wanted to be "real." To achieve his goal, he turned to Charles-

Edmond, Charles de La Rounat, Ernest Feydeau, Maurice Schlésinger, Jules Duplan, George Sand, and the Goncourt brothers. He researched socialism and read the abundant revolutionary literature of the 1830s and 1840s, including works by Fourier, Proudhon, and Louis Blanc. Through George Sand, he contacted the dogged anti-monarchist Armand Barbès to ask about his imprisonment following his arrest after the insurrection of 1839. He traveled to Sens, to see the location where his protagonist Frédéric attends collège; to Creil and Montataire, to find a setting for M. Arnoux's faience factory; to the Hôpital Sainte-Eugénie, to observe children suffering from croup, like Marie Arnoux's son in the novel ("It's abominable and I was sorry to be there. But Art comes first!"); to the Jockey Club, to investigate horse races in Paris; and to the forest of Fontainebleau, to decide where Frédéric and Rosanette would spend a few blissful days of sylvan love. He even asked his friend Jules Duplan what would have been on the menu at the tony Café Anglais on Boulevard des Italiens in 1847. As he wrote to Turgenev, he came to Paris "looking for the most stupid information one could imagine: funerals, cemeteries, and undertakers on the one hand, furniture seizures and procedure on the other, etc., etc." He added: "In short, I am shattered by fatigue and boredom. My endless novel is sickening and stupefying me." The need for accuracy sometimes led him to alter his narrative. For instance, he had initially thought that Frédéric would rush home by railroad upon hearing the news of revolution from Paris, putting an abrupt end to his escapade in Fontainebleau. But when he discovered that the Fontainebleau line did not exist in 1848, he wrote to Duplan, "that makes two passages to take apart and redo." He asked Duplan how one traveled from Fontainebleau to Paris at the time, which section of the railroad existed then, and which stagecoaches were available. Everything that could be verified was verified: he was now a historian of the present.

Yet research was not the most time-consuming task. As with his previous novels, he put most of his effort into finding the right word, the ellipsis that provided the proper rhythm, the novel's color and musicality, the description that finally succeeded. "I know them well, the Pangs of Style!" he exclaimed in a letter to George Sand.[7] These pangs caused a "literary anguish" that his correspondent had difficulty understanding, given how easily writing came to her. He worked night and day. When Sand invited him to Nohant for the baptism of her granddaughters, he declined, despite how much he would have enjoyed himself: "I know myself: were I to come to Nohant I'd spend the ensuing month daydreaming about the visit."[8] His friend was disappointed:

"If it was only to go and have a better time somewhere else you'd be forgiven in advance, but it's just to coop yourself up and make yourself miserable, and all for work that you hate."[9] The book moved forward, stagnated, took off again, until the day came when Sisyphus was finally able to put his quill down on a stack of five hundred pages.

When Flaubert told Mlle Leroyer de Chantepie that he was going to write the history of his generation, was it an autobiographical tale he was thinking of? Yes and no. One can judge from the workbook in which Flaubert wrote the initial scenario for the novel in 1863.[10] On page 35 of notebook 19, one finds:

Maître Moreau (novel).

The husband, the wife, and the lover all love each other and are all cowards.

—Crossing on the Montereau boat, an adolescent student.

—Maître Sch.—Monsieur Sch. Me [*moi*].

—development of adolescence—law—obsession virtuous and reasonable woman accompanied by children.

—The husband, nice, initiating ladies of the demimonde ... —costumed ball soirée hosted by the Présid. *Coup*. Paris ... theater, champs élysées ...

adultery mixed with remorse and terrors. Badmouthing of the husband and philosophical arguments of the lover. ends in a rat's tail. all know their reciprocal position and do not dare to say it to each other.—the feelings end by themselves.—they separate. End: they see each other again from time to time—then they die.

Flaubert would not follow this outline to the letter. His heroine would not be Mme Moreau, but Mme Arnoux; Mme Moreau would be Frédéric's mother. But *Sentimental Education*'s foundation in reality is the trio of Mme Schlésinger, her husband, and Flaubert. His "me" reveals a great deal about the work's autobiographical dimension. At the beginning of the novel, Frédéric is the same age as Gustave was when he moved to Paris to attend the law classes that bored him so much. Gustave fell in love with a married woman, whose physical appearance is similar to that of the novel's heroine: hair in black tresses, charcoal eyes, olive skin. The crucial scene of the main characters' meeting on the Montereau boat, in which Frédéric catches the unknown woman's shawl, is inspired by the scene in Trouville when Gustave moved

Mme Schlésinger's coat away from the rising tide on the shore. Frédéric's life in Paris is like Flaubert's: he visits women of the demimonde and attends society parties and masked balls. Yet Flaubert did not create Frédéric in his image. In his notebooks, he judges the young man quite harshly: "A radical lack of imagination, excessive taste—too much sensuality—no determination—too much daydreaming have prevented him from being an artist." Clearly, this failure would have been unacceptable to Flaubert. In the finished novel, Frédéric is "the weakest of men," and when he tries to write a novel or devote himself to painting or music, he doesn't accomplish anything. The author and his character experience similar situations, but their personalities are different.

Impossible Love

The novel's narrative through line is Frédéric Moreau's love for Mme Arnoux. The sentence "It was like an apparition," which introduces the description of Frédéric's first view of Marie Arnoux, is nothing but a hollow promise. There follow Frédéric's excessively timid approaches, hampered by too many obstacles, toward a woman who may be unhappy in her marriage but whose virtue is apparently unshakable. When Marie realizes that she loves Frédéric, she resists all his advances. When she is on the verge of giving in, her son suddenly comes down with croup and she is unable to go to the rendezvous to which she had consented. Later, there seems to be another opportunity for everything to change dramatically and for Frédéric to become Mme Arnoux's lover, but his mistress Rosanette barges in unexpectedly and separates them. Flaubert had changed his mind since writing the initial scenario: "It would be stronger," he wrote in notebook 19, "not to have M. Moreau fuck, and by being chaste in his acts, he would be consumed with love.—She would have had her moment of weakness that the lover had not seen, that he had not taken advantage of." In fact, in the novel, Frédéric is unable to "take advantage" of the moment because the occurrence of an unforeseen circumstance strikes like a twist of fate: a child's illness prevents him from acting. And when Mme Arnoux visits Frédéric years later, a psychological and moral prohibition makes their love impossible once and for all:

> Frédéric suspected that Madame Arnoux had come to offer herself to him; and once again he was filled with desire, a frenzied, rabid lust such as he had never known before. Yet he also had another, indefinable feeling, a repugnance akin

to a dread of committing incest. Another fear restrained him—the fear of being disgusted later. Besides, what a nuisance it would be! And partly out of prudence and partly to avoid degrading his ideal, he turned on his heel and started rolling a cigarette.[11]

Unattainable love is one of the great themes of Romanticism. Flaubert sometimes worried that readers would find too many similarities between his novel and Balzac's *Le Lys dans la vallée* [*The Lily in the Valley*]. In that novel, Mme de Mortsauf experiences a similar reciprocated but impossible love with Félix de Vandenesse. Both women are good Christians, as well as a little superstitious, and they see their children's illnesses as "a warning from Heaven." Yet the irony with which Flaubert depicts Frédéric's great love clearly differentiates *Sentimental Education* from *Le Lys dans la vallée*'s sentimental mysticism. As we have seen, Flaubert was a romantic soul in his youth, but now his novel filled the romantic mold only to show that it was an illusion.

André Vial has pointed out the parallels between *Sentimental Education* and Sainte-Beuve's *Volupté* [*Sensuality*].[12] The latter novel also features a weak-willed young man, Amaury, whose romantic life is divided between four women, including Mme de Couaën, an ideal woman, like Mme Arnoux, for whom one loses one's self in dreams. However, Amaury eventually finds peace on the path to God, while Frédéric will never be saved from his dreary existence.

Of all the characters in *Sentimental Education*, Mme Arnoux is probably the flimsiest. She speaks little, and when she does it is primarily reported in indirect speech. She has only a few appearances in the novel, unlike her husband, who is nearly omnipresent. Frédéric clings to Arnoux to feel closer to his wife; Arnoux is Frédéric's friend, benefactor, and intercessor. To have the icon speak would be to make her common; she has no grand ideas about art and politics, and what little conversation she does make always returns to "the eternal subject of complaint: Arnoux." As refined as an essence, she is raised by Frédéric and his dreams "to a position outside the human condition." Was that not the very place occupied by Élisa in Gustave's memories?

Venal Love

The first scenario of *Sentimental Education* gives the following description of Frédéric: "Not daring to declare his love, he throws himself on the demimondaines." In the novel, the demimondaines are represented by Rosanette, whose nickname, "the marshal," is reminiscent of Aglaé Sabatier as "the president." Flaubert also took character traits from other women of easy virtue, including the actress Suzanne Lagier, Pradier's wife Ludovica, and probably Eulalie Foucaud. These "lorettes" were a well-defined social type described by Baudelaire: "Gavarni created the Lorette. To be sure, she did exist before him, but he perfected her image. I rather believe it was he that coined the word. The Lorette, as has been said before, is not the kept woman, the social phenomenon of the Empire, condemned to live in a funereal tête-à-tête with the moneyed corpse, general or banker, she battened on. The Lorette is a free agent, comes and goes as she pleases, keeps open house, has no master, mixes with artists and journalists, does her best to be witty. I have just said that Gavarni added the final touches to her image; and indeed, carried away by his literary imagination, he invents at least as much as he sees, and for that reason he has greatly influenced manners."[13] While the grisette works as a milliner or seamstress, the lorette lives exclusively off her charm. Once she achieves a certain reputation, she can allow herself to pick and choose her lovers, to dismiss those who tire her, and to conduct several amorous transactions at once. This is the case with Rosanette: when Frédéric meets her, she is Arnoux's mistress, but she is kept by old Oudry, and then by a Russian count, and she denies herself nothing and no one. Gavarni described the behavior of women like Rosanette in the satirical magazine *Le Charivari*. In a drawing he made in 1841, a lorette is having her hair done when her chambermaid announces: "It's the little man with curly hair, I told him, 'Madame is not here' … He's waiting." To which the lorette, who does not want to see the little man with curly hair that day, replies: "Tell him Monsieur is here." The name *lorette* came from the Paris neighborhood of Notre-Dame-de-Lorette, where many of these young women lived. Their dream—which rarely came true—was to become the wife of one of their generous benefactors. Rose-Annette Bon, better known as Rosanette, is one of the lucky ones who gets what she wanted.

The daughter of an alcoholic mother and a silk weaver in Lyon's working class Croix-Rousse quarter, Rosanette is practically sold to a ridiculous old man by her parents. She uses her beauty to make a fairly good career for herself, living in luxury and painting the town red. She is quick on her feet, funny, generally cheerful and spontaneous, sometimes stupid and a little crude, ignorant but eager to learn. She is the embodiment of a sensual, physical love that is the polar opposite of the ethereal love inspired by Mme Arnoux.

Dejected by the fact that Marie is utterly unattainable, Frédéric sets his sights on this pretty girl and enters into competition with Arnoux. Rosanette plays the flirt, resisting and teasing him, until she finally falls into his arms, seeing a promising prospect in this young man who has been living the high life since his inheritance. She becomes attached to him and starts to get in the way. Just as he is about to leave her, she tells him she is pregnant. Since he is not a boor, he stays with her until the child is born. There follows a surprising error in chronology that somehow escaped Flaubert: Rosanette tells Frédéric she is pregnant in 1848 but doesn't give birth until 1851. This rare blunder on the part of the meticulous writer also escaped his punctilious proofreader Maxime Du Camp.

Frédéric's love affair with Rosanette carries the reader into a hedonistic world well known to Flaubert. The 1840s were the heyday of costume balls, which attracted crowds of girls, second-rate artists, ham actors, actresses, over-the-hill seductresses, revolutionary women, grisettes, lorettes, and fortune hunters. The young man from the provinces, freshly arrived from Nogent-sur-Marne, is dazzled by this explosion of color, this profusion of laughter and wild music. "It was," an observer tells us, "a jumble of lunatics, a hue and cry of drunks, jumping up and down, thrashing about, crying, yelling, to the sound of strident, raucous brass music."[14]

When he turns up at Rosanette's costume ball, Frédéric meets a painter, a widower who lets his three sons "run about in rags, while he spends his life at the club," a former actress who is now the mistress of a count, a retired captain "who plays uncle to girls on the make in high society, arranges duels, and dines out at other people's expense," a doctor who writes pornography, a poet, a banker's son, an old buck, a music-hall singer who has become an actor, an unemployed pen-pusher, and, among the fair sex, kept women, emancipated women, and even married women accompanying their husbands. The entire company dances to the deafening racket of an orchestra. Everybody talks at once. Yet some of the laughs are forced, and Frédéric feels distressed in the middle of this gallant party: "He shivered, in the grip of a glacial melancholy, as if he had just caught sight of whole worlds of misery and despair."[15]

There were also many dance-halls at the time. Flaubert introduces the reader to the ball at the Alhambra, a short-lived establishment on the Champs-Elysées. Here we find a cosmopolitan ball attended by girls looking for a protector, a lover, "a piece of gold, or simply for the pleasure of the dance." As for the Palais-Royal, it was famous for its restaurants: to treat your friends to a fine meal, you had to take them to the Trois Frères Provençaux or Véfour. A little farther north, the boulevards were another hub of activity; in *Sentimental Education*, we primarily hear about their theaters (Théâtre des Italiens, des Délassements, des Funambules, the Cirque national, and so on) and its famous restaurants, including the Café Anglais, where Delphine Nucingen dined with Rastignac in Balzac's *Père Goriot* and where Frédéric takes Rosanette at the Vicomte de Cisy's prompting. Among these places of leisure, one must also mention the hippodrome at the Champ-de-Mars, where dandies, courtesans, gawkers, banker, shopkeepers, and industrialists rubbed shoulders with the serious gentlemen of the aristocratic Jockey Club.

In Rosanette, Flaubert tried to deflate the romantic, Balzacian myth of the courtesan with a heart of gold who "advises diplomats" and is eventually redeemed by love.[16] *November* had featured a prostitute of this type, whose downfall was redeemed by her love for the novel's young hero. Those days were over: the courtesan had lost her splendor. Flaubert had already said as much to Louise Colet: "My only complaint about prostitution is that it is a myth."[17]

Rosanette loves Frédéric, but what she wants above all else is to become "a society woman"; once she is able to host soirées, she dreams of marriage. This is when Frédéric begins to tire of her: "Her smile, her voice, the words she used, everything about her came to irritate him, and particularly the look in her eyes, that limpid, vacant, feminine gaze."[18] She also commits the capital offense of denigrating Mme Arnoux, whom she believes to be Frédéric's mistress:

> "And all this for Madame Arnoux!" cried Rosanette through her tears.
> He answered coldly:
> "I have never loved anyone but her."
> This insult stopped her tears.
> "That shows what good taste you've got! A dumpy, middle-aged creature with a complexion like licorice and eyes as big as manholes—and as empty! If that's what you like, go and join her!"[19]

Ultimately, Frédéric brings their relationship to an end, with a decision that is reminiscent of the end of the affair between Flaubert and Louise Colet. Yet if *Sentimental Education* is a roman à clef, one must note the absence of Louise

Colet, the woman writer and intellectual. If she is anywhere to be found in the novel, it would have to be in Rosanette, by far the "sexiest" of Frédéric's four women.

Society Love

The third female figure in Frédéric Moreau's romantic universe is Mme Dambreuse. In this case, the young man is driven to seduce neither by love nor desire. With Mme Dambreuse, Frédéric embraces the Balzacian scheme of success through women. As the wife of a major wheeler-dealer, she is identified as the ideal prey by Deslauriers, who advises his friend Frédéric that "there's nothing like mingling with the rich. Since you own a tailcoat and a pair of white gloves, make the most of them. You must get into that circle. You can introduce me later on. A millionaire—just think of it. Make sure you get into his good books—and his wife's. Become her lover!"[20]

As a white-bread Rastignac far removed from his friend and adviser's voluntarism, Frédéric is slow to follow his advice. It is only after he has received an inheritance from his uncle and returned to Paris as a man of independent means, awaiting a potential appointment to the Council of State, that Frédéric penetrates "that vague, glittering, indefinable thing called *society*." He is finally introduced to Mme Dambreuse, whom he had only glimpsed from a distance during his first stay in the capital. Sitting by the fire surrounded by a dozen guests, she gracefully listens to inanities: "The luxury of the surroundings underlined the triviality of the conversation." Frédéric is not actually drawn to this woman; she is young and very elegant but has "no bloom, like a preserved fruit." Yet her hair, "dressed in corkscrew curls in the English style [is] as fine as silk, her eyes a brilliant blue, her movements graceful."[21]

Dambreuse had married this young woman, née Boutron, the daughter of a prefect with "only a moderate fortune," for her decorative qualities. Flaubert scholars have discovered that the writer had a model for Mme Dambreuse in Mme Gabriel Delessert. She was Mérimée's mistress before she took up with Maxime Du Camp, who then introduced her to Flaubert. In his correspondence, Flaubert mocks Du Camp for being "enchanted to be received chez Mme Delessert."[22] Gustave and Maxime had met her husband, Édouard Delessert, during their trip to the Orient.

Like her model, Mme Dambreuse is twenty years younger than the husband whom she shamelessly cuckolds while keeping up an appearance of absolute propriety. This distinguished coquette is able to attract young men's attention without causing an affront to decency. A skilled hostess, "she [is] at her best in the midst of a score of people talking together—forgetting nobody, provoking the replies she wanted, forestalling dangerous remarks."[23] But in truth, she is bored: romantic intrigues allow her to play a part, to put a little spice in a society life as deadly dull as it is elegant. When Frédéric meets her, she is having an affair with his friend Martinon, who had been introduced to the Dambreuses through his father, a business partner of the financier's. Mme Dambreuse is but a means for the ambitious Martinon to enrich himself: he aims to marry Cécile, the illegitimate daughter whom Dambreuse passes off as his niece. By pulling off this tour de force, Martinon makes way for Frédéric.

Flaubert's moral portrait of the woman in question is merciless. A mask of virtue, religion, and conjugal love hides her true face: coldness, selfishness, hypocrisy, bitterness. "Her spiritualism," writes Flaubert, "did not prevent her from managing her financial affairs with admirable skill." He continues: "She was haughty with her servants; the rags and tatters of the poor left her dry-eyed." And to drive home the point: "She would have been perfectly capable of listening at keyholes, and there could be no doubt that she lied to her confessor."[24] In her defense, she is not a happy woman. She is nothing but a steppingstone for the social and political ambitions of the young people hovering around her sofa. People only care for her because she is the wife of M. Dambreuse, the baron of the new industrial and financial feudalism. While she authoritatively presides over the sumptuous receptions required for a banker of his prestige, she is ultimately just another accessory in the Dambreuse household, on a level with the flashy furniture.

Faced with the impossibility of becoming Mme Arnoux's lover and the constant irritation provoked by the unsophisticated Rosanette, Frédéric becomes a regular guest at this salon of conservatives hungry for revenge for the terrible fright of 1848. His daily visits do not worry the husband, who is apparently not the jealous type but who has, as we find out later, left his wife a nasty posthumous surprise. Frédéric courts the lady of the house without restraint: "When he was with her he did not feel that overwhelming ecstasy which impelled him towards Madame Arnoux, nor the happy excitement which Rosanette had caused him at first. But he desired her as an exotic, inaccessible object, because she was noble, because she was rich, because she was devout."[25] Finally, he is surprised at how easily he gets what he wants. His interests are served: she commits to asking her husband to help him become a deputy. Frédéric becomes a right-hand man to Dambreuse while she "drags him around society."

Nonetheless, his fervor is feigned. "He admitted at that moment what he had refused to acknowledge until then—the disillusionment of his senses. This did not prevent him from feigning ardent passion; but in order to feel it, he had to summon up the image of Rosanette or Madame Arnoux."[26] At this juncture, Dambreuse dies. Without wasting a minute, his widow asks Frédéric to marry her, which should entitle the young man to millions. Bad luck: the banker has left his fortune to his illegitimate daughter. But Mme Dambreuse's personal strongbox would still make a very fine dowry. Nonetheless, the wedding does not take place. Frédéric leaves Mme Dambreuse following an indelicacy on her part: at an auction, she purchases a small chest that Frédéric recognizes as having belonged to Mme Arnoux, which he assumes she has had to sell because of her financial difficulties. Frédéric begs his mistress to abstain; she persists. That settles that—he will not see her again. "His first reaction was one of joy at having regained his independence. He was proud of having avenged Madame Arnoux, by sacrificing a fortune to her; then he was astonished at what he had done, and a feeling of infinite weariness overwhelmed him."[27]

Flaubert deflates another Balzacian myth: the hero has won over the grande dame, but for naught. "*Sentimental Education*," writes André Vial, "is intended as an entire human comedy unto itself. But it primarily aims to be a checkmate to *The Human Comedy*, a sort of negative image of Balzac's world."[28] Unlike Rastignac, Frédéric does not become a minister in the government. He remains an inconsequential bourgeois, who could even resign himself to a conventional marriage in his native city.

Bourgeois Love

Frédéric briefly considers putting all these disappointments behind him by marrying Louise, the only daughter of M. Roque, Mme Moreau's prosperous neighbor and M. Dambreuse's steward. Though Frédéric sees her as a mere child, he is touched by the warmth of this young girl who loves him with a naïve and overflowing love. During a visit to Nogent-sur-Marne, he finds that she has become a woman, notices how moved she is to see him, and tells himself: "You at least will love me!" He peacocks, impresses her with his stories of Paris, and makes her admire him. "The next day Madame Moreau expounded Louise's virtues, and then listed the woods and farms which would eventually be hers. Monsieur Roque had a considerable fortune." For his part, old Roque has big ambitions for his daughter and is betting on Frédéric's future career, impressed by his close ties with the Dambreuses. Roque, the son of a former footman, is also fascinated by the Moreaus' aristocratic connections—Mme Moreau was the daughter of a Comte de Fouvens "and was also related to the oldest families in Champagne."[29] Although no official commitment has been made, Frédéric and Mlle Louise are quickly considered betrothed, the news spreads, and the young woman is convinced it will happen. Here we have everything that Flaubert loathed: bourgeois mores, the obsession with money and marriage. Recall how he spoke of his friend Chevalier: "Good old Ernest! There he is, married, established—and a magistrate to boot. What a perfect bourgeois and gentleman! How much more than ever he'll be the defender of order, family, property!"[30]

Louise does not truly know Frédéric, a young man constantly tossed between his desires, aspirations, and regrets. One night he goes to Mme Dambreuse's and finds there Mme Arnoux and her husband, as well as old Roque and his daughter Louise. His "old love" for Mme Arnoux is reawakened, but the sight of Mlle Roque dismays him: "She had thought it smart to dress all in green, a color which clashed crudely with her red hair. The buckle of her belt was too high; her collar was a poor fit; and this lack of elegance had probably contributed to the coolness of Frédéric's greeting." Mme Dambreuse, who is not yet his mistress, teases him about the young provincial woman's love for him. He denies it: "You're joking! I ask you! An ugly little thing like that!"[31]

After his setbacks and the separation from Mme Dambreuse, he returns to the idea of marrying Louise: it's the "normal order of things," after all. And she loves him. What a good little wife she would make! Alas, it's too late. When he returns to Nogent thinking of marrying her, he passes in front of the church of Saint-Laurent and hears the bells ringing for a wedding. Unbelievable! It is Louise who is getting married. Frédéric is stunned to learn that the lucky groom is none other than his old friend Deslauriers. "Shamefaced, beaten, crushed, he went back to the station and returned to Paris."[32]

The novel could easily have been called *Lost Illusions*, if the title hadn't already been taken by Balzac. Yet Flaubert did not want to abandon his poor hero in the depths of his moral poverty. In the novel's second-to-last chapter, the reader witnesses a kind of epiphany when the invisible icon suddenly reappears in the flesh. It is now 1867, a long time after Frédéric had lost touch with Marie Arnoux. They are both tremendously moved when she confesses that she had secretly shared Frédéric's love. As a result, "his former sufferings were redeemed." He will treasure the lock of white hair she cuts off for him. Yet they will never belong to each other. He watches her leave, full of melancholy. He passed her love by, just as he passed his whole life by. At least this final meeting has revealed to him that they had loved each other with a deep, true love, however impossible.

The "pyramid," as Flaubert referred to a novel's successful construction, has been achieved. But it is a pyramid with two peaks. The epilogue constitutes the second peak—a pathetic one, in which we find Frédéric, having weathered every storm, looking back on adolescent memories with Deslauriers (who has lost Louise to a singer). The best memory scandalized the critics: a visit to a brothel which they had run away from when Frédéric, who had the money, suddenly panicked and bolted: " 'That was the best time we ever had,' said Frédéric. 'Yes, perhaps you're right. That was the best time we ever had,' said Deslauriers."[33]

Flaubert did not want to leave us on a tender note. The novel is concerned with the insignificance of a life, of the two parallel lives of Frédéric and Deslauriers. The story's autobiographical reach thus remains limited. There is no doubt that Flaubert fitted the narrative to the chronological sequence of his own youth. He then constructed his plot by putting to use his "great love" for Élisa Foucault-Schlésinger. He also pulled in his own memories of Paris, the demimonde, and high society. All this makes it difficult to recognize the impersonality he claimed. But at the same time, Flaubert uses irony, the rejection of judgment, and the desire to "imitate God" in his writing—"that is to say, to do and keep quiet," to create a distance between himself and his characters, including his protagonist Frédéric, a distance that disconcerts many readers.

If *Sentimental Education* is the story of a young man who lets his life pass him by, the novel that Flaubert wanted to write is really that of a generation, the representation of a group that reflects the collective destiny. He went so far as to admit that "characters in history are more interesting than characters in fiction."[34] Indeed, Frédéric's adventures would be of limited interest if they were not anchored in social and political reality.

CHAPTER 19

Frédéric Is Us

The generation Flaubert sought to describe in *Sentimental Education* was his own, as well as that of Louis Bouilhet, Maxime Du Camp, Jules Duplan, Frédéric Baudry, Ernest Chevalier, Ernest Feydeau, and his former classmates at the Collège Royal in Rouen and law school in Paris. Born around 1820, these young people were only about ten years old during the Revolution of 1830 and were therefore neither its witnesses nor its beneficiaries—at least not direct beneficiaries.

Alexis de Tocqueville encapsulates the July Monarchy in his *Souvenirs* [*Recollections*]: "In 1830, the triumph of the middle class was decisive and so complete that the narrow limits of the bourgeoisie encompassed all political powers, franchises, prerogatives, indeed the whole government, to the exclusion, in law, of all beneath it and, in fact, of all that had once been above it. Not only was it the sole director of society, but also, one might say, its cultivator. It settled into every office, prodigiously increased the number of offices, and made a habit of living off the public Treasury almost as much as its own industry."[1]

When Flaubert and Frédéric's generation emerged in an eminently bourgeois society, it was too late to make a place for itself, because all the places had been taken following the July Revolution. As for the *pays légal*—the "legal country," defined by the French royalist Charles Maurras as the set of republican institutions imposed on the "real country"—the poll tax limited it to about two hundred thousand voters. This small number, combined with a scattering of electoral colleges that sometimes had no more than one hundred votes, encouraged widespread corruption. François Guizot, the brains and soul of the July regime, developed the theory of census suffrage, which restricted electoral rights to men with *capacités,* that is, the citizens considered most fit to act according to reason. In fact, these citizens were exclusively recruited from the ranks of wealthy landowners, for social status was considered inseparable from political capacity. Members of the intellectual professions who lacked sufficient income, such as teachers, professors, and, most of the time, artists, were thus excluded. The reign of Louis Philippe consecrated the rule of money and government by the property-owners.

In *Sentimental Education*, Flaubert has the industrialist Fumichon recite the property-owners' credo in the Dambreuses' salon:

> "It's a right consecrated by Nature. Children cling to their toys; every people, every animal on earth shares my opinion; the lion itself, if it had the power of speech, would call itself a landowner! Take my case, gentlemen: I started with a capital of fifteen thousand francs. Well, you know, I got up regularly at four o'clock in the morning every day for thirty years! I had the very devil of a job to make my fortune. And now they come and tell me that I can't do what I like with it, that my money isn't my money, that property is theft!"
>
> "But Proudhon ..."
>
> "Oh, don't talk to me about Proudhon! If he were here I think I'd strangle him!"[2]

Fame and fortune was the goal for these young people from the provinces who moved to Paris to go to school, try their luck, get an important job, and scale the heights of artistic or literary success. But they came up against closed doors. The poorest among them believed their only hope for the future was to overthrow the bourgeois regime, through revolution or socialism. It was during the July Monarchy, which saw the real beginnings of the industrial revolution in France, that the "social question" was abruptly raised. Major surveys, such as the one carried out by Louis-René Villermé in 1840, described working-class poverty; new socialist doctrines appeared every day; secret societies spread around the country. Flaubert read Proudhon, Henri de Saint-Simon, Victor Considérant, Pierre Leroux, Charles Fourier, and Étienne Cabet—that riot of authors whom Marx referred to as the "utopian socialists" and whose importance would be revealed by the revolution of February 1848. Flaubert felt caught in a vice between the self-satisfaction of the wealthy and the threat of the socialists.

Disappointed Ambition

Frédéric Moreau's friend Charles Deslauriers is the perfect embodiment of the disappointed ambition of those young men from the provinces who were most determined to follow the path of Balzacian promotion. His insurmountable handicap is that he is poor. Thanks to a partial scholarship, he is able to attend the collège in Sens, where he meets Frédéric. For want of being able to climb the ladder as quickly as he would like to, he becomes his friend's adviser—as well as sponging off him. He has learned from reading Balzac that to succeed in life and society, one only needs a tailcoat and a pair of white gloves. The rest is determination: you set your sights on a "rich home" and you "make sure" you appeal to the millionaire's wife. These are "classic" moves, he says; all you have to do is "remember Rastignac in *The Human Comedy*." Though an admirer of Balzac, Flaubert does not hesitate to poke fun at his mythology when he introduces the character Deslauriers: "He believed in courtesans advising diplomats, rich marriages obtained by intrigue, the genius of criminals, the submissiveness of fortune to a strong will."[3]

After serving as a clerk to an attorney in Troyes, Deslauriers is given the opportunity to dream of his own conquest of Paris thanks to a small inheritance from a relative of his mother. But once in Paris, he leads a life without comfort or grace, despite his will to power: "He wanted . . . to have three secretaries at his beck and call, and to give a big political dinner once a week."[4] His failures convince him that a new regime is needed, a republican regime that will give everyone a chance: he impatiently awaits a new 1789, a major upheaval that he is determined to use to make a niche for himself and find his place in the sun. He vociferates against Louis Philippe and defends a thesis deploring the injustice of testamentary capacity (competency to make a will), which leads him to be held back. He mixes with socialists and grows furious that he has been reduced to a mediocre existence, making a meager living by giving private lessons, writing students' theses, and doing other lowly jobs. He becomes a lawyer, loses his first three cases and, as a result, all his potential future clients. More bitter than ever, he dreams of blowing everything up: "I drink to the total destruction of the existing order, everything called Privilege, Monopoly, Control, Hierarchy, Authority, State."[5] These imprecations are reminiscent of those made by Flaubert in his years of juvenile vehemence: "some day, a day that will come before long, the people will unleash the third revolution: kings' heads will roll, there will be rivers of blood."[6]

In fact, Deslauriers is less a revolutionary than an opportunist. Once the future looks brighter to him, thanks to Frédéric's promise of fifteen thousand francs to found a newspaper, he abandons his radical ideas and decides that the best thing for his paper's success is to have no opinion at all—since all parties are alike in their idiocy (an idea dear to Flaubert): "I see . . . three groups, none of which interests me: those who have, those who used to have, and those who are trying to have. But they are all united in their imbecilic worship of Authority."[7] Gustave repeated this same idea to his correspondents time and time again: "Republicans, reactionaries, reds, blues, tricolored—all are equally inept." The tool for success was a newspaper, and the model to follow was Adolphe Thiers and his paper *Le National*, which had played a major part in the Revolution of 1830 and become a pillar of the July Monarchy. Thiers had himself been a young man of modest means who left to conquer Paris, but he was born in 1797; times had changed. As suggested by the title of his book *De la propriété*, published in 1848, Thiers was an apostle of property who had participated in the straitjacketing of society. Flaubert considered Thiers the politician most representative of the triumphant bourgeoisie under Louis Philippe (the "king of the labor courts"). As he explained to George Sand, it was important to him that his book put this man who had been raised to "the level of a demigod" in his place: "I shall try, in the third part of my novel (when I reach the reaction that followed the June Days) to slip in a panegyric of said gentleman, a propos of his book on property, and I hope he'll be pleased with me."[8]

Finally, the revolution breaks out, and Deslauriers thinks his time has come. After having blithely participated in the February Days, he pesters Ledru-Rollin, a member of the provisional government, to appoint him as one of the provincial commissioners to replace the prefects. But as the new republic is rocked by dramatic events, Deslauriers finds himself caught between the devil and the deep blue sea, equally threatened by the rich, to whom he preaches fraternity, and the socialists, whom he reminds of the need to respect the law. He gets over his lofty ideas: he now hates workers, and, realizing that both the future and the past are in the hands of the conservatives, he changes his tactics and has Frédéric introduce him to M. Dambreuse. Eventually, he marries Louise Roque, after having won over her father "by railing against Ledru-Rollin." A pitiful marriage, as it happens, for Louise will later run off with a singer. The character of Deslauriers is emblematic of those young people whose outsize ambitions were checked by history.

The Rule of Money

In contrast to Deslauriers, whose dogged efforts leave him as poor as when he started out, Frédéric becomes a man of independent means. Many young men dreamed of such a fate, but few achieved it. Flaubert was in the same situation as Frédéric, but he used his private income to devote himself to his work, while his feeble hero is a wastrel who does nothing constructive. Some young people, however, were able to make it to the top of the social pyramid by the sweat of their brow and their genius for intrigue. There is at least one example in *Sentimental Education:* Martinon. The son of a successful farmer, he single-mindedly devotes himself to law school in Paris. He intends to succeed without wasting any time. He adheres to every dominant type of conformism to appeal to millionaires; he fears crowds, secret societies, and the workers who could deal a lethal blow to his ambitions. He is willing to admit that poverty exists, "but neither Science nor Authority can be expected to apply the remedy. It is purely a matter for the individual. When the lower classes make up their minds to rid themselves of their vices, they will free themselves from their wants. Let the common people be more moral and they will be less poor!"[9]

Women play a decisive role in the rise of this "peasant parvenu," as Frédéric describes him. A handsome man, he has won Mme Dambreuse's favors and dreams of becoming the heir to the family fortune by marrying Cécile, M. Dambreuse's "niece," whom he correctly suspects to be the banker's illegitimate daughter. But he is not absolutely certain; he speculates on the inheritance and places his bets on Cécile. He bides his time, prudent and crafty, weighing his chances with the meticulousness of a general peering through his binoculars before he orders the charge. To Mme Dambreuse's disappointment, he decides to marry Cécile, to whom M. Dambreuse does indeed leave his fortune. Score! Martinon is one of the rare characters in Flaubert's novel who triumphs. Having circumspectly supported the Republic of 1848, then enthusiastically joined the Second Empire, he becomes a senator.

Martinon stands apart from the other young men of his generation. From an early age, he has been on the side of the old. Romanticism did not make a dent on him; as far as he is concerned, love is but a ticket to success. He is the synthesis of peasant prudence and bourgeois speculation—in every case a realist, a man on the way up. Flaubert had met a few gentlemen of his type at

Princess Mathilde's salon; he was not sorry to lambaste them in his depiction of this greedy character.

The Dambreuse home, where Martinon makes his battle plans, is representative of those imposing, opulent, pretentious settings in which expensive objects are accumulated to show visitors the power of the master of the house. The *Dictionary of Accepted Ideas* gives an impression of the conversations held during receptions here: guests enthusiastically regurgitate the most worn-out truisms, which also happen to be the most reassuring about the security of the new ruling class—animosity toward republicans, socialists, the press's excesses, and books about the Revolution; praise of property, religion, commerce, industry, and the monarchy. "Footmen loaded with gold braid" listen to these lessons in political wisdom as they come and go.

The birth name of the master of the house had once had an aristocratic particle, but the Comte d'Ambreuse, sensing that the future belongs to industry, trade, and banking, has given up his title. Now, whenever someone addresses him as "Count," he can retort, as Pierre-Paul Royer-Collard was reported to have done to the minister who wanted to ennoble him, "Count yourself!" According to René Dumesnil, the model for M. Dambreuse was Augustin Pouyer-Quertier, a manufacturer from the department of Seine-Inférieure who was at his peak under the Second Empire. But this is of no importance—what Flaubert primarily tried to do was to create a portrait of a typical big businessman of the July Monarchy. Dambreuse heads several companies, notably the General Coal Company of France, whose success is guaranteed by rising coal consumption due to the rapid expansion of the railways, the steamship lines, the ironworks, and the gas companies. There are two matching portraits in his office, one of the republican General Foy, a reminder of a past hostility to the Bourbons, and one of Louis Philippe, which illustrates the logical fate of the revolutionary: to become a conservative. There is no doubt in Dambreuse's mind that the revolution that allowed the bourgeoisie to establish its empire in 1830 is over. Everything has been resolved, and the best possible regime is in place—François Guizot had said as much time and again.

Flaubert's Dambreuse is the quintessence of a member of bourgeois society under Louis Philippe. He is not particularly cultivated but has an admirable practical sense, is at the head of major business initiatives designed for maximum profit, and is a monarchist in so far as the monarchy protects industry and closes French borders to foreign products. Ultimately, he only truly has faith in capital. In him, one sees the beginning of the reign of private property and capitalist business.

After the February Days of 1848, Dambreuse and his friends become sheepish, trembling republicans. They don't understand a thing: "the world was coming to an end!" They echo the ruthless reaction to the workers' uprising in June. Flaubert adopts the tone of social satire to describe the ideas exchanged in the Dambreuse home during the heated hours of the Second Republic. Although the word "bourgeois" appears frequently in his work, we know that he did not use it sociologically. Yet in his depiction of the upper bourgeoisie—personified in *Sentimental Education* by the Dambreuses—he creates a delicious, biting, realistic portrait of a ruling class that triumphed in 1830, was contested in 1848, and recovered under Napoleon III. In this respect, *Sentimental Education* is an essential document: the author's careful observations enrich his investigation of the realities of an era he abhors—his own. The cult of the truth—which in Flaubert requires the use of generalization and exaggeration—is always in competition with his obsession with style. He seeks revenge with the glee of Honoré Daumier.

The Revolutionaries

Despite his hostility toward the bourgeois, Flaubert hardly flatters their opponents. Charles Deslauriers and Frédéric Moreau are republicans or revolutionaries merely by chance. Three of their friends hold far firmer opinions and, when necessary, put them into practice. Their names are Regimbart, Sénécal, and Dussardier. Though they are very different from one another, they share an inextinguishable hatred of Louis Philippe's government.

Citizen Regimbart is one of Flaubert's most colorful characters, a direct descendant of the Garçon and his mechanical pranks. It would be hard to call him a socialist. He is a republican out of hatred for the monarchy, grumbles about the "scurvy tricks of the Government," and makes a fuss when reading the newspapers, though he never suggests the slightest solution—aside from retaking the Rhine. The patriot lives in Montmartre and sponges off his wife, who runs a small sewing shop. He is satisfied to spend his days in the cafés, reading the papers. From the break of day to the deep of the night, he goes from café to bar, from bar to brasserie, driven not by a taste for liquor, but to drown his acrimony. In fact, he speaks little—he uses any occasion to roar, shout, froth, grumble, and fulminate against the authorities and stokes his abhorrence for the rich with the news of the day. His hatred of the nobility makes him seem like an egalitarian Jacobin, and he accepts to serve as Frédéric's second for his duel with the noble Vicomte de Cisy with a "murderous smile." He also claims to know weapons and has his clothes made by the tailor for the École Polytechnique, France's leading engineering school. He has little interest in the social question; a desire for the fall of Louis Philippe constitutes the extent of his diatribes. Yet once the republic is established, he is not entirely satisfied, since there is no mention of the supreme goal of taking back France's natural borders. An eternal malcontent mad for military glory, he is reminiscent of those Napoleonic officers who were pushed aside at the Restoration—like Philippe Bridau in Balzac's *La Rabouilleuse* [*The Black Sheep*]—and spent their time in cafés, waxing nostalgic and feeding their anger. Through the kind of comic twist that he mastered, Flaubert turned this stupid and narrow-minded character into an object of admiration, adulation, and respect both for an important man like Jacques Arnoux and for the owners of the cafés he frequents. The seamstresses who work for his wife love him and consider him "a truly remarkable man." One can sense Flaubert's jubilation in the face of idiocy, which he dramatizes as if he were running a puppet theater.

The character of Sénécal is far more developed. Flaubert saw him as the personification of socialist ideology, which he abhorred. As poor as Deslauriers, Sénécal lives by his wits, working initially as a math tutor, then for a machine manufacturer, then as a foreman in Arnoux's faience factory. He finally becomes an accountant. He is constantly moving on, not because he is incompetent, but because of his moral and political rigor.

Flaubert read an abundance of books on socialism to create this character. In April 1867, he wrote to Louis Bouilhet that in six weeks he had read twenty-seven volumes on the topic. He spared himself nothing of what Sénécal might have read, from the eighteenth-century "prophets of doom" Gabriel de Mably and the abbé Morelly, to Louis Blanc, who was part of the provisional government in 1848. He tackled Rousseau, whose *Social Contract* was a bible for this sans-culotte who naturally hates Voltaire "who-did-not-like-common-people." From these readings, Sénécal has drawn a democratic orthodoxy, which is at once an ethic, an economic dogma, and a policy. The existing regime is anarchical; many suffer while others gorge themselves; the world must return to ancient virtue and, to do so, put an end to social inequality. Sénécal leads a Spartan and upstanding life while waiting for the advent of the future society that will put an end to the reign of the individual and impose moral rectitude for all. The means to that end remain vague: he once mentions "a just division of material goods" and later refers to protecting agriculture and eliminating liberalism everywhere, but in fact we never truly understand what economic system he wants to see established. Ultimately, the change in society will come from the state; Flaubert, who was enraged by the socialist theories regurgitated by Sénécal, summarizes the revolutionary's ideal as follows: "a virtuous democracy, something between a farm and a factory, a sort of American Sparta in which the individual would exist only to serve the State, which would be more omnipotent."

The influence of Christianity is manifest in these hopes for future fraternity. One of the things Flaubert discovered in researching his novel was the Christian sources of the so-called utopian socialists. When necessary, Sénécal even steps in as a champion for Catholicism, declaring that "people had been unfair to the Papacy, which, after all, defended the people; and he called the [Catholic] League 'the dawn of democracy, a great egalitarian movement against the individualism of the Protestants.' "[10] Universal suffrage, which is advocated by Sénécal and all his friends, is "the application of the principles of the Gospel." When the Jesuits are attacked in his presence, he redirects the gathering's anger toward Victor Cousin, whose eclecticism "encouraged selfishness and destroyed solidarity." While the Revolution of 1830 was decidedly anticlerical (against the alliance of the throne and the altar), the Revolution of 1848 was steeped in a religiosity closely observed by Flaubert. "I think part of our problems," Flaubert wrote to Michelet in February 1869, "stem from republican neo-Catholicism."

In reading the socialists, Flaubert came across "the strangest citations. They all talk about religious revelation." He denounced this "enormous and deplorable" influence in his letters to George Sand, citing Louis Blanc, who claimed that his system came from a *divine* source, a "doctrine formulated in the Gospels," "a doctrine of peace, union, and love." The good lady of Nohant defended Louis Blanc a little, but let her "old troubadour" rage against the collusion between neo-Catholicism and these insane doctrines.[11] The individualist and liberal in him took revenge in creating the portrait of the profoundly unlikeable Sénécal.

Sénécal, an indoctrinator of workers, is a member of one of the most important republican secret societies of the time: the Société des Familles. In 1839, he had already participated in the insurrection launched by the leftists Armand

Barbès and Auguste Blanqui. Its failure has not discouraged him. By 1847, seeing that the people are still not taking up arms, he remembers the 1836 assassination attempt on Louis Philippe and begins to think that the most efficient move might be a plot against the sovereign. If the despot falls, the people must naturally rise! He joins the "incendiary bomb conspiracy" as a chemist, but is arrested while on the way to try out the gunpowder in Montmartre. He is eventually released due to lack of evidence.

Flaubert uses Sénécal's character not only to denounce socialism's warped Christian roots, but also, and especially, its authoritarian foundations and hatred of freedom. Sénécal is a doctrinarian without a sense of irony, a dogmatist without subtlety, and an idealist without pity. He is as cold as a mathematician, cherishing humanity but despising people. He is hard on himself but even harder on others, to the point that he goes against his own political convictions when working as a foreman and alienates the workers with his severity. Sénécal's description of the future smallholding of his dreams sounds less like a utopia than a barracks in which an implacable warrant officer brings the grunts into line. "Democracy doesn't mean license for the individual to do as he pleases. It means equality before the law, the division of labor, good order."[12] It is a paradox that he attacks power at the same time that he adulates authority, but the history of revolutions attests to the truth of this paradox: what is good for the people must sometimes be achieved despite them.

Flaubert also took issue with socialism's notion of art. Since 1830, the greatest writers had aligned themselves with literature's *social mission*. In 1834, Lamartine wrote: "Poetry has a new destiny to fulfill: it must be of the people." In 1830, Vigny became a contributor to the liberal Catholic paper *L'Avenir* and, in 1837, the greatest of them all, Victor Hugo, wrote in the preface to his *Voix intérieures* [*Inner Voices*] that "the poet has a serious duty." This gave socialists all the more reason to adopt social purpose and utility as criteria for judging works of art. Thus, in the novel, when the bohemian Hussonnet mocks *Le Chevalier de Maison Rouge* (an Alexandre Dumas play whose revolutionary episodes were much applauded when it was performed in August 1847), Sénécal asks "if the play advanced the cause of democracy." The bohemian answers, "Yes ... I suppose so; but the style ... ." Sénécal interrupts: "Well then, it's a good play. What does the style matter? It's the idea that counts."[13]

In Sénécal, Flaubert includes everything he loathed about the socialist "joke." To take his distaste to its logical conclusion, he eventually shows us the character as an armed accomplice to the coup d'état of December 2, 1851. Sénécal is disappointed in the people, who are still immature and incompetent. "A dictatorship is sometimes indispensable," he says. "Long live tyranny, provided the tyrant does good!"[14] Authoritarian socialism leads him to execute his friend Dussardier, who had remained faithful to the Republic.

Flaubert makes Dussardier the purest figure in the novel. He is a man of the people, a man of '48, but not a proletarian—he is a clerk for a firm of carriers, an employee. But he is uneducated: "His reading was confined to two works, *Royal Crimes* and the *Mysteries of the Vatican*."[15] Inspired by his new friends, he puts together a small library, which includes Eugène Sue's *Mysteries of Paris*, Norvins's *Napoleon*—in which the emperor is not presented as a despot—and the *Fables* of La Chambeaudie, a worker poet whose verses were recited "in every cabaret and several salons in Paris."[16]

Despite his modest social status, Dussardier mixes with the young bourgeois of his age, whom he has met by chance during a protest and whose hatred of the monarchy he shares. His convictions are simple: he is a republican because of his love of the poor and his thirst for justice. His political consciousness was awakened on April 14, 1834, when soldiers massacred the inhabitants of a building on rue Transnonain in retaliation for an antigovernment protest, an episode later immortalized by Honoré Daumier. Dussardier witnessed the scene himself when he was fifteen: "From that time on, he had loathed the Government as being the very incarnation of Injustice. He tended to confuse murderers with policemen."[17]

In conversations with his friends, we always see him express his concern for victims of the police, particularly for Barbès, who had been given a life sentence for the failed insurrection of 1839. Dussardier recalls the inhumane conditions in which Barbès was transferred to his cell. This strapping young fellow has become a republican always ready to defend victims of repression because he has a warm heart: the character's first move upon entering the novel is to throw a punch at a police officer brutalizing a demonstrator. As we see when he cries over the agony of the Poles at the hands of the tsar, his compassion knows no borders. In his room he has a portrait of Béranger, whose song "La Pologne et son peuple fidèle" [Poland and Its Faithful People] had done a great deal to stir pro-Polish sympathy.

Dussardier represents the naïve and generous hope of an ideal republic that will emancipate the oppressed and usher in universal happiness. When the long-awaited day finally arrives, Dussardier is transfigured by joy. Yet the

June Days pose a cruel dilemma for him. He defends the government from the National Workshop insurgents out of his love for the Republic, but he is racked with guilt once he realizes that the victors "hated the Republic!" When Dussardier dies in December while fighting the insurrection out of faith in the Republic, it is by the hand of Sénécal, the ally of the June insurgents and the embodiment of authoritarian socialism. The Revolution of 1848 is at the heart of this big-hearted clerk's tragedy: the jubilation of February, when everything seemed possible; the tragedy of June, when genuine republicans such as Dussardier were torn between faithfulness to the Republic and their compassion for the unfortunate souls of the closed National Workshops; and finally the terrible events of December 2, 1851, which buried yesterday's hopes in blood. Dussardier had to die, for the Republic was in its death throes.

A Generation at Sea

Sentimental Education's social portraiture is not limited to its principal characters. The book's many supporting characters represent different milieus, trades, and sensibilities; they often lack avowed convictions but brush up against the novel's central events. The character of Jacques Arnoux, inspired by Maurice Schlésinger, had previously appeared in *Les Mémoires d'un fou*, where, under another name, he "walked the line between the artist and the traveling salesman." In his store on Boulevard Montmartre, Arnoux shamelessly exploits painters; sells suckers his worthless paintings at blue-chip prices, conning them with fake bills of sale; and turns out pastiches of old masters for "ignorant art-collectors." After his various schemes stop bringing in enough money, he establishes himself as a faience manufacturer, then goes into "a china-clay company as a member of the board," but is tried and sentenced for signing fake reports. He finally sets up as a dealer in rosaries. Not so much a swindler as a devil-may-care, flighty fellow, Arnoux is appreciated for his constant cheerfulness and—when his debts permit—his generosity. His tragedy is that he is not bourgeois enough to really succeed at business, and not artistic enough to have an influence on the art of his time. The title of his newspaper, *L'Art industriel*, "industrial art," summarizes him in a nutshell: he has never been able to choose between art and industry, which will be his downfall.

Among the artists more or less exploited by Arnoux, Flaubert creates Pellerin, a failed painter weighed down with aesthetic theories but with a brush-

1 Gustave Flaubert at nine years of age. Copy by Flaubert's niece Caroline Franklin-Grout (1920) of a drawing by Eustache Langlois (1838).

2 Flaubert's mother. Copy by Flaubert's niece Caroline Franklin-Grout (1920) of a drawing by Eustache Langlois (1831).

3 Flaubert's father, Achille-Cléophas Flaubert, surgeon at the Hôtel-Dieu in Rouen. After a drawing by Joseph Désiré Court.

4 Flaubert's sister, Caroline. Drawing by an unknown artist.

5 Gustave at thirteen years of age (*right*) and his brother Achille (*left*). Drawing by Delaunay (ca. 1835).

6 The pavilion at Croisset, near Rouen. Drawing by Alphonse Lecomte (1905).

7 Alfred Le Poittevin, Flaubert's childhood friend.

8 Élisa Schlésinger with her child. Lithograph by Achille Deveria (ca. 1840).

9 Louis Bouilhet at the age of thirty-two. By Louis Émile Minet (1919), after a pastel by Delarge.

10 Gustave Flaubert. Copy by Flaubert's niece, Caroline Franklin-Grout, of an etching by Eugène Champollion.

11 James Pradier.

12 Louise Pradier.

13 Louise Colet. Drawing
by Victorien Sardou.

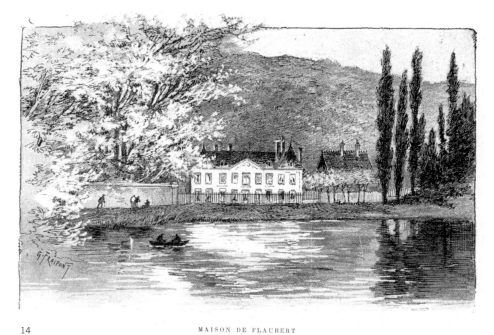

14

MAISON DE FLAUBERT

14 Flaubert's house at Croisset. Drawing by Gustave Fraipont, published in *Les Environs de Rouen* (1890).

15 The writer and caricaturist Henri Monnier dressed up as Monsieur Joseph Prudhomme, a character that he had invented (ca. 1875).

16 *Madame Bovary*. Sculpture by Henri-Michel Jondet (1910).

17 Manuscript page from *Madame Bovary*, part 1, addressed to Louis Bouilhet. Written between August/September 1851 and March/April 1856.

18 Portrait of Flaubert used as the frontispiece for the *Oeuvres de Gustave Flaubert*, Éditions Alphonse Lemerre, Paris, 1885. Engraving by Ernest Friedrich von Liphart (1880).

19 George Sand. Drawing by A. Legrand.

20 *Title:* Monsieur Homais. *Caption:* Flaubert—Ah! my dear girls [Emma and Salammbô]! My POMPOUS IDIOT is even bigger than I thought. Drawing by Lucien Métivet, created on the occasion of the Flaubert centenary for the journal *L'Excelsior* (1921).

21 Flaubert as lieutenant in the National Guard of Croisset during the war of 1870–1871. Copy (1924) of a drawing by Georges Dubosc created for *Le Journal de Rouen* in October 1905.

22 Carte-de-visite portrait of Flaubert by Étienne Carjat (ca. 1860).

23 Portrait of Flaubert's niece, Caroline Commanville, by Albert Witz (1867).

24 Guy de Maupassant. Etching by Paul-Edme Le Rat (1884).

25 Émile Zola. Drypoint by Marcellin Desboutin (n.d.).

26 Charles-Augustin Sainte-Beuve. Lithograph by Bornemann.

27 Caricature of Gustave Flaubert (1922). Copy of a pastel by Eugène Giraud (1868). Flaubert is shown with the Legion of Honor lapel pin (awarded in 1866) during one of the soirées at the Louvre that were organized by Count Alfred Émilien de Nieuwerkerke, then superintendent of the Beaux-Arts Academy.

28

29

30

31

28 *Salammbô*, a five-act opera, opened at the Théâtre de la Monnaie in Brussels on February 10, 1890, and presented at the Théâtre des Arts in Rouen on November 22, 1891, and at the Opéra de Paris on May 16, 1892. This image shows "The feast of the Mercenaries in Hamilcar's garden" from act 1, scene 7, "Salammbô fleeing toward Carthage."

29 The geraniums. Illustration for *Bouvard and Pécuchet* by Paul Gavarni.

30 My cedar of Lebanon. Illustration for *Bouvard and Pécuchet* by Paul Gavarni.

31 The salon of Princess Mathilde. Oil painting by Giuseppe de Nittis (1883).

32 "Homage to the Great Flau! The collection of Homais, Bouvards and other Pécuchets ... specimens of classes, orders, genera, families, and varieties of HUMAN STUPIDITY (stuffed for the Flaubert Museum)." Drawing by Lucien Métivet, created on the occasion of the Flaubert centenary for the journal *Le Rire*, December 24, 1921.

stroke better suited to painting a plate of spinach than a masterpiece. As ridiculous as Pellerin might be, the description of his studio in the Faubourg Poissonière leaves a definite impression that there is some Flaubert in him. Pellerin, who dines "in cheap eating-houses" and has "no mistress," leads an austere life, entirely dedicated to art. Clearly, "his hatred of the vulgar and the mediocre," which finds expression "in sarcastic outbursts of superb lyricism," is shared with Flaubert. His veneration "for the masters" and the sweat he puts into making his constantly revised canvases are surely those of the author prey to the "pangs of style." Further, one recognizes in Pellerin's words the language that his creator used in his own life to celebrate disinterested, "pure art" and reject the artist's social mission. For Pellerin, the Revolution was an abominable period because it "produced nothing in art."

Nonetheless, Pellerin is a loser, a hack. He professes the most beautiful aesthetic theories but is totally incapable of applying them and must accept degrading commissions from the cynical Arnoux to get by. His only greatness is his selflessness, his absolute love of art. His foolishness is the gap between his forceful proclamations and his creative impotence. If he had had the talent of Delacroix, Pellerin could have been heroic; stuck with his own, he is a buffoon. In him, Flaubert exorcized what he could have become had he not written his masterpieces.

Among the revelers, one comes across Cisy, an inept, uneducated, and conformist dandy from an old aristocratic family, whose obsession is with "having tone." He fulfills this ideal after his grandmother's death, donning "his tartan waistcoat, his short coat, the tassels on his shoes, and the admission ticket in his waistband." Nothing is missing from his style, the style of an "Anglomaniac and a musketeer." Seeking emancipation and heavily influenced by *The Mysteries of Paris*, he compares himself to the Austrian Prince Rodolphe, wants to learn French kickboxing, and smokes a short pipe. But these are merely youthful transgressions—he remains attached to his caste. The epilogue puts our mind at rest: "deeply devout and the father of eight children," he has settled "in his ancestral mansion."

As for Hussonnet, he is the perfect bohemian, a glib, cynical scrounger who writes for fashion magazines and short-lived periodicals, supplementing his income as a correspondent for provincial papers. He does not always eat his fill. Having lucked into running a rag called *Le Flambeur*, he fills it with gossip, nasty rumors, and short juicy satires. Like Balzac, Flaubert mocks this world of small papers (which nearly all survived through blackmail) and its bawdy spirit. Though his beginnings are difficult, Hussonnet eventually makes something of himself: he "had an important post which gave him control of all the theaters and the whole of the press." But this is a triumph of the type of journalistic frivolity that Flaubert loathed.

Another typically Parisian type is the ham actor. Delmar, a former music-hall singer who has changed stage names with every bump on his attempted rise to the top, has become an actor. He finally achieves fame by playing "a peasant who lectures Louis XIV and prophesies 1789." From then on, his business consists in "insulting the monarch of every country under the sun." Flaubert had come to know the theater world through his efforts to help Louis Bouilhet in his trials and tribulations with the stage. The roles that turn Delmar into a star remind one of Hugo's 1876 oration over the grave of the great actor and playwright Frédérick Lemaître: "The other actors, his predecessors, represented kings, pontiffs, captains, those we call heroes, or gods, but thanks to the era in which he was born, he was the people. One cannot embody anything that is more fruitful or reaches higher."[18] Delmar represents political theater, the actor convinced of his social mission, to whom Flaubert gives the characteristics of a grotesquely pretentious performer.

Among the supporting characters, we also find Mlle Vatnaz, one of Delmar's admirers. A former provincial teacher, she has also come to Paris looking for success, or better yet a husband. But the unattractive, poor woman does not find a soul mate. Her book *The Young Person's Garland*, "a literary and moral anthology," does not get a publisher. So she leads a mediocre existence, like many others: "She was one of those Parisian spinsters who, every evening, when they have given their lessons, or tried to sell their little drawings or place their pitiful manuscripts, go home with mud on their petticoats."[19] To put an end to this life of scraping by, the well-read Mlle Vatnaz sees only one solution: overthrow everything. The Revolution must lead to the reign of Woman.

Indeed, it was under the July Monarchy that feminism took root in France. New women's papers such as the *Journal des femmes*, headed by Fanny Richomme, and the *Gazette des femmes*, headed by Mme de Mauchamp, were launched, as well as more revolutionary, soon to be well-established feminist periodicals like *Le Globe* and *La Femme libre*, among others. In his notebooks, Flaubert recorded several excerpts such as this passage in favor of women's suffrage from the *Voix des femmes:* "Young women in ancient Gaul had the right to make laws. They were legislators. In some tribes, African women have the right to vote. In England, Anglo-Saxon women participate in legislation. The wives of the Hurons were part of the Council, and the Elders followed their advice."[20] The argument is repeated nearly word for word in *Sentimental Education:* "Mademoiselle Vatnaz maintained that woman ought to have her place in the State. The women of ancient Gaul made laws, as did the Anglo-Saxon women, while the wives of the Hurons belonged to the tribal council. The work of civilization was common to both sexes."[21] Like the socialist and feminist writer Flora Tristan, Mlle Vatnaz believes that "both women and proletarians need to be emancipated," but she goes even further: "the emancipation of the proletariat was only possible through the emancipation of women."

Neither perennial nor interchangeable, these characters all belong to a society transitioning toward democracy. The kings have already been felled, and the emperor who succeeds them will have to call for expanded suffrage to achieve legitimacy. The aristocrats (Cisy) have become ghosts, the democrats and the socialists (Sénécal) are making themselves heard, and the others (Frédéric) lead lives of indecision while feeling their way to where they belong—which explains the characters' changes of opinion, rallying to new causes, and abrupt betrayals. Everyone belongs to the bourgeoisie, whether lower, middle, or upper. The scene is Paris, the peasants are far away; as for the many workers living in the capital, we barely encounter them. *Sentimental Education* is thus a bourgeois novel, in which parvenus jostle for position and money seals fates. The difference between Frédéric and Deslauriers comes down to who does or doesn't have money. Yet they have each found their own way to fail at life. They had dreamed it would be amazing; it has put them in their place.

Like his characters, Gustave Flaubert lived through this economic, political, and social transition, which it would not be an overstatement to say he found hopeless. There was nothing to please him about the advent of the democratic society predicted by Tocqueville. He rejected the universal male suffrage that was demanded and hard won by the Revolution of 1848 because he was wary of the masses. He was exasperated by the nascent socialism that was all in favor of the collective to the detriment of the individual. Culture was being made insipid by inconsequential novels, newspaper serials, and boulevard theater: there was now a "literary industry," just like there was "industrial art." The foundations of this democratic society were in the bourgeois society that had toppled the aristocratic order; its ideology was utilitarianism and profit. What was the way forward between socialists, whose rigid ideals were little different from those of the barracks, and the wheeler-dealers sitting on their bags of money? In his view, there was only one refuge: art. But the artist and writer could only find salvation in solitude or among a limited circle of well-read people: "Any aristocracy that sets itself entirely apart from the people becomes impotent," wrote Tocqueville. "This is true in literature as well as in politics."[22] The same herald of democratic society analyzed the transition that plagued Flaubert:

> In aristocracies, readers are demanding and few in number. In democracies, they are less hard to please, and their number is prodigious. In aristocratic nations, therefore, there is no hope of success without immense effort, and such effort may yield considerable glory, but not much money, whereas in democratic nations, a writer may boast of achieving a modest renown and a substantial fortune at little cost. He does not need to be admired to accomplish this; it is enough if people have a taste for his work.[23]

Flaubert was torn between these two poles of the transition. He wrote as an aristocrat, but he needed an audience. *Sentimental Education* expresses his generation's malaise. The only two characters to succeed are Martinon, a symbol of the parvenu bourgeoisie, and Hussonnet, a hardworking hack in the journalism industry. The others are defeated, either because they missed their chance or because it never came.

The novel about love was a denial of love; the novel about a generation turned out to be about its collapse. *Sentimental Education* was not destined to please its era.

CHAPTER 20

Cold Shower

Louis Bouilhet died before he could read the final two chapters of *Sentimental Education*. For lack of this invaluable reader, Gustave entrusted a copy of the manuscript to the vigilant Maxime Du Camp. As Du Camp reported in his *Souvenirs littéraires*, he had a discussion with Flaubert "that lasted three weeks." "There were times when I was exhausted. I laugh as I remember those struggles, during which, like Vadius and Trissotin, we would hurl blunt truths at each other's heads, without ever causing a wound." Maxime, an extreme purist, found 251 inaccurate expressions and syntax errors; Gustave accepted most, but as he put it, "sent 87 packing": "[Flaubert] claimed, he always claimed a writer is free, according to the demands of his style, to accept or reject the grammatical rules which govern the French language, and that the only laws he must observe are the laws of harmony."[1] In fact, the example provided by the exacting proofreader proves Flaubert right: "For example, he would not have hesitated to say, '*Je voudrais que vous alliez*' instead of '*Je voudrais que vous allassiez*' because the imperfect of the subjunctive does not sound nice." Even in the nineteenth century, the imperfect of the subjunctive sounded unwieldy and old-fashioned. Sometimes Maxime would tell his friend: "You don't give a shit about grammar." The novelist was not entirely resistant to his editor's suggestions; he did accept some, but he rejected the tyranny of syntax.[2] "He said," Du Camp continues, "that style and grammar are two different things; he would quote the greatest writers, who were almost all incorrect, and point out that no grammarian ever knew how to write. On these points we were in agreement, for his opinions were based on irrefutable examples."

Once reread and revised, the manuscript was submitted to Michel Lévy, the publisher of his two previous novels, with whom Flaubert had signed a contract for *Sentimental Education* in 1862. It had been agreed that the author would be paid ten thousand francs for an initial volume of four to five hundred pages, with an additional two thousand francs for every additional hundred pages. After doing the calculations, Michel Lévy paid Flaubert sixteen thousand francs—though the author was expecting twenty—and noted that he was being generous, for at fair value he only owed him fourteen.[3] Flaubert was disappointed; as usual, he did not dare to talk to his publisher about money, but he certainly complained to his friends. This time, George Sand stepped in to help. In May 1869, the lady from Nohant saw Lévy and pleaded Flaubert's cause: the publisher had acquired the book at a bargain price. An agreement is an agreement, replied Lévy, but he would consider paying an additional two or three thousand francs "if the book was successful." While Lévy was within his rights from an accounting perspective, he could have been more generous, given how much money *Madame Bovary* and *Salammbô* had brought in. Lévy might have been taking a short-term risk with the book, but its author was a solid long-term investment. The strategy of building a relationship with a great writer even at the risk of going into the red (which can always be offset, either by the sale of earlier works or the promise of future books) was not yet in practice in the nineteenth century, a period when publishers most often bought manuscripts for a flat fee. *Sentimental Education* was eventually published by Lévy, who did not like its title but had failed to convince the author to change it, at around the same time that Flaubert moved in to a new apartment on rue Murillo, close to the Parc Monceau and not far from Princess Mathilde's home on rue de Courcelles.

From the First Reactions to the Savaging

Flaubert had asked his friends to read the novel or had read it aloud to them himself. They had reacted very favorably. In May, Princess Mathilde had responded to a reading with an enthusiasm "impossible to describe." In November, excerpts from the novel were published in "about thirty papers."[4] On November 17, 1869, Flaubert signed dozens of review copies for the press. He quickly realized that the praise would not be deafening. "People even avoid mentioning my book to me, as if they were afraid of compromising themselves." What few thank-you notes he received were mostly insignificant acknowledgments that the book had arrived, though Jean Bruneau has highlighted a few interesting exceptions.[5] Louis-Bovin Champeau wrote the author that "whoever will want to know the moral and rather sad history of the last fifty years, without having it tarted up, will only need to read your book."

Ernest Chesneau: "Never has irony been wielded with a power both constantly true to form and implacable; never has a society been so cruelly flagellated. How hard you are!" Paul Chéron pointed out a few minor errors: in 1841, for instance, there was no macadam in Paris yet—it was introduced to surface roads there in 1849. Alphonse Cordier sent Flaubert his support: "In fifty years, one will only need to read your book to have an idea, or more than an idea—an evocation of this generation born out of Chateaubriand and Lamartine's woolgathering, a crushed, mongrel generation that did not know how to want and produced nothing." Victor Hugo told him he had "insight like Balzac, but style too."

The most beautiful tribute came from the Goncourt brothers. Jules congratulated him after reading some excerpts in the press, telling him that they were "masterful pieces." On November 24, Edmond sent him a long letter:

Dear old friend,

I've just finished your book, your eight hundred pages that I savored in small sips, and I am eager to tell you how much pleasure, how much *exaltation* reading it has provided me with. Madame Arnoux is deliciously erotic. Monsieur Arnoux is indeed the artist blended with industrialism. Deslauriers, with his envious nature, his back-and-forth between duplicity and friendship, his lawyer's temperament—here is a perfectly depicted variety of the most widespread kind of truly nasty humanity. Frédéric, the failed lover, is admirably positioned with the average level of passion, intelligence, and energy that you wanted for him: in your book, he has all the qualities and flaws that make one fail at life; but you must realize that he will not appeal to women, they'll find he doesn't grab their asses fast enough, and as a consequence that will be detrimental to Gustave in his dealings with courtesans, either honest or dishonest. I will not insult you by complimenting the landscapes and descriptions, we know you've got that down. I will settle for telling you that it is always written in a manly way and is very elevated in thought—the opposition between Rosanette and Madame Dambreuse is charming—the twilight, chiaroscuro figure of Mademoiselle Vatnaz is perfect—Long live Dussardier, down with Sénécal—Pellerin has some great lines—You certainly delivered all the revolutionary jokes and all the conservative jokes à la Prudhomme. By the way, you really have a taste for the verb *saillir* in the imperfect tense; it seems to me to have a really ugly imperfect. All the scenes with the populace swarm tumultuously. In short, do not give a fuck about criticism and squawking: you have written a powerful book, a novel that tells the story of a generation in damn beautiful language. A *jewel* of a scene is the one in which little Louise, one of your most delightful creations, envies the caresses that fish feel all over their bodies; one couldn't be more filthily and childishly sensual, and the *soft cry* (there's an epithet I envy you) that comes out of her throat *like the coo of a dove*. It's sublime. But for me the truly masterpieceful scene—as Gautier would put it—is the last visit [of Mme Arnoux] to Frédéric; I know of no other book with anything so delicate, so touching, so tender, so sad, and without any tricks. Pulling the foot back, what a stroke of genius, and everything, everything they do, everything they say, everything they hint at, there, old man, you hit the jackpot.[6]

Goncourt's praise was sorely needed, given that the first newspaper reviews were not good. While the reviewers certainly recognized that Flaubert's talent was that of a great writer, most considered the novel a failure, and some even found it scandalous.

One important voice was missing: Sainte-Beuve had died on October 13, just before the publication of *Sentimental Education*. The great critic had not spared the author of *Salammbô*, but he knew how to read and report what he saw. He could have set the tone, raised the level. "With whom can one talk of literature?" Flaubert wrote to Maxime Du Camp. "He loved it, and although he wasn't precisely a friend, his death grieves me profoundly. Everyone in France who wields a pen has suffered an irreparable loss."[7] Moreover, he often said that it was partly for Sainte-Beuve that he had written a "modern novel," since the critic had advised him to do so. Now he had died "without knowing a line of it!" Théophile Gautier, who had written an enthusiastic article about *Salammbô*, was on assignment in Egypt for the *Journal officiel* to report on the opening of the Suez Canal; Gustave would not be able to rely on his support. As for Saint-Victor, although he had been so friendly with Gustave at the Magny dinners, he informed Lévy that he would not write about Flaubert's novel because he found it "too poor."

Although many critics shared this negative assessment, their reasons were varied. The first group censured the work for moral reasons, arguing that the author sought to show only the ugliness in the world, along with people's lowness and "cowardly covetousness" (Jules Levallois, *L'Opinion nationale*). "Monsieur Flaubert is merciless regarding any high ambition, any aspiration that aims for anything above the brutal demands of the realities and practicalities of life; he inevitably condemns any character with the slightest pen-chant for romantic love to unremitted disappointment. Anyone who is not a scoundrel is destined to suffer for his honesty, through his loyalty and very sensibility" (Paul Charvet de Léoni, *Le Pays*). "For him, life is nothing but vulgar reality presented in all its details, and considered in the most brutal light" (Adrien Desprez, *La Gironde*). The most merciless critic was himself a great writer—Barbey d'Aurevilly, writing in *Le Constitutionnel:* "The way I see it, the world has enough vulgar souls and vulgar things without adding to the overwhelming number of these sickening vulgarities. But this is not the opinion of M. Flaubert and his school. This is the school that rudely laughs at the ideal in every single thing, both in a moral and an aesthetic sense. This is the school that wants no *sursum corda* ["Lift up your hearts"], whether in the arts or in literature. It is this school that is denying heroism and heroes, contending, with the pens of all its little rascals, 'that there are no more he-roes in humanity' and that all the cowards and dullards of mediocrity are just as good as they are and are even a thousand times more interesting."

As a staunch Catholic, Barbey could only hate Flaubert's "materialism" and his characters' lack of spiritual aspiration. His "love of panache" (Jean Gautier) was offended by the paltry characters in *Sentimental Education*. He was not the first and would not be the last to judge the book's conclusion as "vile." In short, he felt that Flaubert belonged to that guild of "soulless" writers who "despised the Infinite."

A litany of similar complaints was repeated by countless critics. In *Le Journal de Rouen*, Alfred Darcel wrote, "Men are shown by their grotesque side, events from the petty side, and both men and things are drowned in a vast sea of nonsense, which submerges them." Francisque Sarcey believed that *Sentimental Education* had brought him face to face with the Marquis de Sade—though he admitted that he had never read him! He writes: "Reading this book is painful; one comes away with a harsh contempt for humanity, with some kind of aftertaste of degradation" (*Le Gaulois*). This conformist, sen-tentious moral condemnation was repeated from one paper to the next. Flaubert was accused of loving the withered, the filthy, and the mire. Yet the attack from Amélie Bosquet could be said to have come from the left. Speaking on behalf of the women's cause, Bosquet published two particularly hostile articles in *Le Droit des femmes:* "No," she wrote in one of the articles, "this is not art, this process without warmth or sympathy that depresses the soul, dries up emotion, petrifies as it creates, knows no enthusiasm or gaiety, does not refresh life with an atom of virtue or happiness, and seems to have no other goal than to arouse a universal disgust in us." In the second article, she stated that women in Flaubert's novel do not speak, as if the author feared that "by thinking for them" he would be giving them his "intellect." She could not accept Mademoiselle Vatnaz: "The voice demanding the rights of women is Mademoiselle Vatnaz, a matchmaker and thief. I only mention her for the record, for the well-known honorability of our precursors whose names have lived on exempts us from challenging this insult to our cause." Flaubert could only sigh that works of art were being judged on the basis of "religious authority." He was upset by these unkind reviews written by a woman he had helped, defended, and genuinely cared for. Their friendship never recovered.

He initially tried to convince George Sand that the criticism left him unmoved. But nothing could have been further from the truth—the deluge had a powerful effect on him. Particularly since the storm showed no sign of passing: "All we have here," wrote Philarète Chasles in *Le Siècle,* "are thwarted desires and no principles, rough outlines of sensuality, real impotence, desire without will, and empty souls with frivolous minds." "Odious pictures," "a rage to cut down what rises," "lacking a single cry from the heart, a single emotion," "a taste for vulgarity," "the reign of the inept," "a book that damages humanity," "a commitment to disenchanting the world and degrading human nature," "an overall impression of repugnance and ennui."[8] They all let loose with their moral preaching, their humanist sermons, and their denunciations of the pleasure the author took in "expressing the vulgarity of things." Critics on the right called for spirituality, good manners, and modesty, while those on the left requested more positive momentum. In the republican paper *Le Rappel,* Camille Pelletan deplored the book's awful conclusion: "Where are all those great currents that sometimes carry every thought toward some form of beauty or of society?"

Flaubert had expected it: neither the conservatives nor the socialists liked his book. The "author's excursions in the realm of politics" killed the book, according to Amédée de Cesena, who added that "women do not pick up a book to find the declamations made in public meetings." Those who accepted these "excursions" reproached Flaubert for "so rigorously keeping the pans of the balance equal" between the bourgeois and the revolutionaries. Others, like Duranty in *Paris-Journal,* considered that the author had given an unfair picture of the June Days of 1848, "that victory in which heroic bourgeois people, intrepid children of Paris, energetic soldiers, led by the most valiant leaders and associated with the biggest names of old France, set Parisian demagoguery back twenty years." This right-wing criticism was not always explicit, but one can see that Flaubert looked like a dangerous author to the champions of law and order—despite the fact that he was one of them. Criticizing him from the other side, Camille Pelletan reproached the novelist for having deprived the revolution of its "inspiration": "Its entire multitude gesticulates, yells, ripples under our eyes. All it is lacking is the motive, the fine electricity of the riot, the holy enthusiasm of revolt."

While moral condemnation was most frequent, Flaubert was also attacked for his craft. It was generally agreed that *Sentimental Education* was poorly composed—or not at all composed. In a long article in the *Revue des deux mondes*, Saint-René Taillandier went on the offensive: "Without being unaware of the qualities that make M. Gustave Flaubert a writer of some originality, I admire neither his art nor his style unreservedly. What is an art whose result is to do away with composition, to make unity impossible, to substitute a series of sketches for a painting?" Everyone struggled to summarize the book, for the plot—if there was a plot—was diluted in an infinite number of scenes whose uniting connection was difficult to perceive. "Forgive me for saying so," wrote Barbey, "but all in all he is just a bric-a-brac maker." Flaubert had nothing to say, his novel was just a series of tableaus "like those of a magic lantern." Edmond Schérer summarized this objection in *Le Temps:* "If theory has imposed many arbitrary rules on works of art, there is at least one condition that can pass for absolute. This condition is unity. The work must have a center, its lines must be combined, its details must be grouped; it must, in a word, form a whole." Flaubert's obsession with description was denounced in all quarters. An "auctioneer's description, as precise and exact as it is useless" (Adrien Deprez). A "rage to describe, to describe always and anything, about any place and even when out of place" (Francisque Sarcey). Ultimately, wrote Louis Duranty, "the novel's real characters are steamships, rooms, streets, staircases, and landscapes." He added: "M. Gustave Flaubert's book is not a novel, it is a satire, a satire composed of tales, tableaus, episodes that one might think are separate, of characters that get together without connecting, of spare parts that don't fit together, of events without causes or outcomes." In this lack of unity, the excess of descriptive style causes the reader's boredom, "a lethal boredom." Since Flaubert's critics read each other's work, they copied and quoted each other and agreed on the same grievances: an immoral novel, inept characters, a poorly composed story that was cold, repetitive, and boring.

The Masterpiece Recognized

Sales of *Sentimental Education* certainly suffered from these primarily negative reviews. Unlike Flaubert's previous two novels, this one sold poorly—four years later, the initial print run of three thousand had still not sold out.[9] Aside from the reviews, Flaubert was also set back by the general situation in France. The year 1869 was a crucial one for Napoleon III's regime. In May, the republican opposition had come out on top of the legislative elections, forcing the emperor to pass new reforms and, at the end of the year, to appoint Émile Ollivier, a republican who had gone over to the liberal empire, to head the government. The liberalization of the press and public meetings allowed for constant agitation. In January 1870, the murder of the journalist Victor Noir by a distant cousin of the imperial family, Pierre Bonaparte, caused a street demonstration, which the police attempted to confine outside the city, in Neuilly. The polemicist Henri Rochefort, who had been elected a deputy in a by-election on November 25, 1869, let out his battle cry in *La Marseillaise:* "I made the mistake of believing that a Bonaparte could be something other than an assassin!" Rochefort was indicted and sentenced to six months in prison and a two-thousand-franc fine on January 22. In May, the emperor decided to hold a referendum, hoping it would allow him to regain his authority. But on July 19, 1870, war was declared on Prussia. All in all, the novel could have been launched at a better time.

But the public might also have rejected *Sentimental Education* in a different political climate. As the reviews reflect, its first readers were disconcerted. Lovers of novels—starting with women—expected to find in the book all the things that it lacked: a well-structured plot, characters with strong personalities, romantic passion, surprising twists and turns; in short, everything that is generally referred to as "novelistic." *Sentimental Education* is in no sense a novel in the grand tradition. Its characters are bland, contemptible, even horrible people with whom it is difficult to identify. Where are the heroes? Where are the great souls? Where are the evil geniuses, like Balzac's Vautrin? Flaubert had not so much written a dark novel as a grey novel. In *Avenir national*, Louis Asseline described a response shared by many: "To be subjected during the course of two fat volumes to the company of these people who say nothing and do little, whom you can neither love nor hate, to see unfold around you this grey and lifeless saga in which no variation catches your interest, is more than one can bear, and eventually one is outraged by this pointless dilettantism and asks the author to take us back to Carthaginian extravagances." The heroes were missing in action. Poor Frédéric, with his inconstancy, cowardice, and timidity, was hardly the stuff of dreams.

Yet there were a few discordant voices. Though he is quoted above as a detractor, Jules Levallois published an article in *L'Opinion nationale* on November 22, 1869, which his fellow critics would have done well to mull over. Rating Flaubert's talent "above any criticism" and praising his "masterfully written" chapters, Levallois perceived "a secret unity of design" behind the apparent absence of composition, despite the fact that Flaubert's decision to reject "dramatic combinations, adventures, and mystery" had the disadvantage of disappointing an audience eager for thrills. One week later in *Le National*, Théodore de Banville wrote of a work "bearing the indestructible seal of perfection."

On December 7, Flaubert, feeling like a wounded Saint Sebastian, called out to George Sand for help, though he had told her he was not a "sensitive man": "The way they're all jumping on your old troubadour is incredible. People to whom I've sent a copy of my novel are afraid to talk to me about it, either for fear of compromising themselves or out of pity for me. The most indulgent are of the opinion that what I've written is only a series of scenes, and that compositions and patterns are completely lacking. . . . Therefore (you can guess what's coming) if you would care to take [my defense] you'd oblige me. If it embarrasses you, do nothing. No mere indulgence between us." Flaubert knew very well that his dear friend would not need to be told twice. She immediately wrote an article and, having asked Flaubert where to send it, dispatched it to Girardin, the editor of *La Liberté*. The article was accepted but took a long time to appear. Sand and Flaubert grew impatient: "Your article hasn't yet appeared in *La Liberté*. I asked someone to enquire from Girardin what that means: no answer. Politics, I think, is the only reason for this delay. Unless my poor book is the victim of a 'Holbachian conspiracy.'" Flaubert was displaying the classic paranoid conviction of a recently published author that he is being personally attacked. The critics' arrows kept flying; George Sand, always maternal, comforted her friend: "such savage attacks are the inevitable consecration of great merit."[10] Finally, Sand's article was published on December 21.

She had grasped the novel's meaning and lucidly stated it: "This time he has expressed the general state that characterizes times of social transition. Between what is exhausted and what is not yet developed, there is an unknown evil, which weighs in different ways on every existence, which ruins aptitudes and makes what could have been good turn evil; which aborts ambitions both great and small, which erodes, betrays, makes everything go astray, and finally drowns the least bad people in inoffensive egotism. It is the end of the romantic aspiration of 1840 breaking against bourgeois realities, the cunning of speculation, the false ease of down-to-earth life, and the difficulties of work and of the struggle." A finely observed encapsulation.

Yet the most penetrating analysis of the novel was written by Charles Asselineau, a critic unknown to Flaubert, who did not write for the major papers, but for the *Bulletin du bibliophile,* a biannual review for bibliophiles. Asselineau understood the novelty and modernity of a novel whose aim was to depict not "a man's character" but "the character of the time." "It may be," he wrote, "that the time for novels with heroes has passed. This word 'hero,' which demands a heroic time, a time of unity and upward progress, is ridiculous in a fragmented egalitarian society in which individual heroism amounts to the conquest of 'modest happiness.'" The ideas of Tocqueville are manifest here; in fact one could say that Asselineau describes his "individual lost in the crowd." Asselineau insists: "We are no longer capable of the great efforts [we find in Balzac], neither for good nor for evil. Passion is no longer in the study or the salon or the alcove, we are passersby; no longer a society, but a crowd." Asselineau has perfectly understood what Flaubert had always aimed to achieve and had always recommended to Louise Colet and his other "students": "What M. Flaubert sought to depict was the generality. And the generality consisted of precocious young minds, which were consequently blasé, being eclipsed from the outset by the success of those who had preceded them and turning ironic due to their impotence." This explains the apparent flaw in the novel's composition: it is made up of multiple actions, a "mix of adventures and biographies," that describe life as it is—not organized, but fragmented, random, and contingent.

We do not know if Flaubert had the opportunity to read this article. There is no mention of it in his correspondence. He did, however, have the pleasure of reading Émile Zola's review, published in *La Tribune* on November 28, 1869. Zola reminded readers of Flaubert's temperament, which naturally drew him to the epic, and his immoderate effort to resist it: "One can always feel him ready to leap into a burst of lyricism, to lose himself in the expansive heavens of poetry. Yet he remains on the ground; his human reason, his commitment to exact analysis, bind him to the study of the infinitely small. He is a Titan, full of enormous breath, reporting on the customs of an anthill." Zola also describes him as "a poet transformed into a naturalist, Homer turned into Cuvier." But the poet remains, one can feel it in his music—"a sort of continuous bass over which sudden scales of nervous notes sing like the high-pitched whistle of a little flute." Zola praises the book's historical dimension: "The author has made the entire age fit into his work, with its art, its politics, its ways of life, its pleasures, its shamefulness, and its grandeur." As for the descriptions, they are necessary, never gratuitous, because unlike Balzac, Flaubert never proceeds by "reasoned analysis," "but by a series of short scenes bringing the characters and temperaments into play. This inevitably requires descriptions, since it is through the outside that he shows us what is inside." Ten years later, Zola would return to *Sentimental Education* on the occasion of its reissue by Charpentier. Revisiting the grievances voiced by critics upon the novel's initial publication, he states that "the truth is that this only too realistic book is terrifying." He points out the mistake made by those who had denounced the book's faulty composition: the structure was not visible, the framework was not apparent, but the author had nonetheless achieved "a homogenous whole" through his sustained perseverance. Of the protagonist, Zola writes: "Take pathetic Frédéric: his story is ours; and so he arouses anger and pity in me, and I find him so petty, he makes me so scared. An imbecile? Not at all. Misunderstood? Not that either. He's a regular person, like you or me, nothing more. But he shakes me up more than any of the larger-than-life figures in our literature, because this man's moan of impotence screams in every one of my bones."[11]

Having become the leader of a literary school (by this time Zola had published the first volumes of the *Rougon-Macquart* series), Zola enrolled the author of *Sentimental Education:* "This is the model for the naturalist novel, I have no doubt about it. One can go no further in real truth—I am referring to that exact, down-to-earth truth which seems to be the very denial of the art of the novelist."

Whether or not *Sentimental Education* is a naturalistic work, Flaubert had used it to blow up the traditional novel and its demand for the exceptional. Readers were disconcerted by characters too much like the man in the street and were bored by the lack of action. The ironic distance of the author from his characters seemed incongruous and possibly immoral. Today we are better prepared to appreciate the novel, undoubtedly Flaubert's masterpiece, because the literature that followed it abandoned the realm of heroism. Although Balzac's novels feature some apparently insignificant characters, his principal players are always consumed by passion or frenzy—greed, ambition, love, jealousy—which drives their energy to extremes, to ruin or to death. Flaubert's novel sounded the death knell for this kind of novelistic storytelling. In the twentieth century, readers became accustomed to a grey and pessimistic literature inhabited by common people, by the losers and the defeated, that aimed to represent Heidegger's "One." Céline's Bardamu, Camus's Stranger, Roquentin in Sartre's *Nausea*, Cripure in Louis Guilloux's *Le Sang noir* [*Bitter Victory*], the Archambauds and the Gaigneux in Marcel Aymé's *Uranus*, Beckett's Estragon and Vladimir, and Ionesco's little old men, not to mention the "rubes" of the American novel, are all antiheroes in works brimming with derision and abandonment and in which the goal is no longer to tell a story but to describe the tragedy of the human condition. In Flaubert's time, the novel's purpose was to entertain. The field of history was shifting, too, away from the study of great men, great movements, and major events to a focus on anonymous, ordinary people representing a class, a milieu, or a profession. This was a slow process. But at the time that *Sentimental Education* was published, Hippolyte Taine was at work on his *Origines de la France contemporaine* [*Origins of Contemporary France*], in which the masses take precedence over the individual.

Yet Flaubert had not lost sight of the demands of art: he wanted to show that he was not limited to the sublime and the epic, to bright colors and resounding accents, that he could restrict himself to apparently nondescript subjects. Recall what he wrote about *Madame Bovary:* "Common environments disgust me, and it is because they disgust me that I chose this one, which was hyper-common and anti-aesthetic." The challenge that the artist gave himself was to make something beautiful out of something ugly, banal, and quotidian. In *Salammbô*, Flaubert had given free rein to his taste for epics; in *Sentimental Education*, he returned to the trivial, which challenged him to make a masterpiece out of itself.

If one compares *Sentimental Education* with *Madame Bovary*, one can legitimately consider the latter the more successful of the two novels because of the dramatic intensity of its plot, while *Sentimental Education* presents a kind of stasis, monotony, and immobility that frustrates the reader expecting a gripping tale with lots of twists and turns. But one could argue that the true masterpiece is actually this—shall we say—atonal novel that follows the mediocre lives of ordinary humanity. It represents another step away from the ruins of the heroic novel—a genre to which *Madame Bovary* still belonged because of its flamboyant central character. We find nothing of the sort in *Sentimental Education,* which unfolds by the light of half-extinguished fires, under a crepuscular sky, and follows the gloomy experience of a tribe of dead souls. It is politics, more than anything else, that introduces the violence of passion and the cruelty of fate into the story. Once the revolution is quelled, the days go back to the succession of petty intrigues and vague desires required by the return to order. It took the genius of someone like Flaubert to make a novel of a generation by turns frustrated, intoxicated, and finally disillusioned, without drawing moral, philosophical, or political conclusions.

CHAPTER 21

George Sand and the Old Troubadour

A month after the publication of *Sentimental Education*, an exhausted Flaubert, inconsolable following the death of Bouilhet and further saddened by the passing of Sainte-Beuve, entered a profoundly melancholy period of his life. Happily, he could count on the thoughtful affection of George Sand, who invited him to spend Christmas in Nohant. He had long wanted to visit his close friend on her property in the department of Berry, but did not want to be distracted from writing his book. Now, he jumped at the opportunity to enjoy the hospitality of this friend who so dearly wanted him to visit her and her family.

Shortly before Flaubert's arrival, George Sand wrote a long letter to Juliette Adam, an important literary figure in Paris. Its contents, which are reported in Adam's memoirs, tell us a great deal about both Flaubert's disgrace and Sand's friendship: "His artistic refinement and scholarship escape the majority of readers, few people read him, and even fewer recognize what he is really worth. He lacks a little tenderness in art and in life. He is brusque, violent, but infinitely good."[1]

The Nohant Way

On Thursday, December 23, 1869, Flaubert arrived in Nohant accompanied by Edmond Plauchut, an adventurous journalist and friend of George Sand. Along with Flaubert's subsequent thank-you note, George Sand's diaries have left us a detailed account of his visit.[2] Sand's warm welcome allowed the distressed Flaubert to recover his good mood, taste for conversation, and eagerness to tell funny stories. On Christmas Eve, Sand noted that "Flaubert is as happy as a kid." He was solicitous and admiring of Aurore, known as Lolo, the granddaughter of "Mme Sand."[3] One of the highlights of Flaubert's stay was a puppet show. The puppet theater occupied a prominent place in the household and had been built by Maurice, Sand's beloved son and a friend of Flaubert since 1847: "The major appeal of puppets in country life," wrote George Sand, "is to present *stories*, comic, magical, or dramatic novels told over several evenings."[4] The jovial company played various lively games as the Christmas Eve dinner lasted late into the night. On Christmas Day, Flaubert spent over three hours reading out loud his long *féérie*, which he still hadn't succeeded in getting produced. His friends applauded. Later in the evening, having truly regained his good cheer, he displayed his talent for telling stories "that killed us with laughter." He himself was tremendously entertained by an improvisation performed by Maurice in the little theater. On Monday, December 27, with snow piling up outside, Lolo started dancing and "Flaubert dressed up as a woman and danced the cachucha with Plauchut, it was ludicrous, we laughed hysterically." Yet Flaubert did not linger as long as his friend had hoped he would. The next day, he set out for Paris. Though he had been enchanted by this stay with generous friends, he fell back into a deep despondency over the following days. Nothing would be more precious and more comforting to him during these long months of infinite sadness than George Sand's shows of affection, whether during her trips to Paris or in her regular letters.

Yet the friendship that developed between Gustave and George Sand had not been a foregone conclusion. Before meeting Sand, Flaubert did not much admire this author whose prolific output in the *Revue des deux mondes* and elsewhere did not seem compatible with the rigor, effort, and slowness he believed essential to composing a work of art. When he was still sending literary advice to Louise Colet, Gustave would mention George Sand as a counterexample, for her facility went hand in hand with a sentimentality he found exasperating. One had to write with one's head: "In George Sand, one can smell the white flowers; it oozes, and the ideas seep out between the words, as if from between flabby thighs."[5] As we know, he did not approve of an author's presence in the story, and he criticized Louise for "preaching" like George Sand: "You're straying from the principles, you're no longer keeping Beauty and eternal Truth in sight."[6] Additionally, he could not accept Sand's notion of the writer's social and political responsibility. As a spiritual daughter of the political writer Félicité Robert de Lamennais, who was himself a disciple of the socialist Pierre Leroux, she had founded *La Revue indépendante* with Leroux and Louis Viardot in 1841. It was here that she had published *Fanchette*, the appalling true story of an abandoned young girl—a rustic tragedy that inspired Sand to found the local paper *L'Éclaireur de l'Indre*.[7]

Indeed, Sand's political commitments could hardly appeal to an uninvolved writer like Flaubert. After the February Days, which had filled her with enthusiasm, Sand had hurried from Nohant to Paris and put herself at the disposal of the provisional government. She had written editorials for the *Bulletin de la République*, launched the periodical *La Cause du people*, and penned a few lampoons, notably a "letter to the rich" (*Lettre aux riches*), in which she stated that "France will be communist within a century." On April 20, she was on top of the Arc de Triomphe with the members of the government watching the *Fête de la Fraternité*, a huge public ceremony in which soldiers swore allegiance to the new government. Yet she was deeply dispirited by the events of May 15, when demonstrators following Blanqui invaded the Assemblée Nationale, and even more so by the social war of June: "I do not believe in the existence of a republic that begins by killing its proletarians," she wrote to a friend. Having remained faithful to her ideals of equality, solidarity, and a social republic, she began to feel disenchanted. When France voted for a president for the first time—through universal male suffrage, what's more—she struggled to understand the people who had brought Louis Napoléon to power: "The people believe in a name! So they still have the faith we are lacking. They trust promises! So they have a deep instinct for loyalty. They irrevocably condemn those who deceived and oppressed them! So they are not so weak and indecisive after all." But she no longer believed: "I feel no bitterness toward the people, though they appear to be bringing a temporary solution to this revolution, which goes against my wishes."[8] It was at this point that she was overcome by what Michelle Perrot calls "the temptation of Nohant." In 1850, she wrote to Émile de Girardin that "the June Days of 1848 dealt me a blow from which I still haven't recovered, and I've been a misanthrope ever since."

But even after her withdrawal, given Flaubert's poetics and his open contempt for political action, one would not expect that he and Sand would form one of the most beautiful friendships in French literature. For Flaubert, it would be a friendship without ambiguity. Admittedly, when they met in 1859, George Sand was fifty-seven, and the man who had just written *Madame Bovary* was only thirty-seven. This age difference quickly gave George Sand license to address Gustave with the informal "*tu*," while he maintained the more deferential and formal "*vous*." By her own admission, the woman who had experienced stormy relationships with Jules Sandeau, Chopin, Musset, and many others had gone into romantic retirement, though her novel *Dernier Amour* [*Last Love*], published in 1866 and dedicated to Flaubert, had made him the butt of "the most friendly jokes."[9]

Shortly after meeting her, Flaubert wrote to Ernest Feydeau: "I gather you idolize la mère Sand. I find her personally a charming woman. As for her doctrines, expressed in her writings—beware! A fortnight ago I reread *Lélia*. Read it. I beg you, read that book again!"[10] It would take him a while to get over his prejudices.

The friendship began with the publication of *Salammbô*. Sand wrote an admiring review of the novel and sent its author a letter inviting him to Nohant. Flaubert asked Michel Lévy for Sand's address in order to send her his thanks. On January 28, 1863, she replied: "We don't know each other very well. Do come and see me when you have time. It's not far, and I'm always there. But I'm an old woman—don't wait till I'm in my second childhood." By return mail, Gustave thanked her for having called him "Dear Brother": "Dear Madam, It's not that I'm grateful to you for having performed what you call a duty. I was touched by the goodness of your heart; and your sympathy made me proud, that's all. Your letter, which I have just received, adds to your article and goes beyond it, and I don't know what to tell you other than, quite frankly, that I love you for it." Further, he writes: "As for your very cordial invitation, I answer neither yes or no, like a true Norman. Perhaps I'll surprise you some day this coming summer. Because I greatly long to see you and talk with you."[11]

Flaubert and Sand would not meet until a year later, in Paris, and as we have seen, his visit to Nohant would have to wait seven years. In the meantime, the two writers had begun a correspondence. Flaubert now wrote to his "dear Master," an address he sometimes feminized, while she used more variety, addressing him as "dear Flaubert," the mischievous "Monsieur Flobaire," "my dear brave comrade," "my good comrade and friend," "dear friend," "dear comrade," "old man of my heart," "my dear old man," most often "dear friend of my heart," and finally "my troubadour" or "my old troubadour." Their letters became more frequent beginning in 1866, when George Sand started to cautiously participate in the Magny dinners—in fact, the Café Magny became her favorite place to eat when she was in Paris, aside from the Monday night literary gatherings. In her diary, she noted that Flaubert was "passionate and nicer to me than to the others," adding, "I don't know why yet."[12]

The correspondents wrote about their work, told each other their worries, and mentioned the lives of their intimates. George Sand showed Flaubert that strong personality, vigorous mind, and natural optimism that made her letters invigorating and comforting. He described her to Mlle Leroyer de Chantepie: "Our friend Mme Sand visited me for a few days last month [June 1868]. What character! What strength! Yet at the same time there is no one more calming. She passes on something of her serenity." He was seduced, comforted, and stimulated by this woman who did not hesitate to speak to him in a maternal tone. For her part, she considered him very strong and admirably mature. She did not skimp on praising him. After her first visit to Croisset in November 1866, she wrote him: "I was very happy, the week I spent with you. No worries, a comfortable, beautiful landscape, affectionate hearts and your fine, frank and somehow fatherly face. Age has nothing to do with it; there's a protectiveness, an infinite kindness about you; you brought tears to my eyes one evening when you called your mother 'my girl.' " She admired the selfless artist in him: "You are one of the *rare* people who remain sensitive and sincere, who go on loving art uncorrupted by ambition and unintoxicated by success."[13] Yet she worried that he worked too much, she fretted about his isolation, and she was sorry that they lived so far apart: "It's silly not to live next door to those one loves."[14] They were mindful of each other's financial problems and occasionally offered each other help—which they both regularly turned down.

George Sand returned to Croisset in May 1868. But even when they were far apart, they continued their correspondence, talking about everything. Sand did not agree with Flaubert's theory of impersonality: "For my part, I follow my old bent and put myself in my people's shoes. I'm criticized for it, but it doesn't matter." She was surprised by his slow, painful process: "As for style, I don't set as high a value on it as you do." Flaubert insisted on the idea that the novelist "*hasn't a right to express his opinion* on anything whatsoever. Has God ever expressed his opinion? That is why there are so many things that stick in my throat—things I long to spit out, and which I choke down instead. Indeed, what would be the use of uttering them?" She replied: "Not put any of one's heart into what one writes? I don't, I simply do not understand. For my part I don't see how one can put anything else."[15] No matter! Their mutual respect, friendship, and tenderness outweighed any disagreements. In December 1866, he wrote her: "I've taken up *Consuelo*, which I devoured when it ran in the *Revue indépendante*. Once again I'm *charmed* by it! What talent! Mon Dieu, what talent! I keep saying that to myself over and over again 'in the silence of my sanctum.' . . . I can only compare you to some great American river: Vastness and Calm." To which she answered: "And you're reading that stuff? Does it really amuse you? I'll read it again then one of these days, and if you like me I'll like myself."[16]

Politics should have kept apart the former "communist" of 1848 and the man who had been won over by Napoleon III. It did not. George Sand was no longer a "red," but neither had she become a "misanthrope," as she sometimes claimed after June 1848; instead, she was counting the days until the advent of a democratic republic in France. She believed a necessary condition for democracy was to educate the people. How would she react to Flaubert's elitist proclamations? "Axiom," he wrote her: "hatred of the Bourgeois is the beginning of virtue. As for me, I include in the word 'bourgeois' the bourgeois in overalls as well as the bourgeois in a frock coat. It's we, we alone—that is, the educated—who are the People, or, to put it better, the tradition of Humanity."[17] She did not reply directly, but worried about how he would depict the people in *Sentimental Education*. He reassured her: "I told you that I don't flatter the Democrats in my book. But I assure you the Conservatives aren't spared, either. I'm now writing three pages on the abominations committed by the National Guard in June '48, which will make me highly popular with the bourgeois. I'm doing my best to rub their noses in their own turpitude."[18] He raged against Thiers: "Is it possible to find a more triumphant imbecile, a more abject ass, a more turd-like bourgeois?" She applauded him: "At last! At last someone agrees with me about that boor of a politician. It could only be you, *ami de mon coeur*. 'Turd-like' is a sublime expression to describe this kind of 'merdoid' vegetable."[19]

Deep down, George Sand no longer had the spirit of a firebrand, or of a "*pétroleuse*," as the female supporters of the Commune were later contemptuously called. She was able to get along with Flaubert because she had come up with a new philosophy, which she confided to him: "I was young myself once, and subject to fits of indignation. But that's all over! Ever since I started poking my nose into real Nature I've found in it and its revolutions an order, a consistency, a placidity lacking in man, but which man can to a certain extent assimilate so long as he's not too directly embroiled in the difficulties of his own existence. Of course, when those difficulties present themselves again he has to deal with them as best he can, but if he's drunk of the cup of eternal truth he's no longer too passionately engaged for or against the evanescent and relative variety."[20]

Though there were plenty of things to separate them, their desire to find common ground was stronger. There was never the slightest conflict between them. After the happy days spent with Sand and her family during the Christmas season of 1869, Flaubert sank into a new period of sadness, problems, and suffering, primarily caused by the deaths of those he loved.

The Mourning Season

For Flaubert, the death of Louis Bouilhet had been a devastating blow. The publication of his novel did not distract him from his sorrow. He spent the first months of 1870 gathering his friend's final poems for a collection called *Dernières Chansons,* for which he also wrote a preface. After recounting Bouilhet's modest and impoverished life and discussing his poetry and plays, Flaubert described Bouilhet's literary standards—which were also his own. He exalted the labor, research, and exertion necessary to create a piece of literature. "He led an existence completely devoted to the ideal," he wrote of Bouilhet. "He was one of those rare people serving literature only for itself, among the last fanatics of a religion close to death—or already dead."

Life seemed to lead him from one death to the next. After having to separate from his faithful servant, who had been hospitalized for acute articular rheumatism, he witnessed the final days of Jules Duplan, one of his closest confidants, "a wonderful old friend and utterly devoted." Duplan died on March 1, 1870. Gustave and Jules were contemporaries who had been introduced to each other two decades earlier by Maxime Du Camp. Jules had tremendous admiration for Gustave and was very devoted to him. He had often served as his researcher and archivist, gathering articles about his books and answering his requests for details for his novels. Their letters to each other were lighthearted, full of jokes and bawdy tales. His brother Ernest had negotiated Flaubert's contract for *Salammbô* with Michel Lévy. "I grieve for your sorrows," George Sand wrote to Flaubert. "They come too thick and fast." He answered that he had "no one to talk to, no one who *feels,* as you do." He was plagued by physical ailments: flu, eczema, a persistent fever. His friend in Nohant was worried: "How are you, my poor child? I'm glad to be here, surrounded by my family darlings. I'm sorry too, to have left you sad and ill and beset by vexations." Flaubert told her he felt old and complained—it had become a leitmotif—that he no longer saw anyone with whom he could talk.[21]

He was briefly distracted from his melancholy by an incident involving George Sand. He learned that the empress had felt targeted by Sand's latest novel, *Malgré tout* [*Despite It All*], which was being serialized in the *Revue des deux mondes*. In the novel, Mlle d'Ortosa, a character always looking to cause a frisson, makes the following declaration of faith: "I want to marry a rich, young, handsome man, who is hopelessly in love with me, forever devoted to me, and proudly bears an illustrious name in society. I also want him to have power, I want him to be a king, an emperor, or at least the heir apparent to the reigning prince." This passage had been seized upon by the press to stir up a little scandal, and Empress Eugénie had reacted strongly. Flaubert received a telegram from Mme Cornu, a close friend of the empress, asking him to come see her immediately on "urgent business." Hortense Cornu was a childhood friend of Napoleon III whom Flaubert had met through Jules Duplan. She had gone to the trouble of having *Salammbô* translated into German by one of her friends. It therefore fell to her to tell Flaubert that the empress was angry with George Sand. He immediately let his friend know the empress's wishes: "She would like you to write me a letter saying that the Empress was not your model. I am to send your letter to Mme Cornu, who will pass it on to the Empress." Sand replied that she did not write satires, that she did not know the empress, and that her portraits were completely invented: "The public, ignorant of what invention is, always claims to find models. This is a mistake, and demeans art." Flaubert quickly reassured Hortense Cornu and reminded her that all the pharmacists in the Seine-Inférieure had recognized themselves in Homais: "I was quite sure that Mme Sand had no intention of painting a portrait: first because of her high-mindedness, her taste, and her respect for Art, and second because of her character, her sense of decorum and fairness."[22] The incident was closed.

As for George Sand, she again interceded on Flaubert's behalf with Michel Lévy. Flaubert still believed his publisher had paid him four thousand francs less than what he had been promised.[23] She insisted that Flaubert be allowed to see Lévy himself. The meeting was arranged, but Lévy only agreed to give Flaubert an interest-free loan, in exchange for a guarantee that he could have the rights to his next novel. Flaubert, always unable to openly discuss money matters with his publishers, did not send him packing. He was keenly aware that Lévy was also the publisher of the collection of Bouilhet's verse for which he was writing a preface and did not want to jeopardize that project. Sand advised him to be cautious: "Even if he won't shell out 4000 francs, he must at least commit himself to paying 10,000 per volume for the next book. And if he won't do that, then it'll be time enough for you to leave him. But in these days of plebiscite and confusion, which look likely to continue, don't forget that Lévy is the most, if not the only, reliable publisher there is." If Gustave needed money, she continued, he should say so: her latest play, *L'Autre* [*The Other*], was a big success, and she had one thousand francs at his disposal. He thanked her and assured her that he could still put bread on the table and buy himself shirts. He added: "For my part, I'll leave Lévy quite alone—not even answer him. I find such matters intolerable, so atrociously unpleasant that I could scream. I prefer to live less well and not concern myself about money."[24]

The weeks passed. Flaubert could no longer hide his moroseness. He confided in Sand that he no longer had a taste for writing, because too few people liked what he liked. His novel had not been well received by the public, sales were stagnating; now that Bouilhet and Sainte-Beuve were dead, he was terrified he would no longer find anyone in Paris to talk about literature with. It must be said that at this juncture most people were focused on politics. After the worrisome legislative elections of 1869, Napoleon III had hoped to solidify his power by holding a plebiscite on May 8, 1870. The plebiscite cannily asked French voters whether they approved of all the constitutional reforms that were in a liberal, parliamentary vein. The emperor's question had been met with an overwhelming yes, but the situation was made murky by the plebiscitary campaign, strikes, and legal action against the Workers' International. While Flaubert remained indifferent to the agitation, he complained that it distracted people from literature ... and from his novel! He had never felt so lonely in his life: his niece Caroline, whom he loved as if she were his own daughter, lived far away in Dieppe, and his mother was now so old that "any conversation with her (except about her health) is impossible." The little domestic conflicts at Croisset weighed upon him. He confessed to Maxime Du Camp that he was worried he would "turn into a hypochondriac."

Then tragedy struck the Goncourt brothers, with whom he still enjoyed talking, visiting friends, and going to the theater. Jules, the younger of the two brothers, was in a very bad way. Edmond cared for him around the clock, helplessly witnessing his brother's terrifying physical and intellectual deterioration as a result of syphilis. Flaubert was distraught. In a letter dated June 4, Edmond had made a poignant confession: "Please believe me when I tell you that I had decided to end it once and for all, everything had been arranged and prepared—even the letter to the police chief; I would blow his brains out, then mine, but nearly at the very moment I was going to carry out my plan, in a fit of impatience, anger, and despair about I don't know what stupid pig-headedness on his part, I took him by the collar, and my brother, I could say my child, responded to my violence and my gaze with eyes both so surprised and so full of childish terror that my hands let go of him and I felt entirely and forever incapable of killing him.—I say this only to you; not a word to anyone. So we must live."[25] Jules de Goncourt became paralyzed and finally died an agonizing death on June 20. Flaubert wrote: "I'm crammed with coffins, like an old cemetery."[26] He followed the funeral procession from the church in Auteuil to the Montmartre cemetery with a heavy heart, and noted that he had seen Théophile Gautier cry. Once back at Croisset, he wrote to Edmond de Goncourt to invite him to come rest in Normandy. Tired, sick, and devastated, Edmond preferred to visit his family in Bar-sur-Seine before returning to Paris.

Throughout these ordeals, Flaubert was able to rely on George Sand's tender friendship. Whether by seeing her in Paris or reading her letters, he was genuinely comforted by the outstretched hand of this woman who constantly elicited his admiration for her energy, her refusal to enter into any agreement with death, her daily renewed pleasure in life, her ability to accept old age as a happy stage of life, and her tireless generosity. By seeing this elderly woman surrounded by her family at Nohant, so devoted to being a grandmother and enjoying the little pleasures with which she filled her days—teaching her granddaughters, working on her garden, collecting plants, making jam, listening to music, laughing at the puppet theater, savoring the seasonal odors that flooded the garden, admiring the winter landscapes or the return of spring—Flaubert was given a powerful example of what Mona Ozouf calls "the will to give misfortune as little grip as possible."[27] She was able to appease him, comfort him, and give him the courage he had lost. While he did not travel to Nohant as often as he might have wanted, he knew that he had a sweet friend there who would always open her arms to him: "You must come and spend a few days with us if you're going to be in Paris in August. You *did* get a laugh here. We'll do our best to amuse you and stir you up a bit. You'll find the little girls grown taller and prettier. The tiny one is starting to talk."[28] In the "terrible solitude" and "black gloom" he complained of in these years of mourning and literary disappointments, Flaubert was able to lean on this woman who was so denigrated, despised, and slandered by her contemporaries but proved to be the most sensitive confidante: "We all love you, and I love you *passionately*, as you know," she wrote him on August 6, 1869. The letters between the two friends also reveal a kindness we might not expect to find in a master of irony like Flaubert: "I do love you very much," she wrote him, "you know, my dear old man. How perfect it would be to spend a long year living close to such a good and great heart."[29]

Gustave Flaubert and George Sand enjoyed a much-cherished mutual friend, Ivan Turgenev, the author of *Sketches from a Hunter's Album* and the first Russian writer to become truly famous in France. Turgenev, who spent little time on his Russian estate of Spasskoye-Lutovinovo, was usually to be found in Germany, in Karlsruhe or Baden-Baden, where he owned a home, or in France, where he was published by Hachette and Hetzel. Having fallen in love with the opera singer Pauline Viardot in 1843, he lived in a ménage à trois with her and her art historian husband Louis on their estate in Courtavenel-en-Brie (and later in Bougival). The Polish writer Charles-Edmond Chojecki first brought Turgenev to a Magny dinner one evening in February 1863. Jules de Goncourt set eyes on "a charming colossus, a gentle giant who looks like the kindly genie of a forest or a mountain." With blue eyes, thick white hair, a delightful Russian accent, and vast cosmopolitan erudition, he immediately appealed to his hosts, and particularly to Flaubert. A few days later, the Russian writer gave the French novelist translations of *Sketches from a Hunter's Album* and *Rudin*, both of which enchanted Flaubert: "For me, you have long been a Master. But the more I study you, the more I marvel at your talent."[30] Flaubert enjoyed the company of the "gentle giant" whenever he had the opportunity—too rare for his taste—to meet him: "I know few men who are such exquisite conversationalists," he told Princess Mathilde. In November 1868, Turgenev visited him at Croisset. George Sand knew Pauline Viardot and had met Turgenev in Saint Petersburg, but it was really through Flaubert that she got to know him. Early in July 1870, Flaubert wrote to Sand: "Apart from you and Turgenev, I don't know a single mortal with whom I can share the things closest to my heart; and you both live far away."[31] When *Sentimental Education* was published, this most obliging friend informed Flaubert that in Saint Petersburg *The Russian*

Messenger had printed "an enormous article" praising the author and his work. Turgenev added: "Last night in bed I reread the scene of the 'Club de l'Intelligence' and the Spaniard made me laugh out loud." Along with thanking Turgenev for the news, Flaubert made the following confession: "The moments spent with you recently have been the only good times I've had in the last eight months! You can't imagine how isolated I feel on the intellectual front! That's why I seize upon you so avidly, as soon as you turn up."[32]

Unfortunately, Flaubert would not soon see Turgenev again: his Russian friend had returned to Germany shortly before the Franco-Prussian War broke out on July 15, 1870. His melancholy was replaced by worry and fear, but also anger: "I am dismayed by the enthusiasm for war. Why do we fight?"[33]

CHAPTER 22

War!

Yes indeed, why do we fight? Flaubert had his own theory about that, but it wasn't right. His first explanation was philosophical, not to say theological: "because man's natural condition is savagery." Flaubert saw his conviction confirmed in displays of chauvinism, notably in Paris: "I don't know if I'm going to offend your patriotism," he wrote to Edma Roger des Genettes, "but I am *distressed* by the spectacle of my compatriots. Humanity's incorrigible barbarism fills me with a dark gloom. I weep over the bridges felled, the railroads damaged, the waste of so much work! Not to mention the deaths, of which there will be many! I do not see a single *idea* in this war. They are fighting for the pleasure of fighting; I just don't understand."[1] In actuality, the people shouting "To Berlin!" bore much less responsibility than the hunger for power of states and their leaders. Furthermore, only a minority of French citizens were enthusiastic about the declaration of war, as attested by reports filed by prefects around the country. The bellicose may have encouraged the Corps Législatif, France's lower chamber, to vote in favor of military funding by gathering in front of the National Assembly's seat at the Palais Bourbon on July 15, 1870, but that was the extent of their contribution. One does not need to go into the depths of human nature to find the war's causes; look no further than Bismarck and Napoleon III, who both wanted armed conflict between Prussia and France—though the former was markedly more enthusiastic.

War Reviled

Chancellor Bismarck's objective was to unify fragmented Germany under Prussia's domination. With unrivaled diplomatic skill, he had dragged Austria into a war against Denmark, after which the Scandinavian nation had lost its duchies of Schleswig, Holstein, and Lauenburg. Holstein was initially supposed to be administered by Austria, but that did not last. Bismarck's grand scheme was to get rid of the Habsburg Empire; Prussia's victory at the Battle of Sadowa in 1866 allowed it to expand again and form the North German Confederation, a coherent state stretching from the Elbe to the Rhine and a formidable new power under the authority of Prussia. Bismarck now needed to annex the southern states of Bavaria, Baden, and Württemberg. Beginning in August 1866, Bismarck convinced the southern states to sign secret military alliances, which gave him additional power and the promise of unification. France under Napoleon III could not remain passive in the face of such a threat, and Bismarck soon identified France as the next obstacle to be overcome; this would require a war, which would conveniently also serve to cement German unitary patriotism. Convinced that Prussia would enjoy military superiority, after France's disastrous military expedition to Mexico, he provoked France by supporting a candidate to the vacant Spanish throne who was a member of the Hohenzollern dynasty of Prussia. Finally, he humiliated French diplomacy by making public the infamous Ems Dispatch, a truncated version of a message he had received from Wilhelm I, king of Prussia, reporting the French ambassador's demands. Its public release was a terrible affront to France.

In the French camp, the prospect of war with Prussia met with the approval of Napoleon III's entourage, starting with Empress Eugénie. Worried about the regime's liberal and parliamentary turn and wanting to put a stop to the rise of the republican opposition, the emperor's circle considered that a war—which they never doubted France would win—was the best way to reestablish once and for all the political authority that had only begun to be achieved after the successful plebiscite. These advocates of war were unaware of the imperial armed forces' pathetic state and inferiority in numbers. They had been misled by statements such as Minister of War General Leboeuf's declaration that the army was "not missing a single gaiter button." And based on the bellicose demonstrations that outraged Flaubert, they could count on chauvinistic public opinion. The *Marseillaise*, which had been banned since the 1851 coup d'état, was once again sung in the streets of Paris, and cries of "To Berlin!" rose up over the rooftops. Those who argued for peace were physically assaulted.[2]

When war broke out, Flaubert had just gotten back to work on *Saint Anthony*, but he was soon distracted by his obsession with the "frightful butchery" being prepared. He could no longer think of anything but the conflict. Taking the position of a moralist rather than a political observer, he blamed the "incorrigible barbarism of mankind" in a letter to George Sand: "Behold 'natural man'! What price theories now? Extol Progress, enlightenment, the good sense of the Masses, and the sweet nature of the French people! I assure you that anyone who ventured to preach Peace here would get himself murdered." Upon careful consideration, he accepted that the conflict might have geopolitical causes: "But maybe," he wrote to Sand on August 3, "that country [Prussia] was tending to become hypertrophied, like France under Louis XIV and Napoleon." Yet he did not further develop this analysis, opting instead for an elitist interpretation of the consequences of universal male suffrage: "Do you think that if France, instead of being governed, in effect, by the mob, were to be ruled by the 'Mandarins,' we'd be where we are now? If instead of wanting to enlighten the lower classes we'd busied ourselves educating the upper, we wouldn't have M. de Kérary [a deputy in the Corps législatif] proposing the sack of the duchy of Baden—a measure the public finds quite right and proper."[3] This became his hobby horse: government by the "mandarins," by the knowledgeable—that is, by those who know! A lover of Antiquity like himself should have remembered Plato's failure in Sicily: the art of politics does not mix well with science and philosophy.

He was alone at Croisset, fulminating against the masses, the mob, and universal suffrage. He had no idea that in Paris his friend Ernest Renan shared his opinion. Edmond de Goncourt, who had continued writing the *Journal* after his brother's death, reported the discussions of the dining companions who had now moved from Magny's establishment to Brébant's. Renan argued that the German Protestants were superior to the French people, who had been "cretinized" by Catholicism. At times he sounded just like Flaubert: "I'd rather have peasants you kicked in the ass than peasants like ours, whom universal suffrage has made our masters, peasants—the very dregs of civilization, who were responsible for inflicting that government upon us for twenty years."[4]

Beyond the "human butchery" on the horizon, Flaubert had a foreboding that once peace was declared, revolution would follow war. In his letters to Nohant, he bore witness to the ravages caused by war and the growing number of beggars flooding into his region. He predicted the worst: "Soon we'll be moving into *la Sociale*. Which will be followed by a vigorous and lengthy reaction!"[5] Those who know their history will recognize Flaubert's lucidity in predicting a socialist republic followed by a conservative crackdown. But for the time being, news from the border was getting alarming, and Flaubert did not want to remain idle. He would not be a contemplative grouch; he would serve! He initially signed up to be a nurse at the Hôtel-Dieu in Rouen. His disgust with chauvinism and his fits of anger at nationalists were no longer in season. The Prussians had penetrated into Alsace, Marshal MacMahon's French troops had been defeated at Frœschwiller on August 6, and now Strasbourg was under siege. Enemy troops were in Lorraine, where General Frossard, left alone by Marshal Bazaine, was defeated at Forbach. From a distance, Flaubert anxiously followed the Prussians' advance; he had resolved that if they besieged Paris he would go there and fight: "My rifle is ready." On August 18, he sensed that the end of the Empire was now only a question of days, but, as he wrote to Ernest Commanville, "we must defend it to the end." He applauded his brother Achille and the deputy Edgar Raoul-Duval for raising a mobile guard battalion of five hundred men at the city's expense and putting it at the ministry's disposal.

Defending the Homeland

Flaubert's state of mind had changed since the beginning of the war. While he had once professed his indifference to patriotic matters, he now felt like a defender of the French territory: "My sadness," he told Maxime Du Camp, "has turned into belligerent desires. Yes, I stupidly feel like fighting, and I swear on my honor that if I wasn't certain it would kill my mother on the spot, I would go join good [Charles] d'Osmoy, who must now be near Châlons, heading a company of infantrymen." He added: "The idea of peace exasperates me."[6]

He did manage to convince his mother to let him go to Paris "with his rifle over his shoulder" if the capital were besieged. He reported this in a letter on August 26, completely unaware of the military operations that had taken place over the previous eight days. Tragedy was on the horizon. The emperor, who was now a ghost of himself, pale, sick, incontinent, barely able to stay on horseback, had wanted to return to Paris, but Eugénie had persuaded him not to. Acting as regent to try to save the regime, she had formed a new government, replacing Émile Ollivier with Charles Cousin-Montauban, whose entourage was composed exclusively of authoritarian Bonapartists. Fearing that

Paris would revolt if the emperor were to return to the capital defeated, she ordered him to stay with the army, which had been under the supreme command of Achille Bazaine since August 13. While the half of the French army under Bazaine's direct command was besieged in Metz, Napoleon III joined the half under MacMahon, which proceeded to undertake ill-conceived maneuvers and counter-maneuvers. After a series of false victories and serious setbacks, it was defeated once and for all at Sedan on September 1. The emperor, who would not abdicate or sign a peace treaty, was taken prisoner along with eighty thousand men of the defeated army.

In the days leading up to Sedan, Flaubert, who had no doubt that Paris would be besieged, had repeated to all and sundry that he was prepared to go there—that he was disgusted by the idea of peace and was ready to do battle. No defeatist, he wrote to Edmond de Goncourt that it was still possible to turn the situation around. He and his mother had taken in their relatives from Nogent-sur-Seine, the Bonenfants; there were now sixteen people living at Croisset. A full house, but there was still no one to talk to: "Your grandmother," he wrote Caroline, "continues to complain about the weakness of her legs and her deafness. It's all dreadful."[7] Disinformation in the region was such that on August 31, Flaubert rejoiced at "excellent news" from the front: "MacMahon and Bazaine know what they're up to. The latter has been working miracles for two weeks." In fact, it was just the opposite: Bazaine proved an incompetent strategist throughout the entire conflict. But optimism ran so strong that on September 7, Flaubert, still unaware of the disaster at Sedan and the fall of the Empire, sent Princess Mathilde a martial message: "The most peaceable bourgeois such as myself are perfectly resolved to getting killed rather than giving in." He told everyone he was no longer sad and that he wanted to "eat Prussians." As a result, even while getting back to work on *Saint Anthony,* he became a lieutenant of his national guard company; he drilled his men and took lessons in the military arts in Rouen. He told George Sand that everyone he knew was determined to march on Paris if the city were surrounded, and he encouraged his friend to exhort the people of Berry to fight. But he soon learned the truth about the calamity at Sedan and the proclamation of the Third Republic—which he did not much believe in. He took a quick trip to Dieppe, the port from which Princess Mathilde, abandoned by Nieuwerkerke without even a word of goodbye, had embarked for England on the day after the Revolution of September 4. She was accused of having fled with fifty-one million francs in gold in her baggage; Flaubert joined Alexandre Dumas fils in Dieppe to quash this calumny.[8] He returned to Croisset in a lugubrious, depressed state and announced that he was *finished*.

His brother Achille, who had received news from Paris, assured him that the capital was ready to fight. Indeed, Paris did not lack for means of defending itself. Since the 1840s, the city had been heavily fortified, with a twenty-mile-long, thirty-foot-high outer wall surrounded by a ten-foot-deep ditch. Beyond this wall, there were twenty-five solidly armed forts and redoubts within two miles of the city. Faced with the possibility of a siege, many Parisians—those who could afford it—left the city for the provinces. But the city remained well defended by three types of combat units: infantrymen and withdrawn sailors (close to 70,000 men); the Mobile National Guard—the *moblots*—composed of twenty-five- to thirty-five-year-old reservists (about 100,000 men); and the Sedentary National Guard (300,000 men), which had been opened to the population by a decree of August 11, 1870, and was divided by neighborhood. Foundries installed in various establishments provided Paris with the means to make weapons—rifles, cannons, shells. There would be no shortage of food so long as fair rationing was organized (unfortunately, this did not really happen: meat rationing only began on October 16 and bread rationing on January 18). Flaubert was delighted that Paris was determined to resist under the command of its governor, General Trochu.

On September 17, the German armies crossed the Seine at Villeneuve-Saint-Georges. On the 19th, a Prussian offensive drove the French forces out of the heights of Châtillon, taking what would become the key strategic position from which the Germans were able to observe Paris and bomb it. Yet the Prussians did not attack the city's ramparts; rather than an actual siege, they put in place a blockade. Flaubert did not leave for Paris, as he had planned to do, but drilled the men in his militia, remaining every bit as combative, fired up, and hawkish: "Now it's a duel to the death," he wrote to his niece on September 27. "According to the old adage, we must 'fight or perish.' The most craven men have become brave. Tomorrow the Rouen national guard is sending its 1st battalion to Vernon. In 15 days all of France will have risen." Flaubert began night patrols. He made a solemn and "fatherly" declaration to his men: "I informed them that I would run a sword into the belly of the first to falter and ordered them to shoot me should they see me running away."[9] Thrilled by this fervor, he regained his appetite and was even able to get back to his manuscript. He believed that Paris would resist. After all,

Jules Favre, a minister in the Government of National Defense formed in the wake of Napoleon III's capture by the Prussians, had proclaimed that France would not yield "an inch of our territory, nor a single stone of our fortresses." Flaubert also counted on the army of the Loire and other provincial armies to deliver the capital. Now he believed that there would be no civil war, for the bourgeois had become republicans: "I believe *la Sociale* is adjourned," he wrote to Maxime Du Camp. It was late September, and Flaubert was still full of hope—he had faith in the country's resistance. At the same time, he predicted a gloomy postwar period, with the dawn of a new world in which militarism and positivism would prevail. Similar fears were heard at the Brébant dinners: "We are going to be forced to become a serious, well-behaved, reasonable people," noted Edmond de Goncourt. "We will no longer be rich enough to pay tenors, our Opera will be like that of a second-rate city. . . . We are going to be condemned to become a virtuous people."[10]

Early in October, Flaubert began to feel discouraged again. The Prussians were getting closer to Rouen; there was constant talk of the French armies of the Centre region, but they were nowhere to be seen; Strasbourg had surrendered and no one had come to its rescue. "We're just trotting soldiers from one province to the next; that's all." He realized that Paris would not be able to hold out eternally and that within a month the game would probably be up. But that would only be the end of the first act. He began to think, once again, that "the second act will be civil war." Did he know that revolt was already rumbling in Paris? On October 5, while Wilhelm I and Bismarck were taking up residence at Versailles, a demonstration led by Gustave Flourens and swelled by the National Guard battalions from Belleville and Ménilmontant demanded that the government provide good rifles (*chassepots*) and order a mass sortie—that is, an offensive—and municipal elections. Unrest occurred again on October 8, and cries of "Long live the Commune!" began to be heard. The political truce that had been established during the first days of the blockade was now replaced by dissension. The extreme left demanded that the Government of National Defense take appropriate military action. But this government of moderate republicans, including Jules Favre, Jules Ferry, Ernest Picard, and Louis Trochu, the governor of Paris, seemed to fear revolution more than defeat by the Prussians. Jules Favre did not hide the fact: "It was impossible for me not to be both deeply moved and *distressed* by this exhilaration." As for Trochu, he affirmed that he would follow his "plan" to the end, "without revealing it." No one would ever learn whether such a plan actually existed. As a distant witness, Flaubert asked: "Is some abominable intrigue going on in secret? Why such inaction?"[11]

As the Prussians drew closer to Rouen, the Bonenfants went home. Flaubert was bolstered by the news that Minister of the Interior Léon Gambetta had escaped from Paris to Tours by hot-air balloon in hopes of keeping up the fight against the Prussians from the provinces. He grew impassioned as he imagined the war in Paris: "Never in the history of France," he wrote to his niece on October 14, "has there been anything so tragic and so grand.—The siege of Paris! That word alone makes one dizzy, and how it will make future generations dream! No matter, despite it all, I still have hope."

Yet his hope was whittled away with every passing day. He confessed his despair in a letter to the exiled Princess Mathilde: "Here, we're expecting a visit from the Prussians any day now. When will it be? What distress! I am alone with my mother who is aging with every hour amid a *stupid* population, and assailed by packs of beggars. We have up to 400 (I did say 400) a day. They make threats; we're forced to close the shutters in broad daylight. Isn't that lovely? The militia I command is so undisciplined that this morning I resigned." If Bazaine could break loose from Metz, if General Bourbaki could join him, and if the army of the Loire could march on Paris, nothing would be lost, for the Parisians would make a devastating mass sortie! "So long as Paris hasn't been captured, France is still alive!" Even if the Prussians penetrated the city, Flaubert thought, formidable street-fighting would ensue.

The Invasion

The Prussians were on the way, and Flaubert was worried, unable to work. He was sorry that he had not left for Paris as he originally intended to, staying home out of consideration for his mother. Now he was once again overcome with disgust. He was convinced that France was about to enter a "hideous" world: "We will be utilitarian and military, economical, small, poor, abject."

He continued to put his hope in Marshal Bazaine, but on October 29 he learned of the fall of Metz. This was a catastrophe: the German units blocking Metz were now free to move to Paris. The provinces were demoralized. But wouldn't Paris fight furiously? On October 31, the announcement of three pieces of news in quick succession provoked the long-awaited explosion in the capital: Le Bourget, which had been taken from the enemy a few days earlier, had been reoccupied by the Prussians because of a lack of reinforcements;

Thiers, who had been sent to negotiate with Bismarck, had suggested that an armistice was possible; and, most important, Bazaine had surrendered at Metz, a treacherous act that fell like a fatal blow. The battalions from the east of Paris rushed to the Hôtel de Ville yelling, "No armistice! Long live the Commune! Mass uprising!" The insurgents broke open the doors, determined to install a new government committed to all-out war, mass sorties, and the rejection of armistice under any terms. But divisions among the insurgents led to their defeat, and order was reestablished. Nonetheless, the government abandoned any idea of negotiating for an armistice. It organized a plebiscite, in which a majority of participants voted in the government's favor, and held municipal elections by arrondissement. Though he did not know it, Flaubert agreed with the leading demand of the insurgents of October 31: "Ah! If only we had a real victory on the Loire, if Trochu led formidable sorties, things would change. But will they change?"

There is no doubt that Trochu and the entire government—with the exception of Léon Gambetta, who was in the provinces trying to whip up the troops to liberate Paris—wanted to put an end to a fight that they saw as a "heroic folly" and, moreover, one that would risk giving the revolutionaries power by arming them. From Croisset, Flaubert could not understand this refusal to fight by any means possible. He predicted that the Prussians would only have to wait: they would take Paris by famine. The Germans' approach to Rouen drove him to despair. He supposed he would have to accommodate occupying troops. He resolved to refuse. They arrived in mid-December: seven soldiers and three officers to be housed and six horses to be fed. Gustave and his mother took shelter at the Hôtel-Dieu in Rouen: "Oh poor dear child," he wrote to his niece on December 18, "if you could know what it means to hear them drag their swords on the foot path, to have their horses whinny in your face! What a disgrace! What a disgrace!"[12]

In Paris, the patriots' hearts filled with ideas of revolt. Political clubs proliferated. The government was castigated; angry citizens denounced the procrastination of General Trochu, the poor organization of supplies, and the endless lines in the cold, during which women fainted from hunger. Edmond de Goncourt, anything but a leftist, deplored the situation: "The things taking place point to such incompetence up high that the people could easily mistake this incompetence for treason! Yet if it does happen [the Prussians entering Paris], what a heavy responsibility before history will be borne by this government, this Trochu who, with such ample means to resist, with this armed mass of five hundred thousand men, will have—without a battle, without an advantage, without a single small shining action, without even a single big unsuccessful action, finally without anything intelligent, audacious, or stupidly heroic—turned this defense into the most shameful defense in history, that which most eloquently expresses the military void of contemporary France!"[13]

With Caroline safe in England, her husband, Ernest Commanville, traveled to Rouen to offer to take Gustave and Mme Flaubert back to his home in Dieppe. Flaubert turned down the invitation, judging that his mother might be restless in Dieppe, where she knew no one, and that the journey would be too trying for her. As for him, he did not want to go too far from his manservant, who was alone taking care of the Prussians at Croisset: "How will I find my study, my books, my manuscripts? All I was able to put in a safe place were my papers relating to *Saint Anthony*. Émile [the servant] has the key to the study, but they keep asking for it, and go in and take books, which they leave lying around their bedrooms."[14]

In Paris, shortages and the constant threat of famine served as the assailants' best weapons. In order to further sap the population's morale, the Prussians began shelling the city as soon as they finished installing their batteries of Krupp cannons on January 5. The people of Paris now had to protect themselves from a deluge of shells. Flaubert wondered how Parisians would be able to withstand the "horrible bombing." While the shelling of Paris did not play a determining part in the war's outcome, it did result in 750 casualties, including 185 dead. On January 22, after the Battle of Buzenval, a rare sortie launched by the deceitful Trochu to prove the National Guard's incompetence,[15] Paris was rocked by an insurrection demanding a Commune. The riot was overcome. Capitulation was now considered possible; Jules Favre signed the armistice agreement at Versailles on January 28, 1871.

Flaubert described his sadness to Caroline: "The capitulation of Paris, even though expected, has plunged me into an indescribable state. One could hang oneself out of fury. I regret that Paris wasn't burned to the last house, leaving only a great black void. France has fallen so low, is so dishonored, so debased, that I wish she might disappear completely. But I hope that civil war will kill a lot of people for us. Would that I might be included in that number!"[16] He added that as soon as he was able to write Turgenev again, he would ask him what to do to become Russian. Though these were only bitter quips, they expressed the extent of his distress.

There was one small reason to rejoice: after forty-five days of occupation, the Prussians had left Croisset. The house would need to be thoroughly cleaned, though Flaubert said that if it had belonged to him he would have preferred to have it demolished. He did not yet know that there would be more Prussians to quarter in late February. Filled with rage and shame, he decided to stop wearing his Legion of Honor ribbon: "For the words Honor and French are incompatible."

Following Bismarck's demand to negotiate the peace with a legal government, national legislative elections were held on February 8, 1871. Flaubert did not vote. He considered that the newly constituted National Assembly would be cursed from the start: "If it votes for resistance, it will be criticized for its stubbornness; if it comes out in favor of peace, it will be accused of cowardice."

For Flaubert, the Franco-Prussian War was a source of despair tempered by sporadic illusions about a national jolt that never took place. Yet he discovered an aspect of himself that he had thought was entirely lacking: patriotic fervor. However hostile he had initially been to the excesses of militarist passion, once the enemy crossed the border, he was clearly driven by a desire to resist. The artist, so little interested in patriotism, suddenly realized that what was at risk was France's very identity, its civilization and way of life. This only made him more upset by the armies' setbacks, the leaders' negligence, and finally the armistice that spelled defeat. Before the war, he had experienced the bitterness of a misunderstood writer, the misfortune of losing his dearest friend, and the despair of bereavement. Now he was struck with an unfamiliar feeling that he had little hope of ever assuaging: he was suffering from the trouble affecting France itself. For it was not over yet. From the beginning of the conflict, he had expressed his fear of the postwar period. He was particularly convinced of the imminence of a civil war, to be followed by a violent reaction. He could flatter himself that he had been clear-sighted: on March 18, 1871, a popular insurrection broke out. The history of the Paris Commune was underway.

CHAPTER 23

The Paris Commune

On February 8, 1871, the French people elected a monarchist majority to the National Assembly, which was to convene in Bordeaux. They had chosen the "party of peace" over the republicans, who were said to be in favor of continuing the war. After a four-month siege, Paris proved an exception to the rule—its voters were firmly republican. This would be the first sign of division between the capital and the Assembly, which was vested with its powers by the Government of National Defense on February 13. The Grand Théatre de Bordeaux served as its ad hoc legislative palace. Émile Zola, writing for the Paris daily *La Cloche*, astutely chronicled the growing tension between Parisians and the deputies: "No longer able to cry 'Long live the King!' the rural majority now cry 'Long live France!' with exquisite hypocrisy. Who do they hope to fool?"

Flaubert took little interest in the parliamentary debates. In mid-February, he went to live in Neuville, near Dieppe, in the home of his niece Caroline, who had returned from England after the capitulation of Paris. In a letter written on February 18, he told Princess Mathilde of the spiritual pain inflicted on him by the Prussian invasion and the occupation of his home. He added that he had had to bury his family's precious goods and his work notes in the garden. As for politics, he was utterly disillusioned: "So now Father Thiers is President of the Republic! Will he keep her or deliver her to the Orléans? Oh, how my era bores me." Adolphe Thiers, whom Flaubert had long despised, was having his hour of glory. He was seen as a wise old man who had been against the failed war. As a former minister to Louis Philippe, he comforted the majority, who had appointed him "head of executive power" until it was possible to "rule on France's permanent government." Flaubert anticipated that Thiers would be elected president of the republic. He was right, though his prediction would not come true until August 31, 1871.

On August 26, Thiers signed the peace preliminaries with Bismarck at Versailles. Back in Bordeaux two days later, he informed the French people of the conditions of the treaty: "All my life," wrote Zola, "I will remember this astonishing hour. The audience in the public galleries was anxious. You know this treaty: the handover of Alsace, aside from Belfort, the handover of Metz and part of Lorraine, five billion in damages, the occupation of a neighborhood in Paris, the payment of damages in three years, under financial guarantee or the guarantee of a Prussian occupation that would gradually be withdrawn as the payments were made. The entire room was in a painful state of amazement. Rumbles shot across the public galleries. The reading of the treaty ended in dead silence."

On March 1, the Germans marched into Paris with their drums rolling. The city looked deserted, hostile, and silent. Most of the stores were closed, and the windows were draped in black. Thiers had given the Germans the triumphant entry that they had not been able to achieve with their weapons. In exchange, he had been allowed to keep Belfort, a fortified town in northeastern France. But the Parisians were humiliated. In Bordeaux, the treaty was approved despite the resistance of republican orators Edgar Quinet, Victor Hugo, Louis Blanc, and the deputies from the annexed departments. "The struggle was truly disproportionate," wrote Zola. "The Assembly was so committed to peace that it only tolerated with impatience the orators who had signed up to speak against the proposed law. An intolerant majority, and the most upsetting sight of all: France on its knees, under the foreigner's sword, imploring peace and fearful that it would not obtain it, to the point that it no longer wanted to be defended." Once the dismemberment of France was ratified by a vote of 546 to 107, the Germans left Paris, where they had encountered nothing but the ghosts of a city in mourning.

From Dieppe, Flaubert imagined what the Prussians' triumphal entry into Paris must have been like. He wrote to Princess Mathilde: "How I thought of you on Wednesday [March 1]! And how I suffered! All day I saw the Prussians' *faisceaux* [stacked bayonets] shining in the sun on the Champs Elysées. And I could hear their music, their odious music, ringing out under the Arch of Triumph! The man resting in the Invalides [Napoleon I] must have been turning over in his grave, full of rage."

He was profoundly distressed: "No one is more devastated by this catastrophe than I am." It was not only the humiliation of military defeat that afflicted him; he believed that these events would lead to a regression in civilization: "We are witnessing the end of the Latin world," he wrote to his friend Marie Régnier. He told George Sand that he thought he had never been so sad before, so hopeless. He was horrified by the German occupation: "These officers who smash your mirrors with white-gloved hands, who know Sanskrit and fling themselves on your champagne, who steal your watch and then send you their visiting-card, this war for money—these civilized savages horrify me more than Cannibals." A passion for revenge would be born in France: "The government, whatever it may be, will only be able to maintain itself by harping on that passion. Mass murder is going to be the object of all of our efforts—France's ideal!"[1] Flaubert had a point. The seeds of nationalism had been planted. The French, who until their defeat had seen themselves as the leading nation in the world and had conflated patriotism and universalism, had come up against Germany's particularist patriotism, which was transformed into a model by the Prussian victory. Intellectuals like Ernest Renan began to think of using Germany as a source of inspiration to reorganize France and achieve the day of vengeance. Renan was beginning to work on his *Réforme intellectuelle et morale de la France* [*Intellectual and Moral Reform of France*], in which he would deplore the lowering of the nobility: "France's military spirit came from its Germanic side; by violently chasing out the Germanic elements and replacing them with an egalitarian concept of society, France rejected whatever military spirit it had." Edmond de Goncourt was irritated by "the despotic hold on Renan's thought of everything that is said, written, and printed in Germany. Today I heard this righteous person adopting Bismarck's criminal maxim, 'might makes right.'"[2]

The Insurrection

In mid-March, Flaubert left Dieppe to assess the damage the Prussians had done to his home. The soldiers were still there, and the house was "uninhabitable," as was Caroline's apartment in Rouen. "They are behaving *abominably* in Rouen," he wrote to his niece, "and I ask you both not to stay there long, and especially not to walk there at night." A letter from George Sand expressed similar concerns: "I worry lest your awful guests should have ruined Croisset, for they continue to make themselves loathsome and disgusting everywhere in spite of the peace. If I had five billion francs I'd spend it all to get them thrown out!"[3] In the *Journal*, Edmond de Goncourt wrote: "A scatological pamphleteer could write a fiercely witty pamphlet with the title SHIT

AND PRUSSIANS. These disgusting victors have *shit-caked* France with such meticulousness, inventiveness, and imagination that it really deserves a physiological study of that people's taste for excremental business. At Charles Edmond's place, they took down his father's portrait and made a hole where his mouth was. You can guess the rest."[4] Flaubert swore to himself never to spend time with a German again, no matter who he was.

From Rouen, Flaubert traveled to Brussels with Alexander Dumas fils to visit Princess Mathilde. He was in the Belgian capital on March 19 when he learned that there had been fighting in Paris since the previous night. After spending four days with the exiled princess, he embarked at Ostend for London to go and visit Juliet Herbert, whom he had not seen for four years. He stayed at Hatchett's Hotel on Dover Street, which was probably "very expensive."[5] Juliet was a governess for a posh family, the Conants. The reunion must have been brief, for Gustave boarded a boat from New Haven on Monday, March 27, to return to France. Nothing else is known of his visit.

Meanwhile, the revolution was underway in Paris. The Parisians had been exasperated by many of the measures passed by the Assembly in Bordeaux, starting with the decision to make Versailles the new capital of France. The Prussians' entry into Paris on March 1 had only stoked the city's anger at the Assembly of "country people," which was scheduled to move to Versailles on March 20. To avoid an armed conflict between Versailles and Paris, Thiers decided to reclaim the cannons that were in the hands of the National Guard. These cannons had been manufactured in the forges of besieged Paris through fundraising campaigns held in newspapers and public meetings. Many of the cannons had been positioned on the heights of Montmartre before the Germans entered Paris. Thiers's March 17 decree that the cannons would be allocated to the regular army was met with popular resistance and soon set off a general revolt. After a day of violence during which two generals, Claude Lecomte and Clément Thomas, were killed by the mob, the cannons remained in the hands of the National Guard. Thiers and his administration left Paris. The capital fell under the authority of the Central Committee of the National Guard, an organization consisting of battalions from the working-class neighborhoods, which had federated and stood up to the official command even before March 18.

For several days, mediators tried to avoid civil war. These included arrondissement mayors such as Georges Clémenceau, who went back and forth between the Hôtel de Ville in Paris and Versailles, where the National

Assembly was installed on March 20 according to plan. But both sides refused to compromise. On March 26, the Central Committee took the final step into dissidence by organizing elections for a council of the Paris Commune. On March 28, the Paris Commune was proclaimed to enthusiastic cheers. A civil war was looming.

Thus far, Flaubert had only been able to follow these events from a distance, but now he was back in Neuville with his niece and her husband. Did he understand what was going on? In a letter to George Sand dated March 31, he deemed the Commune "a throwback to sheer medievalism." He could not accept that the Commune had decreed that rents should be brought back to October 1870 rates: "Now government meddles in Natural Law and interferes in contracts between individuals. The Commune asserts that we don't owe what we do owe, and that one service is not to be paid for by another. It's monstrous ineptitude and injustice." Reacting in a quintessentially bourgeois manner, Flaubert took a liberal position that paid no heed to the situation of Parisians who had endured four months of a blockade or to the resulting unemployment and poverty and the need for a transition back to normalcy.

Yet he made a genuine effort to understand what was at stake in the civil war. His unfailing patriotism was offended by the Commune because, as he put it, it "deflected our hatred." The bourgeois ranted against the Communards now and had entirely forgotten the Prussians. As for the outcome of the civil war, it would be bleak no matter what happened: "If [the Commune] should defeat the Versaillais and overthrow the government," he wrote George Sand, "the Prussians will enter Paris and 'order will prevail'—as it did in Warsaw. If, on the contrary, it is defeated, the reaction will be fierce and all liberty strangled."[6]

Far from the Barricades

Now that he was finally back at Croisset, Flaubert could breathe again. He felt good. He was happy to return to his study and all his "little belongings." Although he was waiting for the Prussians to leave the region once and for all before he started repairs, he immediately returned to work on *Saint Anthony*. On April 5, he wrote to Caroline about how happy he had been to learn of "the good drubbing" the Versaillais (the regular army) had given "our brothers," adopting the sanctimonious expression that Thiers used in the Assembly to refer to combatants on both sides. The fighting had begun. On

April 2, the regular army took hold of the outpost at Courbevoie; the Commune's troops haphazardly struck back the next day, losing Gustave Flourens, one of the major leaders of the extreme left. General de Galliffet set the tone for the regular army: "I declare war without pity on these assassins!" In his house in Auteuil, Edmond de Goncourt was overcome with enthusiasm: "The Bellevillois [Communards of the Belleville neighborhood] have been defeated! I will savor this jubilation for a long time."

Days passed, and the Commune did not surrender, contrary to Flaubert's prediction that it would not last more than a week. The Versailles army had been reinforced after Bismarck agreed to allow the French troops to be increased, despite the treaty's stipulation that they be limited to 40,000 men. They were increased to 100,000 men, then 130,000, most of whom had recently been released from prisoner of war camps. Thiers, head of the executive, shamelessly declared: "The National Assembly, gathered close around the Government, is sitting peacefully in Versailles, where one of the most beautiful armies that France has ever had is in the final stages of being raised." The Communards did not lack for courage, but indiscipline ruled. Those who were captured were taken to Versailles, where they were abused in every possible way. In his journal, the ethnographer and anarchist Élie Reclus wrote: "These men had their hands bound, and the peacocks who wouldn't have dared to fight them the previous day now spit in their mouths and eyes, and ladies use their parasols to hit these faces bathed in a nervous sweat."[7] War without pity: on April 5, the Communards published a decree declaring that any accomplice of the Versailles government could be taken hostage, and they began arresting priests, most of whom would face the firing squad in the final days of the *semaine sanglante,* the "bloody week" of repression by the regular army. In his diary, Reclus confessed that he "quaked with fear" when he read the decree on hostages posted on the walls: "Any execution of a prisoner of war or of a partisan of the regular government of the Paris Commune will immediately be followed by the execution of three hostages." This did not prevent Reclus from singing the Commune's praises the next day: "For you see, this is truly a holy war of the republic against the monarchies, a holy war of the worker against capital and idleness, a holy war that will give us social renewal."

Flaubert tried as best he could to analyze the situation from a distance. He explained to George Sand that he was "not like the bourgeois" because in his eyes, "after the invasion, there can be no further disaster": "The Prussian war has affected me like a natural disaster, one of those cataclysms that occur every six thousand years; whereas the insurgents in Paris strike me as something very clear, quite obvious and almost simple."[8] In fact, far from understanding the nature of the revolutionary movement in Paris (which was admittedly quite heterogeneous), Flaubert could only see it as a savage throwback to the Middle Ages. His greatest fear was that after the revolution was defeated there would be a reaction, possibly a third empire and undoubtedly a resurgence of "worthy ecclesiastics." Writing to Princess Mathilde, he reiterated his anger toward those who had lost sight of "good Wilhelm's remaining occupying troops" out of fear of the revolution: "France no longer thinks of the Prussians! She no longer even considers the idea of revenge! That's what we've come to!" In his eyes, this was the Communards' greatest crime: he constantly repeated that they had "deflected hate." Growing bombastic, he stated that he would prefer "the complete annihilation of Paris" to the "burning of a single village by these gentlemen, who 'are charming,' etc." He told his friend Edma Roger des Genettes his prognosis: the destruction of the Vendôme column by the Communards[9] "scatters the seeds of a third empire that will later blossom. In about twenty years one of Plon-Plon's [Prince Napoleon's] sons will restore the junior branch. As for socialism, it missed a unique opportunity and is now dead for a long time to come."[10]

Despite her former support for the revolutionaries of 1848, George Sand was even harsher than Flaubert in her assessment of the Commune. In her letters, she referred to "the vile experiment of Paris" and the "infamous Commune." She was in Nohant, far from the theater of operations, probably influenced by the part of the press violently hostile to the Commune. All of the press outside of Paris, including the *Journal des débats*, *Le Figaro*, and *Le Gaulois*, spread the worst stories about the capital's working-class quarters, claiming that pillaging went hand in hand with prostitution and drinking sprees. With Paris a living hell, the army was justified in crushing the insurgents.

At Croisset, Flaubert took stock of his property following the occupation: the Prussians had filched a few unimportant objects—a toiletries bag, some pipes—but all in all "they did no damage." He was pleased to find that the big box of letters he had buried was safe, as were his many notes on *Saint Anthony*. But this did not put a stop to his outrage. In a long letter dated April 30, he told George Sand: "I'm different from all the people I hear lamenting the war in Paris. I find it more tolerable than the invasion, because after the invasion any further despair is impossible—another proof of the depths to which we have sunk. 'Ah, thank God the Prussians are there!' is the universal cry of the bourgeois. I put Messieurs the workers into the same bag, and I'd like to throw the whole lot of them into the river!"[11] He continued with his old hobbyhorse of decrying universal suffrage, because "the people never come of age." He agreed with Renan and Émile Littré in saying that the only salvation for France was "in a *legitimate aristocracy*." As Renan put it, "Essentially blinkered, universal suffrage does not understand the need for science, the superiority of the noble and the scholar." In the meantime, Flaubert thought that in twenty to forty years France would probably see a restoration of the Empire.

Yet based on the principle that no disaster could be worse than the invasion, Flaubert declared that he was now indifferent to public misfortunes. "The callus," he wrote to Princess Mathilde, "has formed over the wound. Good evening! After the Prussian invasion, I drew the shroud over France's face. Let her roll on in mud and blood, it doesn't matter, she is finished. Whatever happens, the government will no longer sit in Paris. Therefore Paris will no longer be the Capital and the Paris we loved will become history." He imagined this future from his lonely retreat, living with a mother who could no longer walk, his sole distraction the Prussian gentlemen taking their constitutionals outside his window. He told Mathilde in passing that he was receiving desperate letters from George Sand "and that her republican faith seemed entirely extinguished."[12]

On May 10, Foreign Minister Jules Favre and Minister of Finance Augustin Pouyer-Quertier traveled to Frankfurt to sign the peace treaty on France's behalf. Inhabitants of the three annexed departments "who intended to keep their French nationality" would have until October 1 to transfer their place of residence to France. Having achieved its unity, Germany became the largest power on the European continent, under the rule of Wilhelm I, who had been crowned Emperor of Germany in the Hall of Mirrors at Versailles on January 18, 1871.

On May 22, Flaubert wrote to Élisa Schlésinger. A month earlier, he had learned that Maurice was dead—"Monsieur Maurice," his old friend from Trouville and the model for Jacques Arnoux in *Sentimental Education*. He told her that upon receiving her letter he had hoped she would decide to move back to France. "As for seeing you in Germany," he wrote, "that is a country where I will never voluntarily set foot again. I've seen enough Germans this year to never want to see another, and I cannot conceive that a self-respecting

Frenchman would for one minute deign to find himself with those gentlemen, however charming they may be. They have our clocks, our money, and our land: let them keep them and let that be the end of it! I wanted to write to you with tenderness, and here's the bitterness welling up!"

The *Semaine Sanglante*

In Paris, the war was still raging. On May 21, 1871, the regular army entered the city through the Porte du Point-du-Jour, its drums and bugles preceding the tocsin. As the calls to arms rang out, Edmond de Goncourt rejoiced that "the death throes of the odious tyranny can be heard in Paris." The next day, he reported that he could see the "demoralization" and "discouragement" of the National Guards. Over the following days, the sounds of rifles, machines guns, and shellfire drowned out the harrowing cries of the soldiers and Communards dying in combat. As they withdrew, the Communards adopted a scorched earth policy, setting fire to the streets they abandoned; those who were captured were executed without a trial. It was a brutal massacre: twenty thousand men, women, and children died in the suppression of the Commune, while the regular army lost barely over a thousand men. By May 28, it was all over. Goncourt took an aesthete's delight in the spectacle of the burned-out Hôtel de Ville: "It is a splendid, a magnificent ruin. All pink and ash green and the color of white-hot steel, or turned to shining agate where the stonework has been burnt by paraffin, it looks like the ruin of an Italian palace, tinted by the sunshine of several centuries, or better still like the ruin of a magic palace, bathed in the theatrical glow of electric light."[13] A leopard cannot change its spots.

This time, Flaubert did not directly witness the spectacle, as he had in 1848 and 1851. Unlike the notables sighing with relief all over France, he worried about the days and years to come: "Do you know what frightens me about France's near future?" he asked Princess Mathilde. "*It is the reaction* that will take place. No matter what name it gives itself, it will be anti-liberal. The fear of the *Sociale* will drive us to a conservative regime whose stupidity will be reinforced." Proving exceptionally clear-sighted—only his timeline was a little off—he added: "Since Thiers has just done us a very great service, he will be the most detested man in his country within a month."

Was Flaubert trying to break with a ruthless pack mentality? On May 27, he read an attack on Victor Hugo in the daily *Le Nouvelliste de Rouen*. The former exile in Guernsey had returned to France as soon as the Empire fell and been elected a deputy on February 8, only to step down and join those who sought to avoid a civil war. He had condemned the Parisian insurrection "before enemy fire" but refused to declare his support for Thiers and the Versaillais, who wanted to humiliate Paris. On May 26, he had opened his doors to the defeated Communards, offering them shelter in his home in Belgium—a mob then attacked his house in retaliation, and he was expelled from Belgium. But even before these events, the Rouen paper took to task the writer "who had the talent to earn many thousands of pounds in income from sonorous phrases and fantastic antitheses, a clown poet," "a simpleton." Flaubert's blood boiled; he immediately wrote to his good friend Charles Lapierre, the paper's editor, to tell him he was scandalized: "When you want to attack the personality of a great poet, don't attack him as a poet." While he did not approve of Hugo's policy of not taking sides, Victor Hugo was still Victor Hugo: "as an old Romantic, I was exasperated by your paper this morning. Old Hugo's foolishness pains me too much as it is, without his being insulted in his genius. When our masters demean themselves, we must do as the sons of Noah did, and cover their shame. Let us at least retain our respect for what was great. Don't let's add to our ruins."[14] Flaubert added: "Having gotten rid of the Commune, you will be stuck with the parish!"

While Flaubert was certainly on the side of the victors, he did not join the stampede of anti-Communard journalists and writers. He was probably most pained by the showers of praise raining down on the army that had been victorious in a war between Frenchmen. Edmond de Goncourt was among those who enthusiastically applauded: "All is well. There has been neither compromise nor conciliation. The solution has been brutal, imposed by sheer force of arms. The solution has saved everyone from the dangers of cowardly compromise. The solution has restored its confidence to the Army, which has learnt in the blood of the Communards that it was still capable of fighting."[15] From the *Journal des Débats:* "How honorable! Our army has avenged its disasters with an inestimable victory!" The *Journal de Paris:* "[The army] has done its job admirably; it displayed genuine humanity in carrying out its duty." *Le Figaro:* "How admirable is the attitude of our officers and soldiers! Only a French soldier can pick himself up so fast and so well."

It was as if the commentators were trying to outdo each other in making insolent statements that implicitly revealed their fear of a social revolution that could have spread to the entire country. Francisque Sarcey was one of many who expressed the elites' repressive frenzy: "Madmen like this, in such large numbers, and all in agreement, form such an appalling threat to the society to which they belong that the only possible penalty is radical suppression."[16]

Flaubert returned to Paris for a few days early in June, mostly for the purpose of consulting some books for *Saint Anthony*. He was frightened by the ruins and even more "sickened" by the attitude of bourgeois Parisians, for whom the Prussians no longer existed: "People excuse them," he wrote George Sand, *"admire them!!!"* 'Sensible' people want to be naturalized as Germans." He even suspected that the Prussians had something to do with the burning of Paris. Behind "such a considerable event," there was certainly "envy, hysteria, iconoclasm, and Bismarck." To Ernest Feydeau, he reiterated the "incredible stupidity" of the victorious Parisians: "It is so inconceivable that one is tempted to admire the Commune." He took stock of his feelings: "I have no hatred for the Communards, for the simple reason that I do not hate rabid dogs. But what still rankles me is the invasion of the [Prussian] doctors of philosophy, smashing mirrors with gunshots and stealing clocks; that's something new in history! I have such a deep grudge against these gentlemen that you will *never* see me in the company of *any German whatsoever*, and I am a little mad at you for being in their infamous country now."[17] Gustave was repeating himself. At least he was perfectly clear: he hated the Commune and was glad to see it defeated, but in his view the Parisian insurrection was merely a consequence of the Franco-Prussian War, and he was outraged by the Versaillais' readiness to oblige the Germans. This allowed him to accurately predict what would happen in the years to come: the triumph of *reaction*, better known as the Moral Order.

In his novel *Philémon vieux de la vieille* [*Philémon, the Old Hand*], Lucien Descaves went back over the long list of men and women of letters who had denounced the Commune: "Maxime Du Camp,[18] Louis Blanc, Théophile Gautier, Leconte de Lisle, Jules Simon, Renan, Goncourt, Champfleury, Caro, About, Ernest Daudet, Veuillot, Francisque Sarcey, De Pressensé, Dumas fils, Henri Martin, Paul de Saint-Victor, Mendès, La Sand [*sic*], J. Claretie, Barbey d'Aurevilly, Bergerat, Taine, Littré, Bourget, De Voguë." Flaubert was not on the list. Descaves did note that after the massacre Flaubert had traveled to Paris merely to find a piece of information for *The Temptation of Saint Anthony*. He had learned of this detail in the Goncourt *Journal*, which he quotes: "This cataclysm seems to have passed over him without distracting him for one moment from the impassive making of books."[19] Descaves could also have quoted Maxime Du Camp's account: "Flaubert came running, not so much to see the ruins as to throw his arms around those he loved."[20]

The following year, Flaubert read Victor Hugo's account of the events in *L'Année terrible* [*The Terrible Year*], which expressed some sympathy for the Commune. He criticized Hugo for not having "a finer discernment of the truth," but added: "No matter! what a fine roar that old lion still has!"[21] Even though his admiration was qualified, he wasn't about to join any anti-Communard lynch mob.

CHAPTER 24

"The Being I Loved Most"

Was Flaubert fully aware of the tragedy of the Commune? Did he truly understand the devastating split that had led France into seventy-two days of civil war and class war? In fact, he was only affected by a single phase of the ordeal of that "terrible year": the military defeat, occupation, and continued Prussian presence. While Flaubert was glad to be reunited with Princess Mathilde when she chose to return to Saint-Gratien, he expressed surprise at her decision in a letter to George Sand: "I think she should have remained in exile for a time. That would have been more courageous and shown greater pride. . . . She returned because she is a spoiled child who can't control her passions."[1] When he went to visit her, he was ashamed to have to walk by two German guards posted at her door: "Anything! Anything! (even the Commune) rather than the pointy helmets."[2]

Yet the Commune was not a mere "interlude," as some historians would later claim. At least twenty thousand Parisians were executed during the *semaine sanglante,* and the councils of war sitting in Versailles sentenced more than ten thousand insurgents who had not escaped to Switzerland or England either to the death penalty (95 sentences, of which 23 were carried out) or to deportation and forced labor in New Caledonia. The workers' movement had been decapitated. A census carried out after the Commune showed that the capital had lost approximately 100,000 workers and craftsmen. Though the Prussians had been unable to take the city by storm, it had been devastated by fires. French society was suffering and would long continue to suffer from deep-set divisions, as if civil war was to be France's political mode, with or without bloodshed.

The double tragedy of the foreign defeat and the internal war, at the very time when the fate of France's political institutions was in the balance, raised questions about the reasons for the country's repeated collective upheavals and for the decline of its military. Among writers close to Flaubert, two stood out in this process of collective reflection: Ernest Renan and Hippolyte Taine—"Taine-et-Renan like Tarn-et-Garonne," joked literary critic Albert Thibaudet, referring to the French department. In the aftermath of the national tragedy, the two men shared a conservative pessimism that one would not expect, coming from writers who had no ties to the Catholic faith and were passionate about science. Yet both wrote books—*La Réforme intellectuelle et morale de la France* in Renan's case and *Les Origines de la France contemporaine* in Taine's—that eloquently criticized French democracy and the revolution that had led to it.

Flaubert privately took part in this exercise in repentance and reflection on the nation's fate in his exchanges with George Sand. Their correspondence had never been so political.

Flaubert and Sand: The Truths of Reason and the Truths of Feeling

Flaubert was not unhappy with the general situation in the summer of 1871. The National Assembly in Versailles had been elected to decide whether to continue the war or seek peace. Since the revolution of September 4, 1870, France's governmental framework had been republican in principle, but the Assembly had a monarchist majority. The "pact of Bordeaux" had deferred the issue of the constitution, and Adolphe Thiers had been appointed to head the government. France was a republic by default and a monarchy in waiting, enjoying the public calm that followed a slaughter. Flaubert was pleased by the spirit of neutrality that prevailed: "Ah! If only we could get used to *what is*, meaning to living without principles, tricks, or slogans. I believe this is the first time in history that such a thing is possible. Could this be the beginning of positivism in politics? Let's hope so."[3] George Sand thought that she could see the "bourgeois republic" taking shape, adding: "I've no doubt it will be a stupid one, as you predicted." But unlike Flaubert, she believed in the long-term power of educating the people. Flaubert continued to praise the current ideological void: the "lack of edification" of Thiers's shaky regime was possibly a "guarantee of solidity."[4] On the anniversary of the September 4 revolution, he succinctly described his position: "The Republic does not make itself felt. So let's keep it."

By Flaubert's own admission, this apoliticism was due to a profound and renewed aversion for his contemporaries: "Ah! How sick I am of the ignoble worker, the inept bourgeois, the stupid peasant and the odious ecclesiastic!" In that same month of September 1871, Sand did not seem any more optimistic: "I'm ill with the illness of my country and my species. . . . All important ties seem to be loosened, almost broken. It looks as if we're all heading into the unknown." Now it was Gustave's turn to comfort her, to tell her there was nothing new under the sun, and to return to his aristocratic refrain: "As long as no deference is paid to the Mandarins, as long as the Academy of Sciences doesn't take the place of the Pope, all Politics, and Society down to its very roots, will be nothing but an assortment of disgusting humbugs." In his view, all of France's current problems resulted from the Christian idea of equality, which had inspired the Revolution and was antithetical to justice. The French were ready to kill each other for the republic or for the monarchy, which was absurd. The important thing was for science to finally prevail over metaphysics! For that, it would be essential to do away both with the plan for "free and compulsory" education and with universal suffrage, which he described as "an insult to human intelligence." Rule by the people made his skin crawl.[5]

Yet this outpouring of exclamations was more emotional than well-reasoned. What exactly was a government by "mandarins"? And who would appoint it? How could one avoid creating a new caste that operated in isolation? What naïveté he demonstrated in his belief in a politics of "science" and reason, in a positivism of social management. His political thinking seems severely limited, weighed down by resentment of the riff-raff (who were nothing but covetous) and the bourgeois (who were nothing but self-interested).

This time, George Sand bristled at Flaubert's views. She began a private rebuttal, but the letter grew so long that she turned it into an article for *Le Temps:* "This letter 'to a friend' doesn't refer to you even by an initial: I don't want to argue with you in public. In it I give you my reasons for still suffering, still wishing."[6] On October 3, 1871, *Le Temps* published her "Reply to a Friend," in which she explained her position and distanced herself from her "old troubadour":

What! You want me to stop loving? You want me to say that I have been mistaken all my life, that mankind is contemptible, hateful, has always been so and always will be? And you reproach me for my anguish, calling it weakness, childish regret for a lost illusion? You say that the populace has always been savage, the priest always a hypocrite, the bourgeois always craven, the soldier always a brigand, the peasant always stupid? You say you have known all this since youth, and you rejoice in never having doubted it because that has spared you disillusionment in later life. You have never been young, then. Ah! You and I are very different, for I have never stopped being young—if to persist in loving is a sign of youth.

Ever the realist, George Sand tells her anonymous correspondent that his desire to isolate himself from regular people, to save himself for a privileged few and cut himself off from everyone else, is an illusion, a utopia, and a failure to understand the way in which every individual is inextricably connected to others. To have contempt for the people is to pretend not to see that all of us are of the people, even if our roots have been "more or less obliterated": "as for me, on the maternal side my roots spring directly from the people, and I feel them alive in the very depths of my being." She is aware of the limitations of public life and does not believe in an infallible remedy for all of the country's ills, but rejects the idea that all of France's problems are *written*, fated, and normal. "One might as well say, straight out: 'It's all the same to me.' But if you add: 'It doesn't concern me,' you are mistaken."

It is common to distinguish between the political right and left according to anthropological notions: the right is pessimistic about human nature and resigned to finding solutions through authority, conservatism, and hierarchy; the left is optimistic and believes in the perfectibility of the human mind through social progress. If we accept this distinction, George Sand's long article reaffirms the leftist convictions one might have thought she had abandoned since the Commune or even since the failure of the Revolution of 1848. The article shows no such abandonment:

My feelings and my reason contest more than ever the concept of fictitious distinctions, the inequality of condition that is imposed as a right conferred on some, as a loss deserved by others. More than ever I need to raise what is low and lift what has fallen. Until my heart ceases to beat, it will be open to pity, it will espouse the weak, rehabilitate the despised. If today it is the populace who are under foot, I will hold out my hand to them; if they become the oppressor and the executioner, I will say they are cowardly and odious.

What is this or that group of men to me, or these proper names that have become badges, or those personalities that are slogans? I recognize only wise men and fools, the innocent and the guilty.

Fatality rejected! Hope! Fraternity! Public education! "Inaugurate by faith the resurrection of our country"[7]: George Sand was a long way from Flaubert's philosophy. After reading this profession of faith, he kindly admitted that he had been "moved" but not "persuaded." He had freed himself from emotional politics, he proclaimed the superiority of *integrity, justice,* and *science*. He persisted in attacking free compulsory education, which would only serve to increase "the number of imbeciles." Citing Renan, he advocated "a natural aristocracy—that is, a legitimate one." He denied that he despised the masses, but explained that while they must be allowed their freedom, they should not be given power. The most urgent thing was to educate the rich and the bourgeois, who were destined to rule—France would be remade from the top down.

Flaubert was a little stung by the implicit portrait of the "friend" to whom Sand addressed her article: "Your 'friend,' as dimly glimpsed through your article, is a rather disagreeable fellow and a first-rate *HHégoiste* [*sic*]." She reassured him: "Our real discussions must remain between ourselves, like lovers' caresses, only more delightful, since friendship has its own mysteries, untroubled by the storms of personality." She concluded that they needed "to find the link, the reconciliation, between your truths of reason and my truths of feeling. Unfortunately France doesn't agree with either of us. It's on the side of blindness, ignorance and stupidity. Oh, I don't deny it—that's precisely what upsets me."[8]

The controversy between the two friends did not end there. Flaubert continued to rail against universal suffrage, stubbornly refusing to understand the principle and stating: "I am certainly worth twenty other Croisset voters!" He argued for justice. She answered "love," adding: "I've never been able to separate the ideal of justice that you speak of from love." She rejected his accusation of sentimentality; she simply had a passion for good. In short, both stuck to their guns. Flaubert did not change his views on suffrage, despite the fact that it was through universal male suffrage that France had elected the National Assembly with which he was so satisfied—at least for the time being. Sand chose to address the subject in the follow-up to her profession of faith, also published in *Le Temps*. She echoed an idea put forth in Victor Hugo's *Les*

Misérables in her apologia for universal suffrage: "Universal suffrage, that is the expression of the will of all, good or bad, is the safety valve without which you would have nothing but eruptions of civil war." Ultimately, Flaubert wanted to return to a system of census suffrage, supposedly based on *capacity*. But how could this capacity be defined, other than through social class, property, and capital? What guarantee could there be of the *morality* of people with these attributes? No, Sand insisted that universal suffrage was the true source of legitimacy, but she admitted that its future rested on the education of the masses and that much time would be required "before the results could be felt."

All in all, Sand comes out of this exchange looking like a moderate republican who believes in progress aimed at improving the fate of humankind but rejects both the utopia of government by the wise and the utopia of revolution. Flaubert, an admiring reader of Renan's recently published *Réforme intellectuelle et morale,* holds to his aristocratic position based on justice and dreams of administering society by science, against the "illusions" of popular suffrage and education for all. Time would show that of the two discourses, that of the "sentimental" George Sand would take hold as the least capable of being challenged. Unable to repudiate his inveterate elitism, Flaubert could not see the coming democratic transition.

The Energy of Loyalty

Flaubert made several extended stays among the ruins of Paris in the aftermath of the Commune. He had gotten back to work on *The Temptation of Saint Anthony,* for which he assiduously visited the Bibliothèque Impériale—the "imperial library" that would soon become "national"—and the library at the Arsenal. This return to Antiquity was a welcome relief from the vileness of his own era. He saw his friends again, chief among them Princess Mathilde, whom he still admired. Her home on rue de Courcelles had been confiscated as an imperial property, so she had moved her Parisian salon to a townhouse she purchased on rue de Berry. She had also replaced her fugitive lover Nieuwerkerke with another artist, the more unassuming Claudius Popelin, a bearded enamaller. Flaubert was also reunited with the disconsolate Edmond de Goncourt and the declining Théophile Gautier. He dined at the home of Victor Hugo, who was back from exile and whom he continued to esteem despite their political differences. He became closer with Turgenev, the "gentle giant" and "lovable barbarian," as Edmond de Goncourt referred to him, despite the fact that he was constantly coming and going between Edinburgh and Baden. Flaubert's greatest literary and intellectual affinity was probably now with the Russian writer, though his gout-afflicted friend drove him to despair by often missing their appointments. Nonetheless, they had a growing number of opportunities to spend time together. In January 1872, Gustave read him the 115 pages of *Saint Anthony* that he had written and a generous portion of Louis Bouilhet's *Dernières Chansons:* "What a good listener! And what a critic!" he wrote to George Sand. "He dazzled me with the profundity and precision of his judgment. Ah! If all those who take it on themselves to judge books could have heard him, what a lesson! Nothing escapes him. And after listening to a hundred-line poem he could still remember a weak epithet. For *Saint Anthony,* he gave me two or three excellent bits of advice concerning details."[9] Flaubert also discovered the promising talent of Émile Zola, who had sent him *La Fortune des Rougon* [*The Fortune of the Rougons*], the first volume of his *Rougon-Maquart* cycle of novels. Flaubert congratulated Zola, despite what he considered an overly explicit preface. He also appreciated Alphonse Daudet's *Tartarin de Tarascon,* which made him roar with laughter. Yet the main reason for his more frequent and longer stays in Paris was that he wanted to make good on his promise to honor the memory of Louis Bouilhet.

To begin with, there was the play *Mademoiselle Aïssé.* He had promised himself and Philippe Leparfait, the son Louis had adopted in spirit if not on paper, that he would get it staged. This was not to be an easy task. The manuscript needed to be reread, revised, and whittled down. He would have to get a theater manager interested, then relentlessly pursue him. Once his fervent efforts led the play to be accepted, he would have to oversee the direction, the casting, the sets, and the rehearsals. And once the opening was in sight, he would have to invite a vast network of friends and harass the critics to ensure that the play did not meet with indifference. Gustave was at his best in this whirlwind of activity and the exertion of energy required to help his late lamented friend. He did not hesitate to play the field, taking the project both to the Théâtre Français and the Odéon. He decided that *Saint Anthony* would have to wait while he devoted entire days to ensuring the play's success. Finally, *Aïssé* was accepted by the Odéon. Now he spent every afternoon at rehearsals. He fought to cast the best actors, eventually managing to get Edmée Ramelli and Sarah Bernhardt in the lead. He realized that several verses of the manuscript were off and set to work fixing them. "I have had actors hired," he wrote to his friend Marie Régnier. "I personally worked on the costumes at the print room; in short, I haven't had a moment of respite in two weeks and this exasperating and busy little life will continue at the same pace for a good two months."[10] On December 1, 1871, he wrote to Philippe Leparfait that the actors had responded to the reading of the play with "the keenest enthusiasm." He did not let up: he attended every rehearsal and authoritatively corrected the actors' performances. As he put it, he "set their asses on fire in a way they never expected." If he didn't like a set, he had it changed. It seemed nothing could resist him. The play finally opened on January 6, 1872. To the ever-acerbic Edmond de Goncourt, "Bouilhet's characters were more artificial than the set." He explained the applause by "the audience's deference to a dead man's hexameters." Nonetheless, Flaubert was pleased with opening night. Alas, the next day the theater was "more or less empty." Flaubert was indignant. He wrote to George Sand that "the press was for the most part stupid and vile. I was accused of wanting to draw attention to myself by *inserting* an inflammatory speech! I'm supposed to be a Red! [*sic*] You see what we've come to!" He also complained to the Odéon's management: on the day of the opening, he had had to bring the props for the first act. "And at the 3rd performance, I was directing the background actors." He had thought the production would generate income for Philippe, but the young man took home a mere four hundred francs. "All that can be said is that we came honorably out of the affair."[11] After the Odéon run, *Aïssé* was performed at the Théâtre de Rouen; Flaubert fought to the finish.

At the same time that he was busy with Bouilhet's play, Flaubert put great care into gathering his friend's poems together in a collection he entitled *Dernières Chansons*. As we have seen, his preface to Bouilhet's volume explored the aesthetic he had shared with the dead poet: the autonomy of art, the refusal to draw conclusions, the duty to represent rather than to demonstrate, the approach of the real not through the illusory reproduction of reality but through generalization and exaggeration, and of course the principle of impersonality.[12]

He wanted *Dernières Chansons* to be published at the same time that *Aïssé* was performed. He reread, corrected, filled in missing verses, took care of the proofs, alerted critics, and did not hesitate to ask George Sand for an article. She willingly obliged in *Le Temps*.

The publication of *Dernières Chansons* led to a serious disagreement with the publisher Michel Lévy. In March 1872, Flaubert received a letter from the printer, Claye, informing him that Lévy had refused to pay his bill. Flaubert assured him that an agreement had been made according to which Lévy was to advance the printing costs and reimburse himself from the sales revenue. But when confronted by Flaubert, Michel Lévy denied that he had made such an agreement. Lévy wanted to hold on to Flaubert as an author, but did not have the slightest hope of selling Bouilhet's poems. "In short," Flaubert wrote to Claye, "I found him so impudent and full of such hateful contempt for literature that we have separated once and for all. Under no circumstances will I have anything further to do with M. Lévy." He asked the printer for an extension, explaining that Bouilhet's heir was not a rich man. He was furious and humiliated. It would take a year for him to come out of it: "I'm beginning . . . to think less often about Michel Lévy. That hatred was becoming a veritable mania, most disturbing to me. I'm not entirely over it, but the thought of the wretched creature no longer brings palpitations, spasms of anger and outrage."[13]

He had not reached the end of his indignation. As the reader will recall, Flaubert wanted to have a small monument to Louis Bouilhet erected in Rouen. The commission he headed had agreed to his idea of a fountain with a bust, and a fund drive had raised 12,000 francs. Now the city's municipal council needed to vote on the matter. Early in December 1871, while he was busy with *Aïssé* and *Dernières Chansons*, he learned that the Rouen municipal council's commission had ruled against his request by a vote of thirteen to eleven. The report of the meeting during which the proposal had been rejected was published on December 18. The principal reasons given were the project's financing (concern that the funds raised were not sufficient), Louis Bouilhet's geographic origin (he was not born in Rouen), and his debatable literary merit. Beside himself with anger, Flaubert wrote a letter of protest to the municipal council of Rouen ("Lettre à la municipalité de Rouen"), which was intended for publication by his friend Charles Lapierre's *Nouvelliste de Rouen* but ultimately ran in *Le Temps* on January 26, 1872. His attack on the council's decision ended with an indictment of the bourgeoisie. He took particular aim at the council's rapporteur, the lawyer Decorde, who had denied that Bouilhet was an "original" writer: dipping into Decorde's own modest oeuvre and quoting a few of his verses, Flaubert pointed out the amateur critic's incompetence and the poetaster's unconvincing fantasies. He then went beyond the individual to denounce the vast stupidity of the philistines:

> This affair is of little importance in and of itself. But it can be noted as a sign of the times—as a characteristic trait of your class—and it is not you, gentlemen, that I am addressing, but all the bourgeois. So I tell them:
>
> Conservatives who conserve nothing.
>
> It is about time to take another direction—and since we're talking about regeneration and decentralization, change the way you think! Finally take some initiative.
>
> The French nobility was lost because for two centuries its feelings were those of lackeys. The end of the bourgeoisie is beginning because it has those of the populace. I do not see it reading other papers, delighting in different music, having more elevated passions. In both classes, one finds the same love of money, the same respect for the fait accompli, the same need for idols to destroy, the same hatred of any superiority, the same spirit of denigration, the same crass ignorance! . . .
>
> Before you send the people to school, you should go there yourselves! Enlightened classes, enlighten yourselves!
>
> Because of this contempt for intelligence you believe you are *full of common sense, positive, and practical* . . . .
>
> You, practical? Come on! You know how to hold neither a pen nor a gun! You allow yourselves to be dispossessed, imprisoned, and slaughtered by convicts! You no longer even have the instinct of the brute, which is to defend itself, and when it is not only your skin that is at risk, but your purse, which should be dearer to you, you lack the energy to go put a piece of paper in a box! With all your capital and your wisdom, you cannot make an organization equivalent to the International.
>
> All your intellectual effort consists in trembling before the future.
>
> Come up with something else or France will sink further and further between a hideous demagoguery and a stupid bourgeoisie.

Between *Aïssé, Dernières Chansons* and its preface, and his battle with the municipality of Rouen, Flaubert spent two months defending the memory of Louis Bouilhet without once lowering his guard. These daily displays of zeal in the face of fatigue, and the anger aroused by the indifference, obtuse thinking, philistinism, and venality of critics and municipal councilors, give us an idea of Flaubert's devotion to the friend who was no longer around to appreciate it. His affection also manifested itself through his concern for Léonie's son Philippe, Bouilhet's heir. He had thought that the performances at the Odéon and the publication of *Dernières Chansons* would allow Philippe, if not to hit the jackpot, at least to earn a significant sum of money. Unfortunately, Philippe spent more on these endeavors than he made.

Throughout Flaubert's life, friendship was a light that never dimmed; he had just proved it again. Even in his political exchanges with George Sand, in which the two expressed starkly conflicting viewpoints, one sees that the quality of his relationship with the lady of Nohant could not be damaged by political disagreement. If Flaubert caused George Sand to worry, it was for entirely different reasons. She thought that he worked too much and that he lived an excessively austere monk's life. As his maternal elder, she did not hesitate to tell him so: "I beg you not to be so completely absorbed in literature and learning. Travel, move about, have mistresses— or wives, just as you like; and during such phases, don't work. One shouldn't burn the candle at both ends; the thing is to light each end turn and turn about."[14]

When Flaubert received these words of encouragement, he was ill: he had a sore throat, which was soon followed by "an abominable flu" and "swollen glands around the neck." As was often the case, his emotional turmoil was manifesting itself physically. A major source of concern was his mother's health. At sixty-eight years old, she was having more and more trouble putting one foot in front of the other.

A Son's Goodbye

Early in October 1871, Flaubert sent his friend Edma Roger des Genettes a report from Croisset: "My only distraction is to take walks, or rather to drag my mother into the garden. The war made her age a hundred years in ten months.—It is very sad to witness the decline of those we love, to see their strength go away, their intelligence disappear." When Flaubert was not at Croisset, Caroline watched over her grandmother. But as he told his friend, Caroline could barely handle Mme Flaubert, whose character had become "intolerable." Achille's wife suggested that they hire a nun to take care of her mother-in-law and keep her company. Flaubert blew up: it was out of the question for a nun or any other female companion to stick her nose into business at Croisset. "If that were to happen, I'm notifying you that I will get the hell out and go live some place that will be *my own*." So Caroline continued to look after Mme Flaubert when Gustave was in Paris, though this was probably not the best solution. Flaubert finally agreed to look for a female companion—with every passing day his mother became less able to be alone.—He mentioned his problem to George Sand, who immediately began searching for the rare bird. To entertain his mother, he took her to Paris and back. But her spirits dropped again, and she alternated between silence and complaints. He increasingly dreaded his pitiful tête-à-têtes with her. While he was clashing with Lévy early in the spring of 1872, he was also oppressed by constant worries about his "poor mother," who was now an invalid. He spent a few more weeks facing her impending death. On April 6, it was all over: "We have just lost our mother. She died after 33 hours of agony!" He struggled to formulate the brief remarks by which he notified his relatives and friends. George Sand, who was unable to attend the funeral because of her own illness, sent him a sensitive note, opening her "maternal heart" to him. On April 16, he confided in his true friend in Nohant: "I've realized for a fortnight now that my poor dear mother was the being I loved most. I feel as if part of my entrails had been torn out."[15] She had adored Gustave and made him her favorite son, hovering around him since his first epileptic fit, beset by "constant anxiety." For him, her love was sometimes a yoke, but it was a yoke he accepted and often cherished. Before she had become this somewhat bitter and surly old deaf lady, he had found in her an attentive and thoughtful being. She was possessive, yes, but not to the point of preventing him from embarking on his long journey to the Orient or from spending more and more time in Paris. And it was not she who refused to welcome Louise Colet into her home, but almost certainly Gustave who used his mother's demanding presence as an excuse for his stubborn refusal to live closer to his mistress.

Mme Flaubert had been a generous host to friends of her son such as Louis Bouilhet, the Goncourt brothers, Turgenev, George Sand, Mme Schlésinger, and others who could appreciate her hospitality. Yet her reserved personality could make her appear a little cold and fretful, displaying, as Flaubert told Louise Colet, "something imperturbable, icy, and naïve that takes you aback."[16] She was a woman whom life had not spared: an orphan at seven, she later lost her husband and daughter in rapid succession. She probably found a new reason to live in having to raise her dead daughter's own child, also named Caroline. After the death of her husband and daughter, she formed a new three-person family at Croisset with Gustave and Caroline. This was a family fairly emancipated from bourgeois rules—a cocoon, a cell whose primary objective was the comfort of the beloved son of whom she was quietly proud. "She constantly talked to me about him," Caroline recollected of her childhood, "and she would make me pray for him morning and night."[17] She did not hesitate to sell some of her properties to support Gustave and cover his Parisian expenses and debts. She was his protector. Toward the end of her life, she had irritated him; now he felt the void she had left in front of him.

He was fifty years old. What would become of him?

In her will, Mme Flaubert left her oldest son, Achille, the farms in Lower Normandy; she left Caroline all her property in Canteleu and a section of Croisset, with the obligation to let Gustave continue to live there: "I want my son Gustave Flaubert to retain enjoyment of the bedroom and bathroom he occupies in the residential house at Croisset his whole life long . . . and so long as he does not marry."[18] To Gustave, she left the farm in Deauville, which brought in about six thousand francs a year in rent. Thus Mme Flaubert wisely ensured that her youngest son would have a regular income while maintaining his routine at Croisset. Achille was not in need, and Caroline could rely on her husband, Ernest Commanville.[19] Flaubert did not know that Mme Flaubert's will was vehemently contested by his sister-in-law, Julie Flaubert. In a letter dated April 30, 1872, and sent to an unidentified correspondent, she rightly questioned the estate's legality: "we can attack what she [Mme Flaubert] did and send Gve [Gustave] packing without any misgivings, we might be criticized but that would not be hard to bear."[20] Yet her husband, Achille, did no such thing.

Thus, Flaubert's life was not as "completely turned upside down" as he told Ernest Feydeau it would be during the short period during which he was unsure about his material situation. He would be able to continue to live and work at Croisset most of the year. He was now more concerned about the moral solitude to which he was condemned—an "absolute solitude." He was most afraid of mealtimes, when he was "face to face with [him]self" at the empty table. He promised himself to toughen up, to be philosophical, and to get back to work: "For me the future amounts to a stack of white paper that must be covered in black." Among the letters of condolence received, he found one to which he did not reply until May 28, 1872—it was from Élisa Schlesinger, whom he addressed as "my always beloved."

There was no way around it: he had to accept the sorrows of life and ease his pain. "You can't imagine," he wrote to Caroline on April 29, "how lovely and quiet *your* Croisset is. Everything is suffused with an infinite sweetness, and there is a kind of assuagement in the silence. The memory of my poor old lady never leaves me: it hovers around me like a mist—I'm as though enclosed in it."[21]

CHAPTER 25

The Ups and Downs of Melancholy

In the two years that followed his mother's death, politics finally caught up with Flaubert. France was in a tremendous state of uncertainty. Adolphe Thiers was in power, and it had been agreed by the pact of Bordeaux that as long as any French territory was still occupied, no decision would be taken regarding the nation's institutions or about whether France was to be a monarchy or a republic. The nameless regime was headed by a president of the Republic without a republic. But in fact, Thiers—the strongman of the moment, the necessary guide, the indispensable diplomat who had negotiated with Bismarck and handled the payment of five billion gold francs to Germany—had silently made his choice long before it was publicly declared: he was in favor of establishing a "conservative republic" because a republic was "the least divisive regime." Gustave Flaubert shared this point of view. Though he had once called Thiers "a turd-like bourgeois," he now felt represented by this politician whose ideas and projects for reconstruction agreed with his conviction that France needed a regime without ideology, one that was equal parts administrative and patriotic—for since the war, Flaubert had become a patriot. He was pleased that "our great national historian" (he was being ironic, of course) was preparing "to close, for a moment, the era of revolutions."[1]

But the monarchists, who still held the majority in the National Assembly, would have none of it. To beat Thiers to the punch, they attempted a "merger" between the Orleanists and the Legitimists (who supported the Bourbon dynasty): the Comte de Chambord, who was the Legitimist pretender, would be crowned Henri V, but since he had no children, his successor would be the Comte de Paris, grandson to Louis Philippe and heir to the House of Orléans. Unfortunately for the monarchists, the Comte de Chambord had lost his grasp on the realities of France's situation while in exile and proved so inflexible that a compromise between the two royalist branches was impracticable. They would have to bide their time until the liberation of French territory before they could make any attempt at restoration. The death of Napoleon III in January 1873 temporarily put an end to the Bonapartist option. France would thus be either a monarchy or a republic, not an empire.

On November 13, 1872, Thiers finally spoke his mind in an address to the Assembly: "The Republic exists; it is the country's legal government; to want anything else would be another revolution and the most dangerous of all." The monarchists cried treason. Feeling duped, they reacted violently. Flaubert felt fully in league with Thiers's message and pitched into the monarchists: "I won't hide from you," he wrote to one of his correspondents, "that the right's obstinacy will wind up turning me, yes you're reading right, into a *Red*! Not out of sympathy for the brutes that make up this party, but out of disgust for the others."[2]

In fact, Flaubert was mostly upset that the right was playing into the extreme left's hands: "The *right* is doing such a good job that at the next elections many very moderate bourgeois will vote with the Reds.—Then we will enter into the Horrible, and it will be for a long time!"[3] When Théophile Gautier died in October 1872, Flaubert became convinced that he had succumbed to "a disgust with modern life," and he suggested that the proclamation of the Republic on September 4, 1870, had inaugurated a society now corrupted by democracy: "Theo," he wrote to Turgenev, "died poisoned by the filth of modern life. People who are exclusively artists, as he was, have no place in a society dominated by the rabble." The "Muscovite," as Flaubert called Turgenev, replied with a little lesson full of wisdom: "Why should you bother yourself so much about the *rabble* as you call them? They only hold sway over those who accept their yoke. . . . And then is M. Alexander Dumas the younger—the embodiment of 'filth' to use your expression—one of the rabble? And M. Sardou, M. Offenbach, M. Vacquerie and all the rest, are they part of the rabble? They stink none the less. . . . No, my friend, it's not that that's difficult at our age, it's the general '*taedium vitae*,' the boredom and disgust with all human activity; it's nothing to do with politics, which after all is no more than a game; it's the sadness of one's fiftieth year." In other words, do not confuse personal decline with world order. In his reply, Flaubert laid it on thick about the public stupidity that so distressed him: "I feel a wave of relentless Barbarism, rising up from below the ground." He admitted that this was not a question of politics, but rather of the mentality of a society that hated any grandeur and loathed literature. He would never back down from this position; once again he took to signing many of his letters "Polycarp."[4]

Nonetheless, he remained attentive to new political orientations and railed against the right, which heralded the reign of "idiots and clericals." On May 24, Thiers was forced to step down. The next day, Patrice MacMahon, the new president of the Republic, defined his policy: "With the help of God, the devotion of our army, who will always be the slave of the Law, and the support of all honest people, we will continue the task of liberating our territory and reestablishing moral order in our country. We will maintain internal peace and the principles on which our society is founded." "Moral order" is certainly an appropriate description for this period, which was dominated by clerical conservatism. A return of the monarchy was now out of the question. In September 1873, Flaubert wrote to Jeanne de Loynes (formerly Jeanne de Tourbey) that only the "center left" was natural to France's "temperament." Was he being won over by the democratic spirit? In November 1873, he declared his republican convictions to his niece: "How ignorant does one have to be of history to still believe in the effectiveness of a man, to await a Messiah, a Savior? Long live the good Lord and down with the gods! Can one make an entire people reverse course, deny 80 years of democratic development, and return to charters granted by the crown?" Suddenly his invectives against universal suffrage, which he once considered "an insult to human intelligence," were forgotten. At the same time conservative and republican, anticlerical and reactionary, nostalgic for a lost aristocracy of the mind and deeply hostile to democratic society while speaking of its "development" as a necessity, Flaubert is reminiscent of Tocqueville, the man who had predicted the advent of such a society. But Tocqueville, as nostalgic as he was, resigned himself to the new society as a sort of accomplishment of divine will. For his part, Flaubert could not stand it. He continued to suffer from the success of mediocre people and even blamed the proclamation of the Republic for Gautier's death. If he had become a republican, it was to be a republican like Adolphe Thiers.

Filling the Void

In the months that followed Mme Flaubert's death, Gustave experienced a prolonged period of emotional distress. In July 1872, he accompanied his niece to Bagnères-de-Luchon, where her doctor had recommended she take the waters. With Ernest Commanville detained by his business, Flaubert played the "escort" and the "duenna," as he put it. He decided to follow the course of treatment while he was at it. He cherished his Caro, whom he asked to call him her "Old Man," or her "Nanny." He had not seen her as often as he would have liked since she had moved to Dieppe, though they still met quite frequently in Paris or Croisset. Their separation produced a voluminous correspondence, in which the uncle's affection for his niece is always evident. Gustave never missed an opportunity to give her a compliment; he kept her up to date on doings at Croisset, recommended books, and talked politics. It was during these weeks in the Pyrenees, between taking baths or showers and drinking glasses of water, that Caroline told Gustave that her marriage was a failure and that she had been passionately in love with Ernest Leroy (the prefect of upper Normandy), though their relationship had come to an end in the aftermath of the war. Did Flaubert take the opportunity to tell Caroline about his affair with her former governess Juliet Herbert? Herbert's biographer, Hermia Oliver, suggests that he did. She concludes that Caroline reacted with a touch of jealousy, supporting her theory with a statement Flaubert made the following autumn, in a letter dated September 24: "My heart is large enough to contain every kind of tenderness. One does not preclude the other, or others." In the same letter, he mentions the bad weather: "I'm afraid Juliet had a very poor crossing." Juliet had just spent some time in Paris, where Gustave had secretly joined her upon his return from Luchon, lying to "everyone" about his schedule.[5] On September 14, he wrote to tell Caroline that Juliet would stop to see her in her "delightful villa" on her way back to England. In this letter, Flaubert refers to Juliet as "my dear companion" for the first time.

Yet he did not see much of this "dear companion." They would meet again under similar conditions in 1874, 1876, 1877, and 1878. Their relationship remained secret, which is difficult to understand given that they were both free and that he sometimes felt lonely. Always the voice of common sense, George Sand pestered him: "Why don't you get married? Being alone is horrible, deadly, and it's cruel to those who love you, too. . . . Isn't there some woman you love, or whom you'd like to love you? Have her to live with you." Gustave replied: "As for living with a woman, marrying, as you advise, it's a prospect I find fantastic. Why? *I have no idea.* But that's how it is. Perhaps you can explain. The feminine existence has never fitted in with mine."⁶ Years before, he had basically told Louise Colet the same thing. After he ran out of arguments he spoke of money, claiming he did not have enough income to take a wife and explaining that he could not change his way of life—"the force of circumstances has gradually intensified my solitude, until now I am alone, utterly alone."⁷ For her part, Juliet seemed to make do with this irregular relationship, understanding Gustave's fierce desire for independence and his conviction that he could only work in the very solitude that he complained about.

We are missing an important source that would elucidate the nature of the relationship between Flaubert and Juliet: their letters. One can imagine the charm Flaubert exercised on his "companion" through his correspondence, maintaining the long-distance love and admiration of this "English governess"—less demanding than Louise, more of a daydreamer, making poetic plans for meetings with the love of her life.⁸ In 1872, she was forty-three years old.

At this juncture, Flaubert was dividing his time principally between Croisset and Paris. To finish writing *The Temptation of Saint Anthony* and, later, his novel *Bouvard and Pécuchet,* he made numerous trips to the capital to haunt its libraries. But for several months, his heart was not in it. His correspondence is one long complaint about his health and his melancholy. Back at Croisset, he immersed himself in his work, which was the only way to calm his tendency to *"insupportation"*—a term he coined to refer to his habit of finding things unbearable. He railed and shouted, was repulsed by his contemporaries, inveighed against universal stupidity, and sometimes felt as though he would die of loneliness. His friend Edmond Laporte gave him a greyhound he named Julio; now he took his walks with Julio, between writing two pages of his book or before or after a swim in the Seine. When he had to go to Paris, he entrusted the dog to its original owner, who was kind enough to take care of it. On her last trip to France, Juliet (whose name must somehow have inspired the dog's name!) gave Flaubert a splendid dog collar: "My only distraction is to kiss my poor dog," he wrote to Caroline, "to whom I address entire speeches. What a happy mortal! His calm and his beauty would make anyone envious."

Sometimes Flaubert dined in Rouen, though rarely at his brother Achille's place, for he did not much care for his sister-in-law Julie (and he did not even know that she had planned to kick him out of Croisset). For that matter, he was not overly fond of his brother, either. His closest friends in Rouen at the time were Charles and Valérie Lapierre. Charles ran the *Nouvelliste,* and his wife was one of Flaubert's three "angels," along with her sister Léonie Brainne, a widow and a pretty, cultured woman who told him of the "immensity" of her affection,[9] and Alice Pasca, an actress to whom Valérie had introduced him. With Léonie, he maintained a sustained friendship that led to a steady correspondence beginning in 1871. It may even have been more than friendship, judging by the intimate tone of letters such as this one, dated March 31, 1872: "I miss you. . . . Why did I meet you so late? My heart is intact, but my sensitivity is exacerbated here, dulled there, like an old knife sharpened too often, that has notches and is easily chipped. . . . I have found on your lips, my dear beauty, something that will remain deep in my heart, no matter what happens." At the very least, Gustave and "that dear beautiful face" that he wanted to "cover in kisses"[10] shared an amorous friendship—whatever that means.

In Paris, he had rekindled his friendships with "those who were left"— Edmond de Goncourt, Turgenev, and George Sand, when she ventured away from Nohant—as well as younger writers he appreciated such as Émile Zola and Alphonse Daudet. He continued to visit Princess Mathilde, who had braved the fall of the Empire, and became a regular at the home of Victor Hugo, whom he found truly "charming" outside of politics, a subject they carefully avoided. There were still other friends from Magny's (now the Brébant), including Renan, Taine, and Berthelot, but he had fallen out with Saint-Victor, whom he could not forgive for his bad reviews and his silence regarding his latest books. Flaubert had gladly accepted an invitation from the mayor of Vendôme to attend the inauguration of a statue of Pierre de Ronsard and had even told Caroline he would go to the mass in the poet's memory—since "Ronsard was a Catholic"—but gave up on the trip as soon as he learned that Saint-Victor was going to participate in the event. "So I won't go to Vendôme," he told Goncourt. "No, my sensitivity has reached such a pathological level, I am so rattled, that the idea of having a disagreeable gentleman's face across from me on the train is odious, unbearable." He continued by telling Goncourt about his profound boredom, his "discouragement about everything," his "yearning to be dead."[11]

Sullen, melancholy, irritated by everything, Flaubert seemed to his friends to have become fickle, capricious, and strident. In his exercises in psychological and moral dissection, Goncourt is not to be outdone in sheer nastiness. Though Flaubert was considerate, friendly, and even affectionate toward him, and there is no doubt that he appreciated conversing with the author of *Madame Bovary,* Goncourt regularly depicts him in the *Journal* as an oaf. He reports that in restaurants, Flaubert demanded a private room because he hated noise and wanted to take his boots off so as to be completely at ease. During the meal, he often monopolized the conversation, indulging in Norman logorrhea and Gascon boasts, getting drunk on his own vehemence, while his stormy words, proving contagious, created tension, nervousness, and aggressiveness that made his fellow diners uncomfortable and spoiled the meal. Goncourt is relentless: according to him, Flaubert is a boor from the sticks.

Though she never badmouthed her dear "old troubadour," even George Sand was sometimes annoyed by him. In a letter to her children Maurice and Lina, she describes an evening with Flaubert that does not paint him in a particularly flattering light. Having been invited by Flaubert to dine at Magny's with Turgenev and Goncourt, she arrived on time and waited until she was joined by Turgenev. Fifteen minutes later, Edmond de Goncourt arrived and told them that Flaubert was waiting for them at Véfour's.

> "Why!"
> "He says he suffocates here, that the [private] rooms are too small, that he worked all night, that he's tired."
> "But I'm tired too."
> "Scold him; he's a big old boor—but let's go on over there."
> "No, I'm starving, let's stay here and have dinner together."
> We laugh and then Goncourt says Flaubert will go mad. So we all pile into a carriage. . . . We climb three hundred steps at Véfour's to find Flaubert asleep on a couch. I call him a hog, he asks for forgiveness, gets down on his knees, the others are splitting their sides laughing. Finally, we eat very poorly, a kind of cuisine I detest, in a private room much smaller than those at Magny's. Flaubert says he can't take it anymore, that he's dead. . . . But when it comes down to it, he's bellowing with joy, he's enchanted [with the play he's writing]. I've had enough of my little chum. I love him, but he splits my head in four. He doesn't like noise, but he isn't bothered by the noise he himself makes.[12]

One finds similar incidents described in Sand's diaries. In April 1873, at Sand's insistence, Flaubert returned to Nohant, where they were joined by Turgenev a few days later. Apparently everything went well: they played, danced, argued, read their works aloud, and Gustave, though he wasn't shy about his hatred of noise, joined right in. "He is as much of a child as the rest of us," she wrote. "He dances, he waltzes; what a kind and honest man of genius." But once Turgenev arrived, Flaubert did not let him get a word in edgewise. Sand commented: "I am left tired and *aching* by my dear Flaubert. Yet I do love him a great deal and he is excellent but too exuberant in his personality. He breaks you."[13]

Back at home, Flaubert wrote to Sand: "Your friends Turgenev and Cruchard philosophized . . . between Nogent and Châteauroux, as they bowled comfortably along in your carriage behind two good fast horses." Cruchard was none other than Flaubert himself, "Otherwise known as Rev. Fr. Cruchard of the Barnabites, spiritual director of the Ladies of Disillusion."[14] This "spiritual director" was a character Flaubert had made up long ago, like the Garçon and the Old Sheikh, and whom he had revived during his stay in Nohant. In the following months, he entertained his friend by sending her the comic essay *Vie et travaux du RP Cruchard* [*Life and Works of the Rev. Fr. Cruchard*], a parodic biography of an ecclesiastic under Louis XIV, "the leading theologian and heartiest eater of the kingdom." Remaining cheerful into senility, Cruchard utters a last pun on his name, then dies: "I think the jug is going to break once and for all" (*cruche* means "jug" and is also a slang term for "idiot" or "blockhead").[15] Along with Saint Polycarp, Cruchard became one of Flaubert's signatures, leading Sand to call him "Cruchard of my heart."

Until February 1873, the letters he sent out in all directions were brimming with his distress, pessimism, and anger at the human race: "I only want one thing, that is *to croak*," he wrote to Philippe Leparfait, the son of Bouilhet's common-law wife Léonie. "I lack the energy to do myself in. That is the only reason I'm still alive. I am so *outraged by everything* that sometimes my heart beats so fast I think I'll suffocate." The same day, he told Goncourt: "It is outrage alone that props me up! For me, outrage is like the rod that dolls have up their asses, the rod that makes them stand up. When I am no longer outraged, I will fall flat."[16]

In March of 1873, his mood began to change: "I'm beginning to feel myself again. What has been wrong with me these last four months? What was it that troubled me so deeply?"[17] His spirit had been broken by the death of Théophile Gautier so soon after that of his "dear old lady," the failures of his endeavors for Louis Bouilhet, and his conflict with Michel Lévy. He had finished writing *The Temptation of Saint Anthony*, but his sore feelings about publishers, journalists, and the public kept him from publishing it. Yet suddenly, at the beginning of spring, he was full of enthusiasm again.

A Craving for Theater

Flaubert had plenty of projects on which to expend his new-found energy. After finishing *Saint Anthony,* he had started on his next novel, *Bouvard and Pécuchet,* for which he planned to do a heroic amount of reading. But the spring of 1873 would primarily be dedicated to theater. The opportunity was provided by the development of Bouilhet's play *Le Sexe faible* [*The Weaker Sex*]. Bouilhet again! His feeling of obligation to honor his friend's memory still held firm. And he still believed that Bouilhet's plays might generate some income for Philippe.

Flaubert had come across this comedy while looking through Bouilhet's papers and discovered that it had originally been turned down by the Théâtre du Vaudeville. While in Luchon, he had fine-tuned its overall scenario, made radical changes to acts one and three, and decided to offer it to the Vaudeville's new manager, Léon Carvalho. The title *Le Sexe faible* was ironic, as Bouilhet had made clear in a letter to Gustave in 1864: "The main idea is that from one end of the social ladder (sorry!) to the other and from one end of human life to the other, we who are the *stronger sex* are under the heel of women."[18] To show the various kinds of domination by women, Bouilhet came up with a likeable young man of twenty-five, Henry, in the grip of a tyrannical widowed mother who is determined to oversee his life. To escape her, he marries, but quickly falls under the authority of his mother-in-law and into the claws of his wife, who turns into a tigress once she becomes a mother. And so it goes: whether it's the nanny or the chambermaid, every woman, however kind or gentle, exerts her unbearable control over the poor fellow, sometimes brutally but more often softly. For the last act, the author even imagined a chorus of women in the manner of Aristophanes, who act in unison to finally put young Henry on the right track.

Flaubert contacted Carvalho, who was immediately enthusiastic and predicted the comedy would be a "major success" at the Vaudeville. In May 1873, he dropped *Bouvard* and enthusiastically started to rework the script: "It has been a long time (nearly a year) since I wrote," he told his niece, "and making sentences feels pleasant." He informed Philippe that he was spending his days and part of his nights working on the play. By mid-June, he was almost finished. But what would Carvalho think? Flaubert invited him to Croisset to listen to a reading of *Le Sexe faible*. The theater manager seemed delighted and predicted that it would be a success. He promised Flaubert he would schedule the play after the performances of Victorien Sardou's *Oncle Sam*.

This revived Flaubert's taste for theater, as he explained in a letter to Princess Mathilde: "Having gotten in the habit over the last six weeks of seeing things theatrically and thinking through *dialogue,* would you believe that I've effortlessly been constructing the outline for another play, entitled *Le Candidat* [*The Candidate*]*." Soon he had a twenty-page outline. The play told the story of a satirical episode in the life of an electoral candidate, through which Flaubert intended to poke fun at the third and fourth estates, the right and the left, and implicitly, universal suffrage. But he wondered whether any government, no matter its political allegiance, would allow such a representation of political mores. Even the risky nature of the endeavor excited him: "If ever I write it, and it is performed, I will be torn up by the populace, banned by those in power, cursed by the clergy, etc."[19] What Flaubert had not anticipated was that Carvalho would like *Le Candidat* so much that he would choose to produce it before *Le Sexe faible*, though he had accepted the latter play "with enthusiasm." The promise of Flaubert's name on the marquee probably played a part in his decision: at the Vaudeville, a play by Flaubert would be more attractive than a play by Louis Bouilhet that had been revised and updated by Flaubert. But Flaubert had his doubts: in these times of moral order and organized pilgrimages during which hymns were sung in praise of the king and in favor of the alliance between Throne and Altar, he was convinced that *Le Candidat* would not make it past the censor. In any case, he was happy to finish his comedy. He read it to Turgenev, who made Flaubert blissfully happy by telling him he thought it would be "a strong play." The writing here was no longer the carefully honed and whittled prose of his novels, but words that flowed spontaneously from the tip of his pen, as in his letters. In late October, he traveled to Paris to discuss *Le Sexe faible,* for which Carvalho was requesting rewrites, but realized that Carvalho was determined to perform *Le Candidat* first. Finally, the manager of the Vaudeville told him so explicitly.

At this point—in late November 1873—Flaubert learned that Ernest Feydeau had died. His relationship with Feydeau had become strained. Feydeau had been paralyzed on one side by a stroke, but had still managed to write a new book, *Mémoires d'une demoiselle de bonne famille* [*Memoirs of a Well-Bred*

Girl]. The manuscript had outraged Flaubert, who judged it "lewd and indecent," not because of its "lighthearted jolliness" but because he saw nothing else in it. He wrote these remarks in the margin of the manuscript, and the author responded by calling him an imbecile. The old friendship came to an end with a shrug: "The loss of this friend is the least regrettable of all those of the last four years."

On November 22, Flaubert told his niece that *Le Candidat* was finished. A week later, he was in Paris reading his play to Carvalho, who found it excellent. But the next day, the theater manager brought up his requests for changes and additions, which Flaubert found exasperating. He did what he was asked, but confided in his niece that he was, "more than ever, irascible, intolerant, unsociable, *excessive*, Saint-Polycarpian. That kind of thing doesn't get better at my age!" By December, the actors had been hired and Flaubert was able to read them the play. They laughed heartily and declared it would be a success. Flaubert realized his play needed a few more revisions and that his previous readers, Carvalho, d'Osmoy, and Turgenev, had made excellent points. He put the finishing touches to it. Now came the censors' turn. After an initial reading, they asked for only a few changes to the language, primarily in the case of words referring to religion (the words "seminarian," "bishop," "Monsignor," and "priest" had to be replaced). Flaubert conceded everything, because everything was not much, and he was weary. The production began rehearsals. Then Carvalho abruptly left the Vaudeville. Naturally, this was initially a cause for concern, but his successor did not change the program. A rehearsal was planned for the censors; Flaubert asked the deputy Raoul-Duval, a friend from Rouen, to come support him. Everything went well, and the production was given its final permit. The opening took place on March 11, 1874. Unfortunately, it was not the triumph Carvalho had banked on and Flaubert had hoped for, but instead a cold shower; the response was absolutely icy. "It was dismal yesterday," wrote Goncourt, "the sort of ice that fell little by little, during the performance of *Le Candidat*, over that audience waiting in all good faith for sublime tirades, for superhuman witticisms, for world-shaking lines, and faced with nothingness, nothingness, nothingness."[20] Flaubert himself had to admit that the audience, though more than favorably disposed toward him, had only applauded out of politeness. He pulled no punches in his report to George Sand: "If ever there was a Flop!" In his view, the actors had performed perfectly, but "[the] Conservatives were annoyed because I didn't attack the

Republicans and the Communards would have liked me to throw a few insults at the Legitimists."

Flaubert withdrew the play after the fourth performance. "I won't have my actors hissed and booed. The second night, when I saw Delannoy [the lead actor] coming off the stage with tears in his eyes, I felt like a criminal and decided that was enough." Sand comforted him as best she could, but when she read the published script, she had to give him the opinion of an experienced woman: his comedy, which was presumably conceived to amuse, was not funny! "On the contrary, it's depressing. It's so true to life it doesn't make one laugh, and since one can't take an interest in any of the characters one isn't interested in the action." She explained to him that one needed to magnify things for the stage: "The subject lends itself to caricature, as in *M. Prud'homme*, or to tragedy, as in *Richard d'Arlington*. But you treat it *exactly*, which means that the art of theater disappears." Ultimately, Flaubert himself came to the conclusion that "the *subject* was a good one. But I bungled it."[21] Luckily for him, the brand-new *Temptation of Saint Anthony* was flying off the shelves.

Saint Anthony, Finally!

Completed in 1872, *The Temptation of Saint Anthony* was published on March 31, 1874. Flaubert had found a new publisher, Georges Charpentier, who in 1872 had succeeded his father, Gervais Charpentier, the founder of the publishing house and innovator of the Petite Bibliothèque Charpentier, a collection of books in affordable editions. The ever-enthusiastic Georges Charpentier would become one of the major publishers of the fin de siècle, publishing Maupassant, Zola, Joris-Karl Huysmans, Goncourt, Alphonse Daudet, and Octave Mirbeau, among others. This warm, likeable man who regularly welcomed artists and writers to his townhouse on rue de Grenelle immediately appealed to Flaubert, whom he had solicited. Flaubert invited him to Croisset in June 1873. Here, the publisher acquired the rights to *Madame Bovary* and *Salammbô*, which Michel Lévy no longer held. Flaubert and Charpentier agreed that they would reissue *Madame Bovary* with an appendix containing the examining magistrate's summons, Pinard's summing-up for the prosecution, and Sénard's speech for the defense. The arrangement was advantageous for Flaubert, and Charpentier was overjoyed. Back in Paris, Charpentier offered to buy back all of Flaubert's books from Lévy and, of course, to publish *Saint Anthony,* which had been gathering dust in a closet. Gustave was pleased to inform Caroline that all of these deals were made "with excellent terms." The honeymoon between the two men had gotten off to such a great start that Flaubert the unbeliever agreed to Mme Charpentier's request that he be the godfather to the couple's youngest son. "I had to do it," he explained to George Sand, "or seem like a boor." From then on, Flaubert felt it was his duty to end his letters to his publisher by asking for news of his godson and "sending Marcel a kiss." Meanwhile, his new publisher agreed to reissue Bouilhet's works, starting with the collection *Dernières Chansons* with a preface by Flaubert. Things were certainly improving on the publishing front.

Charpentier could be pleased with his new acquisitions: the first printing of two thousand copies of *The Temptation of Saint Anthony* sold out in less than three weeks. Other editions followed as Flaubert won back the audience that had given *Sentimental Education* the cold shoulder. *Saint Anthony* was the fruit of a lifetime of work; he had begun mulling it over as far back as 1845, during his trip to Italy, when he was struck by Brueghel's painting in Genoa. For twenty-seven years, he had pondered this book in a genre even he was uncertain of, a kind of fantastical poem based on the legendary character of the hermit haunted by visions and tempted by the Devil.

The legend is dramatically colorful. Having gone into the desert to find God, the anchorite was assailed by a legion of demons. One night, he thought all the animals in the desert were growling at his door. Yet Anthony was able to resist all these visions and every temptation—the temptations of the flesh, gold, and power. Worship of Saint Anthony subsequently developed with the belief that he was able to cure the disease of "holy fire." Many artists were inspired by his legend: Sassetta, Hieronymus Bosch, Matthias Grünewald, Jacques Callot, Tintoretto, Paolo Veronese, and of course Brueghel, whose work had stunned the young traveler in Italy. For Flaubert, Brueghel's painting resonated with an old story he had seen performed as a child at the annual Saint-Romain fair in Rouen. Every year he went to see old Legrain, a puppeteer who was known as "Père Saint Antoine" because he performed the story of the hermit in the desert. In July 1846, Flaubert had bought an engraving of Saint Anthony by Callot and hung it in his study. Finding additional inspiration in Byron's *Cain,* Goethe's *Faust,* and Quinet's *Ahasuerus,* he wrote the first version of *Saint Anthony* that had been so poorly received by Maxime Du Camp and Louis Bouilhet. Despite the encouragement of his mother, who disagreed with his friends' opinion, he had buried the manuscript before embarking for the Orient. Yet he did not give up on this subject, which had naturally been stoked by his visit to Egypt.

Following his friends' advice, he had turned to *Madame Bovary*, "an antidote to his lyricism," according to Edouard Maynial's expression,[22] but had not forgotten "the mythological and theological blaze of *Saint Anthony*." Indeed, once he completed *Bovary*, Flaubert began work on a radically shortened second version of *Saint Anthony* and even published a few chapters in *L'Artiste*. Public prosecutor Pinard referred to those excerpts to support his argument against Flaubert, leading the author to forgo publishing it in book form for fear that it would lead to further prosecution. He had once again returned to *Saint Anthony* after the publication of *Sentimental Education* in 1869, only to bury the manuscript for safekeeping during the war of 1870. He finally threw himself back into the project in June 1871, working with what he told his friend Edma Roger des Genettes was "frightening exaltation." Nonetheless, he continued to be unsure about the book's quality and had no intention of publishing it. It was his meeting with Charpentier that convinced him otherwise. *The Temptation of Saint Anthony* went on sale in 1874, shortly after the flop of *Le Candidat*.

This third version was noticeably shorter than the previous two, sometimes at the cost of pages of beautiful prose. It also had a new concept and a different structure. Flaubert had entered a reading frenzy to prepare the new version, both to complete his research on the gods of Egypt and Greece and to delve deeper into the works of philosophers such as Spinoza, Kant, and Hegel. He "lost" himself in Antiquity, he told George Sand, the better to forget the contemporary world's wickedness. On a deeper level, *Saint Anthony* found Flaubert returning to an ontological and metaphysical meditation on humankind and on himself. Dedicated to the memory of his friend Alfred Le Poittevin, this third version also marked a return to the questions of his youth.

The book consists of face-offs between the hermit and the successive apparitions that put him to the test, including the Devil. Sections of dialogue alternate with descriptions of the places that Anthony is taken to. At the outset, Anthony has fled the world and taken shelter in the Thebaid desert, wearing a goatskin tunic and living off black bread. Night falls, and the anchorite is flooded with memories of good and bad times. To his family's despair, he had left his home, traveled through many countries, and withdrawn from the world: "To groan away in the desert more than thirty years! With my back bowed, like Eusebius, under eighty pounds of bronze, with my body exposed to the stinging of insects like Macarius, and with never an eye shut for fifty-three nights, like Pachomius; it may well be that the beheaded, the burnt, the pincered have less virtue, since my life is one long martyrdom!"[23] Anthony collapses onto his mat, but the Devil is watching and leads him into incredible hallucinations.

In the course of a single night, he is faced with the thousand demons of temptation, those of the flesh as well as the spirit, embodied by caressing or ecstatic characters whom the future saint heroically resists. This long fantastical poem is a deep investigation of the question of being and nothingness. Representatives of every religion, every sect, and every ancient mythology are summoned to tell their truths. They prove so contradictory that they negate each other's certainties. Anthony then wants to seek shelter in his own faith, but the Devil subjects him to doubt:

THE DEVIL

Do the demands of your reason legislate for things? God is no doubt indifferent to evil since the earth is thick with it!

Is it through impotence that he tolerates it, or through cruelty that he conserves it?

Do you imagine him to be constantly readjusting the world like an imperfect masterpiece, and watching over every creature's every movement, from the butterfly's flight to the mind of man?

If he created the universe, his providence is superfluous. If Providence exists, creation is defective.

But good and evil concern only you—like day and night, or pleasure and pain, or birth and death, which are relative to a corner of extension, to a special milieu, to a particular interest. Since the infinite alone is permanent, there is the Infinite—and that's all!

ANTHONY *cannot see a thing. He feels faint.*

An icy cold grips my very soul. I'm past the point of pain! It's like a death deeper than death. I'm spinning in vast darkness. It's inside me. My conscious self shatters under this dilating void!

THE DEVIL

But things reach you only through the medium of your mind. Like a concave mirror it distorts objects—and you lack the means to make accurate checks.

You will never know the universe in its full extent; consequently you cannot form an idea of its cause, nor have a right notion of God, nor even say that the universe is infinite—for it would first be necessary to know Infinity![24]

Readers of *The Temptation of Saint Anthony* were struck by the erudition of an author who seemed to want to provide an exhaustive catalog of every known fact about Antiquity (populations, customs, gods, and so on). Flaubert uses enumeration to compose a new kind of litany-chant. Here is Apollonius: "We came back through the Aromatic Country, the land of the Gangarides, the Comorian promontory, the district of the Sachalites, the Adramites, and the Homerites—then, crossing the Cassanian mountains, the Red Sea and the island of Topazos, we penetrated into Ethiopia through the kingdom of the Pygmies."[25] Here is Isis: "O Neith, beginning of all things! Ammon, lord of eternity, Ptha the demiurge, Thoth his intelligence, gods of the Amenthi, distinct triads of the Nomes, sparrow-hawks in the blue, sphinx at the edge of the temples, ibis upright between the horns of oxen, planets, constellations, shores, murmuring winds, mirrored lights, tell me where I can find Osiris!"[26] Here is Hercules: "I conquered the Kerkopes, the Amazons and the Centaurs. I killed a lot of kings. I broke the horn of Achelous, a great river, I cut up mountains, I joined oceans. I freed enslaved countries; empty countries I peopled. I traveled all over Gaul. I crossed the thirsty desert. I defended the gods, and made my escape from Omphale. But Olympus is too heavy. My arms are giving way. I shall die!"[27]

A strange beauty emerges from this enumerative mania and luxuriant speech, in which the picturesque and the exotic compete with the lyrical. Flaubert had come a long way from "modern novels" and the blathering of electoral candidates to revive the Romanticism of his youth and that period when he wrote tales of fantasy. Once again, he could say "Saint Anthony is me"—the "me" who had chosen solitude, who never ceased meditating on the finiteness of human existence, whose heart and soul were constantly stirred by desire, who mortified his flesh in the name of his god, Literature. *Saint Anthony* is little read today, but in its time, its lyrical flights, its cosmic dimension, and perhaps even its central questions regarding the existence of God and the enigmas of the universe met the expectations of a reading public that, despite a general indifference to religion, was in search of both transcendence and exoticism.

The Temptation of Saint Anthony was given a warm public reception: it was reprinted three times in Flaubert's lifetime. Most of the reviews, however, were vicious. According to Flaubert, the critics were "pitiful, odiously stupid and inane," with the exception of Édouard Drumont in *Le Bien public* (then unknown, he later wrote the influential anti-Semitic book *La France juive* [*Jewish France*]), Théodore de Banville in *Le National,* who celebrated the "masterpiece," and a few other kind words scattered here and there. Once again, the *Revue des deux mondes* set the tone with a review by Saint-René Taillandier: "Nothing is explained, nothing speaks to us, nothing is alive. It is too clear that the author only sought opportunities for imaginary pictures. . . . He applies himself to degrading the idea of God wherever he can." Once again, Barbey d'Aurevilly tore him to shreds in *Le Constitutionnel:* "No normally put together man will take the slightest interest in these grotesque apparitions, which only make us laugh at the author who came up with them, and which follow each other without a purpose or a moment's rest for close to four hundred pages, cruelly irritating the reader's nerves. I have seen some of these exasperated readers accuse M. Gustave Flaubert of being mad. He is not mad, at least not in terms of ardor and impulse. He is very calm. But men, like literature, eventually reach a stage of childlike foolishness."[28] Flaubert's best friends reassured him: George Sand, who spoke of *Saint Anthony* as a "masterpiece," a "magnificent book"; Turgenev, who tried to get a Russian translation published but came up against tsarist censorship; Renan, who told Flaubert how much he enjoyed reading it, adding that he had loaned the book to professors on the faculty of Protestant theology at Strasbourg, now in Paris, and that they "were delighted with it." But one does not feel overwhelming enthusiasm on Renan's part; in fact he advised Flaubert to return to "what interests everybody." As for Edmond de Goncourt, he had made the usual sour remarks in his diary shortly after Flaubert read him long passages of the text in November 1871: according to him, the book lacked originality and personal invention and was merely intelligently applied bookishness. He jotted down a few brief comments upon receiving his inscribed copy of the book in 1874: "Imagination created with footnotes. Originality always reminiscent of Goethe."

Though he pretended not to care, Flaubert was seriously disappointed. The criticism depressed him. He felt that he was a victim of hatred for his own person, of "willful denigration." He believed that people were resentful of his way of life, his isolation, and the fact that he had been and was still a regular at Princess Mathilde's salon. Both his reputation for being unsociable and the politics of the day worked against him. He admitted he was "worn out." His doctor advised him to spend twenty days in the Swiss Alps to "de-neuroticize" himself. Early in July, he traveled to Kaltbad Rigi, where he had taken a small hotel room facing Lake Lucerne and the peaks of the Rigi. He walked, sweated, gasped for breath, and rested, but soon solitude weighed on him, and he bristled at the prevalence of German tourists. Before he knew it, he was "gigantically" bored. The setting was magnificent, but he was no "man of Nature." He wrote to George Sand that he would give "all the glaciers of Switzerland for the Vatican Museum." Turgenev wrote to him to be brave and "come back to us pale and monochrome, like a line from Lamartine." Finally, on July 18, his friend Laporte joined him in the Alps before he set out for Rouen via Dieppe. In a letter to Turgenev, Flaubert summed up his Swiss rest cure: "My stay (or rather my crass idleness) at the Rigi has stupefied me. One should never rest, for the moment one stops doing things, one thinks about oneself and becomes ill, or one thinks one's ill, which is the same thing."[29]

CHAPTER 26

Financial Ruin and Bereavement

As soon as he got home from the Swiss Alps, where he had been bored "to death," Flaubert tried to return to his project for a new novel, *Bouvard and Pécuchet*. He spent four months working on it in Paris. But he could not slip back into his old routine. "For the past six months especially," he wrote to George Sand in January 1875, "I don't know what's been the matter with me. But I feel profoundly ill, without being able to put my finger on it."[1] Throughout the winter in Paris, he did not emerge from what he referred to as his "hypochondria" and "neurosis." His friend from Nohant recommended that he spend less time thinking about himself, though, unlike her, he did not have the enjoyable distractions of children and grandchildren. His sadness was exacerbated by physical ailments: colds, flu, rheumatism. He treated himself with potassium bromide, which gave him eczema. "Twinges of gout here and there, pains throughout my body, *invincible* depression, a sense of the futility of all things, grave doubts about the book I'm writing—that's what's the matter with me, dear and valiant maître. Add to all that worries about money."[2] For Flaubert had been haunted by fears of bankruptcy since the month of April. He was entering one of the most difficult periods of his life.

The Commanville Bankruptcy

In April 1875, Flaubert learned that the Commanvilles were in a disastrous financial situation. Caroline's husband, Ernest, ran a sawmill close to Dieppe but was more of a merchant than an industrialist: he sold firewood and lumber made from logs that were imported from Norway and Russia and then processed in his sawmill. After the Franco-Prussian War, the price of wood had dropped dramatically as part of a general downturn of prices (the depression would last until 1896). Commanville's investments collapsed. As Caroline later explained it, Ernest had believed that wood prices would rise and had gone into debt to buy "enormous forests." His creditors were now coming after him.[3] The disaster directly affected Gustave. Having entire confidence in his nephew, he had invested part of his fortune in Commanville's business and left him to manage it. Since his mother's death, Flaubert had maintained his standard of living thanks to the income from his farm in Deauville and the money Commanville sent him when he requested it. In December 1871, Commanville had received a 100,000-franc line of credit from a banker in Elbeuf, with Mme Flaubert as his guarantor. After her death, the guarantee was passed on to her children, Achille and Gustave, "who were [thus] unwittingly involved in Commanville's commitments."[4]

Upon learning of Ernest's financial collapse, Uncle Gustave used all his financial assets to buy back his nephew's debts. To cut down on his expenses, he gave notice to his landlord on rue Murillo in May and took a more modest rental at 240, rue du Faubourg Saint-Honoré. His new apartment was adjacent to Caroline's, for, as he told George Sand, he could "no longer tolerate solitude." Above all, the essential was to avoid bankruptcy, an unforgivable failing that would bring shame and infamy to the entire family. Gustave did everything he could to save Ernest and Caroline from this ignominious prospect.

Aside from this potential catastrophe, he was haunted by the threat of another disaster: Caroline might be forced to sell the house at Croisset, which did not belong to him. He could no longer sleep: "the idea of no longer having a roof to call my own," he wrote to his niece, "a *home,* is intolerable. I now look at Croisset like a mother who looks at her consumptive child, asking herself: 'How much longer will he live?' And I cannot get used to the possibility of a permanent separation."[5] He was in a state of extreme anxiety. Fearing that the Commanvilles were not telling him everything, he bombarded his niece with letters and questions. He soon found himself totally unable to continue work on his book. "Do not hide anything from me. Anything is better than uncertainty."

Even though Commanville was ruining him, Flaubert never said a word against him. His harshest criticism was no more than a fatherly remonstrance: "Ah! Your poor husband wasn't born to make me happy!" He quickly added: "But no more of that."[6] Yet one can justifiably question Commanville's honesty as a businessman. After Flaubert's death, Edmond de Goncourt bluntly called Commanville a "crook."[7]

Flaubert's letters are full of expressions of pity for his poor beloved Caro, whom he so wanted to be happy. On July 18, he confided in his friend Léonie Brainne:

> We've now been living with this infernal anxiety for four months! Even if things turn out for the best, we'll barely have enough left to live on (at least for the moment) and I fear that sooner or later we'll have to leave poor Croisset. For me this would be the coup de grâce. At my age, you don't start a new life. You know that I'm not a posturer. Well, I believe I am a doomed man, one doesn't get over a blow like this. Yet if Deauville remains mine, if Commanville does not go bankrupt, if he can work again and we keep Croisset, life will still be possible. If not, no.

He started to think about how he could make money. But what job could he set his sights on, he who had never held a salaried position or agreed to contribute to a periodical? For the time being, he was entirely consumed by the humiliation of his nephew and niece. His fatherly heart was suffering, he told Turgenev. George Sand did what she could, writing to Agénor Bardoux, a deputy and friend of Flaubert who was also the undersecretary of state for justice, to ask whether he could find Flaubert a "lucrative job": wasn't there some way to save him? Bardoux and Raoul-Duval bent over backward to try to get him a pension. Flaubert was touched by their efforts, but refused: "I don't think I should be fed from public funds," he wrote to Bardoux. "Remember: such a pension would be published, printed, and perhaps attacked in the press and in the Assembly."[8] However, he let it be known that he wouldn't turn down a position as a librarian for three or four thousand francs a year, plus housing—the Mazarine or Arsenal libraries would do just fine!

That summer, he traveled to Deauville to put the farm up for sale. Flaubert thought he sold it at a good price: 200,000 francs, the equivalent of 800,000 euros today, minus the mortgage. But he immediately had to pay 50,000 francs to Commanville's principal creditor to avoid bankruptcy. Edmond Laporte, ever the faithful friend, advanced half of that to Caroline, with Raoul-Duval providing the other half. Both men agreed to be guarantors, in order to allow for staggered payments. Flaubert roared triumphantly: "There will be no bankruptcy!" "Honor will be preserved!" He was still interested in a position as a librarian, but only if the conditions were favorable: he did not want to be obliged to be in Paris all year long, and he wanted to earn at least three thousand francs.

Early in October, the liquidation was completed. There would be no bankruptcy, but Flaubert was ruined: "My nephew had devoured half my fortune," he told George Sand, "and with the remainder I indemnified one of his creditors who wanted to put him into receivership."[9] Trying to help Flaubert find something else to sell, his friend in Nohant asked whether there were parts of Croisset available, and if so, offered to buy them with some capital she could transfer. Gustave was touched by his friend's generosity, but turned her down. He would manage. In fact, he would have to live very frugally, but at least he could stay at Croisset.

Flaubert's relationship with money is worth dwelling on for a moment. He affirmed that he did not want to talk about it; he claimed—and was probably sincere in saying so—that he had nothing but contempt for money. Exclusively interested in the purest Art, he invariably refused to stoop to writing to "pay the bills," like his many friends and colleagues who published their prose in newspapers and magazines. He was even loath to discuss money matters with his publisher, always entrusting a third party such as his notary or George Sand to do so. But there was a limit to his detachment, as attested by his break with Michel Lévy, whom he never forgave, even after the publisher died in 1875, for what he saw as his revolting stinginess.

Flaubert could get away with this attitude toward money because of his privileged position. He could allow himself such standards because he did not have to *earn* his money; it turned up in his wallet at regular intervals or whenever he asked for it. He was born a man of independent means, unlike his father, who had made a fortune by working at the hospital his whole life and becoming a famous surgeon, supplementing his professional income with investments. Gustave's brother Achille had followed in his father's footsteps as a great doctor at the Hôtel-Dieu in Rouen. But Gustave had chosen a different path. He did not want to *lower himself*: "I have an *extreme* distaste for accepting a position, for no longer being independent. To me, remunerated employment (of any kind) appears to be a degradation." This set Flaubert apart from the bourgeois: he did not enrich himself through work or saving, or through good investments. He knew nothing about all that and did not want to know. Yet what was thoroughly bourgeois about him was the phobia of falling to a lower station, the dread of lacking resources, and the fear of losing his private income and ultimately going bankrupt—a fear very present in his novels, as

Jacques Lecarme has remarked: "Bankruptcy is the damnation of a name and a tribe, the irreparable stain from which no one can recover."[10] The son of an affluent family, long protected by his mother, an heir who drew on his inheritance without hesitation, he was now confronted with the realities of a society he wished to escape: he would have to come down from the heavens.

One can draw a connection between the aristocratic artist's attitude and his political convictions and loathing of universal suffrage. Flaubert certainly had good reason to fear the democratic society that was being built. It would ultimately do away with private incomes in favor of work, whether self-employed or salaried. While there would probably always remain an independently wealthy few, it would become increasingly difficult to escape the commodification of that which should in theory be priceless: the work of art. In 1875, Flaubert, who was an absolute outsider to the economy's capitalist development and society's egalitarian momentum, saw his privileged status as a financially independent writer falling apart. Writing was becoming more of a profession adapted to a growing market and less of a sacred function or a hobby free from financial considerations. Though he did not participate in this development—in fact he railed against it—Flaubert could not help but denounce the success of the mediocre given the poor sales of some of his own works. For this, he blamed the reign of the "plebes," which stemmed from expanded suffrage. This only goes to show that despite his own contradictions, Flaubert perfectly grasped the norms of the new society he abhorred. As for Edmond de Goncourt, seeing Victor Hugo's election to the Senate as a sign of the rise of the republicans, he wrote: "It is, in the name of the absolute principle of equality, the beginning of the destruction of the aristocracy of intelligence."

In September 1875, Flaubert left Croisset to go relax in Concarneau, Brittany, accompanied by Georges Pennetier, director of the Rouen natural history museum, and fellow naturalist Georges Pouchet of the Paris natural history museum, whom Flaubert knew well and regularly consulted when he was writing his novels. While nervously awaiting the liquidation of Commanville's business, he set off with a heavy heart, haunted by his situation's uncertainty and worried about Caroline. The Breton air calmed him down a little. Staying at the Hôtel Sergent, he took sea baths, saw a pardon at Pont-Aven, breathed in the stench of sardines from the fishing boats, and listened with interest to his traveling companions' lessons in marine biology. Having put aside *Bouvard and Pécuchet,* he had set to work on something new in order not to lose his touch. It was a short story, or rather a tale, based on the legend of Saint Julian the Hospitaller, which was depicted on the stained glass windows of the Rouen cathedral and which he had long been thinking about. The piece was a way of testing whether he was still able to make art. "I *want* to force myself to write *Saint Julian*. I'll do it like a chore, to see what comes of it."

After Pennetier's departure, he and Pouchet stayed on until the end of October. The liquidation agreement, which spared Commanville from bankruptcy, bolstered Flaubert's courage, though the future appeared dark. "Here," he wrote to Edmond Laporte, "I lead a peaceful and idiotic little life. I stuff myself with shrimp and lobster, take walks by the sea, have a snooze on my bed after lunch, go to sleep by nine every night, and chat with good old Pouchet, who dissects fish and mollusks for my education. Today he showed me the genital organs of a ray." But to George Sand, he admitted that he would never recover from this terrible blow; he was demolished. He was feeling calmer, he told Turgenev; his heart was not quite so sick anymore, but no matter how he tried, he always came back to "sad thoughts." Nonetheless, his time in Concarneau perked him up enough that he would have extended his stay if Pouchet hadn't had to return to Paris. They both left for the capital on November 1.

Staying in his new apartment on rue du Faubourg Saint-Honoré, he got back in the habit of hosting Sunday gatherings to which he invited his small circle of friends, now enlarged to include Guy de Maupassant and always enlivened by Alphonse Daudet. The other regulars were Turgenev, Goncourt, and Zola. He did not see George Sand, who no longer left Nohant, but maintained a regular correspondence with her.

The Loss of a Great Voice

With Sand, he now only discussed aesthetics, not politics. His novelist friend criticized him, claiming that his writing stayed on the surface because of his obsession with form. She had given a lot of thought to the failure of *Sentimental Education* and had come to the conclusion that its characters were too distant from themselves, and the author too absent from the story. He answered her with a profession of faith from which he did not want to stray:

> As for my 'lack of conviction,' alas! I'm only too full of convictions. I'm constantly bursting with suppressed anger and indignation. But my ideal of Art

demands that the artist reveal none of this, and that he appear in his work no more than God in nature. The man is nothing, the work is everything! . . . It would be very agreeable for me to say what I think, and relieve M. Gustave Flaubert's feelings by means of such utterances; but of what importance is the aforesaid gentleman?

I do think as you do, mon maître, that Art is not merely criticism and satire. That is why I have never deliberately tried to write either the one or the other. I have always endeavored to penetrate the soul of things and to emphasize universal truths; and have purposely avoided the fortuitous and the dramatic. No monsters, no heroes![11]

He repeated that he did not belong to any school and that the only function of art which he wanted to serve was the search for beauty. And if she reproached him for lacking "a broad and definite view of life," he did not contest it: "The words Religion or Catholicism on the one hand, Progress, Fraternity, Democracy on the other, no longer satisfy the spiritual demands of our time. The brand-new dogma of Equality, preached by Radicalism, is demonstrated to be untrue by Physiology and History. I don't see how it is possible today to establish a new Principle any more than to respect the old ones. Hence I keep seeking—without ever finding—that Idea from which all the rest must proceed."

George Sand did not give up easily. She rejected the way of skepticism, contending that humanity is "on the path that leads upward." She did not delude herself about life, but she wanted to get the best out of it, rather than to curse it. She returned to aesthetics: "I don't say you don't believe. On the contrary: one aspect of your life is all affection, protection of others, graceful and simple kindness, which shows that you're a more convinced believer than anyone. But as soon as you're dealing with literature you insist for some reason or other on being a different person, one who has to disappear or even annihilate himself—one who doesn't exist! What a strange obsession! What misguided 'good taste'! Our work can never be better than we are ourselves."

. Why had *Sentimental Education* been a flop? She came back to it: it was because he did not make clear his point of view about his characters, if only with a preface. She criticized him for not giving his opinion and for leaving the reader to judge, which was also true of *Madame Bovary*. The reader was mystified by the absence of the author—by his detachment and assumed indifference. "Hold on to your worship of form; but pay more attention to content."

Flaubert conceded that he and Sand fundamentally disagreed about one thing, Sand's idealism, which he could not share in—"I, poor wretch, remain glued to the earth, as though the soles of my shoes were made of lead." He continued: "As for revealing my own opinion of the people I bring on stage, no, no! a thousand times no! I don't recognize my *right* to do so. If a reader doesn't draw from a book the moral it implies, either the reader is an imbecile or the book a sham, in that it lacks authenticity."

Twenty-first-century readers are so used to this Flaubertian aesthetic of "impersonality" and the author's silence that we do not always recognize the novelty, strangeness, and modernity of the approach. The traditional novel aimed to educate, explain, and demonstrate; the novel according to Flaubert shows, describes, and lets the reader judge. This is what George Sand could not accept. Yet neither their aesthetic nor political differences could call into question their friendship and mutual affection. "You have never done me anything but good," he wrote to her on February 18, 1876, "and I love you tenderly."

At the beginning of March, George Sand's play *Le Mariage de Victorine* [*The Marriage of Victorine*] was revived at the Théâtre Français, but the author stayed in Nohant. Flaubert hurried to write to her about the audience's warm reception and to let her hear the loud applause: "Your play enchanted me and made me cry my eyes out." Yet one might question his sincerity after reading the following passage from a letter to Edma Roger des Genettes: "Last week I saw *Le Philosophe sans le savoir* [*The Unwitting Philosopher*] and *Le Mariage de Victorine* at the Français. So false! So banal! So trivial! In the end, I was so indignant that I went home and spent the whole night rereading Euripides's *Medea,* to cleanse myself of this pablum. People are so indulgent with third-rate works!"

He had finished "Saint Julian the Hospitaller" and was now hard at work on another tale, "A Simple Heart." As concerned with getting the details right as ever, he went to inspect the story's settings in April, first in Pont-l'Evêque and then in Honfleur, despite the fact that he knew both towns well, and took copious notes. Late in May, he learned that George Sand was very sick. On June 8, he received a telegram from Plauchut: "Mme Sand in a very bad way." He did not have time to rush to her. That very day, the novelist of Nohant died of an intestinal blockage. Shattered, Flaubert attended the funeral on June 10 with Renan and Prince Napoleon, the godfather of George Sand's granddaughter Aurore.

Marie-Sophie Leroyer de Chantepie, a great admirer of George Sand, leapt on the opportunity to write to Flaubert. She told him she was very worried that Sand had been forced to be attended by a priest despite the fact that she was no longer a Catholic; her freedom of conscience had been violated. Flaubert reassured her that Sand had not seen a priest. It was only once she was dead that things had taken a religious turn. Sand's daughter, Mme Solange Clésinger, wanted a Catholic burial; she asked the bishop of Bourges, who did not object. Solange's brother, Maurice, who was devastated, was not opposed to it. "The ceremony was immensely moving: everyone was in tears, I along with the rest."[12]

Turgenev wrote from Russia: "Poor dear Mme Sand! She loved us both—you especially—that was only natural. What a heart of gold she had! Such an absence of all low, petty or false sentiments—what a good fellow she was and what a fine woman! And now all of that is there, in the horrible relentless hole in the ground, silent, stupid—and it doesn't even know what it is it's devouring!"[13]

A great friendship had come to an end, a friendship that was paradoxical in its very existence as well as in its intensity. She celebrated life; he loathed it. She was optimistic and idealistic, while remaining grounded in life's practical matters. He was an old bear without a grasp on material realities. She was a progressive; he was a conservative. Their political, philosophical, and aesthetic notions led to insurmountable disagreements. Yet they still appreciated each other and loved each other with a tender, faithful friendship. With George Sand, Flaubert experienced a moral and intellectual exchange untouched by erotic stimulation. She provided him with maternal support, with advice and reassurance. The few times he had visited her in Nohant, he had found the pleasures and joys of family life with Maurice, his wife Lina, and their daughters Gabrielle and Aurore, which sometimes made him regret that he had never had children. Flaubert's life was truly becoming a cemetery. The loss of his dear friend drove him a little deeper into loneliness. Something had to be done to ward off the rush of dark thoughts.

The late writer's friends agreed to erect a monument in Sand's honor. Alexandre Dumas fils refused to join the ad hoc commission because, as Flaubert wrote in a letter to Léonie Brainne, "she had not left him a Delacroix painting he coveted." Flaubert unleashed his irony on the "great man": "What a fine spirit! What a good heart! What a noble artist's nature!"

CHAPTER 27

"Blue Sky Ahead!"

During the summer of 1876, Flaubert felt less moody and more cheerful. He was full of a renewed enthusiasm. "I am *back at full staff*. I feel like writing," he told his friend Edma Roger des Genettes. After "The Legend of Saint Julian the Hospitaller," he threw himself into "The Story of a Simple Heart." He would confide in Maurice Sand, the son of his late friend George Sand, that he had started the short story "exclusively for her, solely to please her."[1] He explicitly wanted to move the reader, to arouse pity, and to show that contrary to his reputation, he was a sensitive soul, just like the great woman of Nohant.[2]

He was growing increasingly fond of Croisset, where he spent most of the day and a good part of the night hunched over the blank page, stopping to read aloud the sentences he had written—what he called his "*gueulades*," his bellowing—or to walk his dog Julio and take his evening swim in the Seine. "At night," he wrote to Caroline, "the sentences rolling through my brain like the chariots of Roman emperors wake me with a start." He did not receive any visitors or read any papers. He struck out twelve pages to write one and a half. When it came time to tell the story of the parrot belonging to Félicité, the protagonist of "A Simple Heart," he stayed true to his commitment to accuracy and asked his friend Georges Pennetier, the director of the natural history museum in Rouen, to provide him with a stuffed parrot to closely examine.[2]

Though he had regained his self-confidence, he remained worried about his financial affairs. He was living hand to mouth, struggling to pay his new servant Noémie's wages. At Christmas of 1876, he only had twenty francs to his name: "A trickle from the family fortune is indispensable," he wrote to his niece. Overwhelmed by bills, he asked Ernest Commanville to replenish his finances. On January 11, he solicited his nephew again: "*This letter* is only to tell you that I am absolutely without *a franc.*—That's not completely true, because I have *10!* But not a centime more." Ernest sent him 100 francs. Gustave wanted to reassure him: a third tale, "Herodias," was underway; he thought he would be done by mid-February, at which point he would have "some cash." Money! It was becoming a major concern, but he wanted to avoid turning it into an obsession. On January 17, after paying Noémie's wages and buying some groceries, he had six francs left. He sometimes had to forgo taking the boat to La Bouille, a stone's throw from Croisset, because he could not afford a ticket. Scheduled to be published in April, his new book, *Three Tales*, was arriving in the nick of time. Turgenev had gotten the Russian magazine *The Messenger of Europe* to agree to publish a translation, on the condition that the three short stories be published in Russian before the book came out in France. Leading up to the release of the French edition on April 24, "A Simple Heart" was published in *Le Moniteur universel* and "Saint Julian" in *Le Bien public.*

But all this was only a drop in the bucket. In late spring, Flaubert devoted much of his time to helping Commanville attempt to get back on an even keel. Flaubert was somewhat optimistic; he believed they had found a solution. The idea was to found a joint-stock company that would allow Commanville to start a new business. They needed one million francs in capital. The value of the factory in Neuville, near Dieppe, which Commanville still owned, had been estimated at 600,000 francs, including land and equipment, so they needed to raise an additional 400,000 francs from investors. By June 18, 1877, Flaubert could tell Edma Roger des Genettes that they had received 120,000 francs in two weeks: "It's not yet all done, but there is blue sky ahead!" He spared himself no effort, writing to all and sundry and visiting potential investors or acquaintances who might help find funding. His correspondence shows that one of the people he solicited was Marguerite Pelouze, a woman who was separated from her husband and had used her considerable fortune to acquire the Château de Chenonceaux and begin major restorations on it in 1864. It is not known how Flaubert met her; all we know is that after having been received at her Paris townhouse on the rue de l'Université he accepted an invitation to visit her at Chenonceaux in May 1877, and that he returned from there delighted with the prospect that the chatelaine would invest in Commanville's business. The loyal Raoul-Duval, who enjoyed a certain social status, was enrolled in looking for investors. But it was not an easy task: how was one to convince investors to give Commanville their money when he had only just barely avoided bankruptcy? *"Business* is not looking good," Flaubert told Léonie Brainne in July. At that stage, they had less than 150,000 francs in commitments from investors. They made some slow progress over the course of the summer of 1877, but the timing was particularly bad. France was undergoing a major political crisis after MacMahon had dissolved the Chamber of Deputies on June 25, and anticipation of the next elections, to be held in October, only made things worse.

These constant efforts on Commanville's behalf did not prevent Flaubert from working quickly. On April 20, 1877, he signed off on the proofs of *Three Tales*, and three days later Charpentier put the book on sale.

The *Three Tales*

While staying in Concarneau in September 1875, Flaubert, then in the depths of his depression and despairing that he would ever be able to finish *Bouvard and Pécuchet*, thought of writing a short piece, a small novel about chivalry entitled "The Legend of Saint Julian the Hospitaller," which would be taken from the *Golden Legend* by Jacobus de Voragine. As attested by a letter to Louis Bouilhet, he had already thought of the subject as early as 1856, after he had finished *Madame Bovary*.[3] Twenty years later, he wrote to Edma Roger des Genettes that *"Bouvard and Pécuchet* was too difficult, I give up; I'm looking for another novel but haven't discovered anything. In the meantime, I'm going to start writing the legend of Saint Julian the Hospitaller, solely to keep myself busy, to see if I can still make a sentence, which I doubt. It will be very short, maybe thirty pages." By the following February, he had finished writing what he told Léonie Brainne was his "religious-pohetic and medievally rococo little story."

The tale begins like an ancient tragedy, describing how Julian unwittingly fulfills a prediction that he will kill his father and mother. What follows comes from the *Golden Legend:* Julian abandons everything, becomes a beggar, and winds up feeding, sheltering, and warming up a leper by sharing his bed with him. This act of holiness is not without consequence. The leper is revealed to be Jesus Christ: "Then the Leper clasped him in his arms. And all at once his eyes took on the brightness of the stars . . . and Julian rose toward the blue, face to face with Our Lord Jesus Christ, who bore him up to Heaven."[4] The taste for fantasy so prevalent in Flaubert's juvenilia was returning to the fore.

As soon as he finished "Saint Julian," Flaubert began another short story, "A Simple Heart," which recounts the life of Félicité, an old maidservant in Pont-l'Evêque, who is very attached to her employer, Mme Aubain, and her children, Paul and Virginie. Grief-stricken by their successive deaths, she focuses her affections on a parrot, Loulou. Devastated to find the bird has died, she comes up with the idea of having it stuffed: "At last he arrived—looking quite magnificent, perched on a branch screwed into a mahogany base, one foot in the air, his head cocked to one side, and biting a nut which the taxidermist, out of a love of the grandiose, has gilded." From then on, she kneels before the stuffed parrot to say her prayers: "and as she breathed her last, she thought she could see, in the opening heavens, a gigantic parrot hovering over her head."[5]

With "A Simple Heart," Flaubert was diving back into his past, his childhood memories, his vacations in Trouville, and preserving a lively image of Julie, the servant who used to read to him and whom he still saw at Croisset. She was old and sick now, but they still talked about all the distant times and lost faces. In June 1876, he told Edma Roger des Genettes: "It is not at all ironic, as you supposed, but on the contrary very serious and very sad. I want to move sensitive souls to pity, to make them cry—since I am one myself." Meanwhile, he had begun a third tale, "Herodias."

Herodias is the name of another heroine of Antiquity, in the same vein as Salammbô. But the story's central character is Saint John the Baptist. It is set in 28 BCE in Judea, then under the rule of the tetrarch Herod Antipas, who has married Herodias, his half-brother's wife. For denouncing this adulterous relationship, the Jew Jokanaan—also known as John the Baptist—is imprisoned in the citadel of Machaerus. Herodias wants him dead. During a feast for Herod's birthday, the tetrarch is fascinated by an unknown dancer and promises to grant whatever she wishes: she asks for John the Baptist's head. Bound to his promise, he has John beheaded and offers the head to the dancer, who is none other than Salome, Herodias's daughter.

The dance of Salome is a motif frequently found in Christian iconography. Flaubert might have been inspired by the tympanum of one of the doors of the cathedral in Rouen, a twelfth-century sculpture representing Salome dancing in front of Herod while John the Baptist is held prisoner in a tower. Some details were probably taken from his Oriental travel notes, notably on the dance of the *almeh*. As usual, Flaubert cut no corners in researching this story, reading broadly from the Gospels to Flavius Josephus, Suetonius, and archaeology manuals. He drew on friends such as Edmond Laporte and Frédéric Baudry, a librarian at the Arsenal whom he asked for the names of the stars in Hebrew and Arabic.

The stories in *Three Tales* have an unexpected Christian tone. Is it a mere coincidence that on December 24, 1876, Flaubert attended midnight mass at the Sainte-Barbe convent with Noémie and the farmer's wife, Mme Chevalier? "And to tell the truth, I liked it there," he told Caroline the next day. Coming after *The Temptation of Saint Anthony*, the stories of Saint Julian, Saint John the Baptist, and blessed Félicité's simple heart were sure to appeal to the Church: it officially recommended the three tales. Flaubert mentioned this to his dear friend Léonie: "The *Three Tales* by 'good M. Flaubert' are recommended in the catalog of a Catholic bookstore as being appropriate to circulate 'among Families.' I told you I was turning into a Father of the Church!"[6]

It is possible to read the *Three Tales* in a less saintly way; one could say that by recounting the life of Félicité, who confuses the Holy Spirit with a parrot, the author is mocking the faith of "simple people." Flaubert denied this interpretation: it is a sad story, without irony. And indeed, the three short stories all include the telling of a Passion and a Redemption; the tone is that of the Christian marvelous. It is not a revival of Flaubert's faith that one notes—a faith he had abandoned in childhood—but perhaps, as with Renan, an aspiration to spirituality, which was invigorated by the images in churches and the religious chants of midnight mass.[7]

Published on April 24, 1877, *Three Tales* immediately brought praise from his friends. Laure de Maupassant, mother of Guy, applauded from Étretat: "a real marvel, a rare masterpiece!" The compliments poured in. Only Edmond de Goncourt, that inveterate curmudgeon, turned up his nose. After Flaubert read "Herodias" aloud at Princess Mathilde's home in February, Goncourt wrote about the evening in his *Journal*: "This reading made me sad at heart. The fact is, I would like Flaubert to obtain a success, which his morale and his health need so badly. His story certainly contains some good things, some colorful scenes, some delicate epithets; but what a lot of theatrical tricks and what a lot of modern feelings stuck into that gaudy mosaic of archaic notes! For all the reader's bellowing, the whole thing struck me as a playful exercise in Romantic archaeology."[8] The Goncourt brothers always resented other people's talent.

Overall, however, the reviews were unusually good. On April 27, the formidable Francisque Sarcey, who had lambasted *Sentimental Education*, admitted in his weekly literary gathering (reviewed in *Le Moniteur universel*) that he had been "seduced"; in his view, Flaubert showed himself to be a painter and a musician: "His pen has found, in parenthetical clauses, in a punctuation specific to him, and in resounding adverbs, the secret to rendering the sound of voices, the noise made by the wind, the gallop of horses, the timbre of bells, the cry of a dying man." Style! All the critics focused on it: "The style is superb . . . grand, striking images abound, and the descriptions sparkle" (Louis Fourcaud, *Le Gaulois*, May 4, 1877). In a rave review in *Le National*, Théodore Banville remarked that far from hampering him, Flaubert's erudition, which some still complained was too heavy handed, allowed him to "always find the right word, his own, decisive word," making it possible for him "to depict everything, even the most idealized eras and figures, without ever relying on a useless verb or a parasitic adverb" (May 14, 1877). In an article published in *L'Ordre* on May 15, Théophile Gautier fils emphasized Flaubert's musicality: "*Three Tales*—we can't help but think of the collection that Beethoven equally modestly called *Three Sonatas*, and in which his inspiration bursts forth with as much power as in his most majestic symphonies. . . . Flaubert's new book evokes a similar sensation and shows that its author, an absolute master of his talent, can adapt it to every dimension." In the June 12 issue of the *Journal officiel*, Alphonse Daudet's wife Julia, who published under the pseudonym Karl Steen, stated that Flaubert's style is "firm, full of imagery, measured; it is the perfection of our French language. There is not a single word, a single epithet too many. One would not dare to move a single comma, and the artistic satisfaction experienced can only be rivaled by the respect inspired by such a noble talent." Though the review published by Henry Houssaye in the *Journal des débats* on July 21 was not the most flattering, Houssaye recognized that Flaubert's style was "masculine, vigorous, precise, colorful, full of bright strokes and delicate nuances, by turns resounding and harmonious, sauntering or flying, calm or vehement." Yet the purist Houssaye also criticized Flaubert for sometimes letting his dread of repetition muddle his prose: he used pronouns to avoid repeating nouns, but it was sometimes unclear what they referred to.

Aside from the quality of Flaubert's style, critics were struck by the fact that the *Three Tales* highlighted the "three aspects of his marvelous talent as a writer," as Alfred Darcel put it in the May 2 issue of the *Journal de Rouen*. Julia Daudet spelled it out:

It is interesting to note that M. Gustave Flaubert's new work admirably sums up and reminds the reader of his diverse inspirations. Thus "A Simple Heart," with its bourgeois milieu, Norman landscape, and the frank language that lends great poetry to vulgar details, reminds one of *Madame Bovary;* "The Legend of Saint Julian the Hospitaller," with its mixture of the magic and the mystical, veiled in places by reflections of stained glass and the dust of solitude, seems to have emerged from *The Temptation of Saint Anthony;* while "Herodias" makes any man or woman of letters feel the purely artistic emotion, the admiration for a talent that has taken only the picturesque aspects of scholarship, that one felt when reading *Salammbô.*

Aside from the praise, which also included Gaston de Saint-Valry's acclaim for Flaubert's "admirable combination of exactitude and poetry" in the May 8 issue of *La Patrie* and Édouard Drumont's article in the May 23 issue of *Liberté,* there were relatively few spoilsports this time around. One might mention Daniel Bernard, who in the May 20 issue of *L'Union* asked what was so interesting about following the life of the ordinary Félicité and chose not to even mention "Herodias." More remarkable was the nasty article in the *Revue des deux mondes* by Ferdinand Brunetière, soon to be one of the most well-known critics in Paris. Once again, the worst review was in the *Revue,* which remained vicious toward Flaubert even after the death of its editor, Louis Buloz. The article was long but its judgment terse: "'A Simple Heart,' 'Herodias,' 'The Legend of Saint Julian the Hospitaller' are certainly the weakest things he [Flaubert] has yet produced." The critic deplored Flaubert's religion of the artist, his concern with effect, which was not well enough hidden; "the same strain in the style, which is annoying and tiring, and the same obstinately materialist method." For Brunetière, there was no doubt: Flaubert's creativity was "running dry."

Despite these isolated voices, the author of *Three Tales* could revel in a more positive critical reception than any he had ever had. Yet the book did not sell. It appeared in the middle of an enduring political crisis that damaged book sales. On May 21, Flaubert told Agénor Bardoux that Charpentier, who usually moved three hundred volumes a day, had sold only five the previous Saturday. "The war of 1870 killed *Sentimental Education,*" he wrote to Maxime Du Camp, "and now an internal coup d'état is paralyzing *Three Tales.* That's really pushing the hatred of literature to extremes."

Parisian Life

Although his appreciation of the charms of Croisset was growing along with the fear that he might lose it, Flaubert spent several months in Paris in 1876 and 1877. Now fifty-five, he could still make it to the fifth floor of his building on rue du Faubourg Saint-Honoré without getting too out of breath. On Sundays, he regularly hosted his friends—Turgenev (when his gout permitted), Edmond de Goncourt, Alphonse Daudet, Émile Zola, and the young Guy de Maupassant, who saw himself as Flaubert's disciple, as well as other occasional visitors.

That season, talk generally turned to Zola's success. His latest novel, *L'Assommoir* [*The Drinking Den*], was beating sales records after having been serialized in *La République des lettres*. Flaubert read the first few chapters and called it "ignoble." He reproached Zola for having chosen to use the language of thugs. His friend Turgenev thought that Zola displayed "much talent," but that there was "too much stirring of chamber pots."[9] Yet once the book was published, its overall effect led Flaubert to change his mind: "It would be unfortunate," he wrote to his friend Edma Roger des Genettes, "to write too many books like this one; but there are superb parts, a narrative that has great elegance and *incontestable truths*. It stays too long in the same range, but Zola is a powerful fellow and you'll see, he'll be very successful." Flaubert viewed Zola's book as a considerable achievement, and he now defended it against all those who were hostile to it. Nonetheless, he could not stand Zola's attempts to use his weekly column to preach his aesthetic theory and try to form a literary school called "naturalism": "Zola's mistake is to have a system, to want to found a school. His columns in *Le Bien public* outrage me every week." He repeated much the same thing to Turgenev: "This materialism annoys me, and nearly every Monday, I get an attack of irritation when I read dear Zola's serials."[10] One Monday night at Brébant's, Flaubert attacked Zola's profession of naturalist faith. Goncourt reported that far from retaliating, Zola dodged the issue by referring to his social class: "You, you had private means which allowed you to remain independent of a good many things. But I had to earn my living with nothing but my pen, I had to go through the mill of journalism and write all sorts of shameful stuff; and it has left me with—how shall I put it?—a certain taste for charlatanism. I consider the word Naturalism as ridiculous as you do but I shall go on repeating it over and over because you have to give things new names for the public to think that they are new."

Zola drew a distinction between his works (his novels) and his newspaper articles, which were "just so much charlatanism to puff up my books."[11]

Whether it was cynical or not, this "naturalism" got people talking, and word spread to the public. Flaubert rejected both naturalism and realism; though he certainly intended to draw from reality, he made no claim to reproduce it. Aside from Beauty, what he aimed for was Truth, which the artist can only reach through generalization ("Art isn't intended to depict exceptional beings") and the right amount of exaggeration ("One must never fear to exaggerate. All the greats did it, Michelangelo, Rabelais, Shakespeare, Molière"). Despite this, and to Flaubert's great displeasure, Zola was lumped in with Goncourt and Flaubert. The trio was invited to a dinner at Restaurant Trapp on April 16, 1877, by six young writers who described themselves as the "realist, naturalist youth" and recognized these three elders as their masters. The six writers in question were Joris-Karl Huysmans, Henry Céard, Léon Hennique, Paul Alexis, Octave Mirbeau, and Guy de Maupassant. In 1877, the three elders had published *L'Assommoir*, *La Fille Élisa* [*The Girl Elisa*], and *Three Tales*. The dinner stunt had been well prepared by Catulle Mendès, the editor of *La République des lettres*, who by April 13 had announced the menu of this upcoming historical dinner: "soup, Bovary purée; salmon-trout à la fille Élisa; truffled chicken à la Saint Anthony; simple-hearted artichokes; 'naturalist' parfait; Coupeau wine; liqueur de l'Assommoir. M. Gustave Flaubert, who has other disciples, notes the lack of Carthaginian eel and pigeons à la Salammbô." This dinner would later be seen as a founding ceremony of the naturalist school. Though the author of *Madame Bovary* could only be irritated by such talk, he genuinely liked and even admired Zola, aside from his theoretical screeds.

Flaubert participated in other literary gatherings, such as the "dinner for booed authors" that assembled "the society of five" who had experienced theatrical flops; namely, Goncourt, Daudet, Zola, Turgenev—who claimed to have been booed in Russia—and Flaubert. These opportunities for the writers to comfort each other were held at different restaurants, but talk always lasted late into the night. Then, as Zola recalled, "since Flaubert hated to go home alone, I accompanied him through the dark streets and went to bed at three in the morning after having philosophized at every street corner."[12] Flaubert still socialized with Princess Mathilde, both in her salon on the rue de Berri in Paris and in her hôtel particulier at Saint-Gratien, which she had been able to hold on to. Saint-Gratien also sometimes served as an alibi: Flaubert told everyone that he was there, while he was secretly seeing his beloved Juliet Herbert in Paris. "For the average person, I am supposed to be at Saint-Gratien," he wrote to Edmond Laporte in September 1876. He could tell his male friends what was really going on: not a love story that might invite snickering—for men were not supposed to be sentimental together—but standard virile copulation. "*I am supposed to be at Saint-Gratien*," he told Laporte, "but in fact I am in Paris, where I am cleaning the rust off my tool." He was a touch more delicate with Turgenev: "Don't be surprised at my long stay in the capital: I am delayed here (*inter nos*) *Veneris causa* [because of Venus]!!!"[13] He told Goncourt, too, that he was cleaning the rust off his tool and that it was to be kept a secret. Masculine modesty forbade declarations of love: men did not love, they fucked. Yet Hermia Oliver has convincingly shown, using quotes and cross-checking to support her argument, that Flaubert was not sleeping with just any woman of easy virtue. On the contrary: "There is every indication that Juliet was his mistress during these twenty days in 1874 and was so again in 1876, 1877, and 1878." A single sentence by Flaubert explains why the affair had to be kept secret: "the least love affairs may cost a woman, however low, her position, her fortune, even her life."[14]

During this period, Flaubert finally won the battle to have a fountain with a bust of Louis Bouilhet erected in Rouen. Gustave, who knew what he wanted, had continued to move heaven and earth to get the new municipality to agree to his project. Thanks to Laporte, who had been reelected to the Lower Seine's regional council, he had managed to put the issue back on the municipal council's agenda. On May 4, 1877, the report, which was inspired by Flaubert, was approved. Flaubert sent Bardoux the news: "You will be pleased to learn that the mayor of Rouen has agreed to my proposal regarding Bouilhet's monument. We will have a pretty fountain, bearing a bust of him with his name, in a densely populated neighborhood." It was a beautiful victory for friendship. But within two weeks, and for several months, Flaubert found himself caught up in what had previously been relatively foreign to him: politics!

Shit to MacMahon

In December 1876, Flaubert was in the middle of writing "Herodias." He confessed to Caroline that he had no idea what was going on in the world. But by September 17, 1877, he could tell Edma Roger des Genettes: "Never has the anticipation of a Political event troubled me more than that of the Elections."

Between these two pronouncements, Flaubert had been outraged by the May 16 crisis, Marshal MacMahon's "coup d'état." France's climate of political uncertainty had supposedly come to an end in 1875, when the National Assembly passed the constitutional laws that established the Third Republic. Elections for the Senate were held in January of the following year, then for the Chamber of Deputies in February and March. While the Senate was held by the conservatives, the Chamber of Deputies was dominated by a republican majority. Who would have the last word—the right-wing president or the left-wing Chamber of Deputies? An open conflict between the executive and the legislature finally erupted after President MacMahon forced out Jules Simon, who as president of the Council of Ministers was the de facto head of government. The disagreement stemmed from the ultramontanist Catholic agitation that had been calling for restoration of the pope's temporal power since 1870, when Rome had been taken by the Italian patriots. On May 4, Léon Gambetta pronounced the famous slogan "Clericalism, that is the enemy!" Jules Simon, a moderate republican outflanked by the left, was forced to accept the Chamber's order of the day, committing the government to repress "ultramontanist demonstrations." On May 16, 1877, President MacMahon, who was hostile to this decision, wrote a letter disowning the head of the government, thus forcing Jules Simon to resign. Alfred de Broglie, the leader of the Orleanists, was appointed to replace him at the head of the hostile Chamber. This power play forged an alliance among the Chamber's 363 republican deputies, who published a manifesto against "the policy of reaction and speculation" on May 20. It began to seem inevitable that MacMahon would dissolve the Chamber with the support of the Senate. He finally did so on June 25, leaving the ultimate battle to be fought during the October legislative elections. In preparation, Minister of the Interior Fourtou did everything he could to ensure that the right would win the elections, using both legal and illegal means to claim a majority of the vote. His tactics included relocating or dismissing 77 deputies, dismissing 1,743 mayors, suspending municipal councils, seizing newspapers, instituting legal proceedings, prohibiting public gatherings, and closing cabarets, Masonic lodges, and republican clubs. But the republicans proved extremely disciplined as they rallied behind Gambetta: it was known that wherever they ran for election, the 363 deputies would not have any republican opponents.

Flaubert, who had published *Three Tales* only a month before the events of May 16, initially railed against "our modern Bayard" (MacMahon's nickname, after a fifteenth-century knight renowned for his fearlessness), whose "antics" were damaging sales of his book. But he soon forgot about his personal interests and realized the situation's overall significance. What he saw—and dreaded—was that the marshal's behavior would drive many of the conservatives he knew into the "red" camp. Faced with the excesses of the moral order, the stifling of personal liberties, and official propaganda, he now took sides against MacMahon: "I should like to be at the elections," he wrote to Turgenev on July 19, "to see the faces of the Macmahonites. Moral Order in the provinces goes so far as to ban charity meetings that aren't of a clerical nature. Oh Human Stupidity!"[15] He was delighted with the discord in the party of moral order, though he worried about the "republican reaction" that would follow its defeat.[16] He was surprised by his own anger: "But why so indignant? I wonder myself. It is probably that the further I get along, the more Stupidity upsets me. And I know of nothing in history more *inept* than the men of May 16." He was furious at MacMahon ("Where can you find an idiot comparable to the modern-day Bayard?"), at Fourtou, and at Lizot, the prefect of the Lower Seine ("our Prefect prohibits conferences on Rabelais—and *geology!*").

In September, there came an explosive piece of news: Thiers had died. Shortly before his death, he had thrown his support behind the Republic, allying himself with Gambetta and against the conservative reaction. His funeral turned into a massive street demonstration. What did Flaubert do? His first instinct was to worry about a push to the right, "out of fear of Gambetta." But he attended the great man's funeral on September 8, joining at least 100,000 Parisians,[17] many of whom had once hated Thiers, the general of the bourgeoisie and butcher of the Commune. Now he was the symbol of the Republic.

"Well!" exclaimed Flaubert in a letter to Edma Roger des Genettes, "I also saw old Thiers's funeral! And I can assure you that it was splendid. This truly *national* demonstration overpowered me. I did not like that king of the Prud-hommes—no matter! Compared to those who surrounded him, he was a giant.—And he had a rare virtue: Patriotism. No one summed up France the way he did. That explains the huge effect of his death."

In *Choses vues* [*Things Seen*], Victor Hugo wrote: "Thiers's funeral today. I went. Went on foot from the house on place Saint-Georges to Notre-Dame de Lorette; from there to Père Lachaise [cemetery] along the boulevards. Huge crowds." This incredible grand finale was a stunning reversal of history: Thiers was buried in the great Parisian cemetery, less than a thousand feet from the wall where dozens of Communards had been shot, after his body had been carried across Paris while the crowd yelled "Long live the Republic!"

By early October, Flaubert was champing at the bit for the elections. He wrote to Léonie Brainne: "And I thought I was a skeptic!" He was not sure how the elections would turn out, but while trundling around the countryside in a cart to research *Bouvard and Pécuchet,* he had noticed that people were exasperated with Marshal MacMahon. On October 5, he wrote to Turgenev: "My hatred for the Moral Order and our 'Bayard' is choking me and wearing me down."[18] He now signed his letters to Zola and Laporte, "Shit to Moral Order" or "Shit to MacMahon."

The republicans won the October elections but lost some seats: they now held 323 seats, versus 208 for the conservatives. MacMahon briefly thought he could find a way around the republican victory, but eventually he had to give in. Of course, he did not appoint Gambetta to head the government. After a short-lived government headed by the right-wing General Rochebouët, the center-left deputy Jules Dufaure was appointed president of the Council of Ministers. Flaubert's friend Agénor Bardoux became minister of education. The crisis and the republican victory defined how the constitutional laws of 1875 would be interpreted in the future: the Chamber of Deputies had preeminence. President MacMahon was forced to recognize this major turning point in a message he did not personally write but was forced to sign: "The Constitution of 1875 founded a parliamentary republic by establishing my absence of responsibility, while it instituted the individual and collective responsibility of the ministers." The Assembly regime was established as a semi-presidential regime: the president had to submit to the legislature. The real head of the executive was the president of the Council of Ministers.

Flaubert could only be pleased with the "sinking of Bayard."[19] Though he had not entirely adopted the ideas of Victor Hugo, who after being elected to the Senate was leading a campaign to have the Communards pardoned, he often saw the great man, visiting him and exchanging ideas, finding him ever more "charming." In the middle of the feverish month of October 1877, he read Hugo's *Histoire d'un crime* [*History of a Crime*], the first volume of which had just appeared, and which he considered "a *very* beautiful book." He admired Hugo's account of the December 2 coup d'état and exclaimed "what a strapping fellow that man is!" It is unlikely he would have expressed such admiration of Hugo in the days of the Second Empire, when he denounced *Les Misérables.*

That the man who once railed against universal suffrage could be won over to the Republic is representative of a state of mind that spread among most writers during the period of "moral order." Edmond de Goncourt was an exception; he mostly worried that his novel *La Fille Élisa* would be a victim of censorship. Otherwise, his conservative positions were unchanged. The "idolatry" of Thiers during his funeral exasperated him; he would not vote: "I have such an aversion for politics that today, when it is really a duty to vote, I abstain ... I will have lived my whole life without voting a single time." Flaubert had once shared this attitude, but had changed his mind. Berthelot had long since asserted that he was a republican; now Maupassant, Daudet, and Charles-Edmond joined him. For his part, in commenting on the death of Thiers for the Russian readers of *The Messenger of Europe*, Zola stated that the republic had become "the definitive form of our government."[20]

Though he had once been so close to Goncourt, Flaubert had modified his positions thanks to Renan, whom he greatly admired. He told Renan how enthusiastically he had read his "Prière sur l'Acropole" ["Prayer on the Acropolis"], a section of *Souvenirs d'enfance*, his recollections of childhood, published in the *Revue des deux mondes* late in 1876. Flaubert had borrowed the idea of an aristocratic government, the government by the mandarins, from Renan. Now the same Renan who had deplored the death of the king in *La Réforme intellectuelle et morale* proved pragmatic and increasingly aligned himself with the Republic, since the republican regime was no longer the regime of popular fury and organized terror, but a "down-to-earth" regime. Renan also noted in his *Souvenirs* that he was grateful to his mother for having given him "an invincible taste for Revolution—despite everything I said against it." In 1877, Renan had condemned "the May 16 coup" grounded in clericalism; by 1878, he had permanently converted to democracy and the Republic.[21] A sign of the times: the author who had been dismissed from the Collège de France in 1863 for his *Vie de Jésus* was elected to the Académie Française in 1878.

The democratic tradition that had begun in 1830 was coming to an end. The process would be completed in 1879 when the republicans won the majority in the Senate and Marshal MacMahon decided to step down. During the nineteenth century, France had transitioned from a constitutional monarchy to an ephemeral republic, after which the Empire had been restored; once the last bursts of monarchism had died out following the May 16 crisis, the country became a parliamentary republic that would emancipate itself from clerical tutelage once and for all. As Charles-Edmond, editor of *Le Temps* and friend to Renan and Flaubert, put it: "It is certain that France is the country where the last and supreme battle of clericalism versus modern thought will be fought."[22]

Like Renan, Flaubert had followed these developments. The May 16 crisis proved decisive. In both men's view, the monarchists and Bonapartists were the engineers of disorder. They both appreciated the secular barrier that the Republic put up against the tides of clericalism, the storms of moral order, and the waves of a religion that forced consciences—in other words, against every denial of liberty. Flaubert's allegiance was certainly not to the "social state" of Jules Vallès, but to the tempered regime of the moderates who had managed to defeat those who had sought to restore the monarchy.

CHAPTER 28

"Everything Infuriates and Weighs upon Me"

Out of hatred for the "party of order" and for "May 16," when President Mac-Mahon had forced the resignation of Jules Simon, Flaubert had joined the republican camp. He was delighted when Marshal MacMahon stepped down in February 1879 and was replaced by Jules Grévy: "I have found the change of President extremely pleasant. It is full of grandeur 'no matter what they say,' a considerable, novel event in the history of France.—And finally, thank God, we are delivered from these military gentlemen, who know about everything except making war."[1] Now that he was rid of the moral order, the clerical hubbub, monarchical ambitions, and the tyranny of the censors, he could dedicate himself entirely to literature. He could return to his "awful book," *Bouvard and Pécuchet,* an insane, impossible, monstrous novel. Though he was angry at himself for having embarked upon it, he thought it might well be his masterpiece. Unfortunately, he was not able to set his mind to it as soon as he had hoped. It was no longer a question of politics, but rather the ever-lurking money worries that kept him up at night and left him so discouraged. His "affairs," as he referred to his problems following Ernest Commanville's near bankruptcy and his personal ruin, were now a daily hell. For many months, his financial misfortunes drained his strength and turned his days into nightmares, keeping him in a constant state of despondency.

"It Weighs upon Me and Suffocates Me"

As we have seen, Ernest Commanville believed the solution to the family's worries was to raise the funds to open a new sawmill. Flaubert tirelessly strove to help his nephew, not only because it was in his own interest, but because of his overflowing, sometimes blind affection for Caroline. He asked his friend Agénor Bardoux, now a government minister, whether he could find him a "capitalist." He continued to have high hopes in Mme Pelouze and returned to Chenonceaux for five days in May 1878. But he feared she would "inexplicably" back out. He pushed Ernest to write her, but his letter did not yield immediate results. The chatelaine would eventually invest 50,000 francs. In September, he confided in Edma Roger des Genettes that his "affairs" were not improving: "After infinite attempts and countless promises, my nephew has not been able to reopen his sawmill." Since Caroline and her husband had had to rent out their apartment on the rue du Faubourg Saint-Honoré, Flaubert gave them the use of his flat, which adjoined theirs, making it all the more difficult for him to spend time in Paris. Now that he was no longer receiving any money from Ernest, he began to wonder how he could afford to return to the capital, where he needed to complete his research for *Bouvard and Pécuchet* at the national library. He hoped for some income from his publishers, Lemerre and Charpentier, who were to reissue *Madame Bovary* and *Salammbô*. He also counted on "a few sous" from the "old Féerie," which, although it had not been performed, could be published. He felt humiliated: "I have the concerns of a grocer."

Confined to Croisset, he dove into *Bouvard* and tried to reconcile himself to poverty, but despondency took hold. Feeling depressed, he confessed to Turgenev that he "was thinking about croaking."[2] He briefly hoped that Charpentier would reprint *Saint Anthony* in a luxury edition for the Christmas holidays, but the publisher balked—another disappointment. Paul Dalloz, the editor of *Le Moniteur,* appeared ready to publish Flaubert's *féerie, Le Château des coeurs,* then had his secretary curtly notify Flaubert that he had changed his mind. In December 1878, Flaubert found himself "in the depths of despair." His intimates pressed him to ask for a paid position. After all, he had friends in high places. And they themselves could intervene. He bridled at the idea: "You know me well enough," he wrote to Edma Roger des Genettes, "to know my answer: *never*. . . . I'd sooner board at a country inn than be a Gentleman drawing a salary from the national budget." When Princess Mathilde alluded to a position worthy of him, he told Edmond de Goncourt it was "as *useless* as her exhortations that I stand for the Académie Française." He mechanically repeated the phrase "Honors dishonor, titles degrade, employment makes stupid." His pride kept him from accepting the fate of a commoner. At that point, he still believed that Commanville would get hold of somebody interested in buying his defunct sawmill and the adjacent land, but the anticipated sale kept being put off from one week to the next.

To make matters worse, while Croisset was buried in snow during the brutal winter of 1878–1879, he slipped on the ice outside his door and badly twisted his ankle and fractured his fibula. He was immobilized for several weeks. Luckily, he could count on his friend Edmond Laporte, a true "Sister of Charity," who attended to his every need, visiting frequently, caring for him, writing letters that he dictated, and keeping him company. Paris had not forgotten Flaubert: letters flooded into Croisset, to the point that it began to annoy him. All this solicitude, and always the same formulaic expressions. A letter from Ernest Daudet informed him that he had been discussed at length in an article in *Le Figaro* dated February 15, 1879. The paper reported that after the author of *Madame Bovary* "lost nearly his entire fortune in a commercial enterprise he had entered into purely out of kindness for a relative," his friends had tried to get him appointed as Samuel de Sacy's replacement at the Bibliothèque Mazarine. To carry out this mission, the article continued, Turgenev had been introduced to Gambetta, the president of the Chamber of Deputies, by "a great lady of the Republic" (the paper avoided naming Juliette Adam), but Gambetta had rudely turned him down.

Flaubert fumed as he read the article. He could have done without this public show of pity, which poorly concealed the conservative paper's political intention: to show the ungratefulness of the republican regime, and particularly Gambetta, toward the great French writers. Flaubert did not want to risk falling out with Gambetta, to whom he had once been introduced, or Gambetta's muse Juliette Adam, who had declared that she liked him. Yet despite its mocking tone and several inaccuracies, *Le Figaro* was right about Turgenev's undertaking. Flaubert had finally given in to his friends and agreed to apply for the position at the Bibliothèque Mazarine: "I have put stupid pride aside," he had written to Turgenev on February 5, "and I accept. For above all, one must avoid dying of hunger, which is a stupid way to die." The Muscovite had therefore set to work, supported by Zola and Charpentier, both of whom were committed to helping Flaubert in any way they could. Mme Adam had served as a go-between to Gambetta. Alas, on February 13, a telegram from Turgenev arrived at Croisset: "Give up all hope, definitive refusal, letter gives details."[3] The position in question was being held for an old acquaintance of Flaubert's, Frédéric Baudry, then a librarian at the Bibliothèque de l'Arsenal. Aside from his annoyance at the article in *Le Figaro*, Gustave responded philosophically, even with indifference: the position would have required him to live in Paris, which he could not afford, even if accommodations were provided. But he had not taken into account the persistence of his friends, who were determined to come to his rescue.

In his regular letters to his niece, he occasionally let slip a poignant remark: "My strength is exhausted, all I can do now is cry." Meanwhile, his acquaintance Senator Alphonse Cordier, a childhood friend who was city councilor for Rouen, let him know that he had mentioned him to Paul Bert, an adviser to Jules Ferry, the new minister of education, as well as to Victor Hugo, who "then and there wrote a warm letter recommending [Flaubert] to Ferry."[4] Two weeks later, Flaubert told Laporte that there was a plan to create an honorary librarian position with "a literary pension" for him at Mazarine. This kind of "charity," as he called it, "disgusted" him. The plan was also supported by Baudry, who probably wanted to make up for taking the position that his "friend" had hoped for. Flaubert replied: "My family ruined me. So it's up to them to feed me, not the government." For the time being, he was waiting for the sale of the sawmill, which had been announced but was taking a long time. Originally valued at 600,000 francs, it eventually brought in only 200,000. Once the creditors were paid off, there would be nothing left. Aside from the creditors, Flaubert had been the largest contributor, but he agreed to be paid last: "You're right, my dear," he told Caroline, "everything must be done—*everything* not to dispossess our friends." Now Gustave considered asking his brother, who was rich (he estimated that Achille, his wife, and their daughter had about 100,000 francs in private income), for a "small pension" of no more than five thousand francs. Achille was convalescing from a stroke in Nice but had wanted to come home as soon as he learned of his brother's accident, which Gustave had persuaded him not to do. Their fairly chilly relationship had lately become warmer. Once back in Rouen, Achille did not hesitate—he would provide Gustave with at least three thousand francs a year. But he was in a seriously weakened state and sometimes lacked mental acuity—Flaubert referred to his "softened brain." Would he remember his promise? Out of precaution, Gustave asked the notary Florimont to formalize the pension, for he knew that Achille's wife did not look with a favorable eye on her husband's generosity.

His friends' efforts paid off. Victor Hugo's support had weighed the most heavily, while Guy de Maupassant, an employee at the Ministry of Education, served as a good informer. On March 6, 1879, Maupassant wrote: "The Minister [Jules Ferry] has ordered his chief of cabinet to write to you to ask if you would accept an honorific title with a pension described as a salary relating to this title." To spare Flaubert's self-esteem, Maupassant emphasized that the salary should be regarded "as an homage from the government and not as a pension for a man of letters."[5] Flaubert did not fall for it. He felt "invincible repugnance"—it was a "disguised pension," and the news would get out, the papers would talk about it. But he added: "If all that, title and pension, could be kept secret, I would accept temporarily with the intention (or even the promise) on my part of giving it up if my fortune were to improve." Maupassant reassured him that no one would know about the pension. So he resigned himself, "for necessity forces me to." He would accept the arrangement as "temporary help," a "loan," but insisted that *Le Figaro* and the other papers keep quiet. "For it is no laughing matter to live on public assistance!"

In May 1879, Jules Ferry, who had officially replaced Bardoux as the minister of education, officially offered Flaubert a position as an off-site associate librarian at the Bibliothèque Mazarine, with a salary of three thousand francs a year and no obligation to put in an appearance. Though he knew better, he could tell Caroline that this was not a "pension." He and Baudry resumed their relations "on the best of terms." In June, Flaubert went to Paris to thank Jules Ferry, who received him with the utmost politeness. The official announcement would be made in September, and the payments would be applied retroactively, beginning July 1, 1879. Flaubert could now keep his apartment in Paris, which was this pseudo-appointment's greatest benefit. But this governmental favor did not entirely resolve his precarious situation. In August, he wrote to Maupassant that his sister-in-law had "squarely *refused* the small annuity that Florimont had requested" for him.[6] His publishers were dragging their feet in making payments to him, and he had heard that Charpentier was on the verge of closing shop. In the summer of 1879, however, he rejoiced at the news that Commanville had finally raised the necessary funds to open a new sawmill: "Could Fortune be changing?" Even though the situation did improve, Flaubert was haunted to the end of his days by a crushing feeling that he was ruined. This was exacerbated by the summonses he continued to receive as a consequence of the Commanville affair—and which he found incomprehensible. Three months before his death, he was still asking his niece: "When will this pecuniary and moral *devastation* come to an end?"

Throughout this protracted, dramatic collapse, Flaubert continued to treat his niece and nephew with the care of the mythical pelican that sacrifices itself for its young, though he had plenty of reason to complain. In the correspondence, one rarely finds a word against them, though Ernest had literally ruined him. In December 1879, he wrote to Caroline: "Once I've paid the gardener 100 francs the day after tomorrow, my entire fortune will amount to 60 francs!—No comment required, right, my dear? And I keep myself from making one, because I don't want to 'write you anything too harsh.' But I ask you to go down into your conscience and examine the situation of the Old Man, whom everyone owes . . . —and no one pays!" In his *Journal*, Edmond de Goncourt reported: "Sad news of poor Flaubert. It seems that he is completely ruined, and that the people for whom he sacrificed his fortune begrudge him the very cigars he smokes. 'My uncle is a strange man,' his niece is reported to have said, 'he does not know how to endure adversity!' "[7] In fact, Caroline and Ernest called him the Consumer and reprimanded him for the amount of firewood he used.[8] According to Edma Roger des Genettes, Flaubert had given his nephew and niece more than one million francs to save them from bankruptcy.[9] One would think this would have entitled him to a little gratitude. But as his abundant letters to Caroline indicate, Uncle Gustave loved her like a father until the day he died. He was constantly consoling her, for Ernest's business problems had made her anemic. He encouraged the hypothetical career as a painter that she had embarked on, praised her portraits to all the journalists he knew, moved heaven and earth to get her work exhibited, and admired her for "reaching the status of a *great painter*." He was constantly worrying about her—her health, her morale. He imagined the worst when she was late to write him, sent her a deluge of compliments and kisses, and made her reputation with influential people such as Goncourt and Princess Mathilde.

The Commanville business also led Flaubert to lose the friend who had been the most steadfast throughout the disaster, Edmond Laporte. This former owner of a lace factory in Petit-Couronne had not hesitated to serve as one of Ernest's guarantors until he himself had been ruined. His friendship with Flaubert had become proverbial. He took notes for Flaubert's books, did him endless favors, and nursed him when he broke his leg. To return the favor, Flaubert had gone out of his way to get Laporte a job and had finally found him a position as a divisional labor inspector in the Nièvre region in central France, though both men were sorry that Laporte would be so far from Croisset. But the Commanvilles' debacle set the two friends against each other. Caroline vaguely explained the situation in an article published in *La Revue de Paris* on December 1, 1905: "Business difficulties had arisen between M. Laporte and my husband; M. Laporte was worried that he would be held liable for the promissory notes he had guaranteed. This led to a cooling of the relationship between my uncle and M. Laporte, which ended in a permanent falling-out."[10] In a note to the centennial edition of Flaubert's correspondence, René Descharmes expressed his doubts about this story: "This explanation can only be accepted with the strongest reservations; the truth probably has more to do with the 'ungrateful little schemes' that M. Lucien Descaves has referred to—and the ungratefulness was not on the part of Laporte or Flaubert."[11] Indeed, Commanville had asked Laporte for further guarantees in order to avoid any legal protests for nonpayment. Laporte refused because he no longer had the means. Ernest and Caroline misled Flaubert, who had complete faith in them, to believe that Laporte had behaved in an unfriendly manner. Laporte told Flaubert that he had wanted to keep him out of it: "So let me discuss this business with Commanville alone. If some temporary unpleasantness should result, at least you won't have to take sides. You must know, my dear Giant, that I shall always love you with all my heart."[12] According to René Dumesnil, "Commanville and his wife, furious that Laporte had thwarted them, lectured the uncle who had ruined himself for them, and convinced him—God knows with what arguments—that Laporte was failing the duties of friendship by no longer agreeing to the Commanvilles' dubious stratagems."[13] Flaubert resigned himself to the rupture, but it would cast a shadow over the last year of his life. And this affair, in which he appears to have let himself be manipulated by his niece, is certainly not his most glorious moment.

Fertile Friendships

Despite such troubles, Flaubert continued to occasionally experience the joys and pleasures of friendship during these dark years, particularly with a group of five writers whose meetings were as festive as they were intellectually rousing: Turgenev, Goncourt, Daudet, Zola, and Maupassant. The most faithful and devoted of the group—with the exception of the young Maupassant—was probably Ivan Turgenev. The "two giants," as the Muscovite and the Norman were called, shared mutual appreciation and admiration for each other. In Flaubert's eyes, Turgenev had only one flaw: his lack of punctuality. He often announced that he was coming to Croisset, only to cancel at the last minute. Most of the time, it was gout that kept him in Paris or Bougival, but not always. He would also let himself get caught up in constantly conflicting duties, which finally made Flaubert lose his temper: "No, I won't pour invective down upon you; but if you knew the *nervous upset* you cause me, you would feel remorse."[14] But what a pleasure it was when he did show up. Both men thrived on their endless literary discussions, for the Russian's cultural knowledge was as vast as the Frenchman's. They often shared the same enthusiasms and disappointments. They read each other chapters from their works in progress and critiqued and encouraged each other. When they were unable to get together, they wrote back and forth, keeping up on literary events and each other's health, and sent each other presents (Turgenev sent salmon and caviar, much appreciated by Flaubert). Turgenev introduced his friend to *War and Peace* and was delighted to find him swept away by Tolstoy: "It's first rate. What a painter and what a psychologist! The first two volumes are sublime, but the third goes terribly to pieces." Turgenev doffed his hat in agreement: "Yes, he is a man of great talent, and yet you put your finger on the weak spot: he has also built himself a philosophical system, which is at one and the same time mystical, childish and presumptuous, and which has spoilt his third volume dreadfully and his second novel [*Anna Karenina*] . . . But for me the matter is settled: *Flaubertus dixit*."[15] This was the general tone of a correspondence that forms a splendid dialogue between two writers.

Edmond de Goncourt was made of different stuff—and was more easily offended. As we have seen several times, his was an acerbic friendship, and his delicate soul never lost an opportunity to be offended by the sight and sound of Flaubert, whom he considered too booming, too theatrical, and too loud in his intemperance. Admiration did not come naturally to this great literary disparager, who imagined that he and his brother were the two major writers of the century. "I have only met three great minds in my life," wrote the diarist, "three very elevated brains, three inventors of totally original concepts. The first, little old [Paul] Collardez, that satyr with the forehead of a Socrates, buried in a village in the Haute-Marne. The two others were [the illustrator Paul] Gavarni and the chemist Berthelot. Next to those three men, the Renans, the Flauberts and so on are small change."[16] At least he reserved his barbs for his *Journal* and sometimes recognized that "small change" was worth its weight in gold. But Goncourt was a jealous sort and was always ready to downgrade Flaubert, despite the fact that he was truly attached to him. Deep down, he enjoyed his company: "Flaubert, on condition that one leaves the center of the stage to him and resigns oneself to catching cold from all the windows he keeps throwing open, is a very pleasant companion. He has a jovial gaiety and a childlike laugh; and everyday contact develops in him a certain gruff affectionateness which is not without charm."[17] The two of them often met at the home of Princess Mathilde, who had managed to reopen her salon by being accommodating with the well-meaning new regime. They saw each other most often at Saint-Gratien, where Goncourt stayed for extended periods. The Saint-Gratien clique of diplomats and the international elite could be boring sometimes—or often, if one is to believe Goncourt. They traveled to Saint-Gratien primarily for the grande dame, who excelled at gathering artists and writers together and charmed them with her name, her manner, and her plain-spokenness. When he was in Paris, Flaubert still hosted his friends on Sundays—it had become an immutable ritual.

In this company of friends, the cheerful, playful Alphonse Daudet entertained everyone with his Mediterranean pranks, improvisations, bawdy tales, and unstoppable good mood. Flaubert had had a good laugh while reading his *Tartarin* and enjoyed both *Le Nabab* [*The Nabob*] and *Les Rois en exil* [*The Kings in Exile*], though he agreed with Goncourt that "his style is of a minor quality, the quality of a well-written serial." Good old Daudet admitted it himself: he was made to tell stories, while the Flauberts and Goncourts had introduced him to the demands of style. A jovial friend, a fine dining companion who was never envious, he was as charming as could be.

In the late 1870s, the group's most high-profile member was Émile Zola, who was Flaubert's junior by about twenty years. His novels were the talk of the town, applauded by some and hated by others. After *L'Assommoir*, *Nana* was a major success, which Flaubert defended against shocked critics. Zola was not as successful in the theater: Flaubert attended the opening of his *Bouton d'or* [*Gold Button*], but found the play "pitiful." After leaving the Palais-Royal theater, he remarked vindictively: "My friend Zola is becoming absurd. He wants to 'found a school,' being jealous of old Hugo's fame. Success has gone to his head, so much more difficult is it to cope with good fortune than bad. Zola's self-confidence as a critic is explained by his inconceivable ignorance. I think that there is no longer any love of Art, Art in itself. Where is there anyone who relishes a good sentence? That aristocratic pleasure is in the realm of archaeology."[18] This did not prevent him from finding Zola "very strong" and *Nana* "splendid." In this case, Turgenev did not agree with Flaubert: "It is so down-to-earth and painstaking that one almost dies of it." Flaubert replied: "I think you're a bit hard on it. There are some fine things, superb cries of passion and two or three characters (that of Mignon amongst others) that delighted me." When Caroline complained of the novel's "obscene language," Gustave agreed, but added that "it is a tremendous work by a man of genius." His appraisal contrasted sharply with that of Goncourt, who, not surprisingly, considered that Zola was "not an artist in the least." Flaubert wondered why Zola had to be bothered with becoming the pope of "naturalism." What hogwash! Yet he liked this young fellow, who was an audacious, talkative gourmand and drove the bigots crazy. He went out of his way to help him obtain the Legion of Honor—Zola really wanted that red ribbon! When the theatrical adaptation of *L'Assommoir* was a hit in Paris, Flaubert, stuck in bed with a broken leg at Croisset, wrote Zola a joyous message: "Ah, finally something good happens to me.—You can't imagine how happy I am, dear friend!" While he continued to mock his naturalist manifestos, he always sent his compliments when his books were released. As for Zola, who recognized Flaubert as his master, he leapt on the reissue of *Sentimental Education* as an opportunity to express his praise in words that touched Flaubert's heart.[19] Still feeling bruised by his novel's lack of success, the writer was ecstatic. Dear Zola, that "colossus!" Flaubert did not feel the slightest envy toward Zola; his younger colleague's success always pleased him. Naturally, this was not the case with Goncourt, whose *Journal* entry for February 25, 1879, includes this typically venomous note: "Zola is triumphant, he fills the world and makes cartfuls of money; but all this noise and currency make him neither jolly nor friendly."

After acquiring and beginning to restore a property in Médan, now in the department of Yvelines, just west of Paris, Zola had the idea of collecting six stories by authors of the young realist and naturalist school under the title *Les Soirées de Médan* [*Evenings at Médan*]. He chose works by Henry Céard, Joris-Karl Huysmans, Léon Hennique, Paul Alexis, himself, and Guy de Maupassant, the youngest of the writers, whose *Boule de Suif* would attract considerable attention. Flaubert called Maupassant "my disciple" and considered him his "adoptive son." Young Guy had admired Flaubert early on, and the older author had returned the favor by effusively and enthusiastically encouraging his first steps in a literary career: "The declaration of fondness you made to him in my presence," Guy's mother Laure wrote to Flaubert in January 1878, "was so pleasant to me that I took it at face value and I now imagine it requires virtually paternal duties on your part." Guy was suffocating in a mediocre position at the Ministry of the Navy; his mother asked Gustave to help him find "a position to his liking." Flaubert called on all his connections to save the young man from the "hell" in which he was slaving away. He introduced him to Bardoux, who had been appointed minister of education, and bombarded Bardoux with letters: "Do something, that is give him the means to work at Literature in peace." Finally his request was granted: in January 1879, Maupassant became an attaché in the Ministry of Education. Flaubert was his adviser and mentor; as a demanding professor, he taught him the principles of his poetics. He gave him advice about his poems and other manuscripts. He convinced Princess Mathilde to have one of the young man's plays performed in her home, introduced him to Juliette Adam, and recommended him to his publisher, Charpentier. In January 1880, upon reading *Les Soirées de Médan*, he became convinced that Maupassant was a great writer in the making: "*Boule de Suif,* the tale by my disciple," he wrote to Caroline, "that I read the proofs of this morning, is *a masterpiece*. I stand by that word. A masterpiece of composition, comedy, and observation." He did not hide his amazement from Maupassant himself, telling him that he was a "master" and his mother Laure that the story was a "marvel."

Meanwhile, Maupassant was taken to court for immorality at Étampes, where *La Revue moderne et naturaliste* was printed. *La Revue* had republished one of his poems originally printed in *La République des lettres* in 1876, under the new title "Une fille" [A Girl].[20] Flaubert immediately headed up the efforts to defend him, alerting the press, advising Guy whom to solicit for help, and writing an open letter to his protégé to be published in *Le Gaulois*. In this dazzling piece of irony and indignation at censorship, the master broke with his custom and addressed his disciple by the informal "tu":

No matter how you struggle, *the party of order* will find arguments. Resign yourself to that.

But tell the court that it should suppress *all* the Greek and Roman classics, without any exception, from Aristophanes to good Horace and tender Virgil. Then, among the foreigners, Shakespeare, Goethe, Byron, Cervantes. Here at home, Rabelais, "from whom French literature flows" according to Chateaubriand, whose own masterpiece deals with incest; and then Molière (see Bossuet's fury at him), the great Corneille, whose *Théodore* has prostitution as its theme; and old La Fontaine, and Voltaire, and Jean-Jacques etc.—and Perrault's fairy tales! What is *Peau d'âne* [*Donkeyskin*] about? And where does the fourth act of *Le Roi s'amuse* [*The King Has Fun* by Victor Hugo] take place?

After that, they will have to suppress the history books that *sully the imagination*.

The letter appeared in *Le Gaulois* on February 21, 1880, and was reproduced in *Le Petit Rouennais*. Five days later, the public prosecutor asked for the case to be dismissed. Flaubert, that great admirer of Voltaire, had not hesitated for a second to publicly use his name to defend freedom of expression. The author of *Madame Bovary* knew its value.

After the death of his "dear master," Maupassant described their special relationship: "For him, I was a kind of apparition from the Old Days. He drew me toward him, loved me. Of all the people I encountered a little late in life, he was the only one whose deep affection I felt, whose attachment became for me a sort of intellectual tutelage, and who was constantly concerned with being good and useful to me, with giving me all that he could give me of his experience, his knowledge, his thirty-five years of labor, study, and artistic intoxication."[21]

In the spring of 1880, Flaubert invited his friends Goncourt, Zola, Daudet, Charpentier, and Maupassant (Turgenev was not in France) to come to Croisset on Easter Sunday for a "gigantic" party that he would pay for with some funds he had set aside. He also asked his doctor, Fortin, who had taken such good care of him the previous year, to join the festivities. Aside from Suzanne, his regular maid, he had hired two additional servants. Goncourt's *Journal* provides a fairly detailed account of this Homeric feast. As usual, the grumpy diarist cannot prevent himself from taking jabs at his traveling companions, but after declaring that he was "very happy to embrace Flaubert," he writes: "It is really very beautiful, his place—I hadn't remembered it too well. The enormously wide Seine, with the masts of invisible ships passing by as though against a backdrop in a theater; the splendid tall trees, their shapes tormented by the sea winds; the garden with its espaliers, the long terrace-walk facing full south: these all make it a fit dwelling for a man of letters—for Flaubert—after having been, in the eighteenth century, the country house of a community of Benedictines."

Goncourt marvels at the excellent dinner; it is generously accompanied with wine, "and we spend the evening telling broad stories that make Flaubert burst into laughter that is like a child's. He refuses to read from his novel—he can't, he's 'all in.' And we retire to bedrooms that are rather cold and contain a number of family busts."[22]

Flaubert had also developed a second circle of friends composed of writers whom he liked and esteemed. Until the end of his life, he would fervently read Ernest Renan and send him his enthusiastic thanks for each of his books. He did poke a little fun at Renan's desire to be elected to the Académie Française, which finally happened in June 1878: "When you are somebody, why wish to be something?" Like Pascal, Flaubert made a strict distinction between "institutional greatness," which was for the bourgeois, and "natural greatness," which was the only kind that mattered. He also kept up his friendship with Hippolyte Taine, though he was more critical of him and openly laughed at his craving to join the Academy. On a more serious note, he did not appreciate Taine's magnum opus *Les Origines de la France contemporaine,* a fiercely antirevolutionary work of history: "If the Constituent Assembly had been only a pack of brutes and scoundrels," he wrote to Edma Roger des Genettes, "it would have experienced what the Commune of '70 [*sic*] experienced. He does not tell any lies. But he does not tell *all* the Truth—which is a way of lying." He continued with a rather nasty explanation: "His violent fear of losing his private income during 'our disasters' somewhat obliterated his critical sense."[23] But this judgment did not prevent him from considering Taine a thinker of the first importance.

Perhaps the most surprising friendship in Flaubert's second circle of friends was that with Victor Hugo. As we recall, he had had a youthful admiration for the great poet, but he treated *Les Misérables,* that "Catholic-socialist" novel, sarcastically. At the time, Hugo was campaigning in the Senate for the amnesty of the Communards who had been exiled and deported, most of them to New Caledonia, while Clémenceau fought the same battle in the Chamber. Flaubert did not agree in the slightest: in his eyes, amnesty was an injustice—the guilty had to pay for their crimes. Despite this, he often visited Hugo at home, and would have gone more often, he wrote, if the great man had spent less time talking to him of the Académie Française and encouraging him to stand for election to it, when to his mind no one deserved it more than Hugo himself. No matter. He dined at the home of Hugo and Juliette Drouet with great pleasure; they avoided the subject of the amnesty. Flaubert had turned down an invitation to the ceremony for the centennial of Voltaire—despite his unceasing "worship" of the author of *Candide*—but enjoyed reading the speech Victor Hugo gave on the occasion at the Théâtre de la Gaieté when it was published in *Le Rappel* and reissued as a pamphlet. He found it "absolutely" admirable.[24] The adverb "absolutely" is all the more surprising given that in this legendarily eloquent speech, Hugo not only recalled the Calas and de la Barre affairs,[25] but also expressed his faith in progress, revolution, and the people, three causes that Flaubert viewed with a healthy dose of ironic skepticism. This suggests there was more than courtesy between Hugo and Flaubert, and that despite their disagreements, the two men were bound by genuine affinities and a great deal of feeling. In fact, Flaubert was always happy to meet Hugo one-on-one—it was his entourage he dreaded, for the entourage pushed Hugo to talk politics. Other than that, he was "a charming man"—Flaubert often used this admiring expression to refer to the patriarch of the Republic.

Should Maxime Du Camp be included in this second circle? Many details of their relationship at this juncture are lacking. Though the two men agreed to burn their correspondence, there remain a few letters that bear witness to a relationship that was literally more distant (Du Camp lived in Baden-Baden), but not extinguished. Maxime continued to send Gustave his new books, in particular the successive volumes of *Convulsions de Paris*, a detailed account of the Commune. Flaubert lectured him and criticized his naïveté in castigating those involved in the Paris revolution, when he had already shown its harmful effects. Why so many adjectives and author's biases? Why had he failed the historian's duty to remain impersonal? Now Maxime was also after the Académie Française: "Why go in for such nonsense?" In short, the great friendship of their youth had come to an end, but they had eventually gotten back in touch; they still spoke and wrote to each other, they still liked each other well enough, but they were no longer intimates.

Outside of these masculine friendships and the attendant virile gatherings, Flaubert cultivated relationships with some remarkable women after George Sand's death. To the end of his life, he remained a regular at the salon of Princess Mathilde, who was always welcoming and full of zest. They wrote to each other regularly, but with a restraint that prevents the letters from being among the more interesting in Flaubert's correspondence. During his last years, he began a literary friendship with Juliette Adam, a great anticlerical republican and patriot (and future supporter of the radical nationalist General Georges Boulanger), whose salon on Boulevard Poissonière was frequented by the cream of the political and literary worlds. He promised her she could publish *Bouvard and Pécuchet* in her *Nouvelle revue* before it was released in book form. He also sang the praises of Guy de Maupassant and introduced her to him. The most touching of his letters are to Edma Roger des Genettes and Léonie Brainne. He had met the former at Louise Colet's salon. Partially paralyzed, she lived in seclusion at Villenauxe, in the Aube region, where Gustave had visited in 1873 to read her *The Temptation of Saint Anthony*. In their letters, they kept each other up to date on political and literary news, commented on current events, and philosophized. Léonie Brainne was his favorite of the "three angels" of Rouen. Flaubert sent her gallant remarks and tried to soothe her worries. In fact, Flaubert's personality is most apparent in his letters: his development, desires, ideas, obsessions, discoveries, and his manner—or rather manners—of loving. It is a shame we do not have his correspondence with Juliet Herbert, the hidden mistress whom he occasionally saw in Paris, up to and including in September 1879.

The End of Polycarp

To his other acquaintances, Flaubert remained the enduring Polycarp of Flaubertian legend. He still signed many of his letters to his intimates with the name of the ancient bishop of Smyrna. He also continued to hurl abuse at his century and rail against universal foolishness with a prophetic tone. To pay homage to the master of Croisset, demonstrate their friendship, and shake him out of his melancholy, a few of Flaubert's friends decided to hold a celebration of the Feast of Saint Polycarp in his honor. In April 1879, Charles Lapierre, the editor of the *Nouvelliste*, and his wife Valérie (sister to the "angel" Léonie) held the first such gathering at their home on rue de la Ferme in Rouen, which Flaubert, still limping, attended propped up by his maid Suzanne. It was a costumed event, with M. Lapierre dressed as a Bedouin and Mme Lapierre as a Berber. "There was a garland of flowers around my plate and glass.—At dessert, they brought a sponge cake on which was inscribed 'Long live Saint Polycarp!'—toasted with champagne."[26] Alice Pasca recited a poem in doggerel:

> Monsieur Flaubert, your patron saint
> is Polycarp, a saint most famous.
> Everyone says he was a good man,
> But it seems he was not joyous.

And so on.

One year later, the Lapierres struck again—this time, with the participation of Léonie. The dishes on the menu were named after Flaubert's works. After dinner, about thirty whimsical letters and telegrams were delivered to the living Polycarp: "The Archbishop of Rouen, several Italian cardinals, some garbage collectors and members of the floor-waxers' guild, the proprietor of a shop selling religious statuettes, etc.—all sent me their greetings."[27] Flaubert's gifts included a Spanish portrait of Saint Polycarp and ... a tooth (relic of the saint).

The second Saint Polycarp celebration proved to be an unsuspected farewell gathering. Only a week later, on May 8, 1880, Flaubert collapsed at home at Croisset, felled by a stroke. His friend Dr. Pouchet later diagnosed a congestive epileptic fit, contending that the old disease that had long left him in peace had reawakened. Pouchet explained the case to Edmond de Goncourt: "He hadn't had any more [epileptic fits] for sixteen years. But the worry over his niece's affairs brought the trouble back. . . . Yes, with all the symptoms, foam on his lips and so on ... And then his niece wanted to have a cast taken of his hand, but it couldn't be done, the hand was so tightly clenched."[28] *Le Gaulois* reported that two years earlier, in May 1878, Flaubert had had a "terrible blackout" at his Paris apartment, but a Dr. Chevreau had been able to treat it. This time, however, medical care came too late: Flaubert's regular doctor, Dr. Fortin, was on a house call in Grande Couronne.

Dr. Fortin was replaced by Dr. Tourneux, who had a different theory about Flaubert's cause of death: "Flaubert did not have any symptoms of an epileptic fit. On the contrary, his atheroma, his apoplectic appearance, everything suggests he died of a ventricular hemorrhage."[29] His unhealthy lifestyle predisposed him to cardiovascular disease: he smoked and consumed too much coffee, heavy food, and sometimes alcohol. René Dumesnil reports that at thirty-five he already suffered from arteriosclerosis. Other theories were considered, including syphilis. It was hypothesized that he had died due to "syphilitic cerebral arteritis."[30] The question remains open to this day.

Aside from his everyday objects, two Oriental slippers, a tobacco jar, a double-barreled rifle, a flask, a sword, "various Algerian clothes," a painting of Napoleon I, his walking sticks, his pipes, his books, and his manuscripts, he left 2,515 francs in a drawer. The entire inventory (furniture, silverware, jewelry, clothes, bookcases) would be valued at 6,925 francs.[31]

The funeral was held at Croisset on Tuesday, May 11, in the presence of many of his friends, including Goncourt, Turgenev, Daudet, Zola, Maupassant, Théodore de Banville, Huysmans, Paul Alexis, François Coppée, Catulle Mendès, José-Maria de Hérédia, d'Osmoy, and many journalists. "Good old Laporte," who had rushed over as soon as he received the news, was not able to bow before his dear Gustave's body: the family had ordered that he not be allowed in. The funeral procession started toward the church in Canteleu early in the afternoon, then left for the cemetery in Rouen after the mass. Witnesses counted 150 mourners. "Aside from the Municipal Council of Croisset and M. Barrabé, mayor of Rouen," Gastin Vassy wrote in the daily *Gil Blas*, "not one civil servant bothered to come from the city that counts Flaubert as one of its greatest claims to fame. We were told that in Rouen people have always held a grudge against Flaubert for presenting himself as a declared enemy of the bourgeois. Rouen's amour propre as a bourgeois city had been wounded, and Rouen stayed away at a time when a solemn homage was de rigueur." As it crossed the city, the procession passed indifferent bystanders and encountered a "general coldness."

Flaubert was buried next to his father, Achille-Cléophas, and his mother, Caroline Fleuriot, not far from Louis Bouilhet's grave. After the priest said his prayers, Lapierre delivered the final goodbye. Flaubert had always rejected the idea that speeches should be made upon his death. Thus Lapierre spoke only a few sentences, evoking the "immense void" the deceased was leaving behind. He finished his funeral address in tears.

Along with Gaston Vassy, a few journalists from *Gil Blas* had hired a coachman to follow the procession. They asked him if he knew the dead man whose "cart his nag was following":

"Of course," he answered, "it's M. Flaubert, the doctor's brother."
"Oh! And do you also know his daughter, Mme Salammbô?"
"Indeed I do," the Rouen coach driver answered.
And he added, in a sentimental tone of voice:
"She must be so sad!"[32]

CHAPTER 29

Post Mortem

Upon his death, Gustave Flaubert was finally recognized for what he had been and would always remain: a great writer. Now the press sang in unison, with only a few discordant notes here and there. On May 11, the anti-conformist poet Jean Richepin published a long article in *Gil Blas* in which he referred to "the great genius France has just lost" and emphasized the "initial Romanticism" that had left its mark on the writer: "We find it in the vividness of his metaphors, the rhythmic sound of his sentences, the lyricism of his imagination, which even at the height of psychological analysis takes flight like a bird, and especially in his fervent love of style as the only power that could bring works of literature to life." In the May 22 issue of *La Vie moderne*, Émile Bergerat wrote of the modesty of an author "outside of high society and coteries": " 'Yes,' he would cry out in his thunderous voice, 'I am more obscure than the newborn beginner. People take me for the inventor of the Flobert rifle! In Rouen, my native city, which I have never left, we don't sell two *Bovary*s in ten years! I live in obscurity and nothing is known of me, other than that I am the brother of a surgeon. That's all!' Alas, one must admit that what he said was close to the truth. We saw it last Tuesday in Rouen, during that painful procession behind the hearse, where barely a hundred men marked time during this mourning for art. Were there even a hundred of us?"

An anonymous article in *Le Figaro* even credited Flaubert with being the father of naturalism. While this kind of error was common, Flaubert's stature was undiminished by these vague approximations. In the May 9 issue of *Le Gaulois*, Fourcaud wrote that "French literature has just been painfully stricken by the loss of this most elevated novelist, this very male prose writer, this rare and marvelous artist who was Gustave Flaubert." Ferdinand Brunetière contributed a long article to the *Revue des deux mondes* (May–June 1880), in which he analyzed all of Flaubert's writing methods and acknowledged that he had "a rare, fertile inventiveness in terms of form." Yet he could not hold back a final nasty remark: "In literature, like everywhere else, methods only deliver the latent effects they contain if they all converge on an appropriate subject. This subject always eluded Flaubert's grasp; he only attained it once, in *Madame Bovary*." Brunetière stuck to his guns: Flaubert only mattered because of his first novel; what followed was a disaster. Despite his obtuse conclusion, the *Revue*'s biased critic honored Flaubert's work with his detailed analysis. Meanwhile, Flaubert's friends, juniors, and disciples—starting with Maupassant—publicly revered the late great writer.

Maupassant wrote to Zola: "I cannot tell you how much I am thinking of Flaubert, how he haunts and chases after me. The thought of him constantly comes back to me, I hear his voice, I recognize his gestures, I see him all the time standing before me in his big brown robe, with his arms raised as he speaks. It is like a solitude that has been created around me, the beginning of the horrible separations that will continue from one year to the next, carrying away all those we love, in whom our memories live, with whom we could best chat of intimate things. Those blows wound our spirit and leave a permanent sadness in all our thoughts."[1]

His friends were committed to memorializing him in stone: a statue of the writer was needed in his native city. A committee was formed with Edmond de Goncourt as chairman, seconded by vice-chairmen Charles Lapierre and Ivan Turgenev. They contacted the sculptor Henri Chapu, who asked for 12,000 francs for his work. The project began to drag; there were few financial contributors. In five years, the committee raised only 9,000 francs. Turgenev tried to expand the fundraising to Russia, but without success. Charpentier considered it his duty to call on the readers of his periodical *La Vie moderne*. In 1887, Maupassant wrote to Goncourt to tell him that he was adding 1,000 francs to the 11,000 the committee had already raised: "We'll easily find the rest." Then came the polemic. In order to collect the amount necessary, some of Flaubert's friends started planning a performance of excerpts from their works at the Théâtre de l'Odéon. The press caught wind of the project. On January 1, 1887, *Gil Blas* mocked the chairman: "Newspapers are reporting that M. de Goncourt is specially sponsoring the performance in question and that it is being done on his initiative. Frankly, we find it a little difficult to believe them. We have a hard time seeing the tasteful, exquisitely tactful man of letters, whom we easily imagine as the last of the

Goncourts, manning the door of a theater to raise money for erecting a monument to the glory of a dear friend, venerated by all." Offended, Goncourt stepped down. Maupassant pressed him to change his mind. Lapierre admitted that they had proceeded in a disorganized manner but that they needed him, Goncourt, to remain at the head of the committee: "You are the leader of the Modern School and your talent and reputation, like your character, naturally make you suited to be the head of this literary event in honor of our poor 'Flau,' as we called him." Goncourt withdrew his resignation, and many new contributions came in. Finally, on November 23, 1890—it had taken ten years!—the monument was inaugurated in Rouen after a gourmet lunch provided by the mayor. With about a hundred people in attendance, tribute was paid to Flaubert with the oompahs of military music and a series of speeches, the most eagerly anticipated of which was by Edmond de Goncourt. Though the "*bichon*" was known to dislike public speaking, he delivered a memorable homage:

> Now that my poor great Flaubert is dead, people acknowledge his genius, as much as his memory could desire. But is everyone aware that while he was alive the critics were fairly resistant to even granting him some talent? And that it did not stop at "resistance to praise"? ... What did that life full of masterpieces earn him? Denial, insults, moral crucifixion. Ah! One could write a good, vengeful book about all the mistakes and injustices perpetrated by critics of works by everyone from Balzac to Flaubert. I remember an article by a political journalist affirming that Flaubert's prose brought shame upon the reign of Napoleon III; I also remember an article in a literary journal in which he was criticized for an *epileptic style*—you know now what poison that epithet held for the man to whom it was addressed.[2]

Indeed, Maxime Du Camp had given the critics fodder when his *Souvenirs littéraires* were published in the *Revue des deux mondes* in 1881. Du Camp had not only revealed Flaubert's disease, which was known only to his family and close friends, but had added to this indiscretion the suggestion that epilepsy had limited his art, just as it explained his so-called difficulty in writing: "Gustave Flaubert was a writer of rare talent," he stated; "without the nervous disorder with which he was afflicted, he would have been a man of genius."[3] This tactless, restrictive homage had outraged Maupassant and provided unscrupulous journalists with the opportunity to sully the memory of the deceased. Once again, Maupassant lauded Flaubert, the "great master of the modern novel," earning him attacks from Léon Chapron in *L'Evénement*, who reduced Flaubert to the single novel *Madame Bovary*, called *Salammbô* the "novel of a neurotic," declared *Sentimental Education* "a concept as tedious as the rain," and said that the recently published posthumous *Bouvard and Pécuchet* was "the work of a senile man."[4] The writer's death had not disarmed the mean-spirited.

The Enigmatic *Bouvard and Pécuchet*

Flaubert's output did not come to an end with his death. If one is to believe Goncourt, on the very day of the funeral, Flaubert's indelicate nephew alluded to the income he and his wife could derive from his unpublished manuscripts. "Commanville," he writes, "kept talking all the time about the money to be made out of the dead man's books, with such peculiar references to our poor friend's amorous correspondences as to give the impression that he was quite capable of blackmailing the surviving correspondents."[5] But in 1881, before any of this correspondence was released, Lemerre published the unfinished manuscript of *Bouvard and Pécuchet*.

As early as 1863, when he was just starting work on *Sentimental Education*, Flaubert had contemplated the idea for a novel originally entitled *Les Deux Cloportes* [*The Two Woodlice*] or *Les Deux Commis* [*The Two Clerks*]. "It's an old idea that I've had for years," he wrote to Jules Duplan at the time, "and perhaps I should get it off my chest. I'd rather write a book about passion, but one doesn't choose one's subjects: one submits to them."[6] The seed of this idea can be detected in an early short story published in 1837 by *Le Colibri* under the title "Une leçon d'histoire naturelle, genre Commis" [A Lesson in Natural History, Genus: Clerk]. The reader will recall this scathing portrait of an ordinary bureaucrat written by a fifteen-year-old Flaubert in the style of the Garçon. Later, Flaubert may also have been inspired by a short story by a certain Barthélemy Maurice, "Les Deux Greffiers" [The Two Court Clerks], which was initially published in *La Gazette des tribunaux* in 1841 and was reprinted in 1858 in *L'Audience,* a publication he was known to read. Alphonse Daudet's wife, Julia, showed the story to René Descharmes and René Dumesnil, who included it in their book *Autour de Flaubert* [*About Flaubert*].[7] This story is about two court clerks who become friends and retire to the countryside, where they plan to enjoy their passion for hunting and fishing.

Boredom sets in after a while, and finally they find nothing better to do than return to their work as copyists, taking turns dictating to each other: "Thus their last pleasure, their real, their only pleasure, was to fictively return to the dull drudgery that for thirty-eight years had been the occupation and maybe, unbeknownst to them, the joy of their lives."

Flaubert borrowed the basic outline of this story about two retirees, but he gave it the breadth of a real book and a philosophy inspired by his vision of human stupidity. This least novelistic of his novels tells the story of two office clerks who become friends when they discover that they have a certain number of tastes and interests in common. Following an unexpected inheritance, Bouvard convinces Pécuchet to settle with him in the countryside, in Chavignolles in Normandy, where they could once and for all break with the monotony of the office. Unlike the two court clerks in Maurice's story, Bouvard and Pécuchet have ideas and ambition. They begin by dedicating themselves to gardening, then, having acquired a farm, they move into agriculture. This initial foray is nothing but a series of disasters that they bring on themselves, with no help from nature, by following the poorly digested advice of the most scholarly treatises. Their failures inspire a desire to understand and stimulate their will to know. They embark on a frantic quest for knowledge: they want to unravel the mysteries of chemistry, medicine, anatomy, physiology, geology, archaeology, and every other science, but also history, literature, philosophy, magnetism, spiritualism, religion, educational science, and politics. Yet with each new endeavor they come up against the contradictions and approximations of the authors they consult, and when they try out their theories, they discover their inadequacy and mistakes, and they move on to something else. At the end, like the two court clerks, they return to copying, their second nature.

An incongruous, contradictory novel chopped into sections and made even more enigmatic by its unfinished state, *Bouvard and Pécuchet* has steadily attracted attention from exegetes, each more learned than the next, but all incapable of definitively sorting out the author's real intentions.

The two subtitles that Flaubert had planned for his book seem to put us on the right track: first, "Encyclopedia of human stupidity,"[8] and later, "On lack of method in the sciences."[9] What kind of stupidity did he want to assail? One form of stupidity is easily identified and would later be detailed in the *Dictionary of Accepted Ideas*, which Flaubert had constantly added to over many years and was published after *Bouvard and Pécuchet*. This is the stupidity of formulaic language, conversational platitudes, and common prejudices, everything that belongs to the world of "Us," that anonymous mass. Anonymous, but often bourgeois, because the bourgeoisie is at the top and is therefore the class that speaks, writes, and discourses, but is universal. Ironic condemnation of this kind of stupidity is found throughout Flaubert's work, in which nearly every character stands for a particular type of generalized stupidity. In *Bouvard and Pécuchet,* each Chavignollais embodies a specific instance of stupidity, whether it is the vanity of caste, the fear of "reds," superstition, credulity, or ignorance. One has to appreciate these characters in the context—and at the heart of—the Revolution of 1848, for which *Bouvard and Pécuchet* provides a rural counterpart to *Sentimental Education*'s account of revolutionary developments in Paris. People are scared at the initial reports of revolt and rally behind the Republic. The priest blesses a Liberty tree. Then, as news from the capital becomes gradually more alarming and the threat of social war dawns, the notables build a party of order based on all their accumulating fears, the lies that are taken at face value, and the desire to be rid of the masses' demands once and for all. What must happen, happens: "And on December 10, all the citizens of Chavignolles voted for Louis Napoleon." With the following comment: "In short, the plebs were no better than the aristocrats."[10] They rejoice to learn of Proudhon's arrest, cut down Liberty trees, demand that teachers be closely watched; "everyone [calls] for a savior," and finally the entire population applauds the December 2 coup d'état. Flaubert uses Pécuchet as a mouthpiece for his own reaction at the time: " 'Do you want my opinion? . . . Since the bourgeois are vicious, the workers jealous, the priests obsequious, and the masses ultimately accepting of any tyrant, so long as he leaves their snouts in the trough, Louis Napoleon did the right thing! Let him gag the people, crush them underfoot, wipe them out—it would serve them right for their hatred of the law, their cowardice, their ineptitude, and their blindness!' "[11] Flaubert often said that with this book he wanted to unleash his anger, spit on his contemporaries, and cough up his bile, and that he was preparing to vomit "an encyclopedia of modern Stupidity."

Yet throughout the entire episode of the Second Republic, Bouvard and Pécuchet stand out both from the "vile bourgeoisie" and the "vile multitude" in that they have become critical observers of their compatriots. By working, observing, and analyzing their own failures, the two friends who started out as fools eventually take on Flaubert's way of looking at things: "Then their minds developed a piteous faculty, that of perceiving stupidity and being unable to tolerate it." They catch this stupidity in insignificant things, "newspaper advertisements, a burgher's profile, an inane comment overheard by chance,"[12] but also—and this introduces a second form of stupidity—in the hundreds of books they read. For there is also a stupidity of the learned. To write his novel, Flaubert read voraciously—many of the titles are cited—encountering mistakes, unfounded statements, uncertain certitudes, and presumptuous hypotheses. Throughout the writing of *Bouvard and Pécuchet*, and with the faithful help of Edmond Laporte, he put together a vast compendium of stupidities. The *Dictionary of Accepted Ideas* is only a fragment of what he gathered. The compendium contains everyday anonymous stupidity, while the *Dictionary* is a collection of published gems, signed and defended by their authors, some of whom are major names. But how can all that fit into a work of fiction?

The manuscript and related work files left by Flaubert are an endless challenge to literary criticism. Many questions remain open.

The first relates to the characters of Bouvard and Pécuchet. Now proverbial, these two names are among the most illustrious figures of stupidity in French literary history. But if truth be told, they may be more complex than they appear to be. It would be too simple to trace their career as a positive evolution toward intelligence and lucidity. From the first chapter, we learn that the two clerks' minds have been enlightened by their intellectual curiosity: "They learned about discoveries, read prospectuses, and their newfound curiosity caused their intelligence to bloom."[13] But though they acquire an awareness of generalized stupidity, up to the end of the existing manuscript they themselves display a naïveté, gullibility, and lack of common sense that relegates them to the world of stupidity. What are we to make of this?

The principal question concerns the book's general meaning. Is it an attack on science? How do we explain that this writer who advocated the "scientific" novel sought to reduce scientists' learning to nothing?[14] But is it really science in and of itself that is under attack? Isn't it rather the arrogance and self-delusions of science? According to Flaubert, "it is impossible to know the Truth."[15] What Flaubert refutes is scientists' claim to attain the truth. In the compendium of stupidities that was to be included in the novel, one finds this quote taken from Raspail's *Histoire de la santé et des maladies* [*History of Health and Diseases*]: "Popular prejudice will eventually prevail over scientific incredulity, and the observations of old wives will defeat learned theories. When it comes to naïve observations, science, which is too self-important by nature, always lags behind popular common sense." Flaubert's inclusion of such foolishness shows that he does not reject science itself. Rather, he is tackling the discourse of causality. As early as 1857, in a letter to Mlle Leroyer de Chantepie, he exclaimed: "Oh! human pride. A solution! The goal, the cause! But we would be God, if we knew the cause."[16] This was also the position of one of the greatest savants of his era, Claude Bernard, the author of the influential *Introduction à l'étude de la médecine expérimentale* [*Introduction to the Study of Experimental Medicine*], which Flaubert so admired that he attended Bernard's funeral in 1878: "Only the *how* of things is within our reach; the *why* is beyond our understanding." This may suggest a way forward: to accuse causality of being "anti-scientific," one must have a certain respect for science. Indictment of causality, refusal of categorical and definitive conclusions, rejection of all dogmatism. Agreed!

However, Flaubert constantly throws us off balance, for this supposed opposition between real science—that of a Claude Bernard—and pseudoscience stamped with religiosity and presumption is partially weakened by some of the sequences in *Bouvard and Pécuchet*. After all, the two clerks fall for spiritualism, then very fashionable, and participate in table-turning séances. Once they have finished their reading, they learn magnetism and eventually cure a few people, to the great displeasure of Chavignolles' Dr. Vaucorbeil, the representative of official medical science. "In *Bouvard and Pécuchet*," writes Claudine Gothot-Mersch, "everything is organized for the reader to lose his footing."[17]

Finally, many have wondered what we would have found in the "second volume" of *Bouvard and Pécuchet*—that is, the chapters that were never written. Flaubert presented the missing volume as the two clerks' "copy." But what are they copying? The *Bouvard and Pécuchet* work file archived at the Rouen library is an accumulation of disparate items: scenarios, sketches, outlines, rough drafts, notes, quotes, various documents, and the *Dictionary of Accepted Ideas*. In other words, a voluminous file that does not definitively shed light on how the novel would have continued. In a letter to Edma Roger des Genettes dated January 25, 1880, Flaubert asserted that writing the second volume would take him no more than six months: "It's three quarters done, and will consist almost entirely of quotations."[18] With the help of Laporte, Flaubert had collected countless items for his compendium of stupidities, targeting sentences sometimes attributed to famous names: Pius IX, Louis Napoleon, Fénelon, Mgr. Dupanloup, Joseph de Maistre, Béranger, Bernardin de

Saint-Pierre, Alexandre Dumas. The compendium was supplemented by another collection, entitled *L'Album de la marquise* [*The Album of the Marquise*], which focused on the literary world, with quotes from Chateaubriand, Sainte-Beuve, Alexandre Dumas fils, Louise Colet, the Goncourts, Barbey d'Aurevilly, Ernest Feydeau, Balzac, Michelet, Lamartine, Victor Cousin, and George Sand. There would also be a *Catalogue of Fashionable Ideas* to enumerate modish absurdities (Defense of slavery—Of Saint Bartholomew's Day—Making fun of the learned). The *Dictionary of Accepted Ideas,* which Flaubert had started much earlier, was also supposed to be included in this second volume. How would he have used this mass of material? We do not know. Critics get lost in conjecture, but at the same time, as Geneviève Bollème writes, "without this second volume, the first is incomprehensible, unpublishable."[19] We do know, thanks to a letter to Edma Roger des Genettes, that he was planning on a conclusion "of three or four pages."[20] But when the book was prepared for posthumous publication, the conclusion was cruelly lacking. The mystery had not been dispelled. After Flaubert's death, Caroline Commanville entrusted Guy de Maupassant with preparing the second part of *Bouvard and Pécuchet,* but despite his best efforts, he had to face the facts: "I've just spent three months consulting and trying to organize the notes of our poor departed one, to turn them into the book he wanted to write, but I now believe this task cannot be executed. His plan was for these notes to be connected, united by pieces of narrative that featured the two clerks again, and through pieces of dialogue forming commentaries on their reading and their copies. I cannot permit myself to write these parts, and without them the book is unreadable: it is no more than an agglomeration, a disordered heap of quotes whose very meaning will sometimes escape the reader."[21]

Published in 1881 in the state in which Flaubert had left it, *Bouvard and Pécuchet* perplexed critics.[22] They deemed it a novel without a plot, with bland characters and a monotonous narrative—in short, an incomprehensible book. Once again, the fiercest critic was Barbey d'Aurevilly, who began his review in *Le Constitutionnel* dated May 10, 1881, by denouncing the "jackals of literature," the abusive heirs of dead writers who "gather up the lions' scraps to live off them." The Commanvilles had certainly wasted no time in having the unfinished manuscript published, without asking themselves what Flaubert would have wanted. Barbey's entire criticism of *Bouvard and Pécuchet* centers on one idea: Flaubert hated the bourgeoisie, he was "obsessed" with it, he wanted to strike at it with a final blast of hatred and contempt, but he "was not talented enough for this final execution of the bourgeois!" His story of two idiots is "a tale of resounding vulgarity and baseness"; it is "disgusting and odious"; "without cheerfulness, talent, or new observations on worn-out, sucked dry, exhausted types—finally, this book is unreadable and unbearable." In the supplement to *Le Gaulois* dated April 6, 1881, Maupassant wrote that Barbey refused to see that there might be something else in the book. The disciple spoke of a "philosophical novel" inspired by a fundamentally pessimistic view of the world and humanity. In this article, he revealed that what the two clerks had collected and started to copy was "the dossier of stupidities plucked from the works of great men." Émile Faguet, one of the leading arbiters of Belle Époque French letters along with Brunetière and Lanson, judged that the author of *Bouvard and Pécuchet* "does not appear to have absolutely sound good sense"; in any case, he added, "this novel is a failure, given that however you read it, it is boring."[23]

Yet *Bouvard and Pécuchet* proved to be a turning point in the history of literature, just like *Madame Bovary* before it. Flaubert had unwillingly been recognized as the father of naturalism; now his last novel heralded its end. In 1884, his follower Joris-Karl Huysmans published *À rebours* [*Against Nature*], whose structure was reminiscent of that of *Bouvard and Pécuchet*, with each chapter "becoming the extract of a specialty, the sublimate of a different art." For Huysmans, naturalism had had its merits, but it "was condemned to repeat itself, forever getting nowhere."[24] The critic Rémy de Gourmount noted that *Bouvard and Pécuchet* marks a major break in the history of the novel. Yet one had to wait for the great Flaubert scholars of the twentieth century, René Descharmes, René Dumesnil, and Albert Thibaudet,[25] to recognize the importance of *Bouvard and Pécuchet* and, later, for Jorge Luis Borges, Raymond Queneau, and Roland Barthes to rank it among the "masterpieces of Western literature."[26]

The *Dictionary of Accepted Ideas*

The *Dictionary of Accepted Ideas* was first mentioned publicly by Maupassant, in 1884, in his preface to the Charpentier edition of *Lettres de Gustave Flaubert à George Sand* [*Letters of Gustave Flaubert to George Sand*], but it was not published until 1911, in the Conard edition of *Bouvard and Pécuchet*. Even though Flaubert had planned to include the *Dictionary* in *Bouvard*,[27] René Descharmes has made a convincing argument that it inspired parts of his two other "modern" novels, *Madame Bovary* and *Sentimental Education*.[28] Picking up from Descharmes, Claude Digeon explains the function of this collection of platitudes: "The *Dictionary* is an original, coherent work in and of itself. And one could say that it sums up in an abstract form an idea concretely expressed by the characters in all of Flaubert's modern works: *Madame Bovary, Sentimental Education, Bouvard and Pécuchet*. In this sense, the *Dictionary* is Flaubert's most significant work, the one in which he theorizes his creations. What we are dealing with here, rather than stupid characters, is stupidity itself."

This highly original work had been conceived by Flaubert as far back as his trip to the Orient in 1850. He wrote to Louis Bouilhet that this collection of commonplaces, established judgments, statements of the obvious, and trivial recommendations, this bourgeois guide to manners, should be preceded by a substantial preface "in which we would indicate just how the work was intended to reconcile the public to tradition, to order and conventional morality, and written in such a way that the reader couldn't tell whether or not we were pulling his leg—that would perhaps be a strange book, and it might well have some success, for it would be very topical."[29] In an 1852 letter to Louise Colet, he went into greater detail about his intentions, summarizing them as follows:

> Thus we would find in alphabetical order, on every possible subject, *everything that should be said in society to be a respectable, amiable man*. One would find:
>
> ARTISTS: are all disinterested.
> LANGOUSTE: female of the lobster.
> FRANCE: needs an iron hand in order to be ruled.
> BOSSUET: is the eagle of Meaux.
> FÉNELON: is the swan of Cambrai.[30]
> NEGRESSES: are warmer than white women.
> ERECTION: is said only in reference to monuments.

> I think the whole would be terrific as *buckshot*. There should not be a single word of my own invention in the entire book, and once one has read it, one would be afraid to speak, for fear of inadvertently speaking one of the sentences it includes.[31]

For a historian, it is a goldmine. Behind the catalog of dull conventions and the map of beaten tracks one can make out a collective portrait of the bourgeoisie of the nineteenth century, through a sort of satirical version of an ideal. The young bourgeois man, fresh from high school, comes to Paris, where he generally attends law school, with other "young men of good family." If he manages to talk his way into the Polytechnic Institute, he realizes "every mother's dream for her son" (SCHOOLS). Once he finishes his studies, he marries a well-raised young woman, who will have abstained from reading "any kind of book" (GIRLS). Indeed, it is reprehensible to remain a bachelor, and every bachelor is seen as "selfish and immoral" (BACHELORS). For debauchery, there are prostitutes, which is a good thing, a "necessary evil" that "keeps our daughters and sisters safe" (PROSTITUTE).

Once he has settled down, the bourgeois forgets his student pranks and devotes himself to business affairs, which "come before everything" and are "the most important thing in life" (BUSINESS AFFAIRS). He will frequently be tempted to become a deputy, for he dreams of becoming a minister, a position that is discredited but nevertheless envied as "the height of glory" (DEPUTY, MINISTER). Having married well, with his social position firmly established, the bourgeois works but knows how to enjoy himself. He and his wife like theater and sometimes push their desire for exoticism all the way to the Odéon, though it is located far from home, that is to say on the Left Bank (ODEON). But mostly they have a society life, they like conversation. The men get together and talk up a storm about the serious problems of the hour; they talk of commerce and industry, those two noble arts (COMMERCE). They praise the speed of the railroad: "If Napoleon had had them, he would have been invincible!" (RAILROAD); they rail against free trade, the "bane of commerce" (FREE TRADE), which allows them to take a passing swipe at Englishmen, "all rich" (ENGLISHMEN), and to make an incidental allusion to "the unspeakable Malthus" (MALTHUS). Then they feel sorry about the death of agriculture, which is "short of manpower" (AGRICULTURE). The bourgeois bitterly complains about his budget, which is "never balanced" (BUDGET)—Perhaps it would be best to cut down on expenses made simply to keep up appearances? No, because it "confers prestige" and "fires the imagination of the masses" "It's absolutely necessary!" (ETIQUETTE). But the masses allow themselves to be influenced by the republicans and by radicalism, "all the more dangerous for being latent" (RADICALISM). All in all, what the French need is to be governed by a sword! (SWORD). Still, that's an extreme measure, because we favor universal suffrage (SUFFRAGE [Universal]), which put the aristocracy in its place (ARISTOCRACY). Yet the working-class quarters remain dangerous; you should avoid living near a factory (FACTORY). Panhandling should be banned (PANHANDLING), but it is reassuring that policemen, "society's first line of defense," are on the lookout (POLICEMEN); otherwise the fundaments of society, "property, family, religion, respect for authority" would be weakened (FUNDAMENTS OF SOCIETY).

Bourgeois stupidity resides in the contrast between the bourgeois' vulgar defense of his material interests and the solemnity of his speech. The same contradiction is found in religious matters. Religion is "a fundament of society," it is "necessary for the common folk, to a point" (RELIGION). Granted, "a population of atheists could not survive," but one should not be too credulous (ATHEIST). The greatest danger is the Jesuits, who are everywhere and "have a hand in every revolution" (JESUITS). It is suitable to make fun of priests who "sleep with their maids"; everyone knows it, but one must always prudently conclude that "there are good ones" (PRIESTS). The bourgeois goes to mass to set an example, and also because it's in good taste—a way of imitating the aristocracy that is at once so detested and so envied. Which does not prevent this materialist and agnostic bourgeois from proclaiming that spiritualism is "the best philosophical system" (SPIRITUALISM).

This conformist bourgeois, politically in favor of religion but philosophically skeptical of it, a guardian of order who is respectful of power, reaches the height of stupidity when he gets involved in art and literature. He values the Gothic style, which "suits religion"; he likes Victor Hugo, despite the fact that "he was wrong to get involved in politics." He attends concerts: "a subscription to the Conservatory is indispensable." He regrets the "lost secret" of mosaics; finds that windmills "look good in a landscape," as do ruins, which make the landscape "look poetic" and "induce reveries." Is Flaubert reproaching the bourgeois for educating himself? No, what he has against him is that he is sufficiently educated to parrot common stupidities, but not enough to have personal taste. Being distinguished means not distinguishing yourself from dominant ideals, accepted truths, and shared phobias.[32]

The *Dictionary* would become a key to understanding Flaubert's novels. A cavern of accepted ideas, as abstract as Plato's pure ideas, this vast catalog of human stupidity sheds light on the behavior and speech of the characters created by the writer, who each have their own style of participating in the world of stupidity, and all to different degrees. This complement to the novels has left us with a *Flaubertian eye,* whose sensitivity to stupidity should protect us from that of our contemporaries and alert us to our own weaknesses: "We are suffering from one single thing: *Stupidity.* But that one thing is formidable and universal."[33]

The Writer Recognized, the Man Discovered

No posthumous publication of Flaubert's writing has done more to further our understanding of his personality, his aesthetic, and the material and moral conditioning of his work than his correspondence. His heir, Caroline, quickly set about collecting Flaubert's letters, both to serve her uncle's memory and probably to make some money. By 1884, Charpentier had published *Lettres de Gustave Flaubert à George Sand,* which included 122 of Flaubert's letters to Sand (out of the 222 now known to us). It had a beautiful preface by Guy de Maupassant. Three years later, working with the same publisher, Caroline issued the first volume of the general correspondence, the fourth and last volume of which would be published in 1893. She had succeeded in collecting a great many letters but had also been turned down by many correspondents and had to acknowledge countless gaps. Though this edition of the correspondence was no more than a rough draft, with certain letters expurgated, Caroline had allowed the reading public to enter into the intimate world of a writer who had avoided all publicity about himself and his ideas his whole life long. It was prefaced by Caroline's *Souvenirs intimes* and did not include Flaubert's letters to his niece, which she held on to until the publication of *Lettres à sa nièce Caroline* [*Letters to His Niece Caroline*] in 1906. Louis Conard took over the correspondence and published five volumes in 1910. This seriously flawed edition was followed by a third edition, issued in four volumes by the same publisher from 1921 to 1925. It is considered the first scholarly edition. From 1926 to 1933, Louis Conard published a nine-volume edition, which was enriched by the Franklin Grout archive that Caroline left to the Institut de France, and by unpublished letters in the collection of the great collector Spoelberch de Lovenjoul in Chantilly. Countless gaps remained, which Éditions Conard addressed in 1954 by publishing a four-volume supplement to the correspondence that added 1,306 letters to those already available.[34] While this edition was significant, it was often inaccurate, patchy, unreliable for dates, and prudishly censored. It was finally followed by the masterful critical edition of the *Correspondance* published under the direction of

Jean Bruneau from 1972 to 2007 in Gallimard's Bibliothèque de la Pléiade.[35] As the public's attention was gradually drawn to the correspondence, Flaubert's work and personality took on another dimension. These letters, which André Gide and many others considered their bible, inspired René Dumesnil to state: "I am among those who consider [them] Flaubert's masterpiece." Citing Dumesnil's appreciation, Jean Bruneau notes that "nothing could have dismayed Flaubert more than this sentence," so dramatically unfair toward the novels. But it gives us a feeling for the admirable nature of this epistolary opus, an unrivaled source for an understanding both of Flaubert himself and of his era.

Gustave Flaubert's place in French literature was only progressively revealed and recognized. One has to go back to the centennial of his birth, in 1921, to note this belated recognition. After a few ceremonies held in Rouen, the main event was the celebration in Paris, where a bust of the writer by the sculptor Jean Escoula was unveiled in the Luxembourg Gardens on December 12. The president of the Republic, Alexandre Millerand, delegated his chief of staff to attend, but the minister of education was present. Among the speeches delivered, one of the most widely discussed was by a popular novelist of the time, Paul Bourget. The celebrations led to many commentaries on Flaubert and his work. Some detractors had not backed down, including the son of Alphonse and Julia Daudet, Léon Daudet, who explained in *L'Action française* that Flaubert was a "sucker" more comical than Homais, without knowing it. The most remarkable article was written for *La Revue de Paris* by Paul Souday, who was considered the leading literary critic of the period following the Great War and had columns in *Le Figaro, Le Gaulois, La Revue de Paris, Les Nouvelles littéraires,* and the Toulouse paper *La Dépêche,* among others. Souday recalled the snubs, attacks, and contempt the author of *Madame Bovary* had been subjected to throughout his life, and how hostile newspaper critics and the academy had been to him. The masterstroke of this war on Flaubert was that of Ferdinand Brunetière, who wrote: "This deep hatred of human stupidity, this hatred that served him so well in *Madame Bovary* but so poorly, however, in *Sentimental Education,* was nothing more than the projection of his own personal stupidity on the things he could not understand." Souday could rightfully affirm that "this heap of injustices allows us to measure his ascent. For that has now been accomplished, definitively. By throwing stones at him, we finally built him a pedestal. Flaubert has triumphed, and no longer has anything to fear."[36]

At the time of the centennial, the house at Croisset no longer stood. Its owner, Caroline Commanville, had sold it to an industrialist who had it razed to build a distillery. All that remains now is the Flaubert Pavilion, later purchased by the municipal council and turned into a small museum in which one can see Flaubert's goose quills, inkwells, pipes, tobacco jar, a few souvenirs from the Orient, and paintings showing the house in all its splendor. By walking away from the Seine and along the cliff overlooking it, the pilgrim can reach the city hall of Canteleu, whose wedding hall is called the "Salle Gustave Flaubert." Three large cabinets house part of the writer's library, offered by Caroline to the Institut Français, which turned it down. The municipality of Rouen did not much admire the writer while he was alive. Today there are reminders of Flaubert everywhere. The Hôtel-Dieu is now the prefecture, but the Flauberts' former lodgings were turned into a Flaubert museum and a museum of medicine. The wide avenue leading there is the Avenue Gustave Flaubert. In 2008 a new, 2,200-foot bridge was named after the author, as if in reparation. The city's university has become one of the most active centers of Flaubert studies in the world, in a final act of reconciliation between a city and a writer who once thought so little of each other.

CHAPTER 30

Sketches for a Portrait

"There are in me, literally speaking, two distinct persons: one who is infatu-ated with bombast, lyricism, eagle flights, sonorities of phrase and lofty ideas; and another who digs and burrows into the truth as deeply as he can, who likes to treat a humble fact as respectfully as a big one, who would like to make you feel almost *physically* the things he reproduces. The former likes to laugh, and enjoys the animal side of man."[1] There are indeed two persons coexisting in Flaubert—and not only in the writer, as he said to Louise Colet in this letter dated January 16, 1852. His personality, habits, and thought are full of para-doxes. While these do not make him a contradictory being, they suggest that he was more complex than one might initially think. "I like wine, but I don't drink; I am a gambler and I've never touched a playing card; I enjoy de-bauchery and I live like a monk. . . . I am a mystic and I don't believe in anything."

Physically, he looked like an athlete but was actually a constantly ailing colossus. Photographs and portraits of Flaubert are rare. Resistant to any kind of publicity, he did not often agree to pose: "The artist," he wrote to Ernest Feydeau, "must not exist. His personality is nothing. The work! The work! Nothing else."[2] His friends saw him as a "giant." The passport he was issued in 1847 states that he stood six feet tall, which made him significantly taller than most of his compatriots, given that the average height of conscripts in Normandy at the end of the century was five feet four.[3] The same document specifies that his hair was dark brown and receding, his eyes blue, and his com-plexion flushed. A perfect Viking. Sedentary but not stagnant, he swam "like a triton" and loved horseback riding. As a young man, he drew a great deal of feminine attention at the theater in Rouen and, a few years later, electrified Louise Colet before she grew to admire his intellectual qualities. In the meantime—this was in March 1853, when Flaubert was only thirty-one—he declared that he was "hugely deteriorated."[4]

Maupassant describes him as follows: "It is said that he formerly had the Olympian beauty of a Greek god. This physical beauty did not last long. A voyage to the Orient tired him and made him grow heavy, and he became the man that we knew, a big, stout, superb Gaul with an enormous mustache, a powerful nose, and thick eyebrows sheltering and covering a seabird's blue eyes, spotted in the middle with an ever-moving tiny black pupil that looked fixedly, penetrating and unsettling, agitated by a constant tremor."[5]

His health problems began with the onset of his supposed epilepsy. Repeated convulsive fits wore him down, then became less frequent and eventually seemed to go away before reappearing at the end of his life. Before he turned thirty, he contracted syphilis, which was at that time treated with mercury rubdowns and purges, whose effects were as damaging as those of the disease. In August 1854, he confided in Louis Bouilhet that he felt "saturated with mercury": "Terrific mercurial salivation, my dear sir. It was impossible for me to talk or eat—atrocious fever etc. Finally, I am rid of it, thanks to purges, leeches, enemas (!!!) and my 'strong constitution.'"[6] In its initial stages, syphilis is not lethal. Gustave offhandedly kept Louis up to date about his chancres, as if they were a sign of virility, then stopped referring to the subject after a few years. Had the disease entered a latent stage? Unless Flaubert had been cured, in which case one would have to say: despite the mercury.

The Adonis of the theater in Rouen felt that he aged quickly. At twenty-eight, he wrote to his mother from Athens to tell her to expect to see him three-quarters bald. He told his mistress that he was losing his teeth. Throughout his life, his letters would be full of complaints about his multiple ailments. He avoided tuberculosis and cholera, which still claimed lives at Croisset in 1873, but suffered sore throats, bouts of violent flu, attacks of neuralgia, nervous disorders that were treated with potassium bromide, rheumatic fever, abnormal palpitations, shingles, and jaundice. While he was recovering from his broken fibula, he wrote to Edmond de Goncourt: "My leg is doing well. But it swells every night. I cannot walk much farther than 100 feet—and I have to wear a band around my ankles. What's more, I had one of my last molars pulled. What's more, I have lumbago. What's more, blepharitis [inflammation of the eyelids]. And currently, since yesterday, I have been enjoying a boil right in the middle of my face."[7] There is eloquence in the number of times he complains about his boils (on his forehead, cheek, or neck). They were probably caused by the deterioration of his general state, along with his questionable hygiene. Contemporary eating habits did not contribute to his good health. In December 1875, Goncourt described a dinner at Victor Hugo's: "There was rabbit stew, followed by roast beef, after which a roast chicken was brought in." With the overeating, the constant coffee, and lack of physical exercise, for which he was criticized by George Sand, Flaubert was aware that overall the life he led "was not exactly very healthy."[8] Flaubert's multiple ailments were probably also partly psychosomatic effects of his anxiety. At fifty-five, he described himself to Léonie Brainne: "My friend Sarah Bernhardt, whom I went to visit in her atelier . . . told me she found me very beautiful, 'full of character,' an artistic word! . . . I do not agree with my illustrious friend. I find myself slumped, disgusting. I look like an old ham actor and an old butcher at the same time. The heart alone is young, and younger than ever, despite it all."[9] Though Flaubert is being a touch flirtatious in this letter to a woman he found appealing, he was indeed like many of his contemporaries in that he aged very quickly. With his sturdy, tall stature, balding forehead, long hair, and thick mustache, and his weight easily over two hundred pounds, Flaubert at an early age looked like the mature man we know from the portraits by the photographer Carjat and the painter Giraud. Did he at least keep a "young heart"?

Flaubert spent his whole life inseparably bound to melancholy, yet when he was with his intimates, his sadness was masked and he became a colorful character sure to make people laugh with his masterful pranks and jokes. He described himself as "more clownish than cheerful." From his teenage years on, he led what he qualified as "not a madcap existence." Spending most of his time at Croisset, with a mother who became increasingly narrow-minded as the years went by, he frequently stated that he was overwhelmed by the monotony of his existence and his lack of distractions, to the point that he sometimes declared that "despair is my normal state."[10] For the young man who had never believed in happiness, the sense of despair was reinforced by his sickness, the misfortunes of his emotional life, and the deaths of his father, sister, and best friend, Alfred—all the premature bereavements—that deepened his loneliness. At twenty, young Gustave confessed to Maxime Du Camp that he "hated life." He confirmed these feelings in a letter to Louise Colet: "You, you love life; you are a pagan and a southerner; you respect passions and aspire to happiness ... —But I detest Life. I am a Catholic. In my heart, I have something of the green oozing of Norman cathedrals. My proclivities are for the inactive, the ascetics, the dreamers."[11]

His hypochondriac core contrasted with his jovial, lively behavior with friends. He was a buoyant companion, whose volubility shocked the stiffly dignified Goncourt brothers. Yet behind his appearance as an exuberant fellow from the provinces, there hid the sensitivity of a young girl: "Jules de Goncourt," he confided to one of his correspondents, "used to call me 'very sensitive.' What is certain is that my eyes are often wet."[12] He cried at the wedding of Élisa Schlésinger's son in June 1872 and broke down in tears at George Sand's funeral. The jokester was a romantic.

Flaubert was also Janus-faced in being both a country mouse and a city mouse. At Croisset, he made little room for "fun and games," but in Paris, his life expanded to include society soirées, drunken dinners, and a whirlwind of literary and romantic experiences. In Normandy, seventy-five percent of his time was spent "digging away" in solitude, preferably at night. He escaped a little to walk his dog Julio or to dive into the Seine, weather permitting. He sometimes hosted friends: Turgenev, who canceled three out of four times, George Sand, who had more and more trouble getting away from Nohant, and other companions such as Edmond Laporte, his faithful admirer until their sad falling-out. He admitted to his correspondents that his horizon was grey, his spirits morose, and he was haunted by boredom, though he had moments of elation when he finally achieved the long-awaited sentence or paragraph after a ream of crossed-out, darkened pages. But this is how he had wanted it. This was how he conceived of his life as a writer, deliberately choosing art against life. Wearing an African tunic, surrounded by souvenirs from the Orient, he smoked one pipe after another and searched for the next word.

When his mind and body got weary, he took the next train to Paris. He always had things to attend to, spending hours in the libraries accumulating thousands of notes. But Paris also meant coming out of his hermetic shell, seeing his friends, going to the salons of the demimondaines and Princess Mathilde, where the brilliance of his improvisations shone, unless he exasperated his best friends with the violence of his outbursts. This swaggerer who caused a sensation wherever he set foot always put friendship first. He was the faithful, obliging, ever-generous friend who never spoke a word against you and always met you with open arms at his residences on boulevard du Temple, rue Murillo, or rue du Faubourg Saint-Honoré. He liked to talk, listen, comfort, seduce, and amuse. Every Sunday when he was staying in Paris, Flaubert turned into a pampering host. When someone he loved was in trouble, he did everything he could to help to find a job, a publisher, or a theater manager. Always leading the applause on opening nights, he also proved a conscientious literary adviser, spending hours on his acquaintances' manuscripts, suggesting revisions and praising successful passages. As his name became well known and respected, he began receiving texts from unknown authors, which he scrupulously read through before making a detailed report to the writer: page after page, he honestly noted the good and the bad, as if his status as a writer gave him an obligation toward his juniors. Once back at Croisset, having dived back into his work, he continued to make himself felt through letters to all and sundry, worried that he didn't receive enough in return, and constantly stoked the fires of friendships that might otherwise go out.

At Croisset as in Paris, he lived like a bourgeois, but he was a bourgeois in permanent rebellion against the bourgeoisie of his time: "When has the Bourgeois ever loomed larger than now?"[13] In fact, he lived the life of a man of independent means, thanks to capital that he had not personally accumulated. Until his financial ruin, which came late in life, he was an heir. He lived off the money he was given, first by his mother, who paid off his debts, then his nephew Commanville, who managed his assets. After he turned fifty, he never even considered earning money. The artist did not dirty his hands, did not involve himself in industry or commerce or even with the income from his own estate. From this perspective, Flaubert remained an overgrown child. But this did not prevent him from displaying an unexpected bourgeois mentality when it came to Caroline's marriage. He allied himself with Mme Flaubert, wanting as she did to ensure that his niece would have a comfortable future, but not giving much thought to whether or not she loved the wood merchant Ernest Commanville. When the young woman confided in him about her reluctance, he believed it was his duty to convince her of the advantages of a promising matrimonial union. That she might love someone else seemed less important to him than the promise of a financially secure life. Ultimately, he was rather pleased to be highborn and to belong to a family of notables. One recalls the letter he wrote to his brother Achille during the *Madame Bovary* trial: "The only truly influential thing will be the name of *père* Flaubert ... At the Ministry of the Interior, they are starting to regret that they rashly attacked me." When Commanville's bad business dealings threatened to ruin, then really did ruin, the man of independent means, Flaubert's first instinct was to avoid bringing shame and dishonor to the family. As for looking for a remunerated profession, he saw it as a step down as inconceivable as if a marquis were forced into a commoner's livelihood. His friends had to push hard before he finally deigned to accept a disguised pension from the Ministry of Education.

The bourgeoisie he targeted was not a social category. He explained as much to George Sand: "Axiom: hatred of the Bourgeois is the beginning of virtue. As for me, I include in the word 'bourgeois' the bourgeois in overalls as well as the bourgeois in a frock coat. It's we, we alone—that is, the educated—who are the People, or, to put it better, the tradition of Humanity."[14] Reading this, one understands the indictment of Flaubert by Sartre and the Marxist critics: "When Flaubert declares, for example, that he 'calls bourgeois anyone who thinks basely,' he is defining the bourgeois in psychological and idealist terms, that is to say from the perspective of the ideology he claims to reject."[15] From the perspective of class struggle, Sartre is not wrong: Flaubert's anti-bourgeois stance is a moral and cultural critique.[16] But even if this critique comes *from the inside* and does not challenge the dominant position of the bourgeoisie, Flaubert's continuous attacks on the intellectual and spiritual poverty of the rich bear the stamp of an assertion of civilization against their uneducated arrogance. Flaubert accepted the contradiction between his social status and his freedom as an artist: "One must divide one's existence into two parts: to live as a bourgeois and to think as a demigod."[17]

As we have seen, it was not the bourgeoisie that Flaubert detested, but stupidity. At a young age, he became aware of what he called "the ridiculousness intrinsic to human life." Yet far from avoiding stupidity, he tracked it, archived it, and made it his vision of the world. As he wrote: "I like the revolting; it is a lower-rung sublime." He often repeated the word "sublime," and in a letter to his mother he writes of "sublime stupidity." He hunted down stupidity: it was undoubtedly "unshakeable," "immense," and "unbearable," but collecting illustrations of it from daily life, on his trips, and in his reading overjoyed him as much as it disgusted him. Stupidity inspired him! His body of work is full of stupidity and his correspondence overflows with it. It is an essential part of his representation of the world. Stupidity was like a backward idealism for the man who dreamed of an Antiquity full of togas and marble; it defined his era—modernity, the industrial age, and, without any doubt, democratic society, in which fools were as important as scholars.

We do not know whether Flaubert read Tocqueville. He refers to *The Old Regime and the Revolution* in an 1862 letter to Michel Lévy, but the correspondence never mentions *Democracy in America,* which is surprising on the part of this insatiable reader. The prophet of the democratization of mores, politics, entertainment, and literature perfectly described the end of aristocratic society and the triumph of the common and the trivial. But where Tocqueville accepts this major movement of history (albeit without enthusiasm), Flaubert uses Saint Polycarp to hyperbolically denounce the "unbearableness" of his era. While this "modern stupidity," this "universal stupidity," this "flood of cretinism" could affect everyone and every social class—no one had a monopoly on it—it is no coincidence that in Flaubert's eyes and in his writing it is most often conflated with the self-satisfied bourgeoisie of the nineteenth century. He perceived the stupidity in socialist doctrines—we've seen how he mocked socialism—but it was the bourgeois milieus he knew best that he viewed as the chief repositories of stupidity, because they combined the innocent stupidity of the nobodies with the smug stupidity of the opulent. Flaubert did not confuse the naïveté of someone like the maid Félicité in "A Simple Heart" or the idealist Dussardier in *Sentimental Education* with the novel's Dambreuse (a Paris banker) or Père Roque (a wealthy provincial). As a young man, he adopted Henri Monnier's caricature of bourgeois stupidity, Joseph Prudhomme; for many years, he referred to Louis Philippe's minister Adolphe Thiers as "king of the Prudhommes." It was no coincidence: Thiers, the pompous defender of property, was a figure who epitomized the reign of the bourgeoisie after 1830. Flaubert contrasted the striking example of bourgeois stupidity with a lost world. That this idealized world was undoubtedly imaginary explains why he situated his golden age so far away, in Antiquity, or in the desert, where there is nothing human—in an age or a place of eternal grandeur.

When it came to women, the bawdy Flaubert was a romantic. In the context of virile friendships, he outdid his companions in unseemly confessions and cynicism. No feelings allowed between men! Women only supplied a respite for these warriors of the quill. You had to boast of your good fortune, detail your "fucks," and share your recipes for better lays, just like hunters sitting around a table vaunting their aim, the spoils left to the dogs, and the day's tally. At Magny's and elsewhere, the words used to discuss the subject of women would not have been out of place in the crudest barracks talk—except when George Sand was present. This garrison house misogyny was not specific to Flaubert. These were the customs of the period, which are particularly visible among writers, since they left written proof of the profoundly non-poetic license they granted themselves. Flaubert threw his voice into the mix, laying it on thick, and mimicking this formulaic immodesty: "The hymn to the penis—to the 'member'—is fundamental," writes Alain Corbin, "in the dominant representations of masculinity."[18] But this saber-rattling did not fool his fellow revelers. There is a revealing passage from Edmond de Goncourt on the subject: during one of these men's dinners, Daudet launched into a confession of his perversities. Flaubert, wanting to play along, burst out: "But Daudet, I'm also a pig!" Daudet responded: "Come on, you're a cynic with men and a romantic with women!" Flaubert admitted it: "Well, it's true, even with women in a brothel, whom I call *my little angel*." Goncourt concludes: "Flaubert is a false pig, calling himself a filthy pig and affecting to be one to measure up to his friends, the honest-to-goodness filthy pigs."[19] One indeed has difficulty finding the filth in Flaubert. He visited brothels in Rouen, Paris, and Egypt, but ultimately did not much care for them. One does not find much evidence of the great romantic myth of the brothel in his work, except perhaps in *November*. The myth of the majestic prostitute, as in Balzac, is no longer operative. In his correspondence, Flaubert writes about prostitutes without poetry. He tells Louise Colet that "the prostitute is a lost myth" and that he has "stopped frequenting her, out of despair of finding her." In reality, only the first of the two assertions was true. Recommendations of favorite spots, the "discourse of demonstrative virility" (Alain Corbin), and countless allusions to visits to brothels—the trip to the Orient was also a form of sexual tourism—are found throughout Flaubert's letters, as well as those written by Alfred Le Poittevin, Maxime Du Camp, and Louis Bouilhet. But sexual release does not necessarily imply jubilation.

Flaubert stood out from his friends in that he practiced epistolary love—one sometimes even has the feeling that letters were enough to satisfy him. Faced with Louise Colet's demands, he rejected "disorderly loves" and "howling passions," preferring "voluptuous friendships and romantic gallantry." This type of ambiguous relationship, in which casualness satisfied both his taste for women and the pressing tranquility that his work demanded, continued throughout his entire life, whether with demimondaines like Jeanne de Tourbey (who married in 1873 and became the Countess of Loynes) or dear friends like Léonie Brainne. Brainne, the lovely widow who admired his books and called him "My Excessive Friend," may never have been his mistress, but she was the regular beneficiary of a sensual flattery often laced with gallantry: "I find you beautiful, kind, intelligent, witty, sensitive"; "Sincerely yours, with all sorts of desires whose object is not heaven, unless it be the heaven of your bed.—Forgive me! and all my affection."

While Flaubert also encountered and experienced love for a single person, he did so in his own fashion. We'll say no more about the adolescent passion he conjured up in Trouville for Élisa Schlésinger, who drove him to a state of "ecstasy" and inspired the character of Maria contemplated by the protagonist of *Mémoires d'un fou*. Flaubert's "great love" for Élisa has been turned into a monument through a confusion of youthful emotion with the torment of an entire life. To Flaubert, Élisa probably remained the poetic image of his first romantic stirrings. He still referred to Trouville in a letter written to her on October 2, 1856, and, much later, on September 6, 1871, he wrote of his "old tenderness" for this "old and dear friend," an expression he repeated on October 5 of the following year: "My old friend, my old Tenderness." Yet it would be a mistake to see his feelings for Élisa Schlésinger as an obsession. The memory of a first love is a poetic source, which Flaubert was able to employ to marvelous effect. Though it did not entirely disappear, the "apparition" of the beautiful lady at Trouville gave way to other feelings and more tangible pleasures such as the fervent encounter with Eulalie Foucaud, the beauty of Marseille, and, especially, Flaubert's long relationship with Louise Colet. For many years, Flaubert critics cast a harsh light on Louise Colet. They saw her as the avid ogress who bothered him with her whims and upset him with her vehemence.[20] But the way he addresses her in his letters has the authenticity of a man in love. In Louise, he found someone with whom he could exchange ideas and talk about literature. If we are to believe Flaubert, she gave him the opportunity to briefly stop separating "physical love" from *the other kind:* "You are the only woman whom I have both loved and possessed. Until now I used women to satisfy desires aroused in me by other women."[21] And also: "Don't you feel that between us there is an attachment superior to that of the flesh?"[22] But it was also during this romance that began just as he came to understand his vocation as a writer that Flaubert became aware once and for all that his own way of loving was incompatible with the demands of his mistress or with cohabitation with a woman—in fact with any attempt at matrimonial normalization. Before loving Louise, Flaubert was at peace, he could devote himself to his art. Then she came along and disrupted his resolution "not to love." Unlike Louise, who constantly made demands and pestered him to move to Paris, he accepted this physical separation so essential to his artistic output: "I could go a year without seeing or writing to you, still my feeling would not cool by one degree."[23] He told her that two people could love each other without seeing each other for ages. But Louise was all-consuming, exclusive, smothering: "It has been six weeks since I have *known* you (to use a decent expression), and I've done nothing. Yet I have to get out of this." Flaubert expressed his fear of love and "grand passions, exalted feelings, frenzied loves, and howling despairs": he wanted to write![24] Eventually he had to come to the cruel admission of April 1847. Louise and Gustave's romance would last a few more years, but the die was cast. For the rest of his life, Flaubert would never stray from his conception of the "main dish," namely art, to which one must devote everything.

The price to pay was that one had to curb one's passions and not marry or have children. You could see each other from time to time, enjoy the "combination of affection and pleasure," learn to separate "without despair." Louise considered Gustave's attitude selfish, proud, and unhealthy, but he would not relent. He told Mlle Leroyer de Chantepie: "As for love, I have never found anything but distress, rage, and despair in that supreme joy!" The little we know of his relationship with Juliet Herbert suggests that he found with her what Louise could not accept: a long-distance romantic relationship, interspersed with occasional sensual rendezvous, the delightful pleasure of being reunited—and probably writing to each other—and holding on to an affectionate mental image of the beloved. In other words, a "seasoning" added to life that was as necessary as it was safe.

The most unusual thing about Flaubert's relations with women, as we have seen time and again, is not in his romantic exchanges but in the plain and simple friendships he maintained with female correspondents whom he treated as equals.

Admittedly, he was not free of misogyny: he let slip a few generalizations about women, and went so far as to tell Louise Colet: "I have always tried (but I think I failed) to make you a sublime hermaphrodite. I want you to be a man down to the navel; below that, you get in my way, you disturb me— your female element ruins everything."[25] Far more surprising are his epistolary exchanges with women, which, while not lacking in affection or tenderness, do not fall into any strategy of conquest. His correspondence with George Sand is among the most beautiful of the genre, and their discussions on literature and politics are clearly the fruit of a relationship based on mutual respect and enthusiasm. His many detailed letters to Edma Roger des Genettes are full of insights and opinions. Possibly most unexpected is the collection of letters exchanged with the sensitive Marie-Sophie Leroyer de Chantepie, a rambling, constantly outraged zealot. Far from treating her as a tiresome admirer, he replied to her long letters with advice, encouragement, personal memories, and words of affection, though they would never meet in person.

Flaubert was truly not the same man when he wrote to women. Tender with his mother, erotic—or odious—with Louise, in cahoots with George Sand, and as delicate as can be with the provincial spinsters, he covered them in compliments and did his utmost, with restraint, audacity, and lamentation, to create with words a disarming character they could not help but love.

These letters exude a quality one would not necessarily have associated with the bear of Croisset: kindness. "Your letters prove to me," Mlle Leroyer wrote to him, "that your heart is on a par with your intelligence, and the profound esteem, the admiration I feel for their author grows along with that that is inspired in me by the good and sensitive man par excellence." Living in solitude, Leroyer had found a man who was "so good," "so kind" to her soul. She told him so again and again: "Besides the great intelligence that everyone admires, you have a heart, a kindness of which I can fully appreciate the value."[26] George Sand echoed these sentiments: "I do love you very much, you know, my dear old man. How perfect it would be to spend all year living close to such a good and great heart."[27]

He loved his mother deeply, until the very end, patiently putting up with the sourness that came over her as she aged. He transferred his childhood love for his sister lost in the prime of life to his niece Caroline, whom he probably overestimated. He wrote to Edma Roger des Genettes that his niece was "a Woman who is neither Bourgeois nor a Courtesan, which is a rarity." George Sand thought he had paternal instincts. Upon witnessing the jolliness at Nohant, he sighed: "Why do I have none of that? And yet I was born with every capacity for affection. But one doesn't choose one's destiny. One submits to it. I was a coward in my youth. *I was afraid* of Life. Ultimately, all accounts are rendered."[28] To another female correspondent, he admitted: "I adore children and was born to be an excellent papa, but fate and literature decided otherwise!—It is one of the melancholies of my old age that I do not have a little being to love and pet."[29] "Literature" had more to do with it than "fate." During his affair with Louise Colet, the prospect of conceiving a child was "dreadful." He rejoiced when he learned there would be no child: "That's one less unfortunate being on earth. One less victim of boredom, vice, or crime, and certainly of misfortune. It will be a good thing if I have no descendants."

Though he loved solitude and made it the necessary condition of his literary work, his was a relative solitude. It only became real upon his mother's death, at which point it weighed upon him increasingly heavily. Devoted to his art, Flaubert escaped from life, but with time his desertion aggravated the despair that had been natural to him from a young age and which sometimes "submerged" him, as he put it. Then, in the depths of unhappiness, he stood firm: "What supported me through all the storms was Pride, self-esteem."[30]

The contradictions of the *homo duplex* are nowhere more apparent than in Flaubert's take on politics. Throughout his life, in one way or another, he proved a friend of order and an enemy of authority—a conservative anarchist. He detested politics on principle, did not read the papers, and professed abstention: "I believe that whether we do everything we can for the progress of humanity, or nothing at all, makes no whit of difference."[31] But the apolitical stance he espoused at twenty-five had its limits. Between his birth in 1821 and his death in 1880, the century was molded by three major developments: the advent of the bourgeoisie in 1830; industrialization, which gave rise to the "social question" and the development of socialist doctrines; and finally, the democratic transition that found France shifting from a constitutional monarchy with severely restricted suffrage to a democratic republic over the six successive regimes that ruled from 1830 to 1880. All this upheaval could not leave him indifferent. His whole life long, he stood up against the reign of the bourgeoisie, which he denounced in the modern novels and in his correspondence. Yet he also expressed his outrage against socialist theorists: "Isn't the ideal state according to the socialists a kind of vast monster absorbing all individual action, all personality, all thought, and that will rule everyone and do everything?" Though he did not know the working class, he attacked the prophets of the proletarian order as furiously as he attacked the members of the party of bourgeois order. As for the progress of democracy, it only made him suspicious: he showed his hostility by denouncing universal suffrage, which he believed heralded the tyranny of the masses and the majority. He aimed to defend the individual and individual liberty against all the forces threatening or denying them—beginning with the people. "All the flags have been so sullied with blood and shit," he wrote to George Sand in 1869, "that it's time to do away with them. Down with words! No more symbols or fetishes! The great moral of the present regime [the Second Empire] will lie in demonstrating that universal suffrage is as stupid as divine right, even if somewhat less odious."[32]

Do these rejections add up to a political position? No. But they reveal attitudes and a sensibility more or less attuned to the evolution of society and the French government. Flaubert's most common attitude was an anarchist stance, hostility to any form of power, and the defense of the artist against anything that interfered with the production of his work: "In my view, the best [government] is one that is in its death throes, because it will give way to another." Yet Flaubert the anarchist needed public tranquility. He was therefore a friend of order. While he had previously been as deeply liberal as he was anti-democratic, Flaubert threw his support behind Napoleon III because he saw him as a lesser evil. He was undoubtedly not an adulator of the powers that be and was always ready to protest against their abuses, yet even the trial of *Madame Bovary* did not drive him to anti-Bonapartism. He became a regular at the salon of Princess Mathilde, proudly accepted invitations to the Tuileries and Compiègne, and accepted the "dishonoring" Legion of Honor. He was nonetheless more comfortable with the regime's liberal coteries; he sided with Prince Napoleon against clerical influence and congratulated Sainte-Beuve for his speeches in the Senate in favor of freethinking and freedom of the press. One could say that at the time he was a partisan of enlightened despotism, though in his eyes the expression would have been contradictory.

Then he changed. He was transformed by the shock of the war of 1870 and the Prussian occupation. The man who had found the idea of a homeland old-fashioned and felt as Chinese as he was French suddenly became a patriot itching for a fight. He joined the National Guard and made martial declarations. The surrender of Paris and the French defeat plunged him into a dark despair. When the insurrection of the Commune erupted in March 1871, he joined many fellow writers in expressing his outrage against the Communards. But all in all he considered them far less detestable than the spiked Prussian helmets that were tolerated by the bourgeois. "I am so exasperated with the Right," he wrote in January 1873, "that I wonder if the Communards weren't correct to want to burn Paris. For raving lunatics are less abominable than idiots. And their reign is always briefer." He never publicly manifested his hostility toward the Parisian revolutionaries; he considered the war in Paris "more tolerable" than the invasion. Unlike his friend Maxime Du Camp, he never became an ordinary supporter of the Assembly in Versailles.

Nonetheless, the events of the "terrible year" did not push him to join the democratic camp. He espoused a new idea in politics, which he had already partially formulated before the war and which called for a legitimate aristocracy, an aristocracy of the mind, with government by the "mandarins." He wanted to be done with universal suffrage and transform society from the top down: "It is no longer a matter of dreaming of the best form of government, . . . but of ensuring that Science prevails. That is the most pressing matter. The rest will follow of itself. Purely intellectual men have rendered greater service to the human race than all the St Vincent de Pauls in the world! And politics will continue to be nonsense as long as it's not a department of science. A country's government should be a branch of the *Institut*, and the most minor branch at that."[33] The mandarins were the country's experts, its technocrats, the people who knew. As Renan wrote at the time: "Democracy cannot escape its sluggishness without entering into terror. . . . The conscience of a nation resides in the enlightened part of the nation, which leads and commands the rest."[34]

This scientific daydream did not last. From 1871 to 1877, the form that the government was to take was hotly debated in a country divided between monarchists and republicans. Flaubert took a liking to Thiers, who had become the leading hope for a bourgeois republic. On July 2 and 9, 1871, voters in forty-eight departments were called to vote in by-elections resulting from the multiple elections in February. One hundred and fourteen seats were at stake. Flaubert told his niece that he had voted in Bapeaume (municipality of Canteleu). It was contrary to his habits, but he had already broken with tradition by voting in the municipal elections in April. This time, the republicans came out on top, winning close to a hundred seats. The idea of the republic was gaining ground. Even before he pronounced himself on the coming regime, Thiers embodied the project for a conservative republic supported by Flaubert: "Perhaps its very lack of edification is a guarantee of solidity? For the first time, we are living under a government that has no principles. Perhaps the age of Positivism in politics is about to begin?"[35] MacMahon succeeded Thiers and, as an ally to the clericalists, presided over the "moral order" that whipped Flaubert up into a frenzy. Never had he been so concerned with politics. He participated in the battle of May 16, attended Thiers's funeral and vaunted his patriotism, was delighted with the republicans' final victory, and admired Victor Hugo's speech on the occasion of Voltaire's centennial. In short, he increasingly agreed with the new idea of a peaceful republic that was ideologically discreet, socially moderate, and remained secular. He applauded when Jules Grévy replaced MacMahon. Adolphe Thiers had declared that "The Republic will be conservative or it will not be." His prediction had come true. And Flaubert, that virulent foe of the bourgeoisie, went along with it, while admitting that he was "a very measly republican."[36]

Critics on the extreme left have accused Flaubert of being reactionary and antisocialist. To do so is to judge him by the criteria of the century that followed his own. Liberal but antidemocratic, he feared the advent of the era of the masses, while rejecting the traditional—monarchical and clerical—order. From this perspective, he did not side with his era's right wing, or with the left. It makes more sense to label him a right-wing anarchist, an enemy of power—which was necessarily arbitrary—who was nonetheless hostile to any collectivist utopia—which was necessarily authoritarian. Yet labels remain approximate. To my mind, Flaubert's variable political line reflects the states of uncertainty in the century that followed the French Revolution and accompanied the slow formation of a democratic society, a process occasionally interrupted by social and political upheavals. The post-revolutionary era brought a wide range of turmoil: the premonition that a new world was coming into being, lack of stability, passion for equality, modernism in every domain, and the threat that tastes and mores would be reduced to the lowest common denominator. All this caught the writer Flaubert in a vice of contradictions, between the conformism of the victors—the bourgeois—and the threat of social and political democracy. He tried to stay above the fray, to dedicate himself to art, but one cannot discard history the way one discards old clothes. Flaubert was forced to give it its due. He tentatively felt his way, not without a certain coherence. In the end, Tocqueville was the theorist of the great democratic transition of the nineteenth century and Flaubert was its novelist—a melancholy, afflicted, and ironic novelist.

Though he did not get involved in colonial affairs, Flaubert's taste for "the Orient" preserved him from racist prejudices. On his travels, he saved his contempt for colonists and expressed his sympathies for the local people. He wore a fez, learned some Arabic words, followed the customs of the lands he visited, and behaved more like an ethnologist than a conqueror. His taste for order did not extend to the colonial order.[37] And while he detested the masses, the crowd, and the populace seen as a whole, he never displayed any feeling of superiority toward individuals of modest condition. This man who loved the social order could stand up for the Romani people, who were hated by the bourgeois but whom he admired.

As he himself recognized, Flaubert was also divided as a writer. He was born with a lyrical bent, considered himself an "old romantic," and had an "itch for epics," yet he also wanted to emancipate himself from the "blazes," to write "about nothing," and practice impersonality (while writing *Madame Bovary*, he noted that its "subject, character, effect, etc., all of it is outside of me"): he wanted the novel to be sustained solely by the internal strength of its style. The rule was clear: the prose sentence must be perfect. To achieve the sentence that would ultimately be printed, he had to search, dig, turn it backward and forward, and yell it out "in a hundred thousand different ways." Flaubert believed in work rather than inspiration: "Inspiration consists in sitting down at your desk at the same time every day." Contrary to what Maxime Du Camp claimed, his writing was not slowed down by his nervous disorder; if he composed his books slowly, it was not because he was sterile. It was a choice: "when I write something from my guts, it goes quickly. But there lies the danger. When you write about yourself, the sentence can be good in bursts (and lyrical minds achieve the effect easily by following their natural bent), but there is something lacking from the whole; there is an abundance of repetitions, commonplaces, banal expressions."[38] Along with this work on the sentence came the imperative of composition. Nothing was left to chance. He made meticulous outlines of his projected novels, seeking unity. "Unity, unity, that is everything," he wrote Louise Colet. He spoke of an "aesthetic mysticism" and, indeed, he lived his life as a mystic of art, "a quill-man" seeking Beauty as a saint seeks divine ecstasy.

In Flaubert, the religion of art is matched by a concern for truth. This can be seen as a paradox: why bother with the truth if the goal is beauty? But in

Flaubert's eyes, literature must take on "the appearance of science" and aim for impartiality and generality. "If your generality is powerful," he wrote to Louise Colet, "it will overcome or at least do much to compensate for the particularity of the anecdote." When the Goncourt brothers described their character Sister Philomène, he noted: "Next to Sister Philomène, I would have liked to see the generality of the nuns, who are not much like her." This sociological or historical ambition demanded significant research, including mountains of documents, trips to investigate his settings, interviews with specialists, and endless fact-checking; each novel was preceded by voluminous research files. The outlines and rough drafts for *Madame Bovary* alone take up four thousand pages. "For a single word or idea," he told Mlle Leroyer de Chantepie, "I do research, I get lost in endless reading and daydreaming."[39] The word "daydreaming" suggests that documentary research does not stop at the requirement for precision; it is also a source for picturesque images, unexpected visions, and dreams.

The subjects of Flaubert's work alternate between those that remain marked by his romantic nature and his taste for epics (*The Temptation of Saint Anthony*, *Salammbô*, "The Legend of Saint Julian," "Herodias") and those that earned him an unwanted reputation as a realist (*Madame Bovary*, *Sentimental Education*, "A Simple Heart," *Bouvard and Pécuchet*). It was as if he needed to take a rest from contemporary trivialities through the poetry of an imaginary Antiquity: "I am driven to write grand sumptuous things, battles, sieges, descriptions of the fabulous old Orient." Whatever he wrote about, he remained the demanding and perfectionist artist: "What shocks me in my friends Sainte-Beuve and Taine," he wrote to Turgenev, "is that they don't take sufficient account of *Art*, of the work itself, of its construction, of its style, in short of everything that constitutes Beauty."[40]

This imperative he proudly inflicted upon himself is part of a sacerdotal conception of the writer's work. Etymologically, *sacerdos* means "priest" in Latin and comes from *sacer*, "sacred." No writer has elevated the creative function to greater heights. Flaubert did not write to make money. He patiently avoided picking the fruit before it was ripe. His cult of beauty kept him away from any moral, social, or political utilitarianism. The author does not intervene directly, does not preach or come to any conclusions; it is the reader who must find the meaning and moral of a work. Art does not demonstrate, it suggests. Gustave Flaubert created a model for writers, which was misunderstood in his own time and continued to be rejected by many in the following century.

Curiously, one of the main reproaches his successors have made has to do with his style, but in this case style also encompasses his life and the rejection of life. "It remains to be demonstrated," writes Henry Laujol, "whether such an artist really needed to cloister himself to realize his full potential."[41] In any case, Flaubert was certainly unable to see things any other way. What is under attack is not style in and of itself, but the way of life that the artist believes must be adopted to achieve that style. As a faithful disciple of Stendhal, Paul Léautaud criticized Flaubert for his lack of spontaneity, while Paul Claudel doubted his natural talent and Claude Roy condemned "the clumsy stumbling of the writing, the pretentiousness of the images, the impropriety of the terms, the uncertainty of the syntax, the aural awkwardness." Later, proponents of socially engaged literature proscribed a literature that was supposedly impersonal but undoubtedly stuck to its social class. Responding to Sartre's condemnations, the writers of the nouveau roman (Nathalie Sarraute, Alain Robbe-Grillet, Michel Butor, Claude Simon, Robert Pinget) reestablished the prestige of Gustave Flaubert, the writer who put an end to the Balzacian novel and whom they turned into a canonical author.[42]

Beyond this experts' quibbling, posterity has made Flaubert one of the great masters of the French novel. His posthumous glory is attested both by the constant stream of studies of his work in France and abroad and the regular republication and translation of his books. In 1998, the French literary periodical *Magazine littéraire* compiled a list of Flaubert's "heirs" that included Henry James, James Joyce, Ezra Pound, Samuel Beckett, Franz Kafka, Mario Vargas Llosa, and even Sartre. One should add Jorge Luis Borges, Raymond Queneau, Georges Perec, Roland Barthes, Pierre Bergounioux, and countless other twentieth-century writers.[43] It should also be mentioned that in an era—our own—in which the tone is set by narcissistic literature, the model of "auto-fiction," and the power of the media, Flaubert's "intransitive" literature deserves deep consideration. The writer is expected to start from his own experience, but only so long as he can reach beyond it.

Whether repellent or inspiring, Flaubert has become an unavoidable reference. Jean-Paul Sartre devoted close to four thousand pages to laying him bare and still didn't get to the end of his work. Meanwhile, just as the young Victor Hugo declared his wish "to be Chateaubriand or be nothing," unknown novices labor before the blank page and the desk lamp, telling themselves "to be Flaubert or be nothing."

Chronology

1821

December 12. Gustave Flaubert is born in Rouen, to Achille-Cléophas Flaubert, thirty-seven years old, and Anne-Justine-Caroline Fleuriot, twenty-eight.

1824

July 15. Birth of Gustave's sister, Caroline.

1825

Julie begins working as a maid in the Flaubert household. She will remain with the family for fifty years.

1830

July 5. The taking of Algiers.

July 27–28–29. The July Revolution.

1832

May 15. Gustave enrolls at the Collège Royal in Rouen in the *huitième classe.*

1834

Flaubert is in *cinquième,* first literary efforts. Meets Louis Bouilhet.

1836

Meets Élisa Schlésinger in Trouville. Begins *Les Mémoires d'un fou.*

1837

Writes many stories, including "Bibliomanie" and "Une leçon d'histoire naturelle, genre commis," published in the small Rouen paper *Le Colibri.*

1838

Reads Rabelais and Byron. Completes *Les Mémoires d'un fou*, dedicated to Alfred Le Poittevin.

1839

In *classe de rhétorique* (last year of secondary school). Writes many stories, including "Smar, vieux mystère." His brother, Achille, marries Julie Lormier.

1840

In *classe de philosophie* (preparation for university admission). Expelled from the Collège. Prepares alone for the baccalaureate, and passes the exam in August. Travels in the Pyrenees and in Corsica. Meets Eulalie Foucaud de Langlade in Marseille. Writes his travel narrative *Pyrénées–Corse*.

1841

November. Registers at law school.

1842–1843

Studies law in Paris. Spends time with the Schlésingers and the Pradiers.

1842

August. In Trouville, meets an English family, the Colliers, whose daughters Henriette and Gertrude become his long-term friends.

November. Completes *November*.

December. Passes his first law exam.

1843

February. Begins the first *Sentimental Education*.

March. Meets Maxime Du Camp.

August. Fails the second law exam.

November. Meets Victor Hugo in the sculptor Pradier's workshop.

1844

January. First "nervous attack" on the road to Pont-l'Evêque. Drops out of law school.

June. The Flauberts settle at Croisset.

1845

January. Completes the first *Sentimental Education*.

March 3. Caroline, Flaubert's sister, marries Émile Hamard.

April–June. The Flaubert family accompanies the newlyweds on their honeymoon to Italy and Switzerland. In Genoa, sees Brueghel's painting *The Temptation of Saint Anthony* at the Balbi Palace.

1846

January 15. Death of Flaubert's father. Achille succeeds him at the Hôtel-Dieu. Gustave will live with his mother at Croisset and in winter quarters in Rouen, on rue de Crosne-hors-ville.

January 21. Birth of Caroline Hamard, Flaubert's niece.

March 20. Death of Caroline, Gustave's sister.

June. Meets Louise Colet at the home of the Pradiers. Begins an affair with Louise in July. Double marriage in the Le Poittevin family: Alfred marries Mlle de Maupassant, and Alfred's sister Laure marries his bride's brother. Flaubert befriends Louis Bouilhet.

1847

May–August. Travels with Maxime Du Camp in Anjou, Brittany, and Normandy, which inspires their joint effort *Par les champs et par les grèves*. Flaubert writes the odd-numbered chapters.

1848

February 24–25. February Revolution: Louis Philippe abdicates and leaves France.

April 3. Death of Alfred Le Poittevin.

April 23. Elections for the Constituent Assembly.

May. Begins writing *The Temptation of Saint Anthony*.

June 23–26. Insurrection following the closing of the Ateliers Nationaux.

August 21. Flaubert and Louise Colet break up.

November 4. Vote on the constitution of the Second Republic.

December 10. Louis-Napoléon Bonaparte is elected president of the Republic by universal male suffrage.

1849

September 12. Finishes writing *The Temptation of Saint Anthony* (first version). Reads it to Maxime Du Camp and Louis Bouilhet, who judge it unpublishable.

October 29. Sets off for the Orient with Maxime Du Camp.

1850–1851

Travels in Egypt, Syria, Rhodes, Constantinople, Greece, and finally Italy, where his mother joins him.

1851

June. Returns to Croisset.

July. Reunites with Louise Colet.

September. Begins *Madame Bovary*.

December 2. Coup d'état. Flaubert is in Paris.

1852–1854

Passionate correspondence and tempestuous relationship with Louise Colet. Du Camp publishes accounts of the journey to the Orient, outraging Flaubert.

1852

December 2. Advent of the Second Empire under Napoleon III.

1853

Corresponds with Victor Hugo, who is in exile.

1855

Rents an apartment in Paris, at 42 boulevard du Temple.

March 6. Sends his last letter to Louise Colet.

1856

September. *La Revue de Paris*, which is edited by Maxime Du Camp, publishes the first of six installments of *Madame Bovary*. Bouilhet's *Madame de Montarcy* is a smash at the Théâtre de l'Odéon.

1857

January–February. Madame Bovary trial. Fragments of *The Temptation of Saint Anthony* (second version) are published in *L'Artiste*.

April. Madame Bovary is published in book form by Michel Lévy.

September. Begins *Salammbô,* which he initially calls *Carthage.*

1858

April 16–June 6. Living in Paris. Travels to Tunisia and Algeria to do research for *Salammbô.*

1859

October. Publication of Louise Colet's *Lui.*

1860

In Paris, befriends the Goncourt brothers.

1862

April. Completes *Salammbô.* Signs contract with Michel Lévy.

June. Begins writing *Le Château des coeurs* with Louis Bouilhet and the Count d'Osmoy.

November 22. Beginning of the Magny dinners.

November 24. Publication of *Salammbô.*

1863

Begins corresponding with George Sand, the author of an article in praise of *Salammbô.* Meets Ivan Turgenev. Spends a great deal of time with Princess Mathilde. Polemics with the archaeologist Guillaume Froehner.

1864

April 6. His niece Caroline Hamard marries Ernest Commanville.

September. Begins the second *Sentimental Education.*

November. Visits the imperial family in Compiègne, after having been invited to the imperial residence at the Tuileries in March.

1865

February. Attends Prince Napoléon's ball with Louis Bouilhet.

July. Travels to Baden and visits Du Camp.

September. Princess Mathilde gives him a watercolor.

1866

July. Travels to England.

August 15. Receives the Legion of Honor.

November. George Sand stays at Croisset, after a first visit in April.

1867

Praises Sainte-Beuve's liberal speeches in the Senate.

1868

May. George Sand visits Croisset again.

November. Turgenev at Croisset.

1869

May 16. Completes *Sentimental Education.*

July 18. Death of Louis Bouilhet.

August. Moves to 4, rue Murillo.

October 13. Death of Charles-Augustin Sainte-Beuve.

November 17. Publication of *Sentimental Education.* The reviews are vicious.

December. Christmas at Nohant.

1870

June 20. Death of Jules de Goncourt.

July 19. War declared on Prussia.

September 4. Proclamation of the republic. Flaubert is a lieutenant in the National Guard.

September 19. The siege of Paris begins. Croisset is occupied by the Prussians.

Flaubert settles in Rouen in the Commanvilles' apartment on quai du Havre, after burying the manuscript of *Saint Anthony* in his garden.

1871

January 28. Paris surrenders, the armistice is signed.

February 8. Election of the National Assembly, monarchist majority.

March 18– May 28. Paris Commune.

March. Travels to England again.

April. Returns to Croisset and gets back to work on *The Temptation of Saint Anthony*.

1872

January 6. Opening of Bouilhet's *Mademoiselle Aïssé*, a failure. Publication of Bouilhet's *Dernières Chansons*, with a preface by Flaubert.

January 26. *Le Temps* publishes Flaubert's letter to the municipality of Rouen arguing for the monument to Bouilhet.

April 6. Death of Mme Flaubert. Caroline inherits Croisset.

June 20. Finishes writing *The Temptation of Saint Anthony* (third version).

July. Revises Bouilhet's *Le Sexe faible*. Accompanies Caroline to Luchon. Begins work on *Bouvard and Pécuchet*.

October 22. Death of Théophile Gautier.

1873

April. Brief stay at Nohant with Turgenev.

May 24. Adolphe Thiers steps down. Patrice MacMahon becomes president of the Republic. Beginning of the "moral order."

June. Completes *Le Sexe faible*. Charpentier becomes Flaubert's new publisher. First letter to Guy de Maupassant.

October 29. Death of Ernest Feydeau.

November. Completes his play *Le Candidat*.

1874

March 11. Opening of *Le Candidat* at the Vaudeville, a failure.

July. Stays in Switzerland.

1875

January–July. Vote on the constitutional laws.

April–May. Ruin of the Commanvilles' business. Flaubert sells his farm in Deauville. Leaves his apartment on rue Murillo and moves to 240, rue du Faubourg Saint-Honoré.

September. Stays in Concarneau on the invitation of Georges Pouchet. Begins "Saint Julian the Hospitaller."

1876
February. Begins "A Simple Heart."

March 8. Death of Louise Colet.

June 7. Death of George Sand.

1877
February. Completes "Herodias."

April 24. *Three Tales* is published by Charpentier. The book is a critical success but does not sell.

May 16. Jules Simon is forced to step down.

June 25. Dissolution of the Chamber of Deputies.

September. Death and funeral of Adolphe Thiers.

October 14–28. Legislative elections, victory of the republicans.

1878
Works on *Bouvard and Pécuchet*.

1879
January 27. Breaks his fibula.

January 30. MacMahon steps down.

October 7. Jules Ferry finds him a sinecure at the Mazarine library.

October. Falling out with Laporte.

1880
January. La Vie moderne publishes *Le Château des coeurs,* a *féerie* for which Flaubert could not secure a theater.

April 27. The last Saint Polycarp celebration is held at the home of the Lapierres in Rouen.

May 8. Flaubert dies of a stroke at the age of fifty-eight years and four months, leaving *Bouvard and Pécuchet* unfinished.

May 11. Funeral at the Cimetière monumental in Rouen, following a funerary mass at the church in Canteleu.

1881
March. Publication of *Bouvard and Pécuchet* by Lemerre. The property at Croisset is sold by Caroline Commanville.

1882
August 24. Inauguration of the monument to Louis Bouilhet in Rouen.

1884
Charpentier begins publishing Flaubert's correspondence.

1892
May 16. Opening in Paris of *Salammbô*, an opera by Reyer.

1910–1954
Publication of Gustave Flaubert's complete works by Conard, in twenty-six volumes, including thirteen of correspondence.

1921–1925
Centennial edition of the complete works edited by René Descharmes and published by the Librairie de France in fourteen volumes.

2007
Publication of the fifth and last volume of the correspondence in the Bibliothèque de la Pléiade.

A Compendium of Flaubert Quotations

Absolute

Only in the Absolute are we well off. Let us hold fast to that; let us keep climbing.[1] (1853)

One should imitate the fakirs who spend their lives holding their heads up to the sun, while vermin crawls all over their bodies. (1861)

Académie française

Several [of my friends] preach to me that I should stand for the Académie! But I have principles, and I will not expose myself to such ridicule. (1875)

When you are somebody, why wish to be something? (1878)

[On Maxime Du Camp, a candidate] Why go in for such nonsense? What honor is there in being proclaimed an equal to Messrs. Camille Doucet, Camille Rousset, Mézières, Viel-Castel, etc.? (1880)

Admiration

It does one good to have something to admire![2] (1873)

Arab

I love this fierce, persistent, hardy people, the last of the primitive societies, who lie in the shade of their camels' bellies at the noon break and smoke their chibouks while railing against our fine civilization, making it quake with rage. (1846)

Art

The cult of Art gives one pride; no one can have enough of it. Such is my morality.³ (1873)

Where is there anyone who relishes a good sentence? That aristocratic pleasure is in the realm of archaeology.⁴ (1878)

Attila

[Rouen] has beautiful churches and stupid inhabitants, I loathe it, I hate it, I call down upon it all the curses of the heavens because it witnessed my birth. . . . O Attila, you kind humanitarian, when will you come with four hundred thousand riders to set fire to this beautiful France, land of suspenders and trouser straps? And I beg you, please start with Paris and with Rouen at the same time. (1843)

Beauty

I am nothing but a literary lizard who warms himself every day in the great sun of Beauty. (1846)

What is beautiful is moral, that's all and nothing more. (1880)

Contempt for vainglory and profit is the first step to achieving Beauty. (1880)

Bourgeois

Above all else, one must defend Justice, yell at Authority—and stun the Bourgeois. (1867)

Be settled in your life and as ordinary as the bourgeois, in order to be fierce and original in your works. (1876)

Two things keep me going: love of Literature and Hatred of the Bourgeoisie, which is now summed up and condensed in what is called the Great Party of Order. (1877)

Buffoonery

There is nothing—no events, feelings, or people—over which I have not na-ïvely run my buffoonery, like an iron roller to smooth pieces of fabric. (1852)

Camel

If you want to know my secret and unremitting passion, I will tell you: camels. Nothing is as beautiful as those big melancholic animals with their ostrich necks and their slow gait, especially when you see them in the desert moving before you in single file. (1850)

Causality

The search for a cause is anti-philosophical and anti-scientific. I dislike reli-gion even more than philosophy because it claims the opposite. If something is due to a need of the heart, so be it. It is that need which is respectable, and not ephemeral dogmas. (1864)

Concluding

The rage to come to a conclusion is one of humanity's direst, most sterile com-pulsions. (1863)

Elsewhere

When I am somewhere, I try to be elsewhere. (1851)

Excess

Excess of any kind has always attracted me. (1846)

I only like confessions when they are excessive. For a gentleman to interest you by talking about himself, he must be exorbitantly good or bad. Giving the public the details of your life is a bourgeois temptation that I've always resisted. (1879)

Farce

Seeing things as a farce is the only way not to see them in a negative light. (1852)

Future

The future is the worst thing about the present.[5] (1839)

Genital organ

The good old genital organ is at the core of human tenderness; it is not tenderness itself, but its substratum, as the philosophers would say. Never did a woman love a eunuch, and if mothers cherish their children more than the fathers do, it is because they came out of their wombs, and the umbilical cord of their love remains tied to their heart, uncut. (1852)

God

I am repelled by the manner in which all religions speak about God—they treat him with such certainty, such nonchalance and familiarity. I am especially revolted by priests, who have his name on their lips incessantly. It's like a chronic sneeze with them: "God's goodness," "God's anger," "an offense against God." That's the way they talk. It means thinking of him as a man, and, what's worse, as a bourgeois.[6] (1859)

When one wants to *prove* God, that is when stupidity begins. (1879)

Great men

There have never been living great men. It is posterity that has made them. (1870)

Happiness

Happiness is a monstrosity; they who seek it are punished.[7] (1846)

To be stupid, selfish, and in good health, those are the three conditions required to be happy. (1846)

Never think about happiness; it attracts the Devil, for it was he who invented that idea to infuriate the human race. (1853)

Since happiness is not of this world, one must try to have tranquility. (1872)

Hate

Hate is a virtue. (1872)

Head

One writes with one's head. If the heart heats up, all the better, but do not say so. It must be an invisible oven. (1852)

History

Everyone is free to look at history in his own way, since history is nothing but the present's reflection on the past, and this is why it must always be re-written. (1864)

Honors

Honors dishonor, titles degrade, employment makes stupid. (1878)

Seriously, I am sorry to have the star [of the Legion of Honor]. What saves me is that I do not wear it. (1879)

Horse

Alexandria bores the shit out of me. It is full of Europeans; all you see are boots and hats, I feel as though I'm at the gates of Paris, without Paris. Finally, in a few days we'll be in Syria, and once there we'll get in the saddle for a long time! We'll be wearing big boots, galloping into the wind. (1850)

As for horseback riding, it is a talent in which I have considerably improved; I believe I am able to remain several days in the saddle without noticing it, and up until now none of the many nags I have mounted has unseated me; I have become a solid rider, if not an expert one. (1850)

Human, all too human

Lies during the day and dreams during the night, that is man for you. (1852)

Tolerable mortals are so rare! (1867)

For me, this is the principle: *one always has to deal with scoundrels.*—One is always deceived, duped, slandered, scorned. *But one must expect it.* And when an exception appears, thank Heaven. (1869)

More than ever, I feel the need to live in a world apart, at the top of an ivory tower, far above the mire in which the average man wallows. (1871)

Impartiality

When will history finally be written as one should write a novel, that is, without the slightest love or hate for the characters? (1852)

I believe that so far we have barely talked about others. The novel has only consisted of exposing the author's personality. I would even say that is true of all of literature, with the exception of perhaps two or three men. Yet the moral sciences must absolutely take another path and proceed like the physical sciences, with impartiality. (1857)

Individual

No one's individual will has any more influence on the existence or destruction of civilization than on the growing of trees or the composition of the atmosphere. (1852)

Nothing that relates to me appeals to me. . . . A man is no more than a flea. (1853)

[To Hippolyte Taine] I am grateful to you for exalting the individual, so belittled nowadays by democrassness [*démocrasserie*]. (1866)

Ink

Ink is my natural element. (1853)

Come on! Let's make our heads spin with the sound of the quill, and let's guzzle ink. It is more intoxicating than wine. (1861)

Irony

The irony does not detract from the pathetic aspect, but rather intensifies it.[8] (1852)

Liberty

All over the world, there is a general and permanent conspiracy against two things, namely, poetry and liberty. (1852)

Life

Life is something so hideous that the only way to bear it is to avoid it. And one avoids it by living in Art, in the constant search for the Truth rendered by Beauty. (1857)

Life is only tolerable with a hobby horse, some kind of work. As soon as you abandon your chimera, you die of sadness. You have to latch on to it and hope that it carries you away. (1863)

Literary people

Literary people are whores who eventually no longer orgasm. (1852)

Love

All the little stars of my heart converge around your planet, oh my beautiful celestial body. (1846)

As much as I like disorderly loves and howling passions in art, I prefer voluptuous friendships and romantic gallantry in practice. (1847)

The very legitimacy of the legitimate union, which is anti-legitimate, outside nature, and against the heart, is enough to chase love away. (1846)

Luxury

The more conscientiously we work, the less we benefit from it. I maintain this axiom with my head under the guillotine. We are luxury workers; no one is rich enough to pay us. (1866)

Melancholy

I carry within me the melancholy of the barbarian races, with their instinct for migration and their innate disgust for life, which made them leave their countries as if to get away from themselves. (1846)

I'll wind up like the canon of Poitiers mentioned by Montaigne, the one who had not left his room for thirty years "due to the inconvenience of his melancholy." (1879)

Newspapers

I have made a place for myself and I stay in it, making sure it always remains at the same temperature. What would I learn from those much vaunted newspapers you want to see me reading in the morning with a piece of buttered bread and a cup of coffee? What does everything they say mean to me? I have little curiosity about the news, politics bores me, serials plague me. All of that wears me out or irritates me. (1846)

No illusions

Learn once and for all that one should not ask apple trees for oranges, France for sun, a woman for love, and life for happiness. (1842)

Do not regret anything, for wouldn't that be to recognize that there is something good in the world? (1854)

Everywhere you look, you see nothing but tears, misfortune, misery, or else stupidity, infamy, base deeds, the acts of scoundrels, and other inconsequential things [*menus suffraiges*], as Rabelais put it. (1853)

Novel

In my view, a novelist does not have the right to give his opinion on the things of this world.—In his creation, he must imitate God in his own, that is to say, he must make it and keep quiet. (1866)

Nuances

Observe the nuances! The truth is only in the nuances. (1871)

Order

How stupid order is—or rather disorder, for that is nearly always what it is called. (1851)

Poetry

Through the monstrosities of existence, always contemplate the great blue sky of poetry, which is above and remains in place, while everything changes and passes. (1853)

Power

[After a fire] To "maintain order," we called in soldiers who crossed their bayonets against the workers, and cavalrymen who obstructed all the streets in the village. One cannot imagine the element of turmoil spread everywhere by Power. I went home feeling basely democratic. (1866)

What a splendid institution it is, Censorship! Axiom: All governments loathe Literature; one Power does not love another.[9] (1873)

Pride

Pride is a wild animal that lives in caverns and deserts. Vanity, on the contrary, is like a parrot, jumping from branch to branch and chattering in full daylight. (1852)

What has supported me through all the storms is Pride, self-esteem. (1879)

Religion

When the people no longer believe in the Immaculate Conception, they will believe in spinning tables. (1866)

What attracts me before all else is religion. (1857)

The 19th century is destined to see the collapse of all religions. Amen! I weep for none of them.[10] (1875)

Pius IX—the martyr of the Vatican—will prove baleful to Catholicism. The devotions he patronized are hideous: Sacré-Coeur, Saint-Joseph, Mary's womb, Salette, etc. It's like the cult of Isis and Bellona in the last days of paganism. (1879)

Deep down, there's something of the priest in me that no one suspects.[11] (1872)

Well yes, I am exasperated by any dogmatism. In short, materialism and spiritualism both seem irrelevant to me. (1879)

Resistance

We must employ every means to stop the flow of shit that is invading us. (1854)

Ruling element

What we need most of all is a *natural aristocracy*—that is, a legitimate one. Nothing can be done without a ruling element; and universal suffrage as it now exists is more stupid than divine right. You'll see some extraordinary things if it's retained. The masses, the many, are inevitably idiotic. I hold few convictions, but I do hold that one, and strongly. Nevertheless, the masses must be respected, however inept they are, because they contain seeds of incalculable fertility. Give them liberty, but not power.[12] (1871)

Sadness

I want a bitter undertaste in everything—always a jeer in the midst of our triumphs, desolation in the very midst of enthusiasm.[13] (1853)

When I think of my solitude and my worries, I ask myself whether I'm an idiot or a saint. (1864)

Each of us carries his necropolis within him.[14] (1866)

I'm crammed with coffins, like an old cemetery.[15] (1870)

Schools

I do not like doctrinarians of any kind. Down with Wardens! May all those who claim to be realists, naturalists, or impressionists stay away from me. Less talk and more art, you gang of clowns! (1878)

Science

If France is to rise again, she must pass from Inspiration to Science, she must abandon all metaphysics in favor of objective inquiry—that it, the examination of reality.[16] (1871)

Socialism

Neo-Catholicism on the one hand and Socialism on the other have made France stupid. Everything is either the Immaculate Conception or workers' lunches.[17] (1868)

Social mission

If you merely write verse or a novel, carve marble, shame! That was acceptable previously, before the poet had a "social mission." Now every piece of writing must have its moral significance, must teach its lesson, elementary or advanced; a sonnet must be endowed with philosophical implications, a play must rap the knuckles of royalty, and a watercolor contribute to moral progress.[18] (1846)

Stupidity

Stupidity is indestructible; nothing can attack it without shattering against it. It has the nature of granite, hard and resistant. (1850)

Deep down there is something stupid about humanity that is as eternal as humanity itself. (1866)

As for myself, I am frightened by universal Stupidity! It seems like a deluge to me, and I experience the terror that Noah's contemporaries must have felt when they saw the flood reach all the summits one after the other. Intelligent people should build something like the Ark, lock themselves in and live there together. (1874)

Human stupidity staggers me more and more! Which is imbecilic—one might as well be outraged at the rain! (1880)

Style

Style, which is something I take to heart, horribly agitates my nerves, I moan, I agonize. There are days when it makes me sick and at night it gives me a fever. . . . What a strange compulsion to spend your life wearing yourself out over words, and sweating all day long to smooth out the sentences.—There are times, it is true, when one feels excessive pleasure, but it comes at the cost of tremendous discouragement and bitterness. (1847)

May I die like a dog rather than hurry by a single second a sentence that isn't ripe![19] (1852)

Style is like music: what is most beautiful and rarest is the purity of sound. (1852)

My own style, which is natural to me, is the eulogistic and swollen style. (1853)

Style is life! It is the lifeblood of thought! (1853)

I know them well, the Pangs of Style![20] (1866)

The dramatic *style* is beginning to get on my nerves. Those short little sentences, the constant sparkle—it all irritates me; it's like Seltzer water, pleasing at first but soon turning stale.[21] (1873)

At night, the sentences rolling through my brain like the chariots of Roman emperors wake me with a start—by their constant jolting and rumbling. (1876)

Success

Success is a result; it must not be a goal.[22] (1876)

The moment something is profitable to my pecuniary interests, it revolts me as if it were a base act. (1876)

Unsure

Unless one is a moron, one always dies unsure of one's own value and that of one's works.[23] (1852)

Women

Women are too wary of men in general and not wary enough of particular men. (1852)

Only one poet, in my opinion, understood these charming animals—namely, the master of masters, Shakespeare the omniscient. His women are *worse* or *better* than his men. He portrays them as overenthusiastic beings, never as reasonable ones. That is why his feminine characters are at once so ideal and so true.[24] (1859)

As for love, all that I have ever found in that supreme joy is turmoil, storms, and despair. Woman seems an impossible thing to me. And the more I study her, the less I understand her. I have always stayed as far away from her as I could. She is an abyss that attracts and frightens me. (1859)

To get drunk on ink is better than to get drunk on brandy. The Muse, crabbed though she may be, is the source of less grief than Woman! I cannot accommodate the two. There has to be a choice. Mine was made long ago.[25] (1869)

[To Guy de Maupassant] You complain about women's asses being "monotonous." There's a very simple remedy: stop using them. (1878)

A Critical Anthology

Absolute

"The hand-to-hand combat with the sentence, the puffing and panting of a water-bearer as he stayed up all night, the collapse in a stupefied state on his divan over fifteen lines he would strike out at daybreak, that absurd asceticism was the only one within his reach, just as Croisset offered him the only cell where he could live as a recluse, since he had the misfortune of being able to reach for the absolute through the sentence and only through the sentence. *Salammbô* and *The Temptation [of Saint Anthony]* would later appear like enormous tumors of this disease of mysticism without an object."

François Mauriac, *Mémoires intérieurs*, in *Oeuvres autobiographiques*, Bibliothèque de la Pléiade (Paris: Gallimard, 1990), 442.

"The education and background of this dispossessed man prevented him from believing in the God of Isaac, Abraham, and Jacob, in the God of Jesus Christ. He no longer knew where to love or who to love, but he loved, and with all his strength, toward the only light that he could still see shining. Philosophers define God by saying that he is Truth, Beauty, and Good. Truth? Flaubert did not know where it was. Good? To him, all of morality rationally seemed no more than social conventions and human fictions. But Beauty? That he knew. It spoke to his heart. Art, the pursuit of Beauty was his own way, the only one he had left, of believing in what dominates the world, outlives the world, envelops, explains, and accomplishes it. This movement that carried him toward Beauty, so he would create a little more beauty, this momentum into which he threw his entire life, is indeed, literally, a love, his own personal way of accessing the necessary God, his affirmation of the Absolute."

Henri Guillemin, *Flaubert devant la vie et devant Dieu*, with a preface by François Mauriac (Paris: La Renaissance du Livre, 1963), 173–74.

Beauty

"For what is beauty? For Flaubert, it is analogous to absolute purity, to re-nunciation; when Flaubert says in reference to Musset that one must be able to separate poetry from sensations, the painting from the portrait, and music from serenades, and tells Amédée Pommier that the works of art he likes are those in which "*the art exceeds,*" it means not that he worships Beauty in and of itself, but that for him it is conquest, agonizing struggle, effort; it is in this sense that he pursues the style he envisions and that this pursuit is an arduous task, the refusal of any imperfection, of any concession to the author's personality. In a word, it is morality: "The morality of Art consists in its beauty, and I hold in highest regard, first, style, and then Truth." Beauty is only achieved through a struggle, a battle; it is the outcome of the struggle, it is the proof of the value in this battle, just as joy is its emotional standard."

Geneviève Bollème, *La Leçon de Flaubert*, 10/18 (Paris: Union générale d'éditions, 1972), 117–18.

Bourgeois

"Flaubert created more archetypes than anyone else in his century; unfortunately, they are lowly and everything about them is negative. And negative without grandeur. Flaubert was right to be enraged at this vile world, over which the vile biped he called the bourgeois ruled: he carries the bourgeois and puts him down everywhere. If he had painted gods, he would have put Bouvard in the skin of Jupiter and Pécuchet in Apollo. Deep down, there is insulting farce and derision in Flaubert. He has a medical spirit, it is the med student in him and the way he is coarsely connected to matter. That explains why your average doctor likes him so well. Like his art, Flaubert's soul is powerful and very vulgar. The gulf between Flaubert and Stendhal is no smaller than that between a Norman farmer and a Florentine nobleman or between a chalet in Pont-l'Evêque and a little palace in Perugia."

André Suarès, *Portraits et préférences* (Paris: Gallimard, 1991), 138.

"[To] be bourgeois under the Empire, [the bourgeois] must hate in themselves the bourgeois of the July monarchy. So it turns out that the artist, the bourgeois, and the practitioner share the same enemies. Behind the scenes the enemies are, of course, those spoilsports, the manual workers. On the level of ideology, they are embodied by the bourgeois of yesterday, that old man who must be cast off. Thus, when the writer uses a permanent catharsis to deny himself so his work might exist and do harm to the human race, he defines his public at the same time, since to the wealthy and the professionals he represents alienation lived as self-hatred, only *magnified*."

Jean-Paul Sartre, *The Family Idiot: Gustave Flaubert 1821–1857*, trans. Carol Cosman (Chicago: University of Chicago Press, 1994), 5:307.

Democratic insignificance

"What target was Flaubert aiming for [in *Bouvard and Pécuchet*]? . . . Is it a critique of heroes? We know that Flaubert proudly considered himself the first novelist able to mock his leading man and leading lady. Bouvard and Pécuchet provided him an opportunity to depict the true heroes of democratic times: antiheroes unable to drive forward a plot, who discourage any attempt at identification. Yet one should not see in this project a hatred for heroes and the plots that bring them to life, but rather a simple double observation: both heroes and novels become impossible in an era that denies any kind of transcendence. And this is why the book is not 'that novel about nothing' that Flaubert had told Louise Colet he dreamed of writing some day or other. Instead, it is a novel about the neutralization of existence carried out by democracy, on the outcome of this work on equality as according to Tocqueville, which the author had foreseen would also be a work on insignificance."

Mona Ozouf, *Les Aveux du roman* (Paris: Fayard, 2001), 232–33.

Depth

"Romantic in his hatred of the bourgeois, Flaubert was a naturalist in his persistence in describing him. That is also where his pessimism proceeds from. Flaubert's characters are types, one might say, but they are types of the most common reality, insignificant, drab, vulgar figures who have no character in and of themselves and who are in no way distinguishable from the surrounding spinelessness. While the romantics created heroes or monsters, he jealously banned any idealism, that of good but also that of evil. . . . And the triumph of his art is precisely that he gave this banality such depth."

Georges Pellissier, "Flaubert," in Louis Petit de Julleville, ed., *Histoire de la langue et de la littérature française des origines à 1900*.

Encyclopedism

"As an heir to the old tradition of the venerable men of letters who were savants first, he was prodigiously erudite. Aside from his vast library of books, which he knew as if he had just finished reading them, he kept a library of notes that he had taken about every volume imaginable, which he had consulted in public establishments and everywhere he had discovered interesting works. He seemed to know this library of notes by heart; he cited from memory the pages and paragraphs where the sought-after fact would be found, written down by him a decade earlier, for his memory seemed incredible."

Guy de Maupassant, "Gustave Flaubert," *L'Echo de Paris*, November 24, 1890.

"Flaubert was infected by the encyclopedic virus from the beginning. It is obvious in *The Temptation of Saint Anthony*, which is in its own way an essay on the lack of method in terms of religion and is no more anti-religious than *Bouvard and Pécuchet* is anti-scientific. . . . It is not easy to recover from the encyclopedic virus. We know where that left Aristotle, Isidore of Seville, and Leibniz. James Joyce was also afflicted with it, as was Rabelais, and like them, Flaubert dealt with his illness with elegance: aesthetically."

Raymond Queneau, preface to *Bouvard et Pécuchet* (Paris: Livre de Poche, 1959), 10–11.

Generation

"He forbids himself theories. But can you describe a life without a philosophy of life? By this means, the theory slips in despite the narrator. He had formed a conception of the world: universal determinism, dead-end pessimism. Against the "bourgeois" spirit that he abhorred and the romantic spirit he repressed to the depths of his being, he affirmed that true wisdom consisted in killing the illusion in one's self. Thus some have compared *Madame Bovary* and *Don Quixote*. Just as Cervantes mocked the exaggerations of the chivalrous ideal, Flaubert denounced the lies of romantic passion. In doing so, he tells us his own story, his gradual emancipation. But what he tells us even better is the story of his time: his body of work is driven by the spirit of a materialist and scientific generation, one that was hard and sensual, as hard as the heart, as sensual as the flesh of quivering Emma."

Pierre Moreau, "Flaubert," in *Dictionnaire des lettres françaises* (Paris: Librairie Arthème Fayard, 1971), pp. 401–2.

Glory

"Do not reproach Flaubert for the discouragement of his heroes and the disappointments they inevitably all suffer. His ironic pessimism turns away neither from life nor action. It only warns man that however beautiful his desires, they are nearly always unrealizable and that is where their beauty lies. But by a supreme irony, Flaubert's own life refuted this bitter philosophy better than any of his works. He had a goal and he reached it completely. His pride dreamed of becoming a great writer and he died in glory, and since his death his glory has only grown and brightened. Flaubert's glory is solid. It stands tall, beyond the reach even of foolishness, for the fools who would deny him would pay tribute to the greatest discoverer of human stupidity since Molière."

Rémy de Gourmont, *Promenades littéraires* (Paris: Mercure de France, 1963), 2:150–51.

Goodness

"He had no children but looked tenderly on other people's children, and my husband only ever called him good Flaubert; good he was, and pitiable and a faithful friend and above all of the pettiness of the profession."

Mme Alphonse Daudet, *Souvenirs autour d'un groupe littéraire* (Paris: Charpentier-Fasquelle, 1910), 18.

Impersonality

"The artist's work only fully interests me if I feel that it is both in direct and sincere connection with the outside world and in intimate and secret connection with its author. Flaubert made a point of honor of only fulfilling the first of these two conditions; but despite him, his work only moves us deeply in those places where it escapes him, so to speak, and tells us more than he wants to."

André Gide, *Essais critiques*, Bibliothèque de la Pléiade (Paris: Gallimard, 1999), 266.

"He makes me laugh, with his doctrines, his beautiful theories. He writes Louise Colet: 'the more personal you are, the weaker. . . . An author in his book must be like God in the universe, present everywhere and visible nowhere.' That does not prevent Flaubert from being present in all his books, perceptible in all his books, especially in those where he tells stories of the twelfth century. He is also present in all the others, in every sentence, in every word."

Georges Duhamel, "Flaubert," in *Tableau de la littérature française de Madame de Staël à Rimbaud* (Paris: Gallimard, 1974), 271.

Integrity

"Naturally, I cannot be accused of fanaticism when it comes to Flaubert, for all his books with the exception of one [*Three Tales*] exasperated me. Yet everyone knows the infinite toil of this man who was "as courageous as the lions"—as I said in a funeral oration in 1890—but persevered with an imbecilic idea and tried for twenty years to extract from his intestine the seditious and inextricable tapeworm of Inspiration.

Since he was no more than a striver, he was unable to create a work of genius, but he was undoubtedly one of the most *upstanding* writers one has ever seen. He left few books, because he was rarely satisfied with himself, if one can even say he was ever satisfied, and his books, which required such hard effort to write, were not made for the masses.

What would the incorruptible say now if he read *Lourdes* or *La Bête humaine*, seeing the reappearance every twenty pages of those formulaic isochrones of that thoughtless pendulum known as the author, whose perpetual back and forth movement would make even an albatross seasick?

What wouldn't he howl in his *gueuloir*, that stormy martyr to the sentence, if he learned that some slimy servant of the populace or some other messiah of the chamber pot and the toilet paper roll sometimes dared to mention him as a precursor?"

Léon Bloy, "Je m'accuse . . . ," in *Oeuvres* (Paris: Mercure de France, 1965), 4:167.

Literature

"This monk of art became the patron saint of men of letters, and could be the same to artists for comprehensively asking the following question: How can the artist achieve his salvation and attain glory? Here, I take the words salvation and glory purely in their theological sense. Christianity tells us that man only gets there through divine grace. As for the artist, he does not get there. It is his works that get there for him. He can make a masterpiece outside of himself. It rarely happens that he makes his life a masterpiece. But he can try. And it is beautiful to try courageously, and no one tried better than Flaubert.

Just as all of Plato's work centers on the problem of the life of the philosopher—and as that of the mystics centers on religious life—all of Flaubert's precious correspondence deals with the question of the literary life. Here, literature becomes a kind of thing unto itself, like philosophy or religion, next to which the rest does not exist. This is a new element. Gautier might have been the one to connect it with romanticism, but Flaubert was the first to establish it with all its developments and all its consequences. He was the first to put it in a central position."

Albert Thibaudet, *Gustave Flaubert*, Tel Collection (Paris: Gallimard, 1999), 289.

Masterpiece

"What does contribute to the balance and efficiency of *Madame Bovary*, unlike *Sentimental Education* where the mocking spirit definitively submerges the whole monotonously, is that all who affect the heroine closely—not only Léon and Rodolphe, but Justin, Father Rouault, and even Charles—are pulled sooner or later from the ordinary by the glint of a central fire, and surround Emma (for everyone is present throughout, or returns, until the end) with an orbiting ring of weak light that is enough to isolate the unalloyed grotesques that are Homais, Binet, or Bournisien, so that, from one end of the book to the other, she hardly seems to notice them. In rereading the novel, what struck me most was not the miserable failures of Emma's loves and fantasies, on which Flaubert dwells at length, but the intensity of the flame that brings his heroine to life and plants her, like a lit torch, in a sleepy town in the boondocks of Normandy. . . . Finally, in the last scenes (when Flaubert, moreover, clearly takes his heroine's side), the bovine placidity of Yonville is disturbed: this flying spark of errant passion is mere inches from setting fire to a village that is nevertheless so exemplarily fireproof.

It is this fury of a frantic will to live—slow to awaken, smoldering and finally exploding in the torpor of a small town like a time bomb—that for many definitively assures the book's greatness. The sinking down natural to

Flaubert is not consented to this time and with counterbalance, retrieves all its poetic potential. Once again, the lighting of a masterpiece changes with time: *M.L.F.* [the French women's liberation movement], like May 68 ("Think of your desires as realities"), close to a century later, find a deeply reflective surface in Emma Bovary, and make the book, for us today, a novel of awakening as much as a novel of failure: the awakening of the proselyte still in a savage state."

Julien Gracq, *Reading Writing*, trans. Jeanine Herman (New York: Turtle Point Press, 2006).

Model for living

"Once again I commune with Flaubert, the Flaubert revealed to us by the letters, who well knew how your work can benefit from the life you make for yourself. Like him, I need a Croisset where nothing other than my work will occupy the center of my daily life, where there will be nothing unforeseen, where no obstacle will accidentally divert the course of my regular secretion."

Roger Martin du Gard, *Journal* (Paris: Gallimard, 1992), 1:196.

Mystic

"Gustave Flaubert's toil would have been less exhausting if its aim hadn't been to find the 'right expression.' In fact, his was a heroic and difficult asceticism that was to make him experience that state in which the ego, after having broken all ties, returns to its envelope with all its attachments. Flaubert faces chaos and moves through confusion before the trigger of expression completes the operation that will result in a lasting precipitate. It is with a view to this 'mysterious chemistry' that we see him constantly preparing himself, gathering material, emptying his mind, putting himself in a state of expectation. There comes a point where the slightest impression from the outside disrupts him, the slightest disturbance oppresses him. Outside of time and space, he no longer even knows what life he is leading, his intimates turn into ghosts, and he goes into a catatonic state.

Is that the state of a writer in the mere grip of the 'pangs of style'? Isn't it rather that of a mystic awaiting his god, that of the scientist preparing for a discovery? The god may remain deaf to his call, the laboratory experiment may fail. What can he do, other than start again with more faith, more scruples, more meticulousness? What the nonbeliever considers lost forever, dried up or sterile, is the time of maturing, of the path toward light, self-evidence, and harmony."

Maurice Nadeau, *Gustave Flaubert écrivain* (Paris: Denoël, 1969), 327.

Nihilism

"Flaubert had had a double education. While he feasted on the novelists and poets, he was simultaneously subjected to a rigorous scientific discipline. The artist of images was a physiologist, and the lyrical artist was a meticulous scholar. There were too many elements colliding with each other in this complex personality, who was better prepared than any other to release the principle of nihilism that the Romantic ideal had enveloped in him."

Pierre Bourget, *Essais de psychologie contemporaine*, Tel Collection (Paris: Gallimard, 1993), 92.

"There was nothing of the nihilist in Flaubert. If he tried to take revenge on contemporary life by representing its collapse as precisely as possible, it was in favor of another life, one that was more intense, flamboyant, and absolute, of which even the most melancholy loss of illusion still contained the promise and portent. Only art shows the way. But humanity is still starting out and the road will be long."

Pierre-Marc de Biasi, *Gustave Flaubert. Une manière spéciale de vivre* (Paris: Grasset, 2009), 305.

Norman

"I had never seen anything like him in my life. He was tall, his shoulders were broad; he was vast, dazzling, and resounding; he wore a kind of brown sailor coat, a real pirate's garment, with poise; breeches as ample as a skirt hung to his heels. Bald and long-haired, his forehead wrinkled, his eyes pale, his cheeks red, his mustache colorless and drooping, he matched everything we read about the old Scandinavian chiefs, whose blood ran through his veins, but not unmixed.

Born of a father from Champagne and a mother of old Lower Norman stock, Gustave Flaubert was a son of the woman, his mother's child. He seemed entirely Norman, not a Norman of the soil, a vassal of the French crown, a peaceful and degenerate son of the companions of Rolf, a bourgeois or villain, a prosecutor or plowman, of avid and cunning genius, saying neither yes nor *vere*, but indeed a Norman of the sea, a king of combat, an old Dane come by the swans' path, having never slept beneath a plank roof nor emptied the beer-filled horn near a human dwelling, loving the blood of priests and gold taken from churches, tying his horse in palace chapels, a swimmer and a poet, drunk, furious, magnanimous, full of the nebulous gods of the north and keeping his steadfast generosity even when he pillaged. . . .

Gustave Flaubert was very good. He had a prodigious capacity for enthusiasm and sympathy. This is why he was always furious. He went off to war for any reason, constantly having an offense to avenge."

Anatole France, *La Vie littéraire* (Paris: Calmann-Lévy, 1889), 2:18–19.

Reactionary

"We should not be deceived by the facile solution that Flaubert adopted, the 'lump-everyone-together' he used to get himself out of the hornet's nest of his contradictions, and the outrageous fatalism he displayed. Flaubert was a thinker as reactionary as he was flat, who hatefully asked for the blood of the workers in revolt, who was repulsed by universal suffrage, and uttered some of the most atrocious cries that the fear of the people ever inspired in the nineteenth-century bourgeoisie (though there was no shortage of such)."

Claude Roy, *Le Commerce des classiques* (Paris: Gallimard, 1953), 238.

Release

"If Flaubert pursued stupidity as it manifested in certain ways of speaking with such dogged hatred, it is because he had had to significantly fight against it in himself. He sometimes naturally found himself writing the kind of expressions he must have been relieved to expel once and for all by marking them with the stigmatization of reproduction: initially he had some kind of thick coating, some kind of anonymous big vulgarity that shone through in his buffoonery, but not only there. I would not be surprised to learn that he experienced on some other level a tragedy like that of Gogol, who confessed to a friend that he had written *Dead Souls* to be rid of all the vices he felt inside himself by personifying them in as many characters: 'For, Gogol added, I have never liked my vices.' If anyone has a right to claim those words as his own, it is certainly Flaubert."

Charles Du Bos, *Approximations* (Paris: Plon, 1922), 166–67.

Style

"The trip to Rouen gave me the idea to reread *Madame Bovary*. . . . Well, to be frank, it doesn't grab me. I don't remember my impression of long ago. Today what I think bothers me is the style. There is really too much love of the form in there. This results in infinite monotonous passages, in my opinion, something that lacks the liveliness that can be achieved by a rapid, spontaneous, slightly neglectful style. There are also too many details on a single object. . . . I would compare Flaubert's style to varnish, and I don't like varnished things. . . . In all of Flaubert there is a lack of abandon that I find profoundly unpleasant, yes, I think I can say that."

Paul Léautaud, "September 1908," *Journal littéraire* (Paris: Mercure de France, 1986), 1: 651–52.

"Let us now counter-test the models that the masters of our time have provided us with. I will spare my reader and to find examples will not go rustling about in any old scribbler's work, but will take an eminently conscientious and respectable man, but poorly gifted, comparable to those old maids who serve as an example of all the virtues from within an austere sterility. On that note, observe that style is a natural quality like the sound of the voice, it is in no way the prerogative of professional writers. In Isabelle Rimbaud's letters, one finds something like a muffled echo of the fraternal instrument; perhaps a great writer only fulfills a certain tone that has been slowly developed and ripened by a family. In any case, one could take forty letters from butchers demanding payment. We would find ten whose authors have a feel for the French language for every thirty who don't. Flaubert belonged to the latter category; the torment of a deaf man trying to make a note he is unable to hear is one of the most moving agonies in the history of literature. . . . [His] isolated successes can hardly overshadow the dismal poverty, the zinc-lined tone of the whole of his work. My God, how it must have rained in Rouen."

Paul Claudel, *Positions et propositions* (Paris: Gallimard, 1928), 79–80.

"I must admit that I was astounded to see [Thibaudet] claim that there was little talent for writing to be found in a man who by his entirely new and personal use of the simple past, the compound past, the present participle, certain pronouns and certain prepositions renewed our vision of things nearly as much as Kant did with his Categories, his theories of the Knowledge and Reality of the outside world."

Marcel Proust, "À propos du "style" de Flaubert," *La Nouvelle Revue française*, January 1, 1920.

Truth

"Flaubert was very true. People exaggerate when they say his books are exclusively populated with scoundrels and imbeciles. They forget Mme Arnoux, Father Rouault, the old maidservant at the country fair, Justin, and even Bovary's mother. There are a few good people in Flaubert's books. They are a little narrow-minded, scattered here and there, as if they were dispersed through a world of imbeciles and especially scoundrels—in what proportion? In the proportion that may more or less be that of reality. . . . His task was to paint the French lower bourgeoisie, the middle class. Inanity, vanity, selfishness, not at all fierce, but prudent, attentive, and a little cowardly, weak moral sense, absence of any ideal, heavy and numb-skulled idiocy, that is what he has given us, which is more or less the truth. No perversity or genuine roguery, or in very low proportions; that too is sticking to the truth. . . . Balzac's great scoundrels and monstrous deviants are unknown to Flaubert. He does not know them; he has not seen them; that is because he is a good realist, he is the man who only truly sees average humanity, like Le Sage; that is because he is true. Truth was the first of Flaubert's muses, the one that was always one step ahead of all the others."

Émile Faguet, *Flaubert* (Paris: Hachette, 1919), 187–88.

Notes

Chapter 1. The Time and the Place

1. Charles Baudelaire, *Baudelaire: Selected Writings on Art and Artists*, trans. P. E. Charvet (Cambridge University Press, 1981), 225.
2. Philippe Muray, *Le XIXᵉ Siècle à travers les âges* (Paris: Denoël, 1984).
3. Alfred de Musset, *The Confession of a Child of the Century*, trans. David Coward (London: Penguin Books, 2012), 12, 15.
4. Maxime Du Camp, *Souvenirs littéraires* (Paris: Librairie Hachette, 1906), 1:118.
5. Musset, *Confession of a Child of the Century*, 17.
6. Pierre Berteau, "Docteur Achille-Cléophas Flaubert, chirurgien rouennais," *Bulletin Flaubert-Maupassant*, no. 15, 2004.
7. Gustave Flaubert, *Madame Bovary*, trans. Francis Steegmuller (New York: Vintage Books, 1992), 377. Unless otherwise indicated, all quotations from *Madame Bovary* are from this edition.
8. Gustave Flaubert, *Correspondance*, Bibliothèque de la Pléiade (Paris: Gallimard, 1973), 1:560.
9. Jean-Pierre Chaline, *Les Bourgeois de Rouen: Une élite urbaine au XIXᵉ siècle* (Paris: Presses de la Fondation nationale des sciences politiques, 1982), 123. The sum of 800,000 francs is roughly equivalent to 3,200,000 of today's euros, but the difference between the two currencies' purchasing power makes conversion difficult. For a breakdown of the estate, see Hubert Hangard, "L'Inventaire après décès d'Achille-Cléophas Flaubert," *Bulletin Flaubert-Maupassant*, no. 25, 2010.
10. Flaubert, *Correspondance*, 1:370.
11. See Jacques Le Goff and René Rémond, eds., *Histoire de la France religieuse*, vol. 3 (Paris: Le Seuil, 1991).
12. Flaubert, *Correspondance*, 2:376.
13. Gustave Flaubert, *The Letters of Gustave Flaubert, 1830–1857*, trans. and ed. Francis Steegmuller (Cambridge, MA: Belknap Press of Harvard University Press, 1979), 47.
14. See Antoine Prost, *L'Enseignement en France* (Paris: Armand Colin, 1968).
15. François Bouquet, *Souvenirs du Collège de Rouen par un élève de pension (1829–1835)* (Rouen, 1895), 12.

16. Gustave Flaubert, *Les Mémoires d'un fou*, in *Oeuvres de jeunesse*, Bibliothèque de la Pléiade (Paris: Gallimard, 2001), 477. Charles Baudelaire, also born in 1821, had similar feelings during the same period: "How bored we are at school, especially at the *Collège de Lyon*. Its walls are so sad, so grimy, so moist, the classrooms so dark," *Correspondance*, Bibliothèque de la Pléiade (Paris: Gallimard, 1973), 1:22.

17. Flaubert, *Letters of Gustave Flaubert, 1830–1857*, 15.

18. Bouquet, *Souvenirs du Collège de Rouen*, 69. *Antony* was a play by Alexandre Dumas.

19. Departmental archives of the Seine-Maritime, shelf number 1 T 1998 (microfilm 2 Mi 0777).

20. Flaubert, *Correspondance*, 1:5. In the French, Gustave misspells *prierais* (would be grateful) as *prirait*.

21. Flaubert, *Letters of Gustave Flaubert, 1830–1857*, 6.

22. Flaubert, *Correspondance*, May 14, 1831, Supplement, 5:925.

23. Flaubert, *Correspondance*, 1:12–13.

24. Flaubert, *Letters of Gustave Flaubert, 1830–1857*, 6.

25. Ibid., 133.

26. See excerpts of Alfred Le Poittevin's letters to Gustave Flaubert in *Correspondance*, 1:831–32.

27. Ibid., 1:589, 622.

28. Ibid., 2:774.

29. Gustave Flaubert, *The Letters of Gustave Flaubert, 1857–1880*, trans. and ed. Francis Steegmuller (Cambridge, MA: Belknap Press of Harvard University Press, 1982), 33–34.

30. Gustave Flaubert and George Sand, *Flaubert-Sand: The Correspondence*, trans. Francis Steegmuller and Barbara Bray (New York: Alfred A. Knopf, 1993), 180.

31. Edmond and Jules de Goncourt, *Journal*, Bouquins (Paris: Robert Laffont, 1989), 1:551. The *dragonnades* were the forced conversions and persecution of French protestants under Louis XIV.

32. Flaubert, *Correspondance*, 1:641.

33. Flaubert, *Letters of Gustave Flaubert, 1830–1857*, 9.

34. Ibid., 49.

35. Pierre Labracherie, "L'élève Gustave Flaubert au Collège Royal de Rouen," *Bulletin des Amis de Flaubert*, no. 10, 1957, 8.

36. Flaubert, *Correspondance*, 1:56.

Chapter 2. "Oh! To Write"

1. Flaubert, *Oeuvres de jeunesse*, 112.

2. Flaubert, *Correspondance*, 1:254.

3. Flaubert, *Oeuvres de jeunesse*, 9–10.

4. Flaubert, *Letters of Gustave Flaubert, 1830–1857*, 8.

5. Flaubert, *Correspondance*, 1:30–31.

6. Flaubert, *Oeuvres de jeunesse*, 388.

7. Bouquet, *Souvenirs du collège de Rouen*, 32.

8. Flaubert, *Oeuvres de jeunesse*, 305.

9. Flaubert, *Letters of Gustave Flaubert, 1830–1857*, 8.

10. Flaubert, *Oeuvres de jeunesse*, 523. Maurice Barrès's *Du sang, de la volupté et de la mort* [*On Blood, Sensual Pleasure, and Death*] was published in 1894.

11. Flaubert, *Oeuvres de jeunesse*, 293.

12. Ibid., 399.

13. Flaubert, *Letters of Gustave Flaubert, 1830–1857*, 9.

14. Victor Hugo, *La Préface de Cromwell*, in *Victor Hugo critique*, Bouquins (Paris: Laffont, 1985), 18.

15. Flaubert, *Letters of Gustave Flaubert, 1830–1857*, 54.

16. Flaubert, *Oeuvres de jeunesse*, 245.

17. Ibid., 536.

18. Flaubert, *Letters of Gustave Flaubert, 1857–1880*, 180.

19. Charles Baudelaire, *Les Fleurs du mal*, trans. Richard Howard (Boston: David R. Godine, 1982), 13.

Chapter 3. To Love

1. Flaubert, *Correspondance*, 1:790.

2. Gustave Flaubert, *Sentimental Education*, trans. Robert Baldick (London: Penguin Books, 2004), 8–9. Unless otherwise indicated, all quotations from *Sentimental Education* are from this edition.

3. Du Camp, *Souvenirs littéraires*, 2:338.

4. Émile Gérard-Gailly, *Flaubert et les fantômes de Trouville* (Paris: La Renaissance du Livre, 1930); *L'Unique Passion de Flaubert: "Mme Arnoux"* (Paris: Le Divan, 1932); *Le Grand Amour de Flaubert* (Paris: Aubier, 1944).

5. René Dumesnil, *Le Grand Amour de Flaubert* (Geneva: Éditions du Milieu du Monde, 1945), 70.

6. Flaubert, *Correspondance*, 1:761. See also Du Camp, *Souvenirs littéraires*, 2:337–38.

7. Flaubert, *Letters of Gustave Flaubert, 1830–1857*, 182–83.

8. Du Camp, *Souvenirs littéraires*, 2:338.

9. Flaubert, *Letters of Gustave Flaubert, 1830–1857*, 84.

10. Flaubert, *Sentimental Education*, 455.

11. Jacques-Louis Douchin, *La Vie érotique de Flaubert* (Paris: Jean-Jacques Pauvert aux Éditions Carrère, 1984).

12. Edmond and Jules de Goncourt, *Pages from the Goncourt Journal*, ed. and trans. Robert Baldick (London: Oxford University Press, 1962), 49.

13. Flaubert, *Letters of Gustave Flaubert, 1830–1857*, 9.

14. Claudine Gothot-Mersch also quotes René Dumesnil's assessment: literature may not have any "more complete, more exact, more profound [analysis] of the rise of desire in a man still a virgin." See Flaubert, *Oeuvres de jeunesse*, 1481–82.

15. Flaubert, *Correspondance*, 1:70.

16. Flaubert, *Oeuvres de jeunesse*, 660.

17. Ibid., 670.

18. Ibid., 684.

19. Ibid., 707.

20. Goncourt, *Pages from the Goncourt Journal*, 49.

21. Flaubert, *Oeuvres de jeunesse*, 774.

22. Eulalie Foucaud, letter quoted in Flaubert, *Correspondance*, 1:906.

23. Flaubert, *Letters of Gustave Flaubert, 1830–1857*, 50.

24. Flaubert, *Correspondance*, 1:400.

25. Douchin, *La Vie érotique de Flaubert*.

Chapter 4. A Change of Direction

1. Honoré de Balzac, *La Comédie humaine*, Bibliothèque de la Pléiade (Paris: Gallimard, 1976), 4:959.

2. Ibid., 4:1003.

3. See Léon's departure for Paris in *Madame Bovary* (p. 143): " 'Never fear!' said the pharmacist, making a clicking noise with his tongue. 'Think of the gay parties in restaurants, the masked balls! The champagne! Everything will go at a merry pace, I assure you!' "

4. Flaubert, *Correspondance*, 1:56.

5. Flaubert, *Letters of Gustave Flaubert, 1830–1857*, 15.

6. Du Camp, *Souvenirs littéraires*, 1:161. Flaubert was six feet tall.

7. Ibid., 1:168.

8. Flaubert, *Letters of Gustave Flaubert, 1830–1857*, 74.

9. Ibid., 20.

10. Ibid., 188.

11. See Berteau, "Docteur Achille-Cléophas Flaubert, chirurgien rouennais."

12. Flaubert, *Correspondance*, 1:169–70.

13. Ibid., 1:184.

14. Flaubert, *Letters of Gustave Flaubert, 1830–1857*, 22.

15. Du Camp, *Souvenirs littéraires*, 1:181–82.

16. "Flaubert vu par les médecins d'aujourd'hui," *Europe*, Sept.–Nov. 1969, 107–12.

17. René Dumesnil, *Flaubert, l'homme et l'oeuvre* (Paris: Desclée de Brouwer, 1947), 477–95.
18. Jean-Paul Sartre, *The Family Idiot: Gustave Flaubert, 1821–1857,* trans. Carol Cosman (Chicago: University of Chicago Press, 1991), 2:42–43.
19. Flaubert, *Letters of Gustave Flaubert, 1830–1857,* 165.
20. Gustave Flaubert, *The First Sentimental Education,* trans. Douglas Garman (Berkeley: University of California Press, 1972), 132.
21. Ibid., 133.
22. Ibid., 210.

Chapter 5. Death on the Horizon

1. Gustave Flaubert, *Bouvard and Pécuchet,* followed by the *Dictionary of Accepted Ideas* and the *Catalogue of Fashionable Ideas,* trans. Mark Polizzotti (Champaign, IL: Dalkey Archive Press, 2005), 305. Unless otherwise indicated, all quotations from *Bouvard and Pécuchet* and *Dictionary of Accepted Ideas* are from this edition.
2. Flaubert, *Letters of Gustave Flaubert, 1830–1857,* 27.
3. Ibid., 29.
4. Flaubert, *Voyage en Italie,* in *Oeuvres de jeunesse,* 1105. A reproduction of the painting can be found in *Album Flaubert,* Albums de la Pléiade (Paris: Gallimard, 1972), 52–53. The painting, traditionally attributed to Pieter Brueghel the Younger, is now in the Galleria Nazionale di Palazzo Spinola in Genoa.
5. See, for example, René Descharmes, *Flaubert, sa vie, son caractère et ses idées avant 1857* (Paris: F. Ferroud, 1909), chap. 3.
6. Flaubert, *Correspondance,* 1:237.
7. Flaubert, *Letters of Gustave Flaubert, 1830–1857,* 31.
8. Ibid., 33.
9. Ibid., 34.
10. Flaubert, *Correspondance,* 1:249.
11. Flaubert, *Letters of Gustave Flaubert, 1830–1857,* 27.
12. Ibid., 37.
13. Flaubert and Sand, *Flaubert-Sand: The Correspondence,* 137.
14. Flaubert, *Letters of Gustave Flaubert, 1830–1857,* 56.
15. Ibid., 38.
16. Ibid.
17. Flaubert, *Correspondance,* 1:740.
18. Flaubert, *Letters of Gustave Flaubert, 1830–1857,* 40.
19. Flaubert, *Correspondance,* 1:264.
20. Jean Bruneau, *Les Débuts littéraires de Gustave Flaubert* (Paris: Armand Colin, 1962), 580.

21. Flaubert, *Correspondance*, 1:238.

22. "Everything happened because it was fated to happen. Mock my fatalism if you will," he wrote to Louise Colet on August 11, 1846, "and tell me I'm behind the times in being a Turk. Fatalism is the Providence of evil: it is the Providence whose evidence one sees, and I believe in it." Flaubert, *Letters of Gustave Flaubert, 1830–1857*, 56.

23. Flaubert, letter to Louis Bouilhet, June 27, 1855.

Chapter 6. Louise

1. *Memoranda de Louise Colet*, in Flaubert, *Correspondance*, 1:807.

2. Théodore de Banville, quoted (in French) by Joseph F. Jackson in *Louise Colet et ses amis littéraires* (New Haven: Yale University Press, 1937), 121.

3. Sartre, *Family Idiot*, 124. As always with this imposing compendium, one must separate the wheat from the chaff. Sartre's interpretative power cannot leave one indifferent, though it also casts doubt on his most beautiful flashes of brilliance. One must at least keep in mind his hypotheses.

4. Charles-Augustin Sainte-Beuve, *Revue des deux mondes*, December 1, 1839, 709–11.

5. Letter of February 25, 1843, George Sand, *Correspondance* (Paris: Garnier, 1969), 63.

6. Flaubert, *Letters of Gustave Flaubert, 1830–1857*, 47.

7. Ibid., 64.

8. Ibid., 77.

9. Ibid., 72.

10. Ibid., 51.

11. Ibid., 46.

12. Jackson, *Louise Colet et ses amis littéraires*, 123.

13. Flaubert, *Letters of Gustave Flaubert, 1830–1857*, 88.

14. Ibid., 89.

15. Julian Barnes, *Flaubert's Parrot* (London: Jonathan Cape, 1984), 131.

16. Du Camp, *Souvenirs littéraires*, 1:257.

17. Ibid., 1:260.

18. Flaubert, *Letters of Gustave Flaubert, 1830–1857*, 92.

19. On March 11, 1848, Louise Colet also announced her pregnancy to her cousin Honoré Clair, making him believe that her sick husband had followed a course of treatment at Eaux-Bonnes in 1847 and had come home feeling strong: "His return to health had an effect on me which I could have done without. I am referring to a pregnancy already well along and which makes me very ill." Is this also what she told Flaubert? See *Lettres inédites de Louise Colet à Honoré Clair*, in *Cahiers d'études sur les correspondances du XIXe siècle*, no. 9, Clermont-Ferrand, 1999.

20. Flaubert, *Letters of Gustave Flaubert, 1830–1857*, 70.

21. Ibid., 73.

22. Ibid., 93.

23. Du Camp, *Souvenirs littéraires*, 1:264.

24. Flaubert, *Voyage en Bretagne. Par les champs et par les grèves*, introduced by Maurice Nadeau (Paris: Éditions Complexe, 1989), 329.

25. Ibid., 352ff.

Chapter 7. 1848

1. Flaubert, *Letters of Gustave Flaubert, 1830–1857*, 70–71.

2. Ibid., 93.

3. Maxime Du Camp, *Souvenirs de l'année 1848*, 2d ed. (Paris: Hachette, 1892), 69.

4. Ibid., 106.

5. Flaubert, *Letters of Gustave Flaubert, 1830–1857*, 94–95.

6. Alexis de Tocqueville, *Souvenirs* (Paris: Gallimard, 1964), 152.

7. Du Camp, *Souvenirs littéraires*, 1:277.

8. Flaubert, *Correspondance*, 1:801.

9. Du Camp, *Souvenirs littéraires*, 1:288–89.

10. René Dumesnil, *Gustave Flaubert* (Paris: Desclée de Brouwer, 1932), 133.

11. See Alexis François, "Gustave Flaubert, Maxime Du Camp et la révolution de 1848," and Gilbert Guisan, "Flaubert et la révolution de 48," *Revue d'histoire littéraire*, January–March 1953 and April–June 1958.

12. Flaubert, *Sentimental Education*, 298.

13. Ibid., 316.

14. Ibid., 149.

15. Ibid., 327.

16. Ibid., 320.

17. Ibid., 321.

18. Ibid., 334.

19. Flaubert, *Bouvard and Pécuchet*, 135.

20. Ibid., 137.

21. Flaubert, *Sentimental Education*, 327.

22. Victor Hugo, *Les Misérables*, trans. Norman Denny (London: Penguin, 1982), 987.

23. Flaubert and Sand, *Flaubert-Sand: The Correspondence*, 92.

24. Flaubert, *Sentimental Education*, 404.

25. Flaubert, *Bouvard and Pécuchet*, 146.

26. Ibid., 159.

Chapter 8. A Longing for the Orient

1. Flaubert, *Cahier intime de 1840–1841*, in *Oeuvres de jeunesse*, 748.
2. Muhammad Ali, quoted by Jean-Marie Homet in "La longue marche de l'obélisque," *L'Histoire*, no. 262, February 2002.
3. See Jean-Claude Berchet, *Le Voyage en Orient: Anthologie des voyageurs français dans le Levant au XIXe siècle* (Paris: Robert Laffont, 1985).
4. Flaubert, *Correspondance*, 1:505.
5. Du Camp, *Souvenirs littéraires*, 1:300.
6. Léon Letellier, *Louis Bouilhet, 1821–1869: Sa vie et ses oeuvres* (Paris: Librairie Ha-chette, 1919).
7. Flaubert, *Letters of Gustave Flaubert, 1830–1857*, 65.
8. Gustave Flaubert, *Voyage en Égypte*, ed. Pierre-Marc de Biasi (Paris: Grasset, 1991). *Voyage en Égypte* has also been published with Flaubert's notes on the rest of the trip in *Voyage en Orient*, ed. Claudine Gothot-Mersch, with Stéphanie Dord-Crouslé, Folio classique (Paris: Gallimard, 2006). The primary English translation of Flau-bert's writings on his travels in the Orient remains *Flaubert in Egypt*, trans. and ed. Francis Steegmuller (Boston: Little, Brown, 1972).
9. Maxime Du Camp, *Voyages en Orient (1849–1851)* (Messina: Peloritana, 1972).
10. Marie-Thérèse and André Jammes, *En Égypte au temps de Flaubert: Les premiers photographes, 1839–1860* (Paris: Kodak-Pathé, 1976).
11. Flaubert, *Letters of Gustave Flaubert, 1830–1857*, 109.
12. Flaubert, *Correspondance*, 1:766. The total is over 100,000 of today's euros.
13. Flaubert, *Voyage en Égypte*, 49.
14. Du Camp, *Souvenirs littéraires*, 1:320.
15. Flaubert, *Letters of Gustave Flaubert, 1830–1857*, 109.
16. Ibid., 105.
17. Ibid., 103.
18. Flaubert, *Flaubert in Egypt*, 19.
19. Ibid.
20. Du Camp, *Souvenirs littéraires*, quoted in *Flaubert in Egypt*, 24–25.
21. Flaubert, *Flaubert in Egypt*, 21.
22. Flaubert, *Voyage en Égypte*, 165.
23. Maxime Du Camp, *Souvenirs littéraires*, quoted in *Flaubert in Egypt*, 26.
24. Flaubert, *Flaubert in Egypt*, 29.

Chapter 9. From the Pyramids to Constantinople

1. Flaubert, *Letters of Gustave Flaubert, 1830–1857*, 114.
2. Ibid., 126.
3. Flaubert, *Flaubert in Egypt*, 52.

4. Ibid., 92.

5. Ibid., 160.

6. Ibid., 137.

7. Maxime Du Camp, *Le Nil*, quoted in *Flaubert in Egypt*, 138.

8. Flaubert, *Flaubert in Egypt*, 142.

9. Du Camp, *Souvenirs littéraires*, quoted in *Flaubert in Egypt*, 140.

10. Flaubert, *Flaubert in Egypt*, 80.

11. Ibid., 73.

12. Ibid., 86.

13. Ibid., 127.

14. Ibid., 202.

15. Gérard de Nerval, *Voyage en Orient*, in *Oeuvres complètes*, Bibliothèque de la Pléiade (Paris: Gallimard, 1975), 2:143.

16. Flaubert, *Flaubert in Egypt*, 44.

17. Ibid., 130.

18. Alain Corbin et al., *Histoire de la virilité* (Paris: Le Seuil, 2011), 2:124–154.

19. Flaubert, *Flaubert in Egypt*, 159.

20. Flaubert, *Letters of Gustave Flaubert, 1830–1857*, 131.

21. Ibid., 116.

22. Flaubert, *Flaubert in Egypt*, 84.

23. Jean-Paul Sartre, *L'Idiot de la famille* (Paris: Gallimard, 1971), 1:1049.

24. Douchin, *La Vie érotique de Flaubert*, 268.

25. Flaubert, *Voyage en Égypte*, 25.

26. Flaubert, *Flaubert in Egypt*, 129.

27. Ibid., 134.

28. Douchin, *La Vie érotique de Flaubert*, 119.

29. Flaubert, *Voyage en Orient*.

30. Flaubert, *Correspondance*, 1:657.

31. Flaubert quoted in Francis Steegmuller, *Flaubert and Madame Bovary*, corrected edition (New York: Farrar, Straus & Giroux, 1968), 187.

32. Ibid., 187.

33. Flaubert, *Voyage en Orient*, 248.

34. Flaubert quoted in Steegmuller, *Flaubert and Madame Bovary*, 187–88.

35. Ibid., p. 195.

36. Maxime Du Camp, *Souvenirs littéraires*, 1:372–73.

37. Gustave Flaubert, *Voyages et carnets de voyage*, in *Oeuvres complètes de Gustave Flaubert* (Paris: Club de l'Honnête Homme, 1973), 29–30; also Flaubert, *Voyage en Orient*, 349.

38. Flaubert, *Voyage en Orient*, 372.

39. Ibid., 375.

40. Flaubert quoted in Steegmuller, *Flaubert and Madame Bovary*, 204.

41. Ibid.

42. Flaubert, *Letters of Gustave Flaubert, 1830–1857*, 137.

43. Flaubert quoted in Steegmuller, *Flaubert and Madame Bovary*, 165.

44. Flaubert, *Letters of Gustave Flaubert, 1830–1857*, 113.

45. Ibid., 132.

46. Ibid., 123.

47. Ibid., 127–28.

48. Du Camp, *Souvenirs littéraires*, 1:355.

49. Maxime Du Camp, *Égypte, Nubie, Palestine et Syrie: Dessins photographiques recueillis pendant les années 1849, 1850 et 1851* (Paris: Gide et J. Baudry Editeurs, 1852). The book contains 125 photographs (approx. 21 x 16.5 cm [8 x 6.5 inches]) printed from Du Camp's paper negatives, three plates that are reproductions of daguerreotypes by Aimé Rochas, and three engraved maps. It was printed at the Blanquart-Evrard photographic print shop in Lille.

Chapter 10. Louise (Last and Final)

1. Flaubert, *Correspondance*, 2:28–29.

2. Ibid., 2:100.

3. Ibid., 2:113.

4. Ibid., 2:436.

5. Ibid., 2:358.

6. Flaubert, *Letters of Gustave Flaubert, 1830–1857*, 196.

7. Flaubert, *Correspondance*, 2:515.

8. Ibid., 2:529.

9. Flaubert, *Letters of Gustave Flaubert, 1830–1857*, 163.

10. Flaubert, *Correspondance*, 2:200–201.

11. Flaubert, *Letters of Gustave Flaubert, 1830–1857*, 180.

12. Flaubert, *Correspondance*, 2:878.

13. Flaubert, *Letters of Gustave Flaubert, 1830–1857*, 150.

14. Flaubert, *Correspondance*, 2:32.

15. Flaubert, *Letters of Gustave Flaubert, 1830–1857*, 174.

16. Flaubert, *Correspondance*, 2:331. Flaubert used the neologism *"pohétique"* to refer to overwrought lyrical poetry.

17. Ibid., 2:57.

18. Flaubert, *Letters of Gustave Flaubert, 1830–1857*, 192.

19. Flaubert quoted in Steegmuller, *Flaubert and Madame Bovary*, 276.

20. Flaubert, *Letters of Gustave Flaubert, 1830–1857*, 145.

21. Excerpts from Maxime Du Camp's letters to Gustave Flaubert, in Flaubert, *Correspondance*, 2:859.

22. Flaubert, *Letters of Gustave Flaubert, 1830–1857,* 154.

23. Ibid., 155.

24. Flaubert, *Correspondance,* 2:463.

25. Ibid., 2:469.

26. Flaubert, *Letters of Gustave Flaubert, 1830–1857,* 166.

27. Flaubert, *Correspondance,* 2:330.

28. Ibid., 2:540.

29. Ibid., 2:382.

30. Flaubert, *Letters of Gustave Flaubert, 1830–1857,* 170.

31. Flaubert, *Correspondance,* 2:892.

32. Professor F. Regli, "Pathologie psychiatrique et maladie organique," in *Pathographies* (no. 116).

33. P. Rentchnick, ibid.

34. Flaubert, *Correspondance,* 2:416.

35. Ibid., 2:543.

36. Ibid., 2:882.

37. Ibid., 2:447.

38. Louis Bouilhet, letter dated January 14, 1854, *Lettres à Gustave Flaubert,* ed. Maria Luisa Cappello (Paris: CNRS Éditions, 1996), 43. English translation in *Letters of Gustave Flaubert, 1830–1857,* 204.

39. Louis Bouilhet, quoted in Flaubert, *Letters of Gustave Flaubert, 1830–1857,* 205. Bouilhet appears to have had Flaubert's consent for this affair, if one is to judge by this note to Bouilhet in a letter dated December 8, 1853: "Ludovica.—You would be mistaken not to go out with her, she is a better lay than the Muse, inter nos." (Ludovica was Pradier's wife.)

40. Flaubert, *Correspondance,* 2:881.

41. Ibid., 2:282.

42. Ibid., 2:888.

43. Ibid., 2:131.

44. Ibid., 2:897.

45. Flaubert, *Letters of Gustave Flaubert, 1830–1857,* 202.

46. Ibid., 204.

47. Jackson, *Louise Colet et ses amis littéraires,* 221. In a letter to Bouilhet dated May 23, 1855, Flaubert refers to "our two angels."

48. Flaubert, *Correspondance,* 2:557.

49. Flaubert, *Letters of Gustave Flaubert, 1830–1857,* 215 (both Flaubert's letter and Colet's addition).

50. See Émile Gérard-Gailly, *Les Véhémences de Louise Colet* (Paris: Mercure de France, 1934).

Chapter 11. Emma

1. Flaubert, *Correspondance*, 2:1271.
2. Douchin, *La Vie érotique de Flaubert*, 186.
3. Flaubert, *Correspondance*, 2:562.
4. Ibid., 2:579.
5. Ibid., 2:589.
6. Ibid., 2:652.
7. Ibid., 2:600.
8. Flaubert quoted in Steegmuller, *Flaubert and Madame Bovary*, 313.
9. Flaubert, *Correspondance*, 2:643–44.
10. Ibid., 2:652.
11. Ibid., 2:654.
12. Ibid., 1:704. Flaubert also drew inspiration from *Mémoires de Madame Ludovica* [*Memoirs of Mme Ludovica*]—an unpublished manuscript on Pradier's estranged wife that was discovered in Flaubert's files (at the Rouen municipal library) by Gabrielle Leleu and published in its entirety by Douglas Siler in issue 145 of *Archives des lettres modernes* (Minard, 1973). Its unknown author describes Louise Pradier's forbidden loves and extravagant spending. Many correspondences have been established between this manuscript and *Madame Bovary*.
13. Bruneau, *Les Débuts littéraires de Gustave Flaubert*, 558.
14. Flaubert, *Madame Bovary*, 367.
15. Ibid., 224.
16. Flaubert quoted in Steegmuller, *Flaubert and Madame Bovary*, 315.
17. Maxime Du Camp quoted in Flaubert, *Letters of Gustave Flaubert, 1830–1857*, 218–19.
18. Ibid., 221.
19. Editorial note quoted in Steegmuller, *Flaubert and Madame Bovary*, 325.
20. Flaubert quoted in Steegmuller, *Flaubert and Madame Bovary*, 326.
21. Flaubert, *Letters of Gustave Flaubert, 1830–1857*, 195.
22. Stendhal, *Love*, trans. Gilbert and Suzanne Sale (London: Penguin Books, 1975), 141.
23. Flaubert, *Madame Bovary*, 43.
24. Ibid., 46.
25. Ibid., 42.
26. Marie de Flavigny, comtesse d'Agoult, *Mémoires 1833–1854* (Paris: Calmann-Lévy, 1927), 96.
27. Flaubert, *Madame Bovary*, 51.
28. Ibid., 52.
29. Ibid., 60.
30. Ibid., 65.

31. Ibid., 313.

32. Ibid., 342.

33. Descharmes, *Flaubert, sa vie, son caractère et ses idées avant 1857*, 103.

34. Flaubert, *Madame Bovary*, 327.

35. Charles Baudelaire, *Baudelaire: Selected Writings on Art and Artists*, 221. According to translator P. E. Charvet, "The general sense of the remark is that just as Julius Caesar would have been cramped on such a narrow stage as [the small Roman colony of] Carpentras, so Madame Bovary was cramped in her provincial surroundings" (p. 451).

36. Flaubert, *Madame Bovary*, 335.

37. Edmond and Jules de Goncourt, *Journal* (French), 2:641.

38. Flaubert, *Madame Bovary*, 97.

39. Flaubert, *Dictionary of Accepted Ideas* in *Bouvard and Pécuchet*, 320.

40. Pierre-Marc de Biasi, *Flaubert: Les secrets de "l'homme-plume"* (Paris: Hachette Livre, 1995), 66.

41. Flaubert, *Madame Bovary*, 11.

42. Ibid., 378.

43. Georges Pradalié, *Balzac historien* (Paris: PUF, 1955), 73.

44. Flaubert, *Dictionary of Accepted Ideas* in *Bouvard and Pécuchet*, 295.

45. Flaubert, *Madame Bovary*, 72.

46. Jean Cassou, *Quarante-huit* (Paris: Gallimard, 1939), 6–7. The comparison with Cervantes and Molière had previously been made by Montégut, in 1876, in the *Revue des deux mondes*. See Flaubert, *Correspondance*, 5:145.

47. Flaubert, *Madame Bovary*, 103.

48. Ibid., 92–93, 404.

49. Ibid., 255.

50. Ibid., 391.

51. Flaubert, *Letters of Gustave Flaubert, 1830–1857*, 185.

52. Flaubert, *Madame Bovary*, 391.

53. François Mauriac, *Trois Grands Hommes devant Dieu* (Paris: Hartmann, 1947), 88.

54. Flaubert, *Correspondance*, 1:210.

55. Flaubert, *Madame Bovary*, 169.

Chapter 12. Fame

1. Jean-Yves Mollier, *Michel et Calmann Lévy, ou La Naissance de l'édition moderne, 1836–1891* (Paris: Calmann-Lévy, 1984), 341ff.

2. In his *Lettres inédites de Gustave Flaubert à son éditeur Michel Lévy*, Jacques Suffel estimates that in 1862, after four reprints, the total number of copies in print was

29,150. Jean-Yves Mollier "raises these figures by about 20 percent and estimates the publisher's profits at a minimum of 35,000 francs, while the author only made 1,300 francs" (Joelle Robert, "Lettres de Flaubert à Michel Lévy," *Bulletin Flaubert-Maupassant*, no. 14, 2004).

3. Flaubert, *Correspondance*, 2:722.

4. Flaubert quoted in Steegmuller, *Flaubert and Madame Bovary*, 327.

5. Flaubert, *Letters of Gustave Flaubert, 1830–1857*, 224.

6. Yvan Leclerc, *Crimes écrits: La littérature en procès au XIXe siècle* (Paris: Plon, 1991), 141. Quote on "carnality": Flaubert, *Letters of Gustave Flaubert, 1830–1857*, 191.

7. Flaubert, *Letters of Gustave Flaubert, 1830–1857*, 226.

8. Du Camp, *Souvenirs littéraires*, 2:150.

9. Quoted by Jean Bruneau in Flaubert, *Correspondance*, 2:1369. Unless otherwise noted, the quotes from the reviews are taken from the Bibliothèque de la Pléiade edition of Flaubert's correspondence or from René Descharmes and René Dumesnil, *Autour de Flaubert: Études historiques et documentaires* (Geneva: Slatkine Reprints, 2002), vol. 1.

10. Flaubert, *Letters of Gustave Flaubert, 1830–1857*, 231.

11. This statement was utterly unfounded.

12. Flaubert, *Letters of Gustave Flaubert, 1830–1857*, 233.

13. Sainte-Beuve, quoted by Robert Kopp in "Outrageantes *Fleurs du mal* . . . ," *L'Histoire*, no. 323, September 2007.

14. Charles Baudelaire, *Baudelaire: Selected Writings on Art and Artists*, 250.

15. Flaubert, *Letters of Gustave Flaubert, 1830–1857*, 234.

16. Flaubert, *Correspondance*, 2:1382.

17. Article collected in Marie-Sophie Leroyer de Chantepie, *Souvenirs et impressions littéraires* (Paris: Perrin, 1890).

18. Flaubert, *Letters of Gustave Flaubert, 1830–1857*, 230.

19. Jean Bruneau collected Marie-Sophie Leroyer de Chantepie's letters in the Bibliothèque de la Pléiade edition of Flaubert's correspondence.

Chapter 13. Life in Paris

1. Flaubert, *Correspondance*, 3:14.

2. Ibid., 2:855.

3. Letter from Jules Michelet, quoted in Flaubert, *Correspondance*, 3:1119.

4. Edmond and Jules de Goncourt, *Pages from the Goncourt Journal*, 48.

5. Edmond and Jules de Goncourt, *Journal* (French), 1:537.

6. Ibid., 1:500.

7. Edmond and Jules de Goncourt, *Pages from the Goncourt Journal*, 98.

8. Hermia Oliver, *Flaubert and an English Governess: The Quest for Juliet Herbert* (Oxford: Clarendon Press, 1980). French translation: *Flaubert et une gouvernante anglaise: à la recherche de Juliet Herbert* (Rouen: Publications des universités de Rouen et du Havre, 2011).

9. Benjamin F. Bart, *Flaubert* (Syracuse: Syracuse University Press, 1967), 391.

10. Gustave Flaubert, *The Letters of Gustave Flaubert, 1857–1880*, ed. and trans. Francis Steegmuller (Cambridge, MA: Belknap Press of Harvard University Press, 1982), 3–4.

11. Flaubert, *Correspondance*, 2:713.

12. Flaubert, *Letters of Gustave Flaubert, 1857–1880*, 7–8.

13. Ibid., 9.

14. Gustave Flaubert, *Carnet de voyage à Carthage*, ed. Claire-Marie Delavoye (Rouen: Publications de l'université de Rouen, 1999), 64.

Chapter 14. *Salammbô*

1. Mollier, *Michel et Calmann Lévy*, 345.

2. Flaubert, *Correspondance*, 2:727.

3. Albert Thibaudet, *Gustave Flaubert*, Tel Collection (Paris: Gallimard, 1935; reprint, 1982), 136.

4. Gustave Flaubert, *Salammbô*, trans. by A. J. Krailsheimer (London: Penguin Books, 1977), 18. Unless otherwise indicated, all quotations from *Salammbô* are from this edition.

5. Ibid., 233, 234.

6. Ibid., 239.

7. Ibid., 250, 251.

8. See Jean Bruneau's note and citations in Flaubert, *Correspondance*, 3:1207–11.

9. Flaubert, *Letters of Gustave Flaubert, 1857–1880*, 39.

10. Charles Baudelaire, quoted by Jean-Benoît Guinot in *Dictionnaire Flaubert* (Paris: CNRS Éditions, 2010), 60.

11. Flaubert, *Letters of Gustave Flaubert, 1857–1880*, 37.

12. Flaubert and Sand, *Flaubert-Sand: The Correspondence*, 5.

13. Flaubert, *Letters of Gustave Flaubert, 1857–1880*, 38.

14. All Flaubert quotes: Flaubert, *Letters of Gustave Flaubert, 1857–1880*, 39–48.

15. Flaubert, *Letters of Gustave Flaubert, 1857–1880*, 50.

16. The cartographer Christian Théodore Falbe had published a map of the site and ruins of Carthage in 1831 (*Plan du terrain et des ruines de Carthage*), while Adolphe Dureau de la Malle had published his *Recherches sur la topographie de Carthage* [*Research on the topography of Carthage*] in 1835.

17. Flaubert, *Letters of Gustave Flaubert, 1857–1880*, 52.

18. Ibid., 61–62.

19. Flaubert, *Correspondance*, 3:274.

20. The French composer Ernest Reyer, a friend of Bouilhet, had planned to write an opera based on *Salammbô* with a libretto by Théophile Gautier. The libretto was eventually written by Camille du Locle, and the opera was staged at the Théâtre de la Monnaie in Brussels in 1890 and revived the same year at the Théâtre des Arts in Rouen.

Chapter 15. Caroline's Marriage

1. Caroline Franklin Grout, *Gustave Flaubert par sa nièce Caroline Franklin Grout: Heures d'autrefois. Mémoires inédits* (Rouen: Publications de l'université de Rouen, 1999), 155. *Heures d'autrefois* was found by Mme Lucie Chevalley-Sabatier, Caroline's niece. Her memoirs and the *Souvenirs intimes* [*Personal Recollections*] that prefaced the Conard edition of Flaubert's letters were published together in *Gustave Flaubert par sa nièce Caroline Franklin Grout*.

2. Grout, *Gustave Flaubert par sa nièce Caroline Franklin Grout*, 52.

3. Flaubert is referring to the character of the Old Sheikh that he and Du Camp made up during their journey to the Orient.

4. Grout, *Gustave Flaubert par sa nièce Caroline Franklin Grout*, 60.

5. This is Lucie Chevalley-Sabatier's hypothesis; see Grout, *Gustave Flaubert et sa nièce Caroline* (Paris: La Pensée universelle, 1971).

6. Flaubert, *Letters of Gustave Flaubert, 1857–1880*, 74–75.

7. See Jean Bruneau's note in Flaubert, *Correspondance*, 3:1305–6.

8. Ibid., 1301–2. Jean Bruneau mentions the "novel imagined by Gérard-Gailly" about Commanville, and cites Lucien Andrieu's article "Commanville," *AFl.*, no. 41, December 1972.

9. Grout, *Gustave Flaubert par sa nièce Caroline Franklin Grout*, 62.

10. The rate of stillbirths and infants dying before the age of one had dropped from 200 out of 1,000 at the beginning of the nineteenth century to 145 out of 1,000 in 1845, but began rising again under the Second Empire. The percent of women who died within two months of giving birth is estimated at 3 percent from 1800 to 1850.

11. Grout, *Gustave Flaubert par sa nièce Caroline Franklin Grout*, 63.

12. Ibid., 64.

13. Chevalley-Sabatier, *Gustave Flaubert et sa nièce Caroline*.

14. Flaubert, *Dictionary of Accepted Ideas* in *Bouvard and Pécuchet*, 305.

15. Chevalley-Sabatier, *Gustave Flaubert et sa nièce Caroline*, 77.

Chapter 16. The Hermit in White Gloves

1. Flaubert, *Correspondance*, 3:1342.

2. Ibid., 3:488.

3. Flaubert and Sand, *Flaubert-Sand: The Correspondence*, 61.

4. Flaubert, *Correspondance*, 3:343.

5. Edmond and Jules de Goncourt, *Journal* (French), 2:1031.

6. Flaubert, *Correspondance*, 3:414.

7. See André Billy, *Les Frères Goncourt* (Paris: Flammarion, 1954), and, for a slightly fictionalized version, Robert Baldick, *Dinner at Magny's* (Paris: Victor Gollancz, 1971).

8. Edmond and Jules de Goncourt, *Journal* (French), 2:961.

9. Edmond and Jules de Goncourt, *Pages from the Goncourt Journal*, 95.

10. Ibid., 78–79.

11. Flaubert, *Letters of Gustave Flaubert, 1857–1880*, 66.

12. Joseph Primoli, quoted by Jean Bruneau in Flaubert, *Correspondance*, 3:1401.

13. Ibid., 3:523.

14. Flaubert, *Correspondance*, 3:746. Notably, see his letter of May 9, 1868.

15. Flaubert, *Madame Bovary*, 411.

16. Edmond and Jules de Goncourt, *Journal* (French), 2:605.

17. Du Camp, *Souvenirs littéraires*, 2:269.

18. Edmond and Jules de Goncourt, *Pages from the Goncourt Journal*, 77–78.

19. The Goncourt *Journal* quoted in Flaubert, *Letters of Gustave Flaubert, 1857–1880*, 27.

20. Flaubert-Goncourt, *Correspondance*, ed. Pierre-Jean Dubief (Paris: Flammarion, 1998), 115.

Chapter 17. Monseigneur

1. Du Camp, *Souvenirs littéraires*, 2:155.

2. Flaubert, *Correspondance*, 2:329.

3. Edmond and Jules de Goncourt, *Journal* (French), 1:969.

4. Bouilhet, *Lettres à Gustave Flaubert*, 564.

5. Ibid., 544.

6. Edmond and Jules de Goncourt, *Pages from the Goncourt Journal*, 120.

7. Flaubert, *Correspondance*, 4:77.

8. Ibid., 3:383.

9. Bouilhet, *Lettres à Gustave Flaubert*, 647.

10. Flaubert and Sand, *Flaubert-Sand: The Correspondence*, 73.

11. "Mon pauvre Bouilhet," in *Flaubert, Vie et travaux du RP Cruchard et autres inédits*, ed. Mathieu Desportes and Yvan Leclerc (Rouen: Presses des universités de Rouen et du Havre, 2005).

12. Flaubert, *Letters of Gustave Flaubert, 1857–1880*, 131–32.

13. Guy de Maupassant, quoted in Letellier, *Louis Bouilhet, 1821–1869*.

14. See Flaubert's letter of January 28, 1872, to Edma Roger des Genettes, in which he describes how he staged "*Aïssé* alone, absolutely alone."

Chapter 18. Frédéric Is Not Me

1. He wrote to Louise Colet: "I loved one woman from the time I was fourteen until I was twenty" (Flaubert, *Letters of Gustave Flaubert, 1830–1857*, 49). Jean Bruneau and, later, Jacques-Louis Douchin, convincingly contested the myth of the "great love" developed by Émile Gérard-Gailly and repeated by René Dumesnil and others. According to Edmond de Goncourt, this passion "had taken hold of him when he was in the eighth grade, [and he] kept [it] deep in his heart, despite the brothels and banal affairs, until he was thirty-two" (*Journal* [French], 2:560). While Flaubert certainly passionately loved Élisa, his feelings had died out by 1862–1863, the period during which he conceived *Sentimental Education*.

2. Letter to Louise Colet dated November 7, 1847.

3. See Jean Bruneau, *Revue d'histoire littéraire de la France*, June 1983, which describes relations between Flaubert and the Schlésingers from 1851 to 1872. Bruneau also contests Gérard-Gailly's hypothesis that the farewell scene is taken from an actual episode.

4. Flaubert, *Correspondance*, 2:415.

5. Flaubert, *Letters of Gustave Flaubert, 1857–1880*, 72.

6. Ibid., 80.

7. Flaubert and Sand, *Flaubert-Sand: The Correspondence*, 41.

8. Ibid., 124–25.

9. Ibid., 126.

10. Notebooks in the collection of the Bibliothèque historique de la Ville de Paris, published by Marie-Jeanne Durry in *Flaubert et ses projets inédits* (Paris: Nizet, 1950).

11. Flaubert, *Sentimental Education*, 455.

12. André Vial, "De *Volupté* à *L'Éducation sentimentale*," *Revue d'histoire littéraire*, January-March and April–June 1957.

13. Baudelaire, *Some French Caricaturists*, in *Selected Writings on Art and Artists*, 228.

14. Louis Veron, *Mémoires d'un bourgeois de Paris* (Paris: Gabriel de Gonet, 1854), 49–50.

15. Flaubert, *Sentimental Education*, 128–37.

16. André Vial, "Flaubert, émule et disciple émancipé de Balzac," *Revue d'histoire littéraire*, July–September 1948.

17. Flaubert, *Letters of Gustave Flaubert, 1830–1857*, 187.

18. Flaubert, *Sentimental Education*, 422.

19. Ibid., 442–43.

20. Ibid., 21.

21. Ibid., 141–42.

22. Flaubert, *Letters of Gustave Flaubert, 1830–1857*, 160.

23. Flaubert, *Sentimental Education*, 390.

24. Ibid., 420.

25. Ibid., 393.

26. Ibid., 403.

27. Ibid., 448.

28. Vial, "Flaubert, émule et disciple."

29. Flaubert, *Sentimental Education*, 261–62.

30. Flaubert, *Letters of Gustave Flaubert, 1830–1857*, 133.

31. Ibid., 369–75.

32. Ibid., 450.

33. Ibid., 460.

34. Letter to Jules Duplan in Flaubert, *Correspondance*, 3:734.

Chapter 19. Frédéric Is Us

1. Alexis de Tocqueville, *Recollections,* trans. George Lawrence (Garden City, NY: Doubleday, 1970), 5.

2. Flaubert, *Sentimental Education*, 372–73.

3. Ibid., 87.

4. Ibid., 61.

5. Ibid., 152.

6. Flaubert, *Letters of Gustave Flaubert, 1830–1857*, 6.

7. Flaubert, *Sentimental Education*, 192.

8. Flaubert and Sand, *Flaubert-Sand: The Correspondence*, 92.

9. Flaubert, *Sentimental Education*, 255.

10. Ibid., 149–53.

11. Flaubert and Sand, *Flaubert-Sand: The Correspondence*, 110–12.

12. Flaubert, *Sentimental Education*, 214.

13. Ibid., 284.

14. Ibid., 404.

15. Ibid., 153. *Les Crimes des rois de France* [*Royal Crimes;* literally, *Crimes of the Kings of France*], by Louis Lavicomterie, was published during the Revolution and reissued in 1834. I have not found any reference to the *Mystères du Vatican* [*Mysteries of the Vatican*], but a book called *Les Mystères de la papauté* [*The Mysteries of the Papacy*] was published in London (n.d.).

16. Herbert J. Hunt, *Le Socialisme et le Romantisme en France* (Oxford: Clarendon Press, 1935), 325.

17. Flaubert, *Sentimental Education*, 251.

18. Victor Hugo, quoted by Eugène Silvain in *Frédérick Lemaître* (Paris: Alcan, 1930), 157.

19. Flaubert, *Sentimental Education*, 323.

20. Flaubert, quoted by René Dumesnil in his edition of *L'Éducation sentimentale* (Paris: Les Belles Lettres, 1958), 2:359.

21. Flaubert, *Sentimental Education*, 336.

22. Alexis de Tocqueville, *Democracy in America*, trans. Arthur Goldhammer (New York: Library of America, 2004), 541.

23. Ibid., 544.

Chapter 20. Cold Shower

1. Du Camp, *Souvenirs littéraires*, quoted in Flaubert, *Letters of Gustave Flaubert, 1857–1880*, 134–35. Vadius and Trissotin are quarreling poets in Molière's *Les Femmes savantes*.

2. See, in particular, "À propos du style de Flaubert," an article by Marcel Proust reprinted in Flaubert, *L'Éducation sentimentale*, Folio classique (Paris: Gallimard, 2011), 572ff.

3. See Mollier, *Michel et Calmann Lévy*, 401–3.

4. Flaubert, *Correspondance*, 4:127.

5. Jean Bruneau refers to the list of about 100 of these letters of acknowledgment, published by *Le Manuscrit autographe*, 1932, no. 37. See Flaubert, *Correspondance*, 4:1116ff.

6. Edmond de Goncourt, in Flaubert-Goncourt, *Correspondance*, 214.

7. Flaubert, *Letters of Gustave Flaubert, 1857–1880*, 134.

8. I consulted the following publications on the BNF's Gallica website and in the archives of the University of Rouen: *Le Figaro*, *Journal des débats* (two articles), *Le Gaulois* (three articles), *L'Opinion nationale*, *Le Pays*, *La Gironde*, *La Tribune*, *Le Constitutionnel*, *Le National*, *Journal de Rouen*, *Le Temps*, *Le Droit des femmes*, *Le Siècle*, *Paris-Journal*, *Revue des deux mondes*, *La Parodie*, *La Liberté*, *Journal officiel*, *L'Avenir national*, *Le Rappel*, *Bulletin des bibliophiles*, *Le Voltaire*.

9. See Jean-Yves Mollier, *Michel et Calmann Lévy*, 401.

10. Flaubert and Sand, *Flaubert-Sand: The Correspondence*, 168–73. The "Holbachian conspiracy" refers to Rousseau's claim in his *Confessions* that Baron d'Holbach was plotting against him.

11. Émile Zola, *Le Voltaire*, December 9, 1879.

Chapter 21. George Sand and the Old Troubadour

1. George Sand, *Correspondance* (Paris: Garnier, 1986), 21:734.

2. George Sand, *Agendas*, 6 vols., ed. Anne Chevereau (Paris: Jean Touzot, 1993), vol. 4 (1867–1871).

3. George Sand's birth name was Aurore Dupin; she became Baroness Dudevant by marriage. She took the pseudonym Sand (inspired by the name of her lover Jules Sandeau) for the publication of her first novel, *Rose et Blanche*.

4. See George Sand, "Le Théâtre des marionnettes de Nohant," in *Oeuvres autobiographiques*, Bibliothèque de la Pléiade (Paris: Gallimard, 1971), 2:1249–76.

5. Flaubert, *Correspondance*, 2:177.

6. Ibid., 2:856.

7. See George Sand, *Politique et polémiques*, ed. Michelle Perrot (Paris: Imprimerie nationale, 1997), 65–105.

8. George Sand, "À propos de l'élection de Louis Bonaparte à la présidence de la République française," *La Réforme*, December 22, 1848; article reprinted in *Politique et polémiques*.

9. Flaubert, *Correspondance*, 3:514.

10. Flaubert, *Letters of Gustave Flaubert, 1857–1880*, 83–84.

11. Flaubert and Sand, *Flaubert-Sand: The Correspondence*, 5–6.

12. Sand, *Agendas*, 3:334.

13. Flaubert and Sand, *Flaubert-Sand: The Correspondence*, 37. Also see George Sand's letter to Lina, in her *Correspondance*, 20:170.

14. Flaubert and Sand, *Flaubert-Sand: The Correspondence*, 61.

15. Ibid., 43–48.

16. Ibid., 52, 57.

17. Ibid., 73.

18. Ibid., 118.

19. Ibid., 92–94.

20. Ibid., 77.

21. Ibid., 187–88.

22. Flaubert and Sand quoted in Flaubert, *Letters of Gustave Flaubert, 1857–1880*, 144–46.

23. See Yvan Leclerc's study of Flaubert's royalties, "Les Droits d'auteur de Flaubert," *Bulletin Flaubert-Maupassant*, no. 27, 2012.

24. Flaubert and Sand, *Flaubert-Sand: The Correspondence*, 197–99.

25. Flaubert-Goncourt, *Correspondance*, 217.

26. Flaubert and Sand, *Flaubert-Sand: The Correspondence*, 202.

27. Mona Ozouf, *Les Mots des femmes* (Paris: Fayard, 1995), 198.

28. Flaubert and Sand, *Flaubert-Sand: The Correspondence*, 203–4.

29. Ibid., 74.

30. Flaubert, *Letters of Gustave Flaubert, 1857–1880*, 73.

31. Flaubert and Sand, *Flaubert-Sand: The Correspondence*, 204.

32. *Flaubert and Turgenev, a Friendship in Letters: The Complete Correspondence*, ed. and trans. Barbara Beaumont (New York: Norton, 1985), 49–50.

33. Flaubert, *Correspondance*, 4:211.

Chapter 22. War!

1. Flaubert, *Correspondance,* 4:216.
2. See Jules Vallès, *L'Insurgé,* in *Oeuvres,* Bibliothèque de la Pléiade (Paris: Gallimard, 1990) 2:968–69.
3. Flaubert and Sand, *Flaubert-Sand: The Correspondence,* 208.
4. Edmond and Jules de Goncourt, *Pages from the Goncourt Journal,* 171.
5. Flaubert and Sand, *Flaubert-Sand: The Correspondence,* 211.
6. Flaubert, *Correspondance,* 4:225.
7. Flaubert, *Letters of Gustave Flaubert, 1857–1880,* 159.
8. Flaubert and Sand, *Flaubert-Sand: The Correspondence,* 213.
9. Flaubert, *Letters of Gustave Flaubert, 1857–1880,* 162.
10. Edmond and Jules de Goncourt, *Journal* (French), 2:292.
11. Flaubert and Sand, *Flaubert-Sand: The Correspondence,* 215.
12. Flaubert, *Letters of Gustave Flaubert, 1857–1880,* 166.
13. Edmond and Jules de Goncourt, *Journal* (French), 2:365.
14. Flaubert, *Letters of Gustave Flaubert, 1857–1880,* 167.
15. In his 1871 book *Paris pendant le siège,* eyewitness Arnold Henryot wrote: "M. Gambetta galvanized the surfaces, but he was too poorly assisted to stir the country's deep layers; while Sir General Trochu, who had only to direct the patriotic torrent, remained convinced to the end that Paris did not have an army" (pp. 172–73).
16. Flaubert, *Letters of Gustave Flaubert, 1857–1880,* 168.

Chapter 23. The Paris Commune

1. Flaubert and Sand, *Flaubert-Sand: The Correspondence,* 221.
2. Edmond and Jules de Goncourt, *Journal* (French), 2:399.
3. Flaubert and Sand, *Flaubert-Sand: The Correspondence,* 222.
4. Edmond and Jules de Goncourt, *Journal* (French), 2:393–94.
5. Oliver, *Flaubert et une gouvernante anglaise,* 163.
6. Flaubert refers to the Russians' brutal repression of the Polish insurrection of 1863. Flaubert and Sand, *Flaubert-Sand: The Correspondence,* 224.
7. Elie Reclus, *La Commune de Paris au jour le jour* (Paris: Schleicher, 1908), 74.
8. Flaubert and Sand, *Flaubert-Sand: The Correspondence,* 225.
9. On Gustave Courbet's initiative, the Communards had destroyed the Vendôme column commemorating Napoleon's wars.
10. Flaubert, *Correspondance,* 4:310.
11. Flaubert and Sand, *Flaubert-Sand: The Correspondence,* 228.
12. Flaubert, *Correspondance,* 4:318–19.
13. Edmond and Jules de Goncourt, *Pages from the Goncourt Journal,* 193.

14. Flaubert, *Letters of Gustave Flaubert, 1857–1880*, 186.

15. Edmond and Jules de Goncourt, *Pages from the Goncourt Journal*, 194.

16. Francisque Sarcey, quoted by Gabriel Hanotaux in *Histoire de la France contemporaine*, 1871–1900 (Paris: Combet et Cie, n.d.), 203.

17. Flaubert, *Correspondance*, 4:342.

18. Maxime Du Camp wrote a four-volume history of the Commune entitled *Les Convulsions de Paris*. A single passage reveals the overall tone: "The orgy had been the principal concern of most of these men, supporting players in a drama they participated in without really understanding it. These men—and they were in the majority—cared neither for the advent of the proletariat nor for social renewal. They were looking for vulgar pleasure, found it without trouble, adding individual depravation to the general depravation, and considered themselves satisfied" (vol. 4, p. 115).

19. Edmond de Goncourt quoted in Lucien Descaves, *Philémon vieux de la vieille* (Paris: P. Ollendorf, 1914). This translation: Edmond and Jules de Goncourt, *Pages from the Goncourt Journal*, 194.

20. Du Camp, *Souvenirs littéraires*, 2:376.

21. Flaubert, *Correspondance*, 4:526.

Chapter 24. "The Being I Loved Most"

1. Flaubert and Sand, *Flaubert-Sand: The Correspondence*, 246.

2. Flaubert, *Correspondance*, 4:349.

3. Ibid., 4:350.

4. Flaubert and Sand, *Flaubert-Sand: The Correspondence*, 234–35.

5. Ibid., 237–40.

6. Ibid., 242.

7. Sand, "Reply to a Friend," in Flaubert, *Letters of Gustave Flaubert, 1857–1880*, 285–93.

8. Flaubert and Sand, *Flaubert-Sand: The Correspondence*, 243–45.

9. Ibid., 259–60.

10. Flaubert, *Correspondance*, 4:422.

11. Flaubert and Sand, *Flaubert-Sand: The Correspondence*, 255–56.

12. On this text's significance, see Liana Nissim, "La Préface de Gustave Flaubert aux *Dernières Chansons* de Louis Bouilhet," *Bulletin Flaubert-Maupassant*, no. 4, 1996.

13. Flaubert and Sand, *Flaubert-Sand: The Correspondence*, 304.

14. Ibid., 260.

15. Ibid., 271.

16. Flaubert, *Correspondance*, 4:100.

17. Caroline Franklin Grout, *Heures d'autrefois*, 50.

18. Departmental archives of Seine-Maritime, shelf number 2E8/340, and http:// flaubert.univ-rouen.fr.

19. In "Flaubert et Commanville," his contribution to the symposium "Flaubert et l'argent" ["Flaubert and Money"], Claude Vermeille shows that Mme Flaubert's will, which dates from 1871, was inspired by Ernest Commanville. The will was liable to annulment because part of the property of Croisset did not belong to Mme Flaubert, but neither Achille nor Gustave wanted to go against their mother's wishes. However, as specified by her will, Croisset was evaluated for division at the purchase price of 90,000 francs, while Vermeille shows that the valuation of the property must have been closer to 150,000 francs: "By imposing the purchase value of 90,000 francs, the grandmother gave the granddaughter 60,000 francs." One can easily see Commanville's influence in this decision. See *Bulletin Flaubert-Maupassant*, no. 27, 2012.

20. "Lettre autographe de Julie Flaubert, belle-soeur de Gustave, au sujet du testament de Mme Flaubert mère," by Arlette Dubois, *Bulletin Flaubert-Maupassant*, no. 27, 2012.

21. Flaubert, *Letters of Gustave Flaubert, 1857–1880*, 192.

Chapter 25. The Ups and Downs of Melancholy

1. Flaubert, *Correspondance*, 4:578.
2. Ibid., 4:608.
3. Ibid., 4:628.
4. *Flaubert and Turgenev, a Friendship in Letters*, 69–71.
5. Oliver, *Flaubert et une gouvernante anglaise*, 165ff.
6. Flaubert and Sand, *Flaubert-Sand: The Correspondence*, 285–87.
7. Ibid., 289.
8. Herbert's biographer writes: "It is more than likely that it was his letters, the hope of future encounters and the memory of past encounters that softened the sometimes little enviable burden of the governess." Oliver, *Flaubert et une gouvernante anglaise*, 175.
9. Flaubert, *Correspondance*, 4:1192.
10. Ibid., 4:607.
11. Edmond and Jules de Goncourt, *Journal* (French), 2:518.
12. George Sand, *Correspondance*, vol. 23, letter dated May 3, 1873.
13. George Sand, *Agendas*, 5:127–28.
14. Flaubert and Sand, *Flaubert-Sand: The Correspondence*, 310–11.
15. Flaubert, *Vie et travaux du R P Cruchard et autres inédits*, ed. Matthieu Desportes and Yvan Leclerc (Presses des universités de Rouen et du Havre, 2005). This volume includes "Alfred" and "Mon pauvre Bouilhet"—pages from Flaubert's journal written after the deaths of his friends.

16. Edmond and Jules de Goncourt, *Journal* (French), 2:537.

17. Flaubert and Sand, *Flaubert-Sand: The Correspondence,* 304.

18. Bouilhet, *Lettres à Gustave Flaubert,* 507.

19. Flaubert, *Correspondance,* 4:691, 713.

20. Edmond and Jules de Goncourt, *Pages from the Goncourt Journal,* 206.

21. Flaubert and Sand, *Flaubert-Sand: The Correspondence,* 338–341.

22. Edouard Maynial, *Flaubert* (Paris: Éditions de la Nouvelle Revue critique, 1943), 147.

23. Gustave Flaubert, *The Temptation of Saint Anthony,* trans. Kitty Mrosovosky (London: Martin Secker & Warburg, 1980), 69.

24. Ibid., 211–12.

25. Ibid., 149.

26. Ibid., 182.

27. Ibid., 191.

28. Jules Barbey d'Aurevilly, article dated April 20, 1874, in *Le XIXe siècle: Des oeuvres et des hommes* (Paris: Mercure de France, 1966), 237.

29. *Flaubert and Turgenev, a Friendship in Letters,* 91.

Chapter 26. Financial Ruin and Bereavement

1. Flaubert and Sand, *Flaubert-Sand: The Correspondence,* 361.

2. Ibid., 367.

3. Caroline Franklin Grout, *Heures d'autrefois,* 80. See Matthieu Desportes's note in the same volume, p. 210.

4. Vermeille, "Flaubert et Commanville."

5. Flaubert, *Correspondance,* 932.

6. Flaubert, *Letters of Gustave Flaubert, 1857–1880,* 220.

7. See above on Mme Flaubert's will, Chapter 24, and below, Chapter 28.

8. Flaubert, *Letters of Gustave Flaubert, 1857–1880,* 219.

9. Flaubert and Sand, *Flaubert-Sand: The Correspondence,* 375.

10. Jacques Lecarme, "Flaubert entre l'usure et la ruine," *Médium,* no. 16–17, July–December 2008, 107–26.

11. This and subsequent quotations from Flaubert and Sand, *Flaubert-Sand: The Correspondence,* 381–90.

12. Flaubert, *Letters of Gustave Flaubert, 1857–1880,* 234.

13. *Flaubert and Turgenev, a Friendship in Letters,* 102.

Chapter 27. "Blue Sky Ahead!"

1. Flaubert, *Letters of Gustave Flaubert, 1857–1880,* 239.

2. See Julian Barnes, *Flaubert's Parrot* (London: Jonathan Cape, 1984).

3. Flaubert, *Correspondance*, 2:614.

4. Gustave Flaubert, *Three Tales*, trans. Robert Baldick (London: Penguin Books, 1961), 87.

5. Ibid., 49, 56.

6. Flaubert, *Correspondance*, 5:279.

7. In *Flaubert devant Dieu* (Paris: Plon, 1939), Henri Guillemin develops the idea that Gustave Flaubert was an unwitting Christian. One reserves the right not to be convinced.

8. Edmond and Jules de Goncourt, *Pages from the Goncourt Journal*, 237–38.

9. *Flaubert and Turgenev, a Friendship in Letters*, 114.

10. Ibid., 134.

11. Edmond and Jules de Goncourt, *Pages from the Goncourt Journal*, 237.

12. Émile Zola, *Le Messager de l'Europe*, July 1880.

13. *Flaubert and Turgenev, a Friendship in Letters*, 129.

14. Oliver, *Flaubert and an English Governess*, 122.

15. *Flaubert and Turgenev, a Friendship in Letters*, 126.

16. Flaubert, *Correspondance*, 5:275.

17. In a letter to his wife, Jules Ferry reported "a million men, spread out in deep masses along the passage of the funeral procession, standing with their heads bare, reverential, everlasting flowers in their buttonholes." Quoted in Georges Valance, *Thiers bourgeois et révolutionnaire* (Paris: Flammarion, 2007), 397.

18. *Flaubert and Turgenev, a Friendship in Letters*, 130.

19. Flaubert, *Correspondance*, 5:343.

20. Émile Zola, quoted in Henri Mitterand, *Zola* (Paris: Fayard, 2001), 2:394.

21. See Jean-Pierre van Deth, *Ernest Renan* (Paris: Fayard, 2012), 392–404.

22. Charles-Edmond, quoted in ibid., 397.

Chapter 28. "Everything Infuriates and Weighs Upon Me"

1. Flaubert, *Correspondance*, 5:530.

2. Ibid., 5:459.

3. *Flaubert and Turgenev, a Friendship in Letters*, 153, 156.

4. Flaubert, *Letters of Gustave Flaubert, 1857–1880*, 252.

5. Guy de Maupassant, quoted in Flaubert, *Correspondance*, 5:1345.

6. Flaubert, *Correspondance*, 685.

7. Edmond and Jules de Goncourt, *Pages from the Goncourt Journal*, 252–53.

8. Flaubert, *Lettres inédites à Raoul Duval*, ed. Georges Normandy (Paris: Albin Michel, 1950), 231.

9. *Le Figaro*, October 14, 1893.

10. Caroline Franklin Grout, quoted in Dumesnil, *Flaubert, l'homme et l'œuvre*, 293.

11. René Descharmes, quoted in ibid.

12. Ernest Laporte, quoted in Flaubert, *Letters of Gustave Flaubert, 1857–1880*, 295.

13. Flaubert, *Correspondance: Supplément (juillet 1877–mai 1880)*, ed. René Dumesnil, Jean Pommier, and Claude Digeon (Paris: Éditions Louis Conard, 1954), 266–67.

14. *Flaubert and Turgenev, a Friendship in Letters*, 161.

15. Ibid., 174–75.

16. Edmond and Jules de Goncourt, *Journal* (French), 2:781.

17. Edmond and Jules de Goncourt, *Pages from the Goncourt Journal*, 248.

18. Flaubert, *Letters of Gustave Flaubert, 1857–1880*, 242.

19. Zola, *Le Voltaire*, December 9, 1879.

20. See Leclerc, *Crimes écrits*, 387.

21. Guy de Maupassant, "Gustave Flaubert," *L'Écho de Paris*, November 24, 1890.

22. Flaubert, *Letters of Gustave Flaubert, 1857–1880*, 270–71.

23. Flaubert, *Correspondance*, 5:403.

24. Ibid., 5:403. See "Discours pour Voltaire," in Victor Hugo, *Politique*, Bouquins (Paris: Robert Laffont, 1985), 984–91.

25. *Translator's note:* Jean Calas was a protestant merchant in Toulouse accused of murdering his son to prevent him from converting to Catholicism (it appears he was in fact hiding his son's suicide to avoid religious sanctions); Calas was publicly executed in 1762. The Chevalier de la Barre was a French nobleman executed in 1766 for blasphemy and sacrilege. Voltaire fought to get both men's names cleared.

26. Flaubert, *Correspondance*, 5:616.

27. Flaubert, *Letters of Gustave Flaubert, 1857–1880*, 274.

28. Edmond and Jules de Goncourt, *Pages from the Goncourt Journal*, 264.

29. Account collected and quoted by Georges Normandy in *Lettres de Flaubert à Raoul-Duval*, 252.

30. Ibid., 260. *Concours médical*, January 22, 1939.

31. See Daniel Fauvel and Matthieu Desportes, "Inventaire après décès des biens de Gustave Flaubert," *Bulletin Flaubert-Maupassant*, no. 8, 2000.

32. Gaston Vassy, *Gil Blas*, May 13, 1880.

Chapter 29. Post Mortem

1. Guy de Maupassant, *Correspondance*, vol. 1, no. 178.

2. Edmond and Jules de Goncourt, *Journal* (French), 3:497. For the full case file on the history of this monument, see Flaubert-Goncourt, *Correspondance*, 293–315.

3. Du Camp, *Souvenirs littéraires*, 1:185.

4. Léon Chapron, quoted in Nadine Satiat, *Maupassant* (Paris: Flammarion, 2003), 250–51.

5. Edmond and Jules de Goncourt, *Pages from the Goncourt Journal*, 264.

6. Flaubert, *Letters of Gustave Flaubert, 1857–1880*, 72.

7. The story is also included in the appendix to Flaubert's complete works, *Oeuvres complètes*, Bibliothèque de la Pléiade (Paris: Gallimard, 1952), 2:992–97.

8. Flaubert, *Correspondance*, 5:535.

9. Flaubert, *Letters of Gustave Flaubert, 1857–1880*, 263.

10. Flaubert, *Bouvard and Pécuchet*, 146–47.

11. Ibid., 159.

12. Ibid., 205.

13. Ibid., 10.

14. In the *Dictionary of Accepted Ideas*, the entry on "LEARNED (person)" reads: "Make fun of him."

15. Flaubert, quoted in the introduction to the Folio Classique edition of *Bouvard et Pécuchet* by Claudine Gothot-Mersch, p. 22.

16. Flaubert, *Correspondance*, 2:731.

17. Gothot-Mersch, introduction to *Bouvard et Pécuchet*, 36.

18. Flaubert, *Letters of Gustave Flaubert, 1857–1880*, 263.

19. See Gustave Flaubert, *Le second volume de Bouvard et Pécuchet*, ed. Geneviève Bollème, Les Lettres nouvelles (Paris: Denoël, 1966).

20. Flaubert, *Correspondance*, 5:599.

21. Guy de Maupassant, in *Flaubert-Maupassant, Correspondance*, ed. Yvan Leclerc (Paris: Flammarion, 1993), 261.

22. It was not absolutely as he had left it, in fact, for Caroline, probably meaning well, had thought it her duty to correct and modify certain passages. We owe the definitive text to the work of Alberto Cento, in his critical edition of *Bouvard et Pécuchet*.

23. Émile Faguet, *Flaubert* (Paris: Hachette, 1899), 134–36.

24. Joris-Karl Huysmans, "Préface écrite vingt ans après le roman," *À rebours* (Paris: Fasquelle, 1903).

25. In 1909, René Descharmes published his doctoral thesis, "Flaubert, sa vie, son caractère et ses idées avant 1857," the first major scholarly work on Gustave Flaubert. René Dumesnil dedicated a great part of his life to Flaubert scholarship of the first importance, such as his contribution to the centennial edition of the correspondence. He also wrote the biography *Gustave Flaubert*, published by Desclée de Brouwer in 1932. Albert Thibaudet is the author of an enlightening biography (*Gustave Flaubert* [1935]), among other works.

26. Borges: Jorge Luis Borges, "A Defense of *Bouvard and Pécuchet*," *Selected Non-Fictions*, ed. Eliot Weinberger (New York: Penguin, 2000). Queneau: see, among others, *Les Enfants du limon* (Paris: Gallimard, 1938). Barthes: see, among others, *Le Degré zéro de l'écriture* [*Writing Degree Zero*] (Paris: Le Seuil, 1953). "Masterpiece of Western literature": see Yvan Leclerc, "La Spirale et le Monument. Essai

sur *Bouvard et Pécuchet* de Gustave Flaubert," SESDES, Présences critiques, 1988; and Mélanie Leroy, dissertation, McGill University, Montreal, 2009, pp. 12–25.

27. See Flaubert, *Correspondance*, 5:599.

28. See René Descharmes, *Autour de "Bouvard et Pécuchet"* (Paris: Librairie de France, 1921).

29. Flaubert, *Letters of Gustave Flaubert, 1830–1857*, 127.

30. *Translator's note:* Voltaire nicknamed Bossuet, Bishop of Meaux, the "eagle of Meaux" in reference to his fearless manner of standing up to Louis XIV. By contrast, his adversary Fénelon, Archbishop of Cambrai, was nicknamed the "swan of Cambrai" because of his retiring personality.

31. Flaubert, *Correspondance*, 1:208–9.

32. *Dictionary of Accepted Ideas*, in Gustave Flaubert, *Bouvard and Pécuchet*, trans. Mark Polizzotti.

33. Letter to George Sand, November 14, 1871, in Flaubert and Sand, *Flaubert-Sand: The Correspondence*, 251.

34. See Jean Bruneau, preface to Flaubert, *Correspondance*, 1:ix–xxxi, and Yvan Leclerc, "Les Éditions de la correspondance de Flaubert," http://flaubert.univ-rouen.fr/correspondance.

35. Jean Bruneau did not live to complete his task. Work on the fifth volume, which he had begun, was taken over by Yvan Leclerc, with the collaboration of Jean-François Delesalle, Jean-Benoît Guinot, and Joëlle Robert.

36. Paul Souday, "Le Centenaire de Gustave Flaubert," *Revue de Paris*, November–December 1921. See also René Dumesnil, "Flaubert et l'opinion," *Mercure de France*, December 1921.

Chapter 30. Sketches for a Portrait

1. Flaubert, *Letters of Gustave Flaubert, 1830–1857*, 154.

2. Flaubert, *Correspondance*, 2:839.

3. See G. Carlier, "Les Conscrits des cantons d'Evreux-Nord et d'Evreux-Sud," *Bulletin de la Société d'anthropologie de Paris*, 1893, no. 4.

4. Flaubert, *Correspondance*, 2:290.

5. Guy de Maupassant, "Flaubert et sa maison," *Gil Blas*, November 24, 1890.

6. Flaubert, *Letters of Gustave Flaubert, 1830–1857*, 239.

7. Flaubert, *Correspondance*, 5:613.

8. Ibid., 5:764.

9. Ibid., 5:197.

10. Ibid., 2:752.

11. Ibid., 2:478.

12. Ibid., 5:789.

13. Flaubert, *Letters of Gustave Flaubert, 1830–1857*, 127.

14. Flaubert and Sand, *Flaubert-Sand: The Correspondence*, 73.

15. Jean-Paul Sartre, "Qu'est-ce que la littérature?," in *Situations II* (Paris: Gallimard, 1948), 167.

16. With the exception that during the period of moral order, Flaubert summed up the stupidity of the bourgeois "by the great party of Order"; see *Correspondance*, 5:282.

17. Ibid., 2:402.

18. Corbin et al., *Histoire de la virilité*, 2:128.

19. Edmond and Jules de Goncourt, *Journal* (French), 2:700–701.

20. See Gérard-Gailly, *Les Véhémences de Louise Colet*.

21. Flaubert, *Letters of Gustave Flaubert, 1830–1857*, 49.

22. Ibid., 174.

23. Flaubert, *Correspondance*, 1:365.

24. Flaubert, *Letters of Gustave Flaubert, 1830–1857*, 88.

25. Ibid., 215.

26. Flaubert, *Correspondance*, 3:135.

27. Ibid., 3:645.

28. Flaubert and Sand, *Flaubert-Sand: The Correspondence*, 334.

29. Flaubert, *Correspondance*, 5:547.

30. Ibid., 5:694.

31. Flaubert, *Letters of Gustave Flaubert, 1830–1857*, 49.

32. Flaubert and Sand, *Flaubert-Sand: The Correspondence*, 152.

33. Ibid.

34. Ernest Renan, *La Réforme intellectuelle et morale*, 10/18 (Paris: Union Générale d'Éditions, 1967), 108, 109.

35. Flaubert and Sand, *Flaubert-Sand: The Correspondence*, 235.

36. Flaubert, *Correspondance*, 5:402.

37. Aside from the correspondence, see Michel Lambart, "Flaubert et la politique coloniale," *Bulletin des Amis de Flaubert et de Maupassant*, no. 18, 2006.

38. Flaubert, *Correspondance*, 2:416.

39. Ibid., 3:66.

40. *Flaubert and Turgenev, a Friendship in Letters*, 46.

41. Henry Laujol, "Correspondance de Flaubert," *Revue bleue*, January–July 1880.

42. See Anne Herschberg Pierrot, "Flaubert, contemporain," in Herschberg Pierrot, ed., "Écrivains contemporains lecteurs de Flaubert," *Oeuvres et critiques* 34, no. 1, Tübingen, 2009.

43. In her review of Herschberg Pierrot, ed., "Écrivains contemporains lecteurs de Flaubert," Delphine Jayot mentions Italo Calvino, Jean Echenoz, Jean-Philippe Toussaint, Pascal Quignard, and Pierre Michon. See https://flaubert.revues.org /971.

A Compendium of Flaubert Quotations

1. Flaubert, *Letters of Gustave Flaubert, 1830–1857*, 202. *Translator's note:* Notes are provided where published English translations have been used. For quotations with no note, the translations are my own.

2. Flaubert and Turgenev, *Flaubert and Turgenev, a Friendship in Letters*, 76.

3. Flaubert, *Letters of Gustave Flaubert, 1857–1880*, 205.

4. Ibid., 242.

5. Flaubert, *Letters of Gustave Flaubert, 1830–1857*, 8.

6. Flaubert, *Letters of Gustave Flaubert, 1857–1880*, 19.

7. Flaubert, *Letters of Gustave Flaubert, 1830–1857*, 51.

8. Ibid., 172.

9. Flaubert and Sand, *Flaubert-Sand: The Correspondence*, 321.

10. Ibid., 378.

11. Ibid., 287.

12. Ibid., 243.

13. Flaubert, *Letters of Gustave Flaubert, 1830–1857*, 181.

14. Flaubert and Sand, *Flaubert-Sand: The Correspondence*, 35.

15. Ibid., 202.

16. Ibid., 240.

17. Ibid., 118.

18. Flaubert, *Letters of Gustave Flaubert, 1830–1857*, 77.

19. Ibid., 161.

20. Flaubert and Sand, *Flaubert-Sand: The Correspondence*, 41.

21. Ibid., 324.

22. Ibid., 388.

23. Flaubert, *Letters of Gustave Flaubert, 1830–1857*, 170.

24. Flaubert, *Letters of Gustave Flaubert, 1857–1880*, 15.

25. Flaubert and Sand, *Flaubert-Sand: The Correspondence*, 129.

Sources and Bibliography

Manuscripts and editions of Flaubert's works

The best guide is the website of the Centre Flaubert at the University of Rouen, which is headed by Yvan Leclerc: http://flaubert.univ-rouen.fr/index.php. It features a list of Flaubert's manuscripts and where they are located, critical studies, a bibliography, and reviews of French and international studies of Flaubert.

The Institut des textes et manuscrits modernes (ITEM), a research department of the CNRS/ENS (Centre national de la recherche scientifique/École normale supérieure) headed by Pierre-Marc de Biasi, uploads "material traces of the literary process" (the writer's notebooks, rough drafts, corrected proofs etc.) as well as many studies of Flaubert: http://www.item.ens.fr.

On its website http://gallica.bnf.fr, the Bibliothèque Nationale de France provides access to eighty-four manuscripts, most of which are fragmentary. Additional documents (rough drafts, outlines, etc.) can be found at the Bibliothèque Municipale in Rouen.

The collections of the French National Archives include a number of documents relating to Gustave Flaubert, including the catalogs of various booksellers and autograph sales, the manuscripts left by Mme Franklin Grout Flaubert, some letters, some documents regarding the expulsion of the pupil Flaubert from the Collège Royal de Rouen, the administration's correspondence regarding the *Madame Bovary* trial, and Flaubert's appointment as an offsite librarian at the Bibliothèque Mazarine.

The final autograph manuscript of *Sentimental Education* is at the Bibliothèque Historique de la Ville de Paris.

There are many French-language editions of Flaubert's works available. The Club de l'Honnête Homme published a very good edition of the complete works in the 1970s.

Gallimard's Bibliothèque de la Pléiade is currently in the process of issuing the complete works. Aside from the five volumes of the correspondence edited by Jean Bruneau (and by Jean Bruneau and Yvan Leclerc in the case of the fifth volume) and an Index by Jean-Benoît Guinot et al., the Pléaide has already issued the juvenilia (2001) and the first two volumes of the complete fiction (2013). The new edition will eventually replace the 1952 Pléiade edition of Flaubert's works.

English translations of Flaubert's works are cited in the notes.

There have been several French volumes focused on specific areas of the correspondence. These include:

Gustave Flaubert–George Sand, edited by Alphonse Jacobs. Paris: Flammarion, 1981.

Flaubert–Tourgueniev, edited by Alexandre Zviiguilsky. Paris: Flammarion, 1989.

Flaubert–Maupassant, text established, introduced, and annotated by Yvan Leclerc. Paris: Flammarion, 1993.

Flaubert–Goncourt, text established, introduced, and annotated by Pierre-Jean Dubief. Paris: Flammarion, 1998.

Lettres inédites à Raoul-Duval, with commentary by Georges Normandy. Paris: Albin Michel, 1950.

English translations of Flaubert's correspondence are cited in the notes.

Gallimard's paperback Folio classique collection provides works edited, introduced, and annotated by scholars:

Madame Bovary, edited by Thierry Laget.

L'Éducation sentimentale, edited by Samuel S. de Sacy, preface by Albert Thibaudet.

Trois Contes, edited by Samuel S. de Sacy, preface by Michel Tournier.

Salammbô, edited by Pierre Moreau, preface by Henri Thomas.

La Tentation de saint Antoine, edited by Claudine Gothot-Mersch.

Bouvard et Pécuchet followed by *Dictionnaire des idées reçues,* and other texts, edited by Claudine Gothot-Mersch.

Correspondance, selection and presentation by Bernard Masson, text established by Jean Bruneau.

Les Mémoires d'un fou followed by *Novembre, Pyrénées-Corse,* and *Voyage en Italie,* edited by Claudine Gothot-Mersch.

Voyage en Orient, edited by Claudine Gothot-Mersch, notes by Stéphanie Dord-Crouslé.

"GF/Flammarion" paperback editions are also worthwhile, notably *Les Mémoires d'un fou, Novembre, et autres textes de jeunesse,* a critical edition by Yvan Leclerc.

Among recent paperback editions, one should also mention:

Voyage en Egypte, unabridged edition of the original manuscript established and presented by Pierre-Marc de Biasi. Paris: Grasset, 1991.

Carnet de voyage à Carthage, edited by Claire-Marie Delavoye. Rouen: Presses universitaires de l'université de Rouen, 1999.

Vie et travaux du RP Cruchard et autres inédits, edited by Matthieu Desportes and Yvan Leclerc. Rouen: Presses des universités de Rouen et du Havre, 2005.

Studies of Flaubert and His Work

Of the many studies devoted to Flaubert, I list only those that are essential.

NINETEENTH CENTURY

Bouilhet, Louis. *Lettres à Gustave Flaubert,* text established and annotated by Maria Luisa Cappello. Paris: CNRS Editions, 1996.

Bourget, Paul. *Essais de psychologie contemporaine, études littéraires.* A. Lemerre, 1885; reissue, Paris: Gallimard, Tel Collection, 1993.

Colet, Louise. *Lui.* Librairie nouvelle, 1860.

Delabost, Merry. *Laumonier. Les Flaubert. Simple esquisse. Trois chirurgiens de l'Hôtel-Dieu de Rouen pendant un siècle (1785–1883). Lecture faite à l'Académie des sciences, belles-lettres et arts de Rouen.* Evreux: Imprimerie de Charles Hérissey, 1889.

Drumont, Édouard. "Gustave Flaubert," *Figures de Bronze ou Statues de neige par Edouard Drumont.* Paris: Ernest Flammarion, 1900.

Du Camp, Maxime. *Souvenirs de l'année 1848. La Révolution de février, le 15 mai, L'insurrection de juin,* presented by Maurice Agulhon. Geneva: Slatkine Reprints, 1979; *Souvenirs littéraires,* 1822–1850, vols. 1–2. Paris: Slatkine Reprints, 1993. I used the 1906 Hachette edition.

Faguet, Émile. *Flaubert*. Paris: Hachette, 1899.

France, Anatole. "Gustave Flaubert," *La Vie littéraire*. Paris: Calmann-Lévy, vol. 4, 1926.

Franklin Grout, Caroline. *Heures d'autrefois, Mémoires inédits, Souvenirs intimes et autres textes*, texts established, presented, and annotated by Matthieu Desportes. Rouen: Publications de l'université de Rouen, 1999.

Gaultier, Jules de. *Le Bovarysme*. 1892, reissued by Presses de l'université Paris Sorbonne, 2006.

Gautier, Léon. *Portraits du XIXe siècle. I. Poètes et romanciers*. Paris: Sanard et Derangeon, 1894.

Goncourt, Edmond and Jules de. *Journal. Mémoires de la vie littéraire. I—1851–1865* and *II—1866–1886*, unabridged edition established and annotated by Robert Ricatte. Paris: Robert Laffont, Bouquins, 1989.

Hennequin, Émile. *Quelques écrivains français: Flaubert, Zola, Hugo, Goncourt, Huysmans, etc.* Paris: Perrin, 1890.

Houssaye, Arsène. "Théo [Théophile Gautier] et Flaubert," *Les Confessions. Souvenirs d'un demi-siècle, 1830–1890*. Paris: E. Dentu, vol. VI, 1891.

Lapierre, Charles. *Esquisse sur Gustave Flaubert intime*. Evreux: Charles Hérissey, 1898.

Lemaître, Jules. *Les Contemporains: études et portraits littéraires*. Paris: H. Lecène et H. Oudin, 1886–1924.

Maupassant, Guy de. "Gustave Flaubert dans sa vie intime." *La Nouvelle Revue*, Paris, January 1, 1881.

Mignot, Albert. *Ernest Chevalier et Gustave Flaubert, leur intimité, lettres inédites de L'auteur de Madame Bovary, l'affaire X . . . , un scandale judiciaire, révélations, etc., notes biographiques rédigées et mises en ordre par Albert Mignot, son neveu*. Paris: E. Dentu, 1888.

Primoli, Joseph Napoléon. "Gustave Flaubert chez la princesse Mathilde, souvenir d'une soirée à Saint-Gratien," followed by "Gustave Flaubert, par la princesse Mathilde Bonaparte," preface to *Gustave Flaubert, Lettres inédites à la princesse Mathilde*. Paris: Louis Conard, 1927.

Richard, Charles. *Chenonceaux et Flaubert*. Tours: Deslis Frères, 1887.

Sainte-Beuve, Charles Augustin. *Correspondance générale*, vols. 10–18. Paris: Didier, 1960–1977.

Sand, George. *Correspondance*. Paris: Garnier, 1986, and *Agendas*, texts transcribed and annotated by Anne Chevereau, Paris: Jean Touzot libraire-éditeur, 5 volumes, 1994.

Tarver, John Charles. *Gustave Flaubert As Seen in His Works and Correspondence*. Westminster: Archibald Constable and Company, 1895.

Zola, Émile. *Les Romanciers naturalistes: Balzac, Stendhal, Gustave Flaubert, Edmond et Jules de Goncourt, Alphonse Daudet, les romanciers contemporains*. Paris: Charpentier, 1881.

TWENTIETH AND TWENTY-FIRST CENTURIES

Album Flaubert, iconography collected and commented on by Jean Bruneau and Jean A. Ducourneau. Paris: Gallimard, Albums de la Pléiade, 1972.

Auriant [pseud.]. *Koutchouk-Hanem l'almée de Flaubert*. Paris: Mercure de France, 1943.

Bac, Ferdinand. *La Princesse Mathilde*. Paris: Librairie Hachette, 1928.

Barnes, Julian. *Flaubert's Parrot* [novel]. London: Jonathan Cape, 1984.

Bart, Benjamin F. *Flaubert*. New York: Syracuse University Press, 1967.

Berchet, Jean-Claude. *Le Voyage en Orient*. Paris: Robert Laffont, 1985.

Bergounioux, Pierre. *Flaubert et l'autre: communication littéraire et dialectique intersubjective*, thesis defended at EHESS (Paris), 1979.

Biasi, Pierre-Marc de. *Flaubert: Une manière spéciale de vivre*. Paris: Grasset, 2009.

Billy, André. *La Présidente et ses amis*. Paris: Flammarion, 1945, and *Les Frères Goncourt: La vie littéraire à Paris pendant la seconde moitié du XIXe siècle*. Paris: Flammarion, 1954.

Bollème, Geneviève. *La Leçon de Flaubert*. Paris: René Julliard, 1964, and *Préface à la vie de l'écrivain*, 1963.

Borges, Jorge Luis. *Discussion*. Paris: Gallimard, 1966.

Brown, Frederick. *Flaubert*. London: William Heinemann, 2006.

Bruneau, Jean. *Les Débuts littéraires de Gustave Flaubert (1831–1845)*. Paris: Armand Colin, 1962.

Chevalley-Chevalier, Lucie. *Gustave Flaubert et sa nièce Caroline*, preface by Jean Bruneau. Paris: La Pensée universelle, 1971.

Cziba, Lucette. *La Femme dans les romans de Flaubert*. Presses universitaires de Lyon, 1983.

Debray-Genette, Raymonde, ed. *Flaubert à l'œuvre*. Paris: Flammarion, 1980.

Descharmes, René. *Flaubert, sa vie, son caractère et ses idées avant 1857*. Paris: F. Ferroud, 1909, and *Autour de Bouvard et Pécuchet*. Paris: Librairie de France, 1921.

Descharmes, René, and René Dumesnil. *Autour de Flaubert*. Paris: Mercure de France, 1912, and *Les Dernières Années de Flaubert*. Paris: La Revue, 1912.

Douchin, Jacques-Louis. *La Vie érotique de Flaubert*. Paris: J.-J. Pauvert aux Editions Carrère, 1984.

Dumesnil, René. *Gustave Flaubert, l'homme et l'œuvre*. Paris: Desclée de Brouwer, 1932, *En marge de Flaubert*, 1927, and *Le Grand Amour de Flaubert*, Geneva: Editions du Milieu du Monde, 1945.

Duruy, Marie-Jeanne. *Flaubert et ses projets inédits*. Paris: Librairie Nizet, 1950.

Fauconnier, Bernard. *Flaubert*. Paris: Gallimard, Folio biographies, 2012.

Gérard-Gailly, Émile. *Le Grand Amour de Flaubert*. Paris: Aubier, 1944.

Gourmont, Remy de. *Promenades littéraires*, vol. 2. Paris: Mercure de France, 1963.

Guinot, Jean-Benoît. *Dictionnaire Flaubert*. Paris: CNRS Editions, 2010.

Jackson, Joseph. *Louise Colet et ses amis littéraires*. New Haven: Yale University Press, 1937.

Le Calvez, Eric. *Gustave Flaubert: Un monde de livres*. Paris: Les Editions Textuel, 2006.

Le Roy, Claude. *Louis Bouilhet, l'ombre de Flaubert*. Paris: H et D, 2009.

Leclerc, Yvan. *Crimes écrits: La littérature en procès au XIXe siècle*. Paris: Plon, 1991.

Letellier, Léon. *Louis Bouilhet 1821–1869: Sa vie et ses œuvres*. Paris: Librairie Hachette, 1919.

Lottman, Herbert R. *Flaubert*. London: Methuen Publishing Ltd, 1989.

Meynial, Edouard. *Flaubert*. Paris: Éditions de la Nouvelle Revue critique, 1943.

Nadeau, Maurice. *Gustave Flaubert écrivain*. Paris: Denoël, 1969.

Oliver, Hermia. *Flaubert and an English Governess*. Oxford: Clarendon Press, 1980. The French translation includes a preface by Julian Barnes (*Flaubert et une gouvernante anglaise: à la recherche de Juliet Herbert*. Rouen: Publications des universités de Rouen et du Havre, 2011).

Sarraute, Nathalie. *Flaubert le précurseur*. Paris: Gallimard, 1986.

Sartre, Jean-Paul. *L'Idiot de la famille. Gustave Flaubert de 1821 à 1857*, new revised and completed edition. Paris: Gallimard, 3 volumes, 1988.

Starkie, Enid. *Flaubert, jeunesse et maturité*. Paris: Mercure de France, 1967.

Suffel, Jacques. *Gustave Flaubert*. Paris: A. G. Nizet, 1979.

Thibaudet, Albert. *Gustave Flaubert*. Paris: Gallimard, 1935, reissue, Tel, 1982.

Vicaire, François. *Flaubert roi de Carthage,* texts collected and presented by François Vicaire. Paris: Magellan et Cie, 2010.

Other Sources

ON LOUIS BOUILHET

Angot, Albert. *Un ami de Flaubert, Louis Bouilhet; sa vie, son œuvre.* 1885.

Frère Étienne. *Louis Bouilhet, son milieu, ses hérédités, l'amitié de Flaubert d'après des documents inédits.* Paris: Société française d'imprimerie et de librairie, 1908.

Maupassant, Guy de. "Louis Bouilhet." Le Gaulois, 1882.

NEWSPAPERS AND PERIODICALS OF FLAUBERT'S ERA

L'Artiste, Chroniques du journal de Rouen, Le Constitutionnel, Le Figaro, Le Gaulois, Gazette de Paris, Journal des débats, Journal illustré, Journal de Rouen, Le Moniteur, Nouvelliste de Rouen, Le Réalisme, Revue contemporaine, Revue des deux mondes, Le Temps, L'Univers, Le Voltaire.

CONTEMPORARY PERIODICALS

Bulletin Flaubert-Maupassant, annual review published by the Association des amis de Flaubert et de Maupassant.

Revue d'histoire littéraire de la France, Presses universitaires de France.

Romantisme, quarterly, Armand Colin.

Illustration Credits

Illustrations follow page 278

Collections of the Bibliothèque municipale de Rouen: Figs. 1, 2, 3, 5, 6, 9, 10, 14, 16, 17, 18, 19, 20, 21, 22, 23, 24, 25, 27, 28, 32

Archives Gallimard: Figs. 4, 7, 11, 12

Bibliothèque nationale de France/Archives Gallimard: Fig. 8

© Roger-Viollet/The Image Works: Figs. 13, 29, 30

© Albert Harlingue/Roger-Viollet/The Image Works: Fig. 15

Private Collection/Bridgeman Images: Fig. 26

Pinacoteca Giuseppe de Nittis, Barletta, Italy/Bridgeman Images: Fig. 31

Index

stupidity, 14, 28, 88, 131, 134, 413–15, 430; Du Camp's description in *Souvenirs littéraires*, 51; expression of, in correspondence, 77, 83–84, 405, 423; facetious spirit in, 14; impersonality aesthetic, 141–42, 144, 156, 179, 181, 198, 212, 243–44, 254, 266, 301, 340, 372, 440, 473; laudable side of, 209; loathing of reality, 54, 134–35, 154, 158, 180–81, 217, 242, 265, 277, 373; melancholy, 19, 31, 77, 122, 127, 195, 297, 347–64, 436, 482; practice of epistolary love, 432–33; self-limitations on fun in Croisset, 428; self-proclaimed paradoxes, 425; shaping factors, 30, 131

Flaubert, Gustave, satirical works: "Étude sur Rabelais," 29; "Ivre et mort" [Drunk and Dead], 29; "Quidquid volueris," 25, 29

Flaubert, Gustave, sexual education of, 39–45; encounter at Hôtel Richelieu, Marseille, 43–44; recounting of desires in *November*, 39–40; visit to brothel, 39–40

Flaubert, Gustave, short stories: "Agonies", 26; "La Belle Explication de la 'fameuse' constipation" [The Beautiful Explanation of the "Famous" Constipation] 28; "Une leçon d'histoire naturelle, genre Commis" [A Lesson in Natural History, Genus: Clerk], 412; "Passion et vertu" [Passion and Virtue], 26; "La Peste à Florence" [The Plague in Florence], 24; "Smar," 27. *See also* "Un Coeur Simple"; Flaubert, Gustave, satirical works; "Herodias"; "The Legend of Saint Julian the Hospitaller"

Flaubert, Gustave, travel narratives: *Par les champs et par les grèves* [*Over Strand and Field*] (with Du Camp), 84; *Pyrénées–Corse 22 août–1er novembre 1840* [*Pyrenees–Corsica August 22 to November 1st, 1840*], 41, 42–43; *Voyage en Egypte* [*Journey to Egypt*], 108, 118, 130

Flaubert, Gustave, youthful writings, 17–19; biography of Louis XIII, 20; Chéruel's influence on, 20; "Chronique normande du Xe siècle" [Norman Chronicle of the 10th Century], 22; comedies for *Billard*, 18; disgust with life vs. exaltation of writing, 17; *Frédégonde*, 18; hymn to writing in "A Scent to Smell, or The Street Artists", 17; interests in history, historical fiction, 19–23; "Une leçon d'histoire naturelle, genre Commis" [A Lesson in Natural History, Genus: Clerk], 412; *Loys XI*, play, 22; "Rome et les Césars" [Rome and the Caesars], 23; short stories, 27–30; *Les Soirées d'étude* [*Study Evenings*] newspaper, 18; survey papers, 20

Flaubert, Juliette (Gustave's cousin), 216

Flaubert and an English Governess: The Quest for Juliet Herbert (Oliver), 191

Flaubert's Parrot (Barnes), 81

Fleuriot, Jean-Baptiste, 5

Les Fleurs du Mal (Baudelaire), 170, 177

Fleurs du Midi [*Flowers of the South of France*] (Colet), 73

Flourens, Gustave, 315, 326

La Fortune des Rougons [*The Fortune of the Rougons*] (Zola), 339

Les Fossiles [*The Fossils*] (Bouilhet), 244

establishment of bourgeois monarchy, 2, 7, 270; fall of, 89, 97, 101; Flaubert's negative reaction to, 10, 30, 52, 88–89, 126; freedom of the press allowed by, 72; influence of reign of, 268; in *Sentimental Education*, 98, 269, 272, 273

Louis XVIII, 1

Lui (Colet), 151–52

L'Univers (Catholic newspaper), 175

Le Lys dans la vallée [*The Lily in the Valley*] (Balzac), 258

MacMahon, Marshall Patrice de, 312–13, 349, 377, 384–89, 391, 439

Madame Bovary (Flaubert): achievement of masterpiece status, 475; Cassou's critique of, 164; charges against, trial of Flaubert for, 168–73; Charles Bovary (character), 5, 155, 159–60, 162, 163; correspondence with Colet about, 141–42; description of supporting characters, 13, 28, 158–66; Dr. Larivière (character), 4, 163; Emma Bovary (character), 10, 158–60, 162, 176; Herbert's English translation, 190; Homais (character), 13, 28, 163–64; impersonality of, 179; inspirations, sources for, 4, 95, 141–42; last sentence of, 233; Laurent-Pichat's requested cuts, 169–70; legal expenses of, 168; Lemerre and Charpentier's reissue of, 392; Leroyer de Chantepie's praise for, 55, 155, 178–80, 198; money made by, 284; Moreau's comment on, 472; periods of writing, 135, 141–44; Pontmarin's attack on, 205; post-Orient trip work on, 135; post-publication sadness, 166; publication in *Revue de Paris*,

152, 153; publishing contract for, 167–68; reading of, to Bouilhet, 136; reception of, 173–78; *Revue des deux mondes* attack on, 174; *Salammbô*'s comparison to, 198–99, 212; self-imposed obstacles in publishing, 17; *Sentimental Education* comparison, 294–95; sources for, 95; success of, 173–78, 183, 223; trial related to, 168–73; as turning point in the history of literature, 418

Madame de Montarcy (Bouilhet), 153, 167, 183–84, 239–40

Madeleine (play; Colet), 138

Mademoiselle Aïssé (Bouilhet), 187, 248, 250, 339

Magazine littéraire, on literary "heirs" of Flaubert, 442

Magnier, Louis, 9

major works of Flaubert. *See* Flaubert, Gustave, major works

Malgré tout [*Despite It All*] (Sand), 304

Mallet, professor, 14

Maria (character in *Memoirs of a Madman*), 33

Le Mariage de Victorine [*The Marriage of Victorine*] (Sand), 372

Le Mari de la danseuse [*The Dancer's New Husband*] (Feydeau), 229

Marie Arnoux (character in *Sentimental Education*, version 2), 59, 255, 257, 266

Marion Delorme (Hugo), 19

Martin du Gard, Roger, 476

Martinon (character in *Sentimental Education*), 263, 271–72, 282

Les Martyrs [*The Martyrs*] (Chateaubriand), 19

Massacre at Chios (Delacroix), 104

Mathilde, Princess. *See* Princess Mathilde

Maupassant, Gustave de, 11

revolutionaries in, 273–78; Romanticism in, 258, 261–63, 290; Rosanette (character), 98, 101, 188–89, 255, 257, 259–64, 285; rule of money narrative in, 271–73; *The Russian Messenger's* praise for, 307–8; Sainte-Beuve's *Volupté* comparison, 258; Sand's support for, 255, 284, 288, 291; Sand's thoughts on failure of, 371–72; Sénécal (character), 96–97, 99–102, 273–78, 281, 285; significance of Revolution of 1848 in, 95–100, 102; society love narrative in, 262–64; sources of character development for, 95–96; title choice, 254; translation into German, 304; venal love narrative in, 258–62; Zola's review of, 292–93

La Servante [*The Maid*] (Colet), 142

sex, sexuality, erotic life of Flaubert: abstinence, 64, 65, 71–72; depictions of prostitutes, 45, 98, 261, 420, 432; homosexual leanings, 81, 123; impact of health issues on, 143; intimacy with Colet, 77–78, 139, 435; loss of virginity, 39; prostitute visits in Egypt, 121–24; prostitute visits elsewhere, 39, 40, 65, 112, 195, 432; sexual discussions with male companions, 431–32. *See also* Flaubert, Gustave, affairs and romances; Flaubert, Gustave, sexual education of

Le Sexe faible [*The Weaker Sex*] (Bouilhet), 355

sex tourism (Egypt), 121–24

Sismondi, Jean de, 20

Sketches from a Hunter's Album (Turgenev), 307

"Smar" (Flaubert), 27–28

Smyrna, travel to, 127–28

Social Contract (Rousseau), 274

Les Soirées de Médan [*Evenings at Médan*] (Zola), 400

Les Soirées d'étude [*Study Evenings*] (newspaper), 18

solitude of Flaubert: complaints about, 307; effect of family, friends' deaths, 69–70; effect of health problems on, 57, 59; effect of Le Poittevin's marriage on, 68; effect of sister's marriage on, 59–60; inability to tolerate, 366; letter to Lévy about desire for, 173; love of relative solitude, 436; in Normandy, 428; reasons for desiring, 134, 282, 351, 362, 436; self-description in *Memoirs of a Madman*, 8; self-reflection about, 464

The Sorrows of Young Werther (Goethe), 38

Souvenirs [*Recollections*] (Tocqueville), 97, 267

Souvenirs, impressions, pensées et paysages pendant un voyage en Orient [*Memories, Impressions, Thoughts, and Landscapes during a Trip to the Orient*] (Lamartine), 104–5

Souvenirs de l'année 1848 [*Memoirs of 1848*] (Du Camp), 89, 95

Souvenirs intimes [*Personal Recollections*], 422

Souvenirs littéraires (Du Camp), 51, 107, 108, 131, 141, 239, 283, 411

Stern, Daniel (Marie d'Agoult), 95, 159

"The Struggles Between the Priesthood and the Empire" (Flaubert), 20

stupidity, Flaubert's detestation of, 14, 28, 88, 131, 134, 413–15, 430

Suarès, André, 470

Sue, Eugène, 170

suffrage. *See* universal male suffrage

unpublished works, 17–18, 45, 107, 254, 412, vii

utopian socialists read by Flaubert, 268

Vargas Llosa, Mario, 442

Vatnaz, Clémence (character in *Sentimental Education*), 190, 280–81, 285, 288

Veyne, François, 225–26

Vial, André, 258, 264

Viardot, Louis, 298

Viardot, Pauline, 307

Une vie [*A Life*] (Maupassant), 220

Vie érotique de Flaubert [*The Erotic Life of Flaubert*] (Douchin), 190

Vie et travaux du RP Cruchard [*Life and Works of the Rev. Fr. Cruchard*] (Flaubert), 354

Vigny, Alfred de, 18, 19

Villemain, Abel-François, 20, 147

Villermé, Louis-René, 268

Voltaire, 63, 69, 274, 401, 402, 403, 439

Volupté [*Sensuality*] (Sainte-Beuve), 258

"Voyage en enfer" [A Trip to Hell] (Flaubert), 24

Voyage en Orient [*Journey to the Orient*] (Nerval), 105

Voyage en Orient (1849–1851) [*Journey to the Orient (1849–1851)*] (Du Camp), 108

War of 1870. *See* Franco-Prussian War (War of 1870)

Wilhelm I (King of Prussia), 310, 315, 328

The Words (Sartre), 69

youthful writings of Flaubert. *See* Flaubert, Gustave, youthful writings

Yuk (god in "Smar"), 27–28

Zola, Émile: *L'Assommoir* [*The Drinking Den*] 382–83, 399–400; Bouilhet's contact with, 410; *Bouton d'or* [*Gold Button*], 399; correspondence with Flaubert, 400; *Evenings at Médan*, 400; *La Fortune des Rougons* [*The Fortune of the Rougons*], 339; friendship with Flaubert, 352, 382, 383, 397, 399–400; literary successes of, 382, 399–400; review of *Sentimental Education*, 292–93; Sunday gatherings with Flaubert, 370